FORGOTTEN WAR

The Criminal Invasion of the Democratic Republic of Congo

The International Conspiracy Unveiled

Rigobert N. Butandu

PublishAmerica
Baltimore

First printing

ISBN: 1-4137-3082-5
PUBLISHED BY PUBLISHAMERICA, LLLP
www.publishamerica.com
Baltimore

Printed in the United States of America

To Maude, Bokang, Mmusi, Fololo, Keith, Benjamin the King, and Didier Butandu, whose love, understanding, and patience I could not bypass.

PREFACE

Rigobert Butandu has written an impassioned book about the grave difficulties that have plagued a country he loves: the Democratic Republic of Congo. The book is partisan and dramatic. It will challenge all who read it to confront the enormous problems now facing—not only the Democratic Republic of Congo—but Africa and the world.

I do not have first-hand knowledge regarding the events in the Democratic Republic of Congo. I know only what I have read in the newspapers, heard on newscasts, or found on-line during an occasional search on the Internet. The details given by Mr. Butandu differ in important aspects from my previous beliefs. Accordingly, I am quite uncertain regarding the "true state of affairs" in this on-going tragedy. I want additional information. And, I want "appropriate action" (more on these two words shortly) to end the suffering detailed by Mr. Butandu.

That I want to know more, and also want "appropriate action," suggests Mr. Butandu has made a significant contribution to the future of his country. While the book will probably anger some, it will challenge thoughtful readers to reexamine the role of law and the actions of the international community in relieving war, conflict and human suffering. I do not agree with every assertion made by Mr. Butandu, and find some of his legal analyses novel and (frankly) controversial. But, whatever the substantive merit of any of my disagreements, the book certainly made me think.

Mr. Butandu's work demonstrates the grave difficulties faced by Africa—and the world—in giving "reality" to the often-grand words of international commitments contained in such documents as the UN Charter, the Geneva Conventions, countless international treaties, and the statute governing the new International Criminal Court. It is one thing to condemn violence, call for democratic national self-governance, establish legal mechanisms to criminalize aggression, and assert the pre-eminence of fundamental human rights. It is quite another thing to make these aspirations "real." As this book shows, the international community has faced substantial difficulties in realizing its commitments to the Democratic Republic of Congo.

Mr. Butandu understandably complains about the international community's seemingly endless discussions (without effective action) regarding violence, democratic self-governance, aggression and human rights within his native land. The international community has not (at least formally) abandoned the Democratic Republic of Congo. But it has also not moved far beyond my reaction after reading this book: the international community has noted a need for more information and has called for "appropriate action."

I, along with the international community, have given an (apparently) ineffective response. This, at the end of the day, is the most important challenge posed by Rigobert Butandu's efforts: How *should* the international community make its grand commitments to justice "real"? The answer (or answers) ultimately given to this question will frame the success or failure of the 21st Century.

In the meantime, I can give no better tentative answers than those suggested by Mr. Butandu. Democracy (and the effective operation of democratic institutions) must be fostered in the Democratic Republic of Congo—and in Africa generally. While fostering the further development of democratic government, there is a pressing need to create and support responsible, independent judicial forums that are committed to the goals of peace, security and respect for basic human rights. The foreign policy of nations (and America in particular) should be conducted as openly and transparently as possible. (In the case of America, additional congressional involvement and oversight is advisable.) Finally, the citizens of the Democratic Republic of Congo (and of Africa as a whole) must ultimately shoulder the huge responsibility of building stable, decent societies.

The colonial period unquestionably imposed certain injustices upon Africa and its people; those injustices (as Mr. Butandu sets out) may well continue today. But these realities suggest that the citizens of Africa—and particularly the citizens of the Democratic Republic of Congo—must strive, first and foremost, to help themselves. The principles of non-violence, self-governance and respect for human rights will become "real" in the Democratic Republic of Congo only when the citizens of that country unite with Mr. Butandu to make them real.

Richard G. Wilkins
Professor of Law
Brigham Young University
Provo, Utah

ACKNOWLEDGMENTS

Violating human rights in any of its forms is a very easy enterprise. For example, the commission of aggression, genocide, war crimes, crimes against humanity and terrorism, and any crime for that matter, requires two dimensions: first, an intent, and second, an action. But to establish the liability of those involved in the commission of such inhuman actions is a difficult enterprise for, often, bias, partisanism, and politic prevail.

Further, denouncing such atrocities when they are being committed and when one is confronted with conflicting national and international interests, requires courage. But, recording those crimes to educate present and future generations, whereas there is a manifest malicious intent and an international conspiracy from the perpetrators and their allies, as well as the international community, to cover such crimes and their authors, is an act of ultimate sacrifice.

A major part of this volume was first presented in the fall of 1999 as a dissertation paper in an International Human Rights Seminar at J. Reuben Clark Law School at Brigham Young University, Provo, Utah, USA, under the title: "Rwanda and Uganda, Two International Criminal States: The Case of the Aggression and Gross Violations of Human Rights in the Occupied Territories of the Democratic Republic of Congo." For that reason, I owe a great amount of intellectual debt to Professor Cole W. Durham, Jr., who taught me that respecting human rights is the affair of all, while reporting, recording, and finding ways to end impunity is the business of those who have learned to stand for peace and justice.

Professor Lynn D. Wadle deserves great appreciation. He was an advisor, teacher, LLM program director at J. Reuben Clark Law School, Brigham Young University, and mostly supportive of my intellectual adventure. Professor Richard G. Wilkins, who taught me International Organizations at J. Reuben Clark Law School at Brigham Young University, has been very prompt to answer my questions and give me directions during the final phase of the redaction of this book. His insights and contribution to the Preface of this book need acknowledgment.

I appreciate the advice of my friend, Professor André Thomashausen, Director of the Institute of Foreign and Comparative Law at the University of South Africa, Pretoria, South Africa; he insisted that I attend the "International Conference on Armed Conflicts in the Democratic Republic of Congo on the Eve of the Inter-Congolese Dialogue in South Africa: Building a Sustainable Peace in the Great Lakes Region," organized by the African Institute of South Africa and sponsored by the UN in Pretoria in South Africa in February 2002; at which, the audience was pleased to listen to my comments and welcomed my thoughts as constructive. He supports the forthcoming of this volume. I thank Dr. H.O. Kaya, Director of the Department of Peace Studies and International Relations at the University of Northwest, Mmabatho, South Africa, and his students, who had me as a guest lecturer in February 2002, and with whom I shared my insights on the prospects and obstacles in restoring peace in the Great Lakes Region in general, and in the D.R. Congo, in particular. They are looking forward to the publication of this book.

I acknowledge the assistance of Dr. Don Norton and his devoted students of the Department of English at Brigham Young University for revising most parts of this work. Their comments were fair and excellent. I appreciate the clarifications made by Professor Théophile Mbemba, former Governor of Kinshasa and Director of the Office of both Presidents, Laurent Kabila and Joseph Kabila, and actual Minister of Interior of the DR Congo, as well as his Senior Advisor, Bernard Ntendi, during our conversations.

Former US Congresswoman, Cynthia McKinney, of Georgia must be acknowledged for her heroic spirit to defend the truth about US foreign policy in the DR Congo. Together with I. William Zartman, director of African studies and conflict management programs, School of Advanced International Studies, Johns Hopkins University, Washington, D.C., Wayne Madsen, investigative Journalist and the author of *Genocide and Covert Operations in Africa 1993-1999*, and Ellen Ray, President of the Institute of Media Analysis and co-founder and editorial contributor to the *Cover Action Quarterly* and their associates—these individuals stood by the Congolese people, spoke out against the Congolese tragedy, and exposed the international conspiracy to destabilize and balkanize the DR Congo. The Congolese people love them and Mother Africa salutes their zeal in defending human rights and justice.

The following personalities brought more light in the finalization of this book: Mr. Balitha Kohona, Head of the UN Treaty Section, and with whom

I spoke on 20 August 2003, and whose comments made me more determined to seek the truth about the unwillingness of the UN Security Council to intervene timely and efficiently in the Congolese crisis; Mr. Amin Mohsen, of the UN Department of Peace Keeping Operations, Political Affairs Section, whom I interviewed on 26 August and 22 September 2003, and who shared the popular view that the UN took too little measure, too late in dealing with the Congolese tragedy; Mr. Charles Henry Brousseau, in charge of the Africa and Asia Department at the French Permanent Mission to the UN, with whom I spoke on 29 September, 2003, and who advised me on the strategies and tactics that the UN Security Council used in response to the Congolese crisis; Me Zénon Mukongo, Legal advisor at the DR Congo Permanent Mission at the UN, interviewed on 29 September 2003, and who gave me the Congolese official position about the outcome that the Congolese people hope for in relation to the war of occupation of their country by Rwanda and Uganda, and who provided me with the materials that the DR Congo published concerning the aggression and the violations of human rights in the occupied territories; Mr. Pascal Nyamulinda, First Secretary of the Rwanda Embassy to the US, consulted 3 October 2003, and who gave me his government's position regarding the Congolese crisis.

I gratefully acknowledge Edwards Marek, owner of *Your dot com for Africa*, now called *Talking Proud, USA*, for giving me permission to use the articles and pictures related to the Congolese tragedy from his website. His eagerness in denouncing and condemning the illegal occupation of the DRC and the atrocities committed therein needs recognition. I also acknowledge the permission extended to me to reprint excerpts from individuals, publishers, and organizations, whose proper credits are given in this book. The success of this book would have been hindered without their understanding and kind assistance. Thus, Renata Morteo, External Publication Officer at the United Nations Publications Department, Suneeta Kaimal, Associate at Legal & Policy Office at Human Rights Watch, Nina Amster, Project Coordinator at the Executive office at the American Law Institute, Cara Smith, Managing Editor at the American Journal of International Law, Bill Schaap, for the Institute for Media Analysis, Inc., Elizabeth le Roux, Director of Publications and Communications at the Africa Institute of South Africa, Elisa Munoz at the Crimes of War Project, David N. Gibbs, Associate Professor at the Department of Political Science at the University of Arizona, Perry Cartwright at the Rights and Permissions Department at the University of Chicago Press, and Martin Sibson at the

Permission Department at Harcourt Education (UK) deserve special thanks.

I thank Alexis Malumalu who, after reading the original copy of the manuscript of this work, insisted and advised that it also be published in the French language to make it available to the Congolese people at large. I acknowledge the remarks of my friend, Dr. Flory Nkoy, who read the proposal of this book, advised me on certain issues, and has been, for years, waiting for the publication of this work.

The unselfish nature and unconditional love from individuals like Nancy and Del Haws, and Patricia and Paul Whipple always helped me keep my head up in joy and pain, for they gave all and share abundantly. I shall remember them eternally.

Finally, history will not forgive me if I do not acknowledge the valiant Congolese people who defended their nation fiercely with their blood and defeated the imperialist enemies and their allies. The wonderful work of the Angolan, Namibian, Zimbabwean armies, and of all those who—individuals or organizations—directly and indirectly assisted the Congolese people to defend the sovereignty and inviolability of their national territory is appreciated herein.

When all is done, I, therefore, shall remain the sole person responsible for the contents of this book.

TABLE OF CONTENTS

PART THREE: APPLICABLE REMEDIES AT LAW

List of Cases

Democratic Republic of Congo v. Uganda, ICJ, (1 Jul, 2000)

Doe v. Karadzic, 866 F. Supp. 734 (SDNY, 1994)

Doe v. Unocal, 2002 WL 31063976 (9th Cir., Cal., Sep 18, 2002)

Filartiga v. Pena-Irala, 630 F.2d 876 (2nd Cir. 1980)

Forti v. Suarez-Mason, 672 F.Supp. 1531 (ND.Cal. 1987)

Kadic v. Karadzic, 866 F. Supp. 734 (SDNY, 1994)

Ortiz v. Gramajo, 886 F. Supp. 162 (D. Mass. 1995)

Prosecutor v. Furundzija, IT-95-17/1-T (Dec. 10, 1998)

Xuncax v. Gramajo, 886 F. Supp. 162 (D. Mass. 1995)

Introduction

People have long memories. They may remember what happened to them in the last millennium: war, atrocities, injustices ... They can easily remember what happened to them, but they forget to remember what they did to other groups.

—Cole W. Durham, Jr.
Law Professor, J. Reuben Clark Law School,
Brigham Young University, USA

Homo homini lupus[1] says a Latin maxim. While the nations of the world celebrated the entry into a new century with trumpets and drums, their songs, dances, and prayers were only temporary. The question most of them would have asked themselves at the end of the twentieth century is simple: *What have we, as a nation, done to bring lasting peace not only to our own citizens and nation, but also to our neighbors, and by extension into the world?* Many see the twenty-first century as an era of peace on earth, in the true sense of the word, and of goodwill to men. In truth, this century will be an era of more contentions, injustices, human rights violations, aggressions, and wars.

The sad thing about this truth is that some nations of the earth seem to have monopolized the notion of peace. They see peace as their exclusive property right. While they promote and defend peace and human rights at home, they have sow contentions, injustices, human rights violations, aggressions, and wars abroad. In truth, they consider their own citizens, friends, and allies as human beings, while they view others as mere animals or objects made to satisfy their carnal pleasures. The Democratic Republic (DR Congo) of Congo is one of these victim nations.

"Toward the end of the 18 century ... it was said that it was part of God's natural law that no one should harm anybody else in their life, health, liberty, or possessions. These rights could never be given up. The existence of this natural law also established the right to do whatever was necessary to protect such rights."[10] Who may remember or can recall, from the colonial era, a time when the African people in general, and those of the DR Congo in this case, lived as free people in a free land? One takes the world as sole witness of colonization, slavery, neo-colonization, and apartheid in Africa. In the DR Congo, one observes these facts: western sponsored rebellions following the independence; a three-decade reign of terror of one of the American government friends, named Mobutu; and four and half years of invasion and aggression by two American government's friends, Rwanda and Uganda, that cost the lives of three and half million people, and whose negative and destructive effects will be felt throughout the next generations. In all these cases, gross violations of human rights took place somehow with the complicity of the international community.

The aggression of a sovereign state, be it in the name of so-called border security or genocide revenge, is an international crime that should not be sanctioned hypocritically by those organisms mandated to prevent and sanction it, in this instance the UN Security Council. Aggression is an act of barbarism comparable to international terrorism and should be dealt with accordingly. And since there had never been aggression without human rights violations, not speaking out against them and not taking action to stop them is irresponsible, shameful, devilish, a sign of a lack of education. There is no reason why the people of the DR Congo should be victims of aggression and rape, be deprived of decent health care and education, be tortured, and savagely killed while the UN and the international community looked on helpless. What sin has this nation committed to endure such sufferings and international plotting? Do the UN, the USA, and Western powers have another definition of aggression and human rights violations than those applied in the case of Iraq, the former Yugoslavia, and Serbia, to only name these few nations?

If the UN, the USA, and Western powers refused to intervene in the DR Congo to compel Rwanda and Uganda to halt their devilish plan and withdraw their armed forces from the territories of the DR Congo, there can only be one logical explanation to such shameful conduct: they condoned and encouraged the aggression and the violations of human rights committed by their allies in that sovereign and independent state. But why did they do that? Whatever a human does—be he or she under the influence of alcohol, drugs or, be he or she sober of mind—there is a reason for that action. That reason may be a righteous one, or it may be an evil one as in this case.

But, whatever motivated Rwanda and Uganda and their mentors, the war of aggression against the DR Congo was a terrible mistake. This criminal act sets up a precedent for the UN, USA, and Western powers that should allow them to review thoroughly their policy in Africa, specifically in the Region of the Great Lakes, because this war will clearly be long and popular.

Who has never heard or seen a good and rich neighbor, someone always eager and ready to help and assist others and the community, be killed by the same people he or she has been helping and assisting, just because of his or her riches? People are not afraid to shed innocent blood because of power, greed, money, and jealousy. So it is also for nations. "The Democratic Republic of Congo ... is populated by about 50 million people and borders nine other countries. Because of its mineral, agriculture, [forest], and water resources potential, the country has the potential to stabilize economically and politically many of its neighbors, and improves the lives of its citizens and those of its neighbors."[3] But Rwanda and Uganda and their imperialist allies have selfish interests in the DR Congo.

Similarly, because of the same resources, the DR Congo not only attracts the attention of the rest of the world, but it has also signed its death warrant: its Balkanization and destruction by its neighbors, mainly Rwanda and Uganda, with the conspiracy of the international community. "Yet in this conflict," outlines Dr. Moreels, "which has spread across central Africa, the people continue to fight for their lives with courage, resignation, and great creativity. The typical cheeky, smiley look of the Congolese people has turned to one of sadness, for millions have perished. They suffer in silence, their plight not recorded by any cameras."[4] Kristin Connor is right to state that "Africa is one of the few places in the world where four years of fighting that leaves an estimated three million dead can go largely ignored by the international community. This is exactly what has happened in the Democratic Republic of Congo (DRC)."[5]

Human rights are neither marketable, nor negotiable. "Human rights are rights possessed by people simply as, and because, they are human beings."[6] Respecting human rights is a moral imperative. But why had the DR Congo begged the world to bring Rwanda and Uganda to reason and order? How can some nations give themselves permission to invade others and kill innocent people, yet escape intimidation by the international community and criminal charges by the ICC or a like criminal judiciary organ? Is the UN a body of disunited nations? How does one prevent such impunity from a nation or group of nations? Like the UN Secretary-General, Kofi Annan, put it when commenting on enhancing the rule of law, "[t]he new millennium is an appropriate occasion to reaffirm the primary objectives of our Organization and focus on them anew. Establishing the rule of law in international affairs is a central priority"[7] for the people of the world and all nations.

Yet, this new millennium should be an era where impunity should be totally discouraged, and legal remedies efficiently used to establish liabilities for violations of international human rights and humanitarian laws. In many instances, the application of these legal mechanisms will only have a deterrent effect. But, what matters most is that a clear and distinct message is sent to perpetrators of human rights and international humanitarian laws, as well as their allies, that the people of the world and the international community shall no more tolerate impunity for horrendous crimes and shall not leave any stone unturned to bring those responsible of such crimes to justice.

In this book, the reader will learn what Dr. Ronald W. Mortensen, Senior Policy Analyst for the Sutherland Institute and a retired Foreign Service Officer, spoke about as he commented on the unnecessary destruction on human lives and property after visiting, in May 2004, the city of Bukavu in the DR Congo, which was under Rwandan foreign occupation: that "[p]roblems enough arise when an individual elects to ignore the law and does as he sees fit. However, no matter how terrible the individual crime, the scale of the damage is generally limited. On the other hand, when civic leaders take it upon themselves to disregard the rule of law the damage may extend to literally millions of [dead] people,"[*] innocent people who did neither elect nor deserve to die.

This work is divided into three parts. Part one comprises three chapters. The first chapter uncovers the roots of this conflict. The second chapter exposes the deliberate misrepresentation of the invaders' real motives to occupy the DR Congo. Finally, the third chapter outlines the gross violations of human rights—namely aggression, war crimes, crimes against humanity, and terrorism—that the invaders committed in the DR Congo.

Part two contains two chapters. Chapter four describes why the international community was biased in dealing with the Congolese tragedy, while the fifth reveals the controversial politics of the US government in the DR Congo.

[*]Ronald W. Mortensen, *Civic Leaders and the Rule of Law*, Sutherland Journal of Law and Public Policy, the Sutherland Institute, Salt Lake City, Utah, July 15, 2004. Reprinted with Permission.

Part three has two chapters. Chapter six shows the duties of the UN toward the DR Congo and its people and how it breached said duties. This chapter also analyzes the different remedies available to the Congolese people and the Congolese State, both victims of international human rights abuse and international humanitarian law violations. Chapter seven sets forth political and legal mechanisms necessary to establishing a durable and sustainable atmosphere of law and order, and therefore peace in the DR Congo and in the Great lakes Region.

Objectives

An important goal in this book is to speak out. Speak, speak, and speak, no matter what the immediate or future consequences on my person would be. Human experience shows that it is hard for the people of this world to sustain the truth. But, at the same time, the same human experience proves that, without the truth, there is no light, freedom, and respect of human rights, democracy, peace and prosperity, and importantly law and order. Therefore, someone needs to take some risk and acts. That is the essence of this volume.

Another objective, rather a prayer, is to see the international-conscientiousness of the citizens of the world. This awareness should lead to the indictment by the ICC—or whatever court of law that shall be established for that purpose—of those leaders, civilians and army officers, individuals, organizations, or corporations that are directly or indirectly responsible for the gross violations of human rights committed in the occupied territories of the DR Congo during and after of the aggression.

In addition, this book aims to produce an objective insight about this war of aggression and the violations of human rights that invading armed forces and their Congolese allies committed in the occupied territories of the DR Congo. Further, the work is intended to sensibilize the American people about the prejudiced policies of their government in the DR Congo, in particular, and Africa, in general. Joining voices with those who had the courage to expose them before, this book seeks to alert all those who love Africa in general, and the DR Congo in particular, that the real causes of this war of aggression are directly linked to the politics of double standard in the UN and the international community.

The other goal is an invitation to the Great Lakes Region to grow up and to stop the culture of impunity, which is contrary to the African culture. The people of this region, in particular their leaders, must honor the Universal Declaration of Human Rights, and the principles contained in the Charter of the UN, the UA Charter, the African Charter on Human and Peoples' Rights, as well any international human rights norms enacted for these ends.

Finally, this work should serve as an educational instrument to jurists, human rights activists, and political scientists; to both students in the legal, peace studies, human rights, political science, international organization fields, and the like. The general public will benefit to learn that only their active and direct participation in the dealings of their governments shall have the stabilizing effect of maintaining law and order, and consequently peace and justice at home and abroad.

Limits of Scope

Though there is sufficient proof that Burundi also invaded the DR Congo, along with Rwanda and Uganda, Burundi has purposely not been discussed here since this state has officially denied their involvement in the present conflict. Nonetheless, the non-mention of this state does not mean that it did not participate in the aggression against the DR Congo. What matters is the fact that whatever its involvement is, it is no different than what its allies, Rwanda and Uganda, did. When established through a legal process, Burundi will share the same responsibilities with respect to accountability of grave human rights abuse, its armed troops, and/or the like committed in the DR Congo.

In addition, allegations of violations of human rights by the Congolese government are not mentioned here since such an attempt would be beyond the scope of this work. Instead, the discussion is solely about the two states that have officially admitted to directly violating the territorial integrity of the DR Congo, namely Rwanda and Uganda, whose direct and circumstantial evidence links them to the violations of human rights in the territories they controlled during their bloody occupation.

And while the reader is likely to find out that the finger is more pointed toward Rwanda than Uganda, it is because evidence shows that Rwanda swore in its wrath that the end of the aggression is to place a pro-allied government in Kinshasa.

Whenever reference has been made to the violations of human rights within the territories of the invading nations, it is to demonstrate a relation of causality to the crisis in the DR Congo. The debate is presented in an honest and mindful way. The sole intent is to exhibit that someone had received instructions to set his old house on fire and accuse his lovely neighbor as the perpetrator of the tort so that the insurance company may give him a new house. Such act is, indeed, fraudulent ab initio and therefore criminal.

The discussions on international legal remedies are channeled with this objective: to help the Congolese people and the Congolese State—all victims of international human rights and humanitarian laws violations—to explore all the available legal tools that would enable them to pursuit justice in domestic, foreign, and international courts for the wrongs that the occupying armies and their Congolese allies committed on them.

PART ONE

THE CAUSES OF THE AFRICAN FORGOTTEN WAR AND ITS HUMAN RIGHTS VIOLATIONS

...Civilians are no longer just victims of a war—today they are regarded as instruments of war. Starving, terrorizing, murdering, raping civilians—all are seen as legitimate. Sex is no defense nor is age... That's strange, a terrible state of affairs in the year after we commemorated the 50th anniversary of the Universal Declaration of Human Rights.

—Mary Robinson, former President of Ireland and former High Commissioner for Human Rights, United Nations

Chapter I
The Roots of the Present Crisis

The DR Congo is sovereign and an independent state that is recognized as such not only by the AU and UN, but also by the entire international community. There is no, and there had never been, a vacuum of power in Kinshasa, no matter the means by which such power was taken or seized. The Congolese are known throughout the world for their warm friendship and tolerance. In Congo, as long as one does what the law requires, nobody cares about his or her origins. None would ask, *Where are you from, and why are you in this country? That's such a long way from home! When are you going back?* as people do in many other countries of the world, especially here in the United States of America.

Because of its historical hospitality, potential mineral and natural resources, and its strategic location in the heart of Africa, the DR Congo has been, for decades, the home to millions of refugees from neighboring countries. Many of these refugees had forgotten their true origins and had become Congolese nationals. This situation mainly occurs in the eastern part of the DR Congo bordering Burundi, Rwanda, and Uganda, given that these three countries are continually in a state of war combating several rebellions. But, as if being "too" welcoming is an act of weakness, the different groups of refugees housed in the DR Congo have brought political and economical instability to the country for decades now. First, the internal causes will be outlined, then the external ones.

1. The Internal Causes

In 1996, the international community had enough of President Mobutu of the DR Congo (ex-Zaïre). Mobutu was the illegal[8] president of the DR Congo, a dying dictator, and one of the cruelest leaders the twentieth century had known. He systematically and methodologically destroyed the whole infrastructure of the DR Congo inherited from the colonization, and committed gross violations of human rights upon his fellow citizens. With the blessing and protection of the same international community that forced him to relinquish power later, he repeatedly refused to democratize the country.

Between the sixties and the eighties, there was a pocket of rebels led by Laurent-Désiré Kabila in the mountains of the eastern part of the country. In the southeast there were others housed in Tanzania, while those operating in the southern province were in Angola. They all fought to oust Mobutu from power. But not having the protection of the international community, like UNITA of Dr. Jonas Savimbi, for example, these armed groups were not so active. Years prior to 1996, there was also a people's army within the Zairian National Army (FAZ) ready to fight Mobutu's private army, the Presidential Special Division (DSP). But neither the population nor the opposing political leaders wanted a bloodbath in the country.

Having seen that Mobutu could not survive because he suffered from prostate cancer and other health complications, and because he also became cumbersome, annoying, and awkward, the international community looked for another to replace him. Since the leader of internal opposition and long opponent to Mobutu, Etienne Tshisekedi Wa Mulumba, is a radical and nationalist, the international community, and mostly the US, thought he would fail to defend their strategic interests if put in power to take over from Mobutu. But, the US has two allies bordering the DR Congo in the East, namely Rwanda and Uganda. Yoweri Museveni, the president of Uganda, proposed to the US a friend he knew since in the bushes of Tanzania as a guerrilla, before his military coup in 1986. Together with Major-General Paul Kagame, actual President of Rwanda, but then Rwandan vice-president and in charge of the Rwandan army, Museveni convinced President Bill Clinton and his administration that Laurent-Désiré Kabila, his friend, was the only person able to defend the interests of the most powerful nation in the world, the US of America, and allies, as well as those of Rwanda and Uganda.

Given that Mobutu believed nobody other than himself should lead the DR Congo, and seeing that he lost all popularity and legitimacy—even among his own ministers and some generals—the US gave its blessings to Kabila to fight him. Laurent Kabila's military operations were planned from Kigali, and in less than a year he crossed the entire DR Congo national territory from east to west and seized power in Kinshasa (in May 1996) with direct help from Rwanda, Uganda, Burundi, and Angola. Other African and Western countries provided logistical and financial assistance in order to get rid of Mobutu. Soldiers and officers of the People's Army, as well as the whole Congolese nation, welcomed Kabila and made it easy for him to conquer Mobutu's corrupted and undisciplined private army.

What were Rwanda, Uganda, Burundi, and Angola's objectives in helping Laurent Kabila to seize power from Mobutu? The answer to this question is mostly found in the next section. Suffice it to say, however, that each of these countries has accused Mobutu of hosting and arming the rebels who tried to destabilize their governments. Kigali, in particular, wanted a big share of the cake in all of this. They desired to directly control Kinshasa, and they succeeded in doing so for a while.

As for the Western powers, Laurent Kabila was supposed to be a "remodeled" Mobutu; meaning someone who would ignore the sufferings of his people and satisfy only his Western "masters." But this was a big miscalculation for all of them, as they ignored Kabila's résumé. Though, when the war of aggression broke up, they painted him as a Marxist and Communist, Kabila was only a nationalist—a disciple and companion of Emery Patrice Lumumba—who wanted, at all cost, to place the interests of his country above any other. So when, Kampala, Kigali, and Washington found out that Kabila was "uncontrollable," as Museveni stated right after the war broke out, they tried to replace him. Thus, the war of aggression imposed on the Congolese people, with all its inhumane consequences.

2. The External Causes

It is amazing and shameful to see the lightness with which the UN, in particular, and the international community, in general, dealt with the crisis in the DR Congo. If dealt with accordingly and without favoritism, one would discover that this crisis was, in truth, another holocaust. The culture of hatred, exclusivism, and intolerance has been going on for decades now between the Hutus, a majority ethnicity, and the Tutsis, a minority group in the region of the Great Lakes, thus leading Rwanda to become a security state. Those are the two points discussed in the following sub-section.

2.1. For the Ideology of Exclusion

David Matas is of the opinion that "the notion of ideology as a root cause of human rights assumes people move from thought to action. Yet some people act unthinkingly or out of base motives alone. Others move from action to thought. They violate human rights first, and then use an ideology to rationalize what they have done. Certainly this was the experience of the Nazi Germany, where anti-Semitism was widespread during the Third Reich."[9] Whatever the case may be, the actual hatred between these two ethnic sisters, Hutu and Tutsi, has reached a point of non-return. These people are as without any civilization, as they kill for pleasure. Killing has become almost a hobby between the Hutus and Tutsis.

It is, of course, wrong to think that these tribes have always lived this way. Not until a few decades ago did the ideology of exclusion pass through from father to son and mother to daughter. When the Tutsis came to power, they thought they were superior to others and should ipso facto, treat the others as inferior beings and slaves. Thus, when one group leads the country, the other is harassed and looks for refuge in a neighboring country, where they organize themselves into a guerrilla army and seek to take power by force so that they may, in turn, exercise unrighteous dominion and oppression on the other group. Often these groups have found refuge in the eastern regions of the DR Congo, where the local populations always welcomed them.

The Banyamulenge or the so-called Congolese Tutsis originated from Rwanda. They have lived in Congo for decades because of the fratricidal wars in their homeland. Most of them have the Congolese nationality. Mobutu's former (three times) Prime Minister, Léon Kengo wa Dondo, is said to be a descendant of that particular ethnic group. They have been living peaceably in Congo, as long as they were not linked to rebellion in their motherland. However, whenever the Tutsis were in power in Rwanda, the Banyamulenge people in the DR Congo sought to impose their supremacy on the autochonous in the regions where they lived. These latter, not willing to accept a domination of those they had welcomed into their lands, organized themselves into several resistances, the most popular being the well-known Mayi-Mayi or Maï-Maï warriors. The Banyamulenge not only tried to become lords of the land that they did not own, they also sought to allocate lands by force to the other Tutsis from Rwanda who ran away from their country because of continual civil wars. This act was perceived as an invasion by the Mayi-Mayis, who sought to defend their land from the invaders.

In addition, whenever the Tutsis were in control in Kigali, the Hutus who ran for their lives into the territories of the DR Congo fell into ambuscades from the Banyamulenge and Rwandan Tutsis. Thus, perpetual clashes took place between Hutus and Tutsis for years, not only in Rwanda or in the border between Rwanda and the DR Congo, but also inside the territories of DR Congo, resulting almost in the ungovernability of the area bordering these two countries to this day.

It is true that "the causes of the conflicts in the [aforementioned] regions are related to the culture of violence and militarism, ethnic killing mentalities. Ethnic self-serving interests have set the stage for ethnic rivalries and ethnic mutual exclusion or extermination that is, in itself, the heart of genocide between Hutus and Tutsis,"[10] mostly in Rwanda. In 1994, when the Rwandan Hutu President, Juvenal Habyarimana's, plane was shot down—no doubt by Tutsi rebels—killing him and others on board (among whom was the President of Burundi, Cyprien Ntaryamira) Rwanda was the theater of mass killings known today as the Rwandan genocide and attributed falsely[11] to one ethnicity, the Hutu. According to a report of over nine hundred pages of a human rights organization published in Paris in early 2000, the Tutsi Rwanda Patriotic Front, under the supreme command of Paul Kagame, engaged in the organized commission of tens of thousands of killings of civilians who were suspected, mainly, to have participated in the 1994 genocide. These killings occurred not only during the genocide, but also within the months that followed.

With reference to the above, Ellen Ray states that "[a]fter three years of civil war in Rwanda, a power-sharing peace accord was negotiated, only to collapse in 1994, when an airplane carrying Rwanda's Hutu president, Juvenal Habyarimana, was shot down, with all aboard, including President Cyprien Ntaryamira of Burundi, killed. A, still secret, 1997 UN investigation implicates Kagame in the assassinations. Warnings of a coming bloodbath, set off by the attack, were ignored, and a horrendous 89-day massacre of 500,000 Tutsis—and 50,000 Hutus—followed. Kagame's movement, then turned on the Hutu-dominated government and took power. The massacres began again, this time of Hutus. More than a million Rwandan Hutus, both militia and civilians, who escaped the killing, fled to eastern Zaire."[12] Many, indeed, say that the killing of Habyarimana is the major cause of the Great Lakes region turmoil today.

After the Rwandan Tutsis rebels, the RPA, defeated the Hutus army, ex-

FAR, one of the biggest exoduses the twentieth century had known took place. As usual, the Hutus—both civilians and combatants—sought refuge into the DR Congo. During the ADFL war of liberation against Mobutu, the Rwandan Tutsi army backing Laurent D. Kabila aimed "to annihilate the military capacity of the ex-FAR and the Interahamwe who, after 'Operation Turquoise' in 1994, has taken a portion of the Rwandese population hostage and reconstituted their forces and command structures in the Zairian camps. Thus, the refugee camps created by the UN High Commission for Refugees and the international humanitarian organizations were knowingly identified as military targets from the outset. Special RPA commandos within the ADFL forces had a mission to physically destroy all Rwandese refugees suspected of genocide, whether armed, involved in combat, or defenseless civilians, including children, women, and the elderly. From the outset, there was a real intention to physically destroy and annihilate part of the Rwandese refugee population in Zaire,"[13] which aim, the RPA achieved. So, this time, the Tutsi-dominated government not only massively killed the Hutus, but also dispersed them all over Central Africa.

2.2. Rwanda, a National Security State

After reading the situation detailed above, one wonders what groups of people live in Rwanda and what kind of state it is. It is obvious that the Tutsi-led government in Kigali has felt threatened from the day they came into power, a logical consequence of their hatred toward their brothers, the Hutus. Thus, security is their first and unique priority. However, warns David Matas, "[t]he dangers of the primacy of security are something human rights observers see in a prison setting.... When security is given primacy, the state becomes a prison and a prison of the worst sort.... A country should not, after all, become a prison."[14] That is the situation in Rwanda, where innocent people, if not killed, were driven from their homes to concentration camps, without appropriate health care and food, just because the Tutsi government suspected them of a potential collaboration with the Hutu rebels. These people lived as prisoners in their homeland.

For the reasons mentioned above, "a national security state is a security apparatus run wild. The tendency of a national security to view every disagreement with the government as subversive and treasonous is accentuated when the security people control the state. Any threat to the status quo is seen as potentially subversive.... The national security doctrine gave the military both reason for perpetrating human rights violations and a legitimization for human rights violation."[15] What seems curious is the fact that this situation is a choice for Rwanda in particular. The ethnic group that seizes power expects the other to counter-attack and overthrow them, beginning a vicious circle. The sad side of this order of things is that other nations, specifically DR Congo, have paid, and continue to pay, a high cost for the spread of the Rwandan and Ugandan conflicts in their national territories. Therefore, as long as "the general perception is that a national security doctrine means disappearances, torture, unlawful confinement, and extrajudicial executions,"[16] as well as ethnic hatred, ethnic cleansing and other massive violations of human rights, the Rwandan and Ugandan government will be a permanent danger to the whole Great Lakes region.

Chapter II
The Invasion and Aggression of the Democratic Republic of Congo by Rwanda and Uganda

As an introduction to the present chapter, reproduced are some extracts of the speech of Ambassador André Kapanga, Permanent Mission of the Democratic Republic of Congo at the United Nations, given September 10, 1998, at the Great Lakes Policy Forum in Washington DC. This is a well-presented message that correlates with this work.

...Since it is beyond doubt that Rwanda and Uganda have violated Congolese sovereignty, the only question for discussion by the international community and the Congolese people, is whether they were justified in doing so. The governments of Rwanda and Uganda have advanced many reasons to justify an invasion that they say did not happen. I believe that these justifications do not withstand thoughtful scrutiny.

...The US State Department has declared that "countering genocide is in the national security interest of Rwanda and other countries in the region." The failure of my government to prevent Interahamwe, ex-FAR and ADF elements, along with allies among the ex-FAZ, from attacking Rwanda and Uganda are invoked as justification for the invasion...

...It is doubtful that the military strategists of Rwanda and Uganda seriously thought that their forces could subdue a nation of 45 million... Their real goal seems to be the temporary seizure of a "buffer zone" along the border. What is to take place in this buffer zone? Has the international community given any consideration to what the Armée Patriotique

Rwandaise will do to those it considers its enemies within this zone?[17]

The first part of this chapter deals with what Rwanda and Uganda have maintained as reasons for invading a sovereign state, namely, the DR Congo; the second part gives the only true version of the invasion.

1. The Erroneous Version

It is sad—even revolting—that the international community had willingly believed the lies told by Rwanda and Uganda about the crisis and their justification in violating the territorial integrity of the DR Congo. Early in August 1998, President Laurent D. Kabila—who understood what was going on—told the world that the DR Congo was a victim of aggression from Rwanda and Uganda. He outlined: "Rwanda lent its troops to a new rebellion against the DRC government, citing its own security needs and the need to protect Congolese Tutsi from genocide."[18] Endorsing Rwandan official position, the US State Department spokesman reported, "Countering genocide is in the national security interest of Rwanda and other countries in the region. The failure of the Congolese government to deal with border security and citizenship for the Banyamulenge population has undermined regional security."[19] In addition, to justify their occupation of the DR Congo, a sovereign state and Member State of the UN, the aggressors, Rwanda and Uganda, claimed that Laurent D. Kabila had become another Mobutu meaning, a dictator.

1.1. Kabila, Another Mobutu!

Rwanda and Uganda tried to use their store of lies to justify occupation of the territories of the DR Congo. They accused Kabila of promoting tribalism, a word they could not have used if they understood its true meaning. They also charged him of mismanagement and centralization of power, as if Laurent D. Kabila was simply their governor. They claimed Kabila was just another Mobutu. They accused him of doing what, in truth, they themselves, Paul Kagame and Oweri Museveni, are doing in Rwanda and Uganda. At the time, Kabila had only been in power for about fifteen months and had inherited a country whose infrastructures were systematically and totally destroyed by Mobutu. Further, both Rwanda and Uganda had a direct control on the politics, finances, and economy of the DR Congo. It was quite a challenge for Laurent D. Kabila and he knew it, as did his fellow citizens and those who knew the situation of the country. The poor man had an impossible mission to fulfill.

The Congolese people, who supported Kabila during his war of liberation, had at least trusted him and his program of reconstruction and reconciliation, though most of them did not know him. For example, his government of national unity brought down the exchange rate from about 400% to 10%, then to 4%. Kabila knew that he owed more of his victory to his people than to the Rwandan Patriotic Army. Therefore, he was liable to the Congolese, since, were it not for the support of the Congolese people, he could not have won the liberation war of 1996-1997 in the first place. The RPA, though equipped with the most modern weapons of war, could not have fought and won the war against Mobutu themselves alone. The so-called second liberation[20] war is in itself a historical proof of this reality.

After the overthrow of Mobutu's regime, Kabila did not have the military capacity to entirely pacify the country by himself. Rwanda had proposed to train the Congolese army. In truth, Rwanda had the military and political control of the Congolese nation, as shown in the next section. But suffice it to say that, at the time, the Banyamulenge represented a large portion of the active Congolese army as the former National Army, which served under Mobutu, was in military reformation and political re-education. As shown in the previous chapter, whenever the Banyamulenge are mixed with their cousins, the Rwandan Tutsis, there is a higher probability that abuse, crimes, insubordination, exacerbation, and exaction become a reality in the communities where they mingle. Particularly in Kinshasa, people became annoyed with the conduct of these soldiers who behaved as if they owned the Congolese people like their personal property.

This is how one Congolese described, then, the situation in the DRC in 1996-1998, referring to the RPA soldiers: "These guys have never seen cute girls, nice cars and houses, and a big city like Kinshasa, with all that makes it lovely. So they came here and have started raping our sisters, killing us because they do not understand our language, and wear the kind of apparel as the one we have. They have taken our houses, cars, and money. They occupied high administrative posts and treated us as if we were inferior to them."[21] That was the situation just a few months after the ADFL took power in the DR Congo and until the eve of the illegal invasion.

Those foreigners, Rwandans and Ugandans, whom the Congolese people had allowed to come and assist them, seemed to have a second plan. Kabila himself was not at ease or exempt from this uncivilized behavior from the Banyamulenge and Rwandan Tutsis. In 1997, long before this crisis broke out, there were rumors that the Banyamulenge had tried to assassinate Kabila, but that soldiers of the former Congolese National Army rescued him. Unfortunately, four years later they succeeded in doing so. Daniel Simpson, US ambassador to Zaire [DR Congo] was heard saying, "he [Kabila] became obsessed with his personal security [composed mainly of the Banyamulenge and RPA] and became dependent from people from his tribe in the south of the country."[22] What the ambassador failed to say is how he, the ambassador, would have reacted in those circumstances as described herein.

The above situation shows that Kabila's dilemma may be the cause of his disagreement with his Banyamulenge and Rwandese-Tutsis advisors weeks before the war of invasion. The Washington Post reported that, "the fighting [came] amid suspicions within Kabila's government that the Rwanda troops had been plotting against the regime. Kabila had been growing anxious over the presence of Rwanda forces in Kinshasa, and increased security around government buildings weeks before ordering them to leave."[23] Neither Kabila nor the Congolese people were happy during that period. Kabila knew well that losing popularity and legitimacy in Kinshasa might be the end of his reign; if Kinshasa had revolted against him and his government, the RPA machine-guns would not have restored him to power, as a matter of fact.

Thus, Kabila either had to sacrifice a people and nation he dearly loved or to take some drastic measures against the Banyamulenge and their cousins, the Rwandan Tutsis. He opted for the last plan, with all the imminent risks resulting from such action. Hence, the real source of Rwanda and Uganda war of occupation against the DR Congo. Accusation of Kabila's dictatorship was, therefore, a scapegoat and sounded ridiculous from the beginning for those who knew the Congolese situation.

1.2. In the Name of the Banyamulenge, You are Invaded!

In the first chapter, it has been explained how the Banyamulenge population became Congolese by African solidarity, as they have never been granted that nationality officially pursuant to established Congolese legal norms. There is, however, no doubt from the Banyamulenge themselves, the

Congolese autochthonous or the international community that all the Congolese accepted this group and that they were free to live anywhere in the DR Congo. One may ask any Munyamulenge, and he or she shall confirm that it is better for the Banyamulenge to live in the DR Congo than be under a Tutsi ruling in Rwanda. That is an undisputed fact. "Human Rights Watch World Report 1999" outlines that "the Banyamulenge, ethnic Tutsis, settled for generations in South Kivu, had spearheaded the ADFL rebellion in 1996 to assert citizenship rights that Mobutu's government moved to deny them. They again rose in August, this time against their former ally, President Kabila, claiming that he has usurped power and failed to resolve their nationality concerns. Neighboring Rwanda and Uganda intervened on their side, as they did during the first war, exposing a dramatic falling out between them and the man they helped to carry to power."[24]

There are sayings that the Banyamulenge were discriminated against by the other populations. This is not true and the only people who have sustained that claim are those who have fomented the war of aggression in the DR Congo. Be it under Mobutu, who refused them the Congolese nationality, or under Kabila, who was about to give to them citizenship—were it not for their high treason—this people have been more privileged than any other ethnic group in the DR Congo. In truth, under Kabila, until on the eve of the war of aggression, the Banyamulenge were the true and real leaders of the Congolese government, together with their cousins, the Rwandan Tutsis. "In Kinshasa, with Kabila named President, key cabinet posts and the new Congo army and security forces were immediately staffed at the highest levels by Rwandan Tutsis,"[25] pointed out Ellen Ray.

The following is an excerpt of an interview by Colette Braeckman, an internationally well-respected Journalist for the Belgian Journal Le Soir, with the late governor of Sud-Kivu, Mr. Jean-Charles Magabe, who escaped from that occupied territory and had a sufficient knowledge of the Banyamulenge situation:

Question: One of the allegations put forward by the rebellion is that the Banyamulenge Tutsis are still being discriminated against, that their status has not yet been settled while it should have been a priority…

Answer: That's not true; in truth, the Banyamulenge live side by side with other ethnic groups, the Bashis, Bavira, Bafulero, and others, among a total population of 2,600,000 inhabitants. It's true that they had problems in the past, as their Congolese nationality was not recognized. However, we did sensibilize the people so that they may be accepted as any Congolese and we have recorded some progress. As regarding political representation, the Banyamulenge were pretty well positioned unlike the others, because the vice-governor and the mayor of Bukavu belonged to their group, as well as the attorney general, the in-charge of SNEL (the Public Enterprise of Electricity), and the inspector of customs; they did not complain and their situation was improving. We had to calm down the population who thought that Kabila was spoiling them, that they were privileged…"[26]

But, Museveni said on "Tuesday, October 6 [1998] meeting in Rwakitura [that] 'the military presence of Uganda in the DRC is based on genuine and legitimate security interests and its determination to prevent genocide,' [while] Rwanda, too, claimed it was in Congo to stem Interahamwe attacks and stop genocide and ethnic cleansing by Kabila's government."[27] It just sounds laughable to any observer that Kabila was going to exterminate, for unknown reasons for that matter, the same people his government was treating with more honors. Once again this argument by the enemies of the DR Congo was illogical and unreasonable in justifying an invasion of a sovereign state in the name of ethnicity. Sadly, it looks like the Tutsi ethnic group is psychologically unbalanced since "they stand for militarism or military politics, violence, ethnic self-serving interest, and ethnic mutual exclusion or extermination. The sad cycles of genocide and counter-genocide since the 1960s that have occurred between two ethnic groups who hate each other and shocked the world are well known."[28]

It is important that the readers of this book understand, at this stage, that "there are only two ethnic groups (Hutus and Tutsis; the Twa are not included because they are a very small number) in Rwanda and Burundi, whereas Congo is home to 450 ethnic groups. Despite this diversity, killings and genocide mentality is not part of the Congolese people's culture. We are peaceful and very hospitable people. The proof of this is that in time there are hatred killings in Rwanda, Burundi, or Uganda against one of the two ethnic groups involved, that group has always been welcomed in Congo for its survival. The same ethnic group for which Rwanda claimed to have invaded Congo for protection had been represented at every level of the government leadership during the past regime they fought against. They were represented at the level of management in the public as well private sector… This ethnic group, although in minority, was spread all over the country freely because the Congolese people accepted them as part of their society… We also have ethnic groups such as Lunda and Tshokwe spread over Angola, and Lamba and Bemba over Zambia just to name a few. However, no ethnic group has ever made use of external forces for its protection. No neighboring country in Africa has ever invaded another to protect an ethnic group on the basis that group is spread in both countries. This has been possible only with Rwanda where a hatred-killings-mentality is part of the culture."[29]

Here is a list of persons of Banyamulenge and/or Rwanda Tutsi origin that held key positions in the DR Congo, as reported by Congonline. A total of fifty-eight are given here, but there were more.

1. Presidency of the Republic: General Director of Finance (Michael Ruda), Materials Management Officer (Mme Chantal), Secretariat of the President (Mme Kambali Régine), Presidential Press Service (Miss Vicky), Presidential Press Service (Miss Elise Claudine), In-charge of Presidential Security (Karema), Presidential Health Services (Dr. Runyambo wa Bahamba), Managing director of Hospitals attached to the Presidency (name not included), Chief physician (Dr. Gashinge), Advisor to the President (Mutambo Joseph), No specific portfolio (Dugu wa Muleng).

2. **Secretariat of ADFL:** (situation before the June 1998 Cabinet reshuffle): General Secretary (Déogratias Bugera), Logistical officer (Major Rwasibo), Advisor (Munyampenda), ADFL treasurer and Counsel member (Mulinda).

3. **Congolese Army Forces**: Acting Chief of Staff (James Kabarehe), Office of Chief of Staff personnel (only from Tutsi ethnic), N'Djili Airport Commandant (Gakwere), Coordinator for the Chief of Staff and responsible for military security for the President (Daniel "Dan").

4. **Military Detection of Antipatriotic Activity (Military Intelligence)**: Deputy coordinator (Commandant Joachim Ngabo), Criminal Department Director (Commandant Irakiza Gerchom), Director of Counter-Intelligence Department (Commandant Padiri Bahizi), National Director of the School of Intelligence and responsible for the deployment of military Intelligence agents (Commandant Patrick Mucho), Director of Research and Analysis Department (Commandant - name unprinted).

5. Civilian Security: High authority at the Immigration (Mushendimu), Director General of Immigration for the Bas-Congo province (Ruganzu)

6. Government: Foreign Affairs (Bizima Kahara), State Minister at the Presidency (Déogratias Bugera), Office Director for Foreign Affairs (Azarias Ruberwa), Official Representative for Foreign Affairs (M. Ruboneka), Diplomate to the USA (M.Rubosisi), Advisor for the NGO and

United Nations Agencies (Kamanzi), Advisor at the Ministry of mines ("Maneno"), Advisor at the Ministry of Finance (Djamanda), Advisor at the Ministry of Tourism (Rusamira), Financial Advisor at Kinshasa city capitol (Claude B - part of name unprinted), Technical Advisor at the Ministry of Post and Telecommunications (Roger Mun - part of name unprinted).

7. **Public Enterprise**: Chairman and Managing Director of Kilomoto (Makuza), Chairman and Managing Director of Sosider (Rukwiza Magera), Chairman and Managing Director of OBMA (Moïse Nyarugabo), Director General of Afridex (name not mentioned), Health Services at Onatra (Karema), National Programme of Immunization (Rubamba), Agent at the Central Bank (Javier Bwasisi), Ofida-Kin-Areo (Alexis).

8. **Provincial Administration:**

North Kivu: Governor (Kanyamuhanga Gafundi), National Police Coordinator (Annie), National Police Deputy Commandant (Bisengimana), 10th Brigade Deputy Commandant (Sebastien Rugeramana), Masisi County Administrator from Nov.1996 to May 1998 (K - name unprinted), Rutshuru County Administrator (Serubari).

South Kivu: Deputy Governor (Benjamin Serukiza), Mayor of Bukavu (Thadée Mutware Minyongo), Mayor of Bagira (Dieudonné Matunge), Deputy Mayor of Kadutu (name unavailable), Deputy Mayor of Ibanda (name unavailable), Attorney General (Jonas Sebatuzi).

Though this list is not exhaustive, suffice to say that because the Banyamulenge represent only a tiny population of the general Congolese population, comparing them for instance to the Bakongo, Baluba, Balunda, Bangala, Bayaka, Batetela, Bahema, Balendu, Bateke, to name these few, the Banyamulenge were slowly but surely preparing for a colonization of the DR Congo in complicity with the Tutsis. This list is indeed a shocking reality of the Hima empire expansion plans.

1.3. You Have the Duty to Protect Our Borders or Else… You are Invaded!

It is very interesting to see how Rwanda and Uganda justified their aggression of the DR Congo, as they first went from accusing Kabila of being a nepotistic and dictator, then to being Banyamulenge's exterminator, and finally invoking the protection of their borders as the reason behind their invasion of a sovereign and independent state and member of the UN. Although Uganda acknowledged some time after the aggression took place that its soldiers were on Congolese territory, Rwanda repeatedly denied that fact—or better, lied—to the Subcommittee on Africa and to the American Congress and government, all who in any way knew the truth. Even after the DR Congo and allies captured some of its soldiers on the battlefields, Rwanda continued to deny that its army was in the DR Congo.

No wonder that, some three weeks after the war of occupation by Rwanda and Uganda against the DR Congo was under way, the UN Secretary-General reported that "[t]he world has been mercifully free from large-scale regional conflict over the past 12 months. Many local wars have continued, however, new ones have broken out, including, for the first time in this decade, a war over territory between two neighbouring States, Eritrea and Ethiopia. While there have been some important successes for the international community... peace in many parts of the world remains precarious. Moreover, peace processes in several regions, including some to which the United Nations have devoted extensive resources over a long period, show a distressing tendency to unravel. Of particular concern is... the continuing instability and violence in the Democratic Republic of the Congo and the rest of the Great Lakes region..."[30] The UN Secretary-General failed short to say that the DR Congo was under foreign invasion. Whether this failure to denounce or condemn the aggression of the DR Congo by Rwanda and Uganda was purposeful or not, the reader shall judge and indeed find the answer herein.

It was only some four months later, when confronted with the facts and in the presence of President Nelson Mandela of South Africa, that Kagame admitted that the Rwandan army was in the DR Congo for the protection of Rwanda's borders in order to prevent and stop the infiltration of Hutus militias in Rwanda. Even then, Kagame did not admit that his forces were actually fighting for another true reason, (subject debated in the next section). It is humiliating for African politics that this continent still has people who are called "leaders" but whose reasoning is poorer than that of a trained donkey. Even if the derivative sense of "politics" means "lies," a reasonable and responsible person cannot continue to lie when his audience is aware of his lies and does not pay any more attention to what he is saying because they are only pure lies. Only a paranoiac can behave that way.

It is true that for the RPA, the final solution to their concerns is the extermination and extinction of the Hutus ethnicity. One will think that this is not true, but history, experience, and reality have proven that it is. The UN, the US (their ally), the western powers, and the rest of the world know it well. Giving the report of the Tripartite meeting in Lubumbashi, President Robert Mugabe of Zimbabwe outlined that "those who want to secure their borders have the right to do so. But, there are two different things between securing borders and invading or aggressing a neighboring country with a pretext of securing its own borders."[31]

Readers are reminded of some truth here, since this is vital to the comprehension of the Machiavellian plans of Rwanda and Uganda in DR Congo. Time Magazine reported that "it was Kagame, with Uganda's and Burundi's support, who had chosen Kabila to replace Mobutu. In exchange, Kagame made one demand: he wanted Rwandan officers to retrain the Congolese army, as a way to help stop cross-border attacks by Congo based Hutus warriors on Rwanda's Tutsi population."[32] This demand was satisfied: "when President Kabila took power, Rwandase, Burundese, and Ugandan troops took charge of security of Congo including the protection of their borders with Congo. They failed to protect those borders. If so, why then today Rwanda, Uganda, and Burundi are manipulating the USA and the international community telling them that they are in Congo to secure their borders?"[33] The answer to this question is found in the next section.

The following is another excerpt of Ambassador André Kapanga, Permanent Mission of the Democratic Republic of Congo to the United Nations, explaining this problem of border protection and pacification, of an address to the United Nations: "To the extent that my government had any capacity of carrying out this pacification, it resided in its national army, the FAC, which in the eastern provinces was largely integrated by Banyamulenge troops, and commanded by Tutsi—indeed, Rwanda Tutsi—officers. The Chief of Staff of the FAC until one month before the rebellion was a Rwanda Tutsi, and he had a free [hand] in deploying our forces to prevent Interahamwe from attacking Rwanda. The civil administration of the region was also dominated by Congolese Tutsis, for instance the governor of North Kivu, as well as his chief information officer, and the Vice-Governor of South Kivu. Thus, the military might of the nation, as it was, was available to serve the security priorities of the Rwanda government. Indeed, subsequent events have confirmed that these officers and troops owed their primary allegiance to Rwanda. If Rwanda failed to subdue the Interahamwe when they were still at least nominally serving in our national army, why do they think they will be more successful now, when they are perceived as foreign invaders and have aroused the hostility of the Congolese population?

"Rwanda apparently discovered that it is not that easy to pacify the border region. For one thing, the Hutu/Tutsi conflict is not the only one afflicting the area. Decades of brutal dictatorship, grinding poverty, and wars that have displaced millions of people have created a volatile mix of inter-communal tensions, which have been augmented and measurably complicated by the arrival of the ex-FAR and Interahamwe in 1994. It may be that it is not simply possible to launch 'surgical strikes' against suspected genocidaires without widespread collateral damage. In recognition of this, my government convened a summit of peace, security, and development in the Great Lakes Region last May [1998], in an attempt to initiate a peaceful solution to the eastern conflict. It is well-known that the governments of Rwanda and Uganda boycotted this conference, at the urging of some Western powers,"[34] surely since they knew that a politically negotiated solution would have meant the return of the Hutus, majority ethnic, to Rwanda and therefore a real threat to the survival of their government of exclusion.

Similarly to the ambassador exposé, the interview of the former governor of South Kivu by the Belgian, Colette Braeckman, also supports the argument that the Rwandan border protection assertion was both flawed and illogic:

Question: A recurrent problem, raised by Rwanda, is one of security of borders. How to deal with Kigali's worry vis-à-vis to Hutu militias' incursions that have become more and more deadly and that are carried out from Kivu?

Answer: But the Rwandans themselves could not solve this problem! They had their hands free in South Kivu, with a battalion of their army at the airport of Kavumu, another at Nyabibwe, and another again at Bunyakiri. Despite that, they could not stop the incursions of assailants! In any case, it needs to be said that Rwanda was never attacked from South Kivu, and joint meetings were regularly taking place at Bukavu or Cyangugu in order to discuss the security of both states. What more could have been done? We do not forget our obligations toward Rwanda, but Kigali has also obligations toward us..."[35] But this is an obligation that Rwanda is not yet prepared to admit and subsequently honor.

Therefore, one can only wonder why Rwanda and Uganda were fighting the Kabila governments if they were still unable to prevent or stop Hutus infiltrations in both of their countries, not only when they were part of the

Congolese government, but mostly during the war of occupation, when they had control over those particular areas that they falsely and ironically accused Kabila of not being able to secure.

Further, in March 1999, the killings of Western tourists, which shocked the world rather than the thousands of Congolese people being slaughtered by Rwandese and Ugandan armies, and which were attributed to Hutu militias, took place inside the Ugandan territory controlled by the Ugandan army. In addition, it needs to be mentioned that the perpetrators of those killings came curiously from the DR Congo, in particular from an area supposedly being controlled by the Ugandan army. At the same time, Rwanda was also not exempt either from infiltrations or deadly attacks from Hutu militias. Anyone having interest in the Great Lakes Region's politics will observe that these deadly attacks against individuals and other objectives, both in Rwanda and Uganda, had come more to spotlight on the eve of the twenty-first century. Unless they were only maneuvers directed to dissuade their ally the US to officially intervene on their sides, these attacks were proof that these two international criminal states, Rwanda and Uganda, had other well-known and devilish plans for and in the DR Congo.

But as for the borders' protection theory, these "countries can invade the Congo any time they want, but still will not solve their problems because they don't get it. They don't get it because Congo is neither their problem nor their solution. Their solution is their culture and their mentality based on their ethnic mutual exclusion. Unless they break the cycle of violence in their own country by ethnic mutual acceptance of their presence, they will always blame outsiders. We do not need their violence and ethnic mutual exclusion to spread over Congo. So, we need them out now."[36] Unfortunately, this wish and prayer was not heard, as Rwanda, mostly, and Uganda did not immediately leave the DR Congo because they had the blessings of the UN, the US and the international community. Further, the invaders had succeeded in spreading the culture of violence and mutual ethnic exclusion between the Hemas and the Lendus in the territories they occupied in the DR Congo.

2. The True Version

As seen in the previous section, the claims about President Laurent D. Kabila's dictatorship, extermination of Banyamulenge tribe, and failure to protect the eastern borders of the DR Congo were purely lies and did not sustain any truth that might have justified the aggression of a sovereign state by its neighbors Rwanda and Uganda. If a case like this one, which is a criminal act, is set up as a precedent for the UN, whose inaction regarding the matter at hand was very astonishing, then countries like Cuba can also invade the US, invoking a potential threat to Fidel Castro's regime by Cuban national opponents living in the US and who are known to have been constituted into militias to liberate Cuba. Just imagine how disturbing such thoughts may be to the American people, in particular, and the international community, in general.

Thus, in the case of the DR Congo situation, if the reasons advanced by Rwanda and Uganda, and which are with great disappointment shared by the US, the UN, and western countries, have proven to be false and wrong, then there are hidden motivations justifying their illegal occupation. The first portion of this section deals with the so-called rebellion, while the second explores the first real reason of this war of aggression. The last part outlines the second real reason why Kagame and Museveni, with the protection of the international community, invaded the DR Congo.

2.1. A Second "Liberation?"

It has amply been shown in the preceding section that Kabila and the Congolese people were frustrated about an obvious presence of the Rwandan troops (which was increasing in number) and their arrogance and misbehavior. President Laurent Kabila had to either allow a colonization of the DR Congo by Rwanda and Uganda or take a risk and ask them to leave the country. He opted for the second option. Ellen Ray described that "[b]y July 1998, Kabila realized that the Congolese people would not support the excesses of the Rwandan 'foreigners' throughout their government. He also recognized the extent to which he had become a puppet of his Tutsi 'allies,' and after confirmed reports of atrocities by Tutsi military against Hutu exiles in the east, and later in the west of the country, had become too prevalent to ignore, and after he had uncovered an apparent Rwandan plot to assassinate him and stage a coup in Congo, Kabila ordered the Rwandans to leave. Less than a week later, on August 2, 1998, Ugandan and Rwandan regular troops invaded Congo with regrouped, well-trained rebel forces, and began the war to overthrow Kabila..."[37]

Below, plainly explained is how the events took place, to quote the former Congolese minister of foreign affairs, Jean-Charles Okito, addressing the 53rd General Assembly of the United Nations:

"July 27, 1998, the President of the Democratic Republic of Congo, His Excellence M'Zee Laurent-Désiré Kabila, after consultations with his Rwandese and Ugandan peers, takes a sovereign decision to end the Rwandese military technical cooperation and to the presence of foreign troops throughout the entire national territory.

"When the Rwandese leave the Congolese territory, it is being noticed that some Tutsis of Rwandese origin called Banyamulenge follow them.

"A week later, the Congolese towns on the borders with Rwanda, namely Goma, Bukavu, and Uvira are being controlled by armed troops from this neighboring country.

"As from August, begins air traffics between Goma and Kitona on the west of the country, and for that matter, via Kigali, a distance of more than 2,000 kilometers. After killing one of the civilian pilots who refused to obey them, those airplanes have been hijacked from Goma Airport to transport troops and arms to the western part of the country.

"At the same time, columns of armoured vehicles and other military equipment from Uganda cross the border with a pretext to defend their interests in Congo. In their progression, despite protestations from the Congolese government, which asks for their immediate withdrawal, Ugandan troops besieged on Thursday August 13, 1998, the town of Bunia in the Eastern Province. The same day the hydroelectric dam of Inga is occupied by forces of Rwando-Ugandan coalition. These forces sabotage machinery and equipment in order to cut off Kinshasa of electricity and water.

"August 23, 1998, Ugandan troops attack the city of Kisangani, always in the Eastern province, in the North-Eastern part of the country, and will occupy it later..."[38]

When the Rwandese and Ugandan armed forces invaded the DR Congo, they executed all the soldiers and officers loyal to the Congolese Army who did not follow them and obey their instructions to mutiny against the central government. As always, in such a situation, there are those who like that kind of adventure and who did not hesitate to seize the opportunity. The Rwandese and Ugandan then call it "rebellion" and a second "war of liberation" by soldiers unhappy with Kabila's regime. Some selected Congolese army officers made few announcements on the radio in Goma and Bukavu to say they no longer recognized Kabila's government. Days later, a number of DR Congo opportunist citizens met in Kigali to form the political arm of the "rebellion." They came from different African and Western countries. Among these were, of course, all the Banyamulenge and Rwandan Tutsis, as well as former politicians from the Mobutu government who lived in exile. They created what is known today as the "Rassemblement Congolais pour la Démocratie" or RCD.

During all this time, Rwanda completely denied its involvement in the conflict and advocated the theory that what was happening in the DR Congo was purely an internal matter created by Kabila's nepotism, mismanagement, and refusal to democratize the country, as if both Rwanda and Uganda are well-managed and democratic states. While most of the western powers followed Rwanda's lies and believed that what was taking place in the DR Congo was indeed a rebellion, Kabila warned that the so-called rebels were only puppets from Rwanda, Uganda, and their Western mentors, and that his country was invaded by forces from Rwanda and Uganda. This is the true theory today, even if the US and the UN—for unknown reasons—still have not officially accepted yet that "the triggering factor in the second war was president Kabila's decision in late July ordering Rwandan troops home."[39]

It was not until November 6, 1998 that Kagame admitted in front of President Nelson Mandela that Rwandan forces were indeed in the DR Congo, as mentioned previously. But even then, he sustained that Rwanda had nothing to do with this "rebellion" and that his troops were in DR Congo to prevent genocide against the Banyamulenge and to protect their borders. Those who are still in love with justice, peace, law and order, and democracy throughout the world will admit that "though the Rwanda and Uganda governments have characterized the hostilities in my country as a 'rebellion' that is internal to the Congo, no serious observer of the situation would deny the role of Rwanda and Uganda as aggressors. Even Mrs. Emma Bonino, European Commissioner for Humanitarian Affairs, and no friend of my government, has loudly protested this 'outright invasion' by Rwanda. In a welcome acknowledgment of the real facts on the ground, President Nelson Mandela declared this past week that my government was within its rights to call for military help from its allies to protect itself from foreign aggression."[40]

If this so-called second "war of liberation" was a true one, and led by Congolese citizens, two things would have essentially happened: first, it would not have lasted even a month, because of its costs; and second, if it had, the rebels would have had the support of the local populations. It is no secret that the "rebels" and their Rwandan and Ugandan allies were not welcomed in the areas they controlled since the Congolese people in those regions organized a passive resistance. Everything the "rebels" and their Rwandan and Ugandan allies did to involve the populations was done manu militari. In addition, it should be understood that since neither of the so-called rebels, Rwanda and Uganda, had the necessary financial resources to support such a costly and long war, logically and reasonably, such assistance, as well in arms as in ammunition, came from somewhere else.

2.2. The Fight for the Control of Congolese Resources

Contrary to Uganda, which seemed to be in the DR Congo in the first place due to a military pact with Rwanda and then for economic adventurism, Rwanda has hegemonic ambitions in the DR Congo. Flory Kante, a Congolese journalist, in referring to an interview that the Belgian newspaper Le Soir had with Paul Kagame, said that "Paul Kagame has acknowledged to have deployed [in the DR Congo] between 15,000 to 20,000 Rwandan soldiers. The objective assigned to these distributors of death, would be deceptive only to those who are naive: become masters of the scandalous riches of our country. Always according to the strongman of Kigali, 'Rwanda is in Congo and must remain there. She has not been invited so that she may get off some day. She remains in Congo for her security reasons.'"[41] Two days later, on 22 October, 1999, Paul Kagame declared that he would maintain his terrorists and bloodthirsty, armed troops in the DR Congo for the same reasons.[42]

Security reasons, you said? So what were your troops doing more than 1,800 miles from the borders, in the western region of the DR Congo, (right at the extreme opposite of the eastern borders they alleged insecurity and sought protection for) besieging one of the biggest hydro-electric dams in the world, and depriving the legitimate citizens of a sovereign state of electricity and water for days, Paul? And what were you doing in the bushes of Mbuji-Mayi, the DR Congo diamond town, some 600 miles from the presumed borders, Kagame? Rwandans argued that they took preventive measures, politically and militarily, by occupying the western parts of the DR Congo and trying to overrun Kinshasa and Lubumbashi because allegedly the decisions to hurt the security of Rwanda were taken from these towns. What a jerk, indeed!

Rwandan intentions in the DR Congo are clear: self-interest, greed, power, and ambition. Their ambition is to control this vast and strategic country in Central Africa. Thus, Rwanda has a well-planned and long-term goal in the DR Congo. Kagame thought that Kabila would always serve Rwandan interests as a priority when he came to power. But when he found out that Kabila was becoming autonomous from Rwandan and allies' influence, he swore in his wrath to depose him by military means and to control directly this immense and rich territory. "The Rwandan government had demobilized some of its soldiers but after mid-year, it recruited more, some forcibly, to meet the need of troops both in the DRC and Northwestern Rwanda. Human Rights Watch received accounts in August and September [1998] of young men taken by force, trained briefly, and then sent to the Congo,"[43] hundreds and thousands of miles away from their borders, in order to defend the same borders. That is ridiculous, and it does not make any sense, except to Rwandans themselves and those who were supporting them in this shameful and deadly enterprise. This is like Mexico blaming the US for not protecting its borders and sending armed troops to Utah to secure the Mexican frontier with the US.

King Leopold of Belgium made the DR Congo his personal and private property. Belgium has been built from treasures coming from this African country. During the African colonization, France, the United Kingdom, and Portugal, to name only a few nations, left no stones unturned in order to colonize Congo. Those who know the US policy in Central Africa have also noticed that the US of America has done its best to neo-colonize the DR Congo, Mobutu serving that purpose well during the first two decades of his reign, and even afterward. The DR Congo is the richest country in Africa, at least in its potential resources. The uranium used by the US in the fabrication of the first atomic bombs discharged upon Hiroshima and Nagasaki came from the DR Congo. This country is also called a "geological scandal" because of its countless mineral and natural resources.

Keith Snow, a freelance photographer and investigative journalist, is right to argue that "[b]ased on my research, this is a western syndicated proxy war, and like in Sierra Leone, Angola and Sudan, it is a war-as-cover for the rapid and unrestricted extraction of raw materials, and war as a means to totally disenfranchise the local people. Diamonds, gold, columbium tantaline, niobium, cobalt, manganese and petroleum, natural gas and timber, and possibly uranium—are a few of the major spoils being pillaged behind the scenes as war ravages DRC, and some of these minerals are almost solely found in DRC, especially cobalt, niobium, columbium tantaline."[44]

In controlling the DR Congo, Rwanda and Uganda think to solve their problem of the lack of democracy at home and develop their countries, as they would have free access to the rich resources of the DR Congo. There is also personal ambition in this adventure that profits not only Rwanda and Uganda, but also some western powers. A rare, but very precious, mineral was discovered in the eastern regions of the DR Congo under occupation. According to the experts, this mineral, called coltan, is used in the fabrication of high performance jets, computers, and cellular (mobile) phones. While Rwanda and Uganda are running a political and military war, western countries are interested in an economical war, as explained in the next sub-section. In other words, Rwanda and Uganda are paving the way for their western allies, even though they also have stolen much of the DR Congo's riches since their occupation.

For instance, Time Magazine has reported that "Museveni's generosity [toward the so-called rebels] hasn't stopped him from exporting more Congolese gold last year than any other nation in the region-trade he swears was legitimate."[45] If Museveni calls stealing and plundering another independent nation's riches a legitimate act, then the Ugandans need to replace him urgently. It is also known that top Ugandan military officials, including Museveni's own brother, were in charge of carrying out the destruction of the Congolese riches.[46] Some of these officers were "disciplined" for personal enrichment.

In addition, by controlling the DR Congo, Rwanda hopes to completely flush out the Hutus, either by physical extermination or by pushing them into a "Diaspora" all over the world. However, what the Rwanda Tutsis are aiming for is a take over of Central Africa. This may be a hard truth, but this is where the UN and US are failing and miscalculating the present crisis in the Great Lakes region. This is why President Laurent Kabila warned that "this war will be long, popular and exported where it came from."

There is no doubt that should Rwanda and Uganda continue to occupy the territories of the DR Congo, then they had better prepare themselves for or should be prepared for a total war. This type of war is "economic, financial, political, and scientific. It involves the whole economic, political, cultural, and military capacity of the nation. The participants in this war are not just soldiers. They include civilians as well as the military, women, children as well as men. Total war is in time and space. It covers the entire territorial space of the state. It is continual, permanent, without a pre-war or post-war period... The concept of total war focuses on the threat of internal subversion."[47] Whoever instigated this war, for whatever reasons, made a very big mistake, it must be said.

"Yet Rwanda is a tiny, impoverished nation, and Uganda is not much larger or richer, while Congo is one of the largest, richest, and most populous nations in Africa, which at one time had its most powerful army. How did this happen? Could impoverished Rwanda and Uganda have orchestrated, armed, and financed such operations on their own? Is it a coincidence that Rwandan strongman Paul Kagame was trained in the United States? That the Rwandan army received, and continues to receive, training in the US? That the Pentagon has had Special Forces military training missions in Rwanda and Uganda for more than five years? Have those vast segments of the Congolese infrastructure, particularly the mining companies, have been taken over by US and western-linked multinationals, working with the Rwandan and Ugandan rebels and governments?"[48] rightly questioned Ellen Ray.

2.3. The Balkanization of the DR Congo: A Fact?

Western powers have always sustained that the DR Congo is too big of a country to be led by one person. They argued that it should either become a federal state or be divided into small sovereign and independent states in a manner of the former Yugoslavia. The sad thing about all of this is the fact that none of the advocates of this work of evil about the partitioning of the DR Congo have ever asked what the Congolese people think about such a Machiavellian plan. Nobody is interested in consulting the citizens of this country since things are being decided in Washington and New York, and mostly given that this is a mafia operation. Many observers during the invasion of the DR Congo believed that the Balkanization of the DR Congo was effective, facilitated by Rwanda and Uganda with this war of aggression. Alas, their dream was defeated by one unchallenged and more powerful weapon: the Congolese nationalism.

"With the collapse of the Soviet Union," explains Ellen Ray, "Balkanization became a common occurrence, as former 'enemy' states were pushed—attacked and occupied—by the only remaining superpower, sometimes alone, sometimes with one or another of America's allies. The USSR was quickly divided into a dozen new nations: Czecholoslovakia was halved, and then Yugoslavia was shattered, piece by piece. And now, there is a serious effort under way by the western powers to balkanize and further plunder Africa. Indeed, three of the largest nations on the continent, Congo, Angola, and Sudan, for many years have faced violent struggles to divide their territories. Some geo-strategists suggest that Balkanization is not necessary when large targeted nations are led by strong, generally repressive governments installed by, or at least indebted to, the West, especially the US. This may explain why, during most of Mobutu regime, there were no serious efforts to destabilize his government, a US client state for all its three decades.... The nation, now Congo, has ended up on the chopping block, its sovereign territory divided and subdivided by invaders, the prize offered by what the Clinton administration cheerfully dubbed 'Africa's First World War.'"[49]

On February 29, 1996, Me Gérard Kamanda wa Kamanda, then deputy premier minister and minister of foreign affairs of Zaïre (DR Congo), said the following at the Vangu Commission of the old HCR-PT regarding the instability of the populations of the Great Lakes region, as recorded by the forces of ex-Kivu: "The General Secretary of the OAU has already initiated a more advanced file on the profound causes of instability in the region of the Great Lakes. The solution to that problem is to apply, on the ground, a study from a Kenyan professor named Mazrvi and which consists to review the states' boundaries on the basis of ethnic affinity, and which would result in the appearance of the Hima Empire at the East of the African continent. It will first be a matter of bringing together Rwanda, Burundi, Tanzania, and the East of Zaïre under one state. Thus, the Bantus will be put together in one space and the Nilotic also among them."[50]

The report continues that thereafter, Me Kamanda wa Kamanda remembered a very significant sentence stated by M. Boutros Boutros, former UN General Secretary, that "countries like Zaïre and Tanzania, having much space, must think to receive that excessive number of Rwandans, not today but in the future."[51] Well, this is the future spoken about; this is the time that evil plan is being put into action.

The partitioning of the DR Congo into satellite states is what Rwanda, Uganda, and their Western allies were trying to achieve in this war of aggression. And, as said before, many observers believed until the end of 2002 that this partitioning was already a fact. When Emile Ilunga, the former political leader of the RCD (a main ally to Rwanda), visited the US of America in 1999, he, without shame and with all boldness, showed a new map of the actual DR Congo divided into four parts: one occupied by the government and its allies; another by the RCD and Rwanda; another one by RCD-Wamba and Uganda; and the last by the MLC and Uganda. This kind of attitude and behavior from some so-called political leader, a person who even wished to run the DR Congo someday, is another betrayal and sends shivers down the spine. How can a compatriot, an African for that matter, agree for the division of an inherited property just to satisfy personal and foreign gains and interests? Once again, these adventurers, who served the interests of Rwandans, Ugandans, and the international community, may be learned, but they are not educated. They are greedy and self-centered, and a band of terrorists and international criminals.

Indeed, in violation of the UN Charter and the United Nations General Assembly Resolution 2625 (XXV) of 24 October, 1970, on the Declaration on Principles of International Law Concerning Friendly Relations and Cooperation among States in Accordance with the Charter of the United Nations, which stipulates that "[n]othing in the foregoing paragraphs shall be construed as authorizing or encouraging any action which would dismember or impair, totally or in part, the territorial integrity or political unity of sovereign or independent States conducting themselves with the principle of equal rights and self-determination of peoples ... and thus possessed of a government representing the whole people belonging to the territory without any distinction to race, creed, or colour."[52] Thus, "[t]he DRC denounces the Machiavellian plan particularly, which under a masquerade intelligently mounted, puts already into being a process of annexing, nevertheless unrealizable in Sud-Kivu. In fact, on 24 August, 1999, under the forced invitation of the Rwandan government, several Congolese agents went to Kigali to participate in the work in view of twinning the towns of Goma, Kigali, and Bukavu."[53] What could have justified such a "cooperation" by Rwanda rather than a real masquerade to further the real annexing of the occupied territories?

Have a closer look at the African map[54] and spot the DR Congo, Uganda, Rwanda, and Burundi. Now look closely at Rwanda and Burundi and you will see that these two countries do not even have enough space to have their names written on the map inside their countries. The names of their countries are, rather, written inside the DR Congo with an arrow pointing to the locations where the states are situated. Now look again closely at the same map and spot the area where the names of Rwanda and Burundi are written inside the DR Congo. These are the areas that Rwanda wants to acquire and conquer with the complicity of the international community. These areas now cover the provinces of North and South Kivu and a part of the Oriental province. And this is the region rich in rare minerals that are found in few soils on earth. According to the DR Congolese government, this region has a reserve of minerals for future Congolese generations. But the DR Congo is about to lose this inherited treasure if the conspiracy to divide this African State continues. Where are fairness, justice, and respect of sovereignty and territorial integrity of a fellow member of the United Nations?

Now, the question is, what will happen if this partition goes ahead as planned by international lobbyists, the UN, USA, UK, Germany, France, and other western countries? Well, first, the Hima Empire will without a doubt be a fact. Second, the DR Congo, as it is known today, will not exist anymore. Third, Rwanda and Burundi, and a large part of the occupied eastern territories of the DR Congo will be part of one Pirate State. Uganda is also likely to claim, as part of its soil, the territories of the DR Congo that were under its occupation. Fourth, the UN, US of America, and other western powers will have to tell the world about the fate of the minorities living in the new state they would like to create, housing Rwanda and Burundi. Fifth, if that plan of partitioning the DR Congo goes ahead, the UN will have created a pattern—better a precedent—to be followed by other nations of the world. Sixth, Africa will be in a perpetual state of war as nations inside one country will ask for a right to self-determination on the basis of persecutions or unfair treatment from the majority. This is the precedent the UN and the western powers want to leave as a heritage to future generations in Africa and around the world. Seventh, and as a consequence of the above, the UN Charter, as we know it today ought then to be rewritten and/or revised.

As to the fate of the Congolese fighting alongside the Rwandans and Ugandans, an advised observer can easily notice that their actual allies will neutralize them. Rwandan troops, for example, will not hesitate to kill them. The situation these Congolese lived in is a forerunner of what might happen to them tomorrow. Those who were closely following the development of the war know that these so-called rebels were almost hostages of Rwandan troops. Many of their political leaders were in house arrest just because they have expressed an opposite viewpoint of what the Rwandans wanted or sustained.

So, since the Lusaka accords,[55] signed between the DR Congo government and its allies on one part, and the so-called rebels and their allies on the other part is more favorable to the second party, the withdrawal of the invaders would be a partial one only. This means that they would retreat only to set up their buffer zone or state in the territories they occupied, awaiting the official creation of their new state spoken about above. No wonder to this day, nearly two years after the signing of the final peace agreement, following the inter-Congolese Dialogue and the constitution of the so-called government of national unity, the Congolese central government is yet incapable of restoring its authority in the occupied territories. Security is a great issue in the occupied territories for there is neither a national unified army nor police. The warlords are still maintaining their owns militias.

Ray confirms the above in her statement: "Something should be said about the way in which a very shady peace process has furthered African Balkanization, just as it did in Yugoslavia. The Lusaka accord was not a good deal for the Congo government; Kabila was forced by implicit and explict threats of greater assistance to the rebels, and endless war. And in consequence a divided Congo became an accepted, institutionalized reality, a solid line drawn through the country in every map that accompanies every news story. The negotiations, stage-managed by the US, intensified the demands for the pullout of all foreign troops from Congo, neatly equating the Ugandan and Rwandan invaders with the troops from Angola, Namibia, and Zimbabwe, invited by the invaded country to assist in repelling the invasion. There is no moral equivalency here. As President Dos Santos of Angola pointed during the UN debate, the accord did not even recognize the legitimacy of the Kabila government,"[56] nor of the Congolese people.

Chapter III
Human Rights Violations in the Occupied Territories of the DR Congo

The twentieth century has disappointed mankind in regard to the gross violations of human rights. It seems like other people's rights to life and the inviolability of their property is a secondary concern that comes after one individual's personal interests and satisfaction. Thus, one can kill his neighbors and destroy their property just to pay respect to his or her passions and personal ambitions. While this is true about individuals, states are not exempt from this bestial behavior. Of course, states are entities that are governed by individuals who carry out their good or bad behavior on that sphere. Individuals who are state leaders and who do not respect their own family members and neighbors are likely to do likewise in their relations with other states. They can instigate the invasion of another sovereign state, or, if they are not militarily capable of doing so themselves, they may combine with their allies. This has always been the case since the beginning of times. But aggression of another state has several negative repercussions, mostly on the civilian populations of the invaded country, and also on the invaders' own people.

It is understood that "the basis of international law is for nations to respect others' sovereignty and to settle disputes peacefully,"[57] points out Amos Yoder. For, whenever there is aggression of one state by another or others, as was the case with the DR Congo, violations of human rights is not something about what one needs to have a degree in law, international politics, or international relations before noticing it. One does not even need to work at the UN or for an NGO, or be a citizen of the aggressed country, or a victim before acknowledging it. That "a human right is 'natural' in that every one knows them, not because they are subject to any particular system of law or religion or particular administration,"[58] is obvious.

For sure, the concept of human rights as we know it today is new, but it has been around too long for the people of this world not to abide by its precepts. The Universal Declaration of Human Rights was adopted and proclaimed in 1948. Individuals and nations of the world have respected its contents for over half a century. Neither the UN Charter nor it is known of any State constitution that has embodied a Bill of rights for its citizens with provisions stating that respect of human rights is marketable and/or negotiable. If any knows of such provision please let him or her tell the world.

Further, it is an undisputed fact that the "primary responsibility for the promotion and protection of human rights under the UN Charter rests in the General Assembly and, under its authority, in the Economic and Social Council (ECOSOC), the Commission on Human Rights, and the UN High Commissioner for Human Rights (UNHCHR)."[59] But, it is believed that the citizens of the world, as individuals, as well as their nations should do their best to promote those rights; otherwise, this mortal life does not have any real meaning at all. It is not a hard thing to assert that each individual, regardless of social status, should endeavor to secure and protect his or her personal and property rights and respect the same toward others.

"In 1968, at the International Conference on Human Rights in Teheran, the Universal Declaration was once again declared 'a common understanding of the peoples of the world concerning the inalienable and inviolable rights of all members of the human family and constitute an obligation for the members of the international community.'"[60] It is sad and regrettable that in the twenty-first century, some individuals and nations are still behaving like the barbarians of the Roman Empire, treating their fellow human beings like sub-humans. The case of the illegal occupation of the DR Congo by its neighbors, Rwanda and Uganda, with the complicity of the international community and lobbyists, is an illustrative example today.

This is what Jean-Charles Okito, former minister of foreign affairs of the Democratic Republic of Congo, said about violations of human rights resulting from the aggression by Rwanda and Uganda:

"The Democratic Republic of Congo is paying once more a heavy toll because of this war imposed on her by outside, and whose innumerable illustrations are seen by:

- the massacres of thousands of innocent Congolese in the east and west, among whom are religious, women, children, and elderly people. These villainous crimes make us think about the murders committed against Hutu refugees by the same Rwandan Patriotic Army;
- massive deportations of populations from Kivu and whose fate is still unknown;
- summary executions of war prisoners;
- the dismantling, sabotage, and destruction of industrial, port, and economical infrastructures of the country. To this day, damages are evaluated at almost three billion American dollars for the city of Matadi alone;
- power cut and water cut off in Kinshasa, a city of more than six million souls, was a real humanitarian drama, illustrated especially by:

i. Important quantity of foodstuffs declared unfit for human consumption;

ii. Innumerable cases of death pointed out in hospitals, because of lack of means for doctors to intervene in conditions required by the practice of their noble profession;

iii. The report sine die of the immunization campaign against poliomyelitis ordered by the WHO and that, with incalculable consequences on the lives of our children, serious obstacle for the future of the country."[61]

The position of the Congolese people and their government was simple, as from the beginning of the war of aggression: "All Congolese people reject the illegal invasion of our country by the forces of Rwanda ... and Uganda. All Congolese people reject the so-called RCD rebels who have betrayed our country by aligning themselves with the invaders, and who have committed atrocities against intellectuals, NGOs, and church groups in territories they occupy."[62]

The first portion of this section deals with the crime of aggression against the DR Congo. The second section focuses on the crime of genocide against the citizens of the DR Congo, the third analyzes the crime against humanity and the crime of war committed on the Congolese people and its nation, and the fourth considers the question of the crime of terrorism.

1. The Crime of Aggression

The crime of aggression against the DR Congo was never arguable or disputable, since Rwanda and Uganda have both acknowledged having their troops, uninvited, on the Congolese soil, and in a manner inconsistent with the UN Charter. Aggression is unauthorized and proscribed by international laws. That the Congolese government never invited these forces is a fact. Kagame even boasted that his troops would not leave the DR Congo, as they were not invited there in the first place. In other words, for Kagame, the Rwandan forces were in the DR Congo to stay and they could only withdraw when they feel like it. But, what Kagame needs to learn and review again and again is that his résumé is written in red and black. Red because he has bloody hands and black since the blood is of his African Black brothers and sisters whom he killed. Further, Kagame must learn that "military invasion, aggression of one state against another innocent victim state, is unjustifiable.... Murder is unjustifiable ... [even if] his human rights violations have become politicized [at the UN, in the US of America, and in western countries]"[63] in the name of the Tutsis 1994 genocide.

For the purposes hereof, here are some definitions of aggression or crimes against peace. The UN General Assembly Resolution of December 14, 1974, defines aggression as: "the use of armed force against the sovereignty, territorial integrity, or political independence of another state, or any other manner inconsistent with the Charter of the United Nations."[64] At the end of World War II, the London Agreement of August 8, 1945, 59 Stat. 1544, EAS No. 472, in its Article 6 (a), made between the US, USSR, Britain, and France, defines crimes against peace as "namely planning, preparation, initiation, or waging of a war of aggression, or a war in violation of international treaties, agreements or assurances, or participation in a common plan or conspiracy for the accomplishment of any of the foregoing."[65]

The PCNICC, option 1, variation 2, defines the crime of aggression as "[the use of the armed force, including the initiation thereof, by an individual who is in position of exercising control or directing the political or military action of a state, against the sovereignty, territorial integrity, or political independence of a state in violation of the Charter of the United Nations.] Any of the following acts committed by [an individual] [a person] who is in a position of exercising control or capable of directing the political or military action of a State: (a) initiating, or (b) carrying out an armed attack directed by a state against the territorial integrity or political independence of another state when this armed attack was undertaken in manifest contravention of the

Charter of the United Nations with the object or result of establishing a military occupation of, or annexing, the territory of such other state or part thereof by armed forces of the attacking state."[66]

In International law, aggression is defined as "the use of armed force by a country against the sovereignty, the territorial integrity, or political independence of another country, or in a manner inconsistent with the Charter of the United Nations. Acts falling within this definition include declaring war against, invading, attacking, blockading, or landing troops on another country's territory,"[67] while invasion means "a hostile or forcible encroachment on the rights of another, the incursion of an army for conquest or plunder."[68]

Either of these definitions outlines that aggression of one state by another or others is an affront to international laws and norms and is, ipso facto, an international crime. The aggression against the independence and the territorial integrity of the DR Congo by Rwanda and Uganda constitutes "...a manifest violation of norms of international law and contravene the purposes and principles of the Charter of the United Nations and the Constitutive Act of the African Union. It is namely the non-appeal of force, of the peaceful settlement of disputes, of respect of the territorial integrity, of the national sovereignty and political independence of states, and of the intangibility of borders inherited from the colonization."[69]

People have argued, with regard to the opinions expressed in this book, that Rwanda and Uganda did not invade the DR Congo, because when they came into the DR Congo in 1996-1997, the UN and the international community had somehow allowed the action. Though the freedom of speech of those people is respected, it is nevertheless hard to understand this kind of reasoning. That the UN and the international community did not condemn Rwanda and Uganda's previous aggression is not an issue. The issue should be why did they not condemn the first aggression? Still it needs to be determined whether, in truth, the UN did not condemn the first aggression. From the records, there is enough evidence that the UN did impliedly condemn the first aggression against the DRC.[70]

Nevertheless, two premises need analysis while comparing these two aggressions by the same states, namely Rwanda and Uganda. First, in 1996-1997 when the aggression against the DR Congo (known as the AFDL war of liberation) occurred, the whole Congolese nation was already very disenchanted with Mobutu's regime. Mobutu was very unpopular among his fellow citizens and had already lost all legitimacy and had just staged another coup in the DRC resulting in the sabotage of the democratic institution process set up by the Conférence Nationale Souveraine. The unwillingness and sturboness of Mobutu to yield to the pleadings of the Congolese people and of the international community paralyzed all political and economical institutions of the nation. Thus, law and order were absent during that period. A small push was necessary for Mobutu to fall. This sole premisse, as it stands, by itself legitimatized the invasion. Second, the whole international community wanted Mobutu out of power.

As an emphasis, be it known that Mobutu had, since 1990, refused to restore democracy against the wishes of the Congolese people and the international community, and had militarily thwarted any effort by political parties and the Congolese civil society to establish democratic institutions, law and order in the country. Indeed, Mobutu had neither legitimacy nor legality to rule the DR Congo.[71] He did not have reliable and/or trusted allies in and out of the DR Congo, for years preceding his overthrow. Some members of his cabinet, his generals, and even certain members of his own family wanted him to relinquish power. The US, his main ally, abandoned him some years back and had arranged a kind of "honorable exit" for him, an offer that he repeatedly rejected. The French position was confusing and Mobutu knew that he could not count on this latter ally. Mobutu could only rely on a few and very selected number of his personal guards and family members for his protection and survival. To defend the country against the ADFL militias backed by Rwanda, Uganda, Burundi, and Angola, Mobutu hired mercenaries from Eastern Europe who massacred hundreds of innocent civilians. From these facts, one may argue that the first invasion was legitimatized.

In contrast, in the 1998-2002 aggression of the DR Congo by Rwanda and Uganda, the premises mentioned above have not occurred. The Congolese people did not want Rwandan and Ugandan forces on their soil; and they were not disenchanted with Kabila's regime. The Congolese, at large, believed that Laurent Kabila was not given a fair chance to rebuild the country because of the illegal occupation of the DRC by Rwanda and Uganda, countries which were massively involved in the day-to-day dealings of the DR Congo prior to the occupation. The Congolese people did not dispute Kabila's legitimacy, though some jurists (depending on the masters they served) debated the legality of his authority. The Congolese people in the occupied territories were passively resisting the invaders and the so-called rebels.

Further, many of Mobutu's friends and family members who are in exile and who, one would think, could have supported the "rebellion" for vengeance, condemned this barbarous act. Some of them were even allies of Kabila in this war of occupation. Tens of thousands of people voluntarily enrolled in the Congolese army, while the invaders and "rebels" recruited manu militaiy in the territories under their control. The allies of the Congolese government, Angola, Namibia, Chad, and Zimbabwe had militarily intervened while others assisted financially and with arms, weapons, and ammunition. The international community was much divided about this whole issue because of the great interests and involvement of international lobbyists and several western powers in this war of aggression.

One may argue, on the merit of international law, that the 1996-1997 foreign-armed intervention in the DRC violated international law, though the aforementioned premises were reasonable, logical, and legitimate. On the other hand, the argument may be made that the 1998 invasion was in compliance with said law, as far as the presence of allied troops on the Congolese soil is concerned. As Amos Yoder indicates, "there are cases in which the right of intervention is recognized under international law. The right of intervention may be right when it takes place at the explicit invitation of the lawful government of a state."[72] This thesis explains and justifies the presence of the Congolese allies' armed troops from Angola, Chad, Namibia, and Zimbabwe, and condemns the presence of the invading Rwandan and Ugandan armed and criminal forces.

Now, when one takes things out of their context, like many of the observers of the aggression of the DR Congo do, it is easy to conclude that the 1996-1997 intervention violated international law. But when the events are put into perspective, one may understand that there was no violation of established international norms, for Mobutu's ruling government from 1992 to his forced departure in exile in 1997 was illegitimate and illegal, as asserted above. Etienne Tshisekedi, Mobutu's main political opponent, led the legitimate and legal government during the aforementioned period. In 1992 the Conférence Nationale Souveraine democratically elected Tshisekedi as the DR Congo Prime Minister to lead the transitional government. But Mobutu banned this second democratically-elected government in the history of the country.[73]

The illegitimacy and illegality of Mobutu's government was evidenced, amongst others, by the fact he resorted to mercenaries rather than to a foreign government to defend the country[74] against the AFDL and its allies, contrary to what a legitimate and legal government would have done, and in opposite to what he (Mobutu) did in the past when the DR Congo was attacked by Congolese rebels. On the other hand, it is agreed that Tshisekedi signed a secret deal with Laurent Kabila, convinced the Congolese masses to support Kabila's military campaigns, and put pressure on the national army (FAZ) to not fight Kabila's soldiers. This was demonstrated by the fact that Kabila went from victory to victories, better from town to town until he reached Kinshasa, almost without a gunshot, and was publicly welcomed by the Congolese in each locality his troops were seen during his war of liberation.

Regardless of what arguments Rwanda and Uganda may advance in defense of and to justify their invasion of the DR Congo, be it known to all that "the prohibition on the use of force is a universally recognized principle of modern international law which, following the Charter of the United Nations, proclaims the obligation of states in carrying on their international relations, to abstain for the use of force against the territorial integrity or political independence of other states."[75] In addition, there is no justification whatsoever, in international law, for aggression of a sovereign state. Aggression and invasion are morally and legally unnecessary and wrong. Aggression is a crime under the law of nations. The fact that a superpower is behind such action does not make such an international crime a right and legal act.

Furthermore, neither Rwanda nor Uganda had later denied their presence on DR Congo's soil without an invitation from the Congolese government or a mandate from the UN. "Often aggressors make a false claim that they have been invited to intervene—Germany when invading Austria in 1938 and the Soviet Union when invading Afghanistan in 1979. Such intervention, of course, is a flagrant violation of international law."[76] This was the case with Uganda at the beginning of the aggression of the DRC as it argued that the presence of its troops in the Congolese soil was an invitation by Kabila's government.[77] But curiously, when the Congolese government requested that Uganda withdraw its soldiers, the response was a refusal. People may call it whatever they want, but this act is called an illegal invasion, and it constitutes an international crime. Besides, Rwanda and Uganda not only were in the DR Congo, but worse, they were determined to topple a legitimate government and had fought the Congolese forces and their allies for that purpose. Just like some western powers and their allies believe that they are authorized at their own will to change—by any means and at any costs—any government that does not defend their interests.

2. The Crime of Genocide

The dirty war that Rwanda and Uganda spread in the DR Congo is dangerous and has destructive and pernicious effects on the lives of millions of Congolese. "The notion of a dirty war follows from the notion of a total war. Because the threat to security comes from civilians as well as armed combatants, the war must be fought against those enemy civilians.... Since war is omnipresent and permanent, it must be fought everywhere, all the time,"[78] no matter how high the number of human casualties may be. And though, "in the modern age, humanitarian and practical considerations have combined to lead the nations of the world to recognize that respect for fundamental human rights is in their individual and collective interest,"[79] there are still some maniac government leaders who think that exterminating other ethnic groups of people is the ultimate solution to a crisis.

Rwanda and Uganda, in their dirty war of aggression to overthrow the Congolese government, have committed genocide. But in the case of Rwanda and its army, they have yet committed another genocide. The Rome Statute of International Criminal Court, article 6, defines genocide as: "any of the following acts committed with intent to destroy, in whole or part, a national, ethnical, racial, or religious group, such as: (a) Killing members of the group; (b) Causing serious bodily or mental harm to members of the group; (c) Deliberately inflicting on the group conditions of life calculated to bring about its physical destruction in whole or part; (d) Imposing measures intended to prevent births within the group; (e) Forcibly transferring children of the group to another group."[80]

In International law, genocide means, "An act committed with the intent to destroy, in whole or part, a national, ethnical, racial, or religious group. Under the terms of the Geneva Convention of 1948, genocide is a crime (whether committed during war or peace) subject to prosecution either in the nation where the act was committed or by international tribunal having jurisdiction elsewhere."[81] That Rwanda and Uganda committed such international crimes in the occupied territories of the DR Congo is obvious, according to direct evidence and the various reports coming from eastern Congo.

This extract of Ugandan online news, The Monitor, published in October 1998, is very significant with regard to the presence of Rwandan and Ugandan troops on the DR Congo soil: "From what we hear, the Ugandan and

Rwandan-backed Congolese Rally for Democracy rebels are not exactly little angels. They have been implicated in massacres of groups of people in areas they control, allegedly for supporting the Kabila government. In one incident, they slew a group of nuns they alleged supported Kabila's forces. Journalists who have visited the areas they control have reported that they are undisciplined and they are distrusted by the people. These are the type of people we are supporting ostensibly to prevent a genocide. Don't get shocked when, a couple months down the road, Uganda and Rwanda, which are in Congo to 'prevent a genocide,' are implicated in a plot to cover up one. If indeed Kagame and Museveni want to prevent a genocide in Congo, it must be a genocide of a particular group of people, not all Congolese."[82] And yet, Rwandan and Ugandan armies committed genocide in the DRC as well as managed to cover some.

David Matas acknowledges that "the law of war assumes that there are combatants who are taking part in the hostilities, and others who are not. The law sets a higher standard for noncombatants, for civilians, rather than combatants. Combatants may, according to the laws of war, be killed. Willful killing of noncombatants is a violation of the laws of war. In a situation of total war, however, everyone is a combatant. The protections of humanitarian law apply to no one. Women and children, the armed as well as the unarmed, become acceptable targets. The concept of total war is a recipe for genocide."[83] So what Rwanda, in particular, is doing is an ideology that needs to only be spread with blood, mostly innocent civilians' blood. One can easily infer that the RPA philosophy is: kill, kill, kill, and exterminate whatever group resists your domination and stands in your way, as long as the members of that group are not Tutsis.

The group that Rwanda and Uganda are targeting is Congolese, in whole or in part, as long as they are supporters of the Congolese legitmate government and/or resist the invasion of the DR Congo. Hundreds of Congolese children were forcibly deported to Rwanda and their fate is still unknown. That widespread killings of Congolese people took place in the regions controlled by the RPA and UDF is undisputed in this war. Congonline reported on one occasion that "the Tutsis have massacred on August 24, 1998, thousands of Congolese in Kavumu, a town located some one hundred kilometers from Bukavu. The number of dead is today evaluated at 1,096 (one thousand nine hundred and six). The first estimations were of 700 dead. On that day of August 24, 1998, members of a religious order, congregation, and the officiating minister were all killed with extreme brutality. The Tutsis cut off their victims' heads, disemboweled some, and pulled off the legs and arms of others, all this in two hours. The slaughter took place simultaneously in three neighboring towns, namely Kavumu, Kilungtwe, and Kalama. Most seriously, the murderers have taken with them the hearts of their victims, after pulling them out the bodies."[84]

In the regions that Rwanda and Uganda occupied, there was obviously serious bodily and mental harm inflicted on the Congolese people for their refusal to support a so-called rebellion that they knew was merely an illegal occupation of their nation by armed foreign forces. As a punishment for the conduct of the Congolese people who supported the Congolese government, the Ugandan troops allegedly chose a very powerful but slow killer weapon: HIV/AIDS. The UN Security Council was merely "[d]eeply concerned at the increased rate of HIV/AIDS infection, in particular amongst women and girls in the Democratic Republic of the Congo,"[85] as a result of the occupation.

However, according to some reports that came from the occupied territories under Ugandan control, most of the troops the Ugandan army ejected on the DR Congo soil were infected with HIV/AIDS. When those soldiers went around raping Congolese girls and women, or even when having "consensual" sexual intercourse with them, they deliberately infected them with HIV. As one knows, people who have HIV are condemned to death. Such conduct is an international crime. In spite of all the politicized praises about her fight against HIV/AIDS, Uganda has a high number of HIV/AIDS cases still.[86] The willful act of infecting Congolese girls and women with HIV was a deliberate action aimed at creating "conditions of life calculated to bring about its physical destruction in whole or part," which satisfied the definition of genocide.

In the case of Rwanda, this is not the first genocide that the RPA has committed. During the 1996-1997 military campaign that brought Laurent D. Kabila to power, the same Tutsi Rwandan army systematically killed thousands of Hutus, innocent civilians seeking refuge in the refugee camps established by the UN and in the jungle in the northern regions of the DR Congo. While the UN and the international community initially charged Kabila with those killings and tried to isolate him internationally because of that, the same approach was not used against Kagame and his army after it was established that they are, in truth, the true killers of Hutus refugees. The treatment of Hutus refugees who returned to Rwanda was not an exception to the barbarous behavior of Kagame's soldiers. In fact, "the doubts are reinforced by a close analysis of the present civil war situation affecting northern and central Rwanda with its plethora of reprisals against the civilian Hutu population by the RPA following attacks of rebel 'infiltrators.' During these disproportionate reprisals, hundreds of people have regularly been massacred, especially since 1997.»[87]

In other words, the Tutsis have countered their 1994 genocide with two others against the Hutus, first in 1994 and then in 1996-1997. Further, they have committed another one against a largely innocent, sovereign, and independent people, the Congolese, due to the mere fact that this people did not want their rule. The international community is assisting in the slow but sure revision of the UN Charter by Rwanda and Uganda, and their allies. These countries are preaching to others that no state should hesitate to exterminate a nation that resists a foreign and barbarous aggression. This was indeed the UN "legalization" of genocide. And those who still think that the Tutsis were the only group victim of genocide in 1994, are wrong, since the Tutsis' same conduct toward the Hutus first and now the Congolese has simply nullified what the Tutsis were victims of, many people think. If it were a soccer match, then the Tutsis would win by 3-1. In short, the Rwandan-Tutsi-Kagame-led government is criminal today of a triple or three counts of genocide: two against the Hutus and one against the Congolese.

Professor Dr. O. Kaya, Head of the Department of Peace Studies and International Relations at the University of Northwest in South Africa, invited the Author on March 22, 2002 to address the students on the current war situation in the DRC, the Inter-Congolese Dialogue for Peace at Sun City in South Africa, and the obstacles and prospects for success in bringing lasting peace in the DR Congo, in particular, and the Great Lakes Region, in general. In order to put things into context and bring to the mind of the audience the realities surrounding this war, with regard to atrocities and crimes against humanity and war crimes, and other violations of international human rights and international humanitarian laws, the author asked that those in the audience with family and/or friendship affiliation with the following countries to stand: Botswana, Republic of Congo, Gabon, Gambia, Lesotho, Mauritius, and Swaziland. He indicated that according to a population estimation done in 1998, none of the above countries has a population of three million people. These countries had respectively 1,478,454 habitants, 2,658,123 habitants, 1,207,844 habitants, 1,292,858 habitants, 1,970,781 habitants (estimated in 1996), 1,168,256 habitants, and 966,462 habitants.

Considering the premise that the Congolese war of aggression has cost over three and a half million lives in four and a half years, the author pointed out to the audience to accept the assumption that the entire population in each one of the above countries (taken individually) were killed. He then used a mathematical formula to enhance his argument. He said, assume that each one of the populations of those countries taken individually were all decimated because of the war; or a pair of combined populations of Botswana and Congo, Botswana and Gambia, Botswana and Mauritius, Botswana and Swaziland, Congo and Swaziland, Gabon and Gambia, Gabon and Lesotho, Gabon and Mauritius, Gabon and Swaziland, Gambia and Mauritius, Lesotho and Mauritius, Lesotho and Swaziland; or triple combined populations of Gambia, Lesotho and Swaziland, he said, were all killed in an armed conflict.[88]

Therefore, any of these countries separately, or any aforementioned combinations of these countries, would only have existed on the map, but with absolutely no human lives within it or them. There was a long silence in the room. This is the enormity, horrifying, unthinkable number of people who have perished in the Congolese war of occupation that Rwanda and Uganda masterminded, concluded the author. Thus, also is the seriousness of this unrecorded, unspoken, and forgotten war of aggression and invasion against the DRC.

Addressing directly those who were standing, the author stated that they may assume that each person they have known in the abovementioned countries, family member or friend, was killed, a victim of this war. He inquired from the group whether this situation would have affected them, and to that question they responded in the affirmative. Thereafter, speaking to the rest of the audience (those with no direct family or friendship affiliation with the above named countries), the author asked whether they would have been affected if their colleagues whose families or friends were killed were affected. Of course, the rest of the students answered. What about those of your other friends or families who are not present here, inquired the author, would they have also been affected? Yes, the students replied. Another silence followed. The author told the audience that their silence meant that they were already affected by the Congolese tragedy as they now saw things in perspective. He thanked the group that was standing and asked that they please sit down.

The author then requested that all the ladies in the audience stand. He pointed out that, like in any armed conflict, the great numbers of victims are women, girls and children. He told the ladies who were standing to imagine that each woman and girl who was killed in the DR Congo war of occupation was likely a victim of sexual and/or physical assault first. The author inquired from the standing ladies whether this situation affected them. The response was in the affirmative. Then, he asked the rest of the audience whether they were affected in some way, their reply was alike. The author concluded that such were the realities of the atrocities committed by the "rebels," Rwandan and Ugandan soldiers, but recorded by no cameras, in the occupied territories of the DR Congo. He thanked the group that was standing and asked that they please sit down.

Nothing more can be said on this subject other than res accendent lumina rebus![89]

3. The Crime Against Humanity and War Crimes

The line is very thin between a crime against humanity and war crimes. For that reason, these two categories of crimes will be dealt with in one subsection for the purposes hereof. The London Agreement of August 8, 1945, referred to above, defines war crimes as "namely, violations of the law and customs of war. Such violations shall include, but not be limited to, murder, ill-treatment or deportation to slave labor or for any other purpose of civilian population of or in occupied territory, ill-treatment of prisoners of war or persons on the seas, killings of hostages, plunder of public or private property, wanton destruction of cities, towns, or villages, or devastation not justified by military means."[90] In International law, war crime is a "conduct that violates international laws governing war. Examples of war crimes are the killing of hostages, abuse of civilians in occupied territories, abuse of prisoners of war, and devastation that is not justified by military necessity."[91]

The London Agreement defines crimes against humanity as "namely, murder, extermination, enslavement, deportation, and other inhumane acts committed against any civilian population, before or during the war, or persecutions on political, racial or religious grounds in execution of or in connection with any crime within the jurisdiction of the Tribunal, whether or not in violation of the domestic law of the country where perpetrated."[92] In International law, crime against humanity means "a brutal crime that is not an isolated incident but that involves large and systematic actions, often cloaked with official authority, and that shocks the conscience of humanity. Among the specific crimes that fall within this category are mass murder, extermination, enslavement, deportation, and other inhumane acts perpetrated against a population, whether in wartime or not."[93]

For the purpose of the Rome Statute of the ICC, "'crime against humanity' means any of the following acts when committed as part of a widespread or systematic attack directed against any civilian population, with knowledge of the attack: (a) Murder; (b) Extermination; (c) Enslavement; (d) Deportation or forcible transfer of population; (e) Imprisonment or other severe deprivation of physical liberty in violation of fundamental rules of international law; (f) Torture; (g) Rape, sexual slavery, enforced prostitution, forced pregnancy, enforced sterilization, or any other form of sexual violence of comparable gravity; (h) Persecution against any identifiable group or collectivity on political, racial, national, ethnic, cultural, religious, or gender as defined in paragraph 3, or other grounds that are universally recognized as impermissible under international law, in connection with any act referred to in this paragraph or any crime within the jurisdiction of the Court; (i) Enforced disappearance of persons; (j) The crime of apartheid; (k) Other inhumane acts of a similar character intentionally causing great suffering, or serious injury to body or to mental or physical health."[94]

Rwandan and Ugandan forces committed crimes against humanity and war crimes from the day they illegally entered the territories of the DR Congo until their departure. IRIN reported on November 4, 1999, that "the UN Special Rapporteur for human rights situation in the DRC, Roberto Garreton, has said that by the end of the first year of the conflict, it was estimated some 6,000 people had lost their lives, many of them civilians killed in retaliation for Mayi-Mayi or Interahamwe attacks on RCD-controlled towns. Another 500 people remained missing, according to his latest report... Garreton said civilians remained hostile toward the RCD, and an 'atmosphere of terror' prevailed in rebels [controlled] areas. The war was perceived as foreign aggression, 'both within and outside the occupied zone.'"[95]

In February 2000, the UN General Assembly resolution "condemn[ed] all the massacres and atrocities still being committed throughout the territory of the Democratic Republic of the Congo, in particular in the zones held by the armed rebels and under foreign occupation, including Bugobe, Nyatende, Kamisimbi, Lurhala, Nyangesi, Biambwe, Nbingi, Bunyatenge, Kaghumo, Banyuke, and Kirima, Kalemié, Pweto, Rutshuru, Kibumba, Kimia Kimia, Dungo Mulunga and Kasese Bolanga."[96]

Rwandan soldiers and their RCD allies, in particular, killed Congolese in the occupied territories without distinguishing between combatants and civilians. They did not have any respect for human life and their actions were in violation of well-recognized and established international legal norms. As the UN Special Rapporteur for the DR Congo said, most of the victims in the zones of occupation were innocent civilians. Late in December 1999, there was a report that the aggressors of the DR Congo buried alive in the region of Mwenga some 15 women alleged to be collaborating with the Congolese government and allied troops. COJESKI reported that "in date of 15 to 22, November 1999, 15 women were buried alive, after they [their torturers] put chillis all over their bodies, in the farming districts of Bulinzi, Bogombe and Ngando."[97]

The names and localities of these victims, as COJESKI reported it, are as follow: 1. Bitondo Evelyne (village of Bulindji); 2. Mbilinzi Musombwa (village of Bulinzi); 3. Safi Christine (village of Bulinzi); 4. Kungwa Anièce (village of Bulinzi); 5. Nakusu Nakipimo (village of Bulindji); 6. Tabu Wakenge (village of Ilinda); 7. Nyassa Kasandule (village of Ilinda); 8. Mapendo Mutitu (village of Ilinda); 9. Bukumbu (village of Ilinda); 10. Spouse of Mwami Kisali; 11. Mum Sifa; 12. Mum Mukoto; 13. A woman not identified yet (at the time of press); 14. Mukunda (village of Bongombe); and, 15. Mbilinzi Kiandundu (village of Ngando).

How can one imagine that such uncivilized acts, just weeks before the entry into a new millennium, can occur? How can one think to bury alive a fellow human being, be he or she a mortal enemy? What about the laws and customs of war that require strict respect for civilian lives and civilian targets, mostly of Article 76.1 of the Additional Protocol 1 of the Geneva Conventions, which stipulates that women must particularly be protected in time of armed conflicts? When are Kagame and his warriors going to learn that the total war they want to impose on the entire Great Lakes region needs, nonetheless, to be fought respecting international laws of war? How would Beinjin, London, Moscow, Paris, and Washington administrations have reacted had these barbarous criminal acts occurred in their backyards? Even the souls of these poor ladies in their peaceable resting-places may guess the answer.

In fact, on 22 December, 1999, a month after the occurrence of the above atrocities, the government of the DR Congo filed an official complaint[98] to the attention of the UN Security Council, the General Secretary of the UN, the UN High Commission of Human Rights, the Commonwealth, the European Union, and of the Organization of African Unity in the following terms:

The Government of Public Salvation addressed a strong protestation to the attention of the UN Security Council, the General Secretary of the UN, the UN High Commission of Human Rights, the Commonwealth, the European Union, and of the Organization of African Unity following the perpetration by the aggressors, crimes against 15 women buried alive in Sud-Kivu. It was yesterday during the press conference held by the Minister of State of Foreign Affairs and International Cooperation, the Ministers of Human Rights, Leonard She Okitundu, of Social Affairs, Moleko Moliwa, of the Minister of State of Petrol, Victor Mpoyo, of the Minister of Information and Tourism, Didier Mumengi, and of the Director of the Head of the State, George Buse Falay.

Indeed, we read from the protestation, from 15 to 22 November ,1999, at least 15 women have been buried alive in the farming districts of Bulinzi, Bongombe, and Ngando in the region of Mwenga, Sud-Kivu province, after being submitted to unhuman treatments and tortures, just for having been suspected of collaborating with the Maï-Maïs.

The Government of the Democratic Republic of Congo through the ministries of Foreign Affairs and International Cooperation, Information and Tourism, Social Affairs and family, and Human Rights, would like to thank you for its invitation requested this day.

The Government of the Democratic Republic of Congo would like to, once more, take advantage of this opportunity to call, through you, on the international community about the great number of massacres committed periodically on the territory of its state, of which there is an eloquent silence from its part [UN Security Council].

Indeed, in constant and blatant violations of relevant provisions of international instruments such as the United Nations Charter, the Charter of the Organization of African Unity, the Charter of International Human Rights, the African Charter of Human Rights and Peoples' Rights, Geneva Conventions of 1949 and its Additional Protocols, the Convention relative to the Rights of Children, the Declaration on the Protection of Women and Children in Periods of Emergence and Armed Conflict of 14 December, 1974, Rwanda, Uganda and Burundi have besieged since 2 August, 1998 a part of our national territory and illustrate themselves in commission of odious and abominable crimes.

Besides the massacres of Kasika on 24 August, 1998 with more than eight hundred dead, of Kilungutwe in September 1998, of Kitutu on 2 September, 1998, of Makoloba on 31 December, 1998 with a thousand persons killed, mainly women, children and elderly persons, of Ngweshe on 15 February, 1999, of Kamituga on 15 March, 1999, of Lubarisi and Kiumba on 9 May, 1999, common national memory also retains other war and crimes against humanity such as: the massacres of Kasala in the High-Lomami on the night of 27 July to 28 July, 1999 where about forty people, without any distinction of age or sex, were locked in the huts and burnt alive; the massacres of Kongolo in Katanga in the month of August 1999 where the number of victims is estimated at 200 persons; the massacres of Kimbumbu, Nonge, and Sola, and the one perpertrated on 23 October, 1999 at the market of Kalungwe at 40 km of Uvira by Rwandan, Ugandan and Burundian troops.

Since two days ago, the international community has been informed through the dynamism of Congolese youth gathering together within the group, which continues to resist against the aggressors in the east of the country, of the perpetration by the aggressors of crimes practically unimaginable to ordinary people in this ending century.

Indeed, from 15 to 22 November, 1999, at least 15 women have been buried alive in the farming districts of Bulinzi, Bongombe, and Ngando in the region of Mwenga, Sud-Kivu province, after being submitted to unhuman treatments and tortures, just for been suspected of collaborating with the Maï-Maïs.

These odious acts, which have become a daily reality for the Congolese people under occupation, constitute manifest, grave and programmed violations of international humanitarian law, in particular of article 76, paragraph 1 of Additional Protocol 1 to the Geneva Conventions on the Protection of Woman in period of war.

If inhumation or incineration in all dignity of the dead in a war zone constitutes a conventional requirement and moral regulated by the Geneva Conventions and its Additional Protocols, what can be said of a state, as it happens, Rwanda, whose regular troops proceed to the burial of alive persons on an aggressed territory?

Given the seriousness of these facts, the Government of Public Salvation of the Democratic Republic of Congo denounces, once again, the silence, passivity showing certain duplicity, even the complicity of the international community.

The Congolese people through its Government of Public Salvation have, since the beginning of the aggression, respected its international commitments in particular protecting all persons at risk because of the war.

Besides, the Democratic Republic of Congo has totally been involved in the processes of the Lusaka Cease-fire Agreement. Such crimes of which are victims, in a systematic and planned way, Congolese women and children, constitute a grave violation of this agreement, which in its article I, point 3.c., stipulates that "the Cease-fire shall entail ... all acts of violence against the civilian population by respecting and protecting human rights."

The international community should essentially condemn and without unambiguous such blatant and massive violations of fundamental human rights. For, the politic of double standard cannot be justified when it comes to protecting human dignity be it of a Kosovar, Rwandan, or Congolese.

Paradoxically, instead of denouncing and condemning established massacres committed on the territory of the Democratic Republic of Congo by Rwandan, Ugandan, and Burundian troops of aggression against its populations, members of the international community are working on to denounce an alleged genocide against the Tutsis in preparation from the Congolese territory. But what do they wait for to advise these same Tutsi armed troops to withdraw from a territory they injustly occupy, and to work for the restoration of peace, instead of granting them by aids and debt reliefs—which constitute as much as a reward for the aggression, war crimes, and crimes against humanity.

The Government of Public Salvation, however, repeats its urgent demands on the following:

the definite condemnation of the armed aggression against the Democratic republic of Congo; for, it is the origin of all the other human rights and international humanitarian law violations;

the definite condemnation of all massacres in general and the last crimes committed in the Democratic Republic of Congo;

the constitution of an international investigation about the massacres and other crimes.

[Signed by]
The Minister of Social Affairs and Family
Anastasie Moleko
The Minister of Human Rights
Léonard She Okitundu
The Minister of State in charge of Foreign Affairs and International Cooperation
Yerodia Abdoulay Ndombasi

What other legal evidence did the international community and the UN request from the DR Congo to prosecute Rwandan and Ugandan invading troops in the DRC. for the commission of gross violations of international human rights and humanitarian law in the Congolese occupied territories? The truth of the matter is that the UN Security Council never demanded legal proof from the Congolese government and victims of human rights violations because nobody over there wants such evidence. One wonders what the guys at the UN Security Council think of the fact that "...Tutsi soldiers developed a system of execution [killing] consisting of the fact that the person to be executed digs her own tomb. The case of the manager of Brasserie, Mr. Buta, who dug his own tomb to be buried in it."[99] Is there anybody there at the UN Security Council who is prepared to die that way or see his or her loved ones be subjected to such evil and ignoble type of death? In fact, such act is in violation of Article 33, paragraph 3 of the Geneva Conventions IV as well as Article 51.2 of the Additional Protocol I, which state that in any armed conflict, it is forbidden to use acts or threats of violence in which the main objective is to spread terror among the populations.

The Congolese government reported further that, "in addition to HIV, the aggressors have developed other techniques of insidious elimination of civil population in the occupied territories: the technique consisted of immersing the victim in a cask of rusted water for a while."[100] This barbaric and criminal act violates Article 35, paragraphs 1 and 2 of the Geneva Conventions Additonal Protocol I, which stipulates that in any armed conflict, the right of parties to choose methods or ways of war is not limited; and therefore, it is forbidden to use arms, ammunition, and materials that may cause unnecessary damages to civilian populations. Likewise, such criminal conduct is in violation of Article 51, paragraph 1 of the aforementioned Protocol, as well as article 3 of the Declaration of Human Rights, and article 6 of the International Pact Relative to Civil and Political Rights.

The Mail & Guardian,[101] a Johannesburg Newspaper, gave a bright illustration of what was happening until 2001 in the occupied territories of the DR Congo, in terms of sexual violence and crimes committed by the invaders and their Congolese allies:

It was while she was on her way to collect the body of her sister-in-law last year that Christine was raped. She resisted, so her attacker—a member of the main rebel group in eastern Democratic Republic of Congo, she believes—shot her twice in the vagina. "That taught the whole village a lesson," she says, shifting with the carefulness of someone well used to pain. "No one fights back anymore."

Christine (25) could have mistaken her attacker's identity: Congolese, Rwandan, and Burundian armies and rebel armies have all tramped through Kabondozi, close by Lake Tanganyika, in the past four years. "Men in uniform come all the time and when they catch you, they rape you."

...By the middle of last year [2001] 2.5 million people were estimated to have died because of the war in eastern Congo. But there is no better measure of the horror of the conflict than the daily expectation of rape.

"We're talking about thousands of women being raped every day, by everybody," says Claude Jibidar, the United Nations humanitarian coordinator in the area. "For me this is now the most horrific aspect of the war."

Most of eastern Congo is off-limits to peacekeepers and aid workers, making statistical accuracy impossible, but in village after village the stories are the same. In the town of Shabunda last year up to 2,400 women were held hostage by a Rwandan interhamwe militia and repeatedly raped. In Kanyola district, a scattering of villages near Lake Kivu, 28 women were raped in public in February alone, a local human rights group says.

For every woman who admits being raped, according to Héritiers de la Justice, a human rights group, many more choose to stay silent.

Francine (20) does not have the luxury of choice. Three Mayi-Mayi fighters took turns to rape her in front of her family. When done, they killed her parents-in-law and niece. Pregnant at the time, she later miscarried.

During the Rwandan genocide—which spilled over into Congo, sparking the war—Tutsi women were raped systematically to spread terror and Aids. But in eastern Congo rape is the product of the general anarchy ravaging the country, Héritiers de la Justice says.

A senior official of the Rwandan-backed Congolese Rally for Democracy (RCD) confirms this. "There's a lot of insecurity, people are afraid to go to their fields; every day in the bush women are being raped," says Benjamin Serukiza, deputy governor of South Kivu province. "Some of our men could be guilty, though 90% of rapes are committed by the other groups."

There is no way to confirm his figure, but in a grimy hospital in Bukavu, the provincial capital, there is another Francine, this one just 14 years old. Two years ago three Mayi-Mayi fighters killed her father and raped her, after accusing them of growing food for the RCD. Six months later an RCD fighter raped her in the forest after accusing her of supplying the Mayi-Mayi. "The second time, I knew what to expect, so I passed out," says Francine, dandling her baby, Pascal—her last surviving relative, and the product of rape.

...As the violence continues—displacing communities, dividing families, degrading the culture—Héritiers de la Justice says that rape by civilians is beginning to rise as well. "Congo has become infected by violence," says Wakenge. "When the war ends, we will not only need our schools, houses, and roads rebuilding, we will also need our consciences healing."

The other serious illustration of sexual violence in the occupied territories of the DRC comes from the following Human Rights Watch article:[102]

"War continues to rage in eastern Congo. Within that larger war, combatants carry out another war—sexual violence against women and girls," said Alison Des Forges, senior advisor to the Africa division of Human Rights Watch.

The report, which is based on numerous interviews with victims, witnesses, and officials, details crimes of sexual violence committed by soldiers of the Rwandan army and its Congolese ally, the Rassemblement congolais pour la démocratie (RCD), as well as armed groups opposed to them—Congolese Mai Mai rebels, and Burundian and Rwandan armed groups.

These combatants raped women and girls during military operations to punish the local civilian population for allegedly supporting the "enemy." In other cases, Mai Mai rebels and other armed groups abducted women and girls and forced them to provide sexual services and domestic labor, sometimes for periods of more than a year.

Some rapists attacked their victims with extraordinary brutality. In two cases, assailants inserted firearms into the vaginas of their victims and shot them. In other cases combatants mutilated the sexual organs of the women with knives or razor blades. Some attacked girls as young as five years of age and women as old as eighty.

Assailants often attacked women and girls engaged in the usual activities necessary to the livelihoods of their families: cultivating their fields, collecting firewood, or going to market. By doing so, the assailants further disrupted the already precarious economic life of the region.

Medical services in eastern Congo have nearly totally collapsed, leaving most victims of rape and other sexual torture with little hope for treatment of injuries or of sexually transmitted diseases, including testing and post-exposure treatment for HIV/AIDS. Some experts estimate that HIV prevalence among military forces in the region may be higher than 50 percent. Rape in these circumstances can be a death sentence.

The report also documents the rejection of some women and girls by their husbands, families, and wider communities because they were raped or because they are thought to be infected with HIV/AIDS. As one such ostracized woman told Human Rights Watch researchers, "My body has become sad. I have no happiness."

With the collapse of official services, Congolese churches and civil society organizations have used their scarce resources to assist the victims. Local organizations, which have also documented sexual violence in the region, contributed to the report.

It seems that people like Kagame and Museveni will not learn respect for human life while in mortality. They need to be stopped before the entire African continent goes into a costly and irreparable war because of their foolishness and criminally-minded nature. According to article 3 of the International Criminal Tribunal for Rwanda, a court that deals with those who killed Kagame's brothers and sisters (and whose court one prays may judge Kagame one day for the same crimes), murder is a "crime against humanity when committed against civilian population, as a part of widespread or systematic attack."[103] Whenever Rwandan and Ugandan soldiers fighting the DR Congo troops fell into Mayi-Mayi's ambush, they, in reprisal, systematically killed hundreds of innocent civilians living in the surrounding villages where the attack took place. This situation became a pattern since the beginning of the war of aggression in the DR Congo.

In addition, Rwandan and Ugandan invaders forcibly recruited children, who received a brief training of a few weeks and then were sent to the front lines to fight their own brothers, sisters, parents, and nation. Human Rights Watch reported that "the rebels re-enlisted hundreds of former child soldiers they found in transit camps run by humanitarian agencies in Bukavu and Kisangani where they were following skill-upgrading programs prior to their planned reunification with their families."[104] This practice was in violation of international human rights and humanitarian laws, and is indeed a war crime. But Kagame and Museveni probably thought that this state of affairs did not concern them, since they are in a situation of total war against whichever nation stands in their way. Even the UN Special Rapporteur on the human rights situation in the DR Congo is of the opinion that "the use of children in warfare is ... more frequent in the case of the RCD ... There has been no reduction in the number of child soldiers in areas controlled by the RCD or MLC."[105] In this case, children as young as nine years old were used by these predators in order to satisfy their personal, selfish, and bestial ambitions in the DRC.

Dr. Reginald Moreels experienced the following human right abuse related to child soldiers in the occupied territories of the DR Congo: "Throughout the DRC, I came across child soldiers. As a war surgeon, I have operated on many of them. It has always repulsed and saddened me to see [children] with not only amputated limbs but amputated souls. I feel strongly that the arms dealers deserve to be brought to justice, with no mitigating circumstances, before International Tribunals. The reality of the situation, where many children are excluded, represents a crisis of family ethics. A child recruited by the army, thrown out in the road or lured into sorcery is one less mouth to feed. This runs totally contrary to family, and African, values. It is societal cancer hiding behind a shameful level of poverty."[106]

Rwandan and Ugandan invaders in the DR Congo have systematically and completely destroyed the already poor social and economical fabric left by the late dictator Mobutu. IRIN reported that "the UN Humanitarian Coordinator for the DR Congo, Darioush Bayandor, said a UN-NGO-donor team, which visited the areas of Moba, Kalemie, and Nyunzu ... found severe economic depression, acute malnutrition, and deserted towns around the Cease-fire line. 'The existence of 1.1 millions of war-displaced people within the DRC and across its frontiers is just one facet of the humanitarian drama in this country ... We are embarrassed to continue sending out these missions because they create expectations among the badly-hit population that someone is finally coming to their rescue.'"[107]

It is important that the world understands that there are more people displaced in this war, combined with the dramatic situation of former Rwandan, Burundian, and Ugandan refugees, than there were in Kuwait, Kosovo, and East Timor. According to Dr. Réginald Moreels, early last year "there [were] 2,100,000 internally displaced Congolese, 330,000 refugees from neighboring countries and 190,000 Congolese who have fled the country,"[108] because of this war of occupation against the DRC. But, unfortunately, Mother Africa is a forgotten continent, with her wars, tragedies, and human calamities.

In any town or village they passed by, looting, stealing, and destruction of property, as well as burning of villages, became a custom for RPA and

Ugandan soldiers and allies.[109] Such conduct from those who would supposedly have brought "a new and prosperous civilization" to the Congolese people, was in violation of article 50 of the Geneva Convention. The Rwandan and Ugandan armed forces were also the cause of an insane disruption of the polio vaccine in the city of Kisangani, which occurred when both forces turned guns on each other between 14-16 August, 1999, thus undermining the health of the Congolese children, the future leaders of the DR Congo. This armed conflict between Rwandan and Ugandan armies in Kisangani led to the loss of 3 million vaccines, according to the DR Congo government.[110]

Similarly and as already mentioned, the same armies committed crimes of war. For instance, they deliberately cut off power and water supplying the capital city, Kinshasa; this evil act resulted in the death of hundreds of patients in the hospitals, most of them infants and other small children. They destroyed both public and private properties in the occupied zones of the DRC. It is quite true that "death and destruction of homes and property on such a scale would be considered a national disaster in any sane society"[111] and modern civilization, but in the DR Congo.

Here is another excerpt from the late and former governor of North Kivu, one of the DR Congo provinces that was under foreign aggression by Rwanda and Uganda. The interview was conducted again by Colette Braeckman:

Question: Have you noticed violence, exactions, stealing?

Answer: In any case, all the vehicles have disappeared. At my office, for example, we have lost twelve cars. It is the same thing at all the UN agencies, private companies. Since those cars could not have gone to the forest, and as we do not see them anymore in Bukavu, I infer that they have crossed the Rwandan border. Besides, the cellular phones, radiotelephones have been confiscated; all communication with the outside is prohibited. In Uvira, some old scores were settled, kidnapping of suspects. At the beginning of the war, the officers, mostly Rwandans, had personal dungeons in the houses they lived in.

Question: What is the situation on a humanitarian plan?

Answer: Very bad. There is cholera at Shabunda, hospitals do not have medicines, the stocks of Unicef have been looted, the schools are empty because parents do not have money and are afraid that the boys may be enrolled in the army, the enterprises like Pharmakina have stopped working and are selling their land ... Boys are practicing passive resistance against the occupation…"[112] This situation, which is a serious war crime, existed in all the occupied territories of the DR Congo throughout the war.

As one might have noticed, Rwanda and Uganda were determined to fight a total and dirty war in and for the conquest of the DR Congo, a sovereign and independent state, and a Member state of the United Nations. "The concept of a dirty war has the notion of human rights violations built right into it… All war inevitably generates excesses and extremes. The concept of a dirty war justifies and even glorifies these excesses,"[113] to the point that the perpetrators believe that their conduct is normal and humanly acceptable. But, as one can see, this war would indeed be long and popular if Rwandans and Ugandans did not come to their senses and withdraw from the territories of the DR Congo, and abstain for further aggression.

4. The Crime of Terrorism

If there is a crime well spoken about at the beginning of this 21st century, it is the crime of terrorism. Likewise, if there is a crime about which the international community has not yet come into a consensus, it is the crime of terrorism. Nor did the Rome Statute or the coming into effect of the ICC ease the tension between different advocates. While there is an agreement in the use of the term "terrorism" in the case of an international conflict and outside foreign actors, individuals, organizations, and states, the controversy is great when there is an internal conflict. For, what some qualify a "terrorist act;" others take it as a "resistance act." Therefore, it is difficult to characterize "terrorism" as a criminal act in international humanitarian law.

For instance, awhile ago, some authors argued that "one obvious difficulty with using the term [terrorist act] within IHL is that, as has often been pointed out, one man's terrorist is another man's freedom fighter. Apartheid leaders regarded the fight against their policies as terrorism and viewed anti-apartheid activists as terrorists. Anti-apartheid activists regarded themselves as guerrillas fighting an illegitimate regime, something condoned by international law."[114]

Despite differences in the definition of terrorism, the following definitions are retained for the purposes of this work:

Terrorism is "[t]he use or threat of violence to intimidate or cause panic, esp. as a means of affecting political conduct."[115] According to the OAU, a "Terrorist act" means: (a) any act which is a violation of the criminal laws of a State Party and which may endanger the life, physical integrity or freedom of, or cause serious injury or death to, any person, any number or group of persons or causes or may cause damage to public or private property, natural resources, environmental or cultural heritage and is calculated or intended to: (i) intimidate, put in fear, force, coerce, or induce any government, body, institution, the general public, or any segment thereof, to do or abstain from doing any act, or to adopt or abandon a particular standpoint, or to act according to certain principles; or (ii) disrupt any public service, the delivery of any essential service to the public or to create a public emergency; or (iii) create general insurrection in a state; (b) any promotion, sponsoring, contribution to, command, aid, incitement, encouragement, attempt, threat, conspiracy, organizing, or procurement of any person, with the intent to commit any act referred to in paragraph (a) (i) to (iii)."[116]

The United Nations General Assembly defined terrorism as "Criminal acts intended or calculated to provoke a state of terror in the general public, a group of persons or particular persons for political purposes are in any circumstance unjustifiable, whatever the considerations of a political, philosophical, ideological, racial, ethnic, religious, or any other nature that may be invoked to justify them"[117]

President Nelson Mandela asserts that, "a terrorist is a person or group of persons, or a state that targets innocent people in order to accomplish its purposes."[118] Thus, it may be said that a terrorist is an individual or group of individuals, private or public organization, or state, that commits premeditated or non-premeditated acts of violence terror, who or which substantially encourages such acts by advising or assisting materially an individual or group of individuals, private or public organization, or state, or who/which harbors those who he, she, or it knows or has reason to know has conspired to commit such acts, acts which causes terror and whose effect is terror. Terrorism is the result of such act.

At the October 2002 Inter-American Commission on Human Rights it was recorded that "[m]uch of the international law on terrorism has taken the form of multilateral treaties. Major anti-terrorism instruments include the International Convention Against the Taking of Hostages, the Convention for the Suppression of Unlawful Acts Against the Safety of Civil Aviation, and the Convention on the Prevention and Punishment of Crimes Against Internationally Protected Persons, including Diplomatic Agents."[119] These treaties have the following in common: first, legislation should be incorporated in domestic laws so that offenses derivative from terrorist acts are pursued through proper channels in domestic courts; second, states' parties are required to investigate, prosecute, or extradite alleged offenders; third, states' parties must take preventive measures to combat terrorism; and fourth, states' parties need not to consider certain types of crimes as political offenses, or committed with political motives, to enable suspected terrorist criminals to escape justice or to not be totally subject to the full extent of justice.

The Rwando-Ugandan illegal occupation of the DR Congo was entirely an act of terrorism. Similarly, by assisting Rwanda and Uganda in that adventure, all so-called rebels committed terrorism. Likewise, it is no hard argument to assert that any state, organization, or group of people that aided, assisted, gave moral and/or material support to the aggressors of the DRC and their accomplices, while it knew or should have known that such aid, assistance, and/or support was used directly or indirectly to maintain the illegal occupation of the DR Congo and the commission of atrocities on civilian populations, committed terrorism.

As discussed thus far, Rwanda, Uganda, and Congolese "rebels," use[d] ... violence to intimidate or cause panic, [but] especially as a means of affecting political conduct" in the DR Congo during the entire illegal occupation of their armed troops.

Evidence shows that Rwanda, Uganda, and allies' military campaigns in the DR Congo during the 1998-2002 occupation "endanger[ed] the life, physical integrity or freedom of, or cause[d] serious injury or death to, any person, any number or group of persons or cause[d] ... to public or private property, natural resources, environmental or cultural heritage, and [wa]s calculated or intended to: (i) intimidate, put in fear, force, coerce, or induce [the DR Congo] ... government, body, institution, the general public or any segment thereof, to do or abstain from doing any act, or to adopt or abandon a particular standpoint, or to act according to certain principles; or (ii) disrupt any public service, the delivery of any essential service to the public or to create a public emergency; or (iii) create general insurrection in a state; (b) any promotion, sponsoring, contribution to, command, aid, incitement, encouragement, attempt, threat, conspiracy, organizing, or procurement of any person, with the intent to commit any act referred to in paragraph (a) (i) to (iii)."

One may honestly recognize that those "[c]riminal acts [that cost the lives of about three and a half millions innocent civilians and which were] intended or calculated to provoke a state of terror in the general public, a group of persons or particular persons for political purposes [we]re in any circumstance [selfish and totally] unjustifiable [and unreasonable], whatever the considerations of a political, philosophical, ideological, racial, ethnic, religious, or any other nature that may be invoked to justify them." Further, one should acknowledge that "[p]eople committed to justice and law and human rights must never descend to the level of the perpetrators of such acts. That is the most important distinction of all."[120]

Rwanda, through Paul Kagame and his lieutenants, Uganda, through Oweri Museveni and his foxes, and the different "rebel" leaders in the DRC with their subordinates, committed exactly those criminal acts referred to above with the sole political intent of replacing the Congolese government and the like, to destabilize the country and create chaos. In their barbaric military adventure, while committing terrorist acts, these individuals did not leave any stone unturned to accomplish their purposes. They instigated mass killings of innocent civilians, intimidated, put in fear, forced, coerced or induced [the DR Congo] ... government ... the general public or any segment thereof, to do or abstain from doing any act, or to adopt or abandon a particular standpoint, or to act according to certain principles; [and] ... (ii) disrupted ... public service, the delivery of any essential service to the public [and] ... create[d] a public emergency; [but they failed to] ... (iii) create general insurrection in a state," but they miscalculated the degree of Congolese nationalism's power.

Rwanda, through Paul Kagame and his lieutenants, Uganda, through Oweri Museveni and his foxes, and the different "rebel" leaders in the DRC with their subordinates, committed terrorist acts in the DR Congo because they individually and severely acted in a manner that enforced those aforementioned acts that international legislations proscribed. How can one call the hijacking of private civilian commercial planes by Rwandan and Ugandan armed forces in August 1998, planes that were used to transport those troops with arms, ammunition, and other military equipment, from the east of the DRC to the west, crossing the entire country, where these forces committed acts in breach of international human rights and humanitarian laws, with the sole intent to create public emergency, general insurrection, and with the sole aim of affecting political conduct? What is the difference in substance between such acts of violence and the 9/11/01 terror act on US soil?

Indeed, in this case, "the Organization of International Civil Aviation is also called in because the violation by Uganda, Rwanda, and Burundi of the

Montreal Convention of 23 September, 1971 relating to the repression of unlawful acts directed against the security of civil aviation. It is not acceptable that the acts of terrorism and air piracy committed by the aggressors go unpunished. For the record, it should be reminded that, in particular, that on 9 October, 1998 the aggressors shot down a Boeing 727 owned by Congo Airlines after take off from Kindu airport, resulting in the death of the crew as well as of 37 women and children."[121] Only time will tell whether the perpetrators of such uncivilized acts will escape international justice again.

Until the time arrives, in the matter at issue of the illegal occupation of the DR Congo, Rwanda, through Paul Kagame and his lieutenants, Uganda, through Oweri Museveni and his foxes, and the different Congolese "rebel" leaders and their men are likely to be held liable as well for terrorism and must stand trial.

5. The Masquerade of the Lendu-Hema Conflict

Few words need to be said about the Lendu and Hema conflict before concluding this chapter. Today's international media attention in the DR Congo is focused on what is happening in the Ituri province where both Lendus and Hemas are killing each other and are committing serious violations of international human rights. No need to mention to this effect that genocide and crimes against humanity are thus taking place in this region and that accountability shall be established and perpetrators of such atrocities punish to the fullest extent of both Congolese and international laws.

However, few know the origin of this fratricide fighting between the Lendus and the Hemas. This fact is first the result of the manipulation of the international media. In addition, it is because the international community wants the people of the world to learn only fabricated stories and complete lies with regard to the DR Congo's tragedies resulting from the Rwanda-Uganda-led war of invasion.

Suffice to mention that this conflict is not a separate or new hostility from the main war of invasion orchestrated by Rwanda and Uganda. The Lendu-Hema conflict is directly and inherently linked to the Rwandan-Ugandan-led war of occupation in the DRC. As long as the hostilities between Lendus and Hemas shall continue, the Congolese war of aggression has not yet ended.

That is the simple truth, hard to swallow by many for sure.

This conflict was planned and coordinated from Kampala (Uganda) with the sole and clear intent of creating instability and chaos after the so-called pull out of Ugandan forces in the Ituri region. It is no secret that the Lendus are militarily trained and equipped by Uganda. The insecurity created by this conflict gives a justification to Uganda to claim that the DRC central government is unable to bring stability to this border region with Uganda. And since this fighting had negative effects on the other side of the Ugandan border, the UDF at the time appointed will have no choice then to intervene, and as alibi, in order to bring "stability" in the Ituri province.

This evil design only means another well-planned occupation of the DRC. For instance, "...Uganda claims that the withdrawal of the last of its 9,000 soldiers from this area created a security vacuum, renewing clashes between rival militias. Of course, these militias are proxy armies for Ugandan, Rwandan ... forces and tensions between Hemas and Lendus were exacerbated by the occupation of the area by Ugandan forces several years earlier."[122] In addition, Uganda also planned this conflict to demonstrate to the world that the DR Congo is not free from tribal wars, as are Rwanda and Burundi. But the truth is that before the Ugandan army occupies the Ituri province, Lendus and Hemas lived in peace with each other.

Further, the DR Congo war of occupation was characterized as the economic war. For, while the occupying forces aimed at toppling the DR Congo government and replacing it with a more favorable one that will serve their interests and those of their allies, they also plundered systematically Congolese natural, mineral, and forest resources, as well as other forms of wealth to fuel the war and enrich their personal financial accounts. Given that the Ituri region is the very same area where some of those Congolese riches come from, setting up a sophisticated and underground mechanism and network where illegal exploitation and pillage of the Congolese national assets shall continue after the withdrawal of the Ugandan armed forces, therefore rendering that province ungovernable, was part of the malicious aforethought plan of the enemies of the DR Congo and its people.

Thus, Museveni and his lieutenants shall be liable for the current crisis in the Ituri province and shall share responsibility for the breach of peace, and all other international violations of human rights and international humanitarian legal norms committed in the Ituri region, because direct and circumstantial evidence prove the involvement of his armed troops.

6. Some Evidence of Human Rights Violations by Rwandans, Ugandans, and Congolese Allies

The Congolese people, in particular, and those in the world with a sense of justice, still ask as to what other evidence the UN needs to go out after the authors of the horrible crimes the Congolese in the occupied territories of their country suffered, in the hands of Rwanda, Ugandan armies, and their Congolese accomplices. There is, indeed, more evidence to prosecute those who commanded the invading troops, the soldiers who committed human rights violations, both Rwandans, Ugandans, and Congolese "rebels" and their leaders. By the way, the UN was in possession of the official written accounts of these hindering crimes from the DR Congo government since 1999. But to date, they are kept secret instead of being investigated and prosecuted.

6.1. Written Testimonial Evidence

In section 3 above, Christine and Francine's stories of brutal rapes are told. Below are more accounts of other victims of these tragic sexual crimes.

Whereas, the same flawed document imposed on the Congolese government and nation, the Lusaka Cease-fire Agreement, forbids the sexual violence in its article I.3.c, as well, article 27.2 of the Geneva Convention relative to the protection of civilian population states that women shall be specially protected against any violation to their dignity, in particular against rape, enforced prostitution, and any offense against decency, the ten women[123]—some whose accounts are given herein—were raped by Rwandan soldiers at Musanjie village at 12 km from Kabinda in October 1999.

There are: 1. Mwissange Kayaya (19 years old); 2. Kasongo Kasongo (19 years old); 3. Mobeshe Lukueka (55 years old); 4. Ntumba Kasongo (35 years old); 5. Tshita Sapu (60 years old); 6. Lumanu Kasongo (33 years old); 7. Epindu Kalobo (20 years old); 8. Ngoyi Nsomwe (32 years old); 9. Shala Malangu (21 years old); 10. Binienge Tshikudi (20 years old). The testimonies of three of these victimized women are reproduced below. These women were lucky to be alive for some did not escape such felony crimes by Rwandan and Ugandan invading armed forces. That was the case of Ms. Nicole Mikunga, 22 years old, who was repeatedly raped and then killed after being beaten with sticks at the head.

1. Testimony of Mrs. Ngoy Nsomwe, born in 1966, married and mother of six children:

It was on 25 November, 1999 that I was arrested at 35 km from Kabinda. I went to get cassava bread to feed my children and husband. On my way back in the middle of the forest, soldiers surrounded us. There was a small house where the commandant of Rwandan [soldiers] was staying. This was really in the middle of the forest. One of the soldiers holds me on the arm and asks me to show them where the Congolese [soldiers] where hiding. Since I did not want, he put me inside the Commandant's house where several members of Kabinda's district where held, civilians who went hunting and who were sought by their families for some days.

Few minutes later, I see five Rwandan soldiers approaching me and pull me outside. They undress me and throw my child in the field. Two soldiers tie my hands and two others my legs just like on a cross. They were about twenty, in queue, and raped me one after the other. I cried, but it was in vain. Nobody had pity about me. After that group of twenty soldiers, I saw another group coming and that's the time I passed out. I found myself naked at Kabinda's District in front of the MONUC observers and the FAC. I did not know how to walk and they transferred me directly to the hospital.

2. Testimony of Mrs. Mobeshe Lukueka, born in 1954, married, mother of nine children, 2 girls and 7 boys:

When they arrested me, they took me behind the small house and I saw other women being taken into the bush. One woman for twenty Rwandan soldiers. There were about ten groups, given that we were ten [women]. They first hit and tortured me because I clapped one of the Rwandan soldiers.

Then I was tied with a cord like a boar and soldiers of the age of my children raped me. Given my age, I could not support the weight of several men and my genitals gave up. I was bleeding like a tap. Despite the blood, they [Rwandans] were still coming [raping me]. Then around 5 o'clock [AM], they asked me to go back to the village otherwise they would kill me. I crawled until I met the FAC and the Zimbabweans [allied armed forces], before I was taken naked to the MONUC. After this incident, my husband kicked me out of the marital home because I was raped. Today, my children are left to themselves to live up to this sad account.

3. Testimony of Ms. Shala Malangu, born in 1978, single, holder of a High school diploma in Education from Kabinda Institute:

I was arrested at 12 km from Kabinda with my bag of cassava bread that I just bought for my parents. The soldiers took everything I had and threw me in the bush. Five of them followed after me and raped me in turn. Then, they chased us away from the forest. I ran on all fours until 5 km from Kabinda where I found the FAC. I even spent three days at the hospital.

6.2. Photographic Evidence

The pictures below were reproduced with permission and were taken from Ed. Marek's website.[124]

Ellen Knickmeyer of AP and Danna Harman of **The Christian Science Monitor** have sounded the warning klaxon of humanitarian horror in the region of Kabinda, in eastern DR Congo. We have fetched the gruesome pictures, pictures that can stand by those of the Holocaust and, except for the skin color, look much the same…

At the Kigali Airport, former President Clinton said, "No more," No mas. There is more. It is here, and elsewhere in this region. There has to be accountability…

These pictures reflect sin in its worst form, crimes against humanity, against our most helpless humanity, our children. Damn all of you who are responsible for this. Damn you all. We might choose to sacrifice our place in heaven just so we can meet your ass in hell and tear it to shreds.

All photos of May 5, 2001 are credited to a heroine [who] has brought these pictures out, **Christine Nesbitt**, Associated Press. All photos of May 12 and 13 are credited to a hero who brought these pictures out, **Sayyid Azim**, Associated Press. Christine and Sayyid, you'll go to heaven while the rest us of take care of the perpetrators of these horrors in hell.

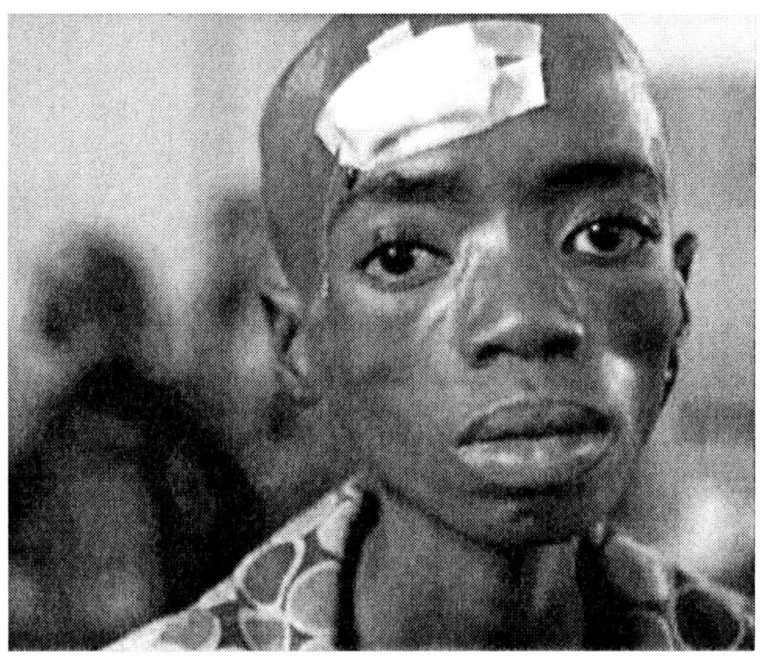

This is the look of horror. Suffering from malnutrition, Motombe Nyeba, 15, sits in the Kabinda Hospital in the Congo, Saturday May 5, 2001. Nyeba came from rebel-occupied territory looking for medical help. Adults and children reaching the front-line hospital in Kabinda told of countless civilians succumbing to disease and hunger in burned, looted villages cut off throughout Congo's 2 1/2-year-old war.

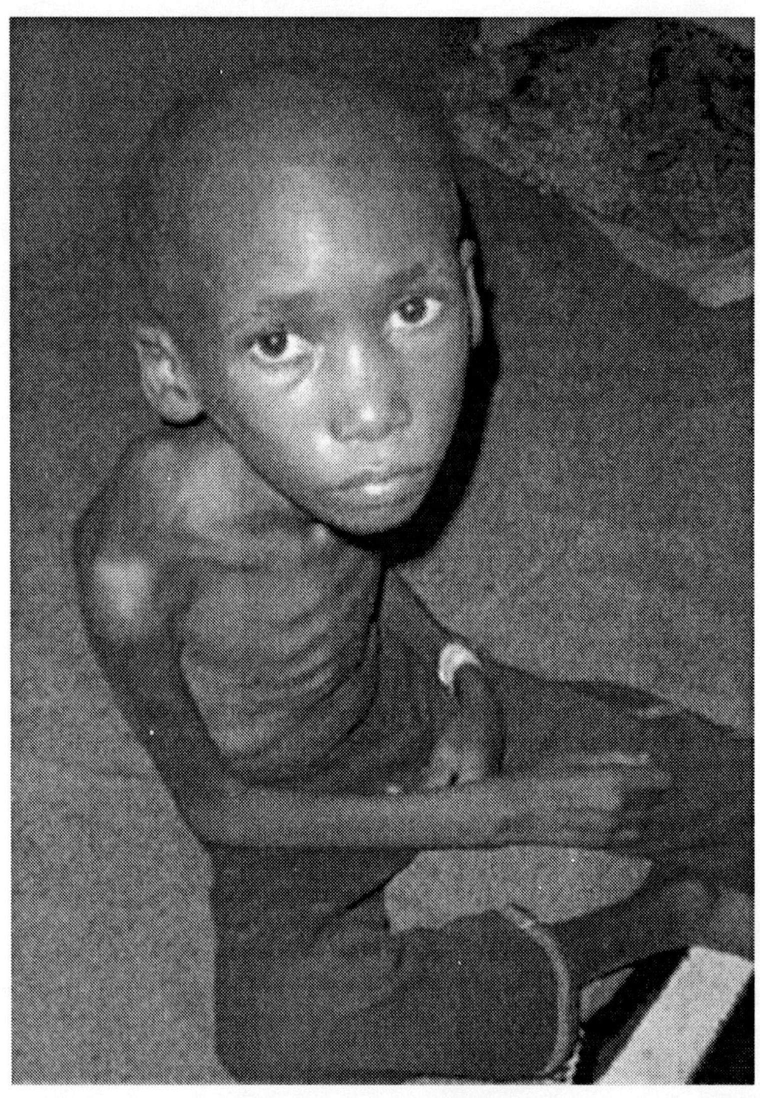

This is the look of utter disbelief. Muganja Kakinga, a 7-year-old malnourished child at Kalemie's main hospital, Sunday, May 13, 2001. The question on young Kakinga's face is, *Why me? What did I do to deserve this?* What's the answer?

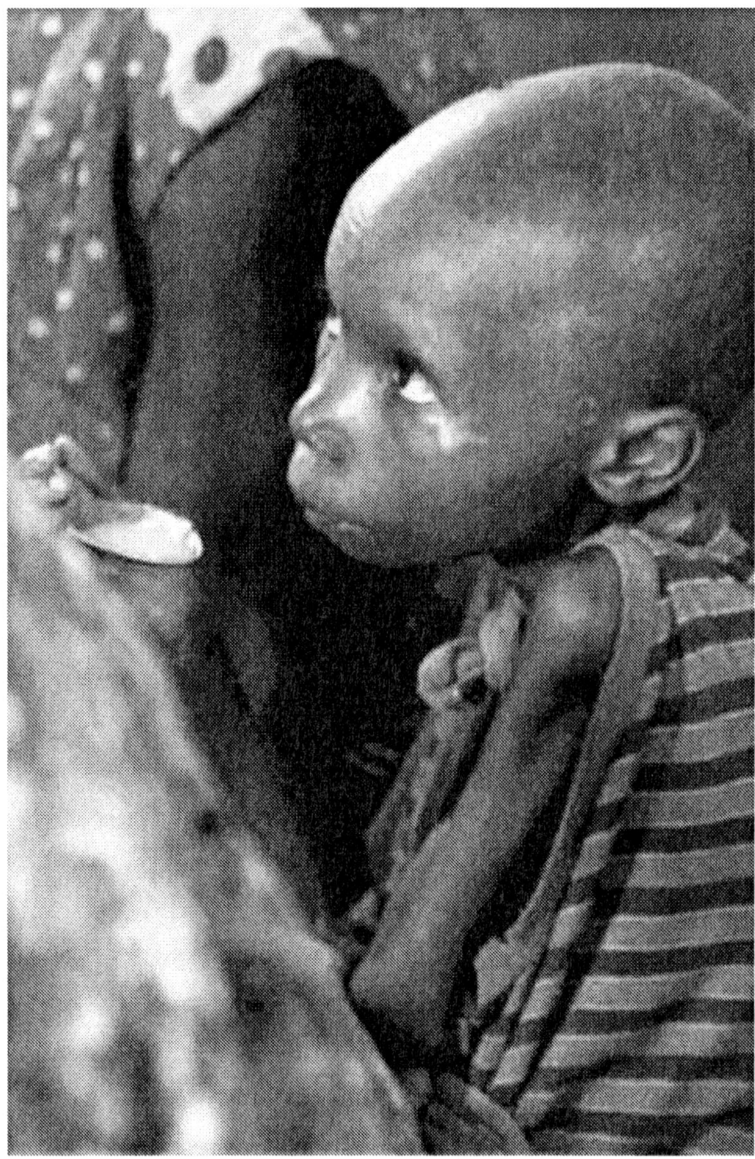

This is the look of disbelief. Suffering from malnutrition, Ngoyi Malango, 8, eats porridge in the Kabinda Hospital in the Congo, Saturday May 5, 2001. The child came from rebel-occupied territory looking for medical help with his father after his mother died.

This is the look of anger. A young boy suffering from malnutrition eats porridge in the Kabinda Hospital in the Congo, Saturday, May 5, 2001.

This is the look of a mother's despair. Her severely malnourished son battles for his life at Kalemie's main hospital on Sunday, May 13, 2001.

This is the look of desperation. A mother washes her daughter who is suffering from severe malnutrition in the Kabinda Hospital in the Congo, Saturday, May 5, 2001.

These are the looks of care. Mbanza Ngoyi washes her 5-year-old daughter, Mbakule Ntambue, who is suffering from extreme malnutrition in the Kabinda Hospital in the Congo, Saturday, May 5, 2001.

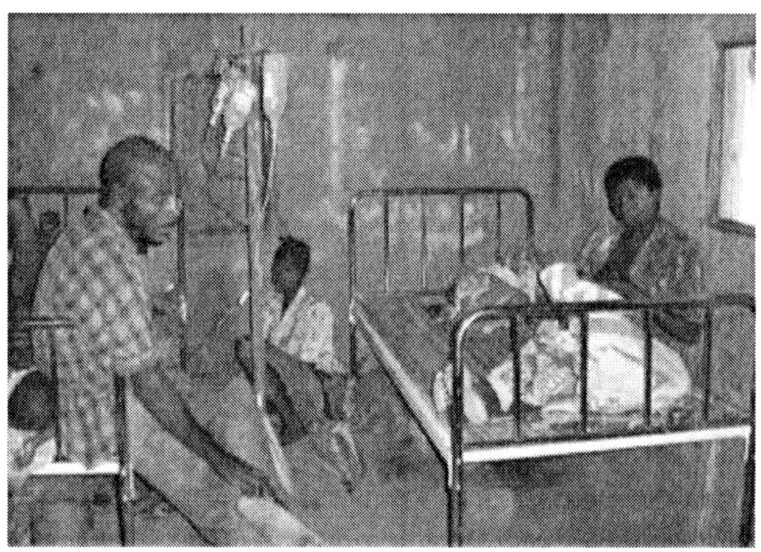

This is the look of a pathetic healthcare facility, and a father who cannot look the camera in the eye. Sleeping in every space available, the young and the old cram the two-bed dispensary in the Congo village of Tobac, an hour drive from the lakeside town of Kalemie on Saturday, May 12, 2001.

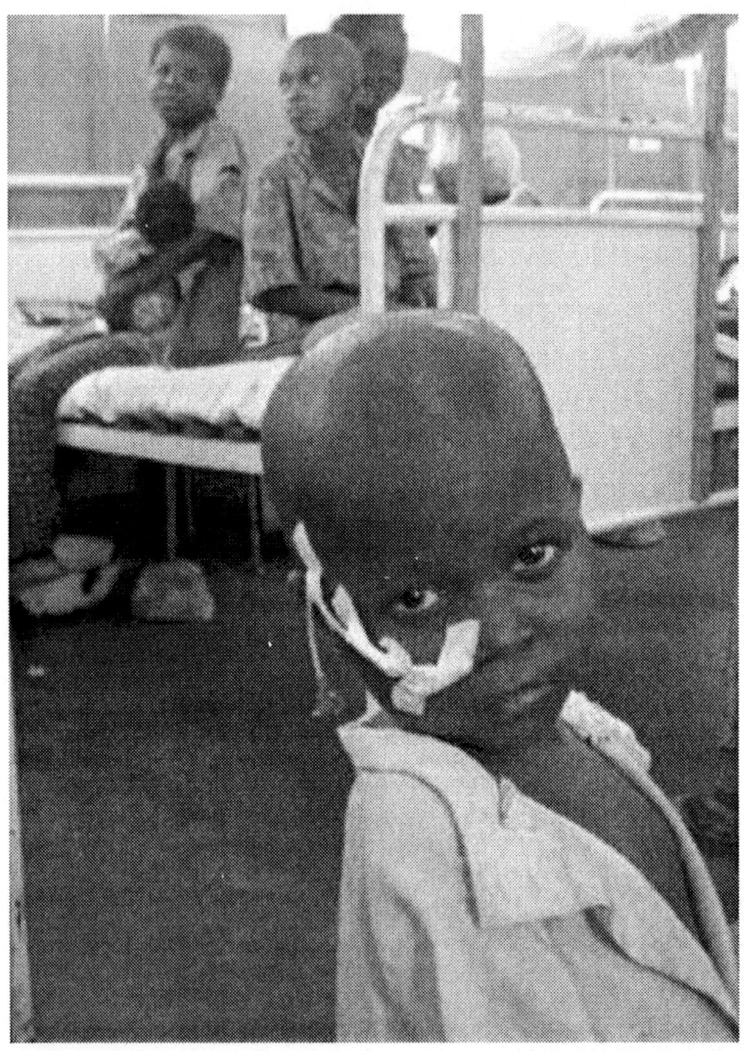

This is the look of, *I'm gonna make it, but I'm gonna remember, too.* Boniface Maskari, a 4-year-old with injuries, waits at Kalemie's main hospital, Sunday, May 13, 2001.

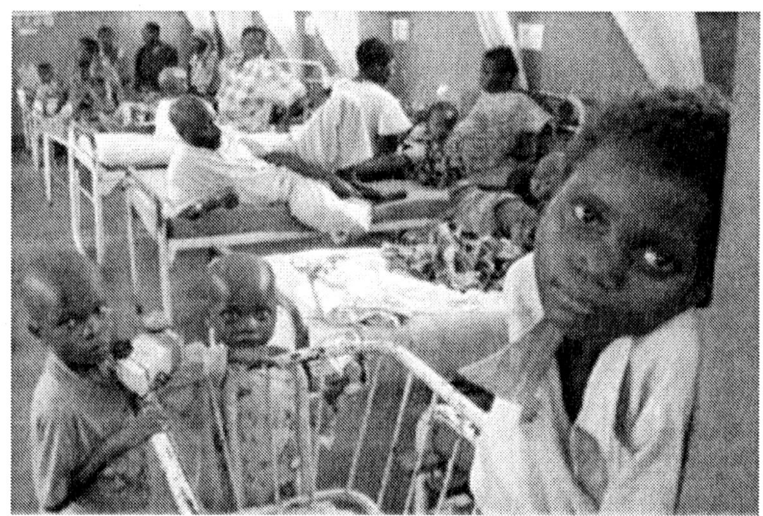

This is the look of, ***Where are you? Where were you?*** Angelan Pelele, right, a 6-year-old malnourished child waits for treatment at Kalemie's main hospital, Sunday, May 13, 2001.

These are the looks of food and help finally received, but accountability still sought. Dozens of malnourished children feed on a high protein diet while seated on mattresses laid out on the floor of Kalemie's main hospital, Sunday, May 13, 2001.

We are only beginning to get a sense for the horror that once again has befallen northeastern DR Congo. That horror is unambiguously carved into the faces of these Congolese.

Members of the Hema ethnic group take shelter at a Roman Catholic mission in Drodro, northeastern Congo, April 10, 2003. Photo credit: Sayyid Azim, AP

Reports are that the region has experienced its worst atrocity since the war in the DR Congo began in 1998, over four years ago. Nearly 1,000 people, the number at present is 966, all Congolese, were killed on April 3 when armed men attacked a Roman Catholic mission in Drodro and 14 surrounding villages, all located about 50 miles northeast of Bunia, near the border with Uganda, and inside the Ugandan zone of occupation.

The UN and the Government of the DR Congo say they are going to launch a thorough investigation. They had better do a good job.

This is a region that has, since 1998, been occupied by Ugandan invasion forces. Uganda still has forces there and has on numerous occasions been implicated in fomenting inter-ethnic violence in the area that has led to violence where previously there was none. Complicating this are Ugandan accusations that Rwandan military forces are now moving back into the area.

The Ugandan and Rwandan invasion and occupation of the DR Congo has achieved only these effects: kill an untold but very high number of Congolese, maim another unknown but very high number of Congolese, destroy an equally unknown but very high number of Congolese lives and Congolese properties, and cause horrific and inexcusable hardship to the Congolese people and their fledgling and struggling government in Kinshasa.

We have only a few photos at present to describe this recent attack... View them closely and imagine what has happened to these defenseless people. Read their faces. We can only pray to our God, whom we know has been suffering with these people through their years of horror, and ask Him to intervene on their behalf.

The photos below are a compilation taken by Antony Njuguna of Reuters and Sayyid Azim of AP. Well done to both, and as the investigations begin, we hope they or others like them can get the images to us. The world must know.

A nun bows in front of a mass grave in Drodro.
Photo credit: Antony Njuguna, Reuters

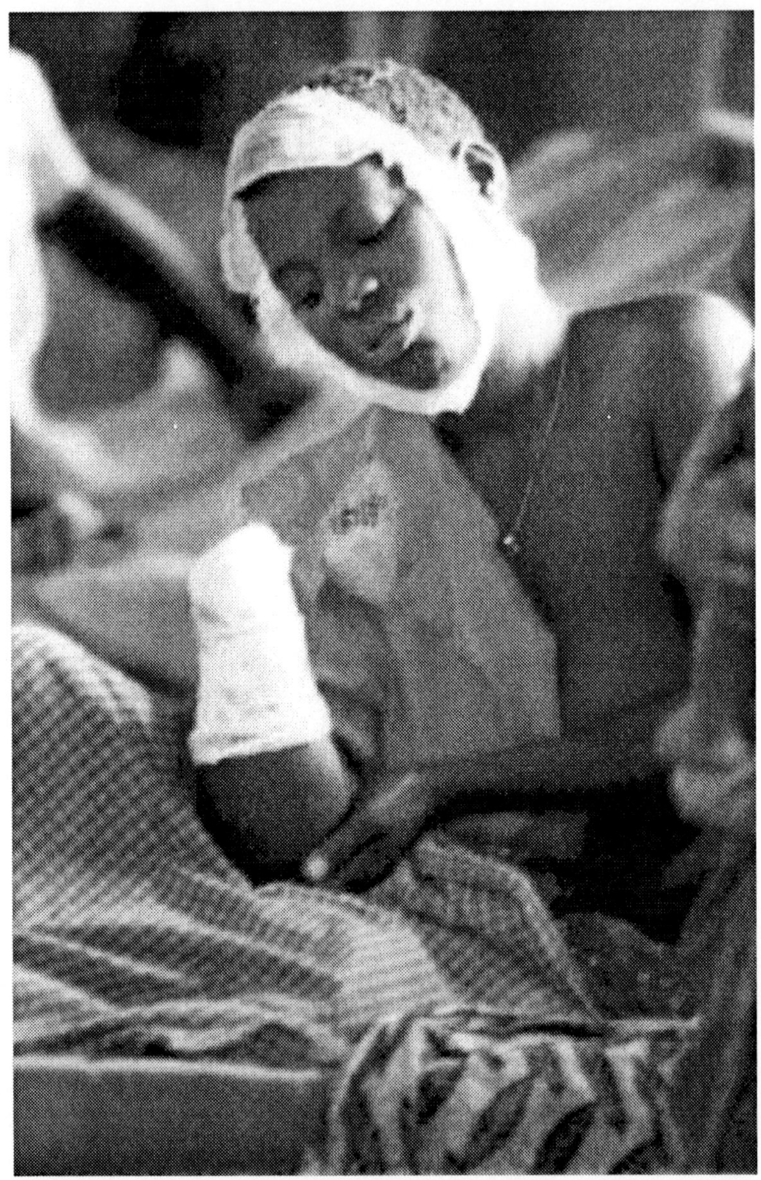

A woman lying in her hospital bed in Drodro, DR Congo, after her hand was chopped off during an attack on April 03.
Photo credit: Marco Longari, AFP

A Hema child stands next to his destroyed home in Drodro, April 9, 2003, after the house was burnt down by attackers. Members of the Hema ethnic group say they were attacked by neighbors from the Lendu ethnic group armed with guns and machetes. **Photo credit:** Sayyid Azim, AP

A Hema family sits next to their destroyed house in Drodro, North eastern Congo, April 9, 2003, after the house was burnt down by attackers. **Photo credit:** Sayyid Azim, AP

Villagers in Drodro in northeastern Congo, April 10, 2003, stand beside a mass grave in which 32 victims of the April 3, 2003 massacres are buried.
Photo credit: Sayyid Azim, AP

Members of the Hema ethnic group take shelter
at a Roman Catholic mission in Drodro, April 10, 2003.
Photo credit: Sayyid Azim, AP

Osama Man! A Hema militia soldier wearing a shirt with the portrait of Osama Bin Laden, greets a girl near the UN compound in Bunia, May 17, 2003. **Photo credit**: Karel Prinsloo, AP. This fighter of Congolese, "rebel" leader Thomas Lubanga identifies himself to Osama Bin Laden.

Pope John Paul (news - web sites) II touches his face during the weekly general audience in St. Peter's Square at the Vatican (news - web sites), Wednesday, April 9, 2003. The pontiff decried reports of mass killings in Congo, appealing Wednesday for efforts at reconciliation among the peoples of Congo, Rwanda, and Uganda. He said the reported massacres and summary executions were "no less worrisome" than the news of "destruction and deaths" in Iraq (news - web sites).
Photo credit: PLinio Lepri, AP

PART TWO

BIAS, POLITICS FROM THE INTERNATIONAL COMMUNITY

...Once you fail to defend human rights in a particular instance, you have given up the defense of human rights and you have accepted another principle to guide your actions.

—Henry J. Steiner and Philip Alston

Chapter IV
The International Community and the Double Standard Doctrine

The Congolese people have a bad memory of the international community, of the UN in particular. Now since the aggression of the DR Congo, a full Member State of the UN as are her aggressors—Rwanda and Uganda—none can convince a Congolese that the UN, the international community, even the USA—the so-called champion of individual and collective liberties, justice, and human rights—can be trusted. How could these governments stand idly looking on while Rwandan and Ugandan armed forces and their Congolese allies were slaughtering thousands of innocent Congolese civilians in the areas they controlled in the DR Congo? How could such a tragedy be willfully ignored by the same foreign powers that mobilized the entire world about the 1991 Kuwait invasion by Iraq, 1994 genocide of the Tutsis, the Bosnian and East Timor wars? Why this vast and international conspiracy against a fellow Member State of the UN and its people? What had the Congolese people or their leaders done—what sin had they committed—in order to find themselves sacrificed and betrayed by those who love to call them brothers and friends (only if sat in front of plates of diamonds, coltan, platinum, copper, uranium, and other minerals)?

Henry J. Steiner and Philip Alston acknowledge that "in the twentieth century the international community has come to recognize the common danger posed by the flagrant disregard of basic human rights...."[125] The African peoples, in general, and the Congolese, in particular, are convinced that the international community is only interested in their riches. If not, and if Steiner and Alston were right, then why did they drag their feet and refuse to stand tall and for the truth during the Congolese crisis? Why did they not condemn the aggression against the DR Congo by Rwanda and Uganda, the genocide, the crimes against humanity, and war crimes that were being committed by their allies?

The UN's attitude is, first deal within this section. The second section points out the ambiguity and imperfections of UN Resolutions relating to the Congolese crisis. Finally, the discussion focuses on the Western powers'attitude with regard to the Congo war of occupation.

This analysis does not include the USA, for it is believed that, for the purpose of this book, this country should not be included with the other Western powers because of her past and actual role in this conflict.

1. The UN and the Conspiracy About the Partition of the DR Congo

The Charter of the United Nations contains the following provisions, which, if applied, would have resulted in both Rwandan and Ugandan forces withdrawing from the DR Congo on the first day of their coward aggression. First, the Preamble of the Charter states that:

We The Peoples of The United Nations Determined to save succeeding generations from the scourge of war ... to reaffirm faith in the fundamental human rights, in the dignity and worth of the human person ... to unite our strength to maintain international peace and security ... to ensure, by the acceptance of principles and the institution of methods, that armed forces should not be used, save in the common interest...

Chapter One has the following provisions regarding the purposes and principles of the UN:

Article 1:

1. To maintain international peace and security, and to that end: to take effective collective measures for the prevention and removal of threats to the peace, and for the suppression of acts of aggression or other breaches of the peace, and to bring about by peaceful means and conformity with the principles of justice and international law, adjustment, and settlement of disputes or situations that might lead to a breach of the peace.

4. To be a center for harmonizing the actions of nations in the attainment of these common ends.

Article 2:

1. The Organization is based on the principle of the sovereign equality of all its Members.

3. All Members shall settle their international dispute by peaceful means in such a manner that international peace and security, and justice, are not endangered.

4. All Members shall refrain in their international relations from the threat or use of force against the territorial integrity or political independence of any state, or in any other manner inconsistent with the Purposes of the United Nations.

Chapter V on the Security Council provides:

Article 24:

1. In order to ensure prompt and effective action by the United Nations, its Members confer on the Security Council's primary responsibility for the maintenance of international peace and security, and agree that in carrying out its duties under this responsibility the Security Council acts on their behalf.

2. In discharging these duties the Security Council acts in accordance with the Purposes and Principles of the United Nations.

Chapter VII On the Action with Respect to The Threats to the Peace, Breaches of the Peace, and Acts of Aggression states:

Article 39:

The Security Council shall determine the existence of any threat to the peace, breach of peace, act of aggression, and shall make recommendations, or decide what measures shall be taken in accordance with Articles 41 and 42, to maintain or restore international peace and security.

Article 41:

The Security Council may decide what measures not involving the use of armed forces are to be employed to give effect to its decisions, and it may call upon the Members of the United Nations to apply such measures. These may include complete or partial interruption of economic relations and rail, sea, air, postal, telegraphic, radio, and other means of communication, and the perseverance of diplomatic relations.

Article 42:

Should the UN Security Council consider that measures provided for, in Article 41, would be inadequate or have proved to be inadequate, it may take such action by air, sea, or land forces as may be necessary to maintain or restore international peace and security. Such action may include demonstrations, blockade, and other operations by air, sea, or land forces of Members of the United Nations.

There is no doubt in the minds of millions of Africans, that the Security Council has a different interpretation of the terms "peace and security" when it comes to applying Articles 39, 41, and 42 to African armed conflicts. If there were impartiality and fairness at the UN Security Council, the articles just referred to would have been applied in the case of the DR Congo in order to force Rwandan and Ugandan armed forces out of this country hours after they invaded it. The DR Congo was under invasion by Rwanda and Uganda, but it amazingly took the UN Security Council months before even being able to officially acknowledge these facts.

Did the UN Security Council doubt that there was actually a threat to peace, a breach of peace, and an act of aggression against a Member State of the UN, namely the DR Congo, by its neighbors, Rwanda and Uganda? Why this unfair treatment from an organization that has for mission to maintain and restore peace and security? Why did the Security Council not drag its feet in the case of Kuwait in 1991 and East Timor later? On October 19, 1999, IRIN reported the DR Congo minister for Human Rights, Leonard She Okitundu, as stating that "the procrastination—not to say, shameful inaction—of the Security Council is at odds with its primary mission and with the scope of the problems to be solved in the war-stricken Congolese provinces."[126]

If the UN failed to fulfill, honor, and respect the provisions contained in Chapter VII of its Charter in the case of the DR Congo, but had applied them in the past with regard to Iraq, for example, then either this international body does not understand its purposes and principles, or the DR Congo does not fall in the category of those members of the UN the Chapter refers to. If the latter hypothesis is the case, then the world needs to know the reasons behind it. Otherwise, the UN is in truth, a true divider and criminal international body, highly politicized and a cause of political instability in developing nations, favoring such or such other state because of its financial contributions to its budget and political might, thus allowing or closing its eyes when such a state and its allies violate international laws and norms of human rights and international humanitarian laws.

Maybe, in the case at hand, the UN is aware of the conspiracy of the partitioning of the DR Congo for the purposes of establishing the "Hima empire" and is satisfying, by the same token, international lobbyists, a financially powerful group of people who know how to influence, in their favor, foreign or domestic politics, be it in Washington, New York, Bonn, Paris, or London. They do so in order to satisfy their personal interests and those of their friends no matter how harmful such actions may be to other fellow human beings or entire nations.

It is known that "the UN back regional initiatives seeking a peaceful resolution to renew Congolese conflict. On August 31, the Security Council issued a presidential statement that expressed alarm at the plight of the civilian population throughout the country and urged all parties to respect and protect human rights and respect humanitarian law. The statement also called for a cease-fire, the withdrawal of foreign forces, and the engagement of a political dialogue to end the war in the Congo."[127] You know what? The Congolese people and its government are of the opinion that the wording of this statement from the UN was simply an insult; and many agree. It was an insult because one can easily read between the lines that the UN, in general, and the Security Council, in particular, had applied Article 7, Chapter I of the Purposes and Principles of the Charter of the UN to the DR Congo situation, which reads as follows:

Nothing contained in the present Charter shall authorize the United Nations to intervene in matters which are essentially within the domestic jurisdiction of any state, or shall require the Members to submit such matters to settlement under the present Charter; but this principle shall not prejudice the application of enforcement measures under Chapter VII.

In short, according to the UN, the situation in the DR Congo was purely an internal matter. That is why, even four years after the aggression the UN was still talking of "the engagement of a political dialogue to end the war in the Congo." That is why the Security Council deliberately failed to condemn officially in words and conduct the aggression of a sovereign state that is a member of the UN, namely, the DR Congo, by its neighbors, Rwanda and Uganda, members of the same international organ. Further, the Security Council was unable to enforce its resolutions against Rwanda and Uganda during the entire illegal occupation period, or a total of four and half years.

The UN should have forced Rwandan and Ugandan invaders out, from the beginning, no matter their justification in occupying the DR Congo. This is why the US had since reasoned like the UN—reasoning that does not surprise any African—and had exercised subtle pressure on the allies of the DR Congo to withdraw their troops from the Congolese soil, without doing the same to its allies, Rwanda and Uganda. That is why, when the person who was, then, under secretary of State for Africa, Ms. Susan Rice, toured Central Africa to investigate the matter at hand, her failure to mention the withdrawal of Rwandan and Ugandan troops from the DR Congo surprised Kagame and Museveni. That is why the rest of the international community did not dare point a finger at Rwanda and Uganda, despite the undisputed facts that aggression was occurring in the DR Congo, and that genocide, crimes against humanity, and war crimes were being committed by the invaders, Rwanda and Uganda, as well as their Congolese allies.

The question that should be asked is who were the UN, the US, and the international community trying to fool? Assuming that what happened in the DR Congo was truly a "rebellion," are the UN, the US, and the international community then setting a precedent with the situation in the DR Congo while Uganda had been in a state of civil war, even before Museveni's coup, nearly two decades ago, and Rwanda, for decades? When is the UN going to ask Rwanda and Uganda to open a political dialogue to end the wars in those countries? Why did the UN try to distract the world with unreasonable, illogical, and demoniac statements instead of taking care of its responsibilities and living up to its principles? What was surprising—even laughable—was the fact that, though Rwanda and Uganda acknowledged having invaded the DR Congo, thus violating the territorial integrity of this country and international laws, still the UN and the international community wanted to protect them. This act was really unthinkable and illegal, and it makes one wonder about the mental state of the people who lead this international body or somehow influenced its politics.

The present experience is only a drop of water in the glass proving that those people constitutes a band of international criminals and terrorists. As argued above, a terrorist is an individual or group of individuals, private or public organization, or state that commits premeditated or non-premeditated acts of violence terror, who substantially encourages such acts by advising or assisting materially, or who harbors those who, he, she, or it knows or has reason to know, have conspired to commit such acts, or those who he, she, or it knows or has reason to know, have committed such acts, acts which cause terror and whose effect is terror. The people of the world are invited to determine whether the UN conduct vis-à-vis to the Congolese tragedy is acceptable in a civilized society and legally reasonable.

It will be repetitious, though it would serve its purpose, to say, "[s]ince Rwandese, Burundese, and Ugandan troops invaded the DR Congo, they have been abusing the Congolese people in the occupied territories. They killed innocent civilians, they rape[d] women, they destroy[ed] the economic infrastructure of the country, they destroy[ed] civilians and culture records of the Congolese citizens, and they impose[d] new settlements and exploit[ed] illegally the Congolese national resources. Their presence [was] a major hindrance for the Congolese democracy. Their criminal presence denie[d] the rights to Congolese people for self-determination, self-governance, and the violation, and a total disregard of the international norms and laws,"[128] violations and disregard which were not tolerated in Kuwait, Bosnia, Kosovo, and East Timor, to name only a few locations, because in those countries there are human beings living therein, while in Africa there are simply animals. Yes, whatever breathes in Africa are undesirable animals that do not need justice, fairness, and protection, but exploitation and extermination only!

Assuming again that, despite the acknowledgment by Rwanda and Uganda that they have invaded the DR Congo for whatever reasons they argued, the aggression—in order to satisfy the UN and the US political thought of the end of the twentieth century—was rather a purely domestic affair, meaning, a "rebellion" not from, but by, Rwanda and Uganda, because these two countries are, according to the records in New York and Washington, provinces of the DR Congo. What suitable plans did the UN and the US have for the withdrawal of Rwandan and Ugandan forces when internal matters in the DR Congo were arranged to meet their wishes? Yes, what reasonable plans did the UN and US have to present to the world to force the two criminal states to leave the DR Congo and never return uninvited and/ or in violation of well-established international legal norms? And what guaranties did they give to the Congolese people that such barbarous acts would neither be repeated nor permitted in the future? Those are some of the questions the Congolese people would want answers to. But for now, until proof to the contrary, the answer is NOTHING. No reasonable, sustainable plans or guaranties were presented either to the Congolese people or the world in general. NOTHING! This simply means that nothing shall stop the invaders to return to the DRC some day singing the same songs and dancing the same dance.

The silence, stupor of mind, inaction of the UN, and the law of the jungle that this westernized and monopolized international organ wants to perpetuate in Africa is dangerous. The tragic situation in the DR Congo has, at least, illuminated the minds of Africans to understand the true face of this international body that many are still trusting. The real intent of the UN, her unwillingness to condemn the aggression of the DR Congo by Rwanda and Uganda, as well as its deliberate misrepresentation to the citizens of the world that Rwandan's ethnic culture of mutual exclusion and hatred, and Ugandan perpetual state of rebellion would likely, and would definitely, be resolved with the holding of a national dialogue about the DR Congo by the Congolese was deceptive yesterday as it is today. The UN approach, which ignores the Congolese genocide and other gross violations of human rights that Rwandan and Ugandan committed in the DR Congo, is an insult to the Congolese people and to human rights lovers, and shows the incompetence of this international body in maintaining and restoring peace and security in Africa.

Furthermore, the UN's attitude shows and confirms the thesis that the partition of the DR Congo would be effective when the US gives its final blessing to the Security Council, by which time, the UN and US hope the redaction of the complete document on the "Bosnialization" of the DR Congo will be finalized. Me Kamanda, former vice-prime minister and minister of foreign affairs of Mobutu, is of the opinion that the actual secretary general of the UN, Kofi Anan, is aware of the report of the Kenyan professor, Mazrvi, about the "Balkanization" of the DR Congo, because he has a copy of the report. Me Kamanda outlined the following about this Machiavellian plan of tearing the DR Congo into pieces: "I have conducted an intense diplomatic activity in Geneva in order to let Mrs. Sadako Ogata understand that the feasible solution for Rwanda, in order to avoid a stalemate of the situation, is the return of refugees to their home. The General Secretary of the AOU, for example, is against this thesis about Zaire [DR Congo] and left even the meeting's room in Geneva. I had to have a private conversation with him in his office for him to understand me. I will find that his Deputy Office Director is a Rwandan, precisely a Tutsi."[129]

The preceding paragraph shows another element of the conspiracy, with the UN's blessing, regarding the partitioning of the DR Congo. "Just as in the case of Hitler's Nazi Germany this criminal conspiracy is aimed at regaining lost colonial territories and countries, the plunder and exploitation of the peoples and the resources of their country, and the perpetuation of a system of amassing fabulous profits for industrial and armaments monopolies. It is a desperate plot of the imperialist second Reich...,"[130] stated a wise man, freedom fighter, and Black African politician.

Thus, the elephant would be shared again, this time with the sole purpose of giving a part to the great devourer and new colonialist, namely, the US. It is agreed that "at its best, the United Nations can offer leadership to the world. At its worst, it exacerbates disputes by bringing states into disputes in which they would otherwise not be involved, and by providing a platform for intemperate vilification."[131] All this is done mostly in order to satisfy personal interests, ambitions, and passions, and as well as ethnic ideology in the case of the DR Congo crisis.

However, the lesson that the UN must learn is that "whether an ideology generates human rights violations or rationalizes them after they are committed, the ideology is equally dangerous. An unjustified violation is much less likely to be replicated than a justified one. A self-justifying violator is going to be more difficult to stop, to bring to justice, than a violator who claims no justification at all. An ideology is as much a root cause for the continuation of violations as it is a root cause for the initiation of violations,"[132] argues David Matas. And may the UN and the people of the world be prepared for that.

The aggression in the DR Congo by Rwanda and Uganda is a legal tragedy. It demonstrates the fragility in the wording of the UN Charter. This Charter, as a whole, contains so many holes that only those countries that are financially and economically powerful can fill them up (holes) to their advantage, in order to better serve their interests and those of their allies. For example, the criteria that categorized such violations of international norms as "international crimes" is so vague, shaky, and looks like a "balloon" that flies only in the direction of the wind. However, one wonders if it is the wind that blows the balloon or if it is the balloon that follows the wind. Such are some of the provisions contained in the Charter of the UN.

Thus, "what qualifies a case for inclusion is not clear. If the criterion for inclusion as a genocide or a genocidal massacre is the commitment of gross violations of human rights that involve a large number of deaths, then one wonders why some cases are while very similar ones are out."[133] In 1994, when the Rwandan-led Hutu government massacred thousands of Tutsis and moderate Hutus, the international community condemned such violations of human rights, calling them genocide. But when the today-led Tutsi government repeated the same scenario, first on the Hutus in 1994, then in 1996-1997, both on Rwandan and Congolese soils, and last on Congolese citizens, the international community had a completely blind eye about these violations. Worst, while Rwanda and Uganda were claiming to have their troops illegally on the Congolese soil, the international community once again led, by their "Chairman and Chief Executive Officer," the UN Security Council, demonstrated a curious and unusual unwillingness to acknowledge these facts.

This attitude of the UN is similar to a TV show on public education shown sometimes in the fall of 1999 on PBS. A certain lady had brought her fourteen-year-old daughter, whom, she complained, was involved in gangs and had been experimenting with drugs and sex. She wanted to know what to do to help her wild teen. While the daughter acknowledged that she was in gangs, using harmful drugs, and had sex several times, the mother kept on insisting that her daughter was a virgin, according to a doctor she took the girl to for a check-up. Her daughter was very surprised to hear that statement and laughed at the mother; but the latter still maintained that her daughter was a virgin. The daughter was shocked by the bold defense of her mother and might probably have said to herself, "Thanks, Mom, for defending my 'virginity,' though I myself and the outside world know that I have dishonored my body."

The above illustrates the UN's attitude toward Rwanda and Uganda. The UN, in particular the Security Council, defended the invaders of the DR Congo in the same manner, as did the mother of that wild teen. In doing so, this institution had set up a very dangerous precedent in its dealing with the DR Congo situation today, and other similar worlds' armed conflicts tomorrow. The UN is busy setting up mines and highly detonable and destructive explosives in each nation of the earth, a shameful enterprise that one should refuse his or her children to learn about. Someone has to stop those fools at the UN before the entire world gets into trouble and crumbles. One can only agree with President Nelson Mandela that, "we believe that this violence [in the DRC], like the system of apartheid ... is a direct challenge to the authority of the [UN Security] council and a subversion of its global tasks of furthering peace and promoting the objectives contained in both the UN

Charter and the Declaration on Human Rights. Failure on the part of the council to act firmly and decisively cannot but undermine its prestige and authority at a time when the council and the United Nations as a whole are called upon to play an even active role in the ordering of world affairs."[134]

In the case of the DR Congo, it is known that for a while, " ...the Security Council has been moving cautiously yet steadily forward. There may not be time for foot-dragging. We've seen it in East Timor how quickly the UN Security Council can act when the P-5 members decide to do so ... The question now is how is it going to work in this instance? Frankly there is some suspicion that Britain, France, and the US may not be in agreement as to the outcome they want to see in the DRC. National rivalries might supersede larger issues of justice, the application of the international law, and the adherence to well-established norms of behavior. This would be more an insult to the Congolese people who've suffered for more than a century at the hands of various external forces, and yet again their fate is in the hands of these global powers and their African allies,"[135] who invaded their country, a sovereign state, and who killed their people and plundered their numerous natural and mineral resources.

The UN "General Assembly in 1978 adopted, without a vote, resolutions calling on nations to refrain from the threat or the use of force, suggesting negotiation of disputes and encouraging the secretary general to exercise his functions fully in the cause of peace and to make use of the International Court. The point is that there is a solid body of precedent and international agreements prohibiting war and requiring nations to settle disputes peacefully. This precedent is routinely supported in UN resolutions by the Security Council and General Assembly in dealing with aggression. This precedent ... has played an important part over the long run in containing and discouraging aggression.... The UN Charter is a flexible instrument and showed the many ways it was used to contain and settle wars. It is even designed to take care of the problem of 'rogue cop' in which one of the permanent members supports aggression. In that case the issue can be transferred to the General Assembly by a procedural vote of the Security Council not subject to veto. In a number of cases beginning with the Korean War, the General Assembly took charge of protecting the victim of aggression,"[136] emphasizes Yoder.

Why did the UN not apply this available body of precedent and protect the DR Congo from humiliation, loss of millions of lives, and systematic destruction of its national assets by its invaders? Why did the UN not settle the problem of "rogue cop" whilst there is enough evidence that the US had supported the aggression of the DR Congo? Ed. Marek was right to say: "By the way, [the US] Rape, Abuse, and Incest National Network offers these recommendations for helping a friend who has been raped:

Listen. Be there. Don't be judgmental.

Be patient. Remember, it will take your friend some time to deal with the crime.

Let your friend know that professional help is available but realize that only your friend can make the decision to get help.

The Government of the DR Congo sought professional help on its own, from the UN Security Council. The UN Security Council did not listen, it was not there for the Congolese people, it couldn't care less how the Congolese people deal with the crimes committed against them, and the council has no intention of dealing with those crimes itself..."[137] That the UN Security Council did not listen is self-evident. But the reason they did not listen to the appeals of the Congolese people was unreasonable, suspicious, irresponsible, and illegal.

2. Ambiguous and Flawed UN Resolutions and Statements

Look at the UN Security Council Resolutions (UN S/RES),[138] and Presidential Statements (UN S/PRST)[139] taken during the invasion of the DR Congo, and you will be outraged that none of them specifically and expressly name Rwanda and Uganda as invaders, and/or condemns the illegal occupation of the DR Congo.

2.1. Some Illustrations

UN S/Res./1234 of 9 April, 1999, the first that the Security Council adopted six months after the illegal invasion of the DRC, went very close to condemn the presence of uninvited forces in the territories of the DR Congo, as reproduced in its entirety below:

RESOLUTION 1234 (1999)
Adopted by the Security Council at its 3993rd meeting, on 9 April 1999

The Security Council,

Recalling the statements by its President of 31 August, 1998 (S/PRST/1998/26) and of 11 December, 1998 (S/PRST/1998/36),

Expressing its concern at the further deterioration of the situation in the Democratic Republic of the Congo and the continuation of hostilities,

Expressing its firm commitment to preserving the national sovereignty, territorial integrity, and political independence of the Democratic Republic of the Congo and all other states in the region,

Recalling that the Assembly of the Heads of State and Government of the Organization of African Unity during its first ordinary session held in Cairo from 17 to 21 July 1964, adopted in its resolution AHG 16(1) the principle of the inviolability of national frontiers of African states, as stated in paragraph 2 of the communiqué of the Central Organ of the OAU Mechanism for Conflict Prevention, Management and Resolution issued on 17 August, 1998 (S/1998/774, annex),

Concerned at reports of measures taken by forces opposing the Government in the eastern part of the Democratic Republic of the Congo in violation of the national sovereignty and territorial integrity of the country,

Expressing its concern at all violations of human rights and international humanitarian law in the territory of the Democratic Republic of the Congo, including acts of and incitement to ethnic hatred and violence by all parties to the conflict,

Deeply concerned at the illicit flow of arms and military material in the Great Lakes region,

Recalling the inherent right of individual or collective self-defense in accordance with Article 51 of the Charter of the United Nations,

Welcoming the appointment by the Secretary-General of his Special Envoy for the peace process for the Democratic Republic of the Congo,

Stressing that the present conflict in the Democratic Republic of the Congo constitutes a threat to peace, security, and stability in the region,

1. Reaffirms the obligation of all states to respect the territorial integrity, political independence, and national sovereignty of the Democratic Republic of the Congo and other States in the region, including the obligation to refrain from the threat or use of force against the territorial integrity or political independence of any state or in any other manner inconsistent with the purposes of the United Nations, and further reaffirms the need for all states to refrain from any interference in each others' internal affairs, in accordance with the Charter of the United Nations;

2. Deplores the continuing fighting and the presence of forces of foreign states in the Democratic Republic of the Congo in a manner inconsistent with the principles of the Charter of the United Nations, and calls upon those states to bring to an end the presence of these uninvited forces and to take immediate steps to that end;

3. Demands an immediate halt to the hostilities;

4. Calls for the immediate signing of a cease-fire agreement allowing the orderly withdrawal of all foreign forces, the re-establishment of the authority of the Government of the Democratic Republic of the Congo throughout its territory, and the disarmament of non-governmental armed groups in the Democratic Republic of the Congo, and stresses, in the context of a lasting peaceful settlement, the need for the engagement of all Congolese in an all-inclusive process of political dialogue with a view to achieving national reconciliation and to the holding of an early date of democratic, free, and fair elections, and for the provision of arrangements for security along the relevant international borders of the Democratic Republic of the Congo;

5. Welcomes the intention of the Government of the Democratic Republic of the Congo to hold an all-inclusive national debate as a precursor to elections, and encourages further progress in this respect;

6. Calls upon all parties to the conflict in the Democratic Republic of the Congo to protect human rights and to respect international humanitarian law, in particular, as applicable to them, the Geneva Conventions of 1949 and the Additional Protocols of 1977, and the Convention on the Prevention and Punishment of the Crime of Genocide of 1948;

7. Condemns all massacres carried out on the territory of the Democratic Republic of the Congo and calls for an international investigation into all such events, including those in the province of South Kivu and other atrocities as referred to in the report submitted by the Special Rapporteur on the situation of human rights in the Democratic Republic of the Congo in accordance with resolution 1999/61 of the fifty-fifth session of the Commission on Human Rights (E/CN.4/1999/31), with a view to bringing to justice those responsible;

8. Condemns the continuing activity of and support to all armed groups, including the ex-Rwandese Armed Forces, Interahamwe, and others in the Democratic Republic of the Congo;

9. Calls for safe and unhindered access for humanitarian assistance to those in need in the Democratic Republic of the Congo, and urges all parties to the conflict to guarantee the safety and security of United Nations and

humanitarian personnel;

10. Welcomes the commitment by the parties to the conflict in the Democratic Republic of the Congo to stop fighting in order to allow an immunization campaign and urges all parties to the conflict to take concrete action in order to provide greater protection to children exposed to armed conflict in the Democratic Republic of the Congo;

11. Expresses its support for the regional mediation process by the OAU and Southern African Development Community to find a peaceful settlement to the conflict in the Democratic Republic of the Congo and calls upon the international community to continue to support these efforts;

12. Urges all parties to the conflict to continue to work constructively through the regional mediation process toward the signing of a cease-fire agreement and settlement of the conflict in the Democratic Republic of the Congo, and calls upon all states in the region to create the conditions necessary for the speedy and peaceful resolution of the crisis and to desist from any act that may further exacerbate the situation;

13. Expresses its support for the Special Envoy of the Secretary-General for the peace process in the Democratic Republic of the Congo, calls upon all parties to the conflict to cooperate fully with him in his mission in support of regional mediation efforts and national reconciliation, as set out in his mandate (S/1999/379), and urges Member States and organizations to respond readily to requests from the Special Envoy for assistance;

14. Reaffirms the importance of holding, at the appropriate time, an international conference on peace, security, and stability in the Great Lakes region under the auspices of the United Nations and the Organization of African Unity, with the participation of all the Governments of the region and all others concerned;

15. Reaffirms its readiness to consider the active involvement of the United Nations, in coordination with the Organization of African Unity, including through concrete sustainable and effective measures, to assist in the implementation of an effective cease-fire agreement and in an agreed process for political settlement of the conflict;

16. Requests the Secretary-General of the United Nations to work closely with the Secretary-General of the Organization of African Unity in promoting a peaceful resolution of the conflict, to make recommendations on the possible role of the United Nations to this end, and to keep the Council informed of developments;

17. Decides to remain actively seized of the matter.

This resolution was the greatest shortfall of all the others that followed in Re: the aggression and invasion of the DR Congo by Rwanda and Uganda armed forces. At this stage of the armed conflict there were substantial evidence that these countries had invaded the DR Congo. So, in lieu of "...the presence of forces of foreign states in the Democratic Republic of the Congo in a manner inconsistent with the principles of the Charter of the United Nations, and calls upon those states to bring to an end the presence of these uninvited forces and to take immediate steps to that end", as stated in Article 2 above, the Security Council were supposed to name Rwanda and Uganda expressly. These two countries were the only foreign states, as history recalls and in the light of this book, whose presence of armed forces in the DR Congo was inconsistent with the principles of the Charter of the United Nations. The Congolese government never invited Rwandan and Ugandan armed forces into the DRC after 28 July, 1998 nor did the UN mandate them. Kagame acknowledged this fact regarding his forces as discussed previously.

The question is why did the Security Council conceal the real identities of Rwanda and Uganda, in spite of ample evidence of their presence in the DR Congo, and whereas the whole world knew that the only uninvited armed forces in the DR Congo were Rwandans and Ugandans? Why did the Security Council dig around the bush if they did not have interest in the illegal invasion of the DR Congo? Why was it a big deal for the Security Council to directly identify Rwanda and Uganda as invaders, order them to immediately leave the territories of the DR Congo instead of using a dark diplomatic approach? Why did the Security Council use the unknown and impersonal language when referring to uninvited forces, calling them "those," when each member of the Security Council knew with clarity and conviction that "those" foreign uninvited armed forces were Rwandans and Ugandans? The only reasonable explanation is that the Security Council was protecting Rwanda and Uganda. The language in the said article 2 is protective, and therefore it was morally and legally wrong for the Security Council to act in that manner. This *modus operandi* is grossly irresponsible given the capital position and solemn mandate of the UN Security Council in restoring and maintaining peace among nations.

UN S/Res./1304 of 16 June, 2000 is the most spoken about resolution, for it gives to the Security Council a sense of honor and a restoration of its international obligations toward the DR Congo, though it is still grossly flawed. Below are excerpts of this Resolution:[140]

Resolution 1304 (2000), Adopted by the Security Council at its 4159th meeting, on 16 June, 2000,

The Security Council,

4. Further demands:

(a) that Uganda and Rwanda, which have violated the sovereignty and territorial integrity of the Democratic Republic of the Congo, withdraw all their forces from the territory of the Democratic Republic of the Congo without further delay, in conformity with the timetable of the Cease-fire Agreement and the 8 April, 2000 Kampala disengagement plan;

13. Condemns all massacres and other atrocities carried out in the territory of the Democratic Republic of the Congo, and urges that an international investigation into all such events be carried out with a view to bringing to justice those responsible;

14. Expresses the view that the Governments of Uganda and Rwanda should make reparations for the loss of life and the property damage they have inflicted on the civilian population in Kisangani, and requests the Secretary-General to submit an assessment of the damage as a basis for such reparations.

It took the Security Council twenty-two months (nearly two years) before expressly and clearly stating "that Uganda and Rwanda, which have violated the sovereignty and territorial integrity of the Democratic Republic of the Congo, withdraw all their forces from the territory of the Democratic Republic of the Congo without further delay," as stated in Article 4(a) above. By this time, when the Security Council explicitly named Rwanda and Uganda as the only invaders of the DR Congo, over two million Congolese had already died as a result of this unwanted and unjust war imposed on them. The Security Council had the obligation to charge Rwanda and Uganda of violating the sovereignty and territorial integrity of the DR Congo just hours after the armed forces of these countries entered the DR Congo soil, but it failed to do so.

In addition, to demonstrate to the world how biased this organ (the UN Security Council) is, two other monumental errors are found in the above article. First, the Security Council asked that the invading Rwandan and Ugandan forces withdraw from the DR Congo "in conformity with the timetable of the Cease-fire Agreement and the 8 April, 2000 Kampala disengagement plan," the Cease-fire Agreement and Disengagement plan from which the Security Council knew or had reason to know that Rwanda,

Uganda, and their puppet Congolese "rebels" thwarted repeatedly, sabotaged from day one, were unwilling to abide by, and above all were designed to deprive the Congolese people of their sovereignty while legitimizing the so-called rebel movements, and which at the most were effective by the end of the year 2002.

By these facts alone, both the Cease-fire Agreement and Disengagement Plan were "already a delay" by their very nature. Thus, the request that Rwanda and Uganda forces withdraw in conformity of those two documents was unknown and ambiguous. The corrupted Cease-fire Agreement never states that the invading armed forces of Rwanda and Uganda, which finally the Security Council acknowledged violated the sovereignty and territorial integrity of the Democratic Republic of the Congo, withdraw unconditionally from the DR Congo. The letter and spirit of that stillborn document puts a conditional withdrawal on the invaders. Rwandan and Ugandan evil armed forces were required, pursuant to this dead document, to only withdraw reciprocally with SADC troops from Angola, Namibia, and Zimbabwe that the Congolese Government legally invited to help counter the invasion. What a reversal of legal norms this was?

For a slow understanding reader, let's put this into perspective: You own a piece of real property—a ranch—lawfully and legally inherited from your parents, and live on it with your family and some extended family members. This property is rich in natural and mineral resources, and other forms of wealth. Suddenly one day, invaders move into your property armed to teeth. You call 911 repeatedly and each time speak to an operator; no emergency help arrives immediately or later in the following days. You plead to your neighbors to intervene and repulse the invasion given that the authorities have totally failed to protect you. By the way, you are a member of the Neighborhood Watch Association (NWA) and all the neighbors you asked for help and who show up on your property to assist you belong to this association.

Meanwhile, the invaders who had been sharing your personal property since day one of the invasion have insiders within your family. Let's say two of your children, nephew, father-in-law, private secretary, and few of your security staff are corrupted and side with the invaders. Surprisingly, instead of calling it an invasion, the media states that there is rebellion within your family. All this aggravated the situation, as you feel deeply betrayed. As weeks and months go on, the invaders gain grounds and half of your property is under their direct control. In passing, they have destroyed and plundered your property, and committed sexual and other forms of violence on your wife, daughters, granddaughters, maids, killed your son, two cousins, brother-in-law, some security staff, and some of your helping neighbors. For sure the intent of these criminals is to deprave you of your property, kill you, and forge your will giving one of your corrupted sons sole ownership of this estate through inheritance. The aim, after all, is to totally control the resources on your property. Once, they launched an attack on your house located at the extreme of the property from where they assembled the bulk of their forces, but you managed to defeat them with the assistance of your loyal family members and allies.

A few weeks later, you are surprised to hear a rich and powerful citizen living in another county offers what he calls the most "viable" solution to the crisis in your property. He states to your amazement that the only way to find a peaceable settlement about the criminal act taking place in your property is to have the members of the NWA, who came to protect you, leave your property. By the way, this rich guy is the principal contributor to the police funds and he sits at the Board of the Police Association. He even dared to send diplomatic missions to your neighbors' families to convince them to withdraw from your property. But the members of the Association knew perfectly that leaving you alone at this stage of the conflict simply means losing you and your property physically. So, they refused to leave. At this time, your suspicions on the hand behind this illegal invasion of your land are confirmed: the rich man has real motive to see the invasion and dark goals linked him to your county. He was found guilty of masterminding the death of your uncle, who owned the ranch before your dad. The rich guy is also assisting the invaders with training and intelligence. Having lost on the diplomatic field, the rich man directly and indirectly threatens you that unless you request that the members of NWA leave your property immediately, he will ensure that the invasion become permanent and that in the process you may lose your life.

To this day, months after the invasion started, the Police never offered any help. Finally, they show up one day and offer to settle the dispute that they call an internal matter. They request and condition the withdrawal of the invaders with the reciprocal withdrawal of your buddies of the NWA and warn that you may take or leave it. You cannot believe that the Police have just legitimized the presence of the invaders on your property and are unwilling to take their responsibilities and to live up to their motto of "To Serve and Protect." Frustrated, robbed, and betrayed, you feel forced to sign the "Cease-fire Agreement," though aware that you're giving up the inviolability notion of your property as well as the fundamental rights of your family. Your buddies have now left, the invaders have also gone after dragging their feet.

However, you are not secured and do not have full control of your property like prior to the invasion because of these two factors: first, though you mingle with your "sold out" family members, you can sense there is still enmity and from time to time they display disobedience toward you. They behave as if your authority was equal to theirs. Second, some members of your family, who lived under occupation, are slaughtering each other, for the occupying forces have sow divisions among them. There is no real peace in your property and you live on your guard knowing that the invaders who are settled just behind your walls may come back any day. By the way, members of your family sometimes report to you that they have seen the invaders trespassing again but disguised as family members. From time to time, you also get such reports from uncorrupted police officers assigned to monitor the application of the "peace" agreement.

You come now to understand with certainty the degree of this conspiracy better than before and warn that this conflict may be long and popular. By the way, the Police gave a blind eye to all the atrocities and gross human rights violations that the invaders and their allies committed inside your property. There is no plan in view to investigate and to prosecute such criminal acts. You cannot legally fight the rich guy and the Police, for they are powerful. Even the thought of suing the invaders brings cold sweat to your brow and armpits. By the way, you have been forced to withdraw the complaint against the invaders at the District court. You are left to yourself to mourn on the loss of your dear ones and the systematic looting of your fabulous resources. Your neighbors and friends tried to comfort you, but that is all they can do, for they do not have the power to do more.

If you understood the essence of the above fictitious story, then you know what happened in the Congo, and take yourself as a graduate in international studies from the University of UNAMERICA, with a major in international politics. By the way, if you feel the pains of the Congolese people and their broken hearts, and you have decided to help to contribute to the policing of this world and to fight impunity, and determined to teach to future generations about respect of human rights at home and abroad, then you have graduated with honors. SALUTE, for you are brave and a true HERO!

Some recapitulation is deemed necessary here to comprehend the second error. In Article 4 (a) of the UN S/Res/1304 of 16 June, 2000, the Security Council requests, "that Uganda and Rwanda, which have violated the sovereignty and territorial integrity of the Democratic Republic of the Congo, withdraw all their forces from the territory of the Democratic Republic of the Congo without further delay, in conformity with the timetable of the Cease-fire Agreement and the 8 April, 2000 Kampala disengagement plan." What is happening here? Truly, the Security Council had to ask "Rwanda and Uganda ... to withdraw without further delay" from the territory of the DR Congo. In passing, it should be mentioned that this sentence was supposed to end there as recorded above without the need to add the following ambiguous terms "in conformity with the timetable of the Cease-fire Agreement and the 8 April, 2000 Kampala disengagement plan." But was it necessary that the Security Council remind us that Rwanda and Uganda "have violated the sovereignty and territorial integrity of the Democratic Republic of the Congo"? Maybe yes; however, the essential terms of the provision are missing here, for Rwanda and Uganda and the entire world knew about this violation.

Here is the missing piece and how sub-section 4 (a) was supposed to be written keeping in mind that the Security Council was acting under Chapter VII of the UN Charter.[141] Two different ways are suggested:

First suggestion: The Security Council,

4. Further condemns in its strongest terms the invasion of the Democratic Republic of Congo, a UN Member State, and demands:

(a) that Uganda and Rwanda, which have violated the sovereignty and territorial integrity of the Democratic Republic of the Congo, an act which is in violation of the UN Charter and all established international legal norms, withdraw all their forces from the territory of the Democratic Republic of the Congo without further delay and conditions;

Second suggestion: The Security Council,

4. Further demands:

that Uganda and Rwanda, which have violated the sovereignty and territorial integrity of the Democratic Republic of the Congo, an act which constitutes an invasion and which it condemns in its strongest terms because in violation of the UN Charter and all established international legal norms, withdraw all their forces from the territory of the Democratic Republic of the Congo immediately and unconditionally.

The missing link is that the Security Council never expressly and explicitly condemns the invasion of the DR Congo. The Council simply asked "that Uganda and Rwanda, which have violated the sovereignty and territorial integrity of the Democratic Republic of the Congo, withdraw all their forces from the territory of the Democratic Republic of the Congo…" Why did the Council make such a demand? Well, because both "Uganda and Rwanda … violated the sovereignty and territorial integrity of the Democratic Republic of the Congo." Now this is where the Article shows it is flawed and where the legal issue lies. Is a crime an unlawful act? Yes. Is a criminal act always illegal? No, for an unlawful act can legally be justified on the grounds of self-defense and public policy, for instance. Is violation of one's state sovereignty and territorial integrity wrong? Yes. Always? No, for international laws and the UN can authorize such acts and history is full of good precedents. Violation of one's state sovereignty and territorial integrity may be legally justified on the grounds of intervention as provided in the UN Charter. For example, the US-led coalition that intervened in Kuwait to kick Iraq out and end the invasion was not illegal, for the UN Security Council authorized the act. Thus, each time the UN intervened in one country or authorized the intervention, such an act is legal pursuant to international legal norms.

Likewise, Rwanda and Uganda might have argued that theirs were the right to violate the DR Congo sovereignty and territorial integrity on the ground of self-defense, for example if such was the case. However, it is well known that nothing might have justified such self-defense in the first place, for Congo never attacked either Rwanda or Uganda nor authorized any armed group or militia to do same. Therefore, violation of the DR Congo sovereignty and territorial integrity was criminal because the act had no legal ground. It was the UN Security Council's responsibility to make it clear in its resolution that both Rwanda and Uganda severely and jointly violated the sovereignty and territorial integrity of the DR Congo because their act was in violation of the UN Charter and all established international legal norms.

Thus, it was not sufficient that the Security Council demands that Rwanda and Uganda withdraw from the Democratic Republic of Congo because they violated the sovereignty and the territorial integrity of the latter. But rather, in order to establish accountability, the Security Council should had asserted the basis or ground on which such violation was illegal. As started above, illegality of Rwanda and Uganda's act of violating the sovereignty and territorial integrity of the Democratic Republic of Congo lies on the fact that neither the UN Charter nor the laws of nations authorized such action. Article 4 (a) of UN S/Res./1304, as put forth by the Security Council, shields out Rwanda and Uganda's liabilities in the commission of this criminal and illegal act of violating the sovereignty and territorial integrity of the DR Congo. Was this missing piece in terms a very deliberate act of the Security Council aimed at defrauding the Congolese people and their nation of their rights to legal remedies? By the end of this book, the reader should already have known the answer to this question and uncovered the truth.

Coming back to UN Resolution 1304 (2000), it is a shame that the UN Security Council went on to charge Rwanda and Uganda only with the loss of lives and property in Kinsagani, as stated in Article 14 above, as if the presence of Rwandan and Ugandan troops in the Bas-Congo, Nord and Sud-Kivu, Kasaï Oriental, Katanga, and Equateur provinces during the war of occupation, was merely a health promenade. The Security Council's irresponsible conduct tells one story: the massacres, atrocities, and pillage theses troops committed in the aforementioned provinces were not grave human rights violations.

Further, Article 13 above was supposed to mention that, until an international investigation on those atrocities is completed, presidents, Kagame of Rwanda and Museveni of Uganda, are personally liable for all violations of human rights their armed forces committed in the DR Congo. This is as well applicable to all "rebel" group leaders like Jean-Pierre Bemba, Wamba dia Wamba, Bizima Kahara, Adolphe Onusumba, Mbusa Nyamwisi, Roger Lumbala, Emile Ilunga, Laurent Nkundabatware and all their foxes. But, the Security Council never had such an open condemnation against the leaders of Rwanda, Uganda, and Congolese "rebel" groups in their agenda.

Although all the Reports of the Panel of Experts on the Illegal Exploitation of Natural Resources and their Forms of Wealth of the Democratic Republic of the Congo have established the direct link between the systematic plundering of the Congolese national assets and the continuation of the war, and unavoidably and consequently, the grave violations of international human rights the Congolese people have suffered in the hands of Rwandan and Ugandan invaders and their Congolese associates, the Congolese people feel that the UN has unfairly treated them. And they have the right to feel so. For instance, the Congolese criticized UN Security Council Resolution S/Res/1457/2003 of 24 January, 2003, mostly the terms of its Article 15 which states: "[The Security Council] *Urges* all states, especially those in the region, to conduct their own investigations, including, as appropriate through judicial means, in order to clarify credibly the findings of the Panel, taking into account the fact that the Panel, which is not a judicial body, does not have the resources to carry out an investigation whereby these findings can be considered as established facts."

The Congolese people think that the UN Security Council, as stated previously, has done too little too late to protect them against the illegal occupation of their country and its dramatic consequences. It is their opinion that the Security Council would have gone with all force and judicial power to halt the pillage of their country's wealth. Instead, the Security Council has given the power to the offenders to be judges and parties, and therefore escape liability, the Congolese people strongly believe. However, as discussed in chapter six below, the recommendations of the Panel of Experts on the Illegal Exploitation of Natural Resources and Other Forms of Wealth of the Democratic Republic of the Congo does not limit the accountability of individuals and companies named in the reports, since the Panel does not have such mandate, neither power nor authority. In fact, "[t]he nature of the Panel and the various mandates that it has been given preclude it from determining the guilt or innocence of parties that have business dealings linked to the Democratic Republic of the Congo. Accordingly, the Panel has restricted itself to the narrower issue of identifying parties where it has information indicating a prima facie case to answer."[142] On the contrary, these reports may serve as the basis for any legal action against the perpetrators of international human rights and violators of humanitarian laws during the criminal occupation of the DRC.

Further, the Congolese people generally agree that of all the reports of the Panel of Experts on the Illegal Exploitation of Natural Resources and Other Forms of Wealth of the Democratic Republic of the Congo sole the Report of 12 April, 2001 given by Mme. Chairperson, Safiatou Ba-N.Daw of Côte d' Ivoire, is the most complete, transparent, real, objective and fair to their cause, while all the others by Ambassador Chairman Mahmoud Kassem of Egypt were primarily aimed at satisfying political demands from various parties. In fact, the UN Security Council replaced Madame Safiatou Ba-N.Daw with Ambassador Mahmoud Kassem for political reasons. Madame Safiatou Ba-N.Daw's report caught many individuals and companies, named therein, off guard since they knew that their evil and illegal activities in the occupied territories of the DRC could never have come to light, maybe not that soon.

2.2. Characteristics of UN Security Council Resolutions Relating to the Congolese Crisis

It is manifest that in this war of aggression against the DR Congo, the latter was the victim. However, the general characteristics of all the UN Security Council resolutions and statements pertaining to this war of occupation do not point out this fact. The main characteristics of those documents are as follow: the sovereignty, territorial integrity, and political independence of the Democratic Republic of the Congo and of all States in the region; the Lusaka Cease-fire Agreement; and the non-personalization of human rights violations. These three elements that typify all the Security Council documents about the almost five-year Congolese tragedy did not unfortunately address the essence of the problem. Because of this failure, any solution in tackling the Congolese crisis shall only be temporary and short.

First, it is wise to predict that the DR Congo will seek, again, the support of SADC and of the international community to repel a third, even fourth Rwandan and/or Ugandan invasion. This will occur because in "trying" to solve its tragedy of 1998-2002, the UN Security Council never focused on and addressed the problem of the aggression directly. For example, why was the Security Council so concerned about "the sovereignty, territorial integrity, and political independence of ... all states in the region" as stated in all its resolutions relating to the Congolese crisis, whereas various reports and records amply show that only the sovereignty, territorial integrity, and political independence of the Democratic Republic of the Congo was the sole issue? Why did the Security Council take preventive measures in protecting other states in the region while it was unable to defend the inviolability of the sovereignty, territorial integrity, and political independence of the Democratic Republic of the Congo, the immediate victim?

By failing to directly protect the sovereignty, territorial integrity, and political independence of the DR Congo, which was a victim of aggression, but wanting to generalize the solution to a problem that did not exist, the Security Council demonstrated that the DR Congo was not a victim, and consequently that the solution to remedy the DRC crisis not a priority. Even if the DR Congo was harboring Rwandan and Ugandan rebels who attacked Rwanda and Uganda, or any rebels from other states in the region for this matter who attacked their homeland, it would be disputable that the sovereignty, territorial integrity, and political independence of either Rwanda, Uganda, or such other state in the region were violated if the DR

Congo itself did not directly aggress Rwanda, Uganda, or such state in the region. The DR Congo never had a hegemonic or expansionist intention or mentality in the Great Lakes region, whereas this had always been the Machiavelli plan of its eastern neighbors, and of Rwanda, in particular.

Second, it must be understood once and for all that the Lusaka Cease-Fire Agreement is not a peace agreement. This was not the intent of the western master-minders who created the idea, though some actors involved in the conflict might have thought that it was a peace agreement. Because the Lusaka Agreement is only a cease-fire agreement, the enemies of the DR Congo knew that they could violate it at will. And since this agreement is not a peace agreement the notion of sending peacekeepers to the DR Congo to keep the peace was not in the UN Security Council agenda. When there is a peace agreement, as the case had been in many armed conflict situations, the UN will send a peace keeping mission. This mission will create a buffer zone to ensure that the different belligerents do not break the peace agreement. The interposition of the UN forces between the parties to the conflict has also a dissuading effect on the parties who signed the agreement to abide to its terms. MONUC was not designed for and is not a peace mission. The composition of its units and equipments evidence this argument.

In the case of the Congolese war of aggression interestingly, the Lusaka Cease-fire Agreement relating the Democratic Republic of Congo of 10 July, 1999[143] became "the most viable basis for the resolution of the conflict in the Democratic Republic of the Congo,"[144] and for which the UN Security Council expressed "its strong support ... insisting that all parties honor their obligations under that Agreement."[145] Why did this entirely-flawed document become the most important text from which the destiny of over 55 million Congolese was decided? And why did the UN Security Council stress the importance of this document and warn the parties to the conflict about its violation, in lieu of a peace agreement?

The above interrogations have the same answer. Two of the Permanent members of the Security, namely the US and the UK, which advocated the Cease-fire Agreement, could not tolerate the presence of their troops on the Congolese soil for a peacekeeping operation. And since they knew that the other UN members were willing to contribute troops, and given that these members were going to require the US and UK to do likewise because of their direct involvement in the conflict, they found that their only and sole legitimate escape was to push for a resolution of the conflict under a cease-fire agreement rather than a peacekeeping agreement. The US, in particular, could not accept a repetition of a shameful failure of another American military mission of the type of Somalia. No, the US said to a peacekeeping mission in the Congolese jungle, where Mother Nature would not shield the US military personnel from obvious ambushes or the like. After all, the US had already a Special Forces personnel on the grounds that might have evaluated the great risk American soldiers would face if sent to the DR Congo. Further, there was no way that the US would have tolerated the presence of French troops on Congolese soil during the conflict while they remained out because unwilling to participate.

Thus, the US put severe pressure on both Kabila's regimes to not even think on refusing to go ahead with the Lusaka Cease-fire Agreement though the content of the text violated the sovereignty and territorial integrity of the DR Congo, and did not reserve to the Congolese people the right to decide on the future of their country and its governmental institutions. Worse, this worthless piece of paper granted to the enemies of the DR Congo, those same individuals and foreign states that planned and executed the aggression of the DR Congo, the right to choose on behalf of the Congolese people the type of political, social, economic, and military institutions that are good for their country.

Furthermore, and embarrassingly, this document legitimatizes the existence of the so-called rebels, confirming the precedent that in Africa, one needs to only take arms against the Central government to force the latter to accommodate the rebels politically. This approach by the UN Security Council to settle the Congolese war of invasion was illegitimate, illegal, and highly irresponsible. Can one imagine that this sort of language be spoken in western countries? No way, never!

No wonder that when this author, sometimes in the summer of 2001, conversed with a high DR Congo political personality and warned him about the content of the Lusaka Cease-fire Agreement, the latter responded humbly that the DR Congo government did not have any choice under current international pressure than to go ahead with the text "as is" and see what strategy it can use during the Inter-Congolese Dialogue in order to cut off the thorny corners. The argument seemed a wise and a better diplomatic approach under the circumstances. But whether the DR Congo had succeeded to remove also the explosives and mines that the stillborn document contains is something to be seen in the long run, for this war is not yet over.

It is hilarious that the UN Security Council, whose primary responsibility is the maintenance of international peace and security, gave, expressly, preference to a cease-fire agreement rather than to a peace agreement in the Congolese case. In truth, this modus operandi was simply an insult to the Congolese people. And as argued previously, nothing will deter both Rwanda and Uganda to not invade the DR Congo for a third or fourth time, for there are no neutral and UN mandated interposition forces between the DR Congo, Rwanda, and Uganda. There are no UN-mandated, dissuading forces in the eastern Congo whose presence will make Rwanda, mostly, think twice before launching another attack on the Congolese soil. The UN Security Council wants it that way, the international community knows this fact, while the DR Congo has both eyes opened and watching.

Further, if the UN Security Council believed that Rwanda had a legitimate cause in aggressing the DR Congo to defend its borders from Rwandan rebels' incursions "harbored" in the DRC, it would have sent peacekeeping operations in the DR Congo to ensure that Rwandan borders are secured permanently. But, not surprising to those who are enlightened that the UN Security Council did not have such items in its agenda because from the beginning Rwandan's accusations against the DRC regarding the security of its borders were false, misleading and a big lie.

Third, the DR Congo is likely to be victim of another invasion mostly from its neighbor Rwanda because all UN Security Council resolutions and statements in relation to the 1998-2002 aggression are so impersonal and general that they do not condemn specifically both Rwanda and Uganda for their roles: first, in violating the sovereign and territorial integrity of the DRC contrary to the UN Charter and other recognized international legal rules, second for fomenting so-called rebellions, and third for committing gross violations of international human rights.

For example, Article 13 "Condemns all massacres and other atrocities carried out in the territory of the Democratic Republic of the Congo, and urges that an international investigation into all such events be carried out with a view to bringing to justice those responsible." But in the next lines of the same resolution, Article 14, the UN Security Council "Expresses the view that the Governments of Uganda and Rwanda should make reparations for the loss of life and the property damage they have inflicted on the civilian population in Kisangani, and requests the Secretary-General to submit an assessment of the damage as a basis for such reparations."

Then almost three years later, in another resolution, the Security Council "Condemns the massacres and other systematic violations of International Humanitarian Law and human rights perpetrated in the Democratic Republic of the Congo, in particular sexual violence against women and girls as a tool of warfare and atrocities perpetrated in the Ituri area by the Mouvement de Libération du Congo (MLC) and the Rassemblement Congolais pour la Démocratie/National (RCD/N) troops, as well as the acts of violence recently perpetrated by the Union des Patriotes Congolais (UPC) forces, and reiterates that there will be no impunity for such acts and that the perpetrators will be held accountable."[146]

The above resolutions expressed the vagueness and ambiguity that characterizes UN resolutions regarding the Congolese crisis. The analysis shows that the UN Security Council shall not expressly name neither Rwanda nor Uganda for their part in the commission of the crime of aggression against the DR Congo, the crime of genocide, the crimes against humanity, war crimes and terrorism, which are crimes in violation of international norms, in spite of proof of direct and circumstantial evidence of the participation of armed forces of those two countries in the perpetration of such crimes.

In addition, the Security Council is making it clear that both Rwanda and Uganda shall be liable only "for the loss of life and the property damage they have inflicted on the civilian population in Kisangani," as expressed above and discussed previously. Whether any legal instrument is planned to establish investigation and accountability is the question those who were innocent during those conflicts are probably asking where they are. Further, whereas there is ample proof that both Rwanda and Uganda (the latter mostly) committed crimes against international humanitarian laws in the Ituri province, the UN has only condemned MLC, RCD/N and UPC's actions. Make no mistake, nobody would dare to minimize the participation of those groups of bandits in the perpetration of human rights violations in the Ituri province and other provinces; however, the fact that the Security Council explicitly failed to mention the RPA and UDF is particularly very choking and misleading.

In light of the above, one will notice that it is only after Uganda withdrew its troops from the Ituri province that the use of terms like massacres and genocide were being consistently and constantly utilized on the international sphere regarding the crisis in the DR Congo. When one observes the UN Security Council dealing, it is noticed the use of the term "massacres" was a new vocabulary within that organ, whereas these atrocities were committed on a gross scale when the UDF maintained a high presence in the Ituri province. To begin with, as mentioned in the previous chapter, who created division between the Lendus and Hemas? Not the DR Congo government obviously, but rather the Ugandan government. These two sister tribes, Lendu and Hema, lived in peace until Museveni's agents came to sow rivalries between them with the intent to have a "good" excuse for returning to the DR Congo uninvited and manu militari. In addition, Uganda's conduct was to show to the world that the DR Congo was not exempt from ethnic war. Museveni and his lieutenants can laugh now for succeeding in this enterprise, but rendez-vous soon at The Hague or to the Congo international criminal tribunal.

The other characteristic, not of less importance, that portrays all UN resolutions and statements relating to the invasion of the DRC by Rwanda and Uganda, is the fact that none of these texts demands solely the withdrawal of Rwanda and Uganda, the invading States. Curiously, whenever the UN Security Council requested the withdrawal of troops from the DR Congo, it referred to the withdrawal of all foreign troops, as discussed previously. For example, sometimes during the war, the Security Council requested "(a) that Uganda and Rwanda, which have violated the sovereignty and territorial integrity of the Democratic Republic of the Congo, withdraw all their forces from the territory of the Democratic Republic of the Congo without further delay, in conformity with the timetable of the Cease-fire Agreement and the 8 April, 2000 Kampala disengagement plan; (b) that each phase of withdrawal completed by Ugandan and Rwandan forces be reciprocated by the other parties in conformity with the same timetable; (c) that all other foreign military presence and activity, direct and indirect, in the territory of the Democratic Republic of the Congo be brought to an end in conformity with the provisions of the Cease-fire Agreement."[147]

The Congolese have deeply criticized this unilateral attitude of the UN Security Council, which they believed deprived them of their sovereign right to defend themselves. Never in the history of the nations has the UN requested that foreign states, invited to help a legitimate government to contain a foreign aggression, be required to pull out their troops before or at the same time as the invaders to facilitate the peace process. The Congolese case was indeed a premiere. The US, in fact, demanded boldly that all the allies of the DR Congo withdraw from the Congolese soil as soon as the Congolese government invited them to intervene. To what end was such a request made, than to help Rwanda and Uganda to put the DR Congo, its people, and its numerous and various resources under the total and direct control of the invaders and their western masters. What an inversion of international legal norm this bold and unjust request was indeed!

3. The Western Powers' Hypocrisy

Africans believed that the Europeans, because of their colonial history in Africa and their relationship with the Africans, would have been the first people to understand them and to defend them in situations like the one in the Great Lakes region. But they have just been disappointed again. In fact, most of the colonial European countries were never for the decolonization of Africa. They have always tried to impose a sort of neo-colonialist system in Africa and are bitter about losing direct control over what they amazingly continue to think is their unborn right: Africa and its immense riches. Somehow, there should be rejoicing in the metropolises of those countries opposed to the decolonization of Africa, when situations like the one in the Great Lakes region take place. Otherwise, "the violation of Congo's sovereignty, territorial integrity, including the gross violation of fundamental rights by invaders should bring an uproar in the international community,"[148] as was the case in Kuwait, Bosnia, Kosovo, and East Timor.

But the silence of the international community in regard to the aggression of the DR Congo is, indeed, a betrayal and demonstrates clearly the doctrine of double standard as preached through the actions of the Western countries. These countries intervened in Kuwait, Bosnia, Kosovo, and East Timor because those are regions where human beings live, while in Africa, they consider its people like simple animals, good only for a safari. Or, because in the first mentioned regions the inhabitants are "whites" and should therefore be protected by all means and at all costs, while in the second region, the inhabitants are "blacks" and do not need protection from the international community since they are only sub-humans.

Thus, when Blacks turn guns against each other, actions that are most of the time incited by western whites, the latter turn their backs away. In other word, Black people's mutual extermination does not concern the Western world. "It is evident that a total disregard for the lives of black people, which is the essence of [the many civil wars and instability in Africa], continues to hold sway at the highest reaches of [western] government[s]."[149] There should be motivations justifying the Western countries' conduct of inaction in the DR Congo, because even a fool has a motivation justifying his or her actions. And the people of Africa would like to know why the international community did not openly condemn Rwanda and Uganda for having invaded the DR Congo, a sovereign and independent state.

Dr. Firoz Osman, quoted in The Star, a South African Newspaper, that former president, Nelson Mandela, in regard to the threat made by the United States of America to attack Iraq (again), that the United States of America "showed up Western hypocrisy when he (president Mandela) said: 'But what we know is that Israel has weapons of mass destruction. Nobody talks about that. Why should there be one standard for one country, especially because it is black, and another one for another country, Israel, that is white.'"[150]

In fact, "one must ask if the International community needed any more evidence than the one the world... "[151] saw happening in the occupied territories of the DR Congo, in order to take up their responsibilities and cease all hypocrisy, condemn Rwanda and Uganda's invasion, ask them to end the massacres and all violations of human rights, and to immediately and unconditionally withdraw their troops from the Congolese soil or face terrible consequences. In early March 1998, when some Western tourists were killed in Bwindi National Park in Uganda (on the borders with Rwanda and the DR Congo), the whole Western world was united and spoke of the matter with indignation, as if it were the end of the world and that it was the first time they have ever heard about massacres in the Great Lakes region. Fortunately, "for the outside world, it was a vivid reminder of the terror that still grips the heart of Africa,"[152] that while the Westerners come to Africa to exploit and cheat the people on the sales of minerals, they have also destroyed their rights and brought animosity, mistrust, and hatred among those people who have been living for centuries as brothers and sisters.

3.1. The Criminal Conspiracy of Western Media

The silence of the Western mass media is also very surprising. Unfortunately many are those Africans who do not understand that it is very easy for the West to manipulate and therefore corrupt their media as it is done anywhere in the world. Those who closely followed the evolution of the crisis in the Great Lakes region, and in the DR Congo, in particular, shall recall some unfair western media reports. For example, when the DR Congo's coalition gained ground on the battlefields, only a much-selected number of international media spoke about it. On the other hand, when the invaders, Rwanda and Uganda, illegally occupy even a small village, the Western media spoke of the fall of a strategic town.

The case of the eight killed Western tourists spoken of above was "a dramatic illustration of the behind the scene management of publicity,"[153] and propaganda from the international media. What about Kassika, where four hundred deaths occurred in August 1998, and Makobola where five hundred were killed in December 1998? Were those weekend or Christmas parties, collateral damages (as General Colin Powell called it) or what? What about Kavumu, Burhinyi, Mwenga, Kamituga, Walangu, and other locations, where more than ten thousand people were massacred by the Rwando-Ugandan coalition? Why was the Western media so silent about situations that would have helped to bring to pass peace and security?

Is this not a conspiracy? Why this conspiracy? The answer is simple for any reasonable person. The Western media, with CNN and BBC at the top of the list, which claim to be democratic, transparent, and impartial, and which are the first to criticize developing countries' so-called anti-democratic practices, are not fair, partial, or incorruptible. Otherwise, why are they the first ones to misinform the international public and to defend the devilish plans of so-called Western democracies? One needs recall the propaganda covering the Anglo-American mission in Kosovo to understand what this is all about. These news media are serving the expansionist and imperialistic ambitions of the countries where they are housed and their allies.

Some time during this war of aggression, the same media made much noise about the illusionary presence of North Korean soldiers in the Katanga province and the acquisition of Scud missiles from Iran by the Kabila government, only to enable their countries to supply Rwanda and Uganda with sol-sol, sol-air missiles, war planes, and sophisticated war weapons for the conquest of the big elephant, the DR Congo. All those allegations were definitely false, and were all intentional public misinformation. Worst of all, the Western media make much publicity, even where people can easily see for themselves that their stories are simply tales. Furthermore, no apology follows their wrong reports, like others would do and even when the public expected it. A little bit of decency and courtesy does not kill nor make a person, a group of persons, institution, or government weak or inferior. On the contrary, it proves maturity, respect, and a sense of civilization. But, the Western media prefer to keep quiet, after they have spread lies, as long as they have satisfied the interests of some governments and international lobbyists and achieved their devilish goals.

Ellen Ray's comment[154] is a good illustration of the case at hand. She noted that, "When a nation is a target for Balkanization, the justification for the overt and covert operations such campaign entails is almost always a 'humanitarian' effort to control inter-ethnic strife. The media generate public confusion by fabricating, or exaggerating, ethnic, tribal mini-wars, often stirred up and paid for by the agents of the would-be Balkanizers. For example, nearly every article about the invasion of the Democratic Republic of Congo by the US-supplied and trained armies of Uganda and Rwanda referred to the invaders' local paid agents as oppressed Congolese ethnic groups or former members of Mobutu's army rebelling against the Kinshasa government. The articles often described 'tribal warfare' in breathless detail, citing mini-wars like those being fostered by outsiders between the Hema and the Lendu.

"The severe destabilization of a targeted nation or area of the world," continues Ellen, "is a logical and necessary prerequisite to Balkanization. The media help to promote that destabilization by their demonization of targeted leaders. Such campaigns often carry over stones of ethnic persecution, along with accusations of corruption, communism, terrorism, or (but only when it suits the US) fundamentalism. Even though the western press could not, in the end, boost Mobutu, their grudging recognition of Kabila was at best cautious, suspicious, and extremely short-lived. After Kabila threw out the Tutsi officers (Rwandan and Ugandan) who had been installed in most key military and intelligence posts, usually over the strong objections of the local people, the press' honeymoon with Kabila was over. As Kabila heard the complaints of the Congolese people about Tutsi-led terror against Hutu refugees, as he traveled to independent nations like China, Libya, and Cuba, he began to be vilified as 'corrupt,' as a 'thug.'"

By the same token, the Western media targeted the main ally of the DR Congo, namely Zimbabwe, in this war of aggression against Rwanda and Uganda. This country is, despite an international conspiracy to crash President Robert Mugabe, well better off than are Rwanda and Uganda. Its road, transport, telecommunication, educational, and medical infrastructures [until before the conspiracy] were one of the well-developed in Africa and could not be compared to struggling countries like Rwanda and Uganda. Zimbabwe had about eleven thousand soldiers in the DR Congo fighting alongside their allies, Namibians and Congolese. Rwanda had almost double that number, about twenty thousand.

3.2. The Illegal Abatement of International Financial Institutions

It was ironic and surprising to see all the publicity from the Western media about Zimbabwe's economic struggles at home because of its involvement in the DR Congo war, while that same publicity was not heard about in either Rwanda or Uganda, countries which are still getting millions of US dollars from international financial institutions, mainly, the IMF and the WB, despite their aggression and illegal invasion of the DR Congo. When looking at the situation very closely, one induces the following attitude from the international community toward Zimbabwe: You have halted the progression of our allies in the Congo and therefore thwarted our plans. Now, life will get tough at home for you because you are using your own money to help your ally, the DR Congo, contrary to Rwanda and Uganda, which are being supported by us financially and militarily. Without military and financial support form Western countries, it was impossible for Rwanda and Uganda to sustain a four-and half-year military campaign in the DR Congo. They do not have the nerves, frankly speaking!

To illustrate the above financial aid from those world finance organizations, it is worth to record the following: "...in November 1998 Mr. Awori[155] charged that the Ugandan government had procured some $32 million in military supplies, including 62 Russian made tanks. He said he had pictures of the tanks and that he had information from the defense ministry that the tanks were to be airlifted to Goma, DR Congo, three to four at a time. He also charged that Ugandan military involvement in the Congo, and in Sudan, was a breach of the constitution and urged impeachment of President Museveni. The major defense procurement was occurring, by the way, at the same time Uganda was convincing the World Bank and IMF that it needed some $700 million in debt relief under the Highly Indebted Poor Countries (HIPC) debt relief initiative, an award achieved in September 2000, the first such award made on the African continent."[156] These financial institutions cannot deny that they did not know that their aid to Uganda was diverted or utilized by the latter in the acquisition of weaponry used in the invasion of the DRC, the maintenance of Ugandan control in the occupied territories of the DR Congo, and the commission of international human rights violations and humanitarian laws, for they knew or had reason to know how and to which ends was the financial assistance granted to Uganda used.

Keith Snow also provides a good substantiation while demonstrating the link between African wars and international monetary entities. He argued that "[t]hese wars are prosecuted by local warlords, military dictators, and their elite intelligence and security networks, typically armed, funded, and trained by western intelligence and/or ex-military and/or private security companies. And these networks are particularly ruthless. However, again, they are directly associated with in-country western military and intelligence advisors and their programs. That includes Israel, US, British, German, and French. But IMF/WB and OPIC and ADB funds continue to flow, and they support selective interests and projects and infrastructure, which helps their related industries further expropriate the resources and the people and the institutions. Uganda provides a good example. Uganda is at war on three fronts and a significant percentage of the IMF/WBW funding that has gone into Uganda has been diverted for military objectives. The banks, which fund Uganda through the international monetary institutions, are often associated with the multinationals involved in the plunder of raw materials. Uganda has supported the SPLA war in Southern Sudan, and I took testimony from Uganda dissidents who insist that US military advisors have worked with the SPLA and UPDF against Khartoum."[157]

Further, the WB has done something that should irritate any Congolese who knows and would like to know what really happened during this war of aggression, to more substantiate the hypocrisy of western powers. "The World Bank has praised Uganda for its economic performance and the reforms under the structural adjustment program as a success story and has promoted its case for the new debt relief program, the Highly Indebted Poor Countries ... this economic performance was driven in part, especially over the past three years, by the exploitation of the resources of the Democratic Republic of the Congo. Notes exchanged between World Bank staff clearly show that the Bank was informed about a significant increase in gold and diamond export from a country that produces little of these minerals or exports quantities of gold that it could not produce.... Internal discussions of the World Bank staff also confirm this knowledge of the situation: in one of those internal exchanges, a staff member warned his colleague that the World Bank silence would blow up in the Bank's face.

"In the case of Uganda," the report goes on, "and its exploitation of natural resources of the Democratic Republic of the Congo, the World Bank never questioned the increasing exports of resources and in one instance a staff member defended it ... [in] Uganda, the representative of the Bank dismissed any involvement of Uganda in the exploitation of those resources. The Bank not only encouraged Uganda and Rwanda indirectly by defending their case, but equally gave the impression of rewarding them by proposing these countries for the Highly Indebted Poor Countries debt relief initiative. The Bank's shadow on the conflict in the Democratic Republic of the Congo is even more apparent on the budget. The balance of payments of both Uganda and Rwanda shows a significant increase in long-term borrowing in support of the budget. The defense balance however has increased in absolute terms, allowing Uganda and Rwanda to continue the conflict. There seems to be a precedent for the Bank's behavior. During the Cambodian crisis in the 1980s, the Bank turned a blind eye to the illicit exploitation of Cambodian timber; the question is whether it is World Bank policy to ignore broad governance issues (hard or soft) while dealing with its clients."[158]

But the general public does not see and know the true face of this band of international terrorists and their criminal activities. These criminals killed by often using war weapons, but also by using very destructive but slow killing weapons like starvation, allowing deadly epidemics, HIV/AIDS, lack of adequate clean water and hygienic, and educational facilities. They support the aggressors and invaders, but they condemn the victims. They are both parties and judges, violate international legal norms, and get away with crimes.

In Africa, as illustrated in the DR Congo's case, this situation occurred because of the Western powers direct or indirect involvement in all the armed conflicts, solely for business opportunities. As Bruce Hendrickson noted, "there seems to be a myth out there that the UN is an independent international body led by Secretary-general Kofi Annan, and if the UN fails yet again, 'they' will be to blame. Of course, the UN is a body comprised of member-states led by the P-5 members of the Security Council. Nothing happens in the area of security issues or military operations without their approval as outlined in Article 39 of Chapter VII of the Charter. One assumes that Russia and the People's Republic of China have no interest in preventing the UN from protecting the territorial integrity and national sovereignty of the DRC. In this instance the three countries whose decision making will be decisive are Britain, France, and the United States—the same three countries that failed to act in Rwanda in 1994. Success or failure will be determined in Washington, Paris, and London—not in New York."[159]

It is true that the European Union had contacts with the leaders of the Great Lakes region. For instance, in its presidential statements of August 11 and 27, 1998, the EU expressed its concern about the growing crisis in the Congo, called for a political dialogue among all the parties involved, and strongly condemned human rights violations by all the forces involved. The EU's special envoy to the Great Lakes, Aldo Ajello, toured the trouble region in what was called an evaluation mission in September of 1998 calling for a solution that would guarantee the long term security of the Congo and its neighbors in his public statements. But alas, like the UN, he did not condemn the cause of the violations of human rights in the eastern territories of the DR Congo nor the aggression of the DRC by Rwanda and Uganda.

Hence, the EU cannot make statements contrary to those of the Security Council since they all have mutual interests in the DR Congo, namely, the fall of the Kabila government and the "Balkanization" of the country so that they may satisfy their economic and imperialistic appetites. Thus, confirming the sayings of the French Alain Minc that "the war [cold war] has left the political field and will take place on the economic spheres."[160]

The truth is that the international community is scared of something: some emerging power in central Africa, namely, the DR Congo. Their argument is always that, if they place another Mobutu in power—a person who will put foreign interests in the DR Congo before those of his own citizens—then they will be at peace. They are reasoning as follows: the bigger and richer a nation is, the more powerful it becomes, and the more influence it has over the politics of its neighbors. Consequently, such a country is likely to become independent and threaten the interests of some superpowers. There is no doubt that the international community does not want to see or hear about that powerful country rising like the morning star. Thus, the implementation of the well-known philosophy: divide to better reign!

Now, no matter what the fate of the Congolese people will be, one thing will stand: the truth. The Congolese people recall this song by Maïtre Franco Luambo Makiadi, a legend of the Congolese music: "The white man has made guns to kill people, but not to kill the truth."[161] The truth, and only the truth, will stand and persist through the ages and will endure all conspiracies against the African people, in general, and the Congolese, in this case. One's tradition is not conquered like a town or like a country. This is a reality that western powers shall not grasp and comprehend in all their imperialistic conquests. They failed to understand it yesterday, cannot comprehend it today, and shall not master it tomorrow. And he, who speaks of tradition, speaks of Africans. The African tradition shall remain a metaphysic subject in the Western Hemisphere.

If the international community does not act quickly, for something that is already too late anyway (for not having done it early and prudently), they shall reap their reward, for this war shall be long, popular, and exported to where it came from. Either the world, as a body, stands for fairness, justice and peace for all, or they stand for destruction and war. For, "[we] too have noticed how the international community is biased against the DR Congo and the majority of Congolese people ... the international community is biased against the government and the Congolese people, very much in favor of Rwanda and Uganda, and very fearful about another massacre against the Tutsi, but blind to the many massacres committed against the Congolese people at large."[162]

One inspired westerner, with first hand experience in the Congolese tragedy, made the following pleading: "Currently in the sub-region of the DRC, the people are taking control of their destiny, at the cost, however, of great bloodshed and tears. So let us turn our attention once again to our black brothers and sisters who we have ignored for so long. We have an obligation to go beyond rhetorical declarations and intentions and to reinvest in the country in a culture of respect that respects Congolese culture. At the same time we must push for peace."[163] Unfortunately, the international community refused to listen to and ignored this call, which is the call of all the Congolese, in particular, and Africans, in general.

Chapter V
The United States of America's Controversial Politics in the DR Congo

The Congolese people know that the US of America had a great interest in this war of aggression by Rwanda and Uganda against their motherland, as they assisted the armies of these two countries with military training, arms and ammunition, intelligence, either directly or indirectly. In addition, the people of the DR Congo do not have a good memory of the US government for having facilitated the assassination in 1961 of their first democratically-elected Premier Minister. They are aware that "The United States' involvement in Congo since before independence from Belgium in June 1960 has been steady, sinister, and penetrating. Most notable was the CIA's role in the overthrow (September 1960) and later assassination (January 1961) of Congo's first Prime Minister, the charismatic (and socialist), Patrice Lumumba,"[164] as emphasized Ellen Ray.

Further, the US government had supported the dictatorship of the late Mobutu for more than three decades. Mobutu's reign was one of terror, wide violations of human rights, misappropriation, nepotism, tribalism, mismanagement, institutionalization of corruption, inversion of moral values, looting of private and public properties, and many other vices that have led to the total and complete collapse of the state's infrastructures. Last, not least, the Congolese people do not appreciate the arrogance of the American government, its open-sided politics, unfairness, injustice, cowardice, and promotion of violations of human rights and war of aggression against their dear nation by its allies, Rwanda and Uganda.

1. The Might of the United States of America

The strength of the American government is its foreign policy. But one always wonders how many Americans know or are interested in their foreign affairs. One also wonders whether, if Americans were somehow more interested in the way their government behaves outside of their "home," this world would not have become more peaceable and united. In the past years, "Former president Nelson Mandela condemned 'the attitude of the United States of America (as) a threat to world peace..."[165]

American politics in Africa, in general, and, in the DR Congo, in particular, are just a joke. If one tells a less-enlightened American that his government promotes war and human rights abuse in Africa, in the name of economic and other interests, that person will probably think that the one uttering those words is insane and a fool. Why? Well, because, this kind of thought and conduct is almost unthinkable and unacceptable in American domestic affairs. However, "...no foreign policy can be sustained [in this country] without the informed consent of the American people. We learned that lesson in Vietnam...,"[166] warned the wise Senator, Joe Biden.

Let no one make any mistake. Contrarily to the ignorance they show about their foreign affairs policies, and a general and traditional arrogance that they display, Americans are lovely people. They are, indeed, some of the few people in the world one would like to have as neighbors. On the other hand, it worries more than one that Americans often show a blind fanaticism and submission toward their leaders, in particular, their president. If you ask them, for example, why do you hate the Democratic Party? They will generally reply that it is because of their liberalism. If asked, for instance, what's wrong with liberalism, you will get an unsound and vague answer.

It is obvious that Americans hate Saddam Hussein. If you inquire about the reasons behind this hatred, why did they go to war in 1991 and 2003 against Iraq, the response is often ambiguous, irrational and even puerile. The general answer in this case is that Saddam Hussein is a bad guy, evil. If you ask them, do you know the US made Saddam Hussein, they are surprised and suddenly stop the discussion. Then, the ignorance is demonstrated. What they know, in fact, is what TV channels portray, and what they believe is what they hear their president say, and repeat over, and over, and over again. There is rarely critical and positive thinking. So when the American president says, "We need to attack Iraq and remove Saddam Hussein from power because of human rights abuse and proliferation of weapons of mass destruction," everyone cheers, very few question his real motives, in this instance, the control of Iraqi oil. It is unfortunate that this ignorance does allow them to condemn guys like Saddam Hussein for their dictatorship and lack of democracy; for if Americans looked closely at the history of their foreign policy with regard to this subject, they will be stunned and ashamed.

Mondli Makhanya, a South African journalist with the Sunday Times, recorded the following, in line with the above: "IT WAS author James Baldwin who once commented that he loves America 'more than any other country in this world, and exactly for this reason, I insist on the right to criticize her perpetually.' If only Baldwin countrymen had adopted his approach to patriotism then maybe the world would be spared the monster that its only power is turning out to be. In a very odd way, the nation that portrays itself as the bastion of liberty and enlightenment has now become the enemy of these values. The philosophy of Americans is that they are right and their rightness gives them the right to bully the world. It is therefore likely that very soon, American warplanes will be bombing Iraq and tanks will be trundling through the desert. Back home in the US, there will be frenzied flag-waving and anthem-singing sessions as Americans follow the war live on television. There will be very little in the way of questioning the motives of the US government. What President George W. Bush and his posse of securo-crats say will be gospel truth. The more extreme their war talk, the more appreciative the American audience will be. And the louder their shrieks, the louder the applause will be among Americans baying for Arab blood. It is an enviable position that Bush is in. Many world leaders would give an arm and a leg to be able to manipulate their domestic audiences like that. Even the likes of Robert Mugabe and Pakistan's Pervez Musharraf get tougher opposition from their populations for decisions they take. Only absolute despots like Muammar Gaddafi—and yes, Saddam Hussein—receive louder adulation than American presidents.

"Americans have given their rulers carte blanche to do as they wish—so long as they invoke the name and spirit of the 'founding fathers.' America has reached the point at which patriotism becomes totally dangerous. The rhetoric and arrogance emanating from the US, both from ordinary as well as political leaders and opinion-formers, sounds eerily like the noises made in the fascist states in the 1930s and 1940s. When reputable newspapers and powerful broadcasters begin to sound like state-controlled media in dictatorships, you have to worry. Were it not for the fact that the US is a modernized state, one could easily draw comparisons between its psyche and that of the infant fascist republics of the past century. But the US is democratic and prosperous, and generally takes good care of its citizens. It pronounces freedom of thought and expression among its core values. The problem is that the society has been so "dumbed down" that Americans eschew these liberties and parrot whatever the official line is at a particular time. Even the two parties, which compete for political power every four years, are almost replicas of each other. The little political divergence that occurs takes place on the distant fringes of society. It is the form of racist extremist groupings and charismatic black religious leaders. Otherwise, Americans think uniformly."[167]

One also needs to know, with regard to American foreign politics, that "the principle of the defense of human rights cannot be consistently applied in foreign policy because it can and must come in conflict with other interests that may be more important than the defense of human rights in a particular instance ... that the defense of human rights must be woven into the fabric of American foreign policy is, of course, an attempt to conceal impossibility of consistently pursuing the defense of human rights. And once you fail to defend human rights in one instance, you have given up the defense of human rights and you have accepted another principle to guide your actions,"[168] a principle which is anti-democratic and criminal, and therefore, dangerous for the maintenance of peace and stability in the world.

For instance, "[t]the State Department encourages 'African solutions to African problems,' but when the involved countries' chief concern is sustaining their power in their own countries, chaos in the Congo is a solution to their problems. While the United Nations shrinks from instigating change, the United States prefers to remain uninvolved and continues to have ties with Uganda and Rwanda," two modern terrorist countries they know have committed more atrocities and violations of all imaginable international human rights and humanitarian laws in the DR Congo, than Saddam Hussein ever committed on his own people and neighbors throughout his entire reign.

The following is a reproduction of a copy of a letter written by Congresswoman Cynthia McKinney on 31 August, 1999, and addressed to American President Clinton:[169]

Honorable William Jefferson Clinton
President, United States of America
The White House
Washington, DC 20515

Mr. President:

I have just returned from the Democratic Republic of Congo, meeting with committed individuals from a myriad of walks of life. Unfortunately, I feel compelled to report to you that crimes against humanity are being committed in the Democratic Republic of Congo and throughout Africa, seemingly with the help and support of your Administration. I would suggest to you that US policy in the Democratic Republic of Congo has failed and it is another example of our policy failure across the continent. One only has to point out to diplomatic duality in Ethiopia and Eritrea, indecisiveness and ambivalence in Angola, indifference in the Democratic Republic of Congo, the destruction of democracy in Sierra Leone, and inflexibility elsewhere on the Continent. The result is an Africa policy in disarray, a Continent on fire, and US complicity in crimes against humanity.

Mr. President, everywhere, people whisper it, but are too "polite" to say it out loud: your Africa policy has not only NOT helped to usher in the so-called "African Renaissance," but has contributed to the continued pain and suffering of the African peoples.

Meanwhile, thousands of people die unnoticed each day from poverty, disease, and war. This is not the legacy that you want to leave for all of us who have supported you and who also care very deeply for Africa. And I am convinced that you don't want the "drift" of your Africa policy to inflict more suffering among the world's most vulnerable people as you wind down your last days in the White House.

In addition, your failure to intervene and stop the illegal invasion of the Democratic Republic of Congo by your allies, Uganda and Rwanda, has directly led to the commission of crimes against humanity by their troops in the Democratic Republic of Congo.

Even now, you ask the world to "shadow kiss" this outrageous policy by calling these two countries uninvited when the world knows both Uganda and Rwanda are military aggressors deep in the territory of the Democratic of the Congo, far away from their borders. The atrocities being suffered daily by all the people of this region are outrageous and are compounded by bad US policy and indifferent US leadership.

Finally, Mr. President, you must take personal charge of our policy. The current policies have boomeranged against us and have bankrupted us in the eyes of our victims and the world. How could you justify leaving Africa in flames as you leave the White House?

It is now time for you to personally engage on these important issues. I stand ready to be your ally on the Hill for all these important issues. We all know that when you get involved in a concerted push of peace it does make a difference. The time for your personal engagement is now.

Thank you, Mr. President for your consideration of this request. Now more than ever, your attention is needed to help Africa climb out of this vicious downward cycle.

Sincerely,
/Signed/
Cynthia McKinney, Member of Congress and member of the House Committee on International Relations and Committee on National Security

On April 16, 2001, Congresswoman Cynthia McKinney organized a roundtable discussion at the Rayburn House Office Building to discuss American foreign policy toward Africa. The following are extracts of her Opening Statement[170] at the occasion:

...The activities of Western governments and Western businessmen in post-colonial Africa provide clear evidence of the West's long standing propensity for cruelty, avarice, and treachery. The misconduct of Western countries in Africa is not due to momentary lapses, individual defects, or errors of common human frailty. Instead, they form part of a long-term malignant policy designed to access and plunder Africa's wealth at the expense of its people. In short, the accounts you are about to hear provide an indictment of Western activities in Africa.

That [the] West has, for decades, plundered Africa's wealth and permitted, and even assisted in slaughtering Africa's people. The West has been able to do this while still shrewdly cultivating the myth that much of Africa's problems today are African made. We have all heard the usual Western defenses that Africa's problems are the fault of corrupt African administrations, the fault of centuries-old tribal hatreds, the fault of unsophisticated peoples rapidly entering a modern high technology world.

But we know that those statements are all a lie. We have always known it.

...At the hearts of Africa's suffering is the West's, and most notably the United States', desire to access Africa's diamonds, oil, natural gas, and other precious resources... The West, and most notably the United States, has set in motion a policy of oppression, destabilization, and tempered, not by moral principle, but by ruthless desire to enrich itself on Africa's fabulous wealth. While falsely pretending to be the friends and allies of many African countries, so desperate for help and assistance, many western nations, and I'm ashamed to say most notably the United States, have in reality betrayed those countries' trust, and instead, have relentlessly pursued their own selfish military and economic policies. Western countries have incited rebellion against stable African governments by encouraging and even arming opposition parties and rebel groups to begin armed insurrection. The Western nations have even actively participated in the assassination of duly elected and legitimate African Heads of State and replaced them with corrupted and malleable officials. Western nations have even encouraged and been complicit in the unlawful invasions by African nations into neighboring countries.

These accounts today are public indictment of European and American governments and businessmen. Something must be done to right these wrongs. Something must be done to restore Africa to peace and prosperity...

A month later, Congresswoman Cynthia McKinney addressed the US Congress Committee on International Relations, Subcommittee on International Operations and Human Rights,[171] on the Congolese crisis as recorded below in its entirety:

IMMEDIATE RELEASE
Statement of Ranking Member Congresswoman Cynthia McKinney
Subcommittee on International Operations and Human Rights
Committee on International Relations
Suffering and Despair: Humanitarian Crisis in the Congo

May 17, 2001

Madam Chair,

This hearing today is vitally important because we have the opportunity to set the record straight as to what has been happening in the Democratic Republic of Congo for the last 3 years. We have the opportunity to be able to draw together the varying investigations and reports of experts who have examined the DRC War and place in the public record the truth about what Rwanda, Uganda, and their rebel allies have done to the people of the DRC. We have the opportunity to pass judgment on the Clinton legacy and make a finding as to exactly what Madeleine Albright and her foreign policy team has done to the Great Lakes region.

I think it's also important to point out at the outset that the US and Belgium deserve special condemnation for the 37 years of suffering in the DRC because it was their intelligence services who conspired to assist in the murder of the democratically elected President, Patrice Lumumba. The west chose Mobuto to replace him and for the next 3 generation's Zaire, as it was then known, was placed in the grip of a corrupt and evil leadership. Despite the mining of billions of dollars of minerals and other resources DRC was left by Mobuto nearly bankrupt and on the brink of collapse. The corporations and the western businessmen who traded with Mobuto never once called him to order, instead they celebrated in his fabulous homes and enriched themselves at the expense of the Congolese people.

Rwanda, Uganda, and their rebel allies began a war in August 1998 in the DRC under the claim of fighting the Hutu interahamwe, the Rwandan militia responsible for much of the killing during the 1994 Rwandan Genocide. President Museveni of Uganda and President Kagame of Rwanda have always maintained that by fighting in the DRC they will defeat the interahamwe, and in so doing secure their borders and prevent another Rwandan type genocide from occurring. They continue to maintain this position until this very day. But this Rwandan/Ugandan explanation for their invasion of DRC is a lie, it's a bright shining lie.

This is not a noble war about saving civilians from genocide or about protecting democracy from tyranny, instead this is a war about self-interest and greed. Despite limp and totally ineffective protestations by the United Nations, the world community has largely stood idly by and allowed these two men to prosecute what can only be described as the most vicious, senseless, and bloody wars being fought in the world today.

The cost of their actions to the DRC and its people is almost beyond measure.

The scale and savagery of the crimes committed by the Rwandan and Ugandan armies in DRC compares to the abhorrent actions of the Nazi assault upon Eastern Europe.

The International Rescue Committee has just released a 2001 Survey of the Death Toll in DRC's war. For the 32-month period from August 1998 until the end of March 2001 an estimated 2.5 million civilians have died in the DRC. Of those 350,000 people have died from violence and 2.2 million have died from disease and malnutrition arising from the adverse effects of the war on the region. IRC estimates that on average 77,000 civilians have perished each and every month in the DRC. That's almost 2,500 civilians dying each day for almost the last 3 years. Compare those numbers with the lost lives in Kuwait 10 years ago and the world's response to Iraqi aggression. The world sent 350,000 troops to the gulf to defend Kuwait. In 100 days the combined military, naval, and air forces of the Western world had reduced the Iraqi military, one of the world's powerful armies, to a burning hulk. And then compare DRC's suffering with the 2 thousand lost lives in Kosovo two years ago. The combined air forces of NATO pounded Belgrade into submission and then indicted Milosevic for war crimes. We all remember how the western world responded to the Iraqi and Kosovo humanitarian disasters and flooded them with food, medicines, shelter, and other aid.

Madam Chairwoman, I am ashamed to say that the western world has treated DRC like it has treated all the other African disasters—too little too late. In January 2001 the World Food Program issued a worldwide appeal for $110 million for urgent food aid to Congo. As of May the World Food Program had received less than one third of this amount. Similarly, UNICEF had asked for $15 million in essential drugs and therapeutic feeding, and to date UNICEF has received less than one tenth of that amount. Incredibly, the principal aid sent by the US to the region has been in the form of military aid to the warring parties. What we do know is that US Special Forces and US funded private military companies have been arming and training Rwandan and Ugandan troops to deadly effect. I think it's appalling that the US tax payer should be directly assisting the military efforts of Rwanda and Uganda, the aggressors in this tragic conflict and who have confirmed by Amnesty International and Human Rights Watch as the authors of terrible atrocities against Congolese civilians. Our efforts in Africa have amounted to nothing more than bank rolling belligerents and mass murders.

What makes this conflict particularly sickening is the role of US and European corporations together with Rwanda and Uganda in the plunder of DRC's resources. The recent UN Report on the Illegal Exploitation of Natural Resources from the DRC made a series of important findings. Before going on let me first commend Madam Safiatou Ba-N'Daw and other UN panelists for their work in preparing the UN Secretary General with a truly first rate investigative report on the theft of DRC's resources.

The report concluded that "there is a mass scale looting, systemic exploitation of Congo's resources taking place at an alarming rate by the armies of Burundi, Rwanda, and Uganda." For example the report finds that "DARA Great Lakes Industry of which DARA Forest is a subsidiary is in collusion with the Ministry of Water, Land and Forests of Uganda to export timber from eastern Congo by falsifying its origins. The countries actively buying this uncertified timber included USA, China, Belgium, Denmark, Japan, Kenya, and Switzerland. In May 2000 DGLI (the parent of DARA Forest) signed a contract for forest stewardship certification with SmartWood and the rogue Institute for Ecology and Economy in Oregon in the United States." This program amounted to nothing more than a scheme to facilitate the certification and extraction of illegally acquired timber from the DRC.

The same large scale theft of DRC's resources has been committed with respect to cobalt, gold, diamonds, coltan, silver, zinc, uranium, and numerous other minerals. Significantly, DRC has some of the world's largest deposits of Coltan, an important mineral critical for maintaining the electric charge in the computer chip industry. The price of Coltan varies from $100 to $200,000 a ton varying on quality and availability. Business in Coltan is booming but its not the Congolese who are getting rich.

Madame Chairwoman, there is an additional and very disturbing report from MISNA, the Catholic News Agency regarding Rwanda's actions with respect to the theft of DRC's resources. MISNA reported in February this year that the Rwandan Army is now setting up "concentration camps" in the Numbi area south of Kivu in order to have sufficient labor on hand to extract Coltan and other precious minerals. It was this enslavement of innocent civilians and captured prisoners of war that drew some of the harshest criticisms against the Nazi and Japanese leadership from the Nuremberg and Tokyo War Crimes Tribunals.

In response to the findings by the UN Special Panel the Rwandans have had the audacity to say that the Congolese people are benefitting from the mining trade in eastern Congo with improvement in their welfare, security, health, education, and infrastructure. Madame Chairwoman, that's almost like saying that the peoples of Eastern Europe who were enslaved in quarries, underground mines, and forced to work in dangerous conditions in automotive and munitions plants benefitted from the Nazi occupation of their countries.

Mr. Robert Raun, President of Eagles Wings resources, a US based company which trades in Coltan, was reported to have described the growing trade in east Congo's Coltan as "Capitalism in its purest form." I say it's capitalism trading in misery.

Madame Chairwoman, we need to support the recommendations of the Ba-N'Daw UN Special Report on the Illegal Exploitation of the Natural Resources from the DRC.

We need to end all military support for the Rwandan / Ugandan military forces.

Our government should publicly condemn the governments of Rwanda and Uganda for their criminal actions in eastern Congo, and we should demand that an International Tribunal be established in the Great Lakes Region to investigate and prosecute the violations of international law.

We need to urgently increase US aid to the peoples of Congo and ensure that they receive adequate food, health care, medicines, and shelter.

We should call on our allies and the entire international community to join us ending the conflict in DRC.

I would end with this. Is it that US military bases in Uganda and Rwanda and easy access to DRC's resources are worth all of this? Thank you, Madam Chair.

The above letter and statements from Congresswoman McKinney are reproduced to show that both the US administration and US Congress knew about the Congolese tragedy from its very beginning. In this case, it should be understood, mostly by the Americans, that the US government was at the top of the war of aggression and invasion against the DR Congo. Further, as the statements prove, the US policy in Africa is the basis of bloodshed between different nations, and thus a risk factor for peace on the African continent. If the aforementioned letter and statements came from a foreign government, institution, or media, Americans would not hear them. They will call them fabricated stories aimed at undermining democracy and the freedom the Founding Fathers fought for. But would they doubt or dispute the involvement of their government in African tragedies, in general, and Congolese, in particular, now that the evidence is as direct as presented by their own elected representatives?

Why would a High-Ranking Member of the US Congress publicly accuse her government of supporting militarily aggression and invasion in the DR Congo if these facts were not substantiated by hard evidence and were true? Furthermore, how would the US government today label another government that supports an aggressor and invader foreign army which terrorizes and commits gross violations of human rights in the occupied territories, and organizes unpopular rebellions with the aim of destabilizing the occupied country? Would the sticky label "terrorist government" or "terrorist state" be appropriate? And if such a label were truly appropriate, would not the US government be also called a terrorist government using the same argument, the same causes giving the same effects? Let one judge it for him or herself.

Or, should one maybe reason like Socrates:[172] if in international law terrorism means "the use or threat of violence to intimidate or cause panic, especially as a means of affecting political conduct,"[173] or if a terrorist is an individual or group of individuals, private or public organization, or state that commits premeditated or non-premeditated acts of violence terror, who substantially encourages such acts by advising or assisting materially individual or groups of individuals, private or public organizations, or states, or who harbors those who he, she, or it knows or has reason to know have conspired to commit such acts, acts which cause terror and whose effect is terror, or if "a terrorist is a person or group of persons, or a state that targets innocent people in order to accomplish its purposes;"[174] and given that, the US government's military assistance to Rwanda and Uganda, two States that aggressed and invaded the DR Congo, and assistance that the US government knew or had reason to know was used to commit genocide, war crimes, crimes against humanity and terrorism in the occupied territories of the DRC, satisfied the aforesaid definitions, should one thus conclude that the US government is a terrorist regime for displaying such conduct under the circumstances? May those who have come to a different logical and reasonable conclusion that does not support the evidence Congresswoman McKinney has shown, and upon which evidence an average reasonable person would come to a fair and just conclusion, demonstrate it.

But, the world knows, as far as the aggression of the DRC is concerned, that "The USA is ... deeply involved in the military support, through instructors, advisers, and the supply of equipment to their allies in Africa. Before 1994, the USA supported the pro-American regime of Yuweri Museveni in Uganda, who in turn—with the green light of the USA—supported the Rwandan Patriotic Front's guerrilla warfare against the neighboring pro-French regime in Rwanda. The co-operation proved successful, as the RPF managed to take over from the extremists, Hutus. Then, as acknowledged officially in 1997, US involvement in the region carried on, with the training of Rwandan armed forces and Kabila's troops in the war against Mobutu's regime in Zaire, in 1996-1997, a period during which both committed grave human rights violations. An impressive and highly sophisticated system of communication was put in place to spy on the whole region, with two US transmission stations in Uganda and Rwanda, and a third on a US military boat off the Congo's coast. The training of Rwanda troops by US military instructors, to be sent to flight in the DRC, continued in 1998 and 1999 at least,"[175] points out Xavier Renou.

From now on, the argument that the American administration backed Rwanda and Uganda up in their war of aggression against the DR of Congo should be neither debatable nor disputable. The question should not be whether they did it but rather, why did they do that? It is believed that the US supported the war due to some sort of a guilty conscience about the Rwandan 1994 genocide. But one needs to understand that the US engagement in the DRC is to defend their national security, for various financial and economical interests, and finally, in order to establish regional power and control in Africa. These are the other four sections dealt with in this chapter.

2. A Guilty Conscience?

Rwanda has never been an ally to the US, but it was to France. The DR Congo has been one of the strongest American political allies in Central Africa and in the entire Great Lakes Region since the sixties; and it successfully helped the US stop the spreading of a dangerous "disease" in Africa called communism. Rwanda, ordinary people say, became an ally of the US by sympathy due to the inaction of the latter to help stop the killings during the 1994 genocide. Thus, the thesis that the US acted on the sides of Rwanda in invading the DR Congo because of a guilty conscience. However, as the lines below explain, there is enough evidence that the US supported the military campaigns of the RPF and was in favor of the 1994 Rwandan genocide.

The US—as is the case today with the DR Congo—was the first country to refuse not only the deployment of UN's peacekeeping force in Rwanda to prevent the 1994 genocide, but also an increase in number while there were already warning signs and alarming reports that a genocide was about to be committed, and was thereafter being committed. According to a Human Rights Paris-based report released on the dawn of the fifth anniversary of the Rwandan genocide, "the United States, Belgium, France, and the UN Security Council all had prior warning about plans for the 1994 genocide in Rwanda and could have prevented it ... even worse, foreign leaders reacted timidly and tardily once the killing began... The Americans were interested in saving money, the Belgians were interested in saving face, and the French were interested in saving their ally, the genocidal government."[176]

Xavier Renou records the following about the 1994 Rwandan genocide that "when the full magnitude of the tragedy became apparent, Boutros-Ghali [then UN Secretary-General] requested the deployment of 5,500 UN peacekeeping troops, as initially suggested by France, which was even prepared to send its own soldiers. Such an intervention would indeed have prevented the US-backed RPF from taking control of the whole country. It would have forced both sides to negotiate, which means that the Hutu extremists would have had to be part of any transitory government. To allow the necessary reconciliation, the launching of the genocide would have had to be officially 'forgotten' or forgiven. Rwanda would not have fallen to the 'Anglo-Saxons,' and conditions for a future take-over by pro-French elements would have been preserved. For the USA, this proposal was unacceptable. The RPF had to take over from the extremists, Hutus. As a result, the UN were at a standstill, and France sent its own troops in Operation Turquoise. The USA, with the RPF firmly in power, authorised the deployment of 7,500 UN troops to organize humanitarian relief operations."[177]

Now instead of learning from the irreparable mistake they made, the same Clinton administration repeated the same stupid mistake by influencing the UN Security Council to give little consideration to the aggression of the DR Congo by her allies, Rwanda and Uganda. Worst of all, the same government supported victims of yesterday's genocide in committing another genocide, not only on innocent Congolese people, but also on the Hutus. The American administration's illogical logic is a demoniac reasoning that one can interpret this way, as referring to the Rwandan Tutsis' criminal actions in the occupied territories of the Democratic Republic of Congo:

We do not know how to say sorry for letting the Hutus kill thousands of *you*r people without preventing such awful conduct, though we knew about such plan. Now it is your turn. So pursuit your killers within and outside of your national territories, mostly in the DR Congo; kill and even exterminate them by all means—summary execution, massacre, starvation, drowning—and make sure to control the Congolese government; and if the Congolese are not submissive in this conquest, do not even hesitate to massacre them, do all this without any fear and regret like the Hutus did to those of your families that had fallen, and lo, we will be with you always, even unto the end of the world, and promise that no action will be taken against you at the UN Security Council, since your actions will be called 'rebellion,' border protection, prevention of another genocide, but never an aggression and invasion of a sovereign state. And, your big brother, Uganda, shall assist you in your adventure. Good luck, kill, kill and kill, do not forget to rape also, and plunder their mineral and natural resources, burn their villages, be merry, for tomorrow we die and all is well!

Not surprising that when Susan E. Rice met with Kagame, she did not even debate the presence of Rwandan troops on DR Congo soil. In fact, she was heard asking if the "obsessions of the Congolese government on the aggression of the DR Congo by Rwanda and Uganda made sense." The Congolese people understand that without the involvement of the US on the sides of Rwanda and Uganda in the invasion of their country, two things might have happened: first, Rwanda and Uganda would not have dared attack the DR Congo, or, even if they had, the war would have ended long ago with their defeat; second, the aggression would also have ended, either by a voluntary or negotiated withdrawal, with the help of African leaders. But the US, more than Rwanda and Uganda, wanted the illegal occupation of the DR Congo to continue for strategic reasons. One hopes that Kagame and Museveni soon understand that Mobutu, Savimbi, Saddam Hussein, Noriega, and many others around the world, used to be great allies to Washington before they [Kagame and Museveni] became such, and their fate is well-known today.

So, it is easy to understand that the US is simply using Kagame and Museveni, or taking advantage of the crisis in the Great Lakes region, to make it look like they are concerned about the safety of the Tutsis. Where were Clinton and his administration in 1994, when the threat of genocide in Rwanda was so apparent and then became a reality? It is ridiculous and, indeed, shameful that "in the DR Congo, the Clinton administration has allowed its remorse for its failure to prevent the genocide of 1994, its desire to see a shining economic star in central and eastern Africa, and its obsession with Sudan's sponsorship of international terrorism to blind it to the Ugandan and Rwandan invasion and occupation of sovereign territories. Rather openly and insistently condemning those actions, the US has covered them under the cloak of President Kabila's failures to democratize and build an inclusive society. The net result of this net policy has been that the Congo was occupied and divided yesterday, it is so today, and it will be tomorrow. But even worse, some 800,000 or more, Congolese have been displaced by war and the Congolese people are now thwarted from every angle to pursue their destiny and improve the quality of their lives. Had the United States spent more time pressing Uganda and Rwanda stay out of the Congo, and less time worrying about the capacity of the Congolese people to get a grip on their leadership, everyone involved would have been a lot better off."[178] But the US is a Hercules, and they want war today, war tomorrow, and war forever in Africa.

The annoying thing about the American government is their arrogance in believing that they are the only people who think right on this earth, and therefore, they have the right to make any decision on behalf of any nation in the world. So they can and must forcibly remove any foreign leader who does not embrace their bestial policy and replace him with one of their choice. This is an insult and a demonstration that the US has been practicing international terrorism, long before the world became accustomed to the use of that word. The other irritating thing is the fact that, because of their arrogance, they always have some excuses to justify their mistakes, for the same wrongdoings for which other countries would be classified as human rights violators and terrorist states. By the same token, they use the same strategy to justify their allies' gross violations of human rights. Thus, it follows that "the discourse of human rights violations has become politicized. Political opponents are criticized as human rights violators. Violations by allies are met with silence,"[179] and even with applause.

As for the Congolese people, if the US owes some kind of compensation to the Rwandan Tutsis for their failure to prevent the 1994 genocide and protect them during the genocide, the US should look for a modest, civilized, and human way of doing it. Maybe the US government can also fly the Tutsis orphans to the Us and help them enjoy the blessings of the "land of the free and the home of the brave," as they did with the children of Kosovo whose parents died during the war. After all, there is also much space in the US of America, and Rwandan Tutsis will gladly appreciate it if the children of those who died during the genocide were taken to the US for their care and education.

To that end, one thing is true and needs to be emphasized. All the Congolese "are very disappointed by the failure of the United States Government to condemn the invasion, aggression, and pillage of [their] country by the Rwandese, Ugandan, and Burundese armies. [They] fail to understand how the USA Administration can fall for the lies being told by those governments, especially Rwanda, about the need to invade the DR Congo, to overthrow the government, and to carve up the Congo—all in the name of border security. It boggles the mind to think the American Administration is falling for this smoke screen... The Administration has said that they never encouraged the invasions, and never condemn them... But, you know... when the United States fail to condemn, it is understood as encouragement. In this case, the US failure to condemn Rwanda, Burundi, and Uganda is tantamount to encouragement."[180] Period, for anything more or less is a lie.

3. In the Name of National Security!

The study of international human rights can broaden one's knowledge about international relations and politics, and enlighten one on how hypocritical are the relations between Western countries and the rest of the world, in general, and the so-called third world, in particular. For example, "in the 1980 United States presidential campaign, the strategic use of human rights was a campaign issue. Presidential candidate Ronald Reagan argued that President Jimmy Carter, by pursuing respect for human rights in Iran and Nicaragua, had destabilized the regime in place, both of which were friendly to the US The destabilization has led to their replacement by regimes, which were unfriendly to the US. Again here, the debate was not about what can be done to promote human rights, but rather the trade off between politics and human rights. These debates about the strategic use of human rights have given the notion of strategy in pursuit of human rights a bad name. The notion of strategy conjures up images of a debate about whether to pursue respect for human rights, about allowing economical or political to rump human rights concerns."[181]

The US Human Rights and Security Assistance, Sec. 502B of the Foreign Assistance Act of 1961, as amended, 22 USCA §2304 has in the implementation requirements section the following provisions regarding the observance of human rights as the principal goal of foreign policy:[182]

(1) The United States shall, in accordance with its international obligations as set forth in the Charter of the United Nations and in keeping with the constitutional heritage and traditions of the United States, promote and encourage increased respect for human rights and fundamental freedom throughout the world without distinction as to race, sex, language, and religion. Accordingly, a principal goal of the foreign policy of the United States shall be to promote the increased observance of internationally recognized human rights by all countries.

(2) Except under circumstances specified in this section, no security assistance may be provided to any country the government of which engages in a consistent pattern of gross violations of internationally recognized human rights ... unless the President certifies in writing ... that extraordinary circumstances exist warranting promotion of such assistance....

(3) In furtherance of paragraphs (1) and (2), the President is directed to formulate and conduct international security assistance programs of the United States in a manner which will promote and advance human rights and avoid identification of the United States, through such programs...

What constitutes extraordinary circumstances is debatable and is entirely left to the discretion of the US president. Thus, a foreign government receiving such assistance from the US may invade another country, massacre (on a gross scale) the people of the invaded country, and commit all kinds of gross violations of international human rights. As long as the extraordinary circumstances' "requirements" are met, all is well with the American administration in the name of national security. This is the case with Rwanda and Uganda, two international criminal states that benefit from US assistance and that invaded a sovereign and independent country, the DR Congo, and which are likely to escape liabilities for grave violations of human rights and international humanitarian laws in the occupied territories of the DRC because of secret combinations with their imperialistic allies.

These two countries will continue to benefit from American assistance, in accordance to paragraph (2) of Sec. 502B of the Foreign Assistance Act of 1961, as amended, 22 USCA §2304, until true leadership leads the USA. It is quite hard to understand how can a government like that of the US, without any shame and concern for its own citizens who deserve better management of the res publica, believe and apply such a policy in its dealings with foreign states? Where are, then, the American values brilliantly and proudly spoken of, if the US government closes its eyes when some allies are violating international, well-established human rights, and humanitarian laws that are universally acceptable by all, just to preserve certain security interests? One can easily infer from this that national security prevented US intervention in Rwanda in 1994, and the same motivate them to not even dare condemn the aggression of the DR Congo by Rwanda and Uganda. One can also observe that the US government's today policy and assistance toward Rwanda and Uganda are in open conflict with the above paragraph (3) of the aforementioned Foreign Assistance Act. Whether a government violates human rights at home or abroad is the same in the eyes of the world, for victims are human beings. A violation of internationally recognized human rights is an international crime that should be sanctioned fairly.

This "policy of the United States came under increasing attack in many parts of Africa, with many voices—including heads of state like Robert Mugabe of Zimbabwe—accusing the US of supporting the Rwandan and Ugandan actions in Congo. The former Assistant Secretary of State for African Affairs, Susan Rice, responded to such allegations in testimony before the House Subcommittee on Africa on September 15, 1999, calling them 'specious and ridiculous.' She reiterated that the US 'fully understands their legitimate security interests in countering insurgents' attacks from the Congolese soil,' and shared 'regional and international frustration with the Kinshasa government's failures with respect to both democratization and human rights.' Nevertheless, she contented that foreign intervention to overthrow the government was 'not acceptable.' Rice said nothing about reports that Rwandan or Ugandan troops might have, themselves, been implicated in rebels' abuse against civilians. She went on to state that 'the US considered Angolan, Namibian, and Zimbabwean intervention as 'destabilizing and very dangerous as well.'''[183] One hopes that Rice underwent a psychiatric evaluation before joining the Brookings Institute in Washington DC, for her reasoning was irresponsible.

How can one react to this type of childish and demagogic reasoning from a person, especially one who holds a high office for that matter? But, one conclusion is reasonable: only one who is drunk with morning's strong wine can argue that way, as Susan Rice did. One wonders what Susan E. Rice thinks of Congresswoman Cynthia McKinney's letter to President Clinton and her statement to the US Congress Committee on International Relations, Subcommittee on International Operations and Human Rights, both that are reproduced in the first section of this chapter, and many others not reproduced in this book. One can only take the world for a witness that neither Susan Rice nor the American administration ever contradicted substantially the statements of Congresswoman McKinney and of others who revealed US involvement in the illegal occupation of the DR Congo.

As mentioned previously, the American government's shameful policy toward the DR Congo dates from the days of independence of this state from Belgium. When the Congolese Premier Minister, Emery Patrice Lumumba, opposed Belgium's efforts to back the secession of the Katanga province, "in this conflict the United States supported Belgium. The Eisenhower administration had encouraged Belgium to form a neo-colonial relationship with the Congo ... Dwight D. Eisenhower himself disdained African nationalism.... Given these attitudes, it should not be surprising that the United States favored Belgium intervention in the Congo. When the Belgium paratroopers intervened, USA welcomed the action.... The United States did not protest against Belgian excesses, even after the Matadi massacres and the Katanga secession ... Most importantly, the Eisenhower administration favored the Katanga secession, which ... was a bulwark for the Belgian interests."[184] As one may notice, the time and people have changed, but American politics toward the DR Congo remain amazingly the same today as they were four decades ago. As to say, no need to change a policy that "works."

And history may sometimes repeat itself, as in the case at hand. The Eisenhower administration hated Lumumba and did not have any intention of supporting him to end of the Katanga secession, though Lumumba had some hope that the American government will help solve the Congolese crisis. He was falsely called a Marxist-communist, as was Laurent Kabila called, for just having been a disciple to Lumumba and a nationalist. "Lumumba also sought support from the United Nations force, but these were unavailing, since UN policy was nearly identical to American policy.... The UN Command refused to become involved in the Katanga controversy, insisting that it was an internal matter. When the UN troops came ... they failed even to enter Katanga province.... UN avoidance of Katanga is surprising. The United Nations force was sent to restore order in the Congo, and there is no doubt that the regional secessions fomented disorder. The UN's lethargy was apparently caused at least in part by the United States,"[185] as was the case with the invasion of the same country by Rwanda and Uganda.

After the US and the UN refused to intervene to halt the secessions in the DR Congo, Lumumba sought support from the Soviet Republic. From that time on, the CIA, in its wrath, sought to kill Lumumba. Gibbs argued that "these events disturbed American officials.... The Central Intelligence Agency, now determined to overthrow Lumumba. The CIA role requires some further discussion. Available evidence suggests that the agency was financing the Congolese National Army and funneling the payments through Joseph-Désiré Mobutu, a young and politically connected army officer.... On September 14, Colonel ... Mobutu staged a coup d'état ... Lumumba's removal as prime minister was reconfirmed ... The United States was involved in the coup ... During July and August [1960], the United Nations policy in the Congo was almost exactly the same as that of the United States. The UN failed to take actions against the regional secessions, while it undermined Prime Minister Lumumba."[186] That President Laurent D. Kabila might have been killed with the complicity of the same CIA is not surprising from the record read since the beginning of this war of aggression. Those who recall the dirty and clandestine works of the CIA all over the world will not also take this thought lightly, in the name of American national security.

Lumumba had strong and popular support from all Congolese, both from civilians and those in the armed forces. His removal made the country more ungovernable as the army and civilians wanted his reinstatement. History recalls that any country where a democratically-elected government had been toppled becomes chaotic, since democratic principles, the right rule of law, good governance, and the respect of human rights suffer a terrible setback. "Finally, on January 17, 1961, Lumumba was assassinated ... the CIA working with Mobutu and Tshombe probably played a role in the murder. With the removal of Lumumba, the Eisenhower administration accomplished its principal objective in the Congo.... The most distinctive feature of US policy was the deep hostility toward Patrice Lumumba. An explanation of US policy must account for the hostility. In their memoirs, Eisenhower-era officials justify the policies in anticommunist terms. The Soviet Union, they argue, seriously intended to take over Congo and its valuable resources. The United States had to remove Lumumba from power, since he was serving the soviet interests.... The United States was acting essentially to preclude Soviet expansion and to protect Western security.... The interpretation is not well supported. There is no evidence that the Soviets actually sought to take control of the Congo. Even if the Soviets did intend to seize power, it is very doubtful that they could have done so.... There is little evidence that Lumumba was a communist, and this point was recognized by American officials.... Lumumba sought American and UN aid several weeks before he accepted Soviet aid.... The Western security argument, moreover, fails to explain US Support for the Katanga secession....US support for the Katanga helped cause the Soviet involvement. Why then did the USA support Katanga? The Western security approach provides no answer."[187]

Thus, ended the life of a well-respected, intelligent, competent, loved, and the first democratically-elected Congolese Prime Minister, assassinated only to satisfy the demands of American national security. The DR Congo shall have several Lumumbas who may also be killed today and tomorrow in the name of American national security, if their actions are somehow found to be against such security interests in the DR Congo. This is very strange indeed and is not different from what authoritarian regimes are doing. Well, come what may, in the name of fairness, justice, peace, and democracy! Has the American policy of 1960-1961 in the DR Congo changed today? History and the experience say no! Does the American government care about the welfare of the Congolese? Even those who have died because of this devilish US policy in the DR Congo will not forget that the answer is no.

Is the American administration really interested in the protection of the Rwandan Tutsis to the point of justifying its shameful silence about the aggression of a sovereign state and the gross violations of human rights by its allies, Rwanda and Uganda, in the DR Congo? The answer is debatable. However, those who are enlightened say no since the same American administration had never explained why it failed to protect that ethnic group during the 1994 genocide. In addition, Kagame and Museveni do not even know their fate after their adventure ends. They are only milking cows. After they have been sucked and cannot produce milk, they will be given to the abattoir. They can rub their shoulders today with high US government officials and feel proud about themselves. Hopefully they do remember that there is a season to everything under heaven. They better converse with Mobutu and Savimbi in the spirit world as nothing precludes another better marriage—mutatis mutandis—between the American government and the Congolese government.

What does the US government want exactly in the DR Congo? The next sections will attempt to answer to this question.

4. Our Financial and Economical Interests First, Sirs!

In the DR Congo, the Congolese learn two realities that they carry with them through the ages and will never forget. They learn the first one at school and the second just in society. First, they learn and then know that the DR Congo is the third potentially richest country in the world, after the US and Russia. Well, one may think that this is nonsense talk. But studies have proved it. For example, "...Eastern Congo, virtually annexed by Uganda and Rwanda, is one of the most mineral-rich areas in the world ... Gold and diamonds and rare strategic minerals [that] are flowing into the two countries [Rwanda and Uganda], earning vast sums for their treasuries,"[188] are also found in that region. Second, without hurting anybody's feelings, Africans have also learned that when the American government gives you a chicken with one hand, it takes from you ten cows with the other hand. Here, the emphasis is on the capitalistic and materialistic culture and style of life. There is nothing for nothing, in other words. And that is the same principle that governs the relationship of the states in the world. Through that principle, alliances are made and broken off.

That the DR Congo is a potentially rich country is a fact. That is why it is called a "geological scandal." And the American government knows this fact better than any other earthly institution. It is believed that American satellites discovered numerous, important, rare, and precious minerals in the DR Congo decades ago. And the American government only knows the locations of those resources. This is like a kind of classified document, and it may be so until the Lord comes again. It is also believed that the lion is not as aggressive as the leopard toward people. He only attacks a human being when provoked; however, the degree of that provocation is left, unfortunately, to its sole discretion. In criminology studies, it is said that a robber does not enter someone's house with the primary intent to kill; otherwise, he is not no longer called a robber. But he kills, or commits felony murder, in two circumstances: first, in order to neutralize the person who discovers him; and second, to wipe away any evidence that may lead to his identification and arrest. Nevertheless, whatever the case, once he kills, he commits felony-murder and becomes a murderer.

Money is the source of all evil, the world says. When someone who looks at money as his master and idol is obstructed in gaining more, that person may not hesitate to kill, instigate conflicts, and incite people to fight and to start war because his pipes or taps are shut off. Those types of people are powerful; they have money; they can influence and even control politics. They also have the power to turn father against son, brother against sister, mother against daughter, and wife against husband. They may be organized into cartels and become even more powerful. They influence the great armies of the world, often bypassing some national and international laws. Everyone likes calling them "my friend" because of their money and power. Politicians mostly are their friends since these people contribute financially to their electoral campaigns. They have done so many good things for the world, but they are also accountable for the destruction of this world. They are called lobbyists. Do not mess with them; otherwise you'll be out of power and even dead. One of these people is Jean-Raymond Boulle.

Now, "who is Jean-Raymond Boulle? Aged forty-seven years old, Boulle is a British citizen native of Mauritius. He lives in Monaco in France. During the AFDL liberation war, reports Forbes, he arrived on March 27, 1997, in Goma, the general headquarters of the rebels. With his associate Joseph Martin, they bought diamonds produced in the occupied territories of Kabila. Thus, in April, they came back with concessions for two important mines... Boulle lent a light flight of the Amf firm to the rebellion of the time and advanced one million US dollars for mining tax purposes. In return, he was granted a contract to rehabilitate the bad lower production of copper and zinc noticed in Kipushi and to develop the exploration of copper and cobalt in Kolwezi. According to Forbes, Boulle has a good relationship with the Clinton administration. A week after the fall of Kinshasa in Kabila's hands, he sponsored the trip to the new Congo for powerful guests from Washington, among whom was a Congresswoman.

"Boss of Amf (American mineral fields) he has the means to do that because he can be allied with political contributions and official favors. He is well introduced in the political arena in Washington. Already, in 1987, he obtained from the then goyernor of Arkansas, who is Bill Clinton, the authorization to exploit an old diamond mine converted into a tourist park. A guest at the investiture of Bill Clinton at the White House, Boulle, who benefits from the misery of African people, does not only have the DRC as his hunting field. His enterprise, Amf, is well established in Angola. Mercenary and money being linked together in Africa, Boulle has connections with mercenaries' contractors. Thus, after the Clinton administration forced the Angolan government to abandon mercenaries they were using in aid of mercenaries approved by Washington, the boss of Amf bought the subsidiary of a security company to emerge, Idas, a company located in Belgium—this, with the rights to diamonds by paying 2.3 million US dollars in shares.... If Jean-Raymond Boulle can finance the war in Angola in order to get treasure, what can't he do in the Congo to get back what Kabila is refusing him after putting off contracts he signed in the past? Concordant sources in the United States link Boulle to what is happening in the Congo. He wants Kabila dead ... judges insufficient the way Kabila paid him back after he got power, comparing to the support he offered him during the liberation war. In addition, Amf does not appreciate that Kabila is about to sign a contract with the giant International conglomerate Anglo-American Corp from South Africa."[189]

That international lobbyists like Boulle have interests in DR Congo minerals is not questionable. Further, that people like Boulle may be one of those financing the aggression of the DR Congo is not surprising either. In addition, that Rwanda and Uganda are only using their human-power in this war against the DR Congo as their financial assistance comes from foreign Western powers is obvious. Furthermore, that the US, by its deliberate failure to condemn its Rwandan and Ugandan allies, which invaded a sovereign country, had only encouraged and supported such actions for obscure interests is a reality.

Finally, it is more than true that some American administration officials might have direct financial interests in the Congo and saw in President Laurent D. Kabila an obstacle to reaching their economic appetites. Otherwise, why this shameful and conspiring silence from people who always speak loudly when their neighbors slaughter animals in their backyard without taking them to the abattoir? If they did not have some financial and economical interests in the war of aggression in the DR Congo by their allies, Rwandans and Ugandans, this conflict would have ceased long ago. These men could not have tolerated that their same allies might commit human, economic, and social atrocities in defiance of all international norms and international humanitarian laws. The world watched how quickly, efficiently and effectively, directly and indirectly the US intervened in Kuwait, Bosnia, Kosovo, and in East Timor. Why in the world did they drag their feet in the DR Congo case, which started even before the East Timor's conflict, if it was not in the name of financial and economical gains?

The US has always had great economical interests in the DR Congo since the independence of this latter country. Gibbs tried to analyze such interests after the national security thesis seemed to be inadequate concerning the US support of the Katangese secession. He said, "[w]e will now consider an economic interpretation of American policy. The interpretation argues that the Eisenhower administration supported the Katanga because it had a financial interest in doing so. Several administration officials had investments in Central Africa... Belgian interests organized the Katanga secession, and the United States, in turn, supported the secession. Patrice Lumumba opposed the Belgians, and the USA sought to overthrow him. Officials justified these policies in terms of national security because American foreign policy is always justified that way. The economic perspective explains the Eisenhower policy quite well... A ... business figure was Maurice Tempelsman. Mr. Tempelsman was the owner of Leon Tempelsman and Son, a diamond trading firm named after his father...

"Beginning in 1961, Tempelsman urged the Kennedy administration to purchase industrial diamonds from the Congolese. The plan called for the following: The US government was to purchase Congolese diamonds to be used in the government's strategic stockpile, and the Congolese, in exchange, were to receive American agriculture commodities. Tempelsman apparently hoped to act as middleman and make a substantial profit... President Kennedy also had some connections. Tempelsman supported Kennedy during the 1960 election and arranged a meeting between Kennedy and Henry Oppenheimer, the famous South African investor. Tempelsman had a longstanding friendship with the Kennedy family, which has continued to this day. Indeed, the late president's son, John Fitzgerald Kennedy, Jr., spent a summer working for Tempelsman in Africa... Most of the major policymakers in the Kennedy administration—including Stevenson, Bowles, Fredericks, Ball, Sorenson, Devlin, Cleveland, McGhee, Harriman, MacArthur—had ties to one of the interested investment groups at the time they entered the government service, or in the familiar 'revolving door' tradition, they established such ties after leaving the government."[190]

The US has considerable economic interests in the DR Congo, as stated previously. And because of those interests, as was the case in the sixties, the American administration is really concerned about who leads the DR Congo. They want to ensure that they continue to benefit of what they need to keep themselves on top of all other countries having the same interests in the DR Congo. For sure, international lobbyists have the same interests, but these people have strong links with the American government to enable them to operate within the American legal framework. But, be it for national security, financial and economic interests, or any other interests, the truth of the matter is that the US did not have part of the share in 1880, when the West partitioned Africa into pieces of lands—dividing families, clans, and tribes—in order to satisfy their passions and ambitions.

Therefore, they want their share now. The US wants to have direct control in Africa so space needs to be created to accommodate them, by all means and at all costs. Thus, this war of aggression against the DR Congo by US allies, Rwanda and Uganda—and other wars like in Sierra Leone, Sudan, Ethiopia, Ivory Coast, and as it was in Angola—to facilitate that economic appetite and ultimately the control of the DR Congo. This is the object of the next section. President Mandela responded to the press, in regard to the American threats to attack Iraq (again), that the US "is motivated by George W Bush's desire to please the arms and oil industries in the United States of America."[191] For instance, where are the WMDs that were at the core of the invasion of Iraq by American-British Coalition? Neither the White House nor the British administration has brought to the world credible and substantial evidence of their whereabouts. Meanwhile, in Iraq, US and British corporations have mushroomed; likewise, any objective observer knows who controls Iraqi's oil industry today.

After the cold war, one would have expected to see the US changing its African policy to one of frank cooperation and development—cooperation aimed at the African masses as the first beneficiaries of any American form of assistance. But, it is sadly observed that US African policy has not changed and it is still characterized by marginalization. As to say, no one changes a team that wins. "With the end of the Cold war, US African policy remained marginal ... But while the marginalization of the continent in the US foreign policy has been widely analyzed, attention has not been paid to whether the American business sector is happy with it or not. Direct US involvement in Africa is also driven by economic interests ... a major objective of US involvement was to maintain access to minerals, at cheap price. Although Western countries rely less and less on raw materials, their level of dependence is still relatively important, as shown by the war waged against Iraq in 1990-1991. These economic interests did not disappear with the collapse of the USSR. Privileged access to raw materials is still a strategic interest as well as a major source of profit for a few American transnational corporations, in the field of telecommunications, transport, mining and oil,"[192] argues Xavier Renou. Perhaps, the recent collapse of Saddam Hussein's regime explains very well this economic interest.

5. For the Establishment of a Regional Power and Control

Except for Liberia and Ethiopia, each African country has been a colony during a particular historical time. In 1880, the settlers, according to their will and wants, divided African nations into colonies. The USA was not present at the time. In the sixties, the US was interested in a number of African states, among others the DR Congo. They, too, wanted to have their share of the cake. But the Belgians would not let them do it. So, the years 1963-1965 will be those of business conflicts between the US and Belgium in the DR Congo. The Kennedy administration was known as an anti-colonialist government and fought Belgian policy of after the independence = before the independence. The US succeeded in overrunning Belgian policy in 1965 by assisting Mobutu stage a military coup d'état.

Gibbs records that "the United States clearly benefitted from the coup. The CIA has supported Mobutu throughout his political career. The agency helped to install him as dictator... The Mobutu era proved a crucial one in the history of international relations in the Congo.... A group of American companies, termed the anti-colonial bloc, sought to displace the established Belgian companies, while the Belgians sought to retain control. This conflict, in turn, decisively influenced the [American] diplomacy of the Congo... "[193] Mobutu had the full support of the US in what was seen as a fight for economic independence, when he tried to cut off all Belgian interests and replaced them with American ones with the implementation of his widely failed nationalization policy. Curiously, the American government praised such nationalization and Africanism from Mobutu since it was in their favor. Having won the economic battle with the help of Mobutu, their ally, the US had control in the great giant DR Congo; from where they directed their African policy in the Central and the Great Lakes regions until a few years before the fall of Mobutu.

However, history is repeating itself. The American administration, by replacing their former friend Mobutu with Laurent D. Kabila, aimed to keep a direct eye in the affairs of the DR Congo. Hence, the US hoped to control, from the DR Congo countries like Angola, Burundi, Rwanda, Uganda, Sudan, Eritrea, and Ethiopia to name only a few. But this time, Laurent D. Kabila's Africanism was regarded as a threat to American national security and economic interests. Mobutu's Africanism and his human rights abuses were supported by the American government because of his blind loyalty toward the US in fighting communism in Africa. Today, however, the Cold War is over, and the US believes that the new Congolese leader should be somebody who has the ability to defend American interests without any alibi.

Thus, either Laurent D. Kabila did it or he was out of power. The objective observer knows why Laurent D. Kabila was assassinated, and the truth shall sooner or later be known to all. The sad thing about this scenario is that, besides the fact that the US—or any other State in this matter—does not have the right to impose a leader on the Congolese people (just like the American people cannot accept that some leaders be arbitrarily imposed on them, although many believe that George W. Bush is the exception to the rule), the US had enforced this modus vivendi with innocent blood by allowing its allies Rwanda and Uganda to invade the DR Congo and providing them with human and material assistance to accomplish this act.

The fight for the control of the DR Congo is the reason why the US had still not accepted publicly that its allies, Rwanda and Uganda, did illegally occupy this independent state. But the US is not alone in that fight. Some other Western states, mainly Belgium, France, the United Kingdom, and Germany to only name a few, are only interested in a share of the DR Congo. Some have argued that Western countries have criticized the American administration for its involvement in the Congolese aggression, as well as its strange and astonishing silence while its allies, Rwanda and Uganda, had systematically violated international human rights norms and humanitarian laws, but that the US would have replied by threatening to freeze its contributions' funds to the UN and other assistance to such states if the international community should openly criticize them. That is why, to this day, though the aggression of the DR Congo by American allies, Rwanda and Uganda, it is a fact none of the Western countries or the UN itself had ever tried to condemn it explicitly in the strongest language.

And the fight for the control of the DR Congo is also the reason why Washington's approach to solving the Congolese tragedy is ambiguous and unrealistic; an approach that does not take into account the realities on the grounds; at the worst, an approach that ignore the rights of the Congolese people and threatens the sovereignty of the republic. This trend advocated by the US government, since Rwanda and Uganda aggressed and invaded the DR Congo, is better illustrated in the lines below. At the White House briefing on the interahamwe and the situation in the DR Congo on August 6, 2002, in the Washington foreign press center, Pierre Prosper, State Department Ambassador-at-large for War Crimes, presented the US official position:[194]

PROSPER: Thank you very much.

Last week I traveled to the Democratic Republic of the Congo to launch the second phase of our aggressive and targeted Rewards for Justice

Campaign. The phase of this campaign targets for apprehension of nine individuals who stand accused of genocide, crimes against humanity, and various war crimes before the International Criminal Tribunal for Rwanda. These individuals are believed to frequent the Congo and they continue to play a destructive role throughout the region.

Our effort is designed not only to bring these individuals to justice, but it is also our part in contribution to the recently concluded peace agreement reached in South Africa.

While in the Congo, I met with President Kabila and many members of his administration. They expressed full support for our program in the pursuit and apprehension of these individuals.

It is our firm belief that a key to ending the war in the Congo between the Democratic Republic of the Congo and Rwanda, and thus bringing peace and stability in the region, is arresting and apprehending these key tribunal inductees, who also play a leadership role in fueling the war. We believe that with their arrests and transfer to Arusha, Tanzania, the seat of the tribunal, an environment will be created that will allow for the disarmament, the demobilization, and the repatriation of the foot soldiers, the ex-FAR/ Interahamwe, which will in turn allow for Rwanda to withdraw from the Congo.

We want to see Rwanda withdraw from the Congo. We also want to see the Democratic Republic of the Congo take steps to address Rwanda's security concerns. We are prepared to help and assist. We welcome the agreement reached in South Africa and hope that it will lead to peace in the region.

We remind all states in the Central African region of their international obligations to cooperate with the Tribunal for Rwanda. This means that all the states in the region, particularly the Democratic Republic of the Congo, the Republic of the Congo, and Angola, must seek and arrest all inductees that may be on their territory. Only through a concerted regional and international effort will we be able to take the steps that are necessary to achieve lasting peace in the region.

Thank you.

Q. Adu-Asare: We have heard from a lot of US officials about the message to Rwanda over the years, repeated, just like we hear the message to the Israelis to leave Palestine, and they don't do it. What are the sanctions that have been put in place to make sure Rwanda actually leaves DRC? I have *a* view that maybe that is what is going to begin the process toward peace in the region. Has the US any intention of applying sanctions to Rwanda for failing to move its troops from DRC?

A. PROSPER: Well, what we have now is an agreement in place where Rwanda has in writing committed to leaving the DRC. At the same time, we have a commitment in writing where President Kabila has committed to addressing Rwanda's security concerns. We will look at this document, and we will hold the parties to the words of the document and the spirit behind the document, believing that it is what is needed to bring peace in the region. We will continue to engage both publicly and privately with the parties to express to them what the desired outcome is and should be. We will also speak to them regarding what we believe the consequences of inaction will be.

I do not want to go into details publicly in that regard, but I think what you can see and can expect to see from the United States is a country that will be engaged with the parties in the region, will work with South Africa as the broker of the peace agreement to find a way to move this process forward. Because, again, the time has come where we need to find lasting peace in the region so that the people of the Congo, as well as the people of Rwanda, no longer suffer.

Q. Jeff Morrissey (sp), Sub-Equatorial Africa Defense Monitor: Hi. There are people—I'm sure many in this room, actually—who say that part of the problem in the region is the lack of democracy in Rwanda itself, and I'm wondering what you've done to address that issue as well.

A. PROSPER: The problem that Rwanda has faced since the genocide has been one that is complex on many levels. Obviously, the security issue is a primary concern, not only for Rwanda but for the region. The justice issue is one that has been of concern for Rwanda, the region, and the international community.

We do want to see continued movement toward democratization of Rwanda. We have been working through our development agencies, USAID and others, to promote the rule of law, promote democracy, promote an electoral process in Rwanda.

At the same time, we recognize the security issues that we are trying to address. We see that it is not something that can be fixed overnight, but we need a concerted effort, working with the government, to make it happen.

We believe that the Rwandans know what our desires are, as far as seeking a full transition into full democracy, and they know that we're willing to work with them.

But one of our primary issues that we want to address immediately is this question of security so that we can bring stability to the region.

Q. Adu-Asare, Africa Newscast: Back to Rwanda/Congo. Is there a time frame within which the rest of the world might expect the movement—departure of Rwandan troops from DRC soil? And while we are trying to do this, would it be reasonable for the UN to station peacekeepers as a buffer between Rwanda and DRC if Rwanda would pull its troops back, then we insert the UN? Would that be a reasonable suggestion to make?

A. PROSPER: Regarding the peacekeepers, we are in the process of studying the role that the MONUC peacekeepers should play. We know that the South Africans are prepared to send personnel into the Congo. We will have to see how that all develops. The peace agreement is still fresh and we are still defining the various roles to play. But this is something that will be taken up and addressed during the month of August, not only in capitals, but in New York.

Regarding the timetable, according to the peace agreement accord that has been reached, the Rwandans are to begin withdrawing at the same time or simultaneous to the government of the Congo taking steps to demobilize and disarm the forces that are in there. So what we want to see—again, recognizing that this is an ambitious agenda that has been set—we want to see a beginning of the process. We want to see a beginning of the disarmament, which will lead to a beginning of the withdrawal. And we will continue to work with the parties to see that this occurs.

Q. Adu-Asare: At the point, at the political moment when Paul Kagame and his forces chased out the Hutu forces from Rwanda, there was a report about missing 200,000 Hutus. I believe this was in 1997 or thereabouts. Up to this point, there hasn't been any definitive message as to what happened to those 200,000 people. Is there a chance that there can be an investigation into this issue?

A. PROSPER: We have called for an investigation into the events in the Eastern Congo, not only the event that you're discussing, but the recent events in Kisangani a month and a half, two months ago. During my trip to Kinshasa, this was an issue of discussion with President Kabila. In Rome, back in middle of July, I met with President Kagame; we discussed this issue.

I do believe that the question of what has taken place in the Eastern Congo and the suffering of the people over the years will be a question that we will need to address as a member of the international community and as the international community and the region as a whole. In order to do that, obviously, we must first bring peace and stability to the Congo; we must end the fighting, end the killing and atrocities that are—have taken place.

Q. If you wouldn't mind, what was Paul Kagame's response during the discussion in Rome that you just mentioned?

A. PROSPER: Well, I'm not going to go into details as to the response. But let me put it this way. He clearly understood the level of concern that we had regarding the events in Kisangani. And we mutually agreed that there needs to be accountability, and that we need to also look at the conduct of the parties within the Eastern Congo, some of the other forces that are there. Beyond that, I'm not prepared to go into details as to what he said, but we did make it clear that we believe there needs to be an investigation, they need to support an investigation, and we need to determine exactly what happened and hold the perpetrators accountable.

Q. In addition to, of course, the governments of Rwanda and Congo, there are Congo rebel groups of considerable power and authority. How essential are they, RCD, Bemba's group also, how essential are they to this roundup of Interahamwe? Because there are alliances that exist between these groups and the ex-FAR and the Interahamwe. And are you in discussion, in fact, with the leadership of these rebel groups, who in many ways are as much a government as Kabila's Kinshasa government?

A. PROSPER: We do believe that the other forces in the Congo are relevant and are essential to—have an essential role to play in bringing peace to the Congo.

That is why we are also looking for an inter-Congolese peace agreement—or agreement that will reach an understanding as far as the structure of the government and the sharing of power within the various groups that are there. So, we're supportive of that. We know that there are steps being taken in that direction. We'll have to see where they end up.

But in order for any of the additional forces that are in the Congo currently to be recognized as a credible participant and a credible player in the process, they have their responsibility. They need to assist in the apprehension and location of these individuals. And we expect that of them. We will send that message. We're not directly engaged with them, but this is a message, an overall message, that we're sending throughout the community.

And again, one of the purposes of our reward campaign was not only to actually get the information to bring these people into justice, but it was to send a strong and powerful message that the situation has changed, that we all must work together to bring these people into custody.

When I was in Kinshasa last week, President Kabila was publicly supportive of this. His minister for human rights joined me in a press conference where he affirmed the government's determination to work with us. They announced that they would create a special war crimes commission to follow this particular issue. And from there, we're going to look to the government in Kinshasa to work with us and help us in persuading the other actors in the region that they have a responsibility and a role to play.

Q. Dobra Kosavic (ph), Belgrade daily Vecernje Novosti: Can you please explain how it comes that the United States is so supportive of ad hoc tribunals like for Rwanda and ex-Yugoslavia and so unsupportive of permanent international crimes court?

A. PROSPER: I think the important point to make here is that we are supportive of seeking accountability for war crimes and atrocities as they occur around the world. I think our commitment cannot be questioned, based on our—not only our—the history of our efforts, but our current efforts globally.

The International Criminal Court is a court—a document, a treaty, with which we have a problem. We believe that it is flawed. We believe, though, that it is—the idea is noble. It was a noble idea. It was a noble effort to bring something into being. But in its implementation and its creation, errors occurred along the way that made it a process that is one that is unchecked, that is ripe for abuse, politicization, and exploitation.

What do I mean by that? When you look at the ad hoc tribunals, they were created after intensive debate in New York and elsewhere as to the appropriateness of creating these ad hoc tribunals and whether or not—or questioning what the timing of launching such a tribunal should be. It took into consideration all the various dynamics that were occurring in the region and internationally. So, it was a thought-out process. The jurisdiction of the courts was thought out.

The problem with the ICC is that it leaves all this power in the hands of an individual. In short, an individual can essentially make the decision as to whether or not to immerse him or herself into a hot spot in the world, into a conflict, without the benefit of the debate that takes place in New York to see whether or not this is the right response and whether or not it will further the objectives of bringing peace and stability rather than harm.

So, in putting this power into the hands of an individual, we have a problem with that. The individual can be one that for his or her own political agenda or personal reasons, he or she may launch an investigation into a particular situation, that is, one that is not based on law and facts, but one that is based on political preferences and bias.

Again, our view is that it is an unchecked process that leaves too much power in the hands of the individual with no oversight. And therefore, we cannot support this institution.

We are prepared, however, to work with the states where these war crimes occur to build the capacity so that they can address these problems themselves. If it's a question of political will, we are prepared to try to change and shape the political will in these various parts of the world.

If there's a clear absence of political will, then we are prepared to act responsibly in the Security Council in order to take measures that will bring not only justice and accountability, but peace and stability.

Q. Adu-Asare: In as far as US interests go, your response is very adequate. But I doubt if the rest of the world would agree to your rationalization of it. Why couldn't US stay in there, be part of it, and attempt to change it from the inside as opposed to staying apart?

A. PROSPER: Well, we tried. We tried from 1995 to change it, up till Rome in 1998 where we were not successful. After Rome of 1998, we again tried; we went to New York for all the preparatory commissions to try to change it. We could not do it. We just did not have a meeting of the minds with the supporters of the ICC.

This year, when the ICC came into force on April 11th with enough—actually, when ICC received enough ratifications on April 11th and came into force on July 1st, the opportunity for the United States or a non-party state to influence the process went away, because now only party states, those who have ratified the treaty, can actually play within the treaty, influence the process, influence the court.

We have always said that before we can send it for ratification, we need to see some changes. President Clinton, before leaving office, he informed—or suggested—to President Bush that he not send it up for ratification. He said—President Clinton clearly said publicly that he believed the treaty to be flawed and that it needs significant changes in order for it to be sent to the Senate, and he recommended that it not be sent.

So therefore, we no longer have the opportunity to influence it. Therefore, we've decided to—rather than wage war against the ICC, we will detach ourselves from the process, we will respect the right of others to belong to the ICC, we just hope they respect our right not to be part of it.

Such was the US government's position since the beginning of the Rwandan-Ugandan war of aggression against the DR Congo. Despite several official and indisputable reports from various international agencies, the DR Congo government, and other foreign governments that Rwanda and Uganda have illegally invaded in the DR Congo and violated the territorial integrity of, that their troops have committed war crimes, crimes against humanity and terrorism, and that they should withdraw unconditionally, the US was—on the contrary—interested in marketing its own strategy.

Likewise, for the US, the top priority in the nation building program of the DR Congo should be the assurance that the latter maximize its human, financial, economic, and military resources to protect Rwandan interests. Obviously, the US does not have any logical and reasonable plan on the table, but rather the US has its index finger pointed to the DR Congo as saying: do whatever it takes, and at all costs, for you have yourself to blame if Rwanda aggresses you again.

It is unnecessary to recall that Rwandan's border protection and halting the Banyamulenge ethnic genocide (which were the first motives in aggressing and invading the DR Congo) were a hoax from day one of their barbarous act. For, first, they never explained why were they unable to protect the same borders when they were in charge of the Congolese armies and security apparatus from 1996 to 1998, until just a week before they aggressed the DR Congo, and whereas they had over four battalions stationed close to the same borders with the DRC.

Second, Kagame's government failed to prove the real intention and presence of its troops airlifted to the Congolese west coast, thousand of miles from the Congolese east coast where Rwanda has its borders with the DR Congo, the same borders for which they justified their illegal occupation of the DR Congo. The question on any sane person's lips was: what were the Rwandans doing on the west coast of the DR Congo, on the outskirts of the capital city of the DR Congo, Kinshasa, close to the diamond mining town of Tshikapa, and other towns located thousands and hundreds of miles from their borders? Had their intention been other than the control of the DRC? Unfortunately, the US government refuses willingly to accept these facts and other evidence, but conditioned the return of peace in the DR Congo with the security guaranties of Rwanda.

Further, Prosper's statement in the introductory remarks of the above interview that, "It is our firm belief that a key to ending the war in the Congo between the Democratic Republic of the Congo and Rwanda, and thus bringing peace and stability in the region, is arresting and apprehending these key tribunal inductees, who also play a leadership role in fueling the war," is ambiguous and deeply embarrassing. Ambiguous because until today, and despite several known and unpublished reports, the US government still thinks the outside world does not know who the real authors of the current crisis in the Great Lakes region are. What justice will the arrest of those stimulating the war bring, while it is known that the authors of the same war are not hiding but never been inducted? Where are the RPA soldiers (Kagame at the head) who shot down Habyaramana's (President of Rwanda) plane, killing him and Ntaryamira (President of Burundi), in 1994, and all those on board? This act was at the very source of the Rwanda genocide and a real cause of the present Great Lakes region crisis. Where are the RPA officers and their mentors who ordered that coward action, and when are they going to be inducted by the ICTR? The statement is embarrassing because Prosper knows that Kagame is one of the few leaders at the source of the Great Lakes region turmoil and tragedies.

Finally, while the US government is so eager in tracking down and bringing to the ICT for Rwanda in Arusha, Tanzania, the perpetrators of the Rwandan genocide, it failed to state what appropriate measures they suggest to be put in place to resolve the Congolese tragedy where evidence clearly shows that millions of innocent people felt, under Kagame's troops and their allies, conventional and unconventional machines of war. Prosper's failure to mention such measures is not only intentional, but demonstrates how little care the US government gives to the Congolese case. This attitude is only a forerunner sign that any effort by the Congolese people to bring to justice those responsible of gross violations of human rights and the plundering of their mineral and natural resources, and the like, during the four and half years of aggression and invasion, shall be thwarted at all costs and by all means by Rwanda, Uganda and their allies, despite numerous direct and circumstantial evidence involving these countries. This demonstrates further that the cause of the Congolese shall not fairly be heard when criminal proceedings to prosecute those responsible for the commission of international human rights and humanitarian laws' crimes in the DR Congo begin.

It is exciting and comforting for the Congolese people, in particular, and Africans, in general, in the case at hand, that there are out there, throughout the US, a number of Americans who are dissatisfied with the US government foreign policy in Africa. It is very encouraging to hear some boldly denouncing that, "American policy in the Great Lakes region of Central Africa has, for a very long time, been seriously flawed, embarrassingly flawed. Watching the present feud between America's two darlings, Comrades Museveni and Kagame, ought to ignite tremendous anger within the American population and should evoke a call by the American public for a prompt policy review and reddress of the way these failed policies have tarnished core principles on which the US was founded. There's bad blood between the two leaders, Messrs. Museveni of Uganda and Kagame of Rwanda, both of whom see themselves as omnipotent in the region, both of whom are continually coddled by the US and Britain. Both leaders are enormously egocentric, in their own manner, very capable, yet very deceptive, very cunning, and very savvy at serving their American and British mentors with pabulum, while they execute their secret master plans in the background. In short, they have successfully duped the US for years, many people have died in the process, and the US has missed the real action in the region, the DR Congo."[195]

In summary, the Africa policy of the American administration today or tomorrow will continue to fail, as it has been in the past, if this government thinks that Africans cannot take care of their own business. As long as African realities are bypassed, the US will never succeed in walking side by side with Africa. In addition, if respects of human rights are only effective and a reality in the US, then whichever American administration leads the US should simply forget about Africa. It is a shame and an insult to the American people that in the name of so-called national security, an American administration should blind its eyes and suddenly become insensitive to the gross violations of human rights committed by its allies, while the violations committed by non-ally countries are brutally suppressed in the name of the same "national security." It is truly an embarrassment to the Americans that their government does not leave any stone unturned within or outside of its territories when it comes to human rights violations and the terrorism hunt, while at the same time it is at the source of many gross human rights abuses elsewhere.

Whether the American people deserve being permanently fooled by their foreign policy makers, when it comes to Africa, is an unanswered question on the lips of their African friends. Commenting on the above White House briefing on the interahamwe and the situation in the DR Congo, Marek acknowledged, "[w]e are very gratified to see the Washington press corps pull off the gloves and start playing hardball with American officials on the

Congo war. It's high time these officials have to stand before the American public and explain themselves. More of this is needed with regard to American foreign policy throughout Africa, which we feel has for too long undergone far too little public scrutiny. That in turn has led to maverick policy making often by rookies who have not been subject to public challenge, in some instances not even subject to senior management challenge."[196]

There is no doubt that only leadership weakness is to blame for the failure of the American policy in Africa, in general, and the DR Congo, in particular. For that reason, Senator Joe Biden is of the opinion that "[i]f we learned one thing last year, it should be that the role of those of us in positions of leadership is to speak the truth to the American people—to lay out the facts to the extent we know them and to explain to the American people exactly what's expected of them in terms of time, dollars, and commitment. Our role as leaders is not to color the truth with cynicism and ideological rhetoric but to animate that truth with the same resilience, the same dignity, the same decency, and the same pragmatic approach the American people have applied to every task and every challenge. It's long past time for the President to address the American people in prime time, to level with us about the monumental task ahead, to summon our support."[197] Amen!

PART THREE

APPLICABLE REMEDIES AT LAW

The laws that forbid the carrying of arms ... disarm only those who are neither inclined nor determined to commit crimes... Such laws make things worse for the assaulted and better for the assailants; they serve rather to encourage than to prevent homicides, for an unarmed man may be attacked with greater confidence than an armed man.

—Thomas Jefferson,
Third President of the
United States of America

Chapter VI Possible Solutions to Human Rights Violations in the Occupied Territories

Pursuant to section 906 of the Restatement Third of the Foreign Relations Law of the United States, "[a] private person, whether natural or juridical, injured by a violation of an international obligation by a state, may bring a claim against that state or assert that violation as defense (a) in a competent international forum when the state has consented to the jurisdiction of that forum with respect to such private claims; (b) in a court of other tribunal pursuant to its law; or (c) in a court or other tribunal of the injured person's state of nationality or a third state, pursuant to the law of such state, subject to limitations under international law."[198]

It is with regret and shame, and sometimes with tears in the eyes, that one looks at the functioning of the UN. This international body, which apparently would have helped to bring peace and justice in the world, is an author of division, war, and atrocities. It also is characterized by a shameful inconsistency between its purposes and principles on the one hand, and their application on the other. And yet, speaking about the challenge to peace today, the UN Secretary-General declared: "How far we have moved from a strictly international world is evidenced by the changed nature of threats to peace and security faced by the world's people today. The provisions of the Charter presupposed that external aggression, an attack by one state against another, would constitute the most serious threat."[199] Alas, this was not the case with the aggression of the DR Congo by Rwanda and Uganda.

The UN has let itself to be "flirted" by prostitutes—moral and physic persons—who have taken advantage of her virginity and sullied her, thus causing her to lose her inner and outer beauty. Those prostitutes and predators are individuals (like lobbyists), but also governments, NGOs, and other international organizations. Rwanda, Uganda, the US, and other mentors of the invasion of the DRC are among them. Nevertheless, whatever their positions, they are international criminals with whom the world needs to deal with accordingly.

And because of her flirt, the UN has also become a prostitute, and therefore she can no longer achieve her objectives. So there is a real need for reformation of this international organ, idea discussed in the first section. Since the UN has a duty of care to protect the DR Congo but failed to do so, she is liable for injuries caused to both the Congolese nation and its people, a subject debated in the second section.

In addition, occupying another state is one problem, whereas living up to its rights and obligations as occupying forces is another story. Just like human experience shows, people tend to claim more rights than they acknowledge they have obligations. Worst, in an armed conflict situation like the one at hand, it seemed that the invaders had only rights and no obligations, as demonstrated in the third section. Further, because the law of impunity for those who have violated international norms would simply mean unfairness and injustice to the victims and to any objective observer, criminals (individuals, private organizations, or states) should be punished for their wrongdoings, as explained in the fourth section.

The fifth section addresses the problematic of sovereign immunities. Is it fairness and justice that an individual who commits serious violations of international human rights and humanitarian legal norms escape prosecution because such individual acted under the color of internal laws and given that he or she still holds public office? Universal jurisdiction has a deterrent effect and is necessary in the fight against impunity for violations of international customs of war, as discussed in the sixth section.

1. The UN: An Urgent Need for Reformation

It is unobjectionable that, "in accordance with the Universal Declaration of Human Rights, the ideal of free human beings enjoying freedom from fear and want can only be achieved if conditions are created whereby everyone may enjoy his or her economic, social, and cultural rights, as well as his or her civil and political rights,"[200] if we are determined to see the humanization of this world. Whilst it is also undisputable that the duty to transform this world to a better place is ours, in general, this responsibility cannot be hijacked from those individuals or organs to whom the mandate is given to be our representatives, who act on behalf of our states, for example, the United Nations.

However, if those individuals or organs deviate from their duties, and particularly when this become a dangerous pattern resulting in perpetual conflicts, unfair treatment to other individuals, nations, or institutions, and serious violations of human rights (thus threatening peace and harmony among peoples and nations), it is then firmly believed that ours is the right to replace such individuals or change the purposes of such organs in order to meet the situations of the time.

The UN was born after the Second World War. Nations wearied by the war reasoned and believed that respect to human life and respect of others' property were true values that needed to be protected at all costs. One positive result is that these nations have set rules and regulations to be followed by all, without any exceptions either to the size or power of one state, financial contribution to the UN's coffers, religion, or race of those living in such states. Fair dealings toward each other should have been the norm. Some fifteen years after its creation, the UN had to take a real test: the decolonization of Africa. The positive result of this undertaking came through a challenge since the major defenders of the UN Charter were also colonizing nations throughout the entire world with various interests that some felt almost impossible to relinquish. The third major positive result of the creation of the UN in the last century was to hold back an imminent threat of a third world war during the Cold War era. The end of apartheid in South Africa was also an accomplishment, though not solely imputable on the UN.

Hence, the thought that the UN was and is a good idea is widely shared today.

As human beings, states the International Covenant on Civil and Political Rights, "we are entitled to freedom of thought, conscience, and religion. We have the right to hold and express opinions. The Covenant prohibits incitement to war, or racial or religious hatred. It guarantees our right to peaceful assembly (with restrictions only for safety, health and others' freedoms), and to freedom of association (including joining trade unions)."[201] This is certainly a good principle that needs to be protected at all times. Indeed, this principle needs major protection today, more than ever.

Similarly, "universal human rights ... have received the support of world nations. Respect for human rights is becoming a universal principle of good government"[202] and good governance.

But the UN has unfortunately become so politicized that only a tabula rasa or radical transformation is needed in order to save this international body. The UN has deviated 120 degrees from its orbit. Instead of bringing peace, this international institution is bringing war to the world today because its policies are ruined and are selectively applied. The exceptions to the law have become general rules and vice-versa. The UN has become a monopoly of the great powers, in particular, the US, because of its huge financial contribution and the UK that blindly followed whatever the former thinks and says. Thus, the officious seat of the UN is Washington, while New York is an honorific or symbolic one. UN conferences are a shame to the elect and the intellectual since they have adopted undemocratic practices and are therefore a permanent danger to all nations that still believe in democracy. The UN itself is moving, slowly but surely, from a body of nations and states to a super nation and state that can influence domestic government policies.

Professor Richard G. Wilkins had a terrifying experience at a UN conference held in Istanbul on Habitat II. He commented, among other things, "[t]he ideological views aired before UN lawmakers have been monolithically left-wing and liberal. Indeed, opposing voices at UN conferences have often been effectively silenced. The new rule that has emerged from this unbalanced and politically unrepresentative UN process ... can supplant contrary domestic policies, whether by executive decree or judicial order.... Current UN lawmaking procedures ... raise the scepter of an international government that ignores competing views, that replaces local policy with international mandates, and that encourages (or at least permits) political 'bait and switch'..."[203] These are the kind of conferences where the life or death of people are being determined, where gross violations of human rights will be acceptable in one state and condemned in another, where aggression and genocide of one group constitute a violation of human rights while the same acts committed by an ally state are regarded as ordinary, accepted and acceptable norms and practices.

UN policies are also heavily influenced by international lobbies, which are, in this case, nothing other than the NGOs. These have for good or bad contributed to certain events that have either choked the world or made it a little bit peaceable. However, it is amazing to see the impact they have on the UN lawmakers. In fact, "NGOs exist, in large measure, precisely to influence the substantive outcome of official UN conference deliberations... The net result is a symbiotic relationship between the UN bureaucracy and the NGO community: NGOs inform and support UN functionaries, who in turn rely upon the NGOs to ensure the ultimate enforcement of their decrees—a classic example of mutual back scratching."[204] This is a dangerous pattern, as shown in the case when Hedi Annabi, who was invited in New York by the Security Council, reported, on unfounded grounds and unsubstantiated evidence, that the Tutsi community faced an imminent threat in the DR Congo, thus adding more oil to the fire that none wanted to extinguish. In truth, those who were being massacred by Rwandan and Ugandan armies and their allies were the Congolese people. Unfortunately, UN officials enjoy listening to and believing these kinds of lies, though, such allegations cannot be sustained with substantial evidence.

The Security Council is the biggest failure of all the organs of the UN, at least as far as African matters are concerned. The UN Security Council is a jerk, a band of losers. It is obvious that it defends mainly American and European interests. "The UN Security Council was chastised ... for failing to support African peace initiatives properly or enforce its own decisions when it attempted to end or prevent conflicts on the continent. Critics ranged from UN members to UN officials,"[205] reported Evelyn Leopold. When Iraq invaded Kuwait years ago, the UN Security Council supported the military intervention leading to the invaders' forced withdrawal.

Today, the world is a powerless witness to a double standard doctrine, as the same Security Council was not even willing to acknowledge the aggression of the DR Congo by its neighbors, Rwanda and Uganda, with the complicity of western countries. Leopold quoted the Secretary-General of the UN, Kofi Annan, as saying that, "one problem was asking African countries to mount peacekeeping operations and other ventures, then not helping them financially. 'Even the Europeans who are better equipped in so many respects have had significant help from others in keeping the peace within their region' ... in an obvious reference to the United States."[206] South Africa's ambassador, Dumisana Shadrack Kumalo, said to the Security Council on the matter: "Look at all the discussions you have had on Africa and review them and see if something concrete has come out of them ... Get your house in order."[207] How then can nations trust such a partial and common divider organ? And, in the first place, why should such an organ continue to function the way it does today?

For all these reasons, and because the UN has been totally diverted from its original purposes, it is suggested the following reforms within this international body that ought to be noble:

First, the UN General Assembly should play a real role of a legislative organ within the UN. In order to avoid any influence from the NGOs (since these are often politically oriented to the point of directing decisions that have an international consequence), the General Assembly must ensure that it has its own special teams (Special Rapporteur or Envoyé) for impartially reporting whatever mission they have been entrusted with. And when it comes time to follow up, or enforcement in the fields of decisions made by the lawmakers, every step should be followed to ensure such application of the law is being done with all fairness, keeping in sight that what is being enforced is contributing to maintaining peace and stability in the world. NGOs should vigorously be discouraged to be turned into the "eyes and ears" of the UN, as is the case today.

Second, the Security Council needs an in-depth transformation. First of all, this organ is the "I will and I won't" of the UN, as it can help to bring either stability or more war between nations in conflict. The case of the DR Congo is more than eloquent about the actions of the Security Council. It is obvious that this organ is very unrepresentative and geopolitically unbalanced, and that the number of permanent members should be doubled to include countries like: Brazil or Argentina and Uruguay in South America; Senegal, Angola, South Africa and Egypt in Africa; India in Asia; and Syria or Iran and Jordan in the Middle East. There is no reasonable and valuable reason why the representation within the Security Council continues to be so westernized. Most of the wars where the UN either intervened on time or too late depended, (or even not at all like the debated conflict in the DRC), on whether the UK, France, and US had interests in saving lives. But since the Security Council considers human beings in Africa as mere animals, it has always intervened too late in all the wars in this region. The Security Council is very unfair in dealing with African conflicts and is not geopolitically constituted. This needs to change, now!

One looks at the ICC with pride and welcomes its arrival. However, this international criminal tribunal would also have played a safeguarding role in the UN. It will be good politics if the ICC were also to ensure that corruption and mismanagement within the UN itself is dealt with accordingly. Article 5 of the ICC stipulates, "the jurisdiction of the court shall be limited to the most serious crimes of concern to the international community as a whole. The court has jurisdiction in accordance with this Statute with respect to the following crimes: (a) The crimes of genocide; (b) Crimes against humanity; (c) War crimes; (d) The crime of aggression."[208] Experience has shown that—at least in the cases of the ICC for the former Yugoslavia and now ICT for Rwanda—those who are perpetrators are being hunted down until such time that they are handed over to the relevant court.

However, there is one aspect that the UN, in particular, and the world, in general, has neglected: dark diplomacy. Officials in New York, Washington, Paris, London, Moscow, and Beijing have somehow manipulated the UN lawmakers to the point that, but for such manipulations, adequate measures would have been taken by the UN to prevent lost lives or the commission of the most serious crimes of concern to the international community as a whole. Individuals found to be implicated in such manipulations should be accountable for such actions and be brought before the ICC for their direct or indirect contribution in the commission of international crimes. It does not matter if those persons are called Bill Clinton, Sharon, Paul Kagame or Tony Blair. What matters is that individuals must be accountable for their actions, and impunity be abolished, if we still believe in justice. The case of Slobodan Milosevic is a good precedent. Take the case of the genocide in Rwanda in 1994 and the actual case of the DR Congo illustrated here; there are people in New York, Washington, Paris, London, or wherever they may be, who have persuaded the Security Council that flies, and not human beings were being killed, massacred in the DR Congo, and that this country was not the victim of a foreign aggression from Rwanda and Uganda.

Therefore, as with the case of Milosevic and its lieutenants, the scope of liability of criminals who fall under Article 5 of the ICC should not have been limited only to combatants and commandants on the war fields, to non-combatants who have committed crimes referred to in this article, or to states' concerned political leaders, but also to those who have knowingly and willingly sabotaged the prevention of war, the results that would have occurred therein, and the maintenance of international peace and security.

It is senseless, foolish, and barbaric that the so-called promoters of peace, justice, and democracy in the world should allow continual massacres of millions of innocent people for a piece of a diamond, a barrel of petrol, or other self-hidden interests in the ambiguous name of national security or border protection. Many have argued that it is to escape such liability that the US refused to ratify the final document establishing the ICC. But, is a man going to allow himself to live in a new millennium with impressive outlets like the latest automobiles, luxurious mansions, expensive jewelry, new technologies, and strive to conquer other planets, while in his or her inner self, his or her greediness and self-centeredness put him or her in a position of a wolf to his neighbor?

2. The UN Responsibility vis-à-vis to the DR Congo

That the UN has a responsibility toward member nations to enforce peace and stability in the world is obvious; and that the UN has totally failed to meet this responsibility toward the DR Congo is an undisputable fact. Why did the UN fail to fulfil its duties was largely discussed in chapters IV and V. But, is the UN going to set a pattern, better a bad precedent about impunity regarding crimes that fall within the ambit of Article 5 of the ICC as Rwanda, Uganda, and allies committed them on the Congolese soil? If yes, then the creation of the ICC does not avail anything, her mission having been robbed by the US, in particular, at least in the DR Congo armed conflict's case. This would constitute a mockery to the science of law, an affront that the citizens of the world should take no more. Further, that the UN was negligent in dealing with the Congolese war of aggression is unquestionable, for the UN has a duty of care toward the DR Congo, which is a full member of this organ. Here, the UN breached this duty of care.

2.1. Duty of Care to Protect the DR Congo

The issue is whether the UN is liable to the DR Congo on the theory of negligence.[209] The UN had the duty of care in protecting the DR Congo against any aggression or invasion of its territories, but it failed to do so. By failure to fulfill this duty, the UN was in breach and had no legal defense whatever to justify its inaction. Therefore, the UN should compensate the DR Congo.

In this case, all the elements of the prima facie case are established. First, there was a duty on the part of the UN to conform to a specific standard of conduct for the protection of the DRC, its national resources, and its citizens and their properties against an unreasonable risk of injury from the invaders, Rwanda and Uganda, and their allies. Second, there was a breach of that duty by the UN. Third, the breach of that duty of care by the UN is the actual and proximate cause of the DR Congo's deepened crisis and of injuries to its citizens and the systematic looting of its resources and other forms of wealth. And fourth, there is damage, for there was violation of the territorial integrity of the DR Congo contrary to the UN Charter and international law, plundering of its national assets, and serious violations of human rights on its citizens by Rwanda, Uganda, and allies.

In torts law, a duty of care is owed to all foreseeable plaintiffs. The extent of the duty is determined by the applicable standard of care. Thus, two interrogations need to be answered in the affirmative. First, was the plaintiff foreseeable? Second, if so, what is the applicable standard of care?

The UN owed a duty of care only to a foreseeable plaintiff. Here, this element is met because the DR Congo is a full member of the UN, an attribute that put her in a foreseeable plaintiff position. Therefore, the UN, under its Charter, owes a duty of care to the DR Congo and its citizens and their properties in protecting them against any violation of their fundamental rights from foreign aggressors.

The standard of care required of an international organ, such as the UN, whose purposes and principles are to maintain peace and restore international order, is that of a reasonably competent international organ. A reasonably competent international organ would have acted on behalf of its member,[210] who is its client within a reasonable time, and with diligence and immediacy and would have first denounced, second condemned, third ordered the unconditional withdrawal of the invading forces, and fourth, used deterrent and/or coercive means to force the aggressors to leave the territories of the invaded state, in accordance to Chapter VII, articles 41 and 42 of the UN Charter, had the aggressors refused to do so peaceably, as was the case in Iraq in 1991.[211]

Moreover, by covenanting with UN Member States, under Chapter V,[212] that it will promptly and effectively deal with any threat to peace and security issues they may encounter given that it acts on their behalf, the UN Security Council represents to its Member States that pursuant to said Chapter and as well as to Chapter VII, it has greater competence or will exercise greater diligence than that normally demonstrated by international institutions undertaking similar matters. Thus, here the UN is held to that higher standard.[213]

In the case at hand, the UN's failure to act within a reasonable time and take appropriate action on behalf of the DR Congo was unreasonable and did not meet the greater competence or greater diligence it represents to its

Member States, nor the high expectation one would have of an international body of average competence whose mission is clearly stated in the Preamble of its Charter in these solemn words:

"We The People of The United Nations Determined to save succeeding generations from the scourge of war, which twice in our lifetime has brought untold sorrow to mankind, and to reaffirm faith in the fundamental human rights, in the dignity and worth of the human person, in the equal rights of men and women and of nations large and small, and to establish conditions under which justice and respect for the obligations arising from treaties and sources of international law can be maintained, and to promote social progress and better standards of life in larger freedom, and for these ends to practice tolerance and live together in peace with one another as good neighbors, and to unite our strength to maintain international peace and security, and to ensure, by the acceptance of principles and the institution of methods, that armed forces should not be used, save in the common interest, and to employ international machinery for the promotion of the economic and social advancement of all peoples, have resolved to combine our efforts to accomplish these aims."[214]

The UN would assert that it did not have any pre-knowledge of the aggression of the DR Congo, violation of its territorial integrity and of serious human rights abuses, and therefore could not have taken appropriate steps in defending the DR Congo against Rwanda and Uganda on a reasonable timely manner. However, the DR Congo would counter that the UN is liable because, as pointed out above, the reasonable, ordinary, prudent international body, such the UN, whose primary mission is to maintain peace and international order, would know or should have known that tensions between the invaders and the DR Congo existed prior to the aggression of the latter.[215]

The DR Congo would also argue that the UN is liable because the reasonable, ordinary, prudent international body, such the UN which represents to its Member States that it has greater competence or will exercise greater diligence in undertaking their matters pursuant to Chapter VII of its Charter, should have known that the DRC's action in ordering Rwandan and Ugandan military personnel to leave its territories, thus ending the military assistance with these countries would bring more tensions to the already distorted situation and would likely lead into an armed conflict, and would have therefore taken preventive measures to ensure that Rwanda and Uganda's anger be contented and controlled. Indeed, the UN Secretary-General himself acknowledged that, referring to deadly conflicts, "[t]here is near-universal agreement that prevention is preferable to cure, and that strategies of prevention must address the root causes of conflicts, not simply their violent symptoms. Consensus is not always matched by practical actions, however."[216]

Thus, the UN is liable for its inaction at the time of the aggression of the DR Congo and during such aggression in failing to compel Rwanda and Uganda to comply with the international legal order.

Further, the UN had affirmative duties to act on behalf of the DR Congo. The UN had a duty to control Rwanda, Uganda, and allies in their aggression against the DR Congo and the commission of serious violations of human rights and humanitarian laws on its soil. In the law of torts, an affirmative duty is imposed if one has the actual ability and authority to control a person's actions, and knows or should know the person is likely to commit acts that would require exercise of this control.

The UN's conduct will be measured against the reasonable, ordinary, prudent international institution under the same or similar circumstances. A reasonable international institution with members known to possess violent propensities, such as Rwanda and Uganda, would exercise care to ensure that others were not injured by such member states' actions and would have warned such state members to abstain in committing such acts. The UN had the actual ability and authority pursuant to articles 1, 2, 24, 39 to 41 of its Charter. In this instance, the UN had the ability and authority to control Rwanda, Uganda, and their allies' actions. The UN has never stated that it did not have such ability or authority. On the contrary, the UN used this ability and authority to silently condone the invasion of the DR Congo by Rwanda, Uganda, and allies.

In addition, when the invaders, Rwanda and Uganda, entered the territory of the DR Congo, the UN knew or should have known that they were likely to commit acts that would require exercise of this control. The UN would have known that there is never a peaceful aggression and that the Congolese army and civilian masses were going to resist by all means to the invasion of their country.

Further, a reasonable international body, such as the UN, would have foreseen that member states with imperialistic ambitions and that serve such interests in the Great Lakes region, namely Rwanda and Uganda, would not have left the territory of the DR Congo without armed confrontation when the DR Congo government ordered them to do so on 28 July, 1998, as noted previously. It was or would have been foreseeable to the UN, after being ordered to leave the DR Congo, that Rwandan and Ugandan troops would refuse to do so or simulate such move, only to return later uninvited and commit the kind of acts those named countries have the propensity of committing, in particular genocide and other serious international crimes. For example, previous acts of genocide, crimes against humanity, and war crimes caused by Kagame's troops on the Rwandan soil between 1994 and 1996, and on the Congolese soil in 1996-1997 should have put the UN on notice that this same army was likely to carry out again such international crimes in the DR Congo.

In view of the above, the UN is liable to the DR Congo because it failed to exercise its ability and authority to control Rwanda, Uganda, and their allies' actions of invading the DR Congo and committing therein crimes of terrorism, crimes against humanity, and war crimes, and genocide.

Where a person's conduct falls short of that level that is required by the applicable standard of care owed to the other person, she has breached her duty. Whether the duty of care is breached in an individual case is a question for the trier of fact, meaning the jury. The main problem relates to the proof of the breach. The DR Congo will assert that the UN breached its duty of care on two theories: first, on the theory of violation of Statute and, second, on the theory of Res Ipsa Loquitur.

On the first theory, the DR Congo will claim that there exists a duty owed to her and breach may be established as a matter of law by proof that the UN violated an applicable statute, which is therefore "negligence per se." On the second theory, the very occurrence of an event may tend to establish a breach of duty. However, the doctrine of Res Ipsa Loquitur requires that the DR Congo shows first that the event that caused injuries to her is a type that would not normally occur unless someone else was negligent, and second that the instrumentality causing such injuries was in the sole control of the UN. In addition, the DR Congo must also establish that she was free from fault on her part at the time of the occurrence. If res ipsa loquitur is established in this instance, the DR Congo has therefore made a prima facie case and no direct verdict may be given for the UN.

As a matter of law, the UN should have applied articles 2, 24, and 39 to 42 of its Charter to prevent Rwanda, Uganda, and their allies from invading the DR Congo and to commit acts of violation of human rights, or any other statute which enables her to use its authority for this purpose. The UN was in breach of the above provisions because it did nothing to apply them and determine the existence of any threat to the peace, breach of peace, act of aggression, and make relevant recommendations, or decide what measures shall be taken in accordance with Articles 41 and 42, to maintain or restore peace and security in the DR Congo, as expressly stated in article 39 of its Charter. The UN was therefore negligent per se because it did not act pursuant to those provisions. In doing so, the UN consequently breached its duty of care to protect the DR Congo against Rwanda, Uganda, and allies' illegal occupation.

Further, as a matter of law, the very occurrence first of the aggression of the DR Congo by Rwanda, Uganda, and allies; second, the commission of gross violations of human rights in the occupied territories of the DR Congo where nearly 3.5 million people died in four and half years of illegal occupation, while the UN remained very passive in whole, should only tend to establish a breach of duty from the latter. Why did the UN not intervene from the very beginning whilst there were ample signs of threat to the peace and breach of peace, or at least at the commencement of the illegal occupation whereas it was obvious that Rwanda and Uganda had invaded the DR Congo? Is the illegal occupation of one state's territorial space, followed by acts of violations of human rights, not called aggression and invasion? Did the occurrences of such events in the DR Congo not speak out for themselves as they happened in Kuwait in 1991 when Iraq invaded that country? What more proof did the UN want before acting while humanitarian laws were violated and massacres of civil populations occurred on a greater scale?

It is the UN Secretary-General, Kofi Annan, who exclaimed with remorse that "[r]ecognition that many states have serious and legitimate concerns about intervention does not answer the question I posed in my report, namely, if humanitarian intervention is, indeed, an unacceptable assault on sovereignty, how should we respond to a Rwanda, to a Srebrenica [to a Congo]—to gross and systematic violations of human rights that offend every precept of our common humanity? In essence the problem is one of responsibility: in circumstances in which universally accepted human rights are being violated on a massive scale we have a responsibility to act,"[217] but mostly to act earlier and fairly.

The DR Congo, in the case at hand, never posed a problem to the UN that would have been interpreted as an obstacle to intervention. On the contrary, several records show that the DR Congo pleaded many times to the UN Security Council for such intervention but her pleas went unanswered and ignored. Perhaps, the nearly 3.5 million Congolese who died as a result of the war of occupation by Rwanda, Uganda, and allies on their motherland do not fall within the "circumstances in which universally accepted human rights are being violated on a massive scale" and in which the UN "have a responsibility to act." If this is the interpretation that the UN Security Council gives to the Secretary-General's above terms, then "in essence the problem is one of [ir] responsibility" on her part.

The grave injuries that the DR Congo and its citizens suffered during the Rwandan-Ugandan war of occupation on their soil are the type that would not normally had occurred unless someone was negligent. The DR Congo and the Congolese suffered those injuries because the UN Security Council refused to act on their behalf in accordance to article 24 of its Charter, an act that was negligent on the part of the UN. Further, the instrumentality causing such injuries was in the sole control of the UN. Only the UN could have enforced its laws or statutes, not the DR Congo. Thus, the UN was in breach, as established previously, because it failed to take suitable measures to protect the DR Congo, its people, and their national assets against Rwanda, Uganda, and allies invaders.

The UN may claim that it was not liable for the aggression of the DR Congo and the violations of international human rights on the latter's territories. But the DR Congo will counter that the UN had the obligation and solemn responsibility to exercise its ability and authority in accordance to its mandate. That the UN failed to honor such mandate in the case of the DR Congo is sufficiently demonstrated herein.

In addition, the DR Congo was not at fault. The DR Congo did nothing that would have prevented the UN to fulfill said mandate nor had the DR Congo impeached the UN effort in restoring peace in its territories. In truth, the DR Congo called on the UN and the international community several times to courageously take their responsibilities, condemn the aggression against its country, and to halt the slaughter of its citizens and the plundering of its natural and mineral resources by Rwanda, Uganda, and allies. Today, history and history alone recalls that the DR Congo's pleas were not honored but totally ignored.

Thus, the UN is also likely to be found liable on the doctrine of Res Ipsa Loquitur for its breach of duty of care in protecting the DR Congo against Rwanda and Uganda invading armed troops.

The UN would argue that both the DR Congo and its people's injuries are not the factual cause of her action, and mostly that the "But For" test or theory has not been established. According to this test, an act or omission is the cause, in fact, of an injury when the injury would not have occurred but for the act. The DR Congo and its people will counteract that the "But For" theory is only one of the tests to show actual cause. In fact, this test applies where several acts, of which each is insufficient to cause the injury alone, combine to cause the injury to the person.

Indeed, the "But For" test is established here to prove that the UN's conduct was the legal cause of the DRC's and its citizens' injuries. That is that those injuries would not have occurred at a large scale and systematically as they did but for the obvious negligence of the UN in refusing to uphold its responsibilities and come to the rescue of the DR Congo and its people. In addition, it is fair to hold the UN liable for unexpected injuries or for expected injuries that happen in unexpected ways.[218]

Further, the DR Congo will claim that the UN is liable on the Joint Causes or Substantial Factor test. This theory applies where several causes bring about injury, and any one alone would have been sufficient to cause the injury; The defendant's conduct is the cause, in fact, if it was a substantial factor in causing the injury to the plaintiff. As noted previously, the UN knew or should have known that Rwanda, Uganda, and allies were likely to invade the DR Congo. And since no peaceful invasion exists, the UN knew or should have known that Rwanda, Uganda, and allies were going to commit human rights abuses in the DR Congo. Only the UN has the burden of proof to show that it did not have such knowledge or should not have known of the occurrence of such action. In addition, the UN's inaction prior to and during the aggression of the DR Congo is a substantial factor that demonstrates that such act caused injury to the DR Congo and its people.

Finally, the UN had both the ability and the authority to enforce its statutes to prevent or stop the aggression of the DR Congo and the commission of serious human rights violations by Rwanda, Uganda, and their allies. The UN here failed totally to fulfill its responsibilities with regard to protecting the DR Congo and its citizens. This failure was a substantial factor sufficient enough to have caused injuries alone to the DR Congo and its people. It is obvious that had the UN intervened from day one in the Congolese war of occupation against the invaders, Rwanda and Uganda, millions of lives would have been saved and Congolese national resources would not have been plundered as systematically and methodologically as they had been. The UN's failure to live to its principles and purposes was interpreted by Rwanda, Uganda, and their allies as a blessing and an encouragement to wrong and rob the Congolese people and pillage the natural and mineral assets of their country.

Thus, the DR Congo is likely to assert that the aforementioned substantial factors alone have established that the UN's actions are the actual cause to the injuries both her and its citizens suffered.

The UN would also argue that even if the DR Congo proves the existence of a factual cause, there is no legal causation to its claim, thus liability does not attach. As a general rule, a person generally is liable for all harmful results that are the normal incidents of and within the increased risk caused by its acts. In other words, the foreseeability test is applicable. Foreseeability implies "the quality of being reasonably able to anticipate."[219] Whether the UN's acts were foreseeable to cause injury to the DR Congo and its people is the issue.

The DR Congo and its citizens will show that the UN's actions were expected to cause them injuries as thoroughly explained thus far in this record. In this case, the UN acts as argued above, meaning its non-conformity to the principles and purposes embodied in its own Charter with regard to the Congolese war of occupation, is a harmful result. This harmful and shameful result increased the risk of seeing the DR Congo ripped off of its national assets and its people slaughtered, raped, deprived of their fundamental rights, and subjected to all other sort of abuses by the invaders and their associates.

Further, the UN cannot claim that Rwanda, Uganda, and allies' actions in the DR Congo were unforeseeable harmful results as far as her liability would be concerned, for the DR Congo situation is a direct cause case. In a direct cause case, where there is an uninterrupted chain of events from the negligent act to plaintiff's injury; the negligent party is liable for all foreseeable harmful results, regardless of the unusual manner or timing of their occurrence. Here, as already noted, the UN knew or should have known that Rwanda, Uganda, and allies were very displeased with the Kabila's regime, which they accused of all evils, even of the lack of democracy as if Rwanda and Uganda are democratic states. In addition, the UN knew or should have known that the decision of the DR Congo to end Rwanda and Uganda military assistance and cooperation would likely fuel the already hot situation between these states. At this stage of the conflict, the UN would have sent diplomatic missions to all these countries to appease the situation as the reasonable, ordinary, and prudent international organ whose mission is to prevent conflicts among state members and to restore international legal order.

In view of the above, Kofi Annan, Secretary-General of the UN, declared the following on the subject of Conflict prevention and peacemaking: "In recent years the international community has agreed that preventing armed conflict is critical to achieving lasting human security. Conflict prevention, as I put it in my millennium report, is where it all begins. Shifting from a culture of reaction to one of prevention is highly cost-effective both in human and in financial terms. In the early stages of a dispute, parties tend to be less polarized and more flexible and, thus, more inclined to settle their disputes peacefully than after violent conflict has become entrenched. Prevention also offers the best possible chance to address the root causes of a conflict, and not just its consequences, thus providing a real opportunity to sow the seeds of a durable peace. Confronting new outbreaks of violent conflict around the world and recognizing the importance of acting proactively, I have continued to strengthen our early warning and conflict prevention capacities. My primary objective has been to make early warning and conflict prevention a day-to-day concern for United Nations staff, both at Headquarters and in the field."[220] These remarks only support the DR Congo's argument that the UN knew or should have known of Rwanda and Uganda's intent and acts.

Finally, the UN knew or should have known that by invading the DR Congo, Rwanda, Uganda, and allies would encounter resistance not only from the Congolese armed forces but also from the civilians. The UN knew or should have known that the invading forces would suppress such resistance manu militari as they did. Similarly, the UN knew or should have known that because there is no pacific aggression, and because of the propensities of Rwanda and Uganda in committing genocide and other serious human rights abuses, these two states were likely to commit such barbarous acts in the DR Congo. At this phase of the conflict, the reasonable, ordinary, and prudent international body, whose mission is to prevent conflict among member nations, would have acted in a reasonable and timely manner to stop the aggression of the DR Congo as it did in other heavens.

But what is known is that the UN failed completely to live up to its principles and purposes. In truth, the UN stood idly looking on while genocide and other grave human rights violations were being committed in the DR Congo. Liability in direct cause is attached here because it was foreseeable that the non-motivation, desire, and intent of the UN to send emissaries to Rwanda and Uganda to control their passion and anger might have led to both these countries invading the DR Congo. Liability in direct cause is also attached in this case because the non-intervention of the UN in a reasonable and timely manner was perceived as encouragement by Rwanda and Uganda and legitimated their course of actions. Finally, liability in direct cause should attach because the UN's inaction furthered the commission of genocide, crimes against humanity, terrorism, and war crimes against both the DR Congo and its citizens.

Thus, the UN is also liable on the proximate cause theory because there was an uninterrupted chain of events from her negligent act that resulted in DR Congo and its people suffering injuries. The unusual manner or timing of these occurrences is irrelevant for the UN had the ability and authority to act reasonably and appropriately, but it knowingly failed to do so.

There is no legal defense on any theory justifying the UN's passiveness, immobility, and inaction to intervene in the war of occupation by Rwanda, Uganda, and allies against the DR Congo. The bottom line is that the UN knew or should have known what was happening. And for that reason the UN knew or should have known what to do but it refused to and chose not to take appropriate actions. This has amply been shown herein. The UN Secretary-General himself is of the opinion that "[b]ut surely no legal principle—not even sovereignty—can ever shield crimes against humanity. Where such crimes occur and peaceful attempts to halt them have been exhausted, the Security Council has a moral duty to act on behalf of the international community. The fact that we cannot protect people everywhere is no reason for doing everything when we can. Armed intervention must always remain the option of last resort, but in the face of mass murder it is an option that cannot be relinquished."[221] But for obscure reasons, the UN Security Council relinquished this option in the case at hand.

Maybe the UN will argue that the DR Congo assumed the risk of being invaded by Rwanda, Uganda, and allies when it terminated their military cooperation. The UN will thus assert that the DR Congo must have known of that risk and voluntarily proceeded in the face of the risk. This reasoning would not only be laughable, but illogical and illegal. Aggression is an international crime punishable by international laws. No state that ends military cooperation with another can assume the risk of being aggressed by the latter nor has such act ever occurred in the history of the world. The only reason Rwanda and Uganda invaded the DR Congo was to satisfy an imperialistic agenda. To infer that any state that terminates, regardless of the manner for this purpose, a military cooperation with another state, assumes the risk of being invaded by the latter is a reversal of the international legal order.

Thus, a prima facie case against the UN has been established on the theory of negligence in the war of occupation against the DR Congo, and therefore the UN is liable to the DR Congo and its citizens for damages.

In fact, four months before the Rwanda-Uganda-and-allies-led war of occupation in the DRC, UN Secretary-General, Kofi Annan, declared to the Security Council: "Early warning mechanisms are widely regarded as serving an important role in conflict prevention but, without early action, early warning is of little use. The United Nations early warning capabilities have been significantly improved in recent years. The critical concern today is no longer lack of early warning of impending crises, but rather the need to follow up early warning with early and effective action. Whether the response involves diplomatic efforts, a peacekeeping deployment, or a humanitarian intervention, the sooner action is taken the more effective it is likely to be."[222] What else can be said than verba volent scripta manent,[223] Mr. Secretary-General? Or should one say that "Verba strictae significationis ad latam extendi possunt, si subsit ratio."[224]

2.2. Duty to Sanction Rwanda and Uganda

First of all, it amazes more than one that both Rwanda and Uganda are not, until today, and this despite the many violations of humanitarian and international human rights laws, under the UN's sanctions. When one looks at the DR Congo case alone, there is no legal justification why these two countries have escaped those sanctions. It is Kofi Annan who argued, "[s]anctions, an integral element of the collective security provisions of the Charter, offer the Security Council an important instrument to enforce its decisions, situated on a continuum between mere verbal condemnation and recourse to armed force. They include arms embargoes, the imposition of trade and financial restrictions, interruptions of relations by air and sea, and diplomatic isolation. Sanctions have had an uneven track record in inducing compliance with Security Council resolutions."[225] In the four and half years of their war of occupation in the DR Congo, Rwanda, Uganda, and their allies committed more genocide, crimes against humanity, and war crimes than those committed in Iraq, Bosnia, Kosovo, and Afghanistan combined.

There should not be any mathematical calculations to enable the UN to condemn and sanction the aggressors of the DR Congo, namely, Rwanda and Uganda. In fact, the UN believes in sanctions because "[s]anctions have had an uneven track record in encouraging compliance with Security Council resolutions."[226] In April 1998, the UN Secretary-General, Kofi Annan, asserted that "[s]anctions, as preventive or punitive measures, have the potential to be an effective tool. The multilateral threat of economic isolation may help to encourage political dialogue, while the application of rigorous economic and political sanctions can diminish the capacity of the protagonists to sustain a prolonged fight. In particular, the imposition of an arms embargo can help to diminish the availability of arms with which to pursue a conflict by making the acquisition of weapons more difficult and more expensive... Better targeting of sanctions is necessary to help ensure that they will achieve their intended purpose. Greater use should be made of sanctions aimed at decision makers and their families, including the freezing of personal and organizational assets as well as restrictions on travel..."[227]

An arms embargo relative to the invasion of the DR Congo should be imposed on Rwanda mostly, but on Uganda also, if peace and security are the UN's concern in the Great Lakes region. Some authors argue that "in the quite rare cases where it is possible to organize a boycott that affects the economic, political, and social life of the offending country, it is likely to prevent the most serious human life violations..."[228] Well, it worked against Iraq, one will assert. But it is unlikely that the UN, as it stands today, may enforce such principles against Rwanda and Uganda. However, it is believed that unless the UN hits Rwanda and Uganda hard for having invaded a sovereign state and for committing gross violations of human rights on the Congolese soil, it would have set a precedent to be followed by any other country that feels like doing so, for one or another reason. Preemptive measures, some strategists in the western world are calling it today, meaning hit the enemy before he attacks you. And since it is so easy to find an alibi to justify an invasion of a foreign country under this new, untested, and ambiguous philosophy, then the UN would have helped in the total destruction of this world.

But the UN should have acted in the Congolese case, for there is already a precedent. What happened in 1991, when Iraq invaded Kuwait? Did the UN, the US, and the rest of the international community just fold their hands, arguing that Iraq's version of the story, that Kuwait was stealing its petrol and that Kuwait was its province, ipso facto, legitimized the aggression of a sovereign state, was correct? Not that one recalls, and according to records. In truth, as far as everyone remembers great publicity and propaganda occurred and was followed thereafter by an armed attack, leading to one of the biggest coalitions ever seen since World War II, and thereby resulting in the eviction of Iraq from Kuwait. In addition, if the international community, and the UN, in particular, still believes in the principle of causality, as many sane people do—that the same causes have the same effects—then the UN should have condemned, and kicked out Rwanda and Uganda from the DR Congo territories. And then the UN should have sanctioned Rwanda and Uganda for violations of international laws and multiple gross violations of human rights, pursuant to Article 5 of the ICC.

Article 5 of the ICC should be easy to enforce because the case with Iraq was the establishment of a legal precedent as far as aggression is concerned, while the Nuremberg Trials, the ICC for Yugoslavia, and today, the ICT for Rwanda are all legal precedents for the crime of genocide, crimes against humanity, and war crimes. Commenting on the international legal order and human rights, UN Secretary-General, Kofi Annan, commented that "[b]y adopting the Rome Statute, states took a decisive step, showing their determination to take concrete measures to enforce the rules of international humanitarian law that have been developed over the course of the last 100 years. They displayed their resolve that those whose deeds offend the conscience of humankind should no longer go unpunished. They made known their conviction that, in the affairs of men and women of all nations, the rule of law should finally prevail."[229]

Nevertheless, if the UN, for political reasons, feels that it cannot follow its own rules and regulations, principles and purposes embodied in its Charter in the Congolese case, then the reasonable people of this world, in general, and those of Africa, in particular, have the right to know what those reasons are and what factors have influenced them. In short, it is more than time that the UN stands tall, be impartial, fair, and just, and be accountable for its double standard policy, or be liable for all the crimes committed by Rwanda, Uganda, and US allies in the DR Congo.

3. Rights and Obligations of Occupying Forces Under International Law

Occupying forces have the rights and obligations toward civilians and non-combatants, private as well as public property in the territories they occupy. These forces must comply with international humanitarian and human rights legal norms during the entire period of occupation, the breach of which may have severe consequences on those individuals found to be violators. This reality was not an exception for Rwandan and Ugandan invading forces in the DR Congo.

"The Annexed Regulations to Hague Convention IV of 1907, the 1949 Fourth Geneva Convention, and customary international law set forth the laws of belligerent occupation applicable in this conflict. Both the Nuremberg Tribunal and a 1993 Report of the UN Secretary-General characterized the Hague Regulations as reflecting customary international law binding on all States."[230] Further, Protocol 1, Additional to the Geneva Convention of 8 June, 1977, which contains the most up-to-date provisions regulating the law of occupation, are applicable in the Congolese case as well.

The DR Congo, Rwanda, and Uganda are all Parties to the 12 August, 1949 Fourth Geneva Convention and the 8 June, 1977 Protocol 1 Additional to the Geneva Convention. The DR Congo became Party to the Fourth Geneva Convention on 24 February, 1961 and to the Protocol 1 on 3 June, 1983. Rwanda became Party to the first on 5 May, 1964 and to the second on 19 November, 1984; whereas Uganda became Party to the former on 18 May, 1964 and to the latter on 13 March, 1991. Given that the DR Congo, Rwanda, and Uganda are all Parties to both the Geneva Convention and the Protocol 1 Additional to the Geneva Convention, these two documents are applicable to this conflict.

During the Congolese war of occupation, the conduct of Rwandan and Ugandan invaders demonstrated that they only had rights and no obligations, if not little, to the civilian populations. Sufficiently written and oral, recorded and unrecorded stories, which came and come from the occupied territories of the DR Congo substantially evidence that civilians living in those territories, including their real and personal property, did not receive any protection from Rwandan and Ugandan occupying armed forces. This conduct per se was contrarily to the letter and spirit of Article 51 of Protocol 1, Additional to the Geneva Convention, which states that:

The civilian population and individual civilians shall enjoy general protection against dangers arising from military operations. To give effect to this protection, the following rules, which are additional to other applicable rules of international law, shall be observed in all circumstances.

The civilian population as such, as well as individual civilians, shall not be the object of attack. Acts or threats of violence, the primary purpose of which is to spread terror among the civilian population, are prohibited.

Civilians shall enjoy the protection afforded by this Section, unless and for such time as they take a direct part in hostilities.

Indiscriminate attacks are prohibited.

Neither the Rwandan nor the Ugandan occupiers during the DR Congo war of aggression comply with the provisions of Articles 52, 54, 55, 56, and 57 of Protocol 1, Additional to the Geneva Convention. For example, various reports from NGOs and other international organizations working in the Congolese occupied territories show that most of the serious violations of humanitarian and human rights laws against Congolese civilians were simply in reprisals to both Mayi-Mayi and/or DR Congo government and allies' attacks on Rwandan-Ugandan coalition and allies.

There is no doubt that the Geneva Convention grants to occupying forces several rights in the territories under their control. Rwanda and Uganda, invaders of the DR Congo during the period of 1998-2002, were not exempt from this law of the nations. In truth, these occupying armed forces exploited these rights to the maximum. However, the exercise of those rights outweighed and exceeded their duties and obligations toward the Congolese civilian populations, which they were to protect at all costs. The only notorious thing that one remembers of Rwandan and Ugandan occupying armed forces in the DR Congo is that they excelled in unnecessary destruction, both of human life and property. Otherwise, how can one explain the lost of nearly 3.5 million human lives and a very high number displaced in less than five years of armed conflict?

Furthermore, could Paul Kagame and Owerri Museveni dare point their fingers at and show to the world today what development and prosperity their occupation had brought to Congolese civilians who lived in their occupied territories. Is there a single road, health clinic, or classroom they built in almost five years of occupation? What is known about their foolish endeavors is that they directed the massacres of innocent civilians; they masterminded the forced separation of families; they hampered the WHO's Polio vaccination campaigns and the like; they commanded armed forces who buried Congolese civilians alive; they instructed troops that had for policy the targeting of civilian populations; they abetted military forces that raped girls and women and sexually abused them in the most horrifying and inhuman way; they ordered the destruction and pillage of both private and public assets in the Congolese occupied territories where their armed forces were present; in short, they are in-charge of armed forces that distributed death upon death on civilian populations and non-combatants in the territories of the DRC under their illegal occupation.

Thus, Rwanda and Uganda were in total breach of the Geneva

Convention and the Protocol 1, Additional to the Geneva Convention, because they systematically violated the law of occupation during the entire war of invasion against the DR Congo by allowing their armed forces to act in a manner inconsistent to the prescribed norm of humanitarian laws and international human rights, acts which—like, deprivation of primary health care, rape and other sexual violence, illegal forced labor, summary executions, destruction of private and public property, individual or mass forcible transfers of populations, as well as deportations of protected persons, and the like—resulted in grave violations of human rights against Congolese civilians and non-combatants, which were not directed at a specific military objective nor were they necessary to achieve any military objective.

Rwanda and Uganda may claim that they did not violate the aforementioned Statutes since they did not conquer the DR Congo or annex in part or whole any Congolese territories. However, in international law, the clock of occupation starts running "...as soon as territory is 'occupied' by adversary forces, that is, when the government of the occupied territory is no longer capable of exercising its authority, and the attacker is in a position to impose its control over that area. The entire country need not be conquered before an occupation comes into effect as a matter of law, and a state of occupation need not be formally proclaimed, as General Eisenhower did in the Second World War. Obligations and rights of the Occupying Power obviously extend only to those areas that the attacking forces actually control. Ultimately, whether territory is occupied is a question of fact. That some resistance continues does not preclude the existence of occupation provided the occupying force is capable of governing the territory with some degree of stability. Moreover, it is not legally relevant that the occupiers claim to be 'liberating' the population; so long as an international armed conflict is underway, the justification for the conflict has no bearing on whether the laws of occupation apply,"[231] argues professor Schmitt. Caryle Murphy goes on that, "[u]nder the laws of war, territory is considered occupied when a foreign power actually controls it."[232]

Records demonstrate that Rwandan troops illegally entered and occupied territories of the DR Congo on 2 August, 1998. They controlled many of the said territories until their simulated withdrawal in 2002. Curiously, it was on 2 August, 1990 that Iraq invaded Kuwait. Was this act a simple coincidence or deliberate action by Rwanda and allies to illustrate the double standard doctrine on how the biased international community was going to respond to their illegal occupation of an independent state, fellow Member State of the

UN? Kagame and his foxes have the answer to this interrogation.

4. Individual Liabilities and International Legal Remedies

Individual accountability, prosecution, and punishment of those leaders who conspired, planned, ordered, executed, aided, abetted and/or assisted in the unlawful occupation of the DR Congo, and of those who perpetrated genocide, war crimes, and crimes against humanity, and terrorism in the occupied territories of the DR Congo is the sole fair and just remedy that all those who love peace and justice are seeking for today in connection with the Congolese tragedy. The first instrument in the achievement of such international justice is the speedy creation of a hoc international criminal court for the Congo. Second, the Doctrine of Superior responsibility is applicable in this case; third, victims of the Congolese tragedies may also make use of the US ATCA and TVPA as legal instrumentalities; and fourth, the discussion focused on the concept of universal jurisdiction and the issue of sovereign immunity.

4.1. Why an International Criminal Court for the Congo?

The DR Congo, Rwanda, and Uganda are Parties to the Rome Statute of the ICC. Contrary to what some legalists may think, the ICC is not the best forum to prosecute and sentence the authors of grave violations of humanitarian and international human rights laws that occurred during the Congolese war of aggression, which the Rwandan, Paul Kagame, and the Ugandan, Owerri Museveni, masterminded and executed with the blessing and assistance of their imperialist allies. Two main reasons support this approach. First, the provisions of the ICC are not retroactive,[233] meaning the ICC does not cover violations of the laws of nations committed before its entry into force. Thus, the jurisdiction of the ICC extends only to international violations of humanitarian and human rights norms that occurred on or after 1 July, 2002 when the Rome Statute entered into force. Whereas, the war of occupation against the DRC, and most of the serious violations of international legal laws linked to the Congolese tragedies, occurred before 1 July, 2002 or between the periods of 2 August, 1998 to 1 July, 2002.

Thus, though the ICC may have jurisdiction over crimes against international humanitarian and human rights laws that were perpetrated on or after 1 July, 2002 in the DR Congo, during the Rwandan and Ugandan illegal occupation, the pursuit of such justice before the ICC would be a quest of partial justice for the Congolese people because this Court does not cover crimes that took place before 1 July, 2002. Having individuals who committed violations of international laws in the DR Congo prosecuted by the ICC, and consequently ignoring genocide, war crimes, and crimes against humanity that occurred before 1 July, 2002 would be an open insult and serious moral injury to the Congolese people who can no longer wait for justice.

Second, the ICC's maximum sentence is life imprisonment. In addition, this international criminal court does not impose the death penalty, whereas the prosecution of certain grave crimes committed in the occupied territories of the DR Congo are likely to request that the perpetrators receive the death penalty. Alas, so far, neither the ICTY nor the ITCR impose the death penalty as a sentence. The Statutes of these two courts provide imprisonment as the highest sentence. In the case of ITCR, the maximum jail time a convicted person may serve is 30 years.

The non-imposition of the death penalty by these international criminal courts results from the fact that today's pressuring international trend is the abolition of the death penalty as a form of punishment, rather than its retention, for violations of both national and international laws. The advocates of this movement believe that the death penalty is, per se, an inhuman form of punishment. Further; it is unlikely that the UN Security Council will be supportive of such an idea, as far as the DR Congo's search for international justice is concerned. This means that it is likely that both the US and UK will use their vetoes to strike down any UN Security Council resolution in favor of empowering an ad hoc UN criminal court in the DR Congo to impose the death penalty. Strangely, even the US, that still practices the death penalty in many of its states, is likely to oppose such a move in the DR Congo because those individuals who are likely to get the death sentence are their allies. Curiously, though, it is probable that the US is going to push for a symbiosis of international criminal court and domestic justice in Iraq. This created, hybrid, court of law shall impose the death penalty as a maximum sentence to Iraqis convicted of international human rights violations, since those to be sentenced are the enemies of the American government.

Nonetheless, the essence of this discussion does not evolve nor sit on the maintenance or imposition of the death penalty as a form of punishment for violators of international humanitarian and human rights laws committed during the Congolese war at issue. Nevertheless, one should take notice that, as a matter of law, the death penalty has an effective, positive, and constructive deterrent effect on the future perpetrators of gross crimes that hurt the human conscience. In addition, the imposition of the death penalty by a UN ad hoc International Criminal for the DR Congo shall positively halt the shameful African culture of impunity. The imposition of the death sentence shall send a clear and distinct message that life is sacred, that one's right to life is a non-negotiable fundamental right, and that pursuant to the UN Declaration of Human Rights and other international legal norms, no one has the right to take anyone's life without any due process of law. Not even Paul Kagame and/or Owerri Museveni, their lieutenants and soldiers, or their puppets, so-called rebel leaders, their commandants and soldiers, had such right against any Congolese soul.

Imagine the thrilling effect the indictment, arrest, conviction, and sentence to death of at least one of the above individuals by an international criminal court of the caliber of a UN ad hoc Criminal Tribunal for the Congo shall have in the entire Great Lakes region. There is no doubt that deterrence shall be the determinant factor here and that potential violators of the custom of laws and international human rights will certainly think twice before engaging themselves in any behavior classified as genocide, terrorism, crimes against humanity and war crimes, and/or the like. The sentencing to death, and the enforcement of such a sentence by a competent penal tribunal for violations of the laws of nations, on an individual who once was a powerful person (for example a president, premier minister, or commandant in chief of the army, rebel leader, or the like) in any African nation, is likely to contribute to the establishment or the restoration of law and order, and peace and justice in such a given state and in the entire region because it will send a clear message that nobody is above the law.

The determination at the UN Security Council of whether to retain the death penalty for an ad hoc International Criminal Tribunal, for the Congo to prosecute and trial violations of humanitarian and human rights laws, will be a political rather than a legal decision. Nevertheless, whatever transpires from the UN Security Council's corridors in the months or even years to come will not deter the realities of the atrocities that Kagame and Museveni's armed troops committed in the occupied territories of the DRC, nor will such action impair on the individual liabilities of those the world knows to be the true perpetrators of such international crimes: Paul Kagame and Owerri Museveni.

Yet from the same corridors of the Security Council, reliable sources have cautioned about the idea of and the establishment of another *ad hoc* UN Tribunal. It seems that the Security Council is no more in the mood to set up another *ad hoc* penal tribunal because the lessons learned from the ICTY and the ITCR, the latter in particular, are that the results of these tribunals are neither reliable nor impressive. Therefore, today, the UN Security Council advocates the idea of the establishment of a hybrid court, which is a combination of a local and international criminal tribunal, like the UN Special Tribunal for Sierra Léone or Cambodia, to prosecute violators of international human rights and humanitarian laws. The UN and the international community will assist with prosecutors, advocates, and judges, while both local and international laws shall be of application throughout the judicial proceedings.

From the same sources close to the UN Security Council, comes out the words that when it appears during the investigations that Rwandans and Ugandans are involved in the atrocities committed during their war of occupation in the DRC, then the governments of Rwanda and Uganda must cooperate with the established Tribunal. These countries must then apprehend and hand over to the Tribunal those individuals suspected of committing such atrocities. From what one hears, the non-cooperation of these countries at that moment shall lead the international community to exercise pressure on them for compliance. Whether these measures will work, one can only wait and see. The great risk with the functioning of such tribunal is independence. While there is no reason why local authorities would interfere with the operations of such a court, there is fear that foreign powers will exercise subtle pressures on the tribunal to have their allies either not be convicted or receive lesser sentences. In the worst scenario, these powers would not leave any stone unturned to hamper the prosecution of their allies.

On the other hand, what emerges from the DRC government's circle is clear, concise, and simple. Whether the UN Security Council decides on establishing *ad hoc* tribunal or a mixed tribunal like in Sierra Léone is not a big issue. What matters the most, according to the DR Congo government, is that those liable for the continuing suffering of the Congolese people, those individuals who committed genocide, terrorism, crimes against humanity, and war crimes in the occupied territories during the war of invasion that Rwanda, Uganda, and their allies created, be brought to justice to answer for their crimes and punished accordingly. The Congolese people and those who love peace and justice widely share this view as being one of the few remedies that will stabilize DRC and the Great Lakes Region in its entirety.

4.2. The Doctrine of Respondent Superior

In the law of torts, this doctrine holds the principal, the superior, or the person-in-charge liable for the tortuous acts of the agent or subordinate inasmuch as such acts are committed within the scope of the work or employment. In international customary law and the law of war, this doctrine is called the command responsibility rule or the doctrine of superior responsibility. The underlining principle is that those commanders, military or civilians, who give orders, instructions, or otherwise command, are accountable for the breach of humanitarian and international laws that result from the execution of their orders, instructions, and commands by their subordinates.

Article 146 of the Geneva Convention states:

The High Contracting Parties undertake to enact any legislation necessary to provide effective penal sanctions for persons committing, or ordering to be committed, any of the grave breaches of the present Convention defined in the following Article.

Each High Contracting Party shall be under the obligation to search for persons alleged to have committed, or to have ordered to be committed, such grave breaches, and shall bring such persons, regardless of their nationality, before its own courts. It may also, if it prefers, and in accordance with the provisions of its own legislation, hand such persons over for trial to another High Contracting Party concerned, provided such a High Contracting Party has made out a prima facie case.

Further, Article 86 of Protocol 1 Additional to the Geneva Convention declares that:

1. The High Contracting Parties and the Parties to the conflict shall repress grave breaches, and take measures necessary to suppress all other breaches, of the Conventions or of this Protocol which result from a failure to act when under a duty to do so.

2. The fact that a breach of the Conventions or of this Protocol was

committed by a subordinate, does not absolve his superiors from penal or disciplinary responsibility, as the case may be, if they knew, or had information which should have enabled them to conclude in the circumstances at the time, that he was committing or was going to commit such a breach, and if they did not take all feasible measures within their power to prevent or repress the breach.

Finally, Article 28 of the Rome Statute of the ICC points out the following regarding the responsibility of commanders and other superiors:

In addition to other grounds of criminal responsibility under this Statute for crimes within the jurisdiction of the Court:

(a) A military commander or person effectively acting as a military commander shall be criminally responsible for crimes within the jurisdiction of the Court committed by forces under his or her effective command and control, or effective authority and control as the case may be, as a result of his or her failure to exercise control properly over such forces, where:

(i) That military commander or person either knew or, owing to the circumstances at the time, should have known that the forces were committing or about to commit such crimes; and

(ii) That military commander or person failed to take all necessary and reasonable measures within his or her power to prevent or repress their commission or to submit the matter to the competent authorities for investigation and prosecution.

(b) With respect to superior and subordinate relationships not described in paragraph (a), a superior shall be criminally responsible for crimes within the jurisdiction of the Court committed by subordinates under his or her effective authority and control, as a result of his or her failure to exercise control properly over such subordinates, where:

(i) The superior either knew, or consciously disregarded information which clearly indicated, that the subordinates were committing or about to commit such crimes;

(ii) The crimes concerned activities that were within the effective responsibility and control of the superior; and

(iii) The superior failed to take all necessary and reasonable measures within his or her power to prevent or repress their commission or to submit the matter to the competent authorities for investigation and prosecution.

Stuart E. Hendin comments in these terms concerning Article 28(a) above: "This Article refers to either a 'military commander' or to a 'person effectively acting as a military commander.' This wording may be interpreted in more then one way. The term 'military commander' is obvious on its face and would be referable to a superior within a military chain of command. The term 'person effectively acting as a military commander' may be applicable to a member of the military outside of the chain of command, and not necessarily superior in rank. Further, the wording may also allow a finding of culpability on the part of a civilian who has assumed de jure command or control of some military force, regardless of the size of the force."[234]

Likewise, Hendin analyses the provisions of the above point (b) as follows: "Article 28(b) appears to be a direct attempt to encompass acts or situations not captured by Article 28(a), and is referable to acts committed in non-militarily capacities. It is arguable that Article 28(b) requires only the establishment of a superior-subordinate relationship. Article 28(a) contemplates a non-military individual assuming the necessary characteristics of effective command or control (with the abilities and authorities attendant to the same). Conversely, Article 28(b) may be interpreted to cover the situation where a military individual will be responsible for the actions of non-military individuals or groups." He then stresses the fact that, "It is arguable that the drafters of the Rome Statute intended a lesser standard to be applied to non-militarily (de jure or de facto) superior-subordinate relationships. It is of note that only the term, 'effective authority and control' is used reflecting an understanding that there may be no formal chain of command existent. The term 'effective authority and control' may have the effect of relieving from culpability those who may exert some form of influence but no control."[235]

From the analysis of the aforementioned articles transpires this liability test regarding violations of the customary rules of war. A commander, military person, or civilian, and regardless of the size of armed personnel under his or her command, is accountable for the wrongful acts of his or her subordinate if either he or she "knew or, owing to the circumstances at the time, should have known" that the said subordinate was "committing or about to commit" such acts, which the commander "failed to take all necessary and reasonable measures within his or her power to prevent or repress their commission," pursuant to the Geneva Convention and Protocol 1, Additional to the Geneva Convention.

In the case at hand, Rwandan and Ugandan soldiers, and their different "rebel" groups, respectively under the high command of Paul Kagame and Owerri Museveni, and of the different "rebel" leaders, committed grave violations of humanitarian and human rights norms within the territories they occupied in the DR Congo from August 1998 to 2002. Owing to the circumstances at the time when they ordered their armies to invade a sovereign state, namely the DR Congo, whereas the Congolese local populations resisted strongly the foreign aggression of their homeland, somewhat with arms and sometimes passively, both these high commanders knew, whereas these populations sustained their national army against foreign invaders, whereas the occupying armed forces suppressed such resistances and allegiance to the Congolese flag manu military, burning and destroying entire villages, massacring civilians, raping, at a large scale, girls and women, and committing all other abuses in breach of the Geneva Convention, due to those circumstances, whereas the invaders were thirsty with Congolese blood and drank Congolese blood in all its forms; due to the circumstances at the time, Paul Kagame and Owerri Museveni "knew or should have known" that their armed forces on the Congolese soil were committing or were about to commit such acts.

In addition, not only did those commanding officers, both military or civilians, knew or had reason to know about the commission of such atrocities, but they "failed to take all necessary and reasonable measures within [their] power to prevent or repress their commission," in accordance to the Geneva Convention and Protocol 1, Additional to the Geneva Convention, and other international legal norms. "Liability may also attach to a commander even if he did not actually know about the acts of subordinates but ought to have known about them and his failure in this respect constituted a dereliction of duty on his part, for example, if he is put on notice but fails to do anything about it," [236]argues Major-General Rogers.

What argument do those leaders, Kagame, Museveni, and their Congolese partners advance to defend this miserable failure of protecting civilians and non-combatants? Assume that they even did try to offer to the civilians and non-combatants in the territories under their occupation minimum and/or maximum security and protection depending on the circumstances; how would they explain the death of almost four million innocent people in the territories under their occupation and millions of displaced persons in the same zones?

"After World War II the international community took a giant step toward accountability when it held individual leaders responsible for gross violations of human rights. Regrettably, it took several steps backward in the following decades by favoring governmental immunity to the Nuremberg precedent. Now, however, the international community is back on the course of accountability,"[237] notes Nicole Barrett. Since last century, the international community is weakening its grasp that individuals in leadership positions, who are guilty of violations of the laws of nations, should not escape justice under the veil of State immunities and/or the like. At least, the cases of General Pinochet indicted by a Spanish court on tortures charges; Hisséne Habré, former President of Tchad indicted by a Senegalese court in February 2000 on torture charges as well as human rights violations; Slobodan Milosevic, ex-President of Yugoslavia prosecuted for war crimes by the ICTY, to name these few, is an example that sufficient precedents have been established to trial former heads of state for violations of international humanitarian and human rights norms that they committed within or outside of their national territories.

Even leaders of powerful nations like the US are not exempt from prosecution and may not escape liabilities for violations of international laws in the long run as the following cases show. "...a group of professors from Osgoode Hall Law School filed a complaint before the Yugoslavia Tribunal outlining a criminal case naming Wesley Clark, the North Atlantic Treaty Organization's (NATO) Commander-in-Chief, and the presidents of the NATO countries as defendants. They charged that NATO's policy of targeting power generation and water systems was illegal under the Geneva Conventions. Louise Arbour, former Prosecutor for the ICTY, surprised the international community by announcing in May 1999 that she was taking the complaint seriously and proceeded to open an investigation.... On the tail of the Osgoode complaint, Jerome Zeifman, former Watergate committee counsel, whose case against Richard Nixon forced the US President from the White House, filed charges on June 8, 1999 at the ICTY against Bill Clinton and US Secretary of Defense, William Cohen, for war crimes and crimes against humanity in ordering US troops to participate in the NATO bombing attacks on the former Yugoslavia."[238]

That is not all. Taking advantage of the 16 June, 1993 Belgian law,[239] which was until a few months ago the champion of Universal Jurisdiction, "...complaints alleging war crimes against Bush [senior], [Colin] Powell, and Vice President, Dick Cheney, were filed on behalf of the families of seven Iraqis killed or injured during the 1991 Gulf War."[240] Likewise, in May 2003, pursuant to the same Belgian law, a group of Iraqis filed a complaint against American commanders in Iraq for alleged atrocities committed during the second Iraqi Gulf war. "The complaint is directed against members of the US armed forces—who are not yet identified— for war crimes ... against the officers who commanded them in as far as those officers have given orders for illegitimate military actions, or have failed to act to the best of their abilities, when they had knowledge about orders given with respect to these violations or of facts indicating the start of their execution while in the ability to prevent their continuation or stopping them. This is particularly the case for Colonel Bryan P. McCoy, commander of the Third Marine Battalion of the 4th Regiment, who has encouraged his men to fire at ambulances and civilians.... This complaint is likewise directed against General Tommy Franks, commander of the US and U.K. forces involved in the recent war on Iraq, during which numerous war crimes ... particularly the massive and repeated use of cluster bombs against civilian targets, couldn't have been committed if not on the orders of the highest commander of the troops. In any case, this commander should have had knowledge about orders given with respect to the execution of such a violation of facts indicating the start of their execution. Being the highest commander, General Tommy Franks could have prevented the continuation of these war crimes or stopped them."[241]

Thus, pursuant to Article 146 of the Geneva Convention, Article 86 of Protocol 1, Additional to the Geneva Convention, and Article 28 of the Rome Statute of the ICC, Kagame and Museveni, as well as all "rebel" leaders whose troops illegally occupied territories of the DR Congo, are accountable for the crime of aggression, genocide, war crimes, crimes against humanity, and terrorism committed by their armed forces because they "knew or, owing to the circumstances at the time, should have known" that their armed forces were "committing or about to commit" such international crimes. Further, pursuant to the aforementioned articles, those commanders are liable for the same crimes because they totally "failed to take all necessary and reasonable measures within [their] power to prevent or repress their commission."

4.3. US ATCA and TVPA as Legal Instrumentalities

According to Section §703 of the Restatement of the Law Third of the Foreign Relations Law of the United States, "[i]n general, individuals do not have direct international remedies against a state violating their human rights except where such remedies are provided by international agreement ... whether they have a remedy under the law of a state depends on that state's law."[242] This is the very essence of both the ATCA and the TVPA. In addition, this section provides that "[a]n individual victim of a violation of a human rights agreement may pursue any remedy provided by that agreement or by other applicable international agreements."[243]

One particular, even very important, aspect of the Congolese war of occupation by its neighbors, Rwanda and Uganda, is the fact that the illegal exploitation and plunder of the Congolese natural and mineral resources fuelled the armed conflict, prolonged the war, and contributed to the loss of lives of more than 3.5 million innocent civilians and millions of displaced persons. It is evident that without the involvement of foreign corporations, with the complicity of Rwandans, Ugandans, and Congolese nationals, or so-called rebels, fighting alongside the invaders, the number of human casualties in this war would not have been as severe as known today. Further, the pillage of Congolese national assets would not have been as systematic as currently presented at the international level if the illegal exploitation of Congolese resources did not stimulate the war. This involvement of foreign corporations, with the complicity and support of Rwandans, Ugandans, and Congolese "rebels" who held any parcel of authority in the affairs of that war and contributed to this plundering of Congolese resources, is an international crime punishable by international rules of law.

The Alien Tort Claims Act (ATCA) of 1789 grants jurisdiction to US Federal Courts over "any civil action by an alien for a tort only, committed in violation of the law of nations or a treaty of the United States."[244] Meaning, "[th]e statute can be read to give US courts jurisdiction over non-criminal abuses that occur anywhere in the world, so long as the alleged wrong would violate international law."[245] In other words, foreign nationals can sue, in US Courts, individuals acting on official capacity and corporations who have violated international rules of law. For nearly 200 years, this Statute was unused until 1980 when Dr. Filartiga,[246] a Paraguayan, sued successfully in US courts a Paraguayan police officer who happened to be in the US and who kidnapped and tortured his son, Joel Filartiga. The Plaintiffs were awarded 10 million dollars. "Subsequent cases have been brought against national leaders, such as former Philippine President, Ferdinand Marcos, and senior army officers from Guatemala, Indonesia, Argentina, Ethiopia and El Salvador, among other countries."[247]

Further, "[wh]en world leaders gathered in New York ... for the Millennium summit at the end of 2000, they expected all of the meetings, speeches, and handshakes that are customary elements of diplomatic practice—but several leaders got something that they did not expect: a summons to appear before US courts to account for crimes committed in their homelands. Li Peng, former Chinese premier, and Robert Mugabe, president of Zimbabwe, were both served with court papers for cases brought by victims. Both faced accusations that they ordered massive human rights violations, including torture and extrajudicial killing. In recent months, the stream of lawsuits has grown even stronger. East Timorese plaintiffs are suing the former chief of staff of the Indonesian armed forces, General Johnny Lumintang, in a District of Columbia federal court. The lawsuit accuses him of masterminding attacks on the population of East Timor, in violation of international human rights law."[248]

Furthermore, "[j]ust weeks before Li Peng and Robert Mugabe were served, a group of women who had been raped in Bosnia concluded their case against Bosnian Serb leader, Radovan Karadzic, and were awarded a multi-million dollar settlement by a Manhattan jury."[249]

While the downfall of the Act begins with the service of charges,[250] and the enforcement of judgment in terms of monetary collection for damages resulting from breaches of international legal norms,[251] the ATCA has a deterrent effect and reminds public officials, who have committed crimes against the laws of nations and who happen to be visiting the US, that the era of impunity for violations of the international human rights is at hand, and that they can run but they will never hide anymore. In truth, the supporters of international human rights shall " … smoke them out of their caves … get them running so [they] can get them"[252] and bring them to justice.

In addition to individual lawsuits, "US Plaintiffs relying on the Alien Tort statute have also sued major multinational corporations for alleged complicity in human rights and environmental violations."[253] Perhaps the biggest lawsuit came from the victims and survivors of the Nazis' Holocaust suing Swiss Banks. The other well spoken case is the Unocal case filled in 1996 by Burmese villagers claiming that Unocal employed the services of Burmese soldiers who violated their international human rights. In September 2002, "the Ninth Circuit Court overturned the dismissal of a trial-court judge and ruled that the company could be sued for such abuses as forced labor, rape, and murder committed by Burmese soldiers guarding the Yadana gas pipeline, if plaintiffs produced evidence showing that the company knew about and benefitted directly from the troops' conduct."[254]

In 2002, relying on ATCA, the Khulumani Support Group filed a lawsuit on behalf of South Africans apartheid victims of international human rights violations. The Group considered the "South Africa's apartheid regime an 'institutionalized system of racial disenfranchisement'"[255] and "seeks a measure of justice from those entities which aided or abetted the commission of this atrocity. Apartheid could not have been maintained in the same manner without the participation of the defendants," they argued. For the records, western multinational corporations directly and/or indirectly assisted the South African Apartheid regime in the continuation of its racial discrimination policies. During which period extra-judicial killings, torture, disappearances, murder, political assassinations, and other atrocities where committed against Black people and other people of color.

Often, international human rights violations from multinational corporations go unnoticed, and in the rare cases where they are noticed, they go unredressed. The reason is that domestic courts do not have an existing or adequate system to deal with such crimes. But in many instances, domestic courts do not have the power to regulate such violations because the governemental system of the host country is set up in a way that they offer protection to those commercial entities. In some occasion, victims are threatened of more violations of human rights and/or death if they dare to speak out. This fact is more real in authoritarian regimes across Latino-America, Asia and Africa. Thus, one may remark that "[f]rom the victims' point of view, ATCA has hardly been a cakewalk to justice. Yet ATCA gives hope to victims that any US corporation complicit in grave human rights abuses anywhere in the world can be held accountable in US courts. Human rights campaigners also believe that ATCA can be an incentive for corporations to ensure that their projects do not perpetuate human rights violations. That, in turn, could help improve the US relationship with communities around the world, to the long-term political and economic benefit of the United States. Indeed, this concern for the US standing in the world was what motivated the passage of ATCA over 200 years ago."[256]

In the case of the DR Congo, various reports from NGOs, international organizations, foreign states, and the Congolese government condemned the rape of Congolese resources and extrajudicial killings of innocent civilians and non-combatants during the war of occupation by foreigners whose sole interest was the continuation of the war to better profit from the chaos and enrich their personal and/or corporations' coffers. A UN sponsored Panel of Experts[257] found the following during their investigation on these matters:

The conflict in the Democratic Republic of the Congo has become mainly about access, control, and trade of five key mineral resources: coltan, diamonds, copper, cobalt, and gold. The wealth of the country is appealing and hard to resist in the context of lawlessness and the weakness of the central authority.

Exploitation of the natural resources of the Democratic Republic of the Congo by foreign armies has become systematic and systemic. Plundering, looting and racketeering, and the constitution of criminal cartels are becoming commonplace in occupied territories. These criminal cartels have ramifications and connections worldwide, and they represent the next serious security problem in the region.

The role of the private sector in the exploitation of natural resources and the continuation of the war has been vital. A number of companies have been involved and have fueled the war directly, trading arms for natural resources. Others have facilitated access to financial resources, which are used to purchase weapons. Companies trading minerals, which the Panel considered to be "the engine of the conflict in the Democratic Republic of the Congo" have prepared the field for illegal mining activities in the country.

Bilateral and multilateral donors have sent mixed signals to Governments with armies in the Democratic Republic of the Congo.

Top military commanders from various countries, for different reasons, needed and continue to need this conflict for its lucrative nature and for temporarily solving some internal problems in those countries, as well as allowing access to wealth. They have realized that the war has the capacity to sustain itself, and therefore has created or protected criminal networks that are likely to take over fully if all foreign armies decide to leave the Democratic Republic of the Congo.

The same panel also declared that:

It is often said that the conflict in the Democratic Republic of the Congo is low-intensity warfare, as armies do not confront each other on a daily basis and battles, or rather serious battles, are not frequent…

Current big battles have been fought in areas of major economic importance, toward the cobalt—and copper-rich area of Katanga and the diamond area of Mbuji Mayi. Military specialists argue that the Rwandan objective is to capture these mineral-rich areas to deprive the Government of the Democratic Republic of the Congo of the financial sources of its war effort… This rationale confirms that the availability of natural resources and their exploitation permits the continuation of the war. This may be true for all the parties. In view of the current experience of the illegal exploitation of the resources of the eastern Democratic Republic of the Congo by Rwanda and Uganda, it could also be thought that the capturing of this mineral-rich area would lead to the exploitation of those resources. In that case, control of those areas by Rwanda could be seen primarily as an economic and financial objective rather than a security objective for the Rwandan borders."[258]

In addition, it's Congresswoman, Cynthia McKenny, addressing the Subcommittee on International Operations and Human Rights, Committee on International Relations on 17 May, 2001, as mentioned previously, who declared that "[de]spite limp and totally ineffective protestations by the United Nations, the world community has largely stood idly by and allowed these two men [Presidents Paul Kagame of Rwanda and Yoweri Museveni of Uganda] to prosecute what can only be described as the most vicious, senseless, and bloody wars being fought in the world today. The cost of their actions to the DRC and its people is almost beyond measure. The scale and savagery of the crimes committed by the Rwandan and Ugandan armies in DRC compares to the abhorrent actions of the Nazi assault upon Eastern Europe."

In her letter to President Clinton on 31 August, 1999, Congresswoman Cynthia McKenny stated that, "Unfortunately, I feel compelled to report to you that crimes against humanity are being committed in the Democratic Republic of Congo.... In addition, your failure to intervene and stop the illegal invasion of the Democratic Republic of Congo by your allies, Uganda and Rwanda, has directly led to the commission of crimes against humanity by their troops in the Democratic Republic of Congo."

These reports and others show that Paul Kagame and Yoweri Museveni, and their respective lieutenants, who were involved in the Congolese military campaign discussed herein, and the different Congolese "rebel" leaders with their associates, are individually liable for crimes against the rules of international customary law in the DR Congo. Under the ATCA, since these individuals—many of whom are named in the reports of the Panel of Experts on the Illegal Exploitation of Natural Resources and Other Forms of Wealth of the Democratic Republic of the Congo—committed such acts, they can be sued in US courts by the victims of those abuses or their relatives the next time they visit the US. It is likely that in these circumstances the court will have both in rem and in personam jurisdictions to hear such cases. Thus, an appeal is being herein sent to all victims of serious atrocities in the hands of the aforementioned persons during the Congolese war of aggression or their families, and/or legal representatives, to courageously come forward and enjoy their right under the US Constitution.

Similarly, it is agreed that corporations that traded arms and ammunition for minerals, timber and/or other Congolese forms of wealth with Rwanda, Uganda, or "rebel" groups during the Congolese war of aggression fueled the war and did so solely with the intent to see the continuation of the war for their own economic interests. In addition, companies that traded said minerals and other forms of wealth in or from the DR Congo, knew or had reason to know that the products they bought or traded for were illegally exploited from the DR Congo and that such exploitation fueled the war of occupation and that their act of commission or omission simply aided or abetted the invading troops and their Congolese allies (rebel groups) in the violations of both human and humanitarian laws in the occupied territories of the DR Congo. Further, it is agreed that without such aid or abatement to Rwanda, Uganda, or "rebel" groups from these corporations; first, the illegal occupation of the DR Congo by Rwanda and Uganda would have been shorter than it was, and second, millions of innocent human lives would have been saved, and third, the pillage of Congolese national assets by Rwanda, Uganda, and allies would not have occurred as systematically as it was. Under the ATCA, a multinational corporation that violated international human rights must have a business nexus with the US for that entity to be sued in US courts.

Moreover, before further discussion, it is worth it to get a closer look at the application of the standard of proof that the Panel of Experts on the Illegal Exploitation of Natural Resources and Other Forms of Wealth of the Democratic Republic of the Congo applied in its investigations. "The Panel is an independent fact-finding body established by the Security Council, which reports and provides recommendations to it. As the Panel has no judicial recourse, it can only gather information from voluntary sources. Over the course of the last three years, it has established an extensive network of information sources both in the Great Lakes Region and in countries with links to the Democratic Republic of the Congo. It does not have the legal powers available to a Government, for example, in a criminal or civil investigation. Consequently, when assessing whether the behavior of an individual or company was inappropriate and therefore warranted inclusion in the annexes, a standard of proof based on 'reasonableness' or 'sufficient cause' was applied. In essence, for any particular party the Panel has acquired information indicating that, prima facie, a party has been engaged in conduct related to business dealings linked to the Democratic Republic of the Congo, either directly or indirectly, that do not meet generally accepted international standards of corporate behavior or governance. The Panel used its judgement in assessing the importance and relevance of that information to come to considered views and opinions."[259]

Now, it is important to note that "[t]he international business community in particular acknowledged that companies could not avoid their responsibilities in a country suffering from conflict, such as the Democratic Republic of the Congo. Investors and financiers took a keen interest in the activities of corporations in the Democratic Republic of the Congo, with which they were dealing. Companies themselves commented that their responsibilities extended further than they had previously acknowledged. Supply chains for raw materials, in particular, came into sharp focus, and prompted some of those named to reassess their activities in the Democratic Republic of the Congo."[260]

The Ba-N.Daw Report established "[t]he link between the continuation of the conflict and the exploitation of natural resources would have not been possible if some entities, not parties in the conflict, had not played a key role, willingly or not. Bilateral and multilateral donors and certain neighboring and distant countries have passively facilitated the exploitation of the resources of the Democratic Republic of the Congo and the continuation of the conflict; the role of private companies and individuals has also been vital. The Panel has gathered information showing that linkages between different actors and stakeholders are very well structured to the point that Governments and large reputable companies operate in confidence.... The importing companies and their facilitators are aware of the real origin of the coltan, however... the Panel also has indications of the direct and indirect involvement of some staff of the embassies and cooperation agencies of developed countries. They have facilitated the purchase of illegal minerals. The United States honorary consul in Bukavu, as he presented himself, Ramnik O. Kotecha, in addition to promoting deals between American companies and coltan dealers in the region, is, himself, Chairman of the Kotecha group of companies based in Bukavu and deals in coltan."[261]

Amazingly, the Kassem Report states as follows regarding certain corporations connected to the DRC war: "...There were those parties that, while having only indirect commercial ties to the Democratic Republic of the Congo, still bore a responsibility to ensure that those links did not, albeit inadvertently, contribute to funding and perpetuating the conflict. They comprise annex III of that report [of 15 October, 2002]. A specific example is that of the export of the mineral columbo tantalite (coltan), from which the metal tantalum is extracted. Tantalum is used, inter alia, in the production of electronic components. In 1999 and 2000 a sharp increase in the world prices of tantalum occurred, leading to a large increase in coltan production in eastern Democratic Republic of the Congo. Part of that new production involved rebel groups and unscrupulous business people forcing farmers and their families to leave their agricultural land, or chasing people off land where coltan was found, and forcing them to work in mines. As a result, the widespread destruction of agriculture and devastating social effects occurred, which in a number of instances were akin to slavery. While the processors of coltan and other Congolese minerals in Asia, Europe, and North America may not have been aware of what was happening in the Democratic Republic of the Congo, the Panel's investigations uncovered such serious concerns that it was decided to raise the awareness of the international business community to those issues through annex III in the context of the OECD (Organization for Economic Cooperation and Development) Guidelines for Multinational Enterprises. The purpose was to bring to the attention of the companies listed in annex III their responsibilities visà-vis the source of their raw materials."[262]

The above report states also that "[c]ompanies listed in annex III, however, were included because of apparent breaches of the OECD Guidelines for Multinational Enterprises, a non-compulsory code of business ethics. It was also a means of characterizing their involvement in exploitation activities that were less directly linked to conflict and therefore involved with more indirect ties to the main protagonists. Such companies appear to have benefitted from the chaotic environment in the Democratic Republic of the Congo through, for example, the acquisition of concessions or other contracts from the Government of the Democratic Republic of the Congo on terms that were more favorable than they might have received in countries where there were peace and stability."[263]

US business entities referred to in the above report are: America Mineral Fields (AMFI) operating in the field of mining; Cabot Corporation (tantalum processing); Eagle Wings Resources International (exploitation of coltan); Flashes of Color (diamond trading); Kemet Electronics Corporation (capacitor manufacture); Kinross Gold Corporation (mining); OM Group, Inc. (mining); Trinitech International, Inc. (coltan trading and exploitation); and Vishay Sprague (capacitor manufacture).

The Congolese people, mostly those victims of violations of human rights during the Rwandan-and-Ugandan-led war of occupation against their motherland, are fortunate that when they shall bring legal action against the aforementioned companies in US courts, the Court will apply neither the "reasonableness" nor "sufficient cause" as the standard of proof, but rather "beyond reasonable doubt"or "preponderance of evidence." For, these companies knew or had reason to know that their activities fueled the war and therefore contributed to the grave violations of international human rights the Congolese people were victims of. It would have been foreseeable for these commercial entities that their activities were illegal, even though somehow "legitimate," and precisely that such doings rather harmed the Congolese masses than promoted social and economical welfare to the Congolese at large.

For instance, a reasonable, average person will not comprehend the argument that the companies listed above and dealing with coltan "may not have been aware of what was happening in the Democratic Republic of the Congo," whereas this mineral is only produced in the DRC, specifically in eastern territories that were under occupation, and whereas suddenly the demand and offer of this mineral sharply climbed on the international market while Rwanda and Uganda illegally occupied the DR Congo. How can these corporations claim that they were not conscious of what was happening in the DRC, whereas they ought to know, had all the reasons in the world to know, and had no reason or justification whatsoever not to know?

How can a multinational corporation that knows or has reason to know that a sharp increase of world price of its product, in this instance coltan, led in the "forcing farmers and their families to leave their agricultural land, or chasing people off land where coltan was found and forcing them to work in mines, resulting in the widespread destruction of agriculture and devastating social effects, which in a number of instances were akin to slavery [which are crimes against the laws of nations]," and which "benefitted from [such] a chaotic environment in the Democratic Republic of the Congo" escape liability both to human and property destruction because of rationalization or the application of a wrong legal standard of proof? By what means would such a company have benefitted from a chaotic environment other than illegal ways? Moreover, why should such means be lowly weighed while evidence shows that they were calculated, deliberate, and premeditated?

For example, in its findings, "[t]he Panel also realized that DARA Great Lakes Industries (DGLI), of which DARA-Forest is a subsidiary, along with a sister company in Uganda, Nyota Wood Industries, is in collusion with the Ministry of Water, Land, and Forests of Uganda in establishing a scheme to facilitate the certification of timber coming from the Democratic Republic of the Congo. In May 2000, DGLI signed a contract for forest stewardship certification with SmartWood and the Rogue Institute for Ecology and Economy in Oregon, United States of America..."[264]

Further, the same Panel found that "[fu]ture plans for beating the international system are already in place. According to internal documents of DGLI, DARA- Forest will import timber from the Democratic Republic of the Congo into Uganda, which will be processed for different types of products in the new plant in Namanve for the saw-milling of hardwood, both imported from the Democratic Republic of the Congo and harvested in Uganda. DGLI partners in this new scheme include DARA Europe GmbH Germany, Shanton President Wood Supply Co. Ltd China, President Wood Supply Co. Ltd Thailand, DARA Tropical Hardwood, Portland, Oregon, United States of America. The distribution of sales of the company is thought to remain the same, about 30 percent to the Far East, China, Japan, and Singapore, 40 percent to Europe and 25 percent to North America."[265]

Thus, in these circumstances, the ATCA may apply since it appears that these multinational corporations are implicated in the pillage of Congolese national assets, and consequently aided in the violations of international human rights during the Rwanda and Uganda-led war of occupation in the DR Congo. These corporations have a business contact with the US, and thus they are likely to be subject to prosecution in a US court when the victims of such human rights abuses or their relatives present in the US, and/or legal representatives bring charges like the victims in the Nazi holocaust, in the Unocal, and in the Apartheid cases.

In Doe vs. Unocal Corp.[266], when reversing in part, affirming in part, and remanding the District Court decision, the 9th Circuit Court decided that Defendant-Appellee was legally responsible for human rights violations for aiding and abetting the Burmese Military government in the commission of these acts. Applying the aiding and abetting test in Furundzija the Court held that "The Furundzija standard for aiding and abetting liability under international criminal law can be summarized as knowing practical assistance, encouragement, or moral support which has a substantial effect on the perpetration of the crime. At least with respect to assistance and encouragement, this standard is similar to the standard for aiding and abetting under domestic tort law."[267]

"[I]n 1992, the Torture Victim Protection Act [TVPA] became law. This law creates a right for victims—even aliens—of state-sponsored torture and summary execution in other countries to sue in federal court here"[268] in the US, states Senator Arlen Specter and a member of the US Senate Judiciary

Committee. The primary objective of this Act is "to permit US victims of certain human rights violations to sue in US courts in a similar manner as aliens were permitted to do under ATCA. However, the act is not restricted to citizens; aliens can use it as well. Some of the TVPA's proponents also believed that it was important for Congress to pass a contemporary statute that would reinforce Filartiga's interpretation of the ATCA in the courts. The legislative history of the TVPA is clear on this point, stating that the ATCA has 'important uses and should not be replaced.'

"However, the TVPA in certain respects is more limited than the ATCA. The TVPA grants a cause of action for only two international law violations: torture and extrajudicial killing.... The TVPA also requires that the defendant act under the authority or law of a foreign nation."[269]

Thus, the TVPA is the other legal instrumentality or mechanism that may be used to bring to justice violators of international human rights of foreign origin. The TVPA is made "[to] carry out obligations of the United States under the United Nations Charter and other international agreements pertaining to the protection of human rights by establishing a civil action for recovery of damages from an individual who engages in torture or extrajudicial killing."[270] This limitation on crimes means that the TVPA "cannot be used as it was, for example, in FORTI, for disappearances, or as it was in Karadzic, for war crimes and genocide."[271]

In order to establish a prima facie civil action under the TVPA,[272] a plaintiff must show:

(a) Liability- An individual who, under actual or apparent authority, or color of law, of any foreign nation:

(1) subjects an individual to torture and shall, in a civil action, be liable for damages to that individual; or

(2) subjects an individual to extrajudicial killing and shall, in a civil action, be liable for damages to the individual's legal representative, or to any person who may be a claimant in an action for wrongful death.

(b) Exhaustion of Remedies- A court shall decline to hear a claim under this section if the claimant has not exhausted adequate and available remedies in the place in which the conduct giving rise to the claim occurred.

(c) Statute of Limitations- No action shall be maintained under this section unless it is commenced within 10 years after the cause of action arose.

It is important to understand as one argues that "[t]he new formulations of the Torture Victim Protection Act convey the message that torture committed under color of law of a foreign nation in violation of international law is 'our business,' as such conduct not only violates the standards of international law but also as a consequence violates our domestic law"[273] and destabilizes any given organized human society. In these circumstances, unlike under ATCA where the statute of limitation is uncertain, TVPA can be used retrospectively.[274] The reason behind this argument is that torture had always been universally denounced and condemned in customary laws long before the coming into effect of the TVPA.

During the four and half years war of occupation that Rwanda and Uganda led in the DRC, torture and extrajudicial killings of civilian populations by Rwandan and Ugandan occupying armed forces and their Congolese "rebel" allies was the policy. Innocent civilians were tortured as a means of getting information or punishment. Further, civilians the invaders and Congolese "rebels" killed without any legal due process, either because the invaders suspected them of supporting the Congolese national army or because they refused to cooperate with the invaders and their associates, were Congolese. Paul Kagame, Yoweri Museveni, and all "rebel" leaders knew or had reason to know that their troops were committing such abuses under color law in open violation of legally well-established and recognized international norms.

It would not be an issue here whether Kagame, Museveni, and their Congolese "rebel" foxes acted or failed to act when their officers and soldiers were violating the laws and customs of war. What matters, and what is widely known and accepted, is the fact that under "actual or apparent authority" from their part, their armies subjected Congolese individuals to torture and extrajudicial killings, acts which are in violation of internationally accepted legal rules, and the TVPA. Here, given that Kagame, Museveni, and their Congolese associates' acts were in breach of the TVPA, they shall be liable for damages to those Congolese they subjected to torture, in a civil action; or they shall be liable for damages to the individuals' legal representatives, surviving spouses or relatives, or to any person who may be a claimant in an action for wrongful death for those Congolese they subjected to extrajudicial killing in a civil action.

Thus, when those Congolese victims or their family members, or their legal representatives shall bring a civil action for torture and/or extrajudicial killings against Kagame, Museveni, and their Congolese "rebel" friends, individually and/or jointly, in any US district court, it is likely that such court shall have original jurisdiction of such civil action for a tort, given that such action was committed in violation of the law of nations, and that Kagame,

Museveni, and their Congolese "rebel" associates shall be found guilty of international human rights abuses under the TVPA.

5. The Problem of Sovereign Immunity: A Fair and Just Law?

Recourse to the ATCA or the TVPA is a powerful legal instrumentality that an alien victim of human rights abuses in his homeland, his relatives, or legal representatives in the US can utilize to bring to justice those leaders who have perpetrated international human rights against his person, or mutatis mutandis, the person of the family member or of the individual that they represent. However, in reality, sovereign immunity may hamper the application of these Acts, leaving those leaders who have committed gross violations of international human rights either untouchable or free from any civil and/or criminal prosecution.

The victims of international human rights, their relatives, and legal representatives, human rights activists asked this question: Should state leaders and officials, with actual or apparent authorities, or acting under the color of law when severe human rights atrocities were committed, escape justice because of the veil of sovereign immunity? Does this mean that they were immune and should not therefore be prosecuted, whereas they acted against the laws of international human rights? Is this universal justice? Should it not be agreed that when people are given, or give themselves as the case in many nations, a parcel of authority and powers to act on behalf of their citizens, "[b]ut … those powers are employed to torture people, judicial abstention is inappropriate[?]"[275]

"In 1625, in De Iure Belli ac Pacis, Grotius confirmed his view that the Law of Nations had long accepted the proposition that if a sovereign, cruelly-abused citizens or subjects, denying them basic human rights, that immunity must give way, and humanitarian intervention by another state or states was just and proper. He referred to specific instances of such action in history from antiquity to his time. He wrote: 'Though it is a rule established by the laws of nature and of social order, and a rule confirmed by all the records of history, that every sovereign is a supreme judge in his own kingdom and over his own subjects, in whose disputes no foreign power can justly interfere. Yet where a Busiris, a Phalaris, or a Thracian Diomede provoke their people to despair and resistance by unheard-of cruelties, having, themselves, abandoned all the laws of nature, they lose the rights of independent sovereigns, and can no longer claim the privilege of the law of nations. Thus Constantine took up arms against Maxentius and Licinius, and other Roman emperors who either took, or threatened to take them against the Persians if they did not desist from persecuting the Christians.' So, the right of a sovereign or sovereign states to claim the cloak of immunity to shield them from humanitarian intervention and the bar of justice for human rights crimes against their own citizens and subjects has long been under challenge."[276]

It is a fact that the problem of immunity will be raised whenever indictment, arrest and/or extradition of an individual in a leadership position, who committed grave violations of human rights, takes place. Indeed, immunity is a serious matter in international law. In principle, "a head of state in function or a diplomat accredited on an official mission will likely not be arrested in a majority of foreign countries where he may be travelling… "[277] It is the spirit of the US Foreign Sovereign Immunities Act of 1976 (FSIA) that "[a]ctions brought against currently serving heads of state, where the state is recognized by the United States, are likely to claim and receive immunity."[278] For instance, in 2000, while attending the UN Millennium Conference, President Robert Mugabe was served with court papers of victims claiming he tortured and abused their human rights. US authorities did not, however, arrest President Mugabe.

That confirms the Common Law Head-of-State Immunity principle: "A head-of-state recognized by the United States government is absolutely immune from personal jurisdiction in United States courts unless that immunity has been waived by Statute or by the foreign government recognized by the United States. A visiting head-of-state is generally immune from the jurisdiction of a foreign state's courts."[279] Similarly, neither France nor Belgium could prosecute the late President Laurent Kabila when in a visit in November 1998 when some Tutsis who fled the DR Congo filed charges against him on a count of torture and the like.

Nonetheless, there are some exceptions. First, when the ICC or one of its ad hoc or special tribunals indicts an individual, that individual—regardless of his state function—must be arrested and presented to such UN tribunal. The UN Special Tribunal for Sierra Léone indicted Charles Ghankey Taylor, former Liberian President, while exercising the function of head of state, for war crimes, crimes against humanity, and other gross violations of human rights committed in the territories of Sierra Léone. "The indictment was announced and a warrant for Taylor's arrest was issued while Taylor was in Ghana for peace talks with Liberian rebels who have been fighting to topple

Taylor's regime for the past three years."[280] Alas, the Ghanan government aided Charles Taylor to flee Ghana and return to Liberia hours after the indictment was served on him. The ICTY and ICTR, where it appears those indicted and arrested for mass violations of human rights respectively in the former Yugoslavia and Rwanda, are good precedents on the matter.

The second exception is of a former head of state. "According to international customary law, a former head of state is immune for official acts committed in his functions of a head of state."[281] Similarly, argues Kirgis, "[a] head of state is normally entitled to immunity from prosecution anywhere, even after he or she is no longer the head of state."[282] Today, however, the trend is to deny such immunity to former heads of state who have committed grave human rights abuses and violated humanitarian international laws. "Immunity, however, is unlikely to be granted in a human rights case to a former head of State, or to a head of an unrecognized government. It is important to note that 'Head of State' immunity now, more clearly than ever, attaches to the head of state, only whilst he or she actually occupies that office, and that it falls away after the office is vacated. I suggest that such immunity has become increasingly difficult to defend, when it involves human rights crimes, which if committed by a non-sovereign head of state would cause him to be regarded as hostis generi humani. 'Head of State' immunity can also be waived by a foreign State, although this is unlikely if the defendant is still in office. This development of course is in line with the House of Lords decision in the Pinochet Case,"[283] comments Pepper.

There are some good legal precedents applicable to the Congolese case from the cases discussed above. Given that to establish a prima facie civil action under the TVPA, a plaintiff must show that the perpetrator of the criminal conduct acted "...under actual or apparent authority, or color of law, of any foreign nation," solves one problem and creates some others at the same time. The problem or equation solved pursuant to this article is that the offender should be a public official acting "under actual or apparent authority, or color of law, of any foreign nation." In simple terms, the public official's torture and extrajudicial acts should be accepted and recognized as regular state official dealings for such individuals, inasmuch as he or she acted under actual or apparent authority or color of law to fall under the scope of the TVPA.

Thus, such an individual can claim immunity and no prosecution may be taken against him or her for any act committed while the individual held a public office and acted under actual or apparent authority or color of law.

This interpretation and understanding disqualify automatically those individuals acting without non-governmental actual or apparent authority, or color of law. In practice, individuals like Jean-Pierre Bemba, Bizima Karaha, Azarias Ruberwa, Emile Ilunga, Adolphe Onusumba, Thomas Lumbala, Jean-Pierre Ondekane, Laurent Nkundabatware, Wamba dia Wamba, Mbuza Nyamwesi, and other so-called Congolese rebels should not qualify for immunity, like the Court held in Kadic, since they never represented any official government when they committed war crimes and crimes against humanity.

The second equation is, how the commission of acts, condemned under international customary law as criminals, can become acceptable and goes unpunished solely because the individuals who committed such acts are state officials who acted "under actual or apparent authority, or color of law?" Should a criminal act become less criminal, or non-criminal, because the individual who performed it is or was a state official acting in an official capacity? Does a criminal act committed by a public official, whatever his or her authority and whatsoever the power under which such authority is exercised, fall only in the category of crimes after such official leaves office?

In the Pinochet precedent, "…the conclusion of the majority clearly was that crimes against international law cannot constitute or amount to acts performed in the exercise of the functions of a head of state. Neither sovereign immunity nor head of state immunity could be applied in such circumstances. Though the Pinochet ruling applied to a former head of state, as discussed above, it is difficult to see why the reasoning would not apply to those officials in office, including serving heads of state. If the protection of ratione materiae does not apply to acts performed by a former official, when out of office, how can it apply to the same acts when he is in office? How is 'non-official' criminal activity ever granted immunity? To do so is obvious nonsense. Eventually of course, Pinochet was released on health reasons by the Home Secretary. At the time of his release there were three other requests for his extradition (Belgium, France and Switzerland) in addition to Spain,"[284] states Pepper.

In application to the Congolese case, it is likely that Kagame, Museveni, and their lieutenants who violated international human rights and humanitarian legal norms during their war of occupation in the DR Congo against defenseless civilian populations, will not benefit from state immunity if charged with such crimes in a neutral country while in office, and while in visit in that state. Alas, Belgium, which had the best legal norms to this effect, was pressurized by the US to change its laws, as discussed previously.

It is logical to agree with Professor Pepper, in relation to the personalization of liability for breach of customary laws, that "[h]uman rights abuses are committed by individuals. The slave traders, torturers, summary executioners, genocidists, pirates, enslavers, rapists, and war criminals of every stripe and their masters are human beings abusing other human beings. It is true that the abusers act pursuant to official orders or under the color of law, but this in no way contradicts the fact that there are individuals involved with the acts or omissions which violate the human rights of others. In reality it is not the polis or the community acting and which, in fact, may be powerless to prevent the abuses—even if they are known. It is not even the amorphous 'state' which, along with its entities, acts only through its government officials and agents. Ultimately, a people and their sovereign state may bear ultimate liability, and there is no doubt, in my view, that immunity should not attach in respect of acts which violate the ius cogens from which no derogation is possible and which are frequently prohibited by treaties and conventions ratified by the very same states."[285]

6. The Concept of Universal Jurisdiction

Who gives the authority and power to a foreign state court to indict, issue a warrant of arrest to a suspected gross human rights violator who is a citizen of another state, and to try the latter in that foreign state court? Certain crimes in international law, namely torture, genocide, crimes against humanity, and war crimes, fall in the scope of the universal jurisdiction. Thus, in international criminal law, when a court of a particular state prosecutes the above international crimes, as provided in international treaties, it is said that such courts of such state have universal jurisdiction to prosecute and try any violator of international customary law, regardless of where the crime was committed and with no regard either to the victims or to the violators' nationalities. So, it is understood that "[t]he notion behind this principle is that the nature of such offenses dictates that all states have an interest in exercising jurisdiction over them."[286]

As with regard to remedies for violations of customary law of human rights, it is understood that "[s]ince the obligations of the customary law of human rights are erga omnes (obligations to all states), any state may pursue remedies for their violation, even if the individual victims were not nationals of the complaining state and the violation did not affect any other particular interest of that state."[287] Such is the central idea of the universal jurisdiction an idea which is very deterrent per se and the application of which would have rendered impunity for serious violations of the laws of the nations unacceptable, regardless of the societal status of the author of such abominable and hinderous acts.

Further, in international customary law, if a court of a foreign state does not want to prosecute and/or try the suspected offender, such foreign courts and states should extradite the suspected criminal to another state. To this end, "Cavallo's extradition marks the first time that one country has extradited a person to another country to stand trial for abuses that happened in a third. Cavallo is also the first serving or former Latin American military officer to be prosecuted by a judge from a third country after being arrested in a country where he had no legal problems."[288]

The following provisions of the UN Convention against Torture and Other Cruel, Inhuman or Degrading Treatment or Punishment[289] give a good insight on the prosecution and extradition of violators of this Convention:

Article 6

1. Upon being satisfied, after an examination of information available to it, that the circumstances so warrant, any State Party, in whose territory a person alleged to have committed any offence referred to in article 4 is present, shall take him into custody or take other legal measures to ensure his presence. The custody and other legal measures shall be as provided in the law of that State but may be continued only for such time as is necessary to enable any criminal or extradition proceedings to be instituted...

Article 7

1. The State Party in the territory under whose jurisdiction a person alleged to have committed any offense referred to in article 4 is found shall in the cases contemplated in article 5, if it does not extradite him, submit the case to its competent authorities for the purpose of prosecution.

Article 8

1. The offenses referred to in article 4 shall be deemed to be included as extraditable offenses in any extradition treaty existing between State Parties. State Parties undertake to include such offenses as extraditable offenses in every extradition treaty to be concluded between them.

2. If a State Party, which makes extradition conditional on the existence of a treaty, receives a request for extradition from another State Party with which it has no extradition treaty, it may consider this Convention as the legal basis for extradition in respect of such offenses. Extradition shall be subject to the other conditions provided by the law of the requested State.

3. State Parties, which do not make extradition conditional on the existence of a treaty, shall recognize such offenses as extraditable offenses between themselves subject to the conditions provided by the law of the requested State.

4. Such offences shall be treated, for the purpose of extradition between State Parties, as if they had been committed not only in the place in which they occurred but also in the territories of the States required to establish their jurisdiction in accordance with article 5, paragraph 1.

Françoise Hampson points out that "[g]enerally, treaties which provide for universal jurisdiction, require the state to try the suspect or to extradite him/her to stand trial elsewhere.... Every state bound by the treaties is under the legal obligation to search for and prosecute those in their territory suspected of having committed grave breaches, irrespective of the nationality of the suspect or victim or the place where the act was allegedly committed. The state may hand the suspect over to another state or an international tribunal for trial. Where domestic law does not allow for the exercise of universal jurisdiction, a state must introduce the necessary domestic legislative provisions before it can do so. That is not enough; the state must actually exercise jurisdiction, unless it hands over the suspect to another country or international tribunal."[290]

Two cases in relation to this Convention merit some attention, though it is not the focus of this book to analyze them in details: Hissène Habré and Augusto Pinochet indictments. The Senegalese court that indicted Hissène Habré, former Chadian president, on 3 February, 2000 acted according to the spirit of the UN Convention on Torture and did well. This court did not recognize Habré's immunity as a former head of state, since immunity could not shield his criminal conduct against his people. However the decision of Senegalese President, Abdoulaye Wade, on 7 April, 2001 allowing Habré to leave Senegal, was politically motivated and against the above provisions of the Convention on Torture.

The Pinochet case shares more light on the matter of state immunity. Kirgis pointed out that "...The British House Lords in the Pinochet case faced the question of whether immunity extends to such universally condemned international crimes as torture committed (or presided over) during the time the person was the head of state. It answered the question in the negative, but held that under British law, Pinochet can be extradited only for torture committed in Chile after December 8, 1988, the date on which the Convention against Torture became effective for the UK. (It had already entered into force for Chile and Spain at that point.) According to the House of Lords, only then Pinochet lost the immunity from prosecution he enjoyed as a former head of state, since only at that point did his role in the torture in Chile become an international crime for purposes of British law as well as of international law."[291]

In spite of the fact that the two above cases (Habré and Pinochet), as well as, Cavallo, and other cases prosecuted by international criminal tribunals (Milosevic and Bosnian war criminals, and Rwandan genocidaires), nevertheless, it is demonstrated clearly that in the success of prosecutions in matter relating to violations of international customary laws, some states around the world are very reluctant to indict those foreign leaders alleged of committing international human rights and humanitarian laws violations for political reasons. These states weigh the risks they may encounter in their relationship with other states, in particular the offenders' states or their allies', and then decide accordingly as to whether they should prosecute or not. "However, the enforcement of human rights remains a duty incumbent on all states, and if prosecutors exercise their discretion prudently, are guided by the evidence, and remain respectful of defendants' rights, these risks can be minimized. Trials by outside states can avoid many of the political tensions of proceedings where the crime occurred…."[292]

Furthermore, the hope of human rights activists is to see that other serious and ignoble crimes against international customary laws fall into the ambit of universal jurisdiction. Thus, hesitant states that either are not willing to indict those suspected of breaking international human rights and humanitarian legal norms whatever the reasons, or those states that do not fully prosecute those crimes and their authors, should wake up and live up to their international legal obligations. Such awareness will strengthen the legal principle that "…if an individual commits a crime for which customary law provides for universal jurisdiction in any state, he should not be able to plead successfully before a decision maker that his action was not an international crime for purposes of nullum crimen sine lege."[293]

Finally, the exercise of the universal jurisdiction pursuant to international treaties proves to be deterrent and sends a clear message that none, no matter what his or her nationality be or the nationality of his or her victim, or the state where the crimes took place, shall willfully violate international human rights and international humanitarian legal norms and then escape international justice. It is to that extent one recognizes that "...if an individual commits a treaty-based crime in a state party to one of the treaties once it is in force for the state, he should not be able to plead successfully before any mechanism responsible for accountability (whether prosecutorial or not), domestic or international, that international law did not recognize his offense as a crime for purposes of nullum crimen sine lege."[294] Universal jurisdiction, whether exercised through foreign state court, like in Habré, Cavallo, and Pinochet cases, or applied by international criminal courts as in the case of the Bosnian war criminals or the Rwandan genocide suspects, is today a widely international human rights movement that need to be advocated and supported as a way of combating impunity.

Chapter VII
Finding a Lasting Peace in a Political and Legal Context

Given that history has witnessed that democracy is the best form of governance, it is being strongly advised, in this last chapter, that the current anti-democratic systems of government in Rwanda and Uganda be replaced, as a matter of urgency, by democratic governments. In addition, in view of the fact that the US government is identified with its allies Rwanda and Uganda as one of the prostitute administrations, it is important that the US Congress knows the degree of involvement of this country in the invasion of the DR Congo and takes speedily constructive steps in order to cure whatever wrongs her government has directly or indirectly done. Furthermore, lasting peace in the DR Congo, in particular, is intrinsic to the setting up of an independent and competent judicial system. Lastly, but not least, the invasion of the DR Congo is an African matter, which should seriously be given consideration by Africans, as discussed in the last section.

1. Democratization of Rwanda and Uganda: An Imperative

One can hardly recall a time in African history when Rwanda and Uganda were functioning democratic states. The last elections in Rwanda do not classify the latter as a democratic state. Nor do the existence on paper of some political parties. The core characteristic of democracy is freedom manifested both through civil and political liberties. Do Rwandans and Ugandans freely enjoy rights that emanate from the exercise of these liberties? Answering in the negative, the only right answer for this matter simply means that no freedom exists in these countries. For instance, how many people were arrested at the last electoral rallies in Rwanda just for tearing apart Kagame's portraits and for trying to express their thoughts, generally contrary to those professed by Kagame and his party? By the way, was it a surprise for anyone that Paul Kagame was going to "win" those flawed and unfair elections? Not from what circulates through the international community.[295]

Authoritarian regimes succeeded one another in both Rwanda and Uganda. While opposition and tolerance are ignored in Rwanda and Uganda, it is not news to the world that "the most comforting finding ... is that democratic states do not commit genocides.... Yes, democratic states do not commit genocides because, if they did, we would not call them democratic,"[296] neither do they commit any other serious crimes defined in Article 5 of the ICC. But this is a lesson that Rwandans and Ugandans need to urgently learn in order to stabilize their countries politically and economically. Further, these two states must understand that the respect of human rights, both at home and abroad, is an internationally acceptable norm that they have to comply with.

It is so strange that some people (the American administration particularly) think that the solutions to the Rwandan and Ugandan internal crises are to be found in the DR Congo, as if instability both in Rwanda and Uganda originated from the DR Congo. Whereas, at the same time, these critics bypass the policy of mutual ethnic and political exclusion that those countries believe in and that they have instituted somewhat in their day-to-day lives. Rwanda and Uganda are not provinces of the DR Congo, and only stable democracies are the solution to their rebellions. Democracies would also help them to respect international human rights, be tolerant, and accept other ethnic groups and political opposition, and consider other nations as sisters rather than eternal enemies. For, "regardless of their origin or justification, human rights are understood to represent both individual and group demands for the shaping and sharing of power, wealth, enlightenment, and cherished values in community process, most fundamentally the value of respect and its constituent elements of reciprocal tolerance and mutual forbearance in the pursuit of all other values."[297]

Unfortunately, experience is sadly showing that Rwanda's road to democracy will be a very long and painful one. Rwandans themselves do not even speak about it; neither does the international community or the UN. Democracy referred to here is democracy = liberty, not democracy à Kagamaise, partisans and allies. The current Rwandan/Tutsi-led government cannot even dare talk of democracy while they are still defending their ideology of national security and culture of mutual exclusion. The Rwandan/ Tutsi government cannot, in any way, dream or speak of democracy while their Hutu brothers and sisters are still scattered all over the world. A truth and reconciliation commission and a general amnesty as sine qua non conditions should first precede whichever democratic process the actual Rwandan government considers. All their refugees should be given an opportunity to willfully return home and participate in the reconstruction of their nation. Political dialogue should be free and tolerated and basic human rights accepted and granted by Kagame's Tutsi-led regime.

Besides, Rwanda needs to learn to wash its duty linen at home. A repeated pattern of violations of human rights should not be tolerated in a civilized society, unless Kagame and his foxes never considered themselves being a civilized people. If so, there are many even inside Rwanda who would be willing to volunteer and to teach them some of the accepted principles of human civilization. In the meantime, "in an increasingly interdependent and interpenetrating global community, any human rights orientation that is not genuinely in support of the widest possible shaping and sharing of all values among all human beings is likely to provoke widespread skepticism. The last half of the 20th century is replete with examples,"[298] and Rwanda is one of those. Rwanda does not need a lesson on that matter since they have lived and are still living that reality today.

No wonder that while Rwanda was busy occupying some eastern provinces of the DR Congo, the UN General Assembly "Expresse[d] deep concern at the continuing serious violations of human rights and international humanitarian law in the country, in particular those associated with the conflict in the north-west, and in regard to conditions of detention and the trial process of those accused of genocide and crimes against humanity."[299] Thus, it seems Rwanda is more concerned about violations of human rights than the setting up of democratic institutions that should facilitate reconciliation, peace, and prosperity in the tiny and poor country in perpetual international welfare state.

Human Rights Watch World Report 1999 recorded that "in an incident in late October that became known only at the end of 1997, RPA soldiers allegedly caused the deaths of hundreds and perhaps thousands of persons who had sought refuge in caves at Kanama. Estimating the number of those killed in the course of the year was difficult. Investigators could not travel freely in the area and witnesses often refuse to speak for fear of reprisals.

Diplomats concluded between 100,000 and 250,000 persons were unaccounted for out of a population of some 1,500,000 in the two prefectures of Gisenyi and Ruhengeri."[300] The Rwandan government not only slaughtered its own citizens, but also committed some abuses against the UN. In fact, "Rwandan authorities suspended the activities of the United Nations Human Rights Field Operation in Rwanda in May and July and refused to allow it to continue monitoring human rights. The Rwandan government wanted the field operation to limit itself to delivering technical assistance. The UN Commissioner for Human Rights, Mary Robinson, who had firmly condemned abuses during a visit at the end of 1997, insisted that the monitoring was essential to the operation. Rather than continue with the mere semblance of a UN human rights presence, she ended it altogether."[301]

Amnesty International 2000 Annual Report gave the following summary: "The number of killings inside Rwanda decreased compared to 1998, but killings of unarmed civilians and "disappearances" were still reported throughout 1999. Meanwhile, thousands of unarmed civilians were killed across the border, in the Democratic Republic of the Congo (DRC), and in an armed conflict involving several governments, including Rwanda, as well as various armed opposition groups, including Rwandese interahamwe militia and soldiers of the former Rwandese armed forces. Around 125,000 people were detained in prisons and detention centers across Rwanda, most accused of participation in the 1994 genocide. Many were held without charge or trial for prolonged periods in conditions amounting to cruel, inhuman, and degrading treatment. Arbitrary arrests were reported. Detainees in local detention centers and in military custody were ill-treated. At least 1,420 people were tried for participation in the 1994 genocide. At least 180 were sentenced to death. A number of detainees who were released were rearrested, including several who had been tried and acquitted. Journalists were perceived as critical of the government and opposition politicians were subjected to various forms of harassment, including arrest."[302]

In its 2001 annual report, Amnesty International records that "Reports of 'disappearance,' arbitrary arrest, unlawful detention, and torture or ill-treatment of detainees continued throughout 2000. A number of killings of unarmed civilians were also reported. An estimated 125,000 people continued to be held in detention, the overwhelming majority accused of taking part in the1994 genocide. Many have been held for prolonged periods without charge or trial in conditions amounting to cruel, inhuman, and degrading treatment. At least 140 people were sentenced to death for crimes committed during the 1994 genocide, some after unfair trials, but no executions took place. Trials of genocide suspects also continued at the International Criminal Tribunal for Rwanda (ICTR) in Tanzania. In eastern Democratic Republic of the Congo (DRC), Rwandese military and allied forces, as well as Rwandese armed groups opposing them, were responsible for massacres of civilians, torture, including rape, 'disappearances' and the systematic harassment of human rights defenders....

The Rwandese Patriotic Front (RPF)-led government retained tight political control of the country. Open political opposition was not tolerated. Despite signs of growing internal dissatisfaction from genocide survivors and from dissident RPF members, no significant political opposition emerged in the country. Both the RPF and the government were criticized for being dominated by members of the Tutsi ethnic group."[303]

In spite of the accounts regarding Rwanda's human rights situation, it is amazing that the American government believes that the security guaranties of Rwanda must be met in order to have lasting peace in the DR Congo. To achieve this purpose, the US government urged the Congolese government to sacrifice its sovereignty to satisfy the security demands of Rwanda. It is ridiculous and unreasonable for the US government to place democracy in Rwanda in a lesser priority order, but to argue that "...our primary issue that we want to address immediately is this question of security so that we can bring stability to the region."[304] This is an unmeasurable dream for the American administration, unless they know that it is simply a lie and purely rhetorical. Does security bring democracy or the other way around? Even if security was brought to Rwanda, it will not be sustained if democratic institutions are lacking.

What Rwanda needs for the establishment of its national unity is a truth commission that the international community should supervise. Rwandans need a legally based forum[305] where victims and offenders would sit together to talk freely about their past, where perpetrators should admit their wrongdoings, and where victims should facilitate reconciliation by forgiving their offenders. But for such a system to succeed and bring healing and reconciliation, it is believed that both nations—the Hutu on one hand and the Tutsi on the other—must have what is called "kamikaze" persons—in other words, people who would be bold enough to take the risk to bring both nations together without fear of reprisals from their own group members. Such structure needs a political will from those in power and in authority. It is firmly believed that, among the rotten potatoes like Paul Kagame and his foxes, there are people of goodwill, both Tutsis and Hutus who are unhappy about this whole ordeal and who would be ready, if given the opportunity, to bring to pass peace, justice, and democracy in Rwanda. Without all these, Rwandan existence will be one of a continual suffering and human torture.

Uganda is mistakenly viewed as another democratic country in Africa. At least this is the impression one has in the US after speaking with American people. This is surely a matter of ignorance and even dupery, and one of concern. The US has such a good relationship with Uganda. This fact induces Americans to believe that Uganda is also a land of liberty and freedom. The visit of President Clinton on March 24-25 of 1998 and of George W. Bush on July 11-12 of 2003 accelerated that belief. Well, maybe the killing of some eight Western tourists in March of 1999 was a sign that things were never well in Uganda. Ed. Marek reported the opinion of some enlightened Americans in these words: "We are especially disturbed by the praise Museveni receives from Washington. Transparency International, an organization not to be viewed lightly, ranks Uganda as the second most corrupt country in Africa. We also don't believe the economic data coming out of Uganda is reliable. The fact is that 50 percent of the Ugandan budget is subsidized by the West. That's no economy. That's a welfare state."[306]

Human Rights Watch Report 1999 states the following about the National Resistance Movement (NRM) of President Oweri Museveni of Uganda:

"Restrictions on political activity prevented those opposed to the government's policies from organizing and canvassing for support to bring change through electoral action, while rebels movements of several years' standing fought in the north and west of the country.... Conflict with rebels continued in many areas of Uganda. Active rebels groups in 1998 included the West Nile Bank Front (WNBF), Uganda National Rescue Front II (UNRF-II), and the Lord's Resistance Army (LRA), all operating from Sudan rear bases, and the Allied Democratic Forces (ADF), operating in the Rwenzori mountains in Western Uganda and Eastern Congo.... The Ugandan army was ... responsible for serious abuses against civilians in ... regions for which individuals were rarely held to account. The Uganda constitution, adopted in 1995, restricted freedom of association and assembly, allowing political parties to exist in name, but prohibiting them from opening and operating branch offices, holding delegates' conferences or public rallies, or sponsoring candidates. The ruling NRM, while effectively operating as a party, was exempt from these restrictions.... ChakaMchaka, the national political education program suspended since the 1996 presidential and parliamentary elections after protests by western diplomats, would resume. ChakaMchaka teaches the NRM's views that political parties are destructive and sectarian organizations for Uganda past woes."[307]

Human Rights Watch recorded in its 2000 Annual Report that "President Yoweri Museveni's National Resistance Movement (NRM), in power since 1986, continued to govern through what it called the 'movement' or 'no-party' system of government, justifying its restrictions on political participation as essential to prevent a return to Uganda's violent past. The NRM's direct access to state resources and the exclusion of its 'movement' structures from the stringent regulations placed on political parties guaranteed the NRM's political dominance, and effectively prevented independent political parties from organizing for change through electoral action. Violent opposition groups of several years standing fought in the north and west of the country, and renewed rebel activity emerged in eastern Uganda. These groups, particularly the Allied Democratic Forces (ADF) in the west, continued to carry out brutal assaults on civilians, brutalizing, killing, looting, and abducting adults and children alike. The Ugandan army was also responsible for serious abuses against civilians in areas of conflict, for which individual soldiers were rarely held to account. The government continued its constitutional ban on independent political activities, prohibiting political parties from holding party conferences, public rallies, sponsoring candidates in elections, and opening branch offices...."[308]

Likewise, "[t]he Ugandan political landscape in 2002 was characterized by continued conflict over the 'movement' system, by which Uganda is governed. As a result, political and civil rights were violated, though on a somewhat lesser scale than during the violent election year 2001. Uganda was a major player in armed conflicts in the region: Continuing during most of the year, the occupation by the UPDF (Uganda's army) of the northeastern part of the Democratic Republic of Congo (DRC) began to be scaled back in September; meanwhile, the UPDF fought a major military offensive against the rebel Lord's Resistance Army in northern Uganda and southern Sudan. In both wars, civilians were victims of widespread abuse.

"Legal restrictions as well as arbitrary arrest and detention were used to suppress political dissent. On May 9, parliament adopted the highly contested Political Organizations Law, which retained current constitutional restrictions on political parties and added new ones. It outlawed most activities normally associated with political parties, such as opening and operating branch offices, and holding delegates' conferences and rallies. Existing political parties would 'legally cease to exist' if they failed to register within six months of the law's entry into force. A parliamentary commission investigating the violence during the 2001 presidential and parliamentary elections unearthed cases of detention of suspected opposition politicians in illegal locations, torture, and state-sponsored violence against opposition supporters. For example, Kidima Mubarak, who had campaigned in 2001 for a parliamentary candidate opposing the brother of army commander James Kazini, testified before parliament in March 2002 about his arrest in June 2001 followed by two months of detention at military barracks in the Ugandan-controlled areas of the DRC."[309]

Thus, as described by two most respected human rights organizations, the type of regime the American government is an ally of. The Ugandan regime of Museveni is characterized by a history of human rights abuses that are tolerated by the US since 1986, for ambiguous reasons. It is a regime that would already have been under UN sanctions for its high disregard of international human rights norms, but that the US and the international community curiously defend to death at the WB and the IMF, from where it gets its funds. This is almost the same policy the US used with Mobutu during those beautiful and glorious years when he was the best ally of the US in Africa. Museveni is apparently playing this role today. Museveni has categorically refused to negotiate with the different rebel groups in Uganda, calling them terrorists. What was disappointing is the fact that the Clinton administration dared to point a finger at Laurent Kabila, accusing him of being a dictator for not opening the political space and instituting democracy, while Museveni, who has been in power for almost two decades, does not have a democratic government. That is silly indeed!

However, whatever assistance Museveni's government receives from the US will not stop the rebellions in Uganda until Museveni is willing to speak with its opponents, civilian as well as military, and he democratizes Ugandan state's institutions. With this in mind, it is also suggested that the same treatment for Rwanda be applied to Uganda. Instead of wasting money, time, and human and economical resources in pursuing ambitious conquests in the DR Congo and fighting its opponents in vain, the Ugandan government should concentrate its efforts in promoting peace, reconciliation, and nation building. However, in order to achieve this, the Ugandan government needs to grant its opponents an amnesty and establish a truth and reconciliation commission in order to enable people to come together, to bury the past, and look to the future with faith, optimism, and confidence by building a democratic society.

While it must be admitted that the whole Great Lakes region needs the urgent implementation of democratic institutions, it should be understood that people who are in the intensive care or the emergency room need more care and treatment than those who are in an Outpatients unit. This only means that, "the search for peace between Hutus and Tutsis has to start at home in Rwanda.... It has to start with ethnic and national reconciliation and unity in Rwanda ... and not in Congo."[310] The war in the DR Congo was being fought on the wrong battlefield. It was merely Rwandan and Ugandan wars that spread over on the Congolese soil. And if the US is serious about the matter and cares about the people of Rwanda and Uganda, they should encourage and help these two countries to create democratic environments, a way of establishing stable democracies, and law and order.

In conclusion, "[i]t is our view that both countries have been overcome by the usual things that overcome even the most well-meaning people in the Great Lakes region, money, power, and greed. Both Rwanda and Uganda are riddled with enormous internal dissent; neither country is a democracy; each country is ruled by a strong, centralized power figure, Museveni in Uganda, Kagame in Rwanda, and each of these leaders has successfully wooed American leaders in both the Clinton and Bush administrations. Each country is terribly corrupt, Uganda more so, perhaps, than Rwanda, and each is enormously deceptive, Rwanda more so, perhaps, than Uganda."[311] And yet, the US, their ally, and the rest of the international community are not willing to openly speak of the establishment of internationally recognized, acceptable, and accepted democratic principles in both Rwanda and Uganda.

2. The Contribution of the US Congress in This Conflict

The US Congress has a role of checks and balances to the US executive branch, led by the president. Because of the scale of the conflict in the DR Congo and the undisputed involvement of the US therein, the American Congress has certain responsibilities to perform. In fact, "[m]ost people familiar with the conflict believe more US involvement could help ease the poverty, malnutrition, fighting, and death. This is how the United States can continue in its role as the world's lone superpower."[312] There is no doubt that the US Congress knows well the roots and the hidden reasons that led to the aggression of a sovereign state, namely, the DR Congo, by its neighbors, Rwanda and Uganda. It would be impossible and a blind lie to say that they do not know them. Congresswoman McKinney was a member of the US Congress when she reported to this federal body the realities concerning the invasion of the DR Congo by Rwanda and Uganda, as well as all of the gross violations of human rights being committed by Rwandan and Ugandan troops on Congolese soil. There is no doubt that many other notable personalities in the US raised their voices regarding the unwillingness of the American administration to act appropriately.

Point (a) of Section 16 of the Foreign Assistance Act of 1961, as amended 22 USCA, states that "no assistance may be provided under subchapter I of this chapter to the government of any country which engages in a consistent pattern of gross violations of internationally recognized human rights ... unless such assistance will benefit directly the needy people of such country."[313]

That both the Rwandan and Ugandan governments are violating international human rights at home and abroad (in the DR Congo) is not a secret to the world. And, the previous chapters of this work have amply established this fact. Now, if, for example, American military personnel were in Rwanda or Uganda, or even on Congolese soil as military technical advisors to the aggressors of the DR Congo, the American people first, and then the world next, need to know how "such assistance benefits directly" the needy Rwandan or Ugandan populations. And if it was assistance in military training, logistics (such as arms and ammunition) or a financial assistance, the American people, as well as the world, should still know how "such assistance will benefit directly" the needy Rwandans and Ugandans. The US Congress should disclose such information, as it was done in the case of Kuwait, Bosnia, and Kosovo. But if such information exists and cannot be disclosed for so-called national security reasons, then may the world know that it is dirty information that is an embarrassment to the American government.

In addition to what Congresswoman Cynthia McKinney, who was part of the American congressional investigative team in the DR Congo, already reported to the US Congress in view of the situation in the occupied territories of the DR Congo, it should be suggested that the US Congress take a more active mental and technical attitude to pacify the Great Lakes region. "The

US Congress should send a delegation to investigate abuses on the ground.... The US Congress should strongly discourage the continued reliance on a mainly military option by the military regimes of Rwanda ... which will result in more bloodshed of innocent lives. The US Congress should firmly initiate a conference for national unity and reconciliation for ... Uganda, and Rwanda."[314] For the sake of peace in the Great Lakes Region, and to ensure that the way the White House is conducting American policy in Africa, in general, and in the DR Congo in particular, where lies the will of all the American people, the US Congress is urged to accept this honorable mission.

The US Congress can only accept this mission because to begin with and as outlined previously, but for the imperialistic ambitions of the US, genocide in Rwanda would not have occurred in 1994. And consequently, there would not have been a Hutu exodus, and Rwanda would not have invaded the DR Congo citing as reasons the protection of their borders and the extermination of Tutsis. Subsequently, if the US did not help the RPF to take power in Rwanda in 1994, it is unlikely that wars would have broken up in the DR Congo, and doubtful that the magnitude and seriousness of human rights violations in the occupied territories of the DRC would have been so fatal and tragic. Had it not been for the US negative and destructive implication in the Great Lakes Region crisis, it is improbable that this crisis would have been so internationalized as it was.

Rwanda and Uganda, US allies, committed genocide in the DRC. Millions of Congolese perished during the four and half years of the war of aggression in Congo. Millions of others are displaced. The invaders and their allies plundered natural and mineral resources in the DR Congo. Civil and military infrastructures are destroyed. African pride and human dignity have once again been sullied. The invaders have sewed and left behind a very deadly weapon: HIV/AIDS. And yet, they are walking around without any punishment for their criminal acts.

The US government must accept part of the responsibilities for the 1994 Rwandan genocide, for the aggression of the DR Congo, and for the other grave violations of human rights committed thereof. Thus, the US Congress must initiate a rapid process for the reparation of damages caused by Rwandan and Ugandan aggressors with the blessings and assistance of the US. This compensation must be in the forms of rehabilitation of socio-economic infrastructures (mainly transportation, health, communication, and education), the tackling of HIV/AIDS epidemics, the promotion of good governance, and the restoration of social justice with a focus on a speedy indictment by the International Criminal Court or such UN mandated criminal tribunal of the perpetrators of grave human rights violations during the Rwanda-Uganda-led war of occupation in the DR Congo. To avoid any ambiguity, this reparation should be financial, technical, and the like.

The US Congress efforts must be focused on the rebuilding of the Congolese nation. There is no doubt that the Congolese people will gladly appreciate such endeavors. By doing so, the US Congress must keep in mind the approach sought by the UN Secretary-General Kofi Annan: "The crucial underlying need in post-conflict peace-building situations is the security of ordinary people, in the form of real peace and access to basic social facilities. In pursuing these peace-building objectives, a number of requirements are clear. First, time is of the essence. Second, a multifaceted approach, covering diplomatic, political, and economic factors, must be adopted. Third, the effort must be adequately financed. Fourth, there must be high-level strategic and administrative coordination among the many actors."[315]

The day will come, and it is not far distant, when the American people would like to know in detail what really happened in the DR Congo and to what extent was their government involved in the Congolese tragedy. They would like to know why was their Government supporting Rwanda, Uganda, and their allies in this perilous and barbarous adventure. On that day, one thing is certain: many questions will be asked, but few reasonable answers given. Some are already arguing about this whole ordeal that "[t]he American government has been misled by faulty analysis, both during the previous administration and this one. Is there anyone out there who seriously believes that President Clinton signed off on a plan that resulted in three million Congolese deaths in the Ugandan and Rwandan zones of occupation, and the displacement of another three million? Not even Clinton would go that low. It is our view that former US Secretary of State, Madeleine Albright, her sidekick Assistant Secretary of State for Africa, Susan Rice, and former UN Ambassador, William Richardson, were deceived by Museveni and Kagame. It is also our view that they were so easily misled because of this intense friction between Washington and Paris. In addition, they simply were not paying close enough attention to what was really happening on the ground in central Africa, for whatever reason... We also believe that for all their charm, grace, and history as rebels with a cause, Museveni and Kagame have ended up to be worse than Mobutu."[316]

But, alas, the damage has been done and now accountability needs to be established at each level of the administration. Both Clinton and Bush saw it and neither dared stop it. Thus, the day will come, indeed, and it is at hand when the American people will want to know who at the White House, State Department, CIA and Pentagon, were the true masterminds of this shameful American legacy. Even if economic and other strategic interests most of the time drive relations between states, the time is coming when the American people would like to know how economically fruitful were the relationship between Rwanda and Uganda, on one side, and the US, on the other. In addition, how positively and constructively did these relations profit to the American people to tolerate such unnecessary bloodshed and the commission of graves and blatant human rights violations that has cost millions of innocent lives in the DR Congo?

Like many Americans believe, "[t]he country we really need to succeed in this region is the DR Congo—55 million people, a large country with a strategic location and an outlet to the sea, a country with untold human and natural resource wealth, a country that has never been given a chance to excel, a country waiting to explode with growth and prosperity, a country always bound, restrained, and constrained by the West, a country that must be set free and helped with meaningful help. Rwanda and Uganda have fine people, we want to be their friends, and we want to see them live in democracy and freedom as well, which they currently do not enjoy, but when you line up your priorities, these two small and landlocked countries have to take a backseat to the Congo. Yet, American policymakers have chosen not to do that, and we have two more bungling, feuding yokes to carry on our shoulders with little chance of a reasonable payoff."[317]

And above all, here is the time when the Americans are going to inquire on how the hell their government sacrificed the DR Congo with its fabulous, human, natural and mineral resources that would have greatly benefitted the American economy in favor of Rwanda and Uganda from where nothing but innocent blood flows. As one put it, "[l]ook, the DR Congo is the big guy on the block. Make no mistake about it. Angola has a lot of oil, but its government is far more corrupt than anything in Kinshasa, and it has only 11 million people. Sudan is big, but it is involved in its own genocide of black Christians and its history of Islamic terrorism against the US is one that will not go away.

The Congo has more natural wealth than Angola could ever dream of, and the Congo's natural wealth far surpasses any amount of gum arabic they have in Khartoum. More important, the Congolese people have been fighting for democracy (for three decades) of Mobutu, and there are 55-60 million of them in a land where the mighty Congo River can drive trains that have not even been designed yet. What, in comparison, will tiny landlocked Uganda and even tinier landlocked Rwanda offer to the equation?"[318]

There is no doubt that the day is coming when the American people will know the truth about what exactly happened in the DR Congo war of occupation, for they are not that dumb and are visibly tired of being fooled. And on that day, if Museveni and Kagame are still alive, Americans will cry in one accord: "drop Museveni and Kagame. Work to build a partnership with the DR Congo and the Congolese people. That's where the real promise of the future is. Uganda and Rwanda will eventually tag along and benefit from being the Congo's neighbors, that's for sure."[319] In due time, one can hope and pray, Americans will boldly argue so, for they cannot afford to think that a part of the legacy they pass to their children is tainted with Congolese innocent blood. This is the very reason why the US Congress, as pointed out earlier, must appoint a commission of inquiry to investigate the involvement of the US government in the aggression of the DR Congo, genocide, crimes against humanity, and war crimes on the Congolese soil during the war of occupation they orchestrated, and that Rwanda and Uganda led. This commission is also intended to help the US government come out clean once and for all.

3. Establishing an Independent and Competent Judiciary in the DR Congo: The Ultimate Key to Restoring Law and Order

The growth of a nation, its development and stability, are intrinsically tied to its judiciary system. One may look at the rise of the Roman Empire or the Greek Republic at the same era to comprehend this simple principle. When the judiciary is independent, able to prosecute offenses and render judgments without the interference of the executive or any governmental branch, or as the case may be in most African countries and many totalitarian regimes, without the meddling of powerful clans, then its legitimacy is not contested and the masses can trust that its decisions are fair, and therefore legal. Powerful states like the US, France, UK, Australia, South Africa, Germany, to name these few, find their stability in their legal system.

It is not enough to have judiciary or law enforcement officers. The main issue begins from the letter and spirit of the Constitution, which is supposed to be the supreme law of the country. The Constitution must stipulate the separation of powers between the Executive, Legislative, and Judicial branches. Unfortunately, history and experience show that this separation of powers is not enough as well. In addition, even most importantly, there should be a political will mostly from the Executive branch to refrain from interfering with the conduct of the Judiciary. If the latter defaults from its duties and functions, there should be well-established mechanisms within the judiciary system itself or the Legislative to remedy to the situation. Likewise, if the Executive is not satisfied with the Judiciary decisions in one or other cases, only well-established laws should direct the course of the events, not the intervention of the head of the state or the army chief of staff, for instance. No one is above the law, should be the sacred code.

It is no news to anyone that in the majority of African states, the judiciary is a private domain of those in power, their families, associates and clans. For instance, Mobutu took the judiciary hostage throughout his entire reign in the DR Congo (ex-Zaïre).[320] Thus, the result is obvious. Africa is far from development because the judiciary is not independent. Even in countries where people have fought valiantly to establish democratic governments, it is sad to notice that the new leaders are far from accepting the separation of powers and mostly to recognize and respect the independence of the judiciary. For instance, Senegal is supposed to be of hope and a model of democracy in Africa. But the decision of President Abdoulaye Wade on 7 April, 2003 to allow Hissène Habré, former Chadian president wanted for torture and extra judicial killings of thousands of people in Chad, to leave Senegal was a political decision that interfered with a judicial decision from a Senegalese judge to fully prosecute Habré pursuant to the UN Convention on Torture and other international legal norms. President Wade's decision has tarnished Senegalese democracy image on the international sphere, though today he speaks of extrading Habré.

In post conflict settings, the judiciary is even called to play a more crucial role in stabilizing the new society, which is in many instances composed of hybrid philosophies and political concepts. In many cases, though a political compromise has been reached as to the accommodation of ex-rebels, freedom fighters, and the like, the issue of accountability for past crimes committed in the name of "liberation war" remains unresolved. Not only do they refuse any investigation regarding their past involvement in human rights abuses, but often they threaten to retake arms and resume the war if any attempt is made to prosecute them. In situations like these, the judiciary has obviously a hard task. Should the courts exercise their role in prosecuting those involved in serious violations of human rights pursuant to both domestic and international legal norms, or should they close their eyes and allow the government to grant a blunt amnesty?

In any case of human rights violations, there are two parties. On one side, there are perpetrators, and on the other, there are victims. When the armed conflict is nothing other than a war of resistance against occupying forces or a war of liberation from the oppressors, like in South Africa a decade ago, the complexity of the applicability of international legal rules for accountability becomes a great issue. But this is not the focus of this book. However, in the case of rebellions (like Savimbi's bushes war against the Luandan government) or the "no-name" war (like the one at issue in the DR Congo) where adventurists, opportunists, and bandits backed foreign troops that violated the sovereignty and territorial integrity of the country, with the intent to replace a legitimate government, and who together with the invaders committed gross violations of human rights and violated humanitarian international laws, strict accountability should not be put aside or be replaced with a general amnesty, since "[p]recedents of accountability, however selective and limited, contribute to the transformation of a culture of impunity that has hitherto implied the political acceptability of human rights abuses."[321]

Now, how to start the process of accountability, in the case of the DR Congo, for violations of international human rights and humanitarian laws committed in the occupied territories during the war of occupation conducted by Rwanda and Uganda. It is worth first mentioning that impunity as to human rights abuses occurring in the occupied provinces of the DRC shall hamper any move to establish democratic institutions and restore the rule of law in the country. The Congolese people and the international community heard, saw, and witnessed those atrocities. So, for that simple reason, they cannot go unpunished. As Jennifer Widner puts it, "[c]onfronting war crimes after a conflict shows that the community finds these abuses wholly unacceptable."[322] Regarding the Congolese tragedy, thousands of victims are still alive and can provide more evidence on the matter at issue.

To begin, the Congolese tragedy has two dimensions. First, foreign-armed troops from Rwanda and Uganda invaded the country, created so-called rebellions, and all these armed forces together violated international human rights and humanitarian established legal rules. Second, the UDF planned, masterminded, nourished, and flourished the division between Lendus and Hemas in the Ituri province to the point of arming militarily one group with the intent to commit genocide on the other.

The first armed conflict was an aggression of the DR Congo by foreign states, whereas the second was an inter-ethnic war. Given that the facts are a bit different, the solutions shall be a little bit different as well. In the first case, the accountability shall follow this procedure: indictment by domestic and/or international courts of law, arrest, trial, and sentence. In the second, there should first be an ADR under the AU or UN supervision (likely mediation and/or arbitration), indictment, arrest, and sentence. The distinction is crucial here between the first and the second case. The Lendu and Hema conflict involves, to a certain extent, an ethnic dispute, although teleguided from Kampala. This is a fight between Congolese nationals.

The aggression of the DRC, on the other hand, was a deliberate act of foreign invasion. Congolese nationals who aided, abetted the invaders, conspired, and assisted in the mass violations of their fellow citizens did so for power, money, and greed. They are traitors who should be brought to justice pursuant to national and international laws. Lendus and Hemas involved in grave violations of international human rights legal norms shall be liable for their deeds, as well, make no mistake about it.[323] However, because this conflict is an internal affair, mediation and arbitration should precede any litigation to enable the two sister ethnic groups to live again side-by-side in peace as in the past.

Alternative dispute resolution proceedings should pave the way to litigation proceedings in the Lendu-Hema conflict, for two main reasons. First, this procedure shall facilitate the cohabitation between the two ethnic groups, as mentioned above. Second, it is a known fact that the judiciary system in the DR Congo needs urgent reformation. So while the central government struggles to set up an independent judicial system, another legal mechanism should be put into place to deal with critical situations on the ground. "[I]n the immediate aftermath of conflict, one of the most important steps is to rebuild neighborhood forums for dispute resolution. These usually stress mediation and arbitration. Without such informal venues, the capacity of any formal judicial system is likely to be overwhelmed. Local forums can help fill the gap while new judges and lawyers are trained, and gutted courthouses rebuilt. Otherwise former combatants and traumatized civilians will probably turn away from fledgling institutions, and even resume the resolution of differences in the street,"[324] stresses Jennifer Widmer.

Similarly, the final Report of the Panel of Experts on the Illegal Exploitation of Natural Resources and Other Forms of Wealth of the

Democratic Republic of the Congo of 15 October, 2003 points out that "[t]he extension of government authority should also be accompanied by a reform of the rule of law sector and the re-establishment of a criminal justice capacity in all its components: police, judiciary, and corrections. MONUC and the international assistance will be vital in that regard, inter alia, by providing technical assistance in the reform of the legislative instruments, including the penal system and the penal procedure codes, with a view to tailoring those instruments to the needs of courts that function effectively and in harmony with the international legal instruments to which the Democratic Republic of the Congo is party. Material support will also be required for the training of a national integrated police force and the rehabilitation of criminal justice facilities."[325]

That the DR Congo has a well-trained body of jurists cannot be disputed. However, when the ability of these lawyers—judges, attorneys, and advocates—to prosecute and hold fair trial is hampered because of the lack of basic equipment and political intervention (political orientation and corruption), the legal training becomes meaningless. The independence and competence of the Congolese judicial system shall be made possible by tackling the issue in two phases. In the first, all Congolese jurists need to be rehabilitated from the viruses of the second and third Republics of Mobutu's era. Mobutu had a total disregard for the respect of law and order. It is not a surprise that certain well-reputed law professors who became his advisors did not turn him into a law-abiding citizen. In truth, they became as corrupt as the mammon master they served.

This rehabilitation should begin with a self-reconciliation to their profession. The legal profession is a noble vocation. Lawyers are defenders of the values of a society, given that any act a man poses has legal consequences that can be good or bad. In any civilized human society, the law starts and ends with lawyers (advocates, prosecutors, or judges). Lawyers are the first to draft and/or review the last draft of the legislation (local, provincial, national, or international). They draft and/or review schools, corporations, hospitals, insurances, road rules or policies, and many others. What lawyers do influences the way the rest of the community, society, nation, and country behave. Thus, the legal profession is aimed to drive human behavior to do good. When lawyers are corrupt, the judicial system suffers tremendously as the ordinary people can only mistrust lawyers and the fairness of courts' decisions is put in doubt.

This does not imply that all Congolese jurists are corrupt. The issue here is that political regimes for nearly four decades in the DR Congo, even in the whole African continent, had sabotaged the role of the judiciary to the point of rendering it dependent to the regime in place and unable to offer justice fairly. The rehabilitation of Congolese lawyers requires that they be subjected to a mandatory continuing education subsidized by the government and/or international organizations. A part of this process should be to reeducate them to honor their fiduciary duties toward their clients and to be loyal to the courts and judicial system. They should abide to the code of ethics or professional conduct and be disciplined when in breach thereof.

Further, ADR must be incorporated in the curriculum of the law faculties. For the practicing lawyers, ADR should be a part of the rehabilitation program. It should be mandatory that legal counsels advise their clients on the possibility of solving their dispute through ADR rather than litigation. ADR is rooted in the African tradition. Mobutu liked to say "le Chef règle les differends de ses sujets sous l'arbre à palable."[326] In Africa, it is tradition that conflicts should be resolved through mediation or conciliation. For many Africans going to court is taking the road to hell. Africans, unlike Westerners, hate litigation because the language spoken in court is foreign to them, and since they often do not comprehend the legal proceedings. In addition, they know that litigation can be costly and the outcome very uncertain. Given that mediation and arbitration is similar and close to the African system of conflict resolution, it is crucial that Congolese lawyers learn how to minimize time, costs, and strengthen societies' ties through ADR techniques.

For instance, as mentioned previously, the Lendu-Hema conflict should begin with resolution through mediation and arbitration. However, the parties need to be advised that the outcome shall be enforceable as if settled in a court of law. Bringing Lendus and Hemas under the umbrella of legal norms will be a difficult task for the Congolese government. But ADR would help ease the tensions since the outlining principle of dispute resolution is to bring together victims and perpetrators around the same table and to let them come into an enforceable settlement of the dispute. While the mediator or arbitrator sets the rules of engagement, facilitates the discussion between the parties, and officially presides over the parties, he does not, however, control the proceedings and outcome of the meeting. While it is awkward to suggest that all issues be resolved through ADR, it is nonetheless important to indicate that all gross violations of international human rights committed during the Lendu-Hema tribal war must be prosecuted. In fact, certain legal violations can only be solved through litigation, and mass breach of the law of nations is one of them.

Of judges in particular, high judicial ethics is required. Therefore, "[t]o protect the public confidence in an honest, independent judiciary, a judge should participate in establishing, maintaining, and enforcing high standards of conduct, and shall personally observe those standards.... The general standard of integrity and independence obviously applies to a judge's conduct on the bench on a judicial capacity. Although judges must be independent, they must also comply with the law.... The duty of integrity and independence also applies to a judge's behavior in his personal life.... A judge must respect and comply with the law and must act in a way that promotes public confidence in the integrity and impartiality of the judiciary ... this duty applies to conduct both on and off the bench. A judge is subject to constant public scrutiny and must therefore accept constraints that would be burdensome to the ordinary citizen. [For example] a judge must not allow family, social, political, or other relationships to interfere with the judge's conduct or judgments.... [Similarily] a judge must not lend the prestige of the judicial office to advance the private interests of the judge or others."[327] Those are the qualities of the required from the new Congolese judge.

The training of lawyers is not the only answer to restoring law and order in the DRC. Judiciary officers and law enforcement agents must also benefit of a solid education. Lawyers do not arrest nor do they guard offenders before, during, and after trial, nor is it their responsibility to monitor prisoners who are on parole. Judiciary police officers and State police officers have a serious duty to keep law and order, and enforce judicial judgments. Their mission is to protect and serve the civilians. Because of this mission, they are on the front lines of the battlefield in the war against crimes. Given that they are on this position, they should get the best training that enables them to accomplish their task in a professional-like manner.

Further, like the legal profession, joining the police forces should be a vocation. The police service, like any armed forces, should not be a receiver of all human residues in a society. Many people joined the police forces to escape from unemployment or to get instruments enabling them to accomplish their evil design. Wearing police uniforms and carrying a gun therefore give them the power to terrorize peaceable civilians. The new police force in the DR Congo should be a morally clean driven force. Men and women in the police should make the pride of the Congolese society. The presence of a police officer nearby should mean to the civilian: "I am at last safe" not "I am subject to abuse soon, both on my person and property."

Unfortunately, the reality in the DR Congo is far from perfection, since the country suffered decades of arbitrary rules under Mobutu, followed by an armed invasion of nearly five years. Laurent Kabila's regime broke the past of undisciplined, corrupt, and criminal police officers inherited from Mobutu. Today, the relationship between the police services and the civil populations is improving because of the determination of the current leaders to change positively the image of the police. However, no police officer can perform his duties efficiently when he does not have the necessary logistics.

In the US, for instance, the simple view of a police officer shows authority and virulent power. The presence of a police office is very deterrent. The officers are well armed and have bulletproof vests. Their cars look almost like a mini war machine, since they have bulletproof windows, have detective devices, a computer system linked to the national database that contains criminal records. Further, American police officers have short guns in addition to their handguns, have a first aid kit in the trunk and other instruments that can help them respond promptly and efficiently to emergency situations, to better serve and protect the civilians. It is also believed that CPR classes are mandatory. In the US no one, for example, would like to be on the FBI's most wanted list or be a subject of investigation by this agency. This law enforcement body has received international renown and its agents are competent and well respected. The Scorpions division, the South African special police unit modeled after the FBI, is doing a wonderful job as well and is gaining the trust of the masses. But above all, be it in the US or South Africa, policing agents are well trained.

It is not expected that the Congolese government produce such law enforcement agencies overnight. However, in order to fulfill their duties, police officers in the DR Congo should be given the necessary equipment to enforce the law and keep order in the country. A student in medical studies is exposed to all kinds of equipment during his residency and internship. But, if he is unable to use such equipment once on the field, he is likely to perform poorly and even be subject to malpractice. Likewise, an officer of the peace who last saw and manipulated policing equipment at the training camps is unable to properly protect civilians, even his or her own person. The officers should be given adequate transportation and equipment to get to the very remote corners of the country and render services to those in need of protection. They should be trained to handle modern communication apparatus and have access to such devices. Officers who have the right equipment and training are proud of their profession, and therefore are motivated to render service as taught in the police academies.

Similarly, the Judiciary Police officers deserve better training and equipment to enable them to accomplish their tasks. They cannot investigate crimes when the only vehicle available is used by a supervisor who is attending to family, ordinary business, or visiting a girlfriend miles from the office. They cannot exercise their functions properly when they are more poorly armed than the criminals they ought to investigate and arrest. It is indeed absurd to expect them to perform well when they lack office supplies and their offices are maintained under poor conditions. The DR Congo counts many thousands of men and women who are ready to take the oath of allegiance to the constitution to defend their nation and serve their fellow citizens to the best of their abilities. But, the government needs to show its part of commitment, first by engaging itself in on a program that is strong enough to deter the enemies of the republic.

Both these police and law enforcement services in the DR Congo need huge financing, both from national and international coffers in equipment and training to facilitate their performance. It is no prophecy that all the cease-fire agreements and peace negotiations will soon be meaningless if those who are assigned to maintain law and order in the DR Congo are not empowered to deliver the services expected of them for lack of logistics. Without the support of well-trained police officers, civilians will become victims of abuses and will not trust the government. Congolese have not yet forgotten the abuses they were subjects to by Mobutu's law enforcement services, the very same officers who were to give them protection. Further, the situation in the eastern provinces shows that only empowered, official law enforcement agents can restore security rather than a band of bandits under the commandment of former "rebel" leaders, as the case is today.

Further, there is no reason why those people who are entrusted with the duty of protecting everyone else should get a meager salary at the end of the month. This is an unfair and unreasonable practice. Bodyguards are heavily paid, not only to motivate them to render unique services, but also to avoid all temptations of having them being corrupted by enemies and betray the person they protect. Then, how unreasonable and absurd it is to expect police officers to better perform their functions, if they are poorly paid and exposed to temptations of being corrupted? The same reasoning can be held for judiciary officials and officers. A judge who is not getting the salary he fairly deserves is likely to become corrupted. But a corrupted judge does not corrupt himself; he corrupts the law. A reasonable government should always refrain to have unreasonable expectation about its agents and employees. Volunteering is a show of patriotism. But it is evil for a government to request perpetual volunteer work from its ordinary citizens while the same is not demanded from those in leadership positions.

Now, if those people who should establish an independent and competent judiciary, and help in the maintenance of law and order are poorly trained or have insufficient training, and are far less in numbers than needed to perform the work efficiently, is it right to speak about general and presidential elections in a near future? In the case of the DR Congo, given the circumstances, it is childish, unreasonable, and erring to call for elections in the next two years. Law and order should precede the holding of any free and fair elections. Similarly, establishing an independent judiciary should be the *sine qua non* condition for the enjoyment of a true democracy in the DR Congo.

It is a miscalculation and a lie to think that elections are possible soon in the DR Congo as many so-called politicians think. All Congolese who have reached the legal age are entitled to freely and fairly vote, regardless of their location in the country. The right to vote is a fundamental right and none should be deprived of it for the sole purpose of satisfying some political agenda and self-centered interest. The Congolese people have seen enough of those manipulations and are physically tired of hearing them. Where are the funds to build roads, telecommunication, and other necessary infrastructures inherent to the holding of a free and fair election? It is better to not hold elections at all than have elections that will be followed with a bloodbath. Nobody is going to be permitted to tell lies to anyone this time in the DR Congo. Those who need free and fair elections soon in the DR Congo must put up their sleeves and shake their pockets of any penny to contribute to the building up or repairing of the necessary infrastructures needed for the circumstances.

For sure, President Joseph Kabila is put on the spot to respect several accords and take the DR Congo to elections. Knowing the type of person he is, no wonder that he will not mind. However, should the international community rush Joseph Kabila and the Congolese nation to elections whereas conditions on the grounds that should pave the way in these given circumstances are uncertain, and even dangerous? Is this good policy or a trap against Joseph Kabila and another international conspiracy to topple him and definitively balkanize the DR Congo? By the way, no foreigner—physic or moral person—can convince the Congolese people that elections will bring democracy and the rule of law in the nation. The Congolese know what they want and should not be pressurized, for nobody needs so badly free and fair elections in the Congo than the Congolese themselves. The Congolese are politically mature and highly manifest such maturity when left alone to decide about the destiny of their nation. They need friends like any other nation on the earth. However, the time of foreign deceivers, liars, manipulators and African bloodsuckers for imperialistic interests is over.

Finally, UN Security Council Resolution, S/RES/1468 (2003)[328] *has the following provisions:*

2. *Condemns* the massacres and other systematic violations of International humanitarian Law and human rights perpetrated in the Democratic Republic of the Congo, in particular sexual violence against women and girls as a tool of warfare and atrocities perpetrated in the Ituri area by the Mouvement de Libération du Congo (MLC) and the Rassemblement Congolais pour la Démocratie/National (RCD/N) troops, as well as the acts of violence recently perpetrated by the Union des Patriotes Congolais (UPC) forces, and reiterates that there will be no impunity for such acts and that the perpetrators will be held accountable;

3. *Stresses* that the military officers whose names are mentioned in the report of the United Nations High Commissioner for Human Rights in connection with serious violations of international humanitarian law and human rights should be brought to justice, through further investigation, and if warranted by that investigation, held accountable through a credible judicial process;

4. *Calls upon* the Congolese parties, when selecting individuals for key posts in the transitional government, to take into account the commitment and record of those individuals with regard to respect for International Humanitarian Law and human rights and the promotion of the well-being of all the Congolese;

5. *Strongly encourages* the Congolese parties forming the transitional government to establish as soon as possible a Truth and Reconciliation Commission charged with determining responsibility for serious violations of international humanitarian and human rights law, as set forth in the resolutions adopted in the framework of the Inter-Congolese Dialogue in Sun City in April 2002;

6. *Reiterates* that all parties claiming a role in the future of the Democratic Republic of the Congo must demonstrate their respect for human

rights, International Humanitarian Law, as well as the security and well-being of civilian populations and emphasizes that the transitional government in the Democratic Republic of the Congo will have to restore law and order and respect for human rights;

7. *Requests* the Secretary-General to increase the number of personnel in MONUC's human rights component to assist and enhance, in accordance with its current mandate, the capacity of the Congolese parties to investigate all the serious violations of international humanitarian law and human rights perpetrated on the territory of the Democratic Republic of the Congo since the beginning of the conflict in August 1998, and requests also the Secretary-General, in consultation with the High Commissioner for Human Rights, to make recommendations to the Council in other ways to help the transitional government in the Democratic Republic of the Congo address the issue of impunity.

Article 6 above puts the emphasis on the current Congolese government to not leave any stones unturned, "to restore law and order and respect for human rights, and end impunity, across the entire country." For this government to accomplish this mission properly, the judiciary system and police forces need reformation, adequate training, appropriate resources, and sufficient funds, as discussed previously. In addition, it is the intent of the Security Council as stated in the first part of Article 6 that "all parties claiming a role in the future of the Democratic Republic of the Congo must demonstrate their respect for human rights, International Humanitarian Law, as well as the security and well-being of civilian populations." Further, Article 4 "*Calls upon* the Congolese parties, when selecting individuals for key posts in the transitional government, to take into account the commitment and record of those individuals with regard to respect for International Humanitarian Law and human rights and the promotion of the well-being of all the Congolese."

Both the letter and spirit of these two articles disqualify all so-called rebel groups now converted into political parties, the Mouvement de Libération du Congo (MLC), the Rassemblement Congolais pour la Démocratie/National (RCD/N), the Union des Patriotes Congolais (UPC) forces, and the Rassemblement Congolais pour la Démocratie/Goma, as well their leaders for being parties in the DR Congo transitional government. The only reasonable way that these "parties must demonstrate their respect for human rights, International Humanitarian Law, as well as the security and well-being of civilian populations," and "the commitment and record of those [leaders] with regard to respect for International Humanitarian Law and human rights and the promotion of the well-being of all the Congolese," is by showing their resumé or *curriculum vitae* to the Congolese people.

A *curriculum vita* explains the past or gives the history of one's past events and current activities. Which of those parties and their leaders currently in the transitional government can demonstrate that either his party and/or him/herself "respect for human rights, International Humanitarian Law, as well as the security and well-being of civilian populations," while just months ago they violated on a gross scale these same international legal norms? These individuals are the very same people who aided and abetted the invaders of the DR Congo, and commanded armed forces that committed genocide, war crimes, crimes against humanity, and terrorism within the territories they occupied in their motherland. How can international criminals be turned, overnight and without accountability and due process of law, nor monitored rehabilitation, into individuals committed to the security and well-being of same civilian populations they have just systematically killed, raped, and submitted to serious abuses, and whose natural, mineral, and other forms of wealth they plundered methodically? Even if Rwandan Tutsis, for instance, are the most forgiving people on earth and wanted reconciliation at all cost with the Hutus, would they accept that those who commanded the 1994 *genocidaires* share in the Rwandan government in lieu of being subject to international justice? Is not this a joke, error of judgment, and great mockery to the science of law for the international community to impose such individuals on the Congolese people?

Now that these individuals are in the current Congolese government, one sees clearly the urgent need for the Congolese people to speedily help in the institution of an independent and competent judicial system and law enforcement services, and for the international community to assist the Congolese people financially and technically to achieve these ends. It is not erring to declare that these individuals are going to help each other to escape both domestic and international justice. Azarias Ruberwa is exactly doing so as he vowed to defend and protect to death a criminal, in the name of Laurent Nkundabatware, who the UN records identified (and is seeking for prosecution) as the person leading RCD's troops that massacred innocent civilians in the town of Kisangani. Thus, they will try to destabilize any effort seeking to establish the rule of law and order in the DR Congo for they fear accountability for their past international crimes.

Those individuals shall attempt anything to sabotage the heroic effort of the Congolese people but they shall always fail. Ba ndoki ba sili te,[329] shall always remember the Congolese people. The events that are happening in those provinces they reigned as masters and kings between 1998 and 2002 are revealing their real intentions.

For instance, in February 2004, the RCD threatened to withdraw from the Transitional institutions if the government did not release the RDC Major, Joseph Kasongo, accused of illegal possession of arms and ammunitions in Bukavu. The famous RCD Colonel, Jules Mutebusi, deputy-commandant of the 10th Military Region and suspended of his duties by the hierarchy, with reinforcement from the dissident General Laurent Nkundabatware from Goma and back up from the Rwandan government occupied the town of Bukavu from June 2-9, 2004 justifying their criminal action in defense of the "extermination" of Banyamulenge in the Sud-Kivu province, allegation proven false by an UN investigative team, which in turn established that these criminal officers and their troops committed grave violations of human rights on innocent civilians during their deadly enterprise in Bukavu. The commandant of the 8th Military Region, General Obedi Rwibasira, with seat in Goma, Nord-Kivu province, and the Governor Eugene Serufuli Ngayabaseka, both members of the RCD, give their allegiance to President Paul Kagame instead of being under the command of the Congolese President Joseph Kabila. For example, neither of them ever responded to invitations from the government to personally report on their functions to Kinshasa. And the Army General Chief of Staff, lieutenant-general Kisempia Sungilanga Lombe, in his visit to the former occupied territories in August 2004 was unable to get to the Nord-Kivu province for security reasons. Instead, he sent the Army Chief of Staff, General Sylvain Buki, also from the RCD. His visit ended in Bukavu, Sud-Kivu province. Not only that these criminals are masterminding the sabotage of real democracy and the rule of law in the DR Congo, but they also have no respect for their Head of the State to whom they show a deliberate insubordination with the aim to provoke another armed conflict. Neither Kagame or Museveni can tolerate such behavior in their government, but President Joseph Kabila is doing so for the sake of the Congolese people.

Should this Congolese government establish a TRC, as stated in Article 5 of the aforementioned Security Resolution, the individuals referred to in the above paragraphs should not suppose that they will receive a blank amnesty. Such thought is an error of a frenzied mind and unacceptable. The Congolese people and the international community see on those individuals purely as international criminals and terrorists. Thus, "[w]hether their downfall comes through political overthrow ... the vigilance of the international criminal justice will ensure that their crimes do not fall into oblivion, undermining the prospect of an easy escape or future political rehabilitation."[330] The Congolese people have always been dumped, but make no mistake they are not dumb. Or if they were once dumped and dumb, the dumb and dumber episode is now declared over.

The Congolese people have spoken. They only desire justice and the end to the culture of impunity in their country. The Congolese of all backgrounds solemnly believe that finding a lasting peace in a political and legal context in the DR Congo requires that individual liabilities for the perpetrators first be established, and those criminals be prosecuted by domestic and/or international independent and competent courts of law. May these offenders not worry about their rights for they shall be secured at all costs. However, the thought of escaping justice should not be a subject of meditation in their mind, for the Congolese people shall smoke them out from their hiding places.

4. The African Solution

Africans, in general, and black African leaders, in particular, need to be serious about the well-being and the welfare of their people. There is enough evidence that Western countries are to be blamed at a large extent for the past and current economic damages and human casualties in Africa. Now, the time is at hand for Africans to be responsible and acknowledge that while they are, in part, accountable for this crisis, they have the power to reverse this ugly situation if they reconsider their ethos.

In order to achieve the African renaissance, Africans must unite and stand together once and for all. For, "the situation in the [continent] today is such that we can't afford to stand divided"[331] or stand idly looking on while basic human rights are violated and natural and mineral resources are plundered both by Africans and foreigners. The new released list by the UN of individuals and companies involved in the systematic destruction of natural, animal, and mineral resources in the DR Congo is illustrative.

4.1. "If They Exploit Us, It is Because We are Exploitable" —Emery Patrice Lumumba

The truth of the matter is that continual charge of Western powers about the crisis in the DR Congo, the Great Lakes region, or any other African region is a continual demonstration of failure for Africans to resolve their problems and to bring peace and development in the continent. The devil does not take possession of one's soul until the soul's owner willfully invites it to appropriate his or her life. One window of opportunity given to the devil may mean the end (spiritual and/or physical) of one's life. It is the same for many African governments and nations that foreign powers exploit systematically because they have shown that they are exploitable and manipulable.

Thus, instead of constantly blaming Western powers for the chaotic economic situation and human rights violations in Africa, Africans must realize that their leaders must take full responsibility for it. For, African leaders are directly or indirectly involved in the exploitation of the continent's human, natural, and mineral resources. It is indisputable that "Zimbabwe's poverty is caused by Robert Mugabe, Zaire's by ex-dictator Mobutu Sese Seko, SA's largely by the apartheid government."[332] Africans had killed themselves in Biaffra, Congo, Ethiopia, Somalia, Burkina Faso, Chad, Angola, Liberia, Lesotho, South Africa, Uganda, Rwanda, and Burundi to name only these few countries. They kill each other at a large scale in the Congo, Algeria, Central Africa, Sierra-Léone, Nigeria, Sudan, Uganda, Ivory-Coast, Rwanda, and Burundi. "It is unfortunate that African leaders seem to act as foreigners. For there is none who loves his/her continent, who could work for its downfall and destruction. The whole [African] continent is in a perpetual state of chaos and suffering."[333] This unnecessary tragedy would have and may well be avoided.

It is purely hypocrisy to claim that African actual tragedy and misery must always be linked to slavery, colonialism, or the like. "More than three decades after African countries gained their independence, there is a growing recognition among Africans themselves that the continent must look beyond its colonial past for the causes of current conflicts. Today, more than ever, Africa must look at itself. The nature of political power in many African states, together with the real and perceived consequences of capturing and maintaining power, is a key source of conflict across the continent,"[334] argued Kofi Annan.

It would be a scapegoat for African leaders to always attach the misery of the continent to non-disputable historical events; likewise, it would simply be ignorance for the African people to swallow such statements. The truth is that "if Africans want to be taken seriously, they must stand up and take some responsibility for their problems and accept complete responsibility for the action to be taken to correct them. What [do] Africans do about these tragedies besides expect the rest of the world do something? ...The problem in the Great Lakes region goes back to when the Tutsis first made themselves the dominant group without having the greatest numbers.... A point of comparison is that Russia's colonization of Eastern Europe only ended in the 1990s, yet those countries do not expect the rest of the world to rescue them without some effort from their side. Africa will be taken seriously—but first it needs to take itself seriously and show the world what it will do to handle tragedies right from when they first show themselves."[335]

Mobutu was a Western product, but he was an African first. He methodically and systematically destroyed the little economic assets that the colonists left in the DR Congo; likewise, he pillaged national, natural, and mineral resources to satisfy personal and imperialistic ambitions. He had less regard for respect of human rights of his people whom he killed and massacred in order to fulfill his passions. Idi Amin's reign of terror in Uganda was one of the cruelest on African soil. He was an African who killed his citizens to satisfy his bestial instincts. Savimbi was a purely American product whose bloody appetites, purposeless war, and greedy nature led to abandonment by his allies, betrayal by his aides, and killing by his enemies. Thousands of innocent Angolans died because of his bush war. In Addition, he foolishly used the Angolan natural and mineral resources in the territories under his control to foster his military campaigns. He was an African, too.

John Garang, like Savimbi, is supported by the US in his irrational war in South Sudan. Thousands of innocent people have died and die because of his unwilling nature to end a long, unnecessary, and costly war. Yet he still fights until he rules Sudan. Nice dream, John! His fate shall be similar to Mobutu and Savimbi. He is another African. Because of General Robert Guei's stubbornness and political immaturity, Ivory-Coast, once one of the prosperous and quiet African countries, has become troublesome. Hundreds of innocent African children died because of his immeasurable ambitions to rule Ivory Coast at all cost. He died, like Savimbi, a shameful death. He, too, was an African. Those who, in Ivory Coast, are today following Guei's footsteps shall soon find themselves without allies if they do not return to their African roots.

The founders and loyal servants of the apartheid regime in South Africa were all Africans, though of a so-called white skin. Yet, they knowingly and willfully imposed on the majority race a discriminatory system that purposely destroyed Black people's pride and dignity and delayed the healing of slavery and colonization wounds of Black people all over the world. They are accountable for thousands of deaths of innocent African people. Unfortunately, some disciples of the apartheid regime still dream of reinstating manu militari, this odious system. They are Africans, it is understood.

All the abovementioned so-called leaders chose to serve foreign interests. In the process, their greed and selfish nature led them to satisfy personal and/or partisan ambitions. Foreign powers exploited them because they have shown that they were exploitable. Western countries used them to accomplish their capitalistic designs. But those leaders, and many others, misused and abused their nation's resources in order to serve imperialistic interests. In the course of their action, they shed innocent blood. It was a choice they made freely. They killed their African brothers and sisters to get, gain, and maintain power; nothing rational can explain their behavior, and therefore no legal defense is on their side.

Though the evidence linked and will always link Western powers to the misbehavior of African leaders, it will be hard evidence to prove that they forced these leaders to massacre innocent people and commit crimes against humanity at home and sometimes abroad. For sure, the West supplies many African governments and rebel leaders with arms, weapons, ammunition, military equipment, instructors, and, at times, intelligence and money. However, the real perpetrators of human rights abuses, both political and economical, remain those who gave instructions, those who pulled the trigger—in short, those who made the choice to kill other human beings, destroy and plunder their nations and/or other foreign nations' resources. And so far, substantiation has proved that these people were and are all Africans.

As long as Africans and their leaders shall not be united, Western powers shall use the same tactics and maneuvers: they will come with money and weapons to buy the souls of some leaders, accomplish their economic interests and the like, sow divisions among peaceable citizens, retreat with caution, and leave behind ungovernable states. It is sad to observe that in their discourses or speeches "African leaders are often made to think that they are free and independent, that they can make personal decisions... It is a great pity that many of them are being manipulated in that way and cannot organize and serve the interests of their own people first. When you are being told what to do and what not to do, it becomes difficult to realize one's growing alienation and to try to strive toward a change of mentality and policies. African countries will only be developed once their leaders are able to say no to any foreign manipulation and dependence..."[336]

Whether some Africans like Paul Kagame, Oweri Museveni, and "rebel" group leaders in the DR Congo, for example, understand the essence of unity and development, is arguable. For, if they knew their detrimental contribution to the destruction of Africa and African lives, they will stand and oppose Western powers' manipulations and exploitations. Whether these leaders know that, after their mentors of evil works upon the continent of Africa have sucked them up, their lives will end up like those of Mobutu and Savimbi, is not debatable. But at the present time, they have one agenda and priority: to carry out the will and protect the numerous interests of Western powers. They will defend these interests at all costs and slay whomever and destroy whatever shall stand in their way. They shall do this for fear of losing power and they must do it as a means of clinging to power, for they perfectly know that after being in power they shall spend the rest of their lives in prisons.

To accomplish this imperialistic objective, leaders like those mentioned above have no regard whatever for respect of human rights, as amply shown herein. They have committed genocide and crimes against humanity both at home and in the DR Congo. They have plundered the natural and mineral resources of the DR Congo, and they have committed the crime of aggression and international terrorism.

Let one recall the story of a woman, an African mother, in the occupied territories of the DR Congo, who stood up and opposed a forced recruitment of her son by the RCD rebels. The woman had already one son in the Congolese national army. When the rebels summoned her to show them her other son's hiding place, she confronted them in these terms: "I have given up John (the son in the Congolese army) and now you want to take Peter (the son in hiding). I cannot do that." The boldness of this African woman teaches any African to react responsibly when faced with degrading situations. The main reason, it is told, this African woman refused to give up her other son was because she could not sustain the idea that her children face each other on the battlefields as enemies rather than brothers.

Indeed, all those Africans who kill each other, be it in the battlefields or the like, or in any other circumstances, are brothers and sisters. Thus, though they dare act in that manner, they ought not to do so. Each African must ponder and live to the fullest these words of an African son, freedom fighter, peace noble, former president, and one of the most respected African and world statesmen, Nelson R. Mandela: " We say: Let us forget the past. We are brothers, we are sisters, we are one flesh and blood; our [continent] is in danger, our people are being killed every day. If there is anything that can be dangerous to the future of... Africa, it is the fact that we should be squabbling amongst ourselves when Rome is burning."[337] Rome has, indeed, been burning for decades because of a crippled and corrupt leadership, Mr. President.

Africans are exploited because they are exploitable; likewise, foreigners will respect Africans' lives when Africans respect their own lives first. "...It is only when Africa decides to treat each life in its lands as precious—and shows the world that it believes in the sanctity of the life of its own people—will its aching tragedies be taken seriously.... Africa must show the world it, too, cares for every single life that passes futilely away, not only in word, but in deed."[338] There is no magic solution about it. It is a matter of doing it or leaving it and continuing to face pernicious consequences. Enough is enough. The shameful exchange of African innocent blood for the sake of power, greed, and self-interest, and imperialistic ambitions should no more be tolerated.

4.2. The African Renaissance: The Answer

The lack of good governance in most African states is the real cause of African tragedies and misery, claimed the West. In the case of the Great Lakes region, for example, one has to look at the history of the past forty years to understand the extensive damages caused by the absence of discipline in the running of the affairs of states. What does colonialism have to do with Mobutu's reign of total misuse of power and anarchy in the Congo? Or it is because of colonialism that the Tutsis and Hutus slaughter each other in Burundi and Rwanda? What does colonialism have to do with the invasion of the DR Congo by its neighbors, Rwanda and Uganda? Unless Africans, in general, and their leaders, in particular, go back to their roots, many human rights will be violated, much blood will be shed, much aggression will take place, tragedies shall succeed tragedies, and only misery shall reign on African soil.

Africans need to go back to their roots to rediscover themselves. This rediscovery, which is meant to be positive and constructive, needs not to be a rejection of positive and constructive foreign values. It needs not to be a mere philosophy, or a totally abstract notion. For, in the past four decades, Africans' brutal subjection and total submission in the hands of their leaders were because of the succession of various demagogic, ambivalent, abstract, and abusive philosophies. It is an undisputed and indisputable fact that "...many of these leaders, instead of following their visions thoroughly, gave empty hopes to their masses, which at the end did not make enough impact on the economy and politics of Africa."[339]

Africans must now understand that the African Renaissance that is advocated and that should be practiced is "a new beginning, a rediscovery of African people to create and provide suitable and conducive socio-political and economic conditions for sustainable economic growth and general development. This approach has to be understood against the background of the urgent need to eliminate mass poverty, gross economic mismanagement, unemployment, corruption, debt, illiteracy, rising crime, wars, and a host of other evils currently driving African states to near collapse."[340] This approach has also to be understood as an appeal to tolerance by Africans, in particular by those leaders, who misuse and abuse power to satisfy some personal, partisan, and/or tribal or ethnic ambitions and passions. For, it should be emphasized that "the success of the African Renaissance relies on strong and capable leadership. For, although there is always a willingness on the part of the African masses to change their miserable lives, they are often powerless in the sense that their voices are not heard and have little impact on the governance of the African states. Indeed, there is need to go back to the African roots and learn the relevant factors that motivated the pre-colonial leaders to look at the well-being of theirs subjects. This is the key issue of the African Renaissance,"[341] argues Dr. Mulemfo. This approach should, indeed, be understood as the ultimate solution to African problems.

For the African Renaissance to succeed, Africans must ensure that, and all efforts should be made in order to avoid that, their leaders monopolize this notion solely for personal fame, political propaganda, and to strengthen their personal power. The African masses, at all levels of society, should be involved in the process. African Renaissance should be part of the African educational curriculum at schools, mostly at the tertiary level. The train of

African Renaissance would be hijacked; its rail tracks and stations will be sabotaged if the African leaders do not speedily address the issue and constructive strategies set up as means of involving their citizens in the affairs of the nations. Empowering the African people should be the purpose and objective, and the essence of the African Renaissance. That is exactly what President Thabo Mbeki,[342] of South Africa, today's advocate of the African Renaissance, is aiming to accomplish.

Nevertheless, as pointed out previously, African nations should practice good governance to move forward into development. The lack of good governance will drain all energies, break all hopes, and dismantle strategies put into place to help Africans rebuild their continent. Good governance should be seen as the main contributing factor of the African Renaissance. Good governance should be understood as the institution of democracy, the establishment of the rule of law, the supremacy of the constitution, the respect of human rights, the restoration of African values, and the promotion of those principles that will pacify and bring stability in Africa. The US, for example, insists that Africans practice good governance if in quest of US assistance. It is believed that corruption alone costs Africa almost $150 billion a year. No wonder that many African leaders are reluctant to endorse the principle of good governance and address the issue of corruption in their homelands. That will be the greatest test of the New Partnership for African Development (NEPAD), while there lays the success of the African Union (AU).

None of the countries in the Great Lakes region practice good governance. The current crisis in this region is unavoidably tied to the lack of democracy and the rule of law. Some individuals, with parcel of authority in the DR Congo, Rwanda, and Uganda, manipulated their masses to accomplish well-designed plans of destroying the already fragile human, cultural, and economical tissues of those countries. Rwanda and Uganda lack of good governance practices led to the aggression of the DR Congo and the fostering of a costly war, both in human and economic resources, in order to satisfy imperialistic ambitions. The absence of respect of human rights in Rwanda and Uganda has led to the total disregard of the same rights by the soldiers of these countries during their military and criminal occupation of the DR Congo. Both Rwanda and Uganda are accountable for genocide, terrorism, wars crimes, and crimes against humanity on the Congolese soil. It is believed that nearly 3.5 million people have died in the DR Congo as a direct result of the aggression by Rwanda and Uganda, while millions are displaced.

The African Renaissance does not advocate the superiority of one tribe or ethnic group against another. It does not foster the hatred of one tribe or ethnic group toward another. Nor does the African Renaissance promote the exclusion of one tribe or ethnic group in one nation. The African Renaissance does not uphold ethnic cleansing, disrespect of human rights, corruption, the plundering of mineral and natural resources, and invasion of another nation whatever the reason may be. The African Renaissance does not encourage the betrayal of African culture to satisfy imperialistic goals. Nor does it nurture the abuse of power to please oneself, a partisan, and tribal or ethnic cause to the disadvantage of the rest of the populations.

The African Renaissance simply promotes the respect of oneself, the respect of others and their properties. "The vision for an African renaissance is therefore the attainment of that growth to meet the basic needs of the African people for a better life; the creation of a society in which conditions of living such as security, peace, stability, sufficiency, satisfaction, and stimulus for growth prevail; and the need to restore African values encompassing social justice and democratic values, human dignity, accountability, and transparency, the lack of which have constrained the development of the African states."[343] Thus, the African Renaissance is at the core of any development and a way to a better future for African people. The African Renaissance will foster the institution of a democratic Africa and the respect of the rule of law.

Conclusion

The invasion of the Democratic Republic of Congo by Rwanda and Uganda was a criminal act. Neither of those countries ever sought the help of the international community, particularly the UN, to solve whatever wrong they accused the DR Congo of doing, before they took it upon themselves to aggress the DR Congo. This aggression is a criminal act because both Rwanda and Uganda acted contrarily to established legal rules of international law. The occupation of the DR Congo by Rwanda and Uganda was a criminal act because both Rwanda and Uganda did not have the mandate nor seek to obtain one from the UN before invading the DR Congo. By occupying the DR Congo, Rwanda and Uganda acted against the letter and the spirit of both the UN and the AU Charters.

Further, the aggression of the DR Congo by its neighbors, Rwanda and Uganda, was a premeditated and deliberate coward and criminal act. This criminal action was against all established international legal norms. This act was therefore illegal. In international law, "[a] state that has violated an international obligation has the further obligation to provide redress for the violation. The obligation to provide redress presupposes that there been an international obligation, that the obligation was violated, and that the violation was not justified or excused under international law."[344]

The illegal occupation of the DR Congo by Rwanda and Uganda has deep roots in Rwanda and Uganda. As discussed in the first chapter, the ethnic culture of mutual exclusion between Hutus and Tutsis in Rwanda is the true cause, not only of the conflict in the DR Congo discussed herein, but also of the actual crisis in the whole Great Lakes region. The DR Congo has more than two hundred ethnic groups than does Rwanda, but this reality has never been a problem for good governance in the DR Congo. The Congolese have been living in peace for decades without any ethnicity daring to exclude others or plot to exterminate others, as is the case in Rwanda. Because of that mistrust, today, Rwanda is a national security state and is fighting a dirty war inside and outside its borders for various reasons.

The invasion and aggression in the DR Congo by Rwanda and Uganda was neither for the protection of the Banyamulenge, a Congolese Tutsi tribe, nor for the fortification of Rwandan and Ugandan borders. The Banyamulenge are not in danger in the DR Congo today nor were they yesterday under Mobutu regime. The International community is well aware of this reality. Today one may well speculate that only the current expansionism vision of the Rwandan/Tutsi government and its miscalculated act of aggression in the DR Congo have ostracized the Banyamulenge.

Furthermore, there is no border separating Rwanda or Uganda from the DR Congo in the bushes of Kasai, in Kindu, Kisangani, Isiro, Matadi, Kitona, and Kinshasa, to name only these few localities. Kasai is more than four hundred miles from Rwanda. And what were Rwandan and Ugandan troops doing in the Lower-Congo province in August of 1998, a distance of about 1,200 miles away from the borders they were supposed and argued to protect? And what were they doing, with arms and ammunition in Kinshasa and its surrounding areas months after the Kinshasa government ordered them to leave?

The truth about this war of aggression, "...is that the fight inside Congo will become a fight for Congo, a struggle to carve up the nation and assign new borders."[345] It is pointed out that the international community, the UN, and the US are all aware of this plan to partition the DR Congo, and that the Congolese war of invasion did not happen by accident. The conspiracy about the Balkanization of the DR Congo exists as the de facto partition was seen during the war. The thesis of this partition is as follows: the richer and bigger a country, the more powerful it becomes, and the more influence it has over its neighbors, politically and economically, to the point that it constitutes a permanent and potential "danger" for the great powers. Therefore, it has to be divided into small states in order to enable the great powers to continue controlling the world.

It is illogical, even ironic, to speak of aggression and not to acknowledge violations of international human rights by the aggressors in the occupied territories. There is no such thing as a peaceful aggression; and if there were one, it will be called anything else but aggression. And this is a fact that cannot be disputed. One case is the aggression of the DR Congo by Rwanda and Uganda that the US and the UN have refused to acknowledge. In the US's government records, this aggression never took place. It was outlined that such attitude is unfair and unjust and is a mockery to the science of law and an insult to the people of Africa. Rwandan and Ugandan troops committed crime against humanity and war crimes in the DR Congo. As for Rwanda, the RPA has also committed a second genocide on the Congolese soil. And for the sake of fairness and justice, "the [Congolese people] maintain that the [Rwandan and Ugandan] government[s] culpability for [gross violations of human rights in the DRC] extends to acts of commission as well as of omission."[346] The international community knows all about these crimes, but together with the US and the UN they have all covenanted to not denounce them in order to achieve their devilish goal of the partition of the DR Congo.

Thus, Rwanda and Uganda knowingly made a false statement of material fact when they claimed that the Banyamulenge were victims of genocide in the DRC, and when they said that they came to Congo to protect their borders from further incursions from Interamwe and ex-FAR. Therefore, Rwanda and Uganda were aware that the statement they made publicly and to the international community was false. Not only they knew that statement was false, but they made it with the sole intent to deceive the international community. Not only they deceived the international community, but their statement led Rwandans, Ugandans, and their Congolese allies, mutatis mutandis, to commit genocide, terrorism, crimes against humanity, and war crimes on the peaceable Congolese people.

It has been argued that it is sad that the UN failed to bring peace and stability in Africa, contrarily to what it strives to do in Europe or in other areas of the world. The UN's silent and non-condemnation in its strongest terms of the illegal occupation of the DRC simply meant a support to the commission of violations of international human rights by Rwanda and Uganda. This UN modus operandi in the DRC constitutes a grave irresponsibility and a breach of its Charter. This inaction caused the death of millions of innocent victims in the DR Congo, and has put in peril the lives of millions of other displaced people, without counting all health hazards today and tomorrow that are directly associated to this illegal occupation, for instance the rapid spread of HIV/AIDS.

It is, in truth, dangerous for world peace and security that "...the UN organs responsible for the promotion and protection of human rights suffer from most of the same disabilities that afflict the United Nations as a whole, in particular the absence of supranational authority and the presence of divisive power politics. Hence, it cannot be expected that UN actions in defense of human rights will be, normally, either swift or categorically effective. Indeed, on the basis of the historical record to date, it may fairly be said that serious UN efforts at human rights implementation and reform are more often thwarted than not, not least at the hands of the major powers. Nevertheless, assuming some political will, the legal obstacles to UN Enforcement of human rights are not insurmountable,"[347] Burns H. Weston points out with regret.

Western media played a negative and destructive role during the illegal occupation of the DRC. Coordinated by international lobbyists, their sole aim was the Balkanization of the DR Congo for economic reasons. Their reports of the DR Congo armed conflict was deliberately false and misleading to better accomplish preconceived objectives. They totally sided with the enemies of the Congolese people and government. This act of commission encouraged Rwandan and Ugandan invaders, and their Congolese associates, to engage in patterns of violations of human rights and international humanitarian laws never seen in any armed conflict. Thus, the Western media attitude was a deliberate criminal conspiracy toward the Congolese and their nation.

International financial institutions of the caliber of the WB and IMF would have abstained to assist both Rwanda and Uganda during their illegal occupation of the DRC, while there already was sufficient evidence that such aid was diverted to support, militarily, the occupation. On the contrary, these monetary funds organizations behaved themselves in a way that clearly evidenced that they abetted and fueled the illegal occupation of the DRC by Rwanda and Uganda. Such action, it has been debated, was merely illegal and irresponsible.

It has been explained that the Western powers and the USA have set up a precedent, together with the UN, for having not condemned in its strongest term the illegal occupation of the DR Congo by Rwanda and Uganda. Such double standard politics have dangerous consequences for the maintenance of peace and security among nations. The US has a great responsibility in this matter because Rwanda and Uganda are its allies. And it is no secret for anyone that when the US fails to condemn violations of human rights by its allies, the only available inference is that they have encouraged such violations to take place. The US policy toward the DR Congo needs to be positively and constructively transformed for the sake of development, democracy, good governance, nation building, restoration of law and order, and the safety of human lives. This American policy in the DR Congo that has not changed in the past fifty years is the main cause of all the suffering the Congolese people have gone through, since the assassination of Prime

Minister Lumumba, throughout the reign of Mobutu, and in today's crisis.

The national security defense that the US brandishes whenever it violates international human rights laws, as was the case in the firing of missiles in Sudan, and whenever it fails to condemn the same violations committed by its allies, is a vague and ambiguous notion and is therefore a false excuse. The US Government should be ashamed of striving to build a better nation at home, while abroad its policy is a violent one that has killed millions of innocent people. For that reason, "the US has an enormous amount of negative baggage to overcome in this regard. The US responsiveness to security and refugees' needs in Kosovo contrast with the weary reaction to Congo. US prevention of military assistance in Rwanda in 1994 and Congo-Brazzaville in 1997 leaves us with blood in our hands. These reactions need to be erased by a forthcoming response to political and security needs in Congo today. It is the US's interest to do so,"[348] I. William Zartman argued. Few would hesitate to call the US a terrorist state, when one looks at the way they enforce their policy in Africa in general, and the DR Congo in particular in order to satisfy political and economic interests.

There is an obvious imbalance of power at the UN Security Council. There is a strong belief that the UN, in general, and the Security Council, in particular, need a complete reformation in order to meet the needs of the people of the world today. This reformation must take place to achieve peace and impartially maintain security in the world. As for Africa, "the UN should take a more active role in ensuring respect for human rights for African citizens. The organization should have a mechanism that enables it to intervene directly to mediate conflicts in Africa... The UN should be increasingly watchful and ready to act in situations of internal crisis. Africa has become such a hotbed of internal strife ... the UN needs to police Africa to ensure that human rights are respected."[349] This is a role that the current prostitute organization cannot achieve, for the world knows whom they serve. It is Secretary-General Kofi Annan who, alas, observed that "[n]o region in the world illustrates the need to prevent conflict, and the costs of the failure to do so, more dramatically than Africa. The dreadful human cost inflicted by conflicts in Angola, the Democratic Republic of the Congo, Eritrea-Ethiopia, Sierra Leone, the Sudan, and elsewhere is self-evident."[350]

The UN liability in failing to protect the DR Congo during the war of occupation led by Rwanda, Uganda, and allies has been established. It has been well argued and demonstrated that the UN owed a duty of care to the DR Congo and its citizens and that the UN was negligent in fulfilling her responsibilities. The UN had the ability and the authority to restore peace and order in the DR Congo in compelling by all means the invaders, Rwanda and Uganda, to withdraw from the territories of the DR Congo unconditionally pursuant to its Charter. In addition, the UN knew or should have known that Rwanda and Uganda have the propensity of committing grave violations of human rights and should have controlled these two countries' activities in the DR Congo and halted them from committing them in the first place. Further, despite the many calls from the Congolese people, their government, some foreign governments, many NGOs, and other organizations that genocide, crimes against humanity, and war crimes were being committed by the invaders and their allies in the DR Congo, the UN remained unwilling to intervene contrarily to what it did in other heavens. The UN acted in grave violation of its own mandate. Thus, the UN was in breach of duty of care and should compensate the DR Congo and its citizens for what they have systematically suffered.

It has been explained that the international community agrees on the efficiency of sanctions in armed conflict situations. Sanctions, in any form, can bring the stubborn government or warring party that refuses to halt hostilities to its knees. Sanctions have been widely used to compel opposing parties to come into peaceful settlements of their disagreements or to force the wrongful party (ies) to respect international customs and laws of war. However, the fact that the same sanctions' principles were not applied in the case of Rwanda and Uganda to compel them to leave the territories of the DRC that they illegally occupied for nearly five years was an irresponsible and unpardonable act from the UN and the international community. Three and a half million Congolese perished because of this inaction and act of omission from both the UN Security Council and the international community.

Occupying forces, it has been debated, do not only have rights, but they also have obligations. Unfortunately, in the case of the invasion of the DRC, Rwandan and Ugandan occupying forces distinguished themselves as troops that had only rights and no obligations toward the Congolese people living in the localities under their control. The question that remained unanswered is: why were sexual crimes, in particular rape (the norm), torture, extrajudicial killings, and other human rights atrocities so severe in the occupied territories of the DR Congo, if Rwanda and Uganda invading forces understood that they had the right to protect civilian populations rather than submit them to inhuman treatments? It is understood that Rwandan and Ugandan occupying forces breach their international legal obligations toward the Congolese people living in the territories under their control. Never in the history of armed conflicts, had women and girls been objects of and systematically subjected to sexual violence as it happened in the occupied territories of the DR Congo.

It has been suggested with vigor that the ICC may play the role of disciplining all those—individuals, organizations, or states—that think that they have the right, because of some secret combinations with their allies, to massacre other human beings without fear and escape justice. Such impunity from the UN toward international human rights violators should be discouraged at all costs. That is why in order "[t]o strengthen protection, we must reassert the centrality of international humanitarian and human rights laws. We must strive to end the culture of impunity—which is why the creation of the International Criminal Court is so important."[351] All those who are directly or indirectly linked to violations of international human rights norms in the DRC, at any degree of such violations, should be punished, so that future potential perpetrators will know what to expect when they engage themselves in practices that are against human rights and humanitarian laws.

The ICC is expected and should play a deterrent role. "In short, we are facing two interrelated problems following this course of discouraging future potential perpetrators. The first one is to bring the offenders to justice; not only the relatively minor ones, but also those in charge. But it is not sufficient to bring them to justice if most are pardoned and only a few receive modest sentences. That would only continue to send a message that gross violations of human rights may be committed with impunity. The second is to bring such judicial proceedings to the attention of the widest possible audience. So far, the media has refused to do this. That makes them conspirators in the continuing massive violations of human rights in [and by] so many countries that have sanctimoniously signed the relevant conventions outlawing them."[352]

Though legal cases are considered on individual basis, it is a recognized legal principle that similar facts or issues must be dealt with similarly. Good lawyers love precedent, a good legal system believes in it, and legal courts rely on it intensively. Thus, one expects that the same legal norms applied to bring Milosevic and his lieutenants to the ICTY at The Hague be speedily used to bring to justice Kagame, Museveni, and their lieutenants, and the so-called Congolese "rebel" leaders with regards to the Congolese case.

In short, the issue should not be whether Kagame, Museveni and their lieutenants, and the Congolese "rebel" leaders and their associates, involved in the commission of genocide, terrorism, crimes against humanity, and war crimes in the DR Congo should be charged. The issue is, rather, why should they not be charged with those crimes when there is more than enough evidence of their involvement? The appropriate criminal tribunal will apply the command responsibility doctrine in charging those individuals with the crimes they knew or should have known that the soldiers under their command have committed.

Thus, to promote justice and fairness, and due process, an appeal is made to the UN Security Council to establish legal mechanisms and a tribunal to speedily indict all those implicated in serious violations of human rights during the Rwanda-Uganda-and-allies-led war of occupation against the DR Congo. These individuals, whatever their positions or ranks, should be charged, convicted, and sentenced according to the laws of penal procedure established and/or applicable to the circumstances. This tribunal should also seek to indict those who have conspired, at the UN's level, to obstruct the restoration of peace and legal order in the DR Congo. The idea that it should be established an ad hoc international criminal tribunal for Congo, similar to the ICTR, must be discouraged because the latter "does not cover violations of laws and customs of war."[353]

In this matter, it has been discussed that whether the UN Security Council set up an ad hoc criminal tribunal that covers violations of laws and customs of war or a mixed penal tribunal, which shall also include Congolese criminal procedure laws, is not an issue for the Congolese people and its government. In truth, what matters is the indictment, arrest, and trial—according to due process—of all those individuals suspected of breaking international human rights laws and international humanitarian norms in the occupied territories of the DRC during its illegal invasion by Rwanda and Uganda.

It has been demonstrated how Congolese victims of international human rights and humanitarian laws can make use of the ATCA and TVPA, as legal remedies, to sue in US federal courts those individuals and corporations who directly or indirectly committed relevant crimes to them and/or their relatives. To this effect, an appeal is hereupon extended to any Congolese victims of international human rights, their relatives, or legal representatives, who happen to be on US soil, to sue those individuals suspected of committing such abuses in the occupied territories of the DRC and who happen to be present in the US. Likewise, the same victims may sue in US courts, corporations charged with violating international human rights in the

DR Congo during the war of invasion discussed in this book, inasmuch as those companies have business nexus with the US. It is agreed that, considering legal precedents, applying ATCA in this situation shall have deterrent effects and play an essential role in combating impunity.

A lot has been said regarding the issue of sovereign immunities. The legal position supported in this book is that international human rights violations, whether committed under color of law or not, and whoever the author of such commission, are crimes under international laws. It has been stressed out that immunity should not shield an individual who has violated the laws of nations and customs of laws in his capacity as a state official, simply because such individual is still holding a public office. Therefore, no violator of human rights should hide under the cloak of an official status. Indeed, an individual who has violated international legal norms while acting under the color of law of his state, evidences by his act that such state law is a bad law, and therefore a crime under international law. Further, the law of the nations requires that such individuals be prosecuted, tried, and punished to the full extent of the law whether he or she holds official position or not. A crime does not become less criminal because the author thereof is still holding a public position, and that considering this circumstance prosecution should be postponed until such time that the alleged criminal leaves office. What if the perpetrator dies in office, delays his or her retirement from office by manipulating the constitution, or simply by refusing to leave office as it is common in Africa? Should justice then be delayed or simply denied to the victims? Is this modus operandi called justice? Is this not an "institutionalized" anarchy?

The discussion on universal jurisdiction focused on the fact that certain international crimes—for instance, genocide, crimes against humanity, war crimes—that shock human conscience fall under this jurisdiction. Under international law, a foreign state exercises international jurisdiction when it prosecutes gross violations of human rights committed by a foreign citizen in another foreign state, whether the victim is a citizen of the same state as the perpetrator or not, and whether the commission of such acts occurred in the victim's state, the perpetrator's state, the foreign prosecuting state, or any other foreign state. International treaties provide that a foreign state that does not want to prosecute an author of international human rights violations and humanitarian laws, must arrest such person and extradite him or her to a third state willing to prosecute and try him or her. That the application of universal jurisdiction is having deterrent effects in international law to end impunity is demonstrated by the successful precedents analyzed herein.

In order to ensure the safety, political and economical stability in the Great Lakes region, Rwanda and Uganda in particular, but also the whole region, need to be democratized as a matter of priority. It is wrong and a great miscalculation that to think and claim that the democratization of the DR Congo would ipso facto lead to the democratization of Rwanda and Uganda. The democratization of the DR Congo is not a magic solution to Rwanda and Uganda decennial social, political, and economical crisis and instability. The democratization of the DR Congo depends on the Congolese people themselves, while Rwanda and Uganda are dependent upon the US, their allies.

Thus, a fervent call is made to the US Congress to help in the democratization of Rwanda and Uganda in order to enable them to learn tolerance, mutual respect of cultures, and mutual acceptance of ethnic groups (like in the DR Congo), the love of peace, and the strict respect of international human rights. This may seem hard and rhetorical, but it is known that there are people out there in Rwanda—both Hutus and Tutsis—who are willing and are ready to sit together and solve their ethnic differences in order to build a new nation based on the principles of democracy and respect of international human rights. Both Tutsis and Hutus are good people, but the Tutsi-Kagame-led government in Rwanda is the dividing factor between these two groups.

Further, it should be mentioned that "the Human Rights situation in Rwanda ... is linked to that of eastern DRC. The fact that the perpetrators of the 1994 genocide have yet to be brought to trial, that thousands wait in prison without even a file on their case or a basic hearing, and that there are frequent violations of Human Rights, all contribute to tension and fuel the conflict. Whilst this situation remains unsolved, whilst basic measures are not taken to improve the justice system in Rwanda ... the war in the east [of] DRC will periodically resurface."[354] The DR Congo needs a new legal order to competently and constructively tackle this matter and restore law and order in the country. But, "[t]here should be no illusion that the Congolese people will be able to carry out that colossal task on their own. Without the active engagement of the international community, the chances of success will be minimal,"[355] it should be emphasized. That is why the US Congress is called on to conduct its own investigation to determine the involvement of the US government in this crisis and to assist the Congolese government to establish a State of law and order.

It is true that Africans are exploited because they want to be exploited. Their leaders are easily influenced by foreign powers to the point of sacrificing national interests. It has been debated that "colonialism is not a valid explanation for economic and political limitations"[356] in Africa, but rather bad governance, lack of democratic principles, and of the rule of law, and the respect of human rights. It is no secret that foreign powers exploit Africans and their nations because the latter have proven to be exploitable. A solemn call is made to all Africans, in general, and African leaders, in particular, to rediscover their ego and honor the African values and tradition. It has been discussed that the solution to the crisis in the Great Lakes Region, in general, and the DRC, notably, lies in the understanding and application of the African Renaissance notions.

Gone are the days when two individuals were stabbing each other to death, while others look on and even encourage them to keep on fighting. Gone are the days when only the most powerful had the right to life, to freedom, to peace, and security because of their money and their powerful friendly association. Likewise, in today's modern society, encouraging one state to invade another and commit gross violations of human rights on innocent, peaceable citizens is a sign of mental illness, and an act of terrorism and barbarism. While history, until lately, has shown that the same crimes were sanctioned in other countries with western affiliation, the fact that the same Western nations kept total silence in the case of the DR Congo, as if nothing wrong and inhumane happened there, is unthinkable. This attitude only evidences the international conspiracy against the DR Congo and its people. It is time that the UN, the US, and the rest of the international community condemn the presence of Rwandan and Ugandan armies on the Congolese soil and the commission of gross violations of human rights on that independent and sovereign nation. In addition, it is time today that they remind Rwanda and Uganda that human rights are not bargained for, and are neither marketable nor negotiable.

Finally, the Congolese "...people ... demand justice as a right, not as charity..."[357] and request that those who have some sort of link, who promoted or furthered, as little as their activities might have been, whoever they may be and wherever they may be, with the war of aggression against the DR Congo, a sovereign state, be accountable for their direct or indirect participation. It is understood that "[t]he United Nations is an association of sovereign states, but the rights that it exists to protect and promote are people's rights. It allows that individuals everywhere have a responsibility to help defend the ideals of human rights. The role of civil society in the establishment of the International Criminal Court was an inspiring example of what can be achieved by people driven by faith in those ideals. The voice of the people brought us to Rome; the voice of the people gives this gift of hope to succeeding generations."[358] Now, and the voice of the people, a peculiar people, the Congolese people, even the voice of the victims of the criminal invasion of their motherland, and of all those who thirst for fairness, is crying for justice saying, "rendezvous à" La Hague, Kinshasa, or wherever, as this war may be long and popular. Indeed, this war is not yet over!

Bibliography

I. Books

1. Ambrose, Brendalyn P., *Democratization and the Protection of human Rights in Africa. Problems and Prospects.* Westport: Praeger Publishers, 1995.

2. Barbri Bar Review, Thomson Company, 2002.

3. Burdick, Francis. M., *The Law of Torts: A Concise Treatise on the Civil Liability at Common Law and Under Modern Statutes for Actionable Wrongs to Person and Property,* Beard Books, 2000.

4. Garner, Bryan. A., *Black's Law Dictionary*, Seventh Ed., West Group, ST. PAUL, MINN., 1999.

5. Gibbs, N. David., *The Political Economy of Third World Intervention. Mines, Money, and US Policy in the Congo Crisis*. Chicago and London: The University of Chicago Press, 1991.

6. Gutman, Roy and Rieff, D., *Crimes of War. What the Public Should Know*, W. W. Norton Company, New York/London, 1999.

7. Jonassohn, Kurt with Björnson, Karin S., *Genocide and Gross Human Rights Violations. In Comparative Perspective*. New Brunswick/London: Transaction Publishers, 1998.

8. Maloka, Eddy, *A United States of Africa?* Africa Institute of South Africa, 2001.

9. Matas, David, *No More. The Bataille against Human Rights Violations*. Toronto/ Oxford: Dundurn Press, 1994.

10. Mulemfo, M.Makanda, *Thabo Mbeki and the African Renaissance*, Actua Press (Pty.) Ltd., 2000.

11. Philip, David, *Nelson Mandela Speaks, Forging a Democratic, Non-racial South Africa*, Pathfinder, 1993 & David Philip Publishers & Mayibuye Books, 1994.

12. Prosser, W., & Al., *Prosser and Keeton On Torts*, Fifth Edition, Horn Series, Student Edition, West Group, 2001.

13. Ratner, Steven.R., and Abrams, Jason S., *Accountability For Human Rights Atrocities in International Law*. Beyond the Nuremberg Legacy, Second Edition, Oxoford University Press, 2001.

14. Restatement of The Law Third, The American Law Institute, *Restatement of the Law, The Foreign Relations Law of the United States*, Volume 2, ST. Paul, Minn., American Law Institute Publishers, 1987.

15. Steiner, Henry J. and Alston, Philip, *International Human Rights in Context. Law, Politics, Morals*. Oxford: Clarendon Press, 1996.

16. Street, Thomas A., *The Theory and Principles of Torts Law*, Beard Books, 1999.

17. Tambo, Adelaide, *Preparing for power, Oliver Tambo Speaks*, Heinnman Educational BooksLtd., 1987

18. Unesco, *Violations of Human Rights. Possible Rights of Recourse and Forms of Resistance*. Paris, 1984.

19. Wydick, Richard C., *Professional Responsibility*, Barbri Bar Review, A Thomson Company, 2003.

20. Yoder, Amos, *The Evolution of the United Nations System*, Third Edition, Taylor & Francis, 1997.

II. Manuscripts

1. Butandu, Rigobert N., *Rwanda and Uganda, Two International Criminal States: The Case of the Aggression and Gross Violations of Human Rights in the Occupied Territories of the Democratic Republic of Congo,* International Human Rights Seminar, J. Reuben Clark Law School, Provo, Utah, Fall, 1999.

2.*The Causes and Legal Consequences of Military Coups d'Etat in Black Africa, and Their Implications on International Law: A Case Study of the Democratic Republic of Congo under Mobutu Regime (1965-1997),* LL.M Thesis, J. Reuben Clark Law School, Provo, Utah, Spring, 2000.

3. Wardle, Lynn D., Rogers, W. Sherman, & S., & Hogue, Lynn L., *Interstate and International Conflict of Laws* (manuscript ed.), Provo, 2000.

http://www.law2.byu.edu/Wadle/International_Conflicts/iicl_casebook/CHI2IJUR.html

4. Wilkins, Richards G., *Bias, Error, And Duplicity. The UN and the Domestic Law*, Manuscript notes, International Organizations Course, J. Reuben Clark Law School, Brigham Young University, 2000.

III. Reports

1. *Human Rights and US Security Assistance. An Amnesty International USA Report with Recommendations to End Human Rights Abuses in Countries Receiving US Security Assistance.* May 1993 Edition.

2. Inter-American Commission on Human Rights, Organization of American States, *Report on Terrorism and Human Rights,* OEA/Ser.L/V/II.116, Doc. 5 rev. 1 corr., 22 October 2002. http:// www.cidh.oas.org/Terrorism/Eng/toc.htm

3. *International Non-Governmental Commission of Inquiry into the Massive Violations of Human Rights Committed in the Democratic Republic of Congo (Former Zaire) 1996-1997.* Report prepared by the International Centre for Human Rights and Democratic Development (Montreal Canada) (ICHRDD) and l'Association Africaine pour la Défense des DRoits de l' Homme en République Démocratique du Congo (Kinshasa) (ASADHO), Cited in Lexique de Géopolitique, Dalloz Paris, 1998.

4. Kofi Annan, *"We The Peoples", The Role of the United Nations in the 21st Century,* Millennium Report of the Secretary-General of the United Nations, New York, April 3, 2000.

5. Madsen, Wayne, *America's covert operations in the Great Lakes Region* http://www2.minorisa.es/inshuti/madsen2.htm

6. McKinney, Cynthia, *Suffering and Despair: Humanitarian Crisis in the Congo,* Hearing Before the Subcommittee on International Operations and Human Rights of Committee on International Relations, House of Representatives, One Hundred Seventh Congress, First Session, May 17, 2001, Serial No. 107–16, US Government Printing Office Washington: 72-638PS 2001. http://www.house.gov/international_relations/107/726638.pdf

—*Accusations, Crimes against Humanity.* http://www.c-df.org/plaintes/mckinney.html

—Covert Action in Africa: A Smoking Gun in Washington, D.C., April 16, 2001. http://www.ratical.com/co-globalize/ CynthiaMcKinney/news/pr010416.htm

7. Moreels, Reginald, *"Boboto – Amani", A Report for Peace, given at the "International Conference on Armed Conflicts in the Democratic Republic of Congo on the Eve of the Inter-Congolese Dialogue in South Africa: Building a Sustainable Peace in the Great Lakes Region"*, Pretoria, February 2002.

8. Preparatory Commission for the International Criminal Court, Working Group on the Crime of Aggression. New York, 16-26 February

1999, 26 July-13 August 1999, 29 November-17 December 1999. *Discussion paper proposed by the Coordinator. Consolidated text of proposals of the Crime of Aggression*, 9 December 1999.

9. République Démocratique du Congo, Ministère des Droits Humains, Cabinet du Ministre, *Livre Blanc, Tome 2, Sur les Violations Massive des droits de l'Homme, des Régles de base du droit International Humanitaire, ainsi que des Normes Relatives à la Protection de l'Environnement par les Pays Agresseurs (Ouganda, Rwanda, Burundi) et leurs Complices Congolais à l' Est de la République Démocratique du Congo, Couvrant la Période du 06 Novembre 1998 au 30 Avril 1999.*

10. République Démocratique du Congo, Ministère des Droits Humains, Cabinet du Ministre, *Livre Blanc, Tome 3, Sur les Violations Délibérées de l'Accord de Cessez-le-Feu de Lusaka du 10 Juillet 1999, de la Charte Internationale des Droits de l'Homme, des Régles de Base du Droit International Humanitaire ainsi que des Résolutions Pertinentes du Conseil de Sécurité de l'ONU par les Aggresseurs (Ouganda, Rwanda, Burundi) et leurs Complices Congolais du RCD et du MLC dans les Territoires Occupés de la République Démocratique du Congo, Couvrant la Période du 11 Juillet 1999 au 31 Décembre 1999*, Kinshasa, Janvier 2000.

11. République Démocratique du Congo, Ministère des Affaires Etrangères et de la Coopération Internationale, Cabinet du Ministre, Mémoire sur les Evénéments de Kisangani, Couvrant la Période d'Août 1999 à Mai 2002, Kinshasa, Septembre 2002.

12. Schmitt, Michael N., *The Law of Belligerent Occupation*, Crimes War Project, April 15, 2003. http://www.crimesofwar.org/

13. United Nations, *Report of the Secretary-General on the work of the Organization*, General Assembly, Official Records, Fifty-fifth session, Supplement No. 1, (A/55/1), New York, August 30, 2000.

14. UN, *Annual Report of the Secretary-General on the Work of the Organization*, A/53/1, par. 26, 27 August 1998.

15. UN, *The causes of conflict and the promotion of durable peace and sustainable development in Africa,* Report of the Secretary-General Kofi Annan to the UN Security Council, April 16, 1998.

16. United Nations General Assembly, Distr. GENERAL, A/RES/53/156, Fifty-third session, par.3, 9 February 1999.

17. UN Report of the Panel of Experts on the Illegal Exploitation of Natural Resources and Other Forms of Wealth of the Democratic Republic of the Congo, April 12, 2001.

18. UN S/2003/1027, Final Report of the Panel of Experts on the Illegal Exploitation of Natural Resources and Other Forms of Wealth of the Democratic Republic of the Congo, 15 October 2003.

19. United Nations, General Assembly, A/RES/49/60, ANNEX, *Declaration on Measures to Eliminate International Terrorism,* 84th plenary meeting, 9 December 1994.

20. United Nations, General Assembly, A/RES/56/173, Distr.: General, Fifty-sixth session, par.2(c) (i) 27 February 2002.

21. United Nations, General Assembly, A/RES/57/233, Distr.: General, Fifty-seventh session, par. 2(b), 28 January 2003.

IV. Documents

1. *Alien Tort Claims Act* http://cyber.law.harvard.edu/torts3y/readings/update-a-02.doc

2. Barrett, Nicole, *Holding Individual Leaders Responsible for Violations of Customary International Law: The US Bombardment of Cambodia and Laos*, 32 Colum. Hum. Rts. L. Rev. 429 (2001). http://www.icai-online.org/kissingerwatch/barrett.pdf

3. *Belgium Court Dismiss War Crimes Cases*, International Justice, Associated Press, September 24, 2003. http://www.globalpolicy.org/intljustice/universal/2003/0924bush.htm

4. Biden Jr., Joseph R., US. Senator, Foreign Relations Committee Ranking Member, *The National Dialogue on Iraq + One Year*, The Brookings Institute, Washington D.C., 31 July 2003. http://biden.senate.gov/pressapp/record.cfm?id=207000

5. *Complaint.* http://www.informationclearinghouse.info/word/Complaint.doc

6. *Convention against Torture and Other Cruel, Inhuman or Degrading Treatment or Punishment* Adopted and opened for signature, ratification and accession by General Assembly resolution 39/46 of 10 December 1984 *entry into force* 26 June 1987, in accordance with article 27 (1). http://www.unhchr.ch/html/menu3/b/h_cat39.htm

7. *Geneva Convention relative to the Protection of Civilian Persons in Time of War.* Adopted on 12 August 1949 by the Diplomatic Conference for the Establishment of International Conventions for the Protection of Victims of War, held in Geneva from 21 April to 12 August, 1949, entry into force 21 October 1950. http://www.unhchr.ch/html/menu3/b/92.htm

8. Gleeson, K., *World influence of the UDHR. Worldwide Influence of*

the Universal Declaration of Human Rights and the International Bill of Rights. http://www.universalrights.net /main/world.html

9. Hendin, Stuart E., *Command Responsibility and Superior Orders in the Twentieth Century - A Century of Evolution,* Murdoch University Electronic Journal of Law, Vol.10 No.1 (March 2003). htt:// www.murdoch.edu.au/elaw/issues/v10n1/hendin101_text.html

10. Human Rights Watch, *Le Précédent Pinochet: Comment les victimes peuvent poursuivre l'étranger les criminels de droit de l'homme. L'affaire Pinochet - Un rappel à l'ordre aux tyrans, une source d'espoir pour les victims.* http://www.hrw.org/campaigns/chile98/ precedent_french.htm

11. King-Irani, L, *On Learning Lessons: Belgium' Universal Jurisdiction Under Threat,* International Justice, Common dreams, June 25, 2003 http://www.globalpolicy.org/intljustice/ universal/2003/0626gut.htm

12. Ladish, V., Liberian *President Indicted for War Crimes,* War Crimes Project, 16 June 2003. http://www.crimesofwar.org/

—Argentine *Military Officer Extraditated To Spain On Genocide Charges,* Crimes of War Project, 10 July 2003. http://www.crimesofwar.org/ onnews/ news-argentina.html

13. Lobe, J., *Attorney-General Attacks Key Law, International Justice,* Inter Press Service News Agency, May 15, 2003. http://www.globalpolicy.org/ intljustice/atca/2003/ 0515AshcroftATCA.htm

14. McKinney, C., *Accusations, Crimes Against Humanity, Letter of August 31, 1999 to President Clinton regarding Uganda/Rwanda military aggression in Congo (DRC).* http://www.c-df.org/ plaintes/mckinney.html

15. NCN 2000, *The Democratic Republic of Congo: The Lusaka Peace Accords and Beyond.* The public hearings of the Subcommittee on Africa, Committee on International Relations, US House of Representatives, Washington, DC. September 28, 1999. *Testimony of Mwabilu L.Ngoyi assisted by DR. Kanyand Matand.* wysigwyg:/255/http://www.marekinc.com/ NCNLegislate092806.html

—*Uganda and Rwanda, two serious American policy failures, November 09, 2001.*

—*Genocide in Central Africa,* White House briefing on the Interhamwe and the situation in the DR Congo, presented in the Washington foreign press center by Pierre Prosper, State Department Ambassador-at-large for War Crimes, on August 6, 2002. www.marekinc.com/LooAds.html

16. OAU Convention on the Prevention and Combating of Terrorism, 1999, Adopted at Algiers on 14 July 1999. Entry into force in accordance

with Article 20. http://untreaty.un.org/English/Terrorism/oau_e.pdf

17. *Organisation des Nations Unies, Mission de la République Démocratique du Congo, 53ième Session de l'Assemblée Générale de l'Organisation des Nations-Unies*, New York, September 23, 1998. Speech of His Excellence Jean-Charles Okito, Minister of Foreign Affairs of the Democratic Republic of Congo.—Organizations des Nations Unies, Mission de la République Démocratique du Congo. Great Lakes Policy Forum, Washington D.C., *Rwanda and Uganda Aggression Against the Democratic Republic of Congo*. http://rdcongo.org/frames/ acp/UN_RDC03.html

18. *Preparatory Commission for the International Criminal Court, Working Group on the Crime of Aggression*. New York, 16-26 February 1999, 26 July-13 August 1999, 29 November-17 December, 1999. *Discussion paper proposed by the Coordinator. Consolidated text of proposals of the Crime of Aggression*, 9 December 1999

19. Rogers, A.P.V., Command Responsibility Under the Law of War. http://www.law.cam.ac.uk/rcil/COMDRESP.doc

20. Rome Statute of the International Criminal Court. *Adopted by the United Nations Diplomatic Conference of Plenipotentiaries on the Establishment of an International Criminal Court on 17 July 1998.*

21. Slaugther, Anne-Marie, and Bosco, David L., *Alternative Justice, Crimes of War*, International Justice, Global Policy Forum, New York. http://www.globalpolicy.org/intljustice/ atca/2001/altjust.htm

22. Schmitt, Michael N., *The Law of Belligerent Occupation*, Crimes War Project, April 15, 2003. http://www.crimesofwar.org/

23. The African Renaissance: Statement of Deputy President Thabo Mbeki http://www.anc.org.za/ancdocs/history/mbeki/1998/tm0813.htm

24. *The Universal Declaration of Human Rights* http://www.un.org/Overview/rights.html

25. *Torture Victim Protection Act of 1991,* H.R. 2092, approved March 12, Public Law No. 102 – 256, *Equipo* Nizkor & Derec hos Human Rights, 9 November 2002. http://www.derechos.org/nizkor/econ/TVPA.html

26. *United Nations Charter.* http://www.un.org/aboutun/charter/

27. Weston, Burns H., *Human Rights. International human rights: prescription and enforcement. Human Rights in the United Nations* (from the Encyclopedia Britannica). http://www.uiowa.edu/~hr98/resources/basics/weston4.html

—Global Focus: Human Rights '98. Human Rights, from the encyclopedia Britannica. Definition of Human Rights. http://www.uiowa.edu/

~hr98/resources/basics/weston2.html

V. Law Journals

1. Akhavan, Payam, *Behond Impunity: Can International Criminal Justice Prevent Future Atrocities?*, American Journal of International Law, Vol. 95:7, 2001.

2.Mortensen, Ronald W., *Civic Leaders and the Rule of Law*, Sutherland Journal of Law and Public Policy, the Sutherland Institute, Salt Lake City, Utah, July 15, 2004.

3. Widner, Jennifer, *Courts and Democracy in Postconflict Transitions: A Social Scientist's Perspective on the African Case*, Vol. 95:64, 2001.

VI. American Society of International Law

1. Kirgis, Frederick L., *The Indictment in Senegal of the Former Chad Head of State*, ASIL Insights, February 2000. wysiwyg://113/http:// www.asil.org/insights/insigh41.htm

2. Ratner, Steven R. and Slaughter, Anne-Marie, American Journal of International Law, Vol. 93 ~ April 1999 ~ No.2, *Symposium on Method in Internationla Law, Introduction, Appraising the Methods of International Law: A Prospectus for Readers.* wysiwyg://129/http:// www.asil.org/ajil/ symposm1.htm

3. Wedgwood, Ruth and Jacobson, Harold K., *Symposium: State Reconstruction after Civil Conflict*, Foreword, from Vol. 95, January 2001, American Journal of International Law. wysiwyg://98/http:www.asil.org/ ajil/recon1.htm

VII. United Nations Security Council Resolutions

1. S/RES/1078 (1996) 9 November 1996.
2. S/RES/1097 (1997)18 February 1997.
3. S/Res./1234 of 9 April 1999.
4. S/Re./1258 of 6 August 1999.
5. S/Res./1273 of 5 November 1999.
6. S/Res./1279 of 30 November 1999.
7. S/Res./1291 of 24 February 2000.
8. S/Res./1304 of 16 June 2000.
9. S/Res./1316 of 23 August 2000.
10. S/Res./1318 of 7 September 2000.
11. S/Res./1323 of 13 October 2000.

12. S/Res./1332 of 14 December 2000.
13. S/Res./1341 of 22 February 2001.
14. S/Res./1355 of 15 June 2001.
15. S/Res./1376 of 9 November 2001.
16. S/Res./1399 of 19 March 2002.
17. S/Res./1417 of 14 June 2002.
18. S/Res./1445 of 4 December 2002.
19. S/Res./1457 of 24 January 2003.
20. S/Res./1468 of 20 March 2003.
21. S/Res./1484 of 30 May 2003.
22. S/Res./1489 of 26 June 2003.
23. S/Res./1493 of 28 July 2003.
24. S/Res./1499 of 13 August 2003.
25. S/Res./1501 of 26 August 2003.

VIII. United Nations Security Council Presidential Statements

1. S/PRST/1998/26 of 31 August 1998.
2. S/PRST/1998/36 of 11 December 1998.
3. S/PRST/1999/17 of 24 June 1999.
4. S/PRST/2000/2 of 26 January 2000.
5. S/PRST/2000/15 of 5 May 2000.
6. S/PRST/2000/20 of 2 June 2000.
7. S/PRST/2000/28 of 7 September 2000.
8. S/PRST/2001/13 of 3 May 2001.
9. S/PRST/2001/19 of 24 July 2001.
10. S/PRST/2001/22 of 5 September 2001.
11. S/PRST/2001/29 of 24 October 2001.
12. S/PRST/2001/39 of 19 Decemebr 2001.
13. S/PRST/2002/5 of 25 February 2002.
14. S/PRST/2002/17 of 24 May 2002.
15. S/PRST/2002/19 of 5 June 2002.
16. S/PRST/2002/22 of 23 July 2002.
17. S/PRST/2002/24 of 15 August 2002.
18. S/PRST/2002/27 of 18 October 2002.

IX. United Nations Security Council Document

1. S/1999/815, Ceasefire Agreement Relating to the Democratic Republic of Congo.

X. Magazines

1. Contra Costa Times.com, Editorials, *Africa's forgotten war*, May 05, 2003

2. Michaels, Marguerite, *The Bleeding Heart of Africa*, Time Magazine, March 15, 1999.

3. Ray, Ellen, *US Military and Corporate Recolonization of the Congo,* CovertAction Quarterly Spring-Summer 2000 #9. http://www.covertaction.org

4. Wilkins, R.G., *Bias, Error, And Duplicity. The UN and the Domestic Law*, The World and I Magazine, Volume 11, Issue 12, December 1996.

XI. Newspapers

1. La Référence Plus, November 12, 1998.
2. Las Cruces Sun – News, July 14, 2003.
3. Le Palmares #1665, October 20, 1999.
4. The Star, Thursday, September 19, 2002 Edition.
5. The Star, Friday, September 20, 2002 Edition.
6. Sunday Times, Letters, September 8, 2002 Edition.
7. Sunday Times, September 15, 2002 Edition.

XII. Other Online Resources

1. Agence France Press, *Rwanda To Resurrect Traditional Justice System*, International Justice, 17 June 2002. http://www.globalpolicy.org/intljustice/general/2002/0617ga.htm

2. *Amnesty International Annual Report 2000*, Rwanda http://web.amnesty.org/web/ar2000web.nsf/countries/7d4208bcf86ce147802568f200552963?OpenDocument

—*2001 Annual Report, Rwanda* http://web.amnesty.org/web/ar2001.nsf/webafrcountries/ RWANDA?OpenDocument

3. Braeckman, Colette, *Politique. Jean-Charles Magabe, Sur la situation qui prévaut dans la province controleé par la rébellion et les sentiments de la population* . . . In Congonline (Le Soir-31/10/98). http://www.congonline.com/Actualite_Politique/Octobre98/Les12.html

4. Bruno, Kenny, *De-Globazing Justice, The Corporate Campaign To Strip Foreign Victims of Corporate Induced in Human Rights Violations of the Right To Sue in US Courts*, Social/Economic Policy, Multinational Monitor, March 2003. http://www.globalpolicy.org/ socecon/tncs/2003/03justice.htm

5. Congonline, *Politique. Compte rendu de la Tripartite de Lubumbashi*

fait par le Président Mugabe. http://congonline.com/Actualite_Politique/Novembre98/ACP01.html

6. Congonline, *Politic. J.R. Boulle: ce chasseur de trésor qui en veut à Kabila. Les dessous des cartes de l' aggression rwando-ougandaise.* http://www.congonline.com/ Actualite_Politique/Octobre98/Potentiel09.html

7. Congonline, Politique. *Solution à la guerre en RDC. Me Kamanda exhorte les Congolais à un ressaisissement.* (La Référence Plus - 12/11/98). http://www.congoline.com/ Actualite_Politique/November98/Refer45.html

8. CNN, *Report: Rwanda genocide could have been prevented.* http://www.cnn.com/WORLD/ africa/9903/31/rwanda01/index

9. Fideri, Kirungi F., DR Congo: Who is Museveni kidding? African News Online. The Monitor - Kampala. http://www.africanews.org/central/c...inshsa/stories/19981010_feat1.html

10. Frankel, Glenn, *Belgium War Crimes Law Undione by Its Global Reach*, International Justice, Washington Post, September 30, 2003. http://www.globalpolicy.org/intljustice/universal/ 2003/0930univjstop.htm

11. *Global Focus: Human Rights* '98. htpp://www.uiowa.edu/~hr98/resources/basics/ weston2.html

12. Human Rights Watch, United Nations Asks Senegal To Hold Ex-Chad Dictator. Victory for Hiss ne Habr 's Victims, April 23, 2001. http://www.hrw.org/press/2001/04/ habrecat0423.htm

13. HUMAN RIGHTS WORLD REPORT 1999, *The Democratic Republic of Congo. The Role of the International Community* htpp://www.hrw.org/hrw/worlDReport99/africa/DRc3.html

—*Rwanda. Human Rights Developments* http://www.hrw.org/hrw/worlDReport99/africa/ rwanda.html

—*Rwanda. Defending Human Rights.* htt://www.hrw.org/hrw/worlDReport99/ africa/rwanda2.html *Uganda Human Rights Developments.* htt://www.hrw.org/hrw/ worlDReport99/africa/uganda.html

—*Uganda Human Rights Developments*, World Reports 2000. http://www.hrw.org/wr2k/Africa-12.htm#TopOfPage

—U*ganda Humna Rights Developments*, World Reports 2003. http://www.hrw.org/wr2k3/africa13.html

14. IRIN, *Democratic Republic of Congo: Bleak picture of life along ceasefire line.* http://www.reliefweb.int/IRIN/cea/countrystories/DRc/19991011.html

—*Democratic Republic of Congo. Government alleges UN inaction.* http://www.reliefweb.int/IRIN/cea/countrystories/ DRc/19991019.html

—*Democratic Republic of Congo: 6,000 deaths in war's first year.* http://www.reliefweb.int/IRIN/cea/countrystories/DRc/19991104.html

15. *Justice & The Generals, US- Law, Background* http://www.pbs.org/wnet/justice/ law_background_torture3.html

16. Kante, Flory, *Le Palmares Politique. Paul Kagame s'accroche aux diamants de la RDC: 20.000 soldats Rwandais largués dans notre pays!* Le Palmares no 1665, p.8, 20/10/1999.

17. La Reference Plus, Politique, *Des soldats tutsi pillent l'archidiocèse de Bukavu et emportent USD 120.000 à Kigali. Des libérateurs pillards.* htpp://www.congonline.com/ Actualite_Politique/Octobre98? Refer33.html

—*Des rwandophones occupaient des postes de d cision importants dans le régime Kabila: en voici la preuve.* htpp://www.congonline.com/ Actualite_Politique/Octobre

—*Autour de l'Aveu de Paul Kagame: cynisme politique ou perversion de l'esprit?* (Visited Nov. 16, 1998) htpp://www.congonline.com/ Actualite_Politique/Novembre98/Refer47.html

18. Leopold, Evelyn, *UN criticizes itself on keeping peace in Africa* http://biz.yahoo.com/rf/991215/bjl.html

19. Le Potentiel, Politique, *J.R. Boulle: ce chasseur de trésor qui en veut à Kabila, Les dessous des cartes de l'aggression rwando-ougandaise.* htpp://www.congonline.com/ Actualite_Politique/Octobre98/Potentiel109.html

20. Le Soir, Politique, *Jean-Charles Magabe.* htpp://www.congonline.com/ Actualite_Politique/Octobre98/Les12.html

21. Mutond, Kamanga, *Congo Imposes Curfew Amid Gunfire.* http://search.washingtonpost.com/wp-srv/WAPO/19980803/V000370-080398-idx.html

22. NCN 2000, *UN says Tutsi community face imminent threat in DRC.* http://www.marekinc.com/Letters122502.html

—*Holbroke should not have gone to Africa.* http://www.marekinc.com/NCNEditornotesREG121001.html *The American political elite has been misled by faulty analysis regarding the Congo*, June 27, 2002.

—*The rape of the Congo, blame the victim, and the rapist walks*, November 27, 2001.

23. Pepper, William F., *The End of Sovereign Immunity in Cases involving Human Rights Crimes of States, their Leaders and Officials*, Oxford, 23June 2001. http://tihrs.org/resources/online/wfp2001.html

24. Raphael, Alison, *Apartheid Victims Sue Global Corporations*, Social/Economic Policy, OneWorldUS, November 13, 2002. http://

www.globalpolicy.org/socecon/tncs/ 2002/1113apartheid.htm

25. Rayner, Moira, *History of human rights. History of Universal Human Rights - Up to WW2*, http://www.universalrights.net/main/histof.html.

26. Specter, Arlen, *The Court of Last Resort, International Justice*, New York Times, 7 August 2003. http://www.globalpolicy.org/intljustice/atca/2003/0807specter.htm

27. UDHR, *History of human rights, world influence of the UDHR*. htpp://www.universalrights.net/main/world.html

28. *US Commander Franks Faces Belgium "Genocide Case,"* International Justice, Expatica, April 18, 2003. http://www.globalpolicy.org/intljustice/general/2003/0418franks.htm

Annexures

A. CEASE-FIRE AGREEMENT RELATING TO THE DEMOCRATIC REPUBLIC OF CONGO

UNITED
NATIONS S

Security Council
Dist. General
S/1999/815
23 July, 1999

LETTER DATED 23 JULY, 1999 FROM THE PERMANENT REPRESENTATIVE OF ZAMBIA TO THE UNITED NATIONS ADDRESSED TO THE PRESIDENT OF THE SECURITY COUNCIL

At the request of my Government, I have the honor to forward to you herewith the Cease-fire Agreement together with its annexures on the Democratic Republic of the Congo, signed by regional leaders at Lusaka, Zambia, on 10 July, 1999.

I should be grateful if you would bring the contents of this letter and the abovementioned Cease-fire Agreement to the attention of the members of the Security Council. Further, it would be appreciated if you would circulate the agreement as a document of the Security Council.

(Signed) Peter L. Kasanda
Ambassador Extraordinary and plenipotentiary
Permanent representative of Zambia
to the United Nations

Annex

CEASE-FIRE AGREEMENT

PREAMBLE

We the Parties to this Agreement;

CONSIDERING Article 52 of the UN Charter on regional arrangements for dealing with matters relating to the maintenance of international peace and security as are appropriate for regional action;

REAFFIRMING the provisions of Article 3 of the OAU Charter which, inter alia, guarantee all Member states the right to their sovereignty and territorial integrity;

REAFFIRMING further resolution AHG/16/1 adopted by the AOU Assembly of heads of states and Government in 1964 in Cairo, Egypt, on territorial integrity and the inviolability of national boundaries as inherited at independence.;

RECALLING the Pretoria Summit Communique dated 23rd August, 1998 re-affirming that all ethnic groups and nationalities whose people and territory constituted what became Congo (now DRC) independence must enjoy equal rights and protection under the law as citizens.;

DETERMINED to ensure the respect, by all Parties signatory to this Agreement, for the Geneva conventions of 1949 and the additional Protocols of 1977, and the Convention on the Prevention and Punishment of the Crime of Genocide of 1948, as reiterated at the Entebbe Regional summit of 25 March, 1998;

DETERMINED further to put to an immediate half to any assistance collaboration or giving of sanctuary to negative forces bent on destabilizing a neighboring country;

EMPHASIZING the need to ensure that the principles of good neighborliness and non-interference in the internal affairs of other countries are respected;

CONCERNED about the conflict in the Democratic Republic of Congo and its negative impact on the country and other countries in the Great Lakes region;

REITERATING the call made at the second Victoria Falls Summit held from 7 to 8 September 1998, as contained in the joint Communiqué of the Summit, for the immediate cessation of hostilities;

COGNIZANT of the fact that addressing the security concerns of the DRC and neighboring countries is central and would contribute to the peace process;

RECALLING the mandate, contained in the Victoria Falls II joint Communiqué, given to the Ministers of Defenses and other officials working in close cooperation with the OAU and the UN to establish the modalities for effecting an immediate cease-fire and put in place a mechanism for monitoring compliance with the cease-fire provisions;

RECALLING the United Nations Security Council Resolution 1234 of 9 April, 1999 and all other Resolutions and Decisions on the DRC since 2 August, 1998;

RECALLING further the summit meeting of Victoria Falls I and II, Pretoria, Durban, Port Louis, Nairobi, Windhoek, Dodoma, and the Lusaka and Gabon Ministerial peace efforts on the DRC conflict;

RECALLING further the peace Agreement signed on 18 April, 1999 at sirte (Libya);

RECOGNIZING that the conflict in the DRC has both internal and external dimensions that require intra-Congolese political negotiations and commitment of the Parties to the implementation of this Agreement to resolve;

TAKING note of the commitment of the Congolese Government, the RDC, the MLC, and all other Congolese political and civil organizations to hold an all-inclusive National Dialogue aimed at realizing national reconciliation and a new political dispensation in the DRC;

HEREBY AGREE AS FOLLOWS:

ARTICLE I
THE CEASE-FIRE

1. The Parties agree to a cease-fire among all their forces in the DRC.
2. The cease-fire shall mean:

a. the cessation of hostilities between all the belligerent forces in the DRC, as provided for in this Cease-fire Agreement (hereinafter referred as "the Agreement");

b. the effective cessation of hostilities, military movements, and reinforcements, as well as hostile actions, including hostile propaganda;

c. a cessation of hostilities within 24 hours of the signing of the Cease-fire Agreement;

3. The Cease-fire shall entail the cessation of:

a. all air, land, and sea attacks as well as all actions of the of sabotage;

b. attempt to occupy new ground positions and the movement of military forces and resources from one area to another, without prior agreement between the partries;

c. all acts of violence against the civilian population by respecting and protecting human rights. The acts of violence include summary executions, torture, harassment, detention, and execution of civilians based on their ethnic origin: propaganda inciting ethnic and tribal hatred; arming civilians; recruitment and use of child soldiers; sexual; violence, training and use of terrorists; massacres, downing of civilian aircraft; and bombing the civilian population;

d. supplies of ammunition and weaponry and other war-related stores to the field;

e. any other actions that may impede the normal evolution of the cease-fire process.

ARTICLE II
SECURITY CONCERNS

4. On the coming into force of this Agreement the Parties commit

themselves to immediately address the security concerns of the DRC and her neighboring countries.

ARTICLE III
PRINCIPLES OF THE AGREEMENT

5. The provisions of paragraph 3(e) do not preclude the supply of food, clothing, and medical support for the military forces in the field.

6. The Cease-fire shall guarantee the free movement of persons and goods throughout the national territory of the Democratic Republic of Congo.

7. On the coming into force of the Agreement, the Parties shall release persons detained or taken hostage and shall give them the latitude to relocate to any provinces within the DRC or country where their security will be guaranteed.

8. The Parties to the Agreement commit themselves to exchange prisoners of war and release any other persons detained as a result of the war.

9. The Parties shall allow immediate and unhindered access to the International Committee of the Red Cross (ICRC) and Red Crescent for the purpose of arranging the release of prisoners of war and other persons detained as a result of the war as well as the recovery of the dead and the treatment of the wounded.

10. The Parties shall facilitate humanitarian assistance through the opening up of humanitarian corridors and creation of conditions conductive to the provision of urgent humanitarian assistance to displaced persons, refugees, and other affected persons.

11.a. The United Nations Security Council, acting under Chapter VII of the UN Charter and in collaboration with the OAU, shall be requested to constitute, facilitate, and deploy an appropriate peacekeeping force in DRC to ensure implementation of this Agreement; and taking into account the peculiar situation of the RDC, mandate the peacekeeping force to track down all armed groups in the RDC. In this respect, the UN Security Council shall provide the requisite mandate for the peace-keeping force.

b. The Parties shall constitute a joint Military commission (JMC) which shall together with the UN/AU Observer group be responsible for executing immediately after the coming into force of this Agreement, peace-keeping operation until the deployment of the UN peace-keeping force. Its composition and mandate shall be as stipulated in Chapter 7 of Annex “A” of this Agreement.

12. The final withdrawal of all foreign forces from the national territory of the DRC shall be carried out in accordance with the calendar of Annex "B" of the Agreement and a withdrawal schedule to be prepared by the UN, the OAU, and the JMC.

13. The laying of mines of whatever type shall be prohibited.

14. There shall be immediate disengagement of forces in the areas where they are in direct contact.

15. Nothing in the Agreement shall in any way undermine the sovereignty and territorial integrity of the Democratic Republic of Congo.

16. The Parties re-affirm that all ethnic groups and nationalities whose people and territory constituted what became Congo (now DRC) at independence must enjoy equal rights and protection under the law as citizens.

17. The Parties to the Agreement shall take all necessary measures aimed at securing the information of the situation along the international borders of the Democratic Republic of Congo, including the control of illicit trafficking of arms and the infiltration of armed groups.

18. In accordance with the terms of the Agreement and upon conclusion of the Inter-Congolese political negotiations, state administration shall be re-established throughout the national territory of the Democratic Republic of Congo.

19. On the coming into force of the Agreement, the Government of the DRC, the armed opposition, namely, the RCD and MLC, as well as the unarmed opposition shall enter into an open national dialogue. These inter-Congolese political negotiations involving *les forces vives* shall lead to a new dispensation and national reconciliation in the DRC. The inter-Congolese political negotiations shall be under the aegis of a neutral facilitator to be agreed upon by the Congolese parties. All the Parties commit themselves to supporting this dialogue and shall ensure that the Inter-Congolese political negotiations are conducted in accordance with the provisions of Chapter 5 of Annex "A."

20. In accordance with the terms of the Agreement and upon the conclusion of the national dialogue, there shall be a mechanism for the formation of national, restructured, and integrated army, including the forces of the Congolese parties who are signatories to this Agreement, on the basis of negotiations between the Government of the Democratic Republic of Congo and the RCD and MLC.

21. The Parties affirm the need to address the security concerns of the DRC and her neighboring countries.

22. There shall be a mechanism for disarming militias and armed groups, including the genocidal forces. In this context, all Parties commit themselves to the process of locating, identifying, disarming, and assembling all members of armed groups, in DRC. Countries of origin of members of the armed groups commit themselves to taking all the necessary measures to facilitate their repatriation. Such measures may include the granting of amnesty in countries where such a measure has been deemed beneficial. It shall, however, not apply in the case of suspects of the crimes of genocide. The parties assume full responsibility of the ensuring that armed groups operating alongside their troops or the territory under their control comply with the processes leading to the dismantling of those groups in particular.

23. The Parties shall ensure the implementation of terms of the Agreement and its Annex "A" and "B," which form an integral part of the Agreement.

24. The definitions of common terms used are at Annex "C."

25. The Agreement shall take effect 24 hours after signature.

26. The Agreement may be amended by agreement of the Parties and any such amendment shall be in writing and shall be signed by them in the same way as the Agreement.

IN WITNESS WHEREOF the duly authorized representatives of the Parties have signed the Agreement in the English, French and Portuguese languages, all texts being equally authentic.

DONE AT LUSAKA (ZAMBIA) ON THIS ......DAY OF..................

[Signature]

....

FOR THE REPUBLIC OF ANGOLA

[Signature]

....

FOR THE DEMOCRATIC REPUBLIC OF CONGO

[Signature]

....

FOR THE REPUBLIC OF NAMIBIA

[Signature]

....

FOR THE REPUBLIC OF RWANDA

[Signature]

....

FOR THE REPUBLIC OF UGANDA

[Signature]

....

FOR THE REPUBLIC OF ZIMBABWE

AS WITNESSES:

[Signature]

....

FOR THE REPUBLIC OF ZAMBIA

[Signature]

....

FOR THE ORGANIZATION OF AFRICAN UNITY

[Signature]

....

FOR THE UNITED NATIONS

[Signature]

....

FOR THE SOUTHERN AFRICAN DEVELOPMENT COMMUNITY

Enclosure I

ANNEX "A" TO THE CEASE-FIRE AGREEMENT

MODALITIES FOR THE IMPLEMENTATION OF THE CEASE-FIRE AGREEMENT IN THE DEMOCRATIC REPUBLIC OF CONGO

CHAPTER I

CESSATION OF HOSTILITIES

1.1. The Parties shall announce a cessation of hostilities, to be effective 24 hours after the signing of the Cease-fire Agreement. The announcement of cessation of hostilities shall be disseminated by the parties through command channels, and it shall concurrently be communicated to the civil population via print and electronic media.

1.2. Until the deployment of United Nations/Organization of African Unity (UN/OAU) Observers, the cessation of hostilities shall be regulated and monitored by the Parties through the joint Military Commission. With the deployment of UN/ONU observers, the responsibility of verification, control, and monitoring of the cessation of hostilities and subsequent disengagement shall be reported through UN/OAU.

1.3. Any violation of the cessation of hostilities and subsequent events shall be reported to the joint Military Commission and to the UN/OAU mechanisms through the agreed chain of command for investigation as necessary.

CHAPTER 2.

DISENGAGEMENT

2.1. The disengagement of forces shall mean the immediate breaking of tactical contact between the opposing Military Forces of the Parties to this Agreement at places where they are in direct contact by the effective date and time of the Cease-fire Agreement.

2.2. Where immediate disengagement is not possible, a framework and sequence of disengagement is to be agreed by all Parties through the joint Military Commission/UN and OAU.

2.3. Immediate disengagement at the initiative of all military units shall be limited to the effective range of direct fire weapons. Further disengagement to pull all weapons out of range, shall be conducted under the guidance of joint Military Commission/UN and OAU.

2.4. The joint Military Commission/UN and OAU shall design wherever disengagement by movement is impossible or impractical, alternative solutions requiring that weapons are rendered safe.

CHAPTER 3

RELEASE OF HOSTAGES AND EXCHANGE OF PRISONERS OF WAR

3.1. Upon the Cease-fire taking effect, all Parties shall provide ICRC/ Red Crescent with relevant information concerning their prisoners of war or persons detained because of the war. They shall subsequently accord every assistance to the ICRC/Red Crescent representatives to enable them to visit the prisoners and detainees and verify any details and ascertain their condition and status.

3.2. On the coming into force of the Agreement, the Parties shall release persons detained because of war or taken hostage, within three days of the signing of the Cease-fire Agreement and the ICRC/Red Crescent shall give them all the necessary assistance including relocation to any provinces within the DRC or any other country where their security will be guaranteed.

CHAPTER 4

ORDERLY WITHDRAWAL OF ALL FOREIGN FORCES

4.1. The final orderly withdrawal of all foreign forces from the national territory of the Democratic Republic of Congo shall be in accordance with Annex "B" of this Agreement.

4.2. The joint Military Commission/OAU and UN shall draw up a definitive schedule for the orderly withdrawal of all foreign forces from the Democratic Republic of Congo.

CHAPTER 5

NATIONAL DIALOGUE AND RECONCILIATION

5.1. On the coming into forces of the Cease-fire Agreement in the DRC, the Parties agree to do their utmost to facilitate the inter-Congolese political negotiations, which should lead to a new political dispensation in the Democratic Republic of Congo.

5.2. In order to arrive at a new political dispensation and national reconciliation arising from inter-Congolese political Negotiations, the Parties agree upon the implementation of the following principles:

a. the inter-Congolese political negotiations process shall include, besides the Congolese parties, namely the Government of the Democratic Republic of Congo, the Congolese Rally for Democracy, and the Movement for the Liberation of Congo, the political opposition as well as representatives of the *forces vives*;

b. all the participants in the inter-Congolese political negotiations shall enjoy equal status;

c. all the resolutions adopted by the inter-Congolese political negotiations shall be binding on all the participants.

5.3. The Parties agree that the Organization of African Unity shall assist the Democratic Republic of Congo in organizing the inter-Congolese political negotiations under the aegis of a neutral facilitator chosen by the Parties by the virtue of his/her moral authority, his/her international credibility, and his/her experience.

5.4. For the success of the all-inclusive inter-Congolese political negotiations leading to national reconciliation, the facilitator shall be responsible for:

a. making the necessary contacts pertaining to the organizations of the inter-Congolese political negotiations within an environment, which will cater to the security of all participants;

b. organizing, in conjunction with the Congolese parties, consultations with a view to inviting all the major organizations and groups of the recognized representative, political opposition as well as the main representatives of the *forces vives*;

c. conducting, in accordance with the timetable, the discussions leading to the establishment of new political dispensation in the Democratic Republic of Congo.

5.5. Without prejudice to other points that may be raised by the participants, the Congolese Parties shall agree:

a. the timetable and the rules of procedure of the inter-Congolese political negotiations;

b. the formation of a new Congolese National army whose soldiers shall originate from the Congolese Armed Forces, the armed forces of the RCD, and the armed forces of the MLC;

c. the new political dispensation in the DRC, in particular the institutions to be established for good governance purposes in the DRC;

d. the process of free, democratic, and transparent elections in the RDC;

e. the Draft of the Constitution which shall govern the DRC after the holding of the elections.

5.6. The calendar of the inter-Congolese political negotiations shall be as follows:

i. Selection of a facilitator: D-Day +15 days
ii. Beginning of national dialogue: D-Day +45 days
iii. Deadline for the close of national dialogue: D-Day +90 days
iv. Establishing of new institutions: D-Day +91 days

CHAPTER 6

RE-ESTABLISHMENT OF THE STATE ADMINISTRATION OVER THE TERRITORY OF THE DEMOCRATIC REPUBLIC OF CONGO

6.1. In accordance with the terms of the Agreement and upon conclusion of the Inter-Congolese political negotiations, state administration shall be re-established throughout the national territory of the Democratic Republic of Congo.

6.2. On the coming into force of the Agreement, there shall be a consultative mechanism among the Congolese parties which shall make it possible to carry out operations or organizations or actions throughout the national territory which are of general interest, more particularly in the fields of public health (e.g. national immunization campaign), education (e.g. marking of secondary school leavers' examinations), migrations, movement of persons and goods.

CHAPTER 7

THE JOINT MILITARY COMMISSION

7.1. The joint Military Commission shall be answerable to a political committee composed of the Minister of Foreign Affairs and Defense or any other representative duly appointed by each Party.

7.2. The Joint Military Commission shall be a decision making body composed of two representatives from each Party under a neutral Chairman appointed by the OAU in consultation with the Parties.

7.3. The joint Military Commission shall reach its decisions by consensus.

7.4. The mandate of the Joint Military Commission shall be to:

a. establish the location of Units at the time of the Cease-fire;

b. facilitate liaison between the Parties for the purpose of the Cease-fire;

c. assist in the disengagement of forces and the investigation of any cease-fire violations;

d. verify all information, data, and activities relating to military forces of the Parties;

e. verify the disengagement of the military forces of the Parties where they are in direct contact;

f. work out mechanisms for disarming armed groups;

g. verify the disarmament and quartering of all armed groups;

h. verify the disarmament of all Congolese civilians who are illegally armed;

i. monitor and verify orderly withdrawal of all foreign forces.

7.5. The Parties commit themselves to providing the JMC with any relevant information on the organization, equipment, and locations of their forces, on the understanding that such information will be kept confidential.

CHAPTER 8

UNITED NATIONS PEACE-KEEPING MANDATE

8.1. The UN in collaboration with the OAU shall constitute, facilitate, and deploy an appropriate force in the DRC to ensure implementation of this Agreement.

8.2. The mandate of the UN force shall include peacekeeping and peace enforcement operations as outlined below:

8.2.1. Peacekeeping:

a. work with the JMC/OAU in the implementation of this Agreement;

b. observe and monitor the cessation of hostilities;

c. investigate violations of the Cease-fire Agreement and take necessary measures to ensure compliance;

d. supervise disengagement of forces of the Parties as stipulated in chapter 2 of this Annex;

e. supervise the re-deployment of forces of the Parties to Defensive Positions in conflict zones in accordance with Chapter 11 of this Agreement;

f. provide and maintain humanitarian assistance to and protect displaced persons, refugees, and other affected persons;

g. Keep the Parties to the Cease-fire Agreement informed of its peace-keeping operations;

h. Collect weapons from civilians and ensure that the weapons so collected are properly accounted for and adequately secured;

i. In collaboration with JMC/OAU, schedule and supervise the withdrawal of all foreign forces;

j. verify all information, data, and activities relating to military forces of the Parties.

8.2.2. Peace Enforcement:

a. tracking down and disarming Armed Groups;

b. screening mass killers, perpetrators of crimes against humanity, and other war criminals;

c. handing over "genocidaires" to the International Crimes Tribunal for Rwanda;

d. repatriation;

e. working out such measures (persuasive or coercive) as are appropriate for the attainment of the objectives of disarming, assembling, repatriation, and reintegration into society of members of the Armed Groups.

8.3. Composition of the UN Peace-keeping forces shall be selected from countries acceptable to all the Parties.

8.4. The Joint Military Commission shall, immediately upon the coming into force of the Agreement, be responsible for executing peace-keeping operations until the deployment of the UN Peace-keeping force.

CHAPTER 9

DISARMAMENT OF ARMED GROUPS

9.1. The JMC with the assistance of the UN/OAU shall work out mechanisms for the tracking, disarming, cantoning, and documenting of all armed groups in the DRC, including ex-FAR, ADF, LRA, UNRF11, *Interhamwe*, FUNA, FDD, WNBF, UNITA, and put in place measures for:

a. handing over to the UN International Tribunal and national courts, mass killers and perpetrators of crimes against humanity; and

b. handling of other war criminals.

9.2. The Parties together with the UN and other countries with security concerns, shall create conditions conducive to the attainment of the objective set out in 9.1 above, conditions which may include the granting of amnesty and political asylum, except for genocidaires. The Parties shall also encourage inter-community dialogue.

CHAPTER 10

FORMATION OF A NATIONAL ARMY

10.1 In accordance with the terms of the Agreement and following the inter-Congolese political negotiations, there shall be a mechanism taking into account, among others, the physical check of troops, the precise identification of troops, the precise identification of all elements with regard to their origin, date of their enlistment, the units to which they belong, as well as the identification of terrorists and the count of weapons of war distributed in the framework of irregular ("parallel") civil defence groups, for the formation of a national army, restructured and integrated, including the forces of the Congolese Parties signatories to the Agreement, on the basis of negotiations between the Government of the Democratic Republic of Congo, the Congolese Rally for Democracy, and the Movement for the Liberation of the Congo.

CHAPTER 11

RE-DEPLOYMENT OF FORCES OF THE PARTIES TO DEFENSIVE POSITIONS IN CONFLICT ZONES

11.1. Following disengagement, all forces shall re-deploy to defensive positions.

11.2. The positions where units are located shall be identified and recorded by the JMC/OAU and UN.

11.3. Upon re-deployment to defensive positions, all forces shall provide relevant information on troop strength, armaments, and weapons they hold in each location, to the JMC, OAU, and UN mechanisms.

11.4. The JMC shall verify the reported data and information. All forces shall be restricted to the declared and recorded locations and all movements shall be authorized by the JMC, OAU, and UN mechanisms. All forces shall remain in the declared and recorded locations until:

a. in the case of foreign forces, withdrawal has started in accordance with JMC/OAU, UN withdrawal schedule; and

b. in the case of FAC and RCD/MLC forces, in accordance with their negotiated agreement.

CHAPTER 12

NORMALIZATION OF THE SECURITY SITUATION ALONG THE COMMON BORDERS BETWEEN THE DEMOCRATIC REPUBLIC OF CONGO AND ITS NEIGHBORS

12.1. Normalization of the security situation along the common borders between the Democratic Republic of Congo and its neighbors requires each country:

a. Not to arm, train, harbor on its territory, or render any form of support to subversive elements or armed opposition movements for the purpose of destabilizing the others;

b. To report all strange or hostile movements detected by either country along the common borders;

c. To identify and evaluate border problems and cooperate in defining methods to peacefully solve them;

d. To address the problem of armed groups in the Democratic Republic of Congo in accordance with the terms of the Agreement.

CHAPTER 13

CALENDAR FOR THE IMPLEMENTATION OF THE CEASE-FIRE AGREEMENT

The Calendar for the implementation of the Cease-fire Agreement is contained in annex B.

ANNEX "B" TO CEASE-FIRE AGREEMENT: CALENDAR FOR THE IMPLEMENTATION OF THE CEASE-FIRE AGREEMENT

Cease-fire Events	Proposed Calendar
1. Formal signing of the Cease-fire	D-Day
2. Announcement of and dissemination of information on cease-fire by all Parties	D-Day + 24 hours
3. Cessation of Hostilities, including cessation of Hostile Propaganda	D-Day + 24 hours
4. Release of hostages	D-Day + 3 days
5. Establishement of Joint Military Commission and Observer Groups	D-Day + 0 hours to D-Day + 7 days
6. Disengagement of Forces	D-Day + 14 days
7. Selection of a facilitator	D-Day + 15 days
8. Redeployment of the Forces of the Parties in the conflict Zones	D-Day +15 days to D-Day + 30 days
9. Provide information to the JMC, OAU, and UN Mechanism	D-Day + 21 days
10. Mobilsation of OAU Observers	D-Day + 30 days
11. Release/Exchange of Prisoners of War	D-Day +7 days to D-Day + 30 days
12. Beginning of National Dialogue	D-Day + 45 days
13. Deadline for the closure of the National Dialogue	D-Day + 90 days
14. Establishment of New Institutions	D-Day + 91 Days
15. Deployment of UN Peace Keeping Mission	D-Day + 120 days
16. Disarmament of Armed Groups	D-Day + 30 days to D-Day + 120 days

11. Release/Exchange of Prisoners of War	D-Day +7 days to D-Day + 30 days
12. Beginning of National Dialogue	D-Day + 45 days
13. Deadline for the closure of the National Dialogue	D-Day + 90 days
14. Establishment of New Institutions	D-Day + 91 Days
15. Deployment of UN Peace-keeping Mission	D-Day + 120 days
16. Disarmament of Armed Groups	D-Day + 30 days to D-Day + 120 days
17. Orderly Withdrawal of all Foreign Forces	D-Day + 180 days
18. Verification and Monitoring	D-Day + 7 days to D-Day + 180 days (renewable)
19. Re-establishment of State Administration	D-Day + 90 days to D-Day + 270 days
20. Disarmament of Non-Military Personnel	D-Day + 360 days
21. Measures to normalize the security situation along the International borders	D-Day + 30 days to D-Day + 360 days

ANNEX "C" TO THE CEASE-FIRE AGREEMENT: DEFINITIONS

Armed groups: forces other than Government forces, RCD and MLC that are not signatories to this agreement. They include ex-FAR, AFF, LRA, UNRF II, NALU Interahamwe militias, FUNA, FDD, WNBF, UNITA, and any other forces.

Forces of the Parties: the forces of the signatories to the Agreement.

Parties: signatories to the Agreement.

Great Lakes region: the group of states within or bordering the Great Rift Valley system of East and Central Africa.

National Dialogue: the process involving all stakeholders in the inter-Congolese political negotiations with a view to installing a new political dispensation which will bring about national reconciliation and the early holding of free and fair democratic elections.

Forces vives: all the stakeholders' representatives of the civil society such as the churches, Trade Unions etc.

Cease-fire Agreement: this document and its Annexes.

Interahamwe: armed militias who carried out genocide in Rwanda in 1994.

ABBREVIATIONS

ADF	Allied Democratic Forces
Ex-FAR	Former Rwandan Armed Forces
FDD	Forces for the Defense of Democracy in Burundi
FUNA	Former Uganda National Army
LRA	Lord's Resistance Army
UNRF II	Uganda National Rescue Front II
UN	United Nations Organization
PAU	Organization of African Unity
RCD	Congolese Rally for Democracy
MLC	Movement for the Liberation of Congo
SADC	Southern Africa Development Community
DRC	Democratic Republic of Congo
JMC	Joint Military Commission
ICRC	International Committee of the Red Cross/Red Crescent
FAC	Congolese Armed Forces
WNBF	West Nile Bank Front
UNITA	National Union for the Total Independence of Angola
NALU	National Army for the Liberation of Uganda

B. THE ILLEGAL EXPLOITATION OF THE CONGOLESE NATIONAL ASSETS

Letter dated 12 April, 2001 from the Secretary-General to the President of the Security Council

I wish to refer to the presidential statement dated 2 June, 2000 (S/PRST/2000/20) in which the Security Council requested me to establish a Panel of Experts on the Illegal Exploitation of Natural Resources and Other Forms of Wealth in the Democratic Republic of the Congo for a period of six months. The Council also requested that the expert panel, once established, submit to the Council, through me, its final report at the end of the mandate.

Further to my letter dated 2 April, 2001, I have the honor to transmit to you the report of the Panel, submitted to me by the Chairperson of the Panel. I should be grateful if you would bring the report to the attention of the members of the Security Council.

(*Signed*) Kofi A. Annan

Report of the Panel of Experts on the Illegal Exploitation of Natural Resources and Other Forms of Wealth of the Democratic Republic of the Congo

CONTENTS

I. Introduction

1. By the statement of its President of 2 June, 2000 (S/PRST/2000/20), the Security Council requested the Secretary-General to establish an expert panel on the illegal exploitation of natural resources and other forms of wealth of the Democratic Republic of the Congo, for a period of six months, with the following mandate:

–To follow up on reports and collect information on all activities of illegal exploitation of natural resources and other forms of wealth of the Democratic Republic of the Congo, including in violation of the sovereignty of that country;

–To research and analyze the links between the exploitation of the natural resources and other forms of wealth in the Democratic Republic of the Congo and the continuation of the conflict;

–To revert to the Council with recommendations.

2. The Secretary-General, in his letter to the President of the Security Council dated 31 July, 2000 (S/2000/796), notified the President of the Security Council that the composition of the Panel was as follows:

Mme Safiatou Ba-N'Daw (Côte d'Ivoire) (Chairperson);
Mr. François Ekoko (Cameroon);
Mr. Mel Holt (United States of America);
Mr. Henri Maire (Switzerland);
Mr. Moustapha Tall (Senegal).

3. The Panel was assisted by a technical advisor, an associate political officer, an administrator and a secretary.

A. Summary

4. Illegal exploitation of the mineral and forest resources of the Democratic Republic of the Congo is taking place at an alarming rate. Two phases can be distinguished: mass-scale looting and the systematic and systemic exploitation of natural resources.

5. **Mass-scale looting**. During this first phase, stockpiles of minerals, coffee, wood, livestock, and money that were available in territories conquered by the armies of Burundi, Rwanda, and Uganda were taken, and

either transferred to those countries or exported to international markets by their forces and nationals.

6. **Systematic and systemic exploitation**. Planning and organization were required for this phase. The systematic exploitation flourished because of the pre-existing structures developed during the conquest of power of the Alliance of Democratic Forces for the Liberation of Congo-Zaire. These pre-existing structures were improved over time and new networks for channeling extracted resources were put in place. However, the systemic exploitation used the existing systems of control established by Rwanda and Uganda. In both cases, exploitation was often carried out in violation of the sovereignty of the Democratic Republic of the Congo, the national legislation and sometimes international law, and it led to illicit activities. Key individual actors including top army commanders and businessmen on the one hand, and government structures on the other, have been the engines of this systematic and systemic exploitation.

7. The consequence of illegal exploitation has been twofold: (a) massive availability of financial resources for the Rwandan Patriotic Army, and the individual enrichment of top Ugandan military commanders and civilians; (b) the emergence of illegal networks headed either by top military officers or businessmen. These two elements form the basis of the link between the exploitation of natural resources and the continuation of the conflict. Other contributing factors however exist—the roles played by some entities and institutions, and the opportunistic behavior of some private companies and influential individuals, including some decision makers in the Democratic Republic of the Congo and Zimbabwe. Some leaders in the region bear a direct responsibility. The Panel concludes that tough measures must be taken to bring to an end the cycle of exploitation of the natural resources and the continuation of the conflict in the Democratic Republic of the Congo.

8. The Panel's recommendations revolve around six broad themes: (1) sanctions against countries and individuals involved in the illegal activities; (2) preventive measures to avoid a recurrence of the current situation; (3) reparations to the victims of the illegal exploitation of natural resources; (4) design of a framework for reconstruction; (5) improvement of international mechanisms and regulations governing some natural resources; and (6) security issues.

B. Methodological Framework

9. **Methodology**. Owing to the nature of the work and the complexities of the issues, a methodology that allows flexible data collection was essential in order to complete this project. The Panel has therefore utilized:

(a) Primary data collection. Official documentation from ministries and other institutions as well as recorded minutes of meetings involving various relevant actors;

(b) Secondary sources. Reports, workshop proceedings, published and unpublished literature;

(c) Interviews. Structured, semi-structured, and open interviews as well as interviews resulting from various network referrals.

10. A vast amount of data was obtained from three essential sources:

(a) Countries and other entities involved in the conflict in the Democratic Republic of the Congo, namely: Angola, Burundi, the Democratic Republic of the Congo, Namibia, Rwanda, Uganda, Zimbabwe, RCD-Goma, and RCD-ML;

(b) "Third-party" sources such as Belgium, Cameroon, China, Denmark, France, Germany, Kenya, the Netherlands, the United Kingdom of Great Britain and Northern Ireland, the United Republic of Tanzania, the United States of America, Switzerland, various United Nations agencies, the International Monetary Fund, the World Bank, the World Trade Organization, OECD, the International Coffee Organization, De Beers, the Diamond High Council, the International Diamond Manufacturers Association, the University of Maryland, the World Resource Institute, and CIFOR;

(c) Various individual actors and stakeholders who expressed an interest for various reasons in sharing their knowledge and understanding with the Panel.

11. The production and export data series available for the analysis covers the period 1995-2000. Data was systematically analyzed separately and then compared with one another. Comparative analysis thus contributed to the Panel's ability to develop a good understanding of the issues. In addition, the Panel sought to cross-check every item of information received. In relation to this and to the extent possible, Panel members attempted to speak to individuals against whom serious allegations were made. When

access to those key witnesses or primary actors was denied, Panel members often relied on their closest collaborators for insight. The Panel, however, faced a problem of imbalance in the acquisition of data. Indeed data was abundant for Rwanda, Uganda, RCD-Goma, RCD-ML, and MLC. This is partly due to the high number of insiders living in the Democratic Republic of the Congo and in Europe who were directly involved with those entities, and who offered to share almost everything they knew or had experienced or gathered as documentation while they were involved with them. The same quantity and quality of data were not available for Angola, Namibia, or Zimbabwe, although the Panel visited those countries. This constraint can be felt in the report. Overall the report was written using the empirical method combined with the economic analysis of data collected, supported by elements of evidence.

12. **Establishing boundaries**. Geographically, data was gathered for occupied and non-occupied territories within the Democratic Republic of the Congo as well as for any country involved in the conflict or of other strategic importance, geographic, financial, or other. With respect to natural resources, the Panel focused on minerals, forest and agricultural products, and other forms of wealth, primarily taxes. Given the high number of natural resources found in the Democratic Republic of the Congo, the high level of exploitation by numerous parties, and the limited time and resources available to the Panel, the following criteria for the selection of resources to be examined were developed:

- The commercial value of the resources in absolute terms;
- The interest of parties in the resources;
- The scale of exploitation.

13. Based on these criteria, three categories of products were of primary consideration: (a) mineral resources, primarily coltan, diamonds, gold and cassiterite; (b) agriculture, forests and wildlife, including timber, coffee and ivory; and (c) financial products, mainly in regard to taxes. Copper, cobalt, livestock, gorillas, okapis, tobacco, tea, palm oil and land allocation deserved to be among the resources and products to be studied. Some did not meet established criteria, however, and for others, such as copper and cobalt, time constraint was the main reason for a lack of study. These resources are touched upon in the report for illustrative purposes, but were not systematically studied.

14. **Defining the key concepts**. In determining the parameters of the project, the definition or interpretation of illegality and exploitation was vigorously debated.

15.*Illegality*. The most contentious concept in the mandate has been the term "illegality" with regard to exploitation. Almost all actors in the conflict and observers requested a clear definition of illegality. In the Panel's view, the understanding of illegality is underpinned by four elements all related to the rule of law, namely:

(a) Violation of sovereignty. The first element is based on the Security Council's understanding of illegality as described in the Panel's mandate (see the statement of the President of the Security Council of 2 June, 2000 (S/PRST/2000/20)). This posits that all activities—extraction, production, commercialization, and exports—taking place in the Democratic Republic of the Congo without the consent of the legitimate government are illegal. This interpretation suggested that only non-invited forces and their nationals are carrying out illegal activities in the Democratic Republic of the Congo.

(b) Respect by actors of the existing regulatory framework in the country or territory where they operate or carry out their activities. The Panel considers that if authorities exerting effective power and control over their sovereign area recognize or set up a regulatory framework to govern the use or exploitation of resources, this framework shall be respected. Failure to do so may lead to the infringement of the law and, therefore, activities considered illegal or unlawful. In this case, the Panel deems illegality to be the carrying out of an activity in violation of an existing body of regulations.

(c) The discrepancy between widely accepted practices in trade and business and the way business is conducted in the Democratic Republic of the Congo. In this category, the Panel has considered that the use and abuse of power by some actors fall into the category of illegality. This includes forced monopoly in trading, the unilateral fixing of prices of products by the buyer, the confiscation or looting of products from farmers, and the use of military forces in various zones to protect some interests or to create a situation of monopoly.

(d) The violation of international law including "soft" law. The Panel considers that business activities carried out in violation of international law are illegal.

The Panel utilized the aforementioned elements in a complementary manner, refusing to be exclusive or to focus on one single element. On the basis of discussions with different members of the Security Council, the Panel has interpreted the wish of the Security Council to be a broad interpretation of the concept of illegality.

16.*Exploitation.* The Panel opted for a broad understanding and interpretation of exploitation. Exploitation was used beyond the mere consideration of production and extraction. It was viewed as all activities that enable actors and stakeholders to engage in business in first, secondary and tertiary sectors in relation to the natural resources and other forms of wealth of the Democratic Republic of the Congo. The broad interpretation enabled the Panel to look into extraction, production, commercialization and exports of natural resources and other services such as transport and financial transactions.

C. Overview

17. This section offers a general overview of the report. Initially, the Panel examined the pre-existing structures that have facilitated the illegal exploitation of natural resources in the Democratic Republic of the Congo. These elements encompass the financial/commercial links and the transportation networks that essentially laid the foundation for the current situation of illegal exploitation.

18. The Panel then reviewed the primary processes by which the natural resources are physically exploited by the occupying forces, primarily Rwanda and Uganda, in conjunction with their respective rebel counterparts in the Democratic Republic of the Congo. Subsequently, the current structures of exploitation were discussed in order to demonstrate the evolution of the process to its present state. Selected individuals were then profiled to illustrate the extent to which this is an organized and embedded venture. Economic data were then analyzed to confirm the findings described above.

19. The focus then moved to exploring the complexities of the links between the continuation of the conflict and the exploitation of resources through the use of specific country examples. The aim is to demonstrate the varying means by which power structures can manipulate situations for the

most favorable outcome. This section is directly linked to the previous one and, in some cases, information overlapped. This was unavoidable because of the intricate nature of the problem at hand.

20. The report goes on to discuss more incidental elements in this exploitation, which are nonetheless important and relevant: official and non-official fronts utilized as well as the facilitators or passive accomplices within the processes. The report concludes with a summary of the findings and recommendations for action.

D. Background

21. The Democratic Republic of the Congo is located in the heart of equatorial central Africa and has an area of 2,267,600 square kilometers and a current population estimated at 50 million. The Democratic Republic of the Congo is endowed with a unique bio-diversity, vast mineral and forest resources, and rich soils conducive to agriculture (see map). These favorable conditions, concentrated in the eastern regions, are the setting for the current ongoing occupation and struggle to exploit these natural resources.

22. The initial disruption, predominantly affecting the eastern Democratic Republic of the Congo, began with the 1994-1995 refugee crisis in the region, spawned by the war in neighboring Rwanda. The sudden influx of hundreds of thousands of refugees, including members of the Interahamwe, created a new demographic dynamic in the subregional population, abruptly disturbed the delicate balance of the ecosystems and generated a new security situation along the border between the Democratic Republic of the Congo and Rwanda.

23. The situation further deteriorated in 1996 with the war between the Zairian forces and the Alliance of Democratic Forces for the Liberation of Congo-Zaire (AFDL), the rebel movement led by the late Laurent-Désiré Kabila and supported by the Angolan, Rwandan, and Ugandan forces. This AFDL-led conquest of then eastern Zaire fundamentally altered the composition of the regional stakeholders and the distribution of natural resources. Previously, the distribution norm was (via legal and illegal channels) through locally based Congolese, mostly civilian-managed, business operations. However, these traditional modes were quickly

overtaken by new power structures. Along with new players came new rules for exploiting natural resources. Foreign troops and their "friends" openly embraced business in "liberated territories," encouraged indirectly by the AFDL leader, the late President Kabila.

24. In August 1998, fighting erupted again in the northern, western, and eastern parts of the Democratic Republic of the Congo, this time between Rwandan and Ugandan troops and the Congolese army, with the assistance of Angolan, Namibian, and Zimbabwean armies, as well as Sudanese and Chadian forces. The last two countries have since withdrawn their soldiers from the Democratic Republic of the Congo.

II. Illegal Exploitation of Natural Resources and Other Forms of Wealth

25. The illegal exploitation of resources by Burundi, Rwanda, and Uganda took different forms, including confiscation, extraction, forced monopoly, and price-fixing. Of these, the first two reached proportions that made the war in the Democratic Republic of the Congo a very lucrative business. Prior to defining the type and manner of illegal exploitation, however, it is important to examine the pre-existing structures which facilitated this process.

A. Pre-existing Structures That Facilitated Illegal Exploitation

26. Illegal exploitation[359] by foreigners aided by the Congolese began with the first "war of liberation" in 1996. The AFDL rebels, backed by Angolan, Rwandan and Ugandan soldiers conquered eastern and south-eastern Zaire. As they were advancing, the then AFDL leader, the late Laurent-Désiré Kabila, signed contracts with a number of foreign companies. Numerous accounts and documents suggest that by 1997 a first wave of "new businessmen" speaking only English, Kinyarwanda and Kiswahili had commenced operations in the eastern Democratic Republic of the Congo.[360] Theft of livestock, coffee beans and other resources began to be reported with frequency. By the time the August 1998 war broke out, Rwandans and Ugandans (top officers and their associates) had a strong sense of the potential of the natural resources and their locations in the eastern the Democratic Republic of the Congo. Some historians have argued that Ugandan forces were instrumental in the conquest of areas such as Wasta,

Bunia, Beni and Butembo during the first war.

27. Numerous accounts in Kampala suggest that the decision to enter the conflict in August 1998 was defended by some top military officials who had served in eastern Zaire during the first war and who had had a taste of the business potential of the region. Some key witnesses, who served with the Rally for Congolese Democracy rebel faction in early months, spoke about the eagerness of Ugandan forces to move in and occupy areas where gold and diamond mines were located. Other sources informed the Panel that, late in September 1998, they were already engaged in discussions with General Salim Saleh on the creation of a company that would supply the eastern Democratic Republic of the Congo with merchandise, and on the import of natural resources. The project never materialized in this form, but the sources reportedly also discussed this and other business venture possibilities with the President of Uganda, Yoweri Museveni.

28. There are strong indications that, if security and political reasons were the professed roots of the political leaders' motivation to move into the eastern Democratic Republic of the Congo, some top army officials clearly had a hidden agenda: economic and financial objectives. A few months before the 1998 war broke out, General Salim Saleh and the elder son of President Museveni reportedly visited the eastern Democratic Republic of the Congo. One month after the beginning of the conflict, General James Kazini was already involved in commercial activities. According to very reliable sources, he knew the most profitable sectors and immediately organized the local commanders to serve their economic and financial objectives.

29. Financial and commercial links. During the early months of the rebellion, the financial setting and networks were already in place. At the heart of the financial setting is the Banque de commerce, du développement et d'industrie (BCDI) located in Kigali. According to some sources, there was an understanding between the President of Rwanda, Paul Kagame, President Museveni, and the late Laurent-Désiré Kabila on the collection and use of financial resources during the time of the AFDL rebellion. This collaboration led many sources to believe that the three leaders were shareholders in BCDI. But this was not the case.

30. The following example illustrates the nature of the financial

transactions and links involving BCDI, Citibank New York as a corresponding bank, and some companies and individuals. In a letter signed by J. P. Moritz, General Manager of Société minière de Bakwanga (MIBA), a diamond company, and Ngandu Kamenda, the General Manager of MIBA ordered a payment of US$3.5 million to la Générale de commerce d'import/export du Congo (COMIEX),[361] a company owned by late President Kabila and some of his close allies, such as Minister Victor Mpoyo, from an account in BCDI through a Citibank account. This amount of money was paid as a contribution from MIBA to the AFDL war effort.

31. Transportation networks. Illegal activities also benefitted from the old transportation network that existed prior to the 1998 war. This network consists of key airlines and trucking companies, a number of which aided AFDL troops in their war against the Mobutu regime. The pattern of transport remains similar today: merchandise or arms are flown in and natural resources or their products are flown out. For example, Aziza Kulsum Gulamali, a businesswoman operating within the region for some time, utilized this network even in the 1980s. She contracted Air Cargo Zaire to transport arms to the FDD Hutu rebels in Burundi and smuggled cigarettes on the return flight. Since 1998, aircraft also fly from the military airports at Entebbe and Kigali, transporting arms, military equipment, soldiers, and, for some companies, merchandise. On the return flights, they will carry coffee, gold, diamond traders and business representatives, and, in some cases, soldiers. The Panel concludes that these pre-existing networks and structures constitute the basis for the current exploitation of the natural resources of the Democratic Republic of the Congo.

B. Mass-scale Looting

32. Between September 1998 and August 1999, occupied zones of the Democratic Republic of the Congo were drained of existing stockpiles, including minerals, agricultural and forest products, and livestock. Regardless of the looter, the pattern was the same: Burundian, Rwandan, Ugandan, and/or RCD soldiers, commanded by an officer, visited farms, storage facilities, factories, and banks, and demanded that the managers open the coffers and doors. The soldiers were then ordered to remove the relevant products and load them into vehicles. The Panel received numerous accounts and claims of unlawful removal of products by Rwandan or Ugandan armies

and their local RCD allies. The Panel has chosen to illustrate this point with some examples.

33. In the mining sector, SOMINKI (Société minière et industrielle du Kivu) had seven years worth of columbo-tantalite (coltan) in stock in various areas. From late November 1998, Rwandan forces and their RCD allies organized their removal and transport to Kigali. Depending on the sources, between 2,000 and 3,000 tons of cassiterite and between 1,000 and 1,500 tons of coltan were removed from the region between November 1998 and April 1999. A very reliable source informed the Panel that it took the Rwandans about a month to fly this coltan to Kigali. The Panel, however, received official documents including one in which RCD acknowledged removing 6 tons of coltan and 200 tons of cassiterite from SOMINKI for a total of US$722,482.

34. Late in late August 1998, General Kazini's soldiers absconded with the stockpiles of timber belonging to the logging company Amex-bois, located in Bagboka. In December that year, the same General ordered the confiscation of all the stocked timber belonging to the logging company La Forestière. General Kazini was reportedly seen in the area at least twice during the period when the looting occurred and temporarily established his headquarters in the area.

35. Then, in January 1999, in Equateur Province, Jean-Pierre Bemba and General Kazini organized a large operation for the confiscation of coffee beans. Mr. Bemba initiated, encouraged, and perpetuated such practices in the Province. In a written letter to one of his commanders, he urged him to release a bigger vehicle he was using because it was needed urgently. The source indicated that this was later used to carry away tons of coffee beans. A participant in this operation, who has since left the movement, explained that two months were required to remove the enormous quantities of coffee. In the past, this province produced 60 percent of the country's robusta coffee. The localities of Bumba, Lisala, Bosonzo, Binga, and Mindembo for a year did not have coffee stocks to export because of these seizures. The Société congolaise du café, the largest owner of coffee stocks in the area, went bankrupt. The mass-scale looting reached such levels that, in one instance, Mr. Bemba seized 200 tons of coffee beans from the SCIBE company, which was owned by his father, Saolona Bemba. The matter remains unresolved in

court.

36. In some cases, factories were dismantled or machinery spare parts were taken away, as in the case of the sugar factory of Kaliba in South Kivu. When the Panel asked about the dismantling of some factories, the RCD cabinet replied that investors were free to dismantle their factories and relocate wherever they wanted. In essence, RCD recognized the phenomenon, but explained it in terms of the investors' decision to relocate the factories while taking the raw materials from the Democratic Republic of the Congo. Cars and other items were apparently also taken from the country, as statistics on Ugandan registered cars reflected an increase of about one quarter in 1999.

37. The financial sector was not left untouched either. A defector from RCD who participated in some looting informed the Panel that Rwandan soldiers systematically targeted local banks as soon as they conquered a town. In many cases, they would use the RCD soldiers to collect the money while those who were armed would surround the bank. For example, the Kisangani Bank, a branch of the central bank, received a visit of RCD staff accompanied by Rwandan soldiers. Depending on the source (central bank in Kinshasa or eyewitness), anywhere between $1 million and $8 million worth of Congolese francs was taken. The Panel was told that the operation took place a couple of days after the central bank and Ministry of Finance officials deposited money to pay civil servants and old Congolese franc notes were replaced by new ones.

38. Under the escort of soldiers, the money was taken to the Palm Beach Hotel. The hotel management recalled that bags full of money were stored in one of the rooms and that during those few days armed soldiers who could not speak Lingala (the most commonly spoken Congolese language) guarded the hotel premises. Could such an operation involving a number of armed soldiers be carried out without the knowledge and consent of the highest Rwandan commander in the Democratic Republic of the Congo?

39. Aides of Jean-Pierre Ondekane (an RCD leader) reportedly collected the money from the Palm Beach Hotel, flew with it to Goma and handed it over to Emmanuel Kamanzi (former chief of the Finance Department of RCD), who then flew on to Kigali. The Panel could not identify the final

recipient of the money or how much disappeared between Kisangani, Goma, and Kigali. However, some sources told the Panel that Mr. Kamanzi was imprisoned briefly at some point after this transaction. According to the same sources, he had apparently helped himself to the money he was ordered only to transport. Mr. Kamanzi told friends that he simply took a break of two months in Kigali.

40. During the period when this operation was under way, in Equateur Province, Mr. Bemba's men visited several banks. According to a reliable source Mr. Bemba's instructions to his soldiers were to systematically empty the bank once a town was captured. His troops took an equivalent of $400,000 from the Banque commerciale du Congo branch in Bumba, $500,000 in Lisala, and approximately $600,000 in Gemena.

41. The pilfering was also occurring in Kinshasa. The Panel has evidence of a widespread practice by which the late President Kabila would by proxy have companies give a certain percentage of their profits. For example, certain oil companies in the Democratic Republic of the Congo, under the umbrella of taxe parafiscale, were delivering sums of money, in hard cash, daily or weekly to the late President via his Minister, friend, and right-hand man, Mr. Mpoyo. Other companies, such as MIBA, were asked to hand over part of their profits to the late President's regime, and all parastatals and important private companies were invited to open bank accounts in the Banque de commerce et du développement (BCD) (see para. 78).

42. However, over time the mass-scale looting described above diminished and theft by individual soldiers became more visible. For example, in Bunia, during Panel discussions, local non-governmental organizations, eyewitnesses, and victims mentioned cases in which Congolese civilians were injured or murdered for resisting the attempted seizure of property by the RCD rebels and foreign soldiers. In Bukavu, individuals have told Panel members how Rwandan soldiers confiscated their life savings in dollar notes and some of the gold they were buying and keeping as monnaie refuge in the face of the repeatedly devalued Congolese franc. Partially, this has contributed to the increasing resentment felt by the Congolese population toward foreign soldiers and some rebels.

43. The looting of manufacturing plants, stocks, and private property

were not only acts of isolated individual soldiers but were encouraged, sometimes organized and coordinated, by the highest army commanders of both Rwanda and Uganda.

44. General Kazini used the same method to facilitate looting activities. He would appoint loyal commanders and reliable civilian Congolese in the civil administration in areas potentially rich in natural resources in order to secure his networks. This was exactly the case in Ituri, where he appointed Adele Lotsove in 1999 (see para. 71). In turn, these top layers of collaborators, colonels and majors utilized their right-hand men to carry out the actual looting.

45. The Panel has strong indications after talking to numerous witnesses (key and others) that key officials in the Governments of Rwanda and Uganda were aware of the situation on the ground, including the looting of stocks from a number of factories. In some cases, the level of production of mineral resources would have alerted any government, such as those of gold for Uganda and coltan for Rwanda (from 99 tons in 1996 to 250 tons in 1997).

C. Systematic and Systemic Exploitation

46. **Extraction phase**. The mass-scale looting carried out on many levels within the Democratic Republic of the Congo by rebels and foreign soldiers overshadowed with extraction activities during the first 12 months of the second war. When resource stockpiles were looted and exhausted by occupying forces and their allies, the exploitation evolved to an active extraction phase. Both Congolese (civilians and soldiers) and foreigners (civilians and soldiers) became involved in the extraction of natural resources. This section highlights one particular case study rather than offering a number of shorter illustrative examples. The study will in effect demonstrate how a company used illicit business practices and complicity with occupying forces and the Government as well as its international connections to exploit the natural resources of the Democratic Republic of the Congo.

47. **DARA-Forest case study**. A Ugandan-Thai forest company called DARA-Forest moved to the Ituri area late in 1998. In March 1998, DARA-Forest applied for a licence to carry out logging activities in the Democratic

Republic of the Congo, but was denied a forest concession by the Kinshasa authorities. In 1999, the company began to buy production by hiring individuals to harvest timber and then sell it to the company. Initially, these individuals were Congolese operating in partnership with Ugandans. The same year, DARA engaged in industrial production with the construction of a sawmill in Mangina. By 2000, it had obtained its own concession from RCD-ML. Analysis of satellite images over a period of time reveals the extent to which deforestation occurred in Orientale Province between 1998 and 2000. The most harvested forests in the areas were around Djugu, Mambassa, Beni, Komanda, Luna, Mont Moyo, and Aboro. This logging activity was carried out without consideration of any of the minimum acceptable rules of timber harvesting for sustainable forest management or even sustainable logging.

48. Timber harvested in this region, which is occupied by the Ugandan army and RCD-ML, has exclusively transited or remained in Uganda. Our own investigation in Kampala has shown that mahogany originating in the Democratic Republic of the Congo is largely available in Kampala, at a lower price than Ugandan mahogany. This difference in price is simply due to the lower cost of acquisition of timber. Timber harvested in the Democratic Republic of the Congo by Uganda pays very little tax or none at all. In addition, customs fees are generally not paid when soldiers escort those trucks or when orders are received from some local commanders or General Kazini. Timber from the Democratic Republic of the Congo is then exported to Kenya and Uganda, and to other continents. The Panel gathered from the Kenyan port authorities that vast quantities of timber are exported to Asia, Europe, and North America.

49. The Panel also discovered during its investigation that individual Ugandan loggers violated forestry legislation, recognized by their ally RCD-ML, by logging (extracting) the timber directly. According to the Congolese legislation on the *permis de coupe*, only individual Congolese nationals are allowed to harvest timber and only in small quantities. Foreigners must apply for the larger concessions. Initially, Ugandans operated in partnership with a Congolese permit holder. Soon, the Ugandans began to pay the Congolese to sub-lease the permit and, subsequently, to obtain the licence in direct violation of the law.

50. Timber extraction in the Democratic Republic of the Congo and its

export have been characterized by unlawfulness and illegality. Besides extracting timber without authorization in a sovereign country and in violation of the local legislation, DARA-Forest consistently exported its timber without any certification procedure. It tried to approach some certification bodies licensed by the Forest Stewardship Council. These bodies requested documentation and elements that the company failed to provide. Yet DARA-Forest exported timber in violation of a normal procedure generally required and accepted by the international forest community and gradually considered to be international "soft law." Companies importing this uncertified timber from DARA-Forest were essentially in major industrialized countries, including Belgium, China, Denmark, Japan, Kenya, Switzerland, and the United States of America.

51. The Panel also realized that DARA Great Lakes Industries (DGLI), of which DARA-Forest is a subsidiary, along with a sister company in Uganda, Nyota Wood Industries, is in collusion with the Ministry of Water, Land, and Forests of Uganda in establishing a scheme to facilitate the certification of timber coming from the Democratic Republic of the Congo. In May 2000, DGLI signed a contract for forest stewardship certification with SmartWood and the Rogue Institute for Ecology and Economy in Oregon, United States of America. On 21 March, 2000, the Director of the DARA group, Prossy Balaba, sent a letter to the Commissioner asking him to allow an official of SmartWood to visit certain forests, such as Budongo and Bugoma; he was due to visit the region in mid-April. The visit was meant to deceive the official by presenting those forests as the ones for which certification was sought and to convince SmartWood to work for the certification of their timber. Indeed, when the visit took place, from 14 to 16 April, the DARA group had not even applied for the concession of the Budongo forest (Uganda). It was only on 5 July, 2000 that John Kotiram of the DARA group wrote to the Commissioner to request the concession on the Budongo forest.

52. The idea behind this is to use Budongo forest as a model of forests from which timber is harvested and which comply with the international requirements for certification, in order to certify timber coming from the Democratic Republic of the Congo for which basic elements of certification do not exist. Future plans for beating the international system are already in place. According to internal documents of DGLI, DARA-Forest will import

timber from the Democratic Republic of the Congo into Uganda, which will be processed for different types of products in the new plant in Namanve for the sawmilling of hardwood, both imported from the Democratic Republic of the Congo and harvested in Uganda. DGLI partners in this new scheme include DARA Europe GmbH Germany, Shanton President Wood Supply Co. Ltd China, President Wood Supply Co. Ltd Thailand, DARA Tropical Hardwood, Portland, Oregon, United States of America. The distribution of sales of the company is thought to remain the same, about 30 percent to the Far East, China, Japan, and Singapore, 40 percent to Europe and 25 percent to North America. DARA Great Lakes Industries shareholding and management is between Thai and Ugandan nationals, among them John Supit Kotiran and Pranee Chanyuttasart of Thailand and Prossy Balaba of Uganda. Some unconfirmed information indicates that members of President Museveni's family are shareholders of DGLI, although more investigation is needed.

53. The DARA group also established another scheme to carry out fraudulent activities in the Democratic Republic of the Congo. The objects of DGLI range from logging to financial and industrial activities. Because of the confusion created between DARA-Forest, which received a concession from RCD, and DGLI, DARA-Forest has also been dealing in diamonds, gold, and coltan. The Panel has received reports from the custom posts of Mpondwe, Kasindi, and Bundbujyo of the export from the Democratic Republic of the Congo of minerals such as cassiterite and coltan in trucks. During the Panel's visit to Bunia it was reported that other products were loaded in trucks which are supposed to carry timber only; it is likely that coltan and cassiterite were these products. Moreover, the fraud extends to the forging of documents and declarations "originating" in Kinshasa.

54. The logging rate was alarming around Butembo, Beni, Boga and Mambassa. The RCD-ML administration acknowledged its lack of control over the rate of extraction, the collection of taxes on logging activities and the customs fees at the exit points. On the basis of eyewitness accounts, satellite images, key actors' acknowledgments and the Panel's own investigation, there is sufficient evidence to prove that timber extraction is directly related to the Ugandan presence in Orientale Province. This has reached alarming proportions and Ugandans (civilians, soldiers, and companies) are extensively involved in these activities. In May 2000, RCD-ML attributed a

concession of 100,000 hectares to DARA-Forest. Since September 1998, overall DARA-Forest has been exporting approximately 48,000 m^3 of timber per year.

55. **Other extraction schemes**. Burundians and Rwandans have also extracted timber or have been associated with Congolese loggers. Roads to evacuate timber from places deeper in the forest are in a very bad state. Yet Congo timber, as it is referred to in Bujumbura, is readily available in Burundi and Rwanda. Some Burundians, however, are also involved in the harvesting of bark from prunus Africana. This tree is known and used in medicine for prostate treatment. Statistics gathered from the Tanzanian Port Authority clearly indicate that Burundi exported those barks in 1998 and 1999. Prunus Africana is not found in Burundi, however, but rather in the forests of South Kivu.

56. **Mining sector**. In the mining sector, direct extraction was carried out in three ways, namely (a) by individual soldiers for their own benefit; (b) by locals organized by Rwandan and Ugandan commanders; and (c) by foreign nationals for the army or commanders' benefit.

57. The Panel came across a number of cases in which soldiers were directly involved in mining in Watsa. In September 1999, the UPDF local commander demanded the extraction of gold on the pillars of the Gorumbwa mine galleries in which dynamite was used. On 9 September, the galleries collapsed, leading to the death of a number of Congolese miners. Some months later, Ugandan soldiers who came to mine in the same area contracted respiratory disease. Other returning UPDF soldiers have themselves told friends how they operated in order to acquire the gold. From these accounts, it appears that, even when the local commanders were informed about these activities, there was an acceptable level of tolerance. Although the Panel qualifies this behavior as passive complicity on the part of some commanders, it is not clear whether soldiers shared the acquired minerals with their allies.

58. Local Congolese have been mining for years for their own benefit. The novelty of their involvement lies in the fact that some of them were used as "convincible labor" to mine gold, diamonds or coltan. In the Bondo locality within Equateur Province, young men from 12 to 18 years were

recruited by Jean-Pierre Bemba. The Ugandan allies trained the recruits and shared with them the idea that the Ugandan army was an "army of development" that aimed at improving ordinary people's living conditions. After the one-hour morning physical training session, they were sent to gold mines to dig on behalf of the Ugandans and Mr. Bemba. According to eyewitnesses, in Kalima, RPA commander Ruto enrolled two teams of local Congolese to dig coltan; these Congolese worked under the heavy guard of Rwandan soldiers.

59. In the Kilo-Moto mineral district, Ugandan local commanders and some of the soldiers who guarded the different entry points of the mining areas allowed and encouraged the local population to mine. The arrangement between the soldiers and the miners was that each miner would leave at the entry/exit point one gram of gold every day. A key informant of the Panel indicated that on average 2,000 individuals mined this large concession six days a week. This source, confirmed by other sources, informed the Panel that it was so well organized that the business ran smoothly. On average 2 kg of gold are delivered daily to the person heading the network.

60. The last pattern of organized extraction by the occupying forces involves the import of manpower for mining. Occupying forces brought manpower from their own countries and provided the necessary security and logistics. In particular, Rwanda utilized prisoners to dig coltan in exchange for a sentence reduction and limited cash to buy food. The Panel was recently informed that there is a presence of 1,500 Rwandan prisoners in the Numbi area of Kalehe. According to the same report, these prisoners were seen mining coltan while guarded by RPA soldiers. Human Rights Watch also reported the same information in March 2001. This recent report confirms numerous other reports and eyewitness accounts of the involvement of prisoners, some of whom are former refugees.

61. **Impact on wildlife**. Wildlife has also suffered a great deal from the conflict. Numerous accounts and statistics from regional conservation organizations show that, in the area controlled by the Ugandan troops and Sudanese rebels, nearly 4,000 out of 12,000 elephants were killed in the Garamba Park in north-eastern Democratic Republic of the Congo between 1995 and 1999. The situation in other parks and reserves is equally grave, including Kahuzi-Biega Park, the Okapi Reserve and Virunga Park. The

number of okapis, gorillas, and elephants has dwindled to small populations. In the Kahuzi-Biega Park, a zone controlled by the Rwandans and RCD-Goma and rich in coltan, only 2 out of 350 elephant families remained in 2000. There is serious concern among conservationists that the rest fled of their own accord or were killed, as two tons of elephant tusks were traced in the Bukavu area late in 2000. Already by April 2000, about three tons of tusks were temporarily seized by RCD-ML in Isiro. After strong pressure from Uganda, the cargo was released and transferred to Kampala.

62. The Panel has indications that, in most cases, poaching of elephants in violation of international law (Convention on International Trade in Endangered Species of Wild Fauna and Flora (CITES)) was well organized. Either soldiers hunted directly with the consent of the commander or they provided equipment and protection to local villagers to execute the task with the objective of collecting elephant tusks. For example, in August 2000, UPDF Colonel Mugeni and a crew of his soldiers were discovered with 800 kg of elephant tusks in their car near Garamba Park. The Government of Uganda received detailed notification of this incident. Eyewitnesses reported to the Panel several incidents that involved Rwandan soldiers in the trading of elephant and buffalo meat. In the Bukavu and Goma areas, there appears to be a pattern: high commanders take the tusks, soldiers negotiate the wholesale price with some locals, and the locals sell the meat in the market place as retailers.

63. Harvesting of coffee by non-owners has been another feature of the exploitation of natural resources. Jean-Pierre Bemba, the leader of MLC and now the President of the Front de libération du Congo, a partner in the coffee business with General Kazini, has been harvesting coffee directly from plantations he does not own. During our visit to Gbadolite, some locals mentioned that coffee was harvested by Mr. Bemba's men from some private plantations that belonged to individuals who had fled the region.

64. **Monopolies and price-fixing.** In addition to looting and extracting resources, rebels and Rwandan and Ugandan troops have abused the commerce and trade system. In some cases, they forced locally owned and some foreign-owned businesses to close down. The methods used varied from looting to harassing the owners. The end objective was to gain control of local commerce. The result is unprecedented control of the economy of the

eastern and north-eastern Democratic Republic of the Congo. During its field visit, the Panel noted that consumer goods and other merchandise found in Gbadolite and Bunia originated mostly in Uganda. During its field visit to Bunia, the Panel members witnessed the unloading of beer crates from an aircraft coming from Uganda. In Gbadolite, most cigarettes, beverages, toilet paper, etc. are imported from Uganda. Equally, goods in Kisangani, Bukavu, and Goma come mainly from Burundi or Rwanda. Imported goods for the occupied zones arrive via the ports of Mombasa and Dar es Salaam. This was confirmed during the Panel's visit to the customs services (Internal Revenue Authority) in Kampala. Furthermore, depending on the importer of the goods, taxes are not paid. The failure to pay taxes, especially in Orientale Province, was acknowledged to the Panel by RCD-ML during our discussions in Bunia in October 2000.

65. Rwandan and Ugandan troops and their Congolese allies have also been exploiting local farmers. They have imposed prices and conditions on the farmers. In one instance, a farmer living near the Ubangi River, 20 km from Gbadolite, explained to a member of the Panel how he is dependent on the coffee dealers for the supply of the bags imposed by the coffee collectors (buyers). Failure to use these bags leads to an automatic reduction in the price of the coffee. These bags are not produced in the eastern Democratic Republic of the Congo and they have to buy them.

66. In another instance, one woman explained how she and her husband could no longer sell their palm oil to the neighboring Central African Republic or ship it to Kinshasa for a better price. The control of trade and other business networks for commercial crops, such as coffee and palm oil, is almost total within the occupied zones. This translates into a de facto monopoly like the one Jean-Pierre Bemba has on coffee exports in Equateur Province. The locals who desperately remain in the villages work more for less, if anything at all. Humanitarian organizations working in the occupied zones told the Panel stories of a number of women in some villages who have simply stopped taking their children to the health centers because they no longer possess simple items of clothing to preserve their dignity.

67. Exploitation of resources becomes even more questionable, as some of the players not only produce counterfeited Congolese francs, but use them to purchase natural resources. According to reliable sources, the Victoria

Group, whose key shareholder is General Khaleb Akandwanaho, alias Salim Saleh, he was involved in the making of counterfeit Congolese francs. These notes are used for the purchase of commercial crops, primarily coffee. A very reliable source told the Panel that in mid-1999 Jean-Pierre Bemba ordered the production of 100-franc Congolese notes. Simultaneously the Victoria Group also produced counterfeit Congolese francs. By the end of 1999, Equateur Province was flooded with counterfeit Congolese currency so that Mr. Bemba decided to suspend all 100-franc notes, including the ones he had produced, so as to stop inflation in the areas he controlled.

68. The Panel has evidence that the illegal exploitation of natural resources goes beyond mineral and agricultural resources. It is actively occurring also in respect of financial transactions, taxes, and the use of cheap labor, which our mandate qualified as other forms of wealth. Local banks and insurance companies operating in Goma, Bukavu, Kisangani, Bunia, and Gbadolite deal directly with Kigali or Kampala. A system of tax collection—enforced in some cases—has been implemented by MLC, RCD-ML and RCD-Goma with their established Ugandan and Rwandan counterparts. In the rebels' own words, these taxes are aimed at "financing or supporting the war effort." Indeed, part of the funds collected is sent to Kigali (in the case of RCD-Goma). In the case of the former RCD-ML and MLC, not only was part of the taxes sent to Kampala but also individual colonels would claim direct payment from RCD-ML. In Bunia and Bukavu, people protested, demonstrated, and denounced this practice of abuse. In areas controlled by Mr. Bemba, peasants carrying palm oil on bicycles have to pay taxes on the bicycles.

69. The use of child labor is also rampant in the occupied territories. Some children are reportedly mining gold in the Kilo Moto mines. In Equateur Province, some children were seen in the diamond mines. The Panel members witnessed the presence of young MLC recruits at Gbadolite airport and in the city. They were at the airport waiting for a flight, having recently completed their military training.

70. The aforementioned demonstrates that the procedures and processes for exploiting the natural resources of the Democratic Republic of the Congo are continuously evolving. Occupying forces began with the easiest method, looting stockpiles. As the wells ran dry, they developed efficient means of

extracting the additional resources necessary to keep the coffers full. Eventually, any means necessary was recognized as a legitimate mode of acquisition. From all the evidence offered above, it appears that this process will continue to evolve as is deemed necessary.

D. Current Structures of Illegal Exploitation

71. **Administrative structures**. The illegal exploitation of natural resources is facilitated by the administrative structures established by Uganda and Rwanda. Those countries' leaders directly and indirectly appointed regional governors or local authorities or, more commonly, appointed or confirmed Congolese in these positions. Typical examples are, on the Ugandan side, the appointment of the Governor of Ituri Province. On 18 June, 1999, Ugandan General Kazini appointed as Governor of this Province, Adele Lotsove, a Congolese who had already been employed by the Mobutu and Kabila administrations. Information gathered clearly indicates that she was instrumental in the collection and transfer of funds from her assigned administrative region to the Ugandan authorities in 1999. According to some sources, she also contributed to the reallocation of land from Lendus to Hemas. On the Rwandan side, according to one reliable source, Rwandan authorities have helped secure the appointment of Gertrude Kitembo as Governor of Maniema.

72. **Modes of transportation**. Illegal activities have benefitted from the evolution of the means of transportation in the region. Prior to the second war most exchanges of goods and products were conducted through road transportation. To a large extent, smugglers utilized Lake Kivu and Lake Tanganyika to smuggle goods and products to and from the Democratic Republic of the Congo and, in limited circumstances, used aircraft. The shift over the past four years has been noticeable. An increasing number of aircraft are utilized to transport products and arms into the Democratic Republic of the Congo, while transferring out vast quantities of agricultural products and minerals, in particular to Kampala and Kigali. The other novelty of increased air transport has been the use of aircraft leased by the army for commercial and non-military functions. Different categories of people, including soldiers, journalists, and traders, have told the Panel about their journeys in aircraft alongside bags of coffee and other non-military products.

73. This change in mode of transportation was accompanied by a change

in players as well as a redefining of transportation companies. Traditional and well-established companies such as TMK saw their share of the market erode while others simply disappeared (Air Cargo Zaire). At the same time, new companies emerged and expanded, such as Air Navette and Jambo Safari; they are owned or controlled by the relatives and friends of generals, colonels and Presidents. At the other end, outsiders who entered the region with the AFDL "conquest" of Kinshasa during the first war, by transporting troops, remained and consolidated their position; that is the case of Victor Butt, a notorious arms dealer in the region. Most flights to and from Equateur and Orientale Provinces originate from the Entebbe military airport. During a visit to Kampala, the Panel was informed about the concern expressed by the Ugandan Internal Revenue to the Ministry of Defense. This complaint raised the issue of revenue loss to the treasury due to the fact that products entering or leaving the Democratic Republic of the Congo by air to and from Entebbe military airport are not checked, and taxes are not levied by the customs services.

74.On the Ugandan side, three main private companies are involved:

•Air Alexander, whose owner is Jovia Akandwanaho, the wife of Salim Saleh and sister-in-law of President Museveni. Her company mainly operated between Entebbe and Kisangani before the last battle of Kisangani. According to some sources, the company continues to operate in the territory held by Ugandan troops.

•Air Navette has dealings with General Salim Saleh and Jean-Pierre Bemba. The company flies to Gbadolite, Gemena, Kisangani, Bunia, and Kampala. This company uses an Antonov 26 and an Antonov 12.

•Uganda Air Cargo, which mainly deals with the Ugandan Ministry of Defense. Previously, it was using a C-130, but currently uses an Ilyushin 76 and an Antonov 12. This company flies to Entebbe, Gemena, Basankasu, Isiro, and Buta.

The Panel has indications that most private air companies do not own the aircraft they use; the owners are usually people like Victor Butt.

75.On the Rwandan side, a number of private companies operate in the territory. These are:

•New Gomair, which flies to Kisangani-Goma and Kigali. According to some sources, the wife of the current Minister of Finances of Rwanda is a shareholder.

•Air Navette flies to Goma, Bukavu, Kisangani, and Kigali. According to some sources, one of the major shareholders, Modeste Makabuza, also owner of Jambo Safari, is a known figure in the entourage of President Kagame.

•Air Boyoma is a shuttle between Goma and Lodja; according to some sources Mr. Ondekane, former first Vice-President of RCD-Goma, is a shareholder.

•Other companies, such as Compagnie aérienne des Grands Lacs et Cargo fret international, Sun Air Services and Kivu Air Services, operate in the area.

76.Clients and other very reliable sources have indicated that Sabena Cargo is transporting illegal natural resources extracted from the Democratic Republic of the Congo. Sabena Cargo is said to carry coltan extracted from the Democratic Republic of the Congo from Kigali airport to European destinations. The Panel asked to meet with the management of Sabena in Kampala and in Brussels, but no one was made available to speak to the Panel members.

77.**Financial network**. All illegal activities in the eastern Democratic Republic of the Congo, primarily the commercial and trade operations, utilize the financial network to some extent. One of the characteristics of this network has been its ability to quickly adapt to the new political and economic environment. Cities like Kisangani and Goma were already big trading centers for diamonds and consumer goods. Most banks operating in the occupied zones were already in operation in the Democratic Republic of the Congo before the August 1998 war. Their headquarters or corresponding banks were generally in Kinshasa. With the occupation, headquarters and corresponding banks tended to move to Kigali. Some of these banks are:

•Union des banques congolaises. Although the headquarters remains in Kinshasa, it has ongoing operations in areas controlled by Rwanda.

•Banque commerciale du Congo. The headquarters is in Kinshasa and it has branches in the eastern Democratic Republic of the Congo. The Director was transferred to Kigali in order to oversee operations in the eastern Democratic Republic of the Congo. This bank is linked to the Belgolaise, a Belgian bank consortium.

•Banque commerciale du Rwanda. The headquarters is in Kigali, but it has operations in Kisangani, Bukavu, and Goma. The Government of Rwanda is said to be one of the shareholders.

•Banque à la confiance d'or (BANCOR). One of the newest banks in Kigali which started its activities in 1995. It was family-owned until 1999 but early in 2000 a businessman, Tibere Rujigiro, purchased the bank at a very low price according to various sources.

78. **Special cases: BCDI and BCD**. The Banque de commerce, du développement et d'industrie is the newest bank, created in November 1996 and headquartered in Kigali. Its involvement with the Democratic Republic of the Congo dates back to the beginning of the AFDL conquest of the former Zaire. BCDI operated most AFDL financial transactions before Laurent-Désiré Kabila took power. The Panel was told that its shareholders are essentially the Rwandan Patriotic Front, COMIEX, Alfred Khalissa, and some Angolans. The real shareholders are the allies, except Uganda. Some documents, receipts for payments, and authorization for payments made by some large companies in the Democratic Republic of the Congo between early and late 1997 clearly indicate that payments are to be made through BCDI for the contribution to "the war effort." When the late President Kabila came to power, he created the Banque de commerce et du développement, which has the peculiarity of having as shareholders Tristar, COMIEX and Alfred Khalissa of BCDI. The Rwandan Patriotic Front remains, through BCDI and Tristar, a shareholder in BCD in spite of the war situation.

79. **Other private companies**. A number of companies were created to facilitate illegal activities in the Democratic Republic of the Congo. Others have existed in the region for decades and joined the bandwagon to pursue the obvious financial windfalls involved in the exploitation of the country. On the Ugandan, MLC, and RCD-ML side, rebel leaders and/or Ugandan military officials created new companies and businesses using *prête-noms*. Most, if not all, of these companies are privately owned by individuals or a group of individuals.

80. Among the companies involved in the illicit acquisition of natural resources in the Democratic Republic of the Congo, Trinity and Victoria seem to be the most interesting given their modus operandi, activities and respective shareholders. Victoria Group is chaired by Mr Khalil and its headquarters is in Kampala. According to reliable sources, Mr. Khalil deals directly with Mrs. Akandwanaho on diamond issues. Mr. Khalil has two collaborators in the Democratic Republic of the Congo, based in Kisangani

and Gbadolite. Both are said to be from Lebanon, they are Mohammed Gassan and Mr. Talal. During its visit to Gbadolite, the Panel received confirmation of the presence of one of them and his leading role in the purchase of diamonds in the region. A reliable source told members of the Panel that the Victoria Group belongs jointly to Muhoozi Kainerugabe, son of President Museveni, and Jovia and Khaleb Akandwanaho. Victoria Group is involved in trading diamonds, gold, and coffee. The Group purchases these mineral and agricultural products in Isiro, Bunia, Bumba, Bondo, Buta, and Kisangani. The company paid taxes to MLC, but failed to do so with RCD-ML. When counterfeit currencies (Congolese francs and United States dollars) were found in areas where the company buys the natural resources, fingers were pointed at the Victoria Group. Other sources have confirmed to the Panel the involvement of the Victoria Group in the making of counterfeit currency.

81. Trinity is an equally interesting case. Ateenyi Tibasima, second Vice-President of RCD-ML and now the *Commissaire général adjoint* of FLC, was the "manager" of the company. According to reliable sources, Trinity is a fictitious company and a conglomerate of various businesses owned by Salim Saleh and his wife. Its primary purpose was to facilitate their business activities in Orientale Province. To this end, Mr. Tibasima granted a tax holiday to all Trinity activities in the areas controlled by Uganda and administered by RCD-ML in November 1999. Trinity has imported various goods and merchandise and has taken from Orientale Province gold, coffee, and timber without paying any tax. Different individuals, Ugandans as well as Congolese, have taken the opportunity created by the confusion over Trinity to export from the Democratic Republic of the Congo (on behalf of Trinity) various natural resources, also without paying taxes.

82. On the Rwandan side, most companies with important activities related to the natural resources of the Democratic Republic of the Congo are owned either by the Government or by individuals very close to the inner circle of President Kagame. Rwanda Metals, for example, is a company involved in coltan dealing. It purchases coltan and exports it out of the continent. The Panel has strong indications that RPF controls Rwanda Metals. In mid-January 2001, some very reliable sources met with the senior management of Rwanda Metals in Kigali. During these discussions, the Director told them that Rwanda Metals was a private company with no

relation to the army. He further explained that he was expecting key partners that very morning for discussions. As discussions continued, the so-called partners arrived as planned; unfortunately they were in Rwandan army uniforms and were top officers. This incident confirms accounts from various sources indicating that Rwanda Metals is controlled by RPF. Meanwhile there are also indications that RPA is a shareholder of Grands Lacs Metals, a company also dealing in coltan.

83.Jambo Safari is another company whose emergence and growth has raised some eyebrows in Goma and Bukavu. When the August 1998 war started, Modeste Makabuza was buying oil from Kenya and selling it in the eastern Democratic Republic of the Congo. Jambo Safari has benefitted from an internal network of false receipts within RCD-Goma and RPA. According to a very reliable source, Jambo Safari would charge RCD-Goma for three times the quantities of oil delivered and any attempt to question the figures would be suppressed. In a rare attempt to clarify the situation, some members of RCD-Goma during the last General Assembly meeting, in June 2000, requested that a commission be set up to conduct an internal audit. Kigali agreed to send a colonel to conduct the audit along with an RCD team. When the issue of false receipts and overpayment was established, Kigali recalled the colonel and suspended the inquiry. Some sources have confirmed the close ties between Mr. Makabuza, the apparent owner of Jambo Safari, and President Kagame. Jambo Safari has diversified since its original business venture, is now dealing in coffee, recently purchased a fleet of new trucks, and is also involved in air transport with Air Navette.

84.Other minor companies also operate with the protection of some local commanders. For example, Établissement Habier is involved in the distribution of oil and petrol in Goma and Bukavu. This company is said to belong to Ernest Habimana, who is closely linked to RPA, especially to Major Karasira and Mr. Gakwerere. STIPAG, a company owed by Mr. Mbugiye operating in collaboration with Major Kazura (chief of security of the Rwandan Army in the Democratic Republic of the Congo) and Major Gatete, is among those junior companies involved in coffee and diamond dealing. Finally a myriad of small companies was created and their shareholders are invariably powerful individuals in the Rwandan nomenklatura or in RCD structures. That is the case of Grands Lacs Metals, where Majors Gatete, Dan, and Kazura are reportedly shareholders. In other cases, foreign companies incorporate local potentates on their board, as in the case of Gesellschaft für Elektrometallurgie (GFE), with Karl Heinz Albers and Emmanuel Kamanzi as partners, or MDM with Mr. Makabuza.

85. The Panel, on the basis of the data, accounts, and documents received and analyzed, came to the conclusion that the systems of illegal exploitation established by Ugandans and Rwandans differ from each other. In the case of Uganda, individuals, mainly top army commanders, using their hold over their collaborators and some officials in rebel movements, are exploiting the resources of the Democratic Republic of the Congo. However, this is known by the political establishment in Kampala.

86. In the case of Rwanda, things are more systemic. There are linkages and bridges between some key companies, as in the case of Tristar and BCDI and, above all, the relationship between RPA, RPF, BCDI, Rwanda Metals, Grands Lacs Metals, and Tristar. The senior management of these companies seems to report separately to the same people at the top of the pyramid. On the other hand, all key managers have personal relationships with different army commanders who themselves report to the leadership. This pyramidal and integrated structure coupled with the strict discipline of the group has made the exploitation of the resources of the Democratic Republic of the Congo more systematic, efficient, and organized. There is equally a bridge between the internal Rwandan structures of illegal exploitation and the RCD-Goma structures. The Government of Rwanda made arrangements with RCD-Goma to DRain resources from the Democratic Republic of the Congo. There is a case of loans made by BCDI to RCD to pay suppliers whose business is related to RPA. This "financial bridge" is statutory; indeed the RCD statute indirectly recognizes the role of Rwanda in overseeing the finances of the movement and its participation in decision-making and control/audit of finances.

E. Individual Actors

87. The list that follows is not exhaustive, but the Panel's choice was based on the crucial roles played by these persons and their direct involvement in either providing support, entertaining networks, or facilitating the exploitation of natural resources within the Democratic Republic of the Congo. On the Ugandan side, some familiar names surface

frequently, such as Major General Salim Saleh, Brigadier General James Kazini, Colonel Tikamanyire, Jovia Akandwanaho, Colonel Utafire, Colonel Mugeni, Mr. Khalil, Ateenyi Tibasima, Mbusa Nyamwisi, Nahim Khanaffer, Roger Lumbala, Jean-Yves Ollivier, Jean-Pierre Bemba, Adele Lotsove, Abdu Rhaman, and latecomers such as Colonel Muyombo.

88. The Panel has selected to focus on three key actors. First and second are Major General (retired) Salim Saleh and his wife, Jovia Akandwanaho. Khaleb Akandwanaho, alias Salim Saleh, and his spouse Jovia are at the core of the illegal exploitation of natural resources in areas controlled by Uganda. He is the younger brother of President Museveni (very popular in the army) and he pulls the strings of illegal activities in areas controlled by Uganda and allies. James Kazini is his executing arm and his right hand. He controls and protects Mbusa Nyamwisi and Ateenyi Tibasima. In return, they protect his commercial and business interests in regions controlled by the former RCD-ML. He used both the Victoria Group and Trinity for the purchase and the commercialization of diamonds, timber, coffee, and gold. Very reliable sources have told the Panel that behind Salim Saleh there is Jovia Akandwanaho, who is more aggressive on the issue of exploitation of the natural resources of the Democratic Republic of the Congo. She is particularly interested in diamonds. According to very reliable sources, she is at the root of the Kisangani wars. She wanted control of the Kisangani diamond market after having confirmation from Mr. Khalil, "Director" of the Victoria Group, that it was a good idea and that it was feasible to control the Kisangani market.

89. The third is Brigadier General James Kazini, former Chief of Staff of UPDF and former commander of military operations in the Democratic Republic of the Congo. He is the master in the field; the orchestrater, organizer, and manager of most illegal activities related to the UPDF presence in north and north-eastern Democratic Republic of the Congo. He is the right hand of Salim Saleh. He very much relies on the established military network and former comrades and collaborators, such as Colonels Tikamanyire and Mugeni. He has been close to Messrs. Nyamwisi, Tibasima, and Lumbala and to Jean-Pierre Bemba, all of whom have facilitated his illegal dealings in diamonds, coltan, timber, counterfeit currency, gold and coffee, and imports of goods and merchandise in Equateur and Orientale Provinces. He is said to have a good relationship with Mr. Baramoto, a former

general of President Mobutu. In spite of being discharged from his responsibilities as commander of UPDF forces in the Democratic Republic of the Congo, his networks remain in place. The Panel asked to meet with these key actors, but the request was turned down.

90. Actors from Rwanda and RCD-Goma involved in the illegal exploitation of natural resources in the Democratic Republic of the Congo cannot be separated from the structure they serve. Most of these people serve a system. The Panel has, however, noticed a recurrence of some names or the particular role that some individuals have played at a given time and for some operations. In addition to the names mentioned in the paragraphs on main companies, certain names can be highlighted.

91. First, Ali Hussein, who plays a major role in diamond and gold deals in Bukavu and Kisangani. Those who have dealt with him in the past have mentioned the presence of a Rwandan national during commercial negotiations. There are indications that the Rwandan citizen attending the meetings is a civil servant working Bin the President's office in Kigali. Second is Colonel James Kabarebe, who is the RPA facilitator for some deals. According to some sources he has been in contact with Victor Butt [or Bout] for the lease of an Ilyushin 76 that served to carry coltan from the Democratic Republic of the Congo to Kigali. He is said to be a partner to Mohamed Ali Salem, manager of the company Global Mineral. This company is involved in coltan purchasing in Bukavu and Goma. Third, Tibere Rujigiro, member of RPF, who is considered to be one of the main money providers to the party during the 1990-1994 war. He is a major shareholder in Tristar Investment, a company equally close to RPF. He is said to be also involved in the tobacco business.

92.The fourth, Aziza Kulsum Gulamali, is a unique case among key actors in the illegal exploitation of the natural resources of the Democratic Republic of the Congo. Mrs. Gulamali is said to hold several passports. She lives in Bukavu, Brussels, or Nairobi, depending on her schedule. Mrs. Gulamali has acknowledged having been involved in the past in the Burundi civil war. According to reliable sources she armed and financed the Hutu rebels of FDD in Burundi. Yet she built new alliances with the Government of Rwanda and has become a major ally of the Kigali regime and RCD-Goma. Mrs. Gulamali is involved in gold, coltan, and cassiterite dealings in territories controlled by the Rwandans. Prior to that, she was involved in arms trafficking for the benefit of the Burundian Hutus and was equally involved in gold and ivory trafficking. Her name was also mentioned in connection with cigarette smuggling. Very reliable sources told the Panel that she covered her illegal dealings by her cigarette factory, now in bankruptcy. In the coltan business, her clients include Starck, Cogecom, and Sogem; the Bank Bruxelles Lambert handles some of her financial transactions. The Panel requested RCD-Goma several times for a meeting with Mrs. Gulamali and also contacted her aides, but she never arranged a meeting with the Panel.

93. She was recently appointed by RCD-Goma as General Manager of SOMIGL, a conglomerate of four partners, which obtained the monopoly for the commercialization and export of coltan. This monopoly has strengthened her position as a major player in the trade in coltan in the region. RCD-Goma, in an attempt to explain this partnership, said that she is a very useful person and would bring $1 million to RCD monthly. Some sources have told the Panel members that her network of contacts is impressive and that she controls almost every official in RCD-Goma. According to some sources, she is also involved with her daughter, Djamila, in counterfeiting currency. Mrs. Gulamali is famous for forging customs declarations, especially for the products she exports. Confronted recently with a false customs declaration where coltan was declared as cassiterite, she replied, "In this business everybody does that." Her declaration alerted the Panel to the extent to which fraud is prevalent among the companies that export coltan.

F. Economic Data: Confirmation of the Illegal Exploitation of the Natural Resources of the Democratic Republic of the Congo

94. All the empirical evidence provided above is complemented by the economic analysis of data provided by different sources.

Uganda

95. At the request of the Panel, the Ugandan authorities provided extensive data, including production and export values for agricultural products such as coffee, cotton, tea, and tobacco. In terms of minerals, the data also cover gold and coltan production and export figures.

96.The official data contain substantial discrepancies. First, export figures for gold are consistently greater than production values, as shown in table 1 and figure 1.

97.The gap between production and export could originate from the exploitation of the natural resources of the Democratic Republic of the Congo. The Central Bank of Uganda has reportedly acknowledged to IMF officials that the volume of Ugandan gold exports does not reflect this country's production levels but rather, that some exports might be "leaking over the borders" from the Democratic Republic of the Congo. The central bank reported that, by September 1997, Uganda had exported gold valued at $105 million, compared with $60 million in 1996 and $23 million in 1995.

98.Second, the data from the Ugandan authorities are silent with regard to diamond production and export. Several third party sources (WTO, World Federation of Diamond Bourses, Diamond High Council) indicate diamond exports from Uganda during the last three years. These diamond exports are suspicious for many reasons:

(a) Uganda has no known diamond production;

(b) Diamond exports from Uganda are observed only in the last few years, coinciding surprisingly with the occupation of the eastern Democratic Republic of the Congo as shown in table 2 and figure 2;

(c) Finally, these facts corroborate the Panel's findings from field investigation, discussions, and external observers on the need to control the rich diamond zone near Kisangani and Banalia.

99.These figures are understated and there are indications that Uganda exported more diamonds. However, this is not well captured in the statistics because of the loose regulations governing the free zone areas. These regulations permit diamonds originating in any country to be repackaged, and then to be sold from any country as diamonds from a country of origin that is not necessarily the one mentioned in the statistics.

Table 1

Uganda: mineral exports and production, 1994-2000

Year	*Gold*	*Tin*	*Coltan*	*Cobalt*
A. Mineral exports (tons)				
1994	0.22	-	-	-
1995	3.09	-	-	-
1996	5.07	3.55	-	-
1997	6.82	4.43	2.57	-
1998	5.03	-	18.57	-
1999	11.45	-	69.5	67.48
2000	10.83	-	-	275.98
B. Mineral production (tons)				
1994	0.0016	3.704	0.435	-
1995	0.0015	4.289	1.824	-
1996	0.003	0.38	-	-
1997	0.0064	1.81	-	-
1998	0.0082	1.102	-	-
1999	0.0047	-	-	76.74
2000	0.0044	-	-	287.51

Source: Uganda, Ministry of Energy, and Mineral Development. 2000 data are from January to October.

Table 2

Uganda: rough diamond exports, 1997-October 2000

Year	*Volume (carats)*	*Value (United States dollars)*
1997	1 511.34	198 302
1998	11 303.86	1 440 000
1999	11 024.46	1 813 500
2000	9 387.51	1 263 385

Source: Diamond High Council.

Figure 1. Uganda: gold production and exports, 1994-2000

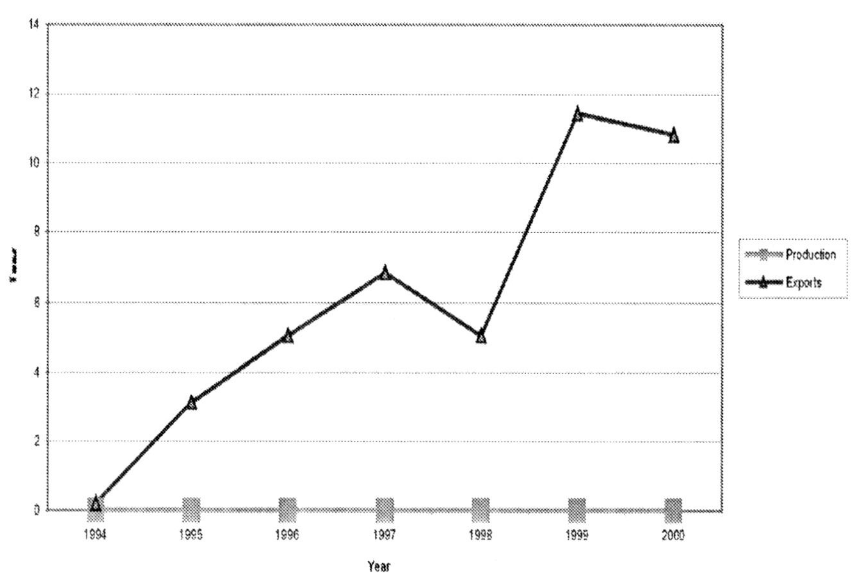

100. Data collected from any third party consistently show that Uganda has become a diamond exporting country; they also show that diamond exports from Uganda coincide with the years of the wars in the Democratic Republic of the Congo, that is from 1997 onward.

101. As far as niobium is concerned, the pattern appears to be the same: no production prior to 1997 followed by a series of increases in exports as shown in table 3 and figure 3.

Table 3

Uganda: niobium exports, 1995-1999 (thousands of United States dollars)

Year	*Niobium*
1995	0
1996	0
1997	13
1998	580
1999	782

Source: World Trade Organization (aggregated data).

102. Third, the Ugandan authorities, in their response to the Panel's questionnaire, stated that there was no record of transit of mineral products. However, the Panel received information from one Ugandan customs post at the border between the Democratic Republic of the Congo and Uganda. Records for 1998, 1999, and 2000 reveal that mineral products as well as other commodities left the Democratic Republic of the Congo and entered Uganda (presumably this would also prove true for the other dozen or so points of entry). The following three examples show an increase in the trans-boundary movement of natural resources between 1998 and 1999.

Coffee 1998: 144,911 bags
1999: 170,079 bags
2000: 208,000 bags
Timber 1998: 1,900 m3
1999: 3,782 m3 and 46,299 pcs
2000: 3,272 m3 and 3,722 pcs
Cassiterite* 1998: None
1999: 30 kgs
2000: 151 Drums

* The sudden increase in the import of cassiterite may also mean an increase in the import of coltan. The Panel discovered that cassiterite is often listed in lieu of coltan, as coltan possesses a higher value, which implies high import taxes in Uganda.

Rwanda

103. In response to the request for statistics by the Panel, the Rwandan authorities provided the following data:

Table 4
Rwanda: mineral production, 1995-2000

Year	*Gold (kg)*	*Cassiterite (tons)*	*Coltan (tons)*
1995	1	247	54
1996	1	330	97
1997	10	327	224
1998	17	330	224
1999	10	309	122
2000	10	437	83

Source: Rwanda Official Statistics (No. 227/01/10/MIN).

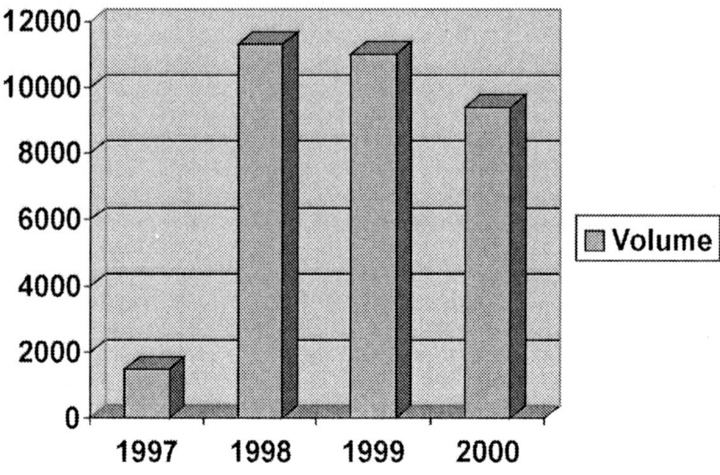

Figure 2. Uganda: rough diamond exports, by volume, 1997 - October 2000

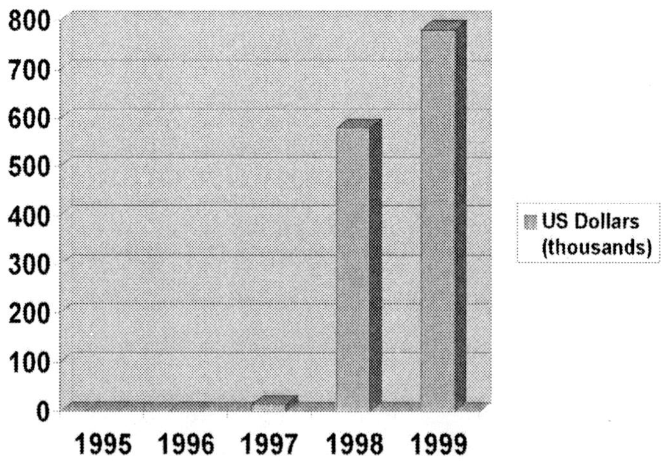

Figure 3. Uganda: niobium exports by volume, 1995-1999

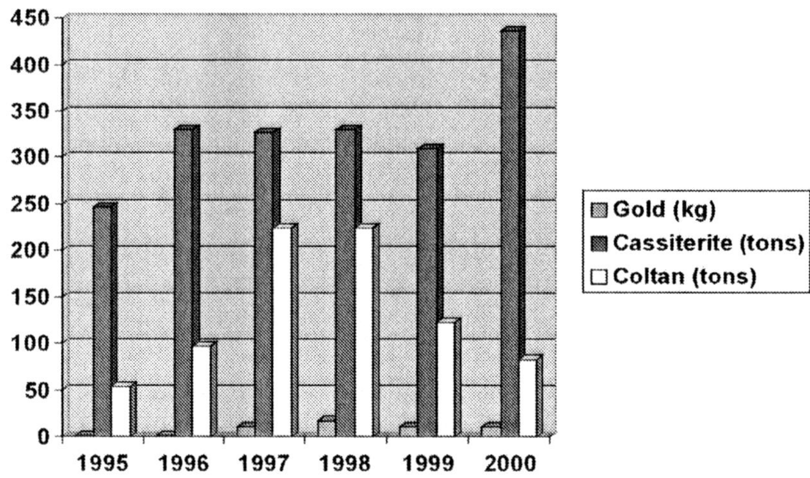

Figure 4.A. Rwanda: mineral production, 1995-2000

Figure 4.B. Rwanda: gold production, 1995-2000 (kg)

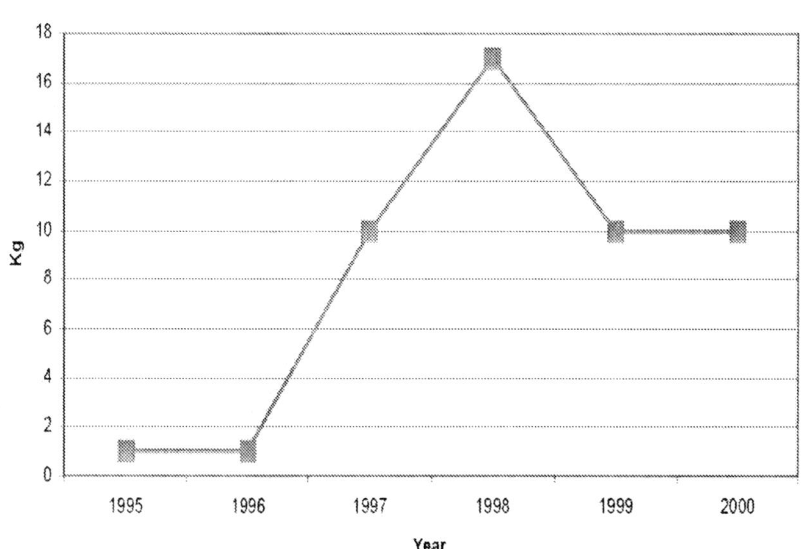

104. The Rwandan authorities also underline the fact that "Rwanda has no production of diamond, cobalt, zinc, manganese, and uranium." However, in spite of this statement, there is substantial evidence that Rwanda has been exporting diamonds. In fact, several organizations such as WTO and the High Diamond Council, and Belgian statistics, have computed import data for selected commodities and provide support for the fact that Rwanda has been exporting diamonds (see table 5 and figure 5). Production figures display some irregular patterns for gold and coltan starting from 1997 (see figures 4.A and B). It is revealing that the increase in production of these two minerals appeared to happen while AFDL, backed by Rwandan troops, was taking over power in Kinshasa.

Table 5

Rwanda: rough diamond exports, 1997-October 2000

Year	*Volume (carats)*	*Value (United States dollars)*
1997	13 060.39	720 425
1998	166.07	16 606
1999	2 500.83	439 347
2000	30 491.22	1 788 036

Source: Diamond High Council.

105. **Burundi**. An IMF office memorandum indicates that "Burundi does not produce gold, diamonds, columbo-tantalite, copper, cobalt, or basic metals." Burundi, however, has been exporting minerals it does not produce. As in the case of Uganda and Rwanda, Burundi's export of diamonds dates from 1998, coinciding with the occupation of the eastern Democratic Republic of the Congo. The coltan exports span a longer period (1995-1999), perhaps suggesting that this might be a regular activity.

106. **Angola, Namibia and Zimbabwe**. Only third party sources were used to determine whether production and export trends in these countries displayed abnormalities. Available production and export statistics relative to Angola, Namibia, and Zimbabwe were fairly normal in terms of trend. They did not reveal any suspicious behavior. Additional data are however needed for a definite stand on the issue. In the case of Zimbabwe, accounts of ongoing and pending deals give clear indications of their potential impact on the balance of payments.

107. The economic and resource-based analysis above, by using the figures given by the respective Governments, reveals that Uganda and Rwanda have been exporting diamonds, and that this activity is hidden and does not appear in the statistics they disseminate. They do not produce diamonds, nor do they officially export this mineral. It is probable that these minerals are coming from the Democratic Republic of the Congo and would constitute the basis for the re-exportation economy.

108. Regarding the Democratic Republic of the Congo, mineral production and export display a declining trend, imputable partly to the occupation of the eastern side of the country. However, the deterioration of the rural infrastructure represents a limiting factor for mining as well as for agricultural activities.

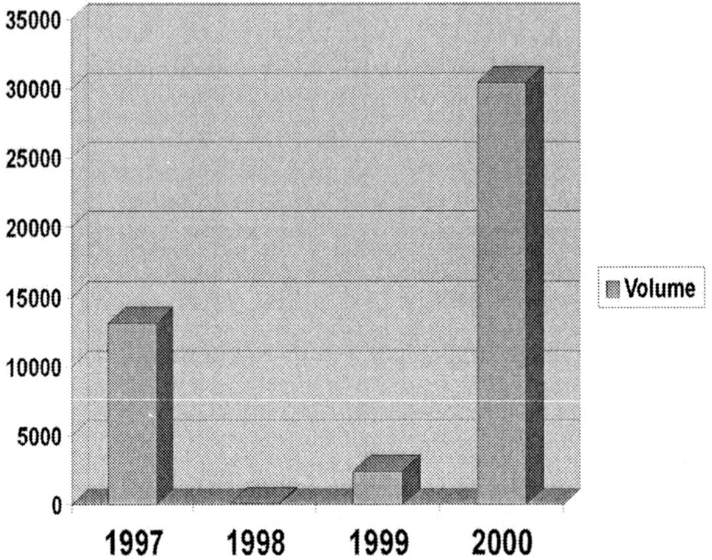

Figure 5. Rwanda: rough diamond exports, by volume, 1997-October 2000

III. Links Between the Exploitation of Natural Resources and the Continuation of the Conflict

109. The following sections explore the links between the exploitation of natural resources and the continuation of the conflict in the Democratic Republic of the Congo. The sections are interrelated, but separated for clarity. The first section outlines the countries' budget allocations for their respective armed forces versus the actual expenditures. It will be demonstrated that military expenditures far outweigh the supposed money allocated for such expenses. The subsequent section will explore, in depth, the means by which these countries find the necessary additional financial resources to continue the war.[362] The panel finds a link between the exploitation of the natural resources of the Democratic Republic of the Congo and the continuation of the conflict.

A. Budgets Compared to Military Expenditures

Rwanda

110. Rwanda spends about 3 percent of its GDP or 29 percent of its annual budget on its defense needs. In the current fiscal year, $70 million was allocated to defense in the national budget. These official figures provided by the Minister of Finance comprise every single expense of the army, including soldiers' pay and bonuses and the maintenance and acquisition of new military equipment.

111. Military specialists with a great deal of experience in the region agreed on the fact that Rwandan soldiers use light equipment, so that expenses on equipment have for a long time been limited. They also recognize that, given the size of the Democratic Republic of the Congo and the portion of the territory under Rwandan control, there is a minimum number of soldiers needed to cover this area, which could be estimated at 25,000 soldiers on average during the period of the conflict. Moreover, the use of aircraft for the transport of troops and some types of equipment and supplies may be costly.

112. An aircraft owner operating in the region has indicated that he charges on average $2,000 per hour. Based on his experience of three rotations per day in a smaller area, the Panel estimates five rotations for Rwanda at an average of six hours each. A simple calculation gives a figure of $1.8 million per month and $21.6 million per year.

113. Based on the minimum number of 25,000 soldiers in the Democratic Republic of the Congo and an average $100 for pay and bonuses, the Panel has calculated a total of $2.5 million per month and $30 million per year. Transportation and pay of troops alone in the Democratic Republic of the Congo amount to $51.6 million per year, which is about three quarters of the total Rwandan official defense budget. By taking into consideration the remaining 20,000 soldiers stationed in Rwanda and their average pay of $50 per month, almost the total defense budget ($63 million) is used on two items. RPA soldiers in the Democratic Republic of the Congo have other basic needs, however, such as ammunition for even their light equipment, and maintenance and replacement of the equipment.

114.All military experts consulted suggested that the official defense *budget of Rwanda cannot alone cover the cost of their war and presence in th*e Democratic Republic of the Congo. The Panel concurs with President Kagame, who described the conflict in the Democratic Republic of the Congo as "a self-financing war."

Uganda

115. Uganda officially spends about 2 percent of its GDP on defense, which is being monitored by the Bretton Woods institutions. For the fiscal year 2000, the defense budget was about $110 million. This budget covers pay of about $70 per month for 50,000 soldiers, 10,000 of whom are stationed in the Democratic Republic of the Congo, pays for the pension of retired soldiers, buys equipment and addresses other needs.

116. According to various sources, UPDF has on average 10,000 soldiers in the Democratic Republic of the Congo out of the 50,000 total. Indeed, the budget line for pay alone for a year is about $41 million for the 50,000 Ugandan soldiers. If a bonus of $20 is paid to each of the 10,000 soldiers, that would amount to $200,000 per month (in 1998 and 1999), a total of $2.4 million per year.

117. On the basis of a rate of $2,000 per hour and six hours on average for a return journey and three rotations a day, UPDF spends on average $12.96 million per year on transportation alone. Other expenses for purchase, maintenance, and replacement of equipment are important. According to some sources, Uganda spent about $126 million on its armed forces in 1999, an overspending of about $16 million.

Democratic Republic of the Congo

118. Of all the warring parties, the Democratic Republic of the Congo presented the greatest challenge as far as defense budget figures and number of troops were concerned. Lack of reliable data and the barely existent State apparatus have made the collection of data very difficult. The country has been at war since 1996 and prior to that the army was already disintegrating. Various military experts that the Panel members met agree on one point: the extreme difficulty of giving an estimate of the Democratic Republic of the

Congo army. Those who try to give an estimate speak of 50,000 to 55,000 soldiers.

119. According to some government sources, the Democratic Republic of the Congo relies on Chinese and Eastern European companies to supply its military arsenal and required equipment. The Panel has strong indications that the Government, despite its economic problems, has invested a great deal in the defense of its territory.

Zimbabwe

120. Zimbabwe's overall defense budget has been decreasing at the very moment ZDF has troops engaged in the Democratic Republic of the Congo. A reduction was announced early in January 2000, lowering the budget from Z$15.3 billion in 2000 to Z$13.3 billion in 2001. Yet, ZDF with approximately 10,000 troops engaged in the Democratic Republic of the Congo spent on average about $3 million per month, a total of $36 million in a year.

Angola and Namibia

121. Angola's presence is smaller than Zimbabwe's in terms of troops. According to some sources, Angolan troops number about 3,000. Namibia's presence is limited to 2,000 troops. The defense budget of N$24 million has remained at the same level since 1999 in spite of the support given to the Democratic Republic of the Congo. However, the emergency or additional budget for the armed forces has decreased from N$89 million in 1999 to N$76 million in 2001.

Rebels

122. The rebel movements MLC, RCD-Goma, and RCD-ML have their own troops. MLC troops are evaluated at 12,000 to 15,000 men. They usually use light military equipment bought from Kampala. In some cases, deals are done between Jean-Pierre Bemba and other traders and businessmen. These deals consist of giving them the opportunities to carry out business activities or granting a mining concession, in exchange for which the beneficiary would supply some military items. In 1999, when Mr. Khalil demanded of

Mr. Bemba a concession for a diamond mine, he obtained a concession in exchange for military fatigues and socks, all made in Uganda.

123. The pay of these soldiers is unknown. The Panel gathered, however, that these young men were not paid, but could receive from time to time some money as "help." The consequence has been their involvement in the exploitation of natural resources. The cost of war appears to be minimal. The war expenses are the purchase of ammunition and light weapons, transport of soldiers by air and the money MLC paid to UPDF and individual top officers for their support. A similar scenario was played out with RCD-ML, which has approximately 3,000 soldiers.

124. The RCD-Goma troops are estimated to be around 12,000 to 15,000. According to some sources, the Rwandan army until recently used to supply the RCD-Goma troops with military equipment. The military budget was not offered to the Panel in spite of its request, and the estimates are very difficult to make. Military equipment and the transport of troops as well as supplies of oil and petrol are the major expenses. Pay is apparently uncertain, so that the soldiers when possible try to survive, even at the expense of the local population and the wildlife. For all parties involved in the conflict in the Democratic Republic of the Congo, this war seems to be expensive by African standards. The question is: how do the different parties finance their war effort?

B. Financing the War

125. There are three primary means of financing this war: (a) purchase of arms and equipment through direct payment; (b) barter (arms for mining concessions); and (c) creation of joint ventures. The economies of Rwanda and Uganda, unlike those of Angola and Namibia, have two varying ways they have financially benefitted from the conflict. Zimbabwe is a special case given the potential of concessions attributed to Zimbabwean companies. Data received from various sources, including the countries involved in the conflict, OECD, and the Bretton Woods institutions, demonstrate that in broad terms the mineral production of those three countries has decreased. However there are some interesting peaks between 1997 and 1999 (see sect. II.F above). Isolated and varied examples of how these countries finance their military presence in the Democratic Republic of the Congo are given below.

Rwanda

126. Rwanda's military appears to be benefitting directly from the conflict. Indeed, the Panel has noted a great integration between the military apparatus, the State (civil) bureaucracy and the business community. RPA finances its war in the Democratic Republic of the Congo in five ways: (a) direct commercial activities; (b) profit from shares it holds in some companies; (c) direct payments from RCD-Goma; (d) taxes collected by the "Congo desk" and other payments made by individuals for the protection RPA provides for their businesses; and (e) direct uptake by the soldiers from the land.

127. Since 1998, the Department of External Relations, through the Congo desk has been receiving substantial amounts of money from various comptoirs. Several diamond comptoirs were operating in Kisangani before the monopoly was given to two in July 2000. According to very reliable sources, taxes were paid directly to the Congo desk. On average, a comptoir with a turnover of $4 million per month would pay $200,000 per month to the Congo desk. Every diamond dealer who intends to purchase diamonds in the eastern Democratic Republic of the Congo or at Kigali would pay 5 percent of the diamond value to the Congo desk before the transaction. This amount is consistent with the so-called mandatory 5 percent of the value of purchased diamonds that the Congo desk takes from the two comptoirs controlling the Kisangani diamond market. Messrs. Nassour and Arslanian, the "conflict diamond dealers" in the eastern Democratic Republic of the Congo, provided, on average, $2 million per year, each directly to the Congo desk. A similar percentage is applied for other mineral resources in the area controlled by RCD-Goma.

128. Before July 2000, monopoly holders used to pay the sum of $200,000 per month in its entirety to Kigali; this has changed slightly since RCD-Goma claimed its share. The larger diamond comptoirs would, therefore, pay $100,000 to the Congo desk and $100,000 to the RCD-Goma authority. The Panel believes that over a period of two years the Congo desk would have received about $4 million as direct payment for granting the authorization to operate in the areas under its control.

129. Some documents point to a direct implication of the Rwandan

Patriotic Army in commercial activities. As mentioned earlier, RPA, through the companies Rwanda Metals and Grands Lacs Metals, has big stakes in the coltan business. Most of the coltan extracted by civilians and prisoners is sold to intermediaries (civilians or soldiers) who in turn sell it to *comptoirs*, some of which are controlled by the Rwandan military. The quasi-totality of this coltan is sent to Kigali, and generally stored in facilities owned by the Government. A good portion goes to Rwanda Metals and the rest is exported directly by some professionals. Rwanda Metals and Grands Lacs Metals, directly or through Congo desk, contact clients on the availability of coltan. Some of the letters sent to potential clients in Europe and the United States of America are signed Dan, who was the head of the Congo desk.

130. Given the substantial increase in the price of coltan between late 1999 and late 2000, a period during which the world supply was decreasing while the demand was increasing, a kilo of coltan of average grade was estimated at $200. According to the estimates of professionals, the Rwandan army through Rwanda Metals was exporting at least 100 tons per month. The Panel estimates that the Rwandan army could have made $20 million per month, simply by selling the coltan that, on average, intermediaries buy from the small dealers at about $10 per kg. According to experts and dealers, at the highest estimates of all related costs (purchase and transport of the minerals), RPA must have made at least $250 million over a period of 18 months. This is substantial enough to finance the war. Here lies the vicious circle of the war. Coltan has permitted the Rwandan army to sustain its presence in the Democratic Republic of the Congo. The army has provided protection and security to the individuals and companies extracting the mineral. These have made money which is shared with the army, which in turn continues to provide the enabling environment to continue the exploitation. The last illustration of how Rwanda finances its war deals with the financial transactions involving Rwandan banks, RPA suppliers and RCD institutions. In these particular cases, Rwanda has used BCDI and SONEX to pay RPA suppliers.

131. SONEX was founded in March 1999 in Kigali. It belonged to RCD-Goma and was managed by Emmanuel Kamanzi, former chief of the Finance Department of RCD-Goma. Its primary purpose was to serve as the commercial and financial arm of RCD, handling most commercial and financial deals. SONEX was dissolved late in 2000, but it had sufficient time

to put in place a pattern for the transfer of resources from RCD to Kigali. The Panel received documents highlighting the financial transactions of SONEX and BCDI. According to those documents, BCDI released $1 million in mid-1999 for SONEX as a loan to pay fuel bills to Jambo Safari. SONEX was to repay this loan with the money obtained from the selling of coltan and cassiterite. By February 2000, $200,000 to $300,000 had already been reimbursed to BCDI. This loan seems to be part of the financial transaction by which money is transferred to Kigali, and some individuals in RCD take their own substantial cut.

132. The same year, SONEX requested another loan of $10 million from BCDI in Kigali, and $5 million was approved. According to one of the actors at the time, the $5 million loan was not physically paid to SONEX. Instead, BCDI ordered Citibank in New York to pay RCD suppliers with the loans technically given to SONEX. This financial arrangement is suspicious in many ways.

133. First, RPF through Tristar is a shareholder in BCDI. Second, the suppliers of RCD are mostly Rwandan companies whose owners are closely acquainted with RPA or RPF. Third, the deal with SONEX is handled by Major Dan, at the Congo desk, who is related by marriage to Mr. Kamanzi, head of the Finance Department and mastermind of the whole operation.

134. The BCDI loans to SONEX could be well-crafted operations to transfer money from BCDI to RPA and to pay RPA suppliers by using SONEX. Paying RPA suppliers is one way of financing the war without taking from the official budget. Reliable sources report that about $700,000 has already been paid back by RCD. According to a RCD-Goma document explicitly detailing how debts should be repaid with money made out of the coltan sale, part of the $1 million per month in taxes that Mrs. Gulamali pays to RCD for the monopoly on coltan could also be used to pay back the BCDI loan.

Uganda

135. Uganda, unlike Rwanda, did not set up an extra-budgetary system to finance its presence in the Democratic Republic of the Congo. The regular defense budget is used and broadly the deficit is handled by the treasury.

However, the Ugandan economy benefitted from the conflict through the re-exportation economy. In turn, the treasury benefitted and this allowed an increase in the defense budget.

136. The re-exportation economy implies that natural resources imported from the Democratic Republic of the Congo are repackaged or sealed as Ugandan natural resources or products and re-exported. That is the case for some gold, diamonds, coltan, and coffee exported by Uganda. The re-exportation economy has had a tremendous impact on the financing of the war, in three ways.

137. First, it has increased the incomes of key businessmen, traders, and other dealers. In the coffee sector, gains have been substantial for the traders in Kampala and Bujumbura. According to an expert in the sector who lives in the region, there is a trick used by coffee exporters in the region. Arabica coffee produced in Bujumbura is of a higher grade than the one produced in Kivu. The difference in price could be in some cases one third. Burundian dealers, by importing Congolese coffee and mixing it then presenting it as Burundian coffee, gain a higher price. The Ugandan traders use the same schemes. In the case of Uganda, the dealers gain both ways. The trader buys inexpensive coffee in the Democratic Republic of the Congo, often with counterfeit currency, eventually mixes it with Ugandan coffee, and then re-exports this coffee as Ugandan robusta, which is of better quality than Congolese robusta.

138. Second, the illegal exploitation of gold in the Democratic Republic of the Congo brought a significant improvement in the balance of payments of Uganda. This, in turn, gave multilateral donors, especially IMF, which was monitoring the Ugandan treasury situation, more confidence in the Ugandan economy. Third, it has brought more money to the treasury through various taxes on goods, services, and international trade. Discussions with the Deputy Commissioner of the Ugandan Revenue Authority revealed that the tax collection level has increased dramatically over the past five years. IMF figures on Ugandan fiscal operations confirm this positive evolution over the past three years. A detailed analysis of the structure and the evolution of the fiscal operations reveals that some sectors have done better than others, and most of those tend to be related to the agricultural and forestry sector in the Democratic Republic of the Congo. Logs, sawn wood, or planks destined for

Uganda, Kenya, or for export out of the continent pay customs duties as they enter Uganda.

139. Between 1998 and 2000, about 1,800 trucks carrying logs, timber, coffee, medicinal barks, cassiterite, pyrochlore, iron ore, tea, and quinina have transited through Uganda. The official figures from the Government of Uganda show an average of 600 lorries per year, all registered by customs officers. As Mrs. Lotsove once noted, the tax exoneration given to the Victoria and Trinity companies represents a net loss of $5 million per month (there are 15 points of entry). The Panel concludes that, given the absence of the exoneration on the Ugandan side, and a higher level of taxes in Uganda, customs duties related to the transiting of Congolese natural resources exploited by Ugandans and some Congolese in Equateur and Orientale Provinces would bring the treasury at least $5 million every month.

140. Another way of financing the presence of the army in the Democratic Republic of the Congo was to purchase military supplies on credit. The Ugandan army has purchased petrol on credit from a number of private companies. The accruing debt is treated as internal debt.

141. The Panel also gathered that the local commanders of UPDF turn a blind eye to soldiers' racketeering among the populations or their involvement in small business. This is seen as a way to pay their bonuses and this has proved to be a very successful method. Information received from friends and relatives of UPDF soldiers who served in the Democratic Republic of the Congo clearly shows that there were elements of self-payment much more satisfactory than the official bonus. Overall, the military, its leaders, and other involved individuals manage to manipulate budgetary and other factors to retain their control in the occupied territories.

142. The Ugandan situation can be summarized as follows: the re-exportation economy has helped increase tax revenues, allowing the treasury to have more cash. Businesses related to the conflict and managed by Ugandans have contributed to an extent to generate activities in the economy in a sector such as mining (gold and diamonds). The growth in these sectors has had a trickle-down effect on the economy and permitted Uganda to improve its GDP in 1998 and maintain it somewhat in 1999.[363] The improvement in GDP has permitted, according to Ugandan officials, an

increase in absolute terms of the military budget while keeping the level of the military budget at the agreed 2 percent of GDP. The apparent strength of the *Ugandan economy has given more confidence to investors and bilateral* and multilateral donors who, by maintaining their level of cooperation and assistance to Uganda, gave the Government room to spend more on security matters while other sectors, such as education, health, and governance, are being taken care of by the bilateral and multilateral aid.

MLC, RCD-Goma, and RCD-ML

143. Officially, the rebel movements receive the bulk of their military equipment through UPDF and RPA. During discussions with the Ugandan Minister of Defense and the Chief of Staff of UPDF, the Panel was informed that weapons seized from the Congolese armed forces are usually given to MLC and RCD-ML. According to other sources, some military equipment is acquired by these groups through direct purchase and barter. The Panel came across a very interesting case in which Mr. Bemba, at the instigation of General Kazini, bargained with the highest authorities of Uganda for the release of some Ukrainian pilots whose Antonov has been captured. A very reliable source told the Panel that in exchange Mr. Bemba received military fatigues, boots, and medical supplies for his soldiers from a third party.

144. RCD-Goma has designed a fiscal system based mainly on the mining sector. About six different forms of tax exist in this sector, and they are applied on approximately eight different types of minerals, including the most important (coltan, gold, and diamonds). From RCD official statistics the Panel notes that in 1999 on average 60 kg of gold were extracted every month from the area controlled by RCD. That is about 720 kg a year. In 2000, the extraction was higher, up to 100 kg a month. With regard to coltan, 27 tons were extracted every month in 1999, while 29 tons were produced every month in 2000. Given the number of comptoirs (19 for coltan), and the six types of tax, the Panel concludes that substantial revenues through tax collection are available to RCD. It is, however, difficult to estimate the figures, although some insiders have told the Panel that the financial situation has been improving since late 2000, and the prospects for a balanced budget are better than two years ago. Information obtained from documents and individuals suggests that, in addition to taxes levied and shares it holds in SOMIGL, RCD-Goma has given a monopoly of coltan to SOMIGL, in

exchange for which it receives $1 million monthly.

145. **Illustration of the commercial activities of RCD**. A preponderance of information obtained from documents and individuals regarding the activities of RCD-Goma in the Democratic Republic of the Congo, Dar es Salaam, United Republic of Tanzania, and elsewhere during the current hostilities, overwhelmingly suggests that RCD-Goma and others are marketing the natural resources of the Democratic Republic of the Congo—gold, diamonds, and timber—through Dar es Salaam. Gold and diamonds belonging to RCD-Goma are shipped through their financial and logistical network, via Dar es Salaam, for sale on the international market. In order to facilitate the movement of the commodities and to give the appearance of legitimacy, RCD-Goma obtains documents to hide or cover their ownership. The documents covering the shipments of gold and diamonds are completed forms of the Democratic Republic of the Congo. The forms indicate issuance from a government organization, complete with the required stamps and signatures indicating approval and issuance in Kinshasa and Lubumbashi. RCD-Goma's representatives in Dar es Salaam coordinate the receipt, forwarding, and sale of gold and diamond shipments. The gold shipments transit through Dar es Salaam international airport for sale to buyers in Sri Lanka and elsewhere. The diamond shipments are held at the Bank of Tanzania before being forwarded to Belgium, the Netherlands, and South Africa.

146. The gold and diamonds are being sold by RCD-Goma in exchange for cash or bartered for armaments and medicines to support continuation of the current hostilities. RCD-Goma's representatives in Dar es Salaam also arrange for the purchase of foodstuffs and other logistical needs for the war effort. In addition, timber resources from the Democratic Republic of the Congo are being shipped through Dar es Salaam to Greece and Belgium. In the case of Greece, the timber transaction is being partially arranged by an import/export business located in Goma. The shipments of gold, diamonds, and timber are also processed in Dar es Salaam in cooperation with RCD representatives by a company believed to be a covert business entity created for the purpose of facilitating support for the financial and logistical operations of RCD-Goma. It is important to note that the activities described above represent an RCD-Goma operation and are exclusive of operations handled by the Government of Rwanda, via Kigali.

147. The Panel concludes on this point that the major rebel groups are gradually becoming autonomous (MLC/FLC and RCD-Goma) in terms of supply of military equipment. They are capable of raising substantial amounts of cash, enough to buy the light equipment they use. Equally they have put in place their own network and contacts, which would allow them to purchase their own equipment when necessary. This growing autonomy has manifested itself recently as RCD-Goma has requested that money usually given to the Congo desk by diamond dealers be shared equally between both entities. Equally, RCD-Goma has initiated some military attacks on RCD-ML positions in order to occupy mineral-rich areas as shown earlier. As the need for an autonomous supply of weapons grows, so does the need to find additional resources, and therefore clashes for the control of mineral-rich areas will be recurrent; so goes the vicious circle of war and exploitation of natural resources on the side of the rebellion.

Democratic Republic of the Congo

148. The Government of the Democratic Republic of the Congo has relied on its minerals and mining industries to finance the war. Between 1998 and early 2001, the strategy for financing the war was based on three pillars, namely (a) search for cash through the attribution of monopolies; (b) direct and indirect uptake of funds from parastatals and other private companies; and (c) creation of joint ventures between parastatals and foreign companies in countries allied with the Democratic Republic of the Congo.

149. **Search for cash**. The late President used different schemes to raise funds. He instituted the *tax parafiscale* (see para. 41) and also implemented schemes such as the creation of a monopoly for the commercialization of diamonds.

150. **Monopoly on diamonds granted to International Diamond Industries (IDI)**. According to government sources, the objective of this monopoly was twofold: first, to have fast and fresh money that could be used for the purchase of needed arms, and address some of the pending problems with the allies. Second, to have access to Israeli military equipment and intelligence given the special ties that the Director of International Diamond Industries, Dan Gertler, has with some generals in the Israeli army.

151. This deal turned out to be a nightmare for the Government of the

Democratic Republic of the Congo and a disaster for the local diamond trade, as well as an embarrassment for the Republic of the Congo, which is currently flirting with illicit diamonds. According to different sources, IDI paid only $3 million instead of $20 million and never supplied military equipment.

152. President Joseph Kabila has expressed willingness to liberalize the diamond trade in the Democratic Republic of the Congo, and IMF and the World Bank are very supportive of this move. IDI is, however, threatening to sue the Government of the Democratic Republic of the Congo. The IDI deal also turns out to be a disaster for the local diamond trade. As the monopoly was granted to IDI, most diamond dealers operating in the Government-controlled area crossed to Brazzaville to sell their diamonds. It is estimated that during the first three months of the monopoly, $60 million worth of diamonds from the Democratic Republic of the Congo were sold on the international market, and the Republic of the Congo was mentioned as the country of origin. This smuggling of diamonds deprived the already ailing economy of the Democratic Republic of the Congo of substantial sums of money and the treasury of substantial tax revenues. This case shows that the desperate need for quick cash to finance the defense of its territory has instead brought other problems to the Government and has paradoxically deprived the treasury of substantial revenue.

153. **Uptaking money from parastatals**. Another way of financing the war has been the direct and indirect uptake of money from parastatals and other private companies, mainly the Société minière de Bakwanga and the Générale des carrières et des mines (Gecamines). The Government has claimed from MIBA since August 1998 on average two fifths of their earnings. The Panel was told that in some cases three fifths, the equivalent of $4 million per sale, was sent to the President's office. The Panel has also confirmation that oil companies gave important sums of money as *taxes parafiscales* to the Government. In most cases, this cash in Congolese francs was delivered to Victor Mpoyo, who then reported to the late President Kabila. This money was used for the salary and bonuses of Congolese soldiers in the battlefield. According to some Congolese officials, the *taxes parafiscales* were never used for the purchase of weapons.

154. MIBA receives from the Government the equivalent of two fifths of its sales of diamonds in Congolese francs changed at the official rate, which

is only one quarter of the black market rate. It is believed that about 75 Congolese francs for each dollar changed is unaccounted for and possibly used for defense needs.[364]

155. The contribution of Gecamines to the war effort appears to be on two levels. On the one hand, one third of the company's profit was taken directly by the Government in 1999 and in 2000. On the other, the Government contributed indirectly to the expenses of the Zimbabwe Defense Forces between May 1999 and October 2000.

A Special Case: Zimbabwe

156. Zimbabwe has financed its involvement in the conflict in two different ways: (a) by using the defense budget—the bulk of Zimbabwe's military expenses seem to be covered by the regular budget; (b) by indirect financing of the war through direct payment by some Congolese entities, mainly companies. According to two very reliable sources, during the tenure of Billy Rautenbach money from Gecamines paid bonuses to the Zimbabwean soldiers. These payments might be linked to the contract between the Government and Ridgepoint. Indeed, part of the rights to exploit Gecamines mines was transferred to Ridgepoint without apparent compensation. According to some sources, the compensation, which is not mentioned in the contract, could be the sharing of profits between the Government of the Democratic Republic of the Congo and Ridgepoint, on the basis of 80 percent for the Government and 20 percent for Ridgepoint. According to some sources, curiously, Mr. Mpoyo, the Congolese minister, signed the contract as one of the officials of Ridgepoint rather than signing on behalf of the Government. Two months after the contract of Mr. Rautenbach as Director of Gecamines came to an end, discontent among Zimbabwean soldiers in Katanga over their lack of bonuses was reported.

157. The Panel has, however, noted a practice which is neither the financing of war nor the provision of direct assistance. The practice is qualified in this report as "incentives for assistance." The former Government of the Democratic Republic of the Congo often used the potential of its vast resources in the Katanga and Kasai regions to secure the assistance of some allies or to cover some of the expenses that they might incur during their participation in the war. Among all of its allies,

Zimbabwean companies and some decision makers have benefitted most from this scheme. The following examples illustrate how different schemes were implemented and benefitted the decision makers, the very group of officials who can decide about ZDF assistance to the Democratic Republic of the Congo. The most utilized scheme has been the creation of joint ventures.

158. Joint ventures. One way of securing the engagement of some allies in the war has been the provision of financial incentives by way of creating business opportunities in the mining sector. At least three features emerged from the scheme: (a) Zimbabwean companies received interesting mining concessions; (b) Zimbabwean companies using their influence with the Government of the Democratic Republic of the Congo developed business partnerships with private companies and parastatals; and (c) in turn, received preferential treatment for their businesses.

159. Sengamines: Example of a joint venture. The Panel gathered that, late in 1998, a private Zimbabwean company, Operation Sovereign Legitimacy (OSLEG), whose shareholders are Lieutenant General Vitalis Musungwa Zvinavashe, Job Whabira, former Permanent Secretary in the Ministry of Defense, Onesimo Moyo, President of Minerals Marketing Corporation of Zimbabwe, and Isaiah Ruzengwe, General Manager of Zimbabwe Mining Development Corporation, got into a partnership with COMIEX; COSLEG was born of this partnership. Through COSLEG, Zimbabwe (ZANU-PF) could exploit and market minerals, timber, and other resources of the Democratic Republic of the Congo.

160. Reliable sources told the Panel that a Zimbabwean delegation headed by the then Minister of Justice, Emmerson Munangagwa, visited the Kasai region to see the various mining concessions given by the late President Kabila to ZDF as barter payment for its military support. The team was composed of the former Permanent Secretary in the Ministry of Defense, Moven Mahachi; the Chief of the Armed Forces, General Zvinavashe; and the President of MIBA, Kadende Muya. President Kabila's gift to the Zimbabwean military was causing a problem, however, as they did not have the financial and technical expertise to exploit their mining concessions. Late in 1998, Thamer Al Shanfari, Chairman of Oryx Natural Resources, was asked to provide the needed financial and technical expertise. Mr. Al Shanfari decided to create Oryx Zimcon, Ltd., a joint venture between Oryx

Natural Resources and COSLEG.

161. Instead of selecting one of the various mines belonging to COSLEG to start its investment, Oryx Zimcon wanted the best mines which initially belonged to MIBA. At the request of ZDF and on the advice of Victor Mpoyo and Mwenze Kongolo,[365] the late President Kabila transferred two of MIBA's richest concessions—the kimberlite deposits in Tshibua and the alluvial deposits in the Senga Senga River, to Oryx Zimcon. Oryx Zimcon and COSLEG together created Sengamines.

162. As promised, Mr. Al Shanfari started investing in Sengamines and used the Breco group of companies of John Bredenkamp to transport mining equipment to the mines. As the technical and financial partner, Oryx was to receive 40 percent, OSLEG 40 percent and COSLEG 20 percent. As the need for money grew, Mr. Al Shanfari decided to launch Oryx on London's Alternative Investment Market under the name Oryx Diamonds. Upon strong objections from various stakeholders, Oryx Diamonds was withdrawn from the market. The new statute of the company does not mention the name OSLEG.[366] The Panel was informed, however, that the increase in the shares of COMIEX as seen in the new statute was meant to preserve the interests of Zimbabweans. The Panel was also told that payment would be made to the Government of the Democratic Republic of the Congo only after the loan taken for this operation (about $25 million) was repaid.

163. The ease with which the Tshibua and Senga Senga River concessions were given to Oryx without due regard for the legal requirements and the preferential treatment given to Oryx show the determination of the former Government of the Democratic Republic of the Congo to reward some of its allies.

Attribution of Concessions

164. According to some sources, a very recent (26 February, 2001) concession of cobalt and copper in Kambove-Kakanda was to be given KMC Group of the Zimbabwean Billy Rautenbach. According to very reliable sources, different ministers had signed the concession two days before the assassination of the late President Kabila and only his signature was missing. The trade unionist of Gecamines has indicated that the cession was

completed, but President Joseph Kabila told the Panel that the deal has not been signed yet. If it is signed, there could be a rapprochement of activities.

165. This case shows rapprochement of the activities and interests of some Zimbabwean businessmen, and a possible link between arms dealing and mining activities in the Democratic Republic of the Congo. Indeed Mr. Bredenkamp is said to have an interest in this venture, although he was alleged to be an arms dealer. In November 2000, a month after the departure of Mr. Rautenbach from Gecamines, Mr. Bredenkamp is said to have established a direct link with Mr. Rautenbach. According to three reliable sources, Mr. Rautenbach, Mr. Bredenkamp, and Mr. Munangwana, the current Speaker of the House of Zimbabwe, Chairman of ZANU-PF and director of many companies belonging to ZANU-PF, met with the late President Kabila to negotiate this contract of the central part of the Gecamines concessions. The Panel does not draw any conclusions, but wishes to highlight the quality of the people involved in the negotiations, their past records, current activities, and position in Zimbabwe.

166. Many other deals are ongoing such as the one concerning the supply of foodstuffs to the Congolese army, for which General Zvinavashe's company is said to have attributed the transport. President Robert Mugabe once told interlocutors that the late President Kabila had given him a mine concession.

167. The Government of the Democratic Republic of the Congo, in its effort to defend its territory and secure the supply of military equipment, has signed a contract worth several million United States dollars with the Government of China. Official sources in Kinshasa, while confirming this deal, have informed the Panel that in exchange a mining concession was awarded to a joint venture between a Chinese company and a parastatal of the Democratic Republic of the Congo.

168. In the same vein, the Government of the Democratic Republic of the Congo has made a deal with the Democratic People's Republic of Korea, which trains troops of the Democratic Republic of the Congo and in exchange, it is believed, has received a mining concession around Shinkolobwe, very rich in uranium. The Americans in the past extracted uranium from this mine. Challenged on this issue, officials of the Democratic

Republic of the Congo mentioned high radioactivity in the area, making it impossible for anyone to work there.

169. According to some officials, the Democratic Republic of the Congo has asked the United States of America to consider addressing the problem of radioactivity in the area, given their historical presence in mining that particular area for uranium. The official denial of a deal between the Democratic Republic of the Congo and the Democratic People's Republic of Korea was based on the fact that the Government of the Democratic Republic of the Congo has sought United States assistance—which it cannot receive if the Koreans are mining the same area.

170. The Panel has enough elements and evidence to suggest that the Government of the Democratic Republic of the Congo, under the late President Kabila, gave strong incentives in the form of access, exploitation, and management of mineral resources. These incentives in turn have "convinced" the Zimbabwean authorities to remain engaged in the Democratic Republic of the Congo. The incentives have, however, been so important that the whole balance of the mining industries is likely to be affected. The question in the region is which course of action will sidelined companies take in the future to guarantee their presence in the mining sector? Will it be another cycle of war or intensification of war in relation to the securing of access to the rich cobalt and copper area of the Democratic Republic of the Congo?

Angola and Namibia

171. These two countries have financed their participation in the conflict with their regular defense budget. In the case of Angola, some deals, minor compared to those of Zimbabwe, have been signed, such as the creation of Sonangol, in which Sonangol Angola has 60 percent of shares and COMIEX 40 percent. Sonangol Angola is a 100 percent state-owned company (Sonangol supplies oil to the Democratic Republic of the Congo). The two countries have also signed a letter of intent to jointly exploit crude oil off their coast when peace returns to the region.

172. In the case of Namibia, the Panel was informed by the Namibian authorities of the existence of a joint venture between a Namibian company

called August 26, whose main shareholder is the Ministry of Defense, an American company and a "company" of the Democratic Republic of the Congo. Other deals involving individuals have been signed. At this point, the Panel has not found substantial evidence that Angola and Namibia have signed commercial deals in the nature of "arms and support for natural resources." Their motivation seems to be solely political and strategic (for Angola). According to very reliable sources, joint ventures proposed to these two countries were a sign of gratitude rather than an incentive for their support and they never pressed for it.

C. Special Features of the Links Between the Exploitation of Natural Resources and the Continuation of the Conflict

173. It is often said that the conflict in the Democratic Republic of the Congo is low-intensity warfare, as armies do not confront each other on a daily basis and battles, or rather serious battles, are not frequent. The Panel noted that the conflict, especially in occupied zones, is fought on three levels:

(a) Government forces and the allies versus the rebels and their Ugandan-Rwandan and Burundian allies;

(b) RCD-Goma and its Rwandan allies versus MLC or RCD-ML and their Ugandan allies;

(c) Rebel movements and their allies (Rwanda or Uganda versus the so-called negative forces: Interahamwe, Maï-Maï, and other dissident groups).

174. Indeed, the conflict in the Democratic Republic of the Congo is being fought on two fronts, official and unofficial. The official front is that of classic warfare—two or more armies confronting each other. This front goes from Pweto to Mbandaka on an uneven line crossing various localities. The unofficial front is concentrated inside zones controlled by rebels and their Ugandan and Rwandan allies.

175. The analysis of battles and skirmishes recorded from mid-1999 to 2001 shows that:

(a) Overall, the number of battles on the official front with the engagement of the army is lower than the number of skirmishes, about 96 between 1999 and 2001;

(b) The number of battles has been decreasing over the years. In the first quarter of 2001, only eight confrontations were reported on the official front line;

(c) Current big battles have been fought in areas of major economic importance, toward the cobalt-and-copper-rich area of Katanga and the diamond area of Mbuji Mayi. Military specialists argue that the Rwandan objective is to capture these mineral-rich areas to deprive the Government of the Democratic Republic of the Congo of the financial sources of its war effort. Without the control of this area, the Government of the Democratic Republic of the Congo cannot sustain the war. This rationale confirms that the availability of natural resources and their exploitation permits the continuation of the war. This may be true for all the parties. In view of the current experience of the illegal exploitation of the resources of the eastern Democratic Republic of the Congo by Rwanda and Uganda, it could also be thought that the capturing of this mineral-rich area would lead to the exploitation of those resources. In that case, control of those areas by Rwanda could be seen primarily as an economic and financial objective rather than a security objective for the Rwandan borders.

176. The number of skirmishes between rebel forces and their allies, and the armed group Maï-Maï has increased. From May to December 2000, about 177 clashes were reported. The battlefields are generally around coltan-and-diamond-mining or coltan-rich areas. The Panel has strong indications that most of the fights between Rwandan soldiers and Maï-Maï have occurred in the so-called "coltan belt." Some areas experienced up to 10 skirmishes in 2000. According to some sources, numerous reports and accounts of eyewitnesses mention the presence of Rwandan and Ugandan soldiers providing security around coltan and diamond mines. Officials of RCD-Goma have confirmed the risk posed by the Maï-Maï and "negative forces" in those areas. A senior RCD official specified that only very well-organized entities with the necessary security infrastructure can carry out the exploitation of coltan in those areas. In this particular case, the Rwandan army is the only institution with that capability in the eastern Democratic Republic of the Congo.

177. Rwanda's "unusual" tactics. The Rwandan forces will attack the same area for two days then pull back. According to our sources, these attacks seem to coincide with the period when coltan has been extracted and put in bags for evacuation by the Maï-Maï. Attacked, the Maï-Maï abandon their

coltan, which is then taken away by small aircraft. The Rwandan soldiers retreat again waiting for the next information on available coltan. In the areas where their grip is weaker, Rwanda, in particular, has designed strategies to retain control within certain echelons of the existing local hierarchies. In those areas controlled by the Interahamwe and Maï-Maï forces, either RPA, from time to time, mounts military operations that allow it to capture the areas temporarily and evacuate the coltan, or else middlemen are used for the purchase of coltan from the Maï-Maï and "negative forces."

178. Battles between rebel movements are also reported in areas rich in mines. On 18 November, 2000, RCD-Goma and its Rwandan allied troops based in Kisangani attacked positions of MLC in Bengamisa, 50 km north-west of Kisangani, and took control of this rich diamond area. On 31 December, 2000, RCD-Goma and its allies launched an attack on the area controlled by RCD-ML and captured Kandole, an area rich in diamonds and with some coltan. Also late in December 2000, RCD-Goma initiated an attack from Lindi to conquer Lakutu, another diamond-rich area.

179. Finally, in areas where the risks are too high, adversaries, if not enemies, become partners in business. That is the case of the Maï-Maï doing business with RPA civilian coltan dealers, who in turn sell to comptoirs controlled by Rwandans and their companies Grands Lacs Metals and Rwanda Metals. The most famous case was when the Maï-Maï chief, General Padiri, informed people in Kigali in November 2000 that he was selling 60 tons of coltan.

180. Strategies to sustain the vicious circle of war and exploitation: The example of Uganda. Top UPDF commanders have essentially used the Hema/Lendu conflict. The Panel has received very reliable information clearly showing how General Kazini and Colonels Kyakabale and Arocha assisted in training different Hema militia, and manipulated those groups to fight each other. Reports clearly showed that while the Kazini camp was helping with the training of the Hemas, the Colonel Peter Karim camp was assisting in training the Lendus—both camps belonging to UPDF. There are strong indications that some UPDF elements may spark violence so as to remain in the region in an attempt to control the gold-rich area and the potentially coltan-rich areas of Nyaleki. There is, therefore, a clear intent of the military commanders to control these mineral-rich areas and keep them

for long-term exploitation. The Nia-Nia confrontation in October 2000, in which UPDF General Kazini and Roger Lumbala fought another UPDF group and RCD-ML is a variation of the fighting inside UPDF for control of coltan-rich areas. According to different sources, Roger Lumbala, of RCD-national, has been used by General Kazini to control the Bafwasende area, rich in diamonds and coltan.

D. Facilitators or Passive Accomplices?

181. The link between the continuation of the conflict and the exploitation of natural resources would have not been possible if some entities, not parties in the conflict, had not played a key role, willingly or not. Bilateral and multilateral donors and certain neighboring and distant countries have passively facilitated the exploitation of the resources of the Democratic Republic of the Congo and the continuation of the conflict; the role of private companies and individuals has also been vital.

182. The Panel has gathered information showing that linkages between different actors and stakeholders are very well structured to the point that Governments and large reputable companies operate in confidence. In the case of coltan, all the needed documentation for its export is provided in Kigali, but there are accomplices in Kinshasa in the Ministry of Mines. The importing companies and their facilitators are aware of the real origin of the coltan, however. According to manifests that the Panel received, Sabena Cargo, as well as SDV of the Bollore group, have been among the key companies in this chain of exploitation and continuation of war. Thousands of tons of coltan from the Democratic Republic of the Congo were carried from Kigali or through the port of Dar es Salaam.

183. The Panel also has indications of the direct and indirect involvement of some staff of the embassies and cooperation agencies of developed countries. They have facilitated the purchase of illegal minerals. The United States' honorary consul in Bukavu, as he presented himself, Ramnik O. Kotecha, in addition to promoting deals between American companies and coltan dealers in the region, is himself Chairman of the Kotecha group of companies based in Bukavu and deals in coltan.

184. On the basis of the facts and their analysis, the Panel reaches the

conclusion that the increase in revenues of the Rwandan army from coltan sales was made easy by three key factors:

(a) The passive role of some private companies such as Sabena and SDV for the transport of coltan, Citibank for the financial transaction as the corresponding bank of BCDI, the self-proclaimed United States honorary consul in Bukavu and some staff in various embassies in Kigali;

(b) The rush to profit of some foreign companies that were ready to do business regardless of elements of unlawfulness and irregularities (see annex I for a sample of companies);

(c) The political legitimization provided by some developed countries. In November 2000 in Kigali, the Panel was told that the illegal exploitation of resources and the financial gains of RPA were justified as the repayment for the security that Rwanda provides.

Bilateral Donors

185. The main bilateral donors to Rwanda and Uganda have been the United Kingdom of Great Britain and Northern Ireland, Denmark, Germany, and the United States of America in various sectors. The analysis of their cooperation shows that sectors benefitting from this assistance are related to poverty, education, and governance. Priority sectors have been water and sanitation, health and governance, including institutional reforms, justice and human rights, especially for Rwanda. In some cases, direct aid to the budget is provided. The balance of payments of Rwanda shows that budget support has steadily increased, from $26.1 million in 1997 to $51.5 in 1999. While such support is legitimate, the problem is that expenditures and services, which were supposed to be provided and covered by the Governments of Rwanda and Uganda and which are covered by the bilateral aid, constitute savings in the national budget. Were these savings used to finance this war?

186. The German Ambassador in Kigali told the Panel about German support to German business dealing in pyrochlore and coltan in the occupied Democratic Republic of the Congo. In this particular case, German cooperation has given a preferential loan of DM 500,000 to Karl Heinz Albers, a German citizen, to expand his coltan business in the Democratic Republic of the Congo (SOMIKIVU) and Mr. Albers' business is guarded by RCD-Goma soldiers.

Multilateral Donors

187. The World Bank has praised Uganda for its economic performance and the reforms under the structural adjustment program as a success story and has promoted its case for the new debt relief program, the Highly Indebted Poor Countries initiative.

188. The Panel has, however, indications that this economic performance was driven in part, especially over the past three years, by the exploitation of the resources of the Democratic Republic of the Congo. Notes exchanged between World Bank staff clearly show that the Bank was informed about a significant increase in gold and diamond exports from a country that produces very little of these minerals or exports quantities of gold that it could not produce (see para. 97). Internal discussions of the World Bank staff also confirm this knowledge of the situation: in one of those internal exchanges, a staff member warned his colleague that the World Bank silence would blow up in the Bank's face.

189. In the case of Uganda and its exploitation of the natural resources of the Democratic Republic of the Congo, the World Bank never questioned the increasing exports of resources and in one instance a staff member even defended it. During the Panel's visit to Uganda, the representative of the Bank dismissed any involvement of Uganda in the exploitation of those resources. The Bank not only encouraged Uganda and Rwanda indirectly by defending their case, but equally gave the impression of rewarding them by proposing these countries for the Highly Indebted Poor Countries debt relief initiative.

190. The Bank's shadow on the conflict in the Democratic Republic of the Congo is even more apparent on the budget. The balance of payments of both Uganda and Rwanda shows a significant increase in long-term borrowing in support of the budget. The defense budget, however, has increased in absolute terms, allowing Uganda and Rwanda to continue the conflict. There seems to be a precedent for the Bank's behavior. During the Cambodian crisis in the 1980s, the Bank turned a blind eye to the illicit exploitation of Cambodian timber; the question is whether it is World Bank policy to ignore broad governance issues (hard or soft) while dealing with its clients.

Transit Countries

191. Countries in the region have indirectly and passively facilitated the cycle of exploitation of the natural resources of the Democratic Republic of the Congo and the continuation of the conflict. This has usually happened without any intent to cover up or protect some interests. That is particularly the case of countries with seaports. Those countries have served as the hub for the export of natural resources. They were bound by regulations and agreements signed within the framework of sub-regional organizations such as COMESA for the seaports of Mombasa and Dar es Salaam and UDEAC/ CEMAC for the port of Douala. Mombasa and Dar es Salaam were the main ports used by Uganda, Rwanda, and Burundi to export some natural resources, such as timber, cassiterite, coffee, and various barks. Douala seaport was also used for coffee from Equateur Province and transported from Bangui.

192. According to some sources, the Government of the Central African Republic was aware of the commercial activities of MLC in Bangui. Jean-Pierre Bemba's friends, Jean-Yves Ollivier, Jean-Pierre Dupont, and Jean-Pierre Saber have all used Bangui as the *arrière-base* for their diamond and coffee deals. The Government never prevented MLC from using the Central African Republic for economic activities. In addition, some individuals were using the territory of the Central African Republic to carry out their illegal activities, as was the case with Victor Butt, who used Bangui airport to load and offload coffee and arms.

193. According to some sources, some countries in the region have been very attractive to Rwandan families with an acceptable level of wealth. Army salaries cannot sustain such lucrative properties and standards of living. How do they sustain these families? Where did the money come from?

194. Kenya has played a different role in the exploitation of the resources of the Democratic Republic of the Congo. It has been the base for the supply of counterfeit United States dollars and also the venue of financial transactions of various traders who export their resources (timber, coffee, and tobacco) through the port of Mombasa.

The Pivotal Role of Leaders

195. This section aims to show how presidents and other decision makers tolerate, organize, or put in place the framework and conditions to maintain the status quo of exploitation and war. The Panel refrains from making allegations about the personal involvement of presidents in the illegal and financial activities until further investigation is carried out. For instance, the Panel received but dismissed, for lack of evidence, allegations of the involvement of President Kagame's family in diamond dealing; it focused rather on the objective elements of the president's political responsibility. In some reports and accounts, the name of President Museveni was mentioned as a shareholder in a specific company. The Panel refrains from citing these accounts until further research is conducted.

196. **President Paul Kagame**. His position in the state apparatus with regard to the exploitation of the natural resources of the Democratic Republic of the Congo and the continuation of the war has evolved, yet his role has remained pivotal. This role can be situated on three levels: his relations with the Rwandan business community operating in the Democratic Republic of the Congo, control over the army, and the structures involved in the illegal activities.

197. According to some reliable sources, President Kagame has close relationships with top Rwandan businessmen. For instance, he maintains good relations with Modeste Makabuza, "owner" of Jambo Safari. He is also close to Alfred Khalissa, the "founder" of BCDI and former manager of BCD. The same sources told the Panel that President Kagame is very close to Tibere Rujigiro, who is known for generous financial support to RPF during the 1990-1994 war. Mr. Rujigiro is one of the shareholders of Tristar Investment, with very close ties to RPF. This close aide to President Kagame has business relationships with Faustin Mbundu, who is known for his arms dealing activities. What all these businessmen have in common is their direct involvement in the exploitation of natural resources in the areas that Rwanda controls. Different sources have told the Panel that each of these businessmen has at a certain point benefitted from the President's "help."

198. President Kagame, when he was Minister of Defense, reorganized or approved the reorganization of the Rwandan army and the Ministry of

Defense, which subsequently led to the creation of the Department of External Relations in which the Congo desk is located. This unit has been the cornerstone of the financial transactions of RPA. The former Minister of Defense should have been aware of the functioning of RPA as well as the daily operations of the army.

199. Two very reliable sources told the Panel that in September 1998 the then Vice-President, during a meeting with various officials of RCD and RPA top commanders, informed the participants that there was a need to raise $50 million to make it possible to reach Kinshasa in two months.

200. Finally, when faced with the question of the involvement of RPA in the exploitation of the resources of the Democratic Republic of the Congo, the President announced in a radio interview that private Rwandan citizens were carrying out commercial activities in the Democratic Republic of the Congo. Was this a deliberate act to mislead various partners or was it translating the President's lack of information on the issue? Meanwhile, the President has admitted in the past that the conflict in the Democratic Republic of the Congo was self-financing. All these elements combined suggest the President's degree of knowledge of the situation, his implicit approval of the continuation of the illegal exploitation of the resources of the Democratic Republic of the Congo, and somehow his complicity as well as his political and moral responsibility.

201. **President Yoweri Museveni**. President Yoweri Museveni's role in the exploitation of the natural resources of the Democratic Republic of the Congo and the continuation of the war can be situated at the following levels: his policy toward the rebel movements, his attitude toward the army and the protection provided to illegal activities and their perpetrators.

202. He has shaped the rebellion in the area controlled by Uganda according to his own political philosophy and agenda. He opted for a more decentralized authority and only intervenes when major problems arise, but he has a very good knowledge of the situation on the ground.

203. Messrs. Mbusa Nyamwisi and Tibasima, former first and second Vice-Presidents close to General Salim Saleh and General Kazini, are more inclined to business and the extraction of natural resources. In December

1999, a report was handed over to the President of Uganda, specifically pointing out the embezzlement of $10 million by Mr. Nyamwisi and $3 million by Mr. Tibasima. Another report was handed to President Museveni in February 2000, specifically denouncing the collusion between Trinity Group and Mr. Tibasima and the impact on the collection of customs duties. President Museveni chose to give the direction of the Congolese Liberation Front to those who are the accomplices of illegal cartels.

204. President Museveni was also informed of the situation on the ground, the exploitation being carried out, and the involvement of officials of MLC and RCD-ML, including the conflict between Hemas and Lendus.

205. The President's family has also been very involved in business in the Democratic Republic of the Congo in the occupied zones. General Salim Saleh and his wife, shareholders in Victoria and Trinity, have confidently carried out their activities, undisturbed.

206. The Panel concludes that when the information is passed to the President and he chooses not to act, when he appoints the very people who carry out criminal activities, and when his family members get away with criminal activities, it becomes overwhelming that the President has put himself in the position of accomplice.

207. **The late President, Laurent-Désiré Kabila**. His role in the continuation of the war has survived his death. On three levels, he bears part of the responsibility for the current situation. First, as the chief of AFDL, he created a precedent in giving a character of "legality" or legitimacy to otherwise illegal operations. During his advance on Kinshasa, he granted concessions even though he did not have authority to do so. These are the same methods being used by some armed groups to fight for power.

208. Second, he allowed and tolerated some unlawful ventures as a way of rewarding allies. He also initiated the barter system in order to defend his territory. This is gradually becoming the normal practice for the rebel groups.

209. Third, he offered a good excuse and a pretext to those who had carefully planned the redrawing of the regional map to redistribute wealth. Many sources have told the Panel how they were approached and asked to

think about the distribution of wealth of the Democratic Republic of the Congo in terms of their personal enrichment.

210. According to the facts, accounts, and information gathered, the pivotal roles of the Ugandan and Rwandan leaders reside in the way in which they diverted the primary mission of their armies from protection of their territory and made them armies of business. By the same token, they indirectly created, within their armies, conditions for top officers to put in place networks that they controlled. These networks are becoming cartels, which will take over the war for natural resources.

211. Presidents Kagame and Museveni are on the verge of becoming the godfathers of the illegal exploitation of natural resources and the continuation of the conflict in the Democratic Republic of the Congo. They have indirectly given criminal cartels a unique opportunity to organize and operate in this fragile and sensitive region. Finally, the attitude of the late President has possibly planted the seeds for another round of war for resources in the Democratic Republic of the Congo. Politicians such as Jean-Pierre Bemba, Mwenze Kongolo, Victor Mpoyo, Adolphe Onusumba, Jean-Pierre Ondekane, and Emmanuel Kamanzi are ready to make any deal for the sake of power or for personal enrichment. Companies such as IDI and Sengamines, some of which reportedly have ties with arms dealers, are likely to create a more troubling situation in the Democratic Republic of the Congo. Equally, joint ventures and concessions given to some allies as rewards may cause some problems given the nature of the shareholders who are either armed forces or powerful and influential politicians. The situation is now deeply embedded and the regional power structures are consequently not stable.

212. The link between the exploitation of natural resources and the continuation of the conflict in the Democratic Republic of the Congo does exist, and it is based on five factors, which are not mutually exclusive. First, the capacity of countries to use their own resources to sustain the war up to a certain stage, as in the case of Angola. Second, the ability of countries to take resources from enemies and use it to fight the so-called "self-sustaining" war, as in the case of Rwanda. Third, the intent of some Governments to take advantage of the war situation and use it to transfer wealth from one country to their national economy, as is the case with Rwanda and Zimbabwe. Fourth,

the will of private citizens and businesses who endeavor to sustain the war for political, financial, or other gains; for example, generals and other top officers in the Ugandan and Zimbabwean army and other top officials and unsavory politicians (Victor Mpoyo, Gaëtan Kakudji, Mwenze Kongolo) in the Government of the Democratic Republic of the Congo. Fifth, the capacity of one of the warring parties to give incentives (mineral and others) to its allies and soldiers, for example the Democratic Republic of the Congo.

IV. Conclusion and Findings

213. The conflict in the Democratic Republic of the Congo has become mainly about access, control, and trade of five key mineral resources: coltan, diamonds, copper, cobalt, and gold. The wealth of the country is appealing and hard to resist in the context of lawlessness and the weakness of the central authority.

214. Exploitation of the natural resources of the Democratic Republic of the Congo by foreign armies has become systematic and systemic. Plundering, looting and racketeering, and the constitution of criminal cartels are becoming commonplace in occupied territories. These criminal cartels have ramifications and connections worldwide, and they represent the next serious security problem in the region.

215. The role of the private sector in the exploitation of natural resources and the continuation of the war has been vital. A number of companies have been involved and have fueled the war directly, trading arms for natural resources. Others have facilitated access to financial resources, which are used to purchase weapons. Companies trading minerals, which the Panel considered to be "the engine of the conflict in the Democratic Republic of the Congo" have prepared the field for illegal mining activities in the country.

216. Bilateral and multilateral donors have sent mixed signals to Governments with armies in the Democratic Republic of the Congo.

217. Top military commanders from various countries, for different reasons, needed and continue to need this conflict for its lucrative nature and for temporarily solving some internal problems in those countries as well as allowing access to wealth. They have realized that the war has the capacity to

sustain itself, and therefore have created or protected criminal networks that are likely to take over fully if all foreign armies decide to leave the Democratic Republic of the Congo.

218. The conflict in the Democratic Republic of the Congo, because of its lucrative nature, has created a "win-win" situation for all belligerents. Adversaries and enemies are at times partners in business (Maï-Maï and Rwandans and Congolese rebels), prisoners of Hutu origin are mine workers of RPA, enemies get weapons from the same dealers and use the same intermediaries. Business has superseded security concerns. The only loser in this huge business venture is the Congolese people.

V. Recommendations

Prerequisite

219. The Panel acknowledges the validity of Security Council resolutions 1304 (2000) and 1341 (2001), as well as the Lusaka Agreement, and puts its report and recommendations within their broad framework. The Panel believes its report and recommendations are consistent with those resolutions.

Follow-up

220. The Panel recommends that the Security Council extend the mandate of the Panel of Experts on the Illegal Exploitation of Natural Resources and Other Forms of Wealth of the Democratic Republic of the Congo, to allow it to conduct a follow-up investigation and report on the structures and networks put in place or facilitated by warring parties to illegally exploit the natural resources of the Democratic Republic of the Congo, including the situation after the withdrawal of foreign military forces.

Sanctions

221. The Security Council should immediately declare a temporary embargo on the import or export of coltan, niobium, pyrochlore, cassiterite, timber, gold, and diamonds from or to Burundi, Rwanda, and Uganda until those countries' involvement in the exploitation of the natural resources of the Democratic Republic of the Congo is made clear and declared so by the

Security Council. All countries should abstain from facilitating the import or export of these resources. Any country breaking this embargo should face sanctions; Governments should take the measures necessary to ensure that companies registered in their territory and individuals breaking the embargo are punished.

222. The Security Council should decide that all Member States without delay should freeze the financial assets of the rebel movements and their leaders. Member States should take the necessary measures to ensure that their public and private financial institutions stop doing business with banks named in this report that are located in Burundi, Rwanda, and Uganda.

223. The Security Council should strongly urge all Member States to freeze the financial assets of the companies or individuals who continue to participate in the illegal exploitation of the natural resources of the Democratic Republic of the Congo immediately after the publication of this report.

224. The Panel recommends that the Security Council declare an immediate embargo on supply of weapons and all military material to the rebel groups operating in the Democratic Republic of the Congo and consider extending this embargo to the States that support or assist those groups.

225. The Panel recommends that the Security Council decide that all military cooperation with States whose military forces are present in the Democratic Republic of the Congo in violation of its sovereignty be suspended immediately until those armies withdraw from the Democratic Republic of the Congo.

Financial and Economic Matters

226. The Panel recommends that the Security Council urge Member States to suspend balance-of-payments support to the countries of the region involved in the illegal exploitation of the natural resources of the Democratic Republic of the Congo, until the Security Council has evidence to its satisfaction that the illegal exploitation of natural resources has stopped.

227. The Panel recommends that the Security Council requests the World Bank and IMF to consider suspending their support to the budgets of these

countries until the end of the conflict. If, within two months after the publication of this report, clear evidence and signs of the disengagement of these countries from the exploitation of the natural resources of the Democratic Republic of the Congo are not given to the Security Council, cooperation between those institutions and the countries involved should be suspended. The World Bank and IMF should design a policy guideline on cooperation between each institution and countries involved in conflicts.

228. The Panel recommends that the Security Council urge Member States sharing a common border with the Democratic Republic of the Congo, or serving as transit countries for goods and natural resources from the Democratic Republic of the Congo, to form a commission to investigate financial and economic activities conducted on their territories in connection with the war in the Democratic Republic of the Congo, and take the necessary action to curb or halt activities that contribute to the continuation of hostilities.

Diamond Business

229. The Security Council should call upon the Democratic Republic of the Congo to take the necessary steps to curb the flow of illicit diamonds by liberalizing the diamond trade. A clear signal in this regard should be sent to all companies that resist and obstruct the liberalization of the mineral markets.

230. All diamond dealers operating in the territories occupied by foreign forces should immediately stop doing business with rebels and Burundi, Rwanda, and Uganda. Failure to do so should lead to action through the World Diamond Council. The Republic of the Congo and the Central African Republic should take the necessary measures to stop abetting the trade in illicit and conflict diamonds.

231. Furthermore, the Panel endorses all the relevant recommendations on diamonds made by the Panel of Experts established by resolution 1306 (2000) in relation to Sierra Leone in its report (S/2000/1195, paras. 155 to 166), in particular:

(a) A certification scheme similar to that adopted by Sierra Leone should be required of the Democratic Republic of the Congo and all other diamond-exporting countries in the region, within a period of six months;

(b) Major trading centers should agree on a recording and public documentation system for rough diamond imports that clearly designate countries of origin and provenance;

(c) All countries importing rough diamonds must apply a "rough control" system whether they have free trade zones or not;

(d) The European Union should have few entry points for diamonds;

(e) The United Nations and the World Diamond Council should form a commission to conduct an annual review of the proper implementation of the certification system;

(f) An annual statistical production report should be compiled by each exporting country and gathered into a central annual report, compiled by the World Diamond Council and/or by the certification body that is expected to emerge from the "Kimberley process."

Forest and Timber

232. The Panel proposes that countries with seaports and those with transit facilities report to the United Nations Forum on Forests on the transit of timber through their territory. As the timber from the Democratic Republic of the Congo transits through the ports of Mombasa and Dar es Salaam, the Governments of Kenya and the United Republic of Tanzania should declare to the Forum on Forests the origins of the timber that is being shipped from their seaports, as well as the certification documents of such timber.

233. The Panel recommends that the United Nations Forum on Forests unifies the different schemes and procedures for timber certification. The certification scheme should be based on the broad framework of principles, criteria, and indicators promoted by the International Panel on Forests and the International Forum on Forests. New criteria on "conflict timber" should be considered. The Forum on Forests should become or designate one single accrediting body for timber certification. The composition of such a body should reflect the diversity of actors and interests as well as the specificity of regions. Such a unified mechanism would prevent some "loose codification" and purely commercial certifying bodies from delivering or attempting to deliver certificates. The Panel urges the Security Council to declare timber and non-timber forest products coming from warring areas, "conflict timber and non-timber forest products." Countries importing non-certified timber should put in place minimum guidelines and sanctions for companies that import timber and non-timber forest products from countries at war or experiencing

civil war related to the allocation or distribution of natural resources.

234. The Panel proposes, following the declaration on the control of illegal logging made by the Group of Eight in 1998, and the ongoing discussions on "conflict timber products," that a mandate be given to the United Nations Forum on Forests:

(a) To compile information in collaboration with various non-governmental organizations on illegal logging and "conflict timber products" in the world;

(b) To publish annually a list of countries involved in illegal and "conflict timber products" trade;

(c) To submit an annual report to the General Assembly of the United Nations.

235. The Panel recommends that countries of transit and final destination of the timber trade request from logging companies certificates of origin for the timber that is transiting through or arriving in their territory. Those countries should send copies of these certificates to Governments of countries of origin within three days. Failure to abide by this should be considered to be complicity on the part of those countries and they should be listed as countries facilitating "illicit timber" and "conflict timber product" trade in the report of the Forum on Forests.

Reparation and Compensation

236. The Panel recommends that individuals, in particular farmers, religious groups, and companies whose properties, livestock, and crops were damaged, looted, or expropriated by the Burundian, Rwandan, or Ugandan armed forces and their allies should be compensated by the states concerned. Properties confiscated should also be returned to their legitimate owners. The Governments of Burundi, Rwanda and Uganda, and their allies should pay compensation to the companies whose properties and stocks of coltan, cassiterite, gold, timber, and other materials which were confiscated or taken between 1998 and 2000. The Security Council may consider how the Office of the United Nations Resident Coordinator in Kinshasa could help in gathering information on the claims.

237. UNESCO, in collaboration with UNEP, the secretariat of CITES and

non-governmental organizations working in the Democratic Republic of the Congo should assess the extent of damage to wildlife in Garamba Park, Kahuzi-Biega Park, the Okapi Reserve, and Virunga Park, and propose sanctions to be taken against those Governments whose soldiers were involved in the mass killing of endangered species.

Framework for Reconstruction

238. The Security Council would give mandate and means to a United Nations commission created to help the Government of the Democratic Republic of the Congo manage the transition in the formerly occupied regions. The Commission will help design and put in place the legal and administrative framework and create an enabling environment for economic activities. The Commission will also help put in place the necessary conditions for the enhancement of State authority and security over its territory.

General

239. The Panel recommends that the Security Council consider establishing an international mechanism that will investigate and prosecute individuals involved in economic criminal activities (such as Khaleb Akandwanaho alias Salim Saleh, Jean-Pierre Bemba, James Kazini, Mbusa Nyamwisi, Ateenyi Tibasima, Roger Lumbala, Aziza Kulsum Gulamali, and others named in this report), companies and government officials whose economic and financial activities directly or indirectly harm powerless people and weak economies.

240. The Panel recommends that the Security Council consider establishing a permanent mechanism that would investigate the illicit trafficking of natural resources in armed conflicts so as to monitor the cases that are already subject to the investigation of other panels, such as those of Angola, the Democratic Republic of the Congo, and Sierra Leone.

241. Member States should be encouraged to adopt legislation that will forbid companies registered in their territory from importing or exporting natural resources to or from invading countries.

Security

242. The Panel urges the Security Council to hold Governments of countries' parties to the conflict in the Democratic Republic of the Congo, rebel movements, and those military representatives cited in the report responsible if any harm is done to any member of the Panel. The Security Council should encourage individual countries to assist the Panel members by providing security to each of them well after the Panel is dissolved. The Security Council should urge the Secretary-General to make the necessary arrangements to ensure the security of the Panel members well after the Panel is dissolved. The Panel has received information of harassment in Bunia and other localities of individuals who may have been in contact with the Panel members. The Security Council should hold the authorities of Rwanda, Uganda, RCD, and FLC responsible for any harm to witnesses who shared their knowledge with the Panel.

Annex I

Sample of companies importing minerals from the Democratic Republic of the Congo via Rwanda.

Company	*Country of Destination*	*Merchandise*
Cogem	Belgium	cassiterites
Muka-Enterprise	Belgium	cassiterites
Issa	Germany	cassiterites
Chpistopa Floss	Germany	cassiterites
Redemi	Rwanda	cassiterites
Banro-Resources Corp.	Malaysia	cassiterites, coltan
	Canada	cassiterites
Bharat	United Republic of Tanzania	cassiterites
Extano-Office	Rwanda	coltan
Coopimar	Rwanda	coltan
Geologistics Hannover	Germany	coltan
Rwasibo-Butera	Switzerland	coltan
Eagleswings	Netherlands	coltan
Veen	Netherlands	coltan
Soger	Belgium	coltan
Patel Warehouse	Netherlands	coltan
Afrimex	United Kingdom of Great Britain and Northern Ireland	coltan
	Netherlands	cassiterites
Chimie Pharmacie	Netherlands	coltan
	Belgium	coltan

Sogem	Belgium	coltan, cassiterites, tin
Cogecom	Belgium	coltan, cassiterites
Cogea	Belgium	coltan
Panalpina	Kenya	coltan
Tradement	Belgium	coltan, cassiterites
Ventro Star	United Kingdom of Great Britain and Northern Ireland	coltan
Raremet	India	coltan
Finconord	Pakistan	coltan
Finiming Ltd	Belgium	coltan
Finconcorde	Russian Federation	cassiterites, coltan
Patel	India	cassiterites
Cicle International	Belgium	coltan
Masingiro	Germany	coltan
Union-Transport	Germany	coltan
Specialty Metal	Belgium	coltan
MDW	Belgium	cassiterites, coltan
Transintra	Belgium	cassiterites

Source: The Rwandan Revenue Authority.

Annex II
Countries visited and representatives of Governments and organizations interviewed.

The Expert Panel on the Illegal Exploitation of Natural Resources and Other Forms of Wealth of the Democratic Republic of the Congo wishes to express its deep appreciation to the government officials, diplomats, non-governmental organizations, individual relief workers, journalists, and others who assisted it in its enquiries and helped to make this report possible.

The Panel further wishes to extend special thanks to the United Nations Organization Mission in the Democratic Republic of the Congo (MONUC), in particular Ambassador Kamel Morjane; to the United Nations Office at Nairobi, in particular Klaus Töpfer and Alexander Barabanov; and to the Office of the Special Representative of the Secretary-General for the Great

Lakes Region of Africa, in particular Ambassador Berhanu Dinka.

Among countries involved in the conflict in the Democratic Republic of the Congo, the Panel would like to make special note of the cooperation received from the Republic of Uganda, which provided the Panel with all information that was requested.

The following list is incomplete in deference to the wishes of those who requested anonymity, in particular Congolese individuals who put their lives at risk in order to provide the Panel with information:

Angola

Government Officials
Vice-Minister of External Relations
Vice-Minister of Finance
Minister of Petroleum
Minister of Geology and Mines

United Nations Agencies and Offices
Representative of the Secretary-General and Head of the United Nations Office in Angola
United Nations Office in Angola

Belgium

Government Officials
Ministry of Foreign Affairs
Ministry of Communications, Civil Aviation Administration
Ministry of Finance
Ministry of Economy and Finance
Cabinet of Deputy Prime Minister and Minister for Foreign Affairs
Department of Customs and Accounts
Office belge du commerce extérieur
Département de douanes et D.R.oits indirects

International Organizations
Eurostat

World Customs Organization

Other
Belgolaise
BHP Diamonds and Minerals
BHV
Diamond High Council
Independent Diamond Valuators
Institute of Politics and Development Management
Langer Diamonds
Nordiska Afrikainstitutet (Nordic Africa Institute)
Royal Museum for Central Africa, Department of Geology and Mineralogy
SwissCargo
World Federation of Diamond Markets

Burundi

Government Officials
His Excellency Major General Pierre Buyoya, President of the Republic of Burundi
Minister of Agriculture and Livestock
Ministry of Finance
Minister of International Relations and Cooperation
Minister of National and Regional Development and Environment
Minister of Transportation, Post and Telecommunications

Representatives of States
Belgium
Democratic Republic of the Congo
France
United States of America

United Nations Agencies and Offices, and International Organizations
MONUC
Office of the Special Representative of the Secretary-General in Burundi
UNDP

World Bank

Democratic Republic of the Congo

Government Officials

His Excellency Major General Joseph Kabila, President of the Democratic Republic of the Congo

Commissariat général du Gouvernement chargé des affaires de la MONUC

Banque nationale du Congo

Banque centrale

Département des Forêts

Direction générale des contributions (DGC)

Direction générale des recettes administratives, judiciaires, domaniales et de participations (DGRAD)

Institut congolais pour la conservation de la nature (ICCN)

Ministre des affaires foncières de l'Environnement, de la conservation de la nature et du développement touristique

Ministre de l'agriculture et elevage

Ministre des D.R.oits humains

Ministre de l'economie, du commerce, et de l'industrie

Ministre de l'energie

Ministre des finances et du budget

Ministère des mines

Ministre d'Etat chargé du pétrole

Ministre des transports et communications

l'Office des douanes et accises (OFIDA)

Representatives of States

Belgium

China

France

Italy

United States of America

Diplomatic Corps of Kinshasa

United Nations Agencies and Offices

FAO

Office of the Special Representative of the Secretary-General
MONUC
Office for the Coordination of Humanitarian Affairs
Office of the United Nations High Commissioner for Human Rights
UNDP
UNHCR
UNICEF
WFP
WHO

Other
COSLEG Holding
Fédération des entreprises du Congo (FEC)
Georges Forrest International
Governor of South Kivu and Provincial Directors
Observatoire gouvernance-transparence (OGT)
Kotecha Group of Companies
Mouvement pour la libération du Congo
Olive Company
RCD-Goma
Rally for Congolese Democracy-ML/Kisangani
Trafca
World Resource Institute

France

Government Officials
Ministry of Foreign Affairs
Ministry of Defense
Ministry of the Economy, Finance and Industry–Department of the Treasury
French Development Agency
Inspector General of Civil Aviation and Meteorology
Direction générale des douanes et D.R.oits indirects – Sous-Direction de l'Union douanière et de la coopération internationale
Bureau of Geological and Mining Research (BRGM)

International Organizations
Organization for Economic Cooperation and Development

Kenya

Government Officials
Minister for Foreign Affairs
Kenya Ports Authority

Representatives of States
Belgium
Democratic Republic of the Congo
France
Japan
Russian Federation
United Kingdom of Great Britain and Northern Ireland
United Kingdom of Great Britain and Northern Ireland Special Representative for the Great Lakes
Zimbabwe

International Organizations
Office of the Facilitator for the peace process in the Democratic Republic of the Congo
United Nations agencies and offices
MONUC
Office for the Coordination of Humanitarian Affairs
Office of the Special Representative of the Secretary-General for the Great Lakes Region
UNDP
UNEP
United Nations Office at Nairobi

Other
International Crisis Group (ICG)

Namibia

Government Officials

Deputy Minister for Foreign Affairs, Information and Broadcasting
Minister of Finance
Deputy Minister of Defense
Minister of Mines and Energy
Minister of Agriculture, Water and Rural Development
Minister of Environment and Tourism

Representatives of States
China
France
Russian Federation
United Kingdom of Great Britain and Northern Ireland
United States of America

Rwanda

Government Officials
His Excellency Major General Paul Kagame, President of the Republic of Rwanda
Chef d'Etat major
Minister of Energy, Water and Natural Resources
Minister for Foreign Affairs
Minister of Finance and Economic Planning
Minister of Agriculture, Forests and Livestock
Minister of Works, Transport and Communications
Minister of Energy, Mines and Water
Minister of Land, Resettlements and Environment
National Bank of Rwanda
Secretary-General of Commerce, Industry and Tourism
Rwanda Revenue Authority

Representatives of States
Belgium
Canada
China
France
Germany

Netherlands
Russian Federation
Switzerland
United Kingdom of Great Britain and Northern Ireland
United States of America
Office of the European Union Delegation

United Nations Agencies and Offices
ECA
FAO
Heads of United Nations agencies represented in Rwanda
International Criminal Tribunal for Rwanda
MONUC
Office for the Coordination of Humanitarian Affairs
UNDP

South Africa

Government Officials
Ministry of Foreign Affairs

Other
Anglo-American
De Beers

Switzerland

Government Officials
Department of Foreign Affairs, Chef de la direction politique
Swiss Federal Administration

International Organizations
World Trade Organization
Other
Société générale de surveillance

Uganda

Government Officials

His Excellency Yoweri Kaguta Museveni, President of the Republic of Uganda

Civil Aviation Authority

Internal Revenue Authority

Minister of Agriculture

Minister of Defence

Minister of Energy and Mineral Development

Minister of State for Environment, Water and Land

First Deputy Prime Minister and Minister for Foreign Affairs

Minister of Finance

Minister of State for Planning and Investment

Ministry of Works, Transport and Communications

Parliamentary Committee on Presidential and Foreign Affairs

Vice-President of the Republic of Uganda

Representatives of States

Belgium

Denmark

France

Italy

Russian Federation

United Kingdom of Great Britain and Northern Ireland

European Union Special Envoy to the Great Lakes

United Nations Agencies

Office for the Coordination of Humanitarian Affairs

UNDP

Heads of United Nations agencies in Kampala

Media

East African

Monitor

New Vision

Radio Uganda

Top Radio

Ugandan Television

United Kingdom of Great Britain and Northern Ireland

Government Officials
Foreign and Commonwealth Office

Other
Cluff Mining
De Beers
The Economist
International Coffee Organization
World Diamond Council

United States of America

Government Officials
Department of State
–Bureau of African Affairs
–Bureau of International Organization Affairs
Congresswoman Cynthia McKinney, Fifth District, Georgia

United Nations Agencies and Offices
UNESCO and United Nations Foundation/White Oak Conference

International Organizations
World Bank

Other
Oregon Certification Group
SmartWood
University of Maryland

Zimbabwe

Government Officials
Senior Secretary for Foreign Affairs
Minister of Energy and Mines
Chief Executive Officer, Civil Aviation Authority

Representatives of States
Belgium
China
France
Russian Federation
United Kingdom of Great Britain and Northern Ireland
United States of America

United Nations Agencies and International Organizations
UNDP
Heads of all United Nations agencies represented in Zimbabwe

Media
Zimbabwe Independent newspaper
Daily News

Other
First Banking Corporation Limited
Zimbabwe Transparency International
ZimTrade

Annex III
Abbreviations

AFDL Alliance des forces démocratiques pour la libération du Congo-Zaïre (Alliance of Democratic Forces for the Liberation of Congo-Zaire)
BCD Banque de Commerce et du développement (Trade and Development Bank)
BCDI Banque de commerce, du développement et d'industrie, Kigali
CEMAC Communauté économique et monétaire de l'Afrique centrale (Central African Economic and Monetary Community)
CIFOR Centre for International Forestry Research Coltan columbo-tantalite
COMESA Common Market for Eastern and Southern Africa
COMIEX (1)Compagnie mixte d'import-export
COMIEX (2)La Générale de commerce d'import/export du Congo
COSLEG COMIEX-OSLEG joint venture
ECA Economic Commission for Africa
FAO Food and Agriculture Organization of the United Nations
FDD Forces pour la défense de la démocratie
FLC Front de libération du Congo (merger of MLC and RCD-ML) Gecamines Générale de carrières et des mines
IDI International Diamond Industries
IMF International Monetary Fund
MIBA Société minière de Bakwanga (Mining Company of Bakwanga)
MLC Mouvement de libération congolais (Congolese Liberation Movement)
MONUC United Nations Organization Mission in the Democratic Republic of the Congo
OECD Organisation for Economic Cooperation and Development
OSLEG Operation Sovereign Legitimacy
RCD Rassemblement congolais pour la démocratie (Rally for Congolese Democracy)
RCD-Goma Rassemblement congolais pour la démocratie, based in Goma RCD-Kisangani Rassemblement congolais pour la démocratie, based in Kisangani, later based in Bunia and referred to as RCD-

	ML
RCD-ML	Rassemblement congolais pour la démocratie—Mouvement de Libération, first based in Kisangani, later in Bunia
RCD-National	Rassemblement congolais pour la démocratie—National, located in Bafwasende
RPA	Rwandan Patriotic Army
RPF	Rwandan Patriotic Front
SOMIGL	Société minière des Grands Lacs (Great Lakes Mining Company)
SOMIKIVU	Société minière du Kivu
SOMINKI	Société minière et industrielle du Kivu
UDEAC	Union douanière et économique de l'Afrique centrale (Central African Customs and Economic Union)
UNDP	United Nations Development Programme
UNEP	United Nations Environment Programme
UNHCR	Office of the United Nations High Commissioner for Refugees
UNESCO	United Nations Educational, Scientific and Cultural Organization
UNICEF	United Nations Children's Fund
UPDF	Uganda People's Defence Forces
WFP	World Food Programme
WHO	World Health Organization
WTO	World Trade Organization
ZANU-PF	Zimbabwe African National Union Patriotic Front
ZDF	Zimbabwe Defence Forces

C. UN SECURITY COUNCIL RESOLUTION 1304 OF 16 JUNE, 2000

Adopted by the Security Council at its 4159th meeting, on 16 June, 2000

The Security Council,

Recalling its resolutions 1234 (1999) of 9 April 1999, 1258 (1999) of 6 August 1999, 1265 (1999) of 17 September 1999, 1273 (1999) of 5 November 1999, 1279 (1999) of 30 November 1999, 1291 (2000) of 24 February 2000 and 1296 (2000) of 19 April 2000, and the statements of its President of 13 July 1998 (S/PRST/1998/20), 31 August 1998 (S/PRST/1998/26), 11 December 1998 (S/PRST/1998/36), 24 June 1999 (S/PRST/1999/17), 26 January 2000 (S/PRST/2000/2), 5 May 2000 (S/PRST/2000/15) and 2 June 2000 (S/PRST/2000/20),

Reaffirming the purposes and principles of the Charter of the United Nations and the primary responsibility of the Security Council for the maintenance of international peace and security,

Reaffirming also the obligation of all States to refrain from the use of force against the territorial integrity or political independence of any State, or in any other manner inconsistent with the purposes of the United Nations,

Reaffirming the sovereignty, territorial integrity, and political independence of the Democratic Republic of the Congo and of all States in the region,

Reaffirming also the sovereignty of the Democratic Republic of the Congo over its natural resources, and *noting with concern* reports of the illegal exploitation of the country's assets and the potential consequences of these actions on security conditions and the continuation of hostilities,

In this regard, *calling on* all the parties to the conflict in the Democratic Republic of the Congo and others concerned to cooperate fully with the expert panel on the illegal exploitation of natural resources and other forms of wealth of the Democratic Republic of the Congo (S/PRST/2000/20) in its investigation and visits in the region,

Expressing its deep concern at the continuation of the hostilities in the country,

Expressing in particular its outrage at renewed fighting between Ugandan and Rwandan forces in Kisangani, Democratic Republic of the Congo, which began on 5 June, 2000, and at the failure of Uganda and Rwanda to comply with their commitment to cease hostilities and withdraw from Kisangani made in their joint statements of 8 May, 2000 and of 15 May, 2000 (S/2000/445), and *deploring* the loss of civilian lives, the threat to the civilian population and the damage to property inflicted by the forces of Uganda and Rwanda on the Congolese population,

Recalling its strong support for the Lusaka Cease-fire Agreement (S/1999/815) and insisting that all parties honor their obligations under that Agreement,

Deploring the delays in the implementation of the Cease-fire Agreement and the 8 April, 2000 Kampala disengagement plan, and *stressing* the need for new momentum to ensure progress in the peace process,

Expressing its deep concern at the lack of cooperation of the Government of the Democratic Republic of the Congo with the Facilitator of the National Dialogue designated with the assistance of the Organization of African Unity (OAU), including the fact that the delegates were prevented from attending the Cotonou preparatory meeting on 6 June, 2000,

Welcoming the report of the Secretary-General of 13 June, 2000 (S/2000/566),

Recalling the responsibility of all parties to the conflict in the Democratic Republic of the Congo for ensuring the safety and security of United Nations and associated personnel throughout the country,

Welcoming the participation in its meetings on 15 and 16 June, 2000 of the members of the Political Committee of the Cease-fire Agreement,

Expressing its serious concern over the humanitarian situation in the Democratic Republic of the Congo mainly resulting from the conflict, and *stressing* the need for substantial humanitarian assistance to the Congolese population,

Expressing also its alarm at the dire consequences of the prolonged conflict for the security of the civilian population throughout the territory of the Democratic Republic of the Congo, and its deep concern at all violations and abuses of human rights and international humanitarian law, in particular in the eastern part of the country, especially the Kivus and Kisangani,

Determining that the situation in the Democratic Republic of the Congo continues to constitute a threat to international peace and security in the region,

Acting under Chapter VII of the Charter of the United Nations,

1. *Calls on* all parties to cease hostilities throughout the territory of the Democratic Republic of the Congo and to fulfil their obligations under the Cease-fire Agreement and the relevant provisions of the 8 April, 2000 Kampala disengagement plan;

2. *Reiterates* its unreserved condemnation of the fighting between Ugandan and Rwandan forces in Kisangani in violation of the sovereignty and territorial integrity of the Democratic Republic of the Congo, and *demands* that these forces and those allied to them desist from further fighting;

3. *Demands* that Ugandan and Rwandan forces as well as forces of the Congolese armed opposition and other armed groups immediately and completely withdraw from Kisangani, and *calls on* all parties to the Cease-fire Agreement to respect the demilitarization of the city and its environs;

4. *Further demands*:

(a) that Uganda and Rwanda, which have violated the sovereignty and territorial integrity of the Democratic Republic of the Congo, withdraw all their forces from the territory of the Democratic Republic of the Congo without further delay, in conformity with the timetable of the Cease-fire Agreement and the 8 April, 2000 Kampala disengagement plan;

(b) that each phase of withdrawal completed by Ugandan and Rwandan forces be reciprocated by the other parties in conformity with the same timetable;

(c) that all other foreign military presence and activity, direct and indirect, in the territory of the Democratic Republic of the Congo be brought to an end in conformity with the provisions of the Cease-fire Agreement;

5. In this context *demands* that all parties abstain from any offensive action during the process of disengagement and of withdrawal of foreign forces;

6. *Requests* the Secretary-General to keep under review arrangements for deployment of the personnel of the United Nations Organization Mission in the Democratic Republic of the Congo (MONUC), as authorized and in conditions defined by resolution 1291 (2000), to monitor the cessation of hostilities, disengagement of forces, and withdrawal of foreign forces as described in paragraphs 1 to 5 above and to assist in the planning of these tasks, and *requests also* the Secretary-General to recommend any adjustment that may become necessary in this regard;

7. *Calls on* all parties, in complying with paragraphs 1 to 5 above, to cooperate with the efforts of MONUC to monitor the cessation of hostilities, disengagement of forces, and withdrawal of foreign forces;

8. *Demands* that the parties to the Cease-fire Agreement cooperate with the deployment of MONUC to the areas of operations deemed necessary by the Special Representative of the Secretary-General, including by lifting restrictions on the freedom of movement of MONUC personnel and by ensuring their security;

9. *Calls on* all the Congolese Parties to engage fully in the National Dialogue process as provided for in the Cease-fire Agreement, and *calls in particular on* the Government of the Democratic Republic of the Congo to reaffirm its full commitment to the National Dialogue, to honor its obligations in this respect and to cooperate with the Facilitator designated with the assistance of the OAU and to allow for the full participation of political opposition and civil society groups in the dialogue;

10. *Demands* that all parties cease all forms of assistance and cooperation with the armed groups referred to in Annex A, Chapter 9.1 of the Cease-fire Agreement;

11. *Welcomes* efforts made by the parties to engage in a dialogue on the question of disarmament, demobilization, resettlement, and reintegration of members of all armed groups referred to in Annex A, Chapter 9.1 of the Cease-fire Agreement, and *urges* the parties, in particular the Government of the Democratic Republic of the Congo and the Government of Rwanda, to continue these efforts in full cooperation;

12. *Demands* that all parties comply in particular with the provisions of Annex A, Chapter 12 of the Cease-fire Agreement relating to the normalization of the security situation along the borders of the Democratic Republic of the Congo with its neighbors;

13. *Condemns* all massacres and other atrocities carried out in the territory of the Democratic Republic of the Congo, and *urges* that an international investigation into all such events be carried out with a view to bringing to justice those responsible;

14. *Expresses* the view that the Governments of Uganda and Rwanda should make reparations for the loss of life and the property damage they have inflicted on the civilian population in Kisangani, and *requests* the Secretary-General to submit an assessment of the damage as a basis for such reparations;

15. *Calls on* all the parties to the conflict in the Democratic Republic of the Congo to protect human rights and respect international humanitarian law;

16. *Calls also on* all parties to ensure the safe and unhindered access of

relief personnel to all those in need, and *recalls* that the parties must also provide guarantees for the safety, security, and freedom of movement for United Nations and associated humanitarian relief personnel;

17. *Further calls on* all parties to cooperate with the International Committee of the Red Cross to enable it to carry out its mandate as well as the tasks entrusted to it under the Cease-fire Agreement;

18. *Reaffirms* the importance of holding, at the appropriate time, an international conference on peace, security, democracy, and development in the Great Lakes region under the auspices of the United Nations and of the OAU, with the participation of all the Governments of the region and all others concerned;

19. *Expresses* its readiness to consider possible measures which could be imposed in accordance with its responsibility under the Charter of the United Nations in case of failure by parties to comply fully with this resolution;

20. *Decides* to remain actively seized of the matter.

D. PROTOCOL OF TWINNING BETWEEN THE TOWNS OF GOMA, BUKAVU, AND RWANDA: A VIOLATION OF THE SOVEREIGNTY AND INTEGRITY OF THE DRC(*)

Whereas negotiations were progressing well at Lusaka, in Kivu, the RCD-Kigali run up new flags as a symbol of the secession of Kivu. For the populations, this act was enough. Thus, on 30 June, 1999 under the aegis of COJESKI (Group of Organizations and Associations of Sud-Kivu Youths) a peaceable march of protestation took place at Bukavu which ended up with the destruction of the flags by the masses. Further, this act [of twinning] is against the African Charter of Human Rights and of the Peoples, and of the constitutive Charter of the UN.

Without many comments, here is, in its entirety, the joint official Communiqué about the protocol of twinning—cooperation between the Province of Sud-Kivu and the prefecture of the town of KIGALI; a veiled annexing of Sud-Kivu to RWANDA by the government of KIGALI:

JOINT OFFICIAL COMMUNIQUÉ OF TWINNING—COOPERATION BETWEEN THE PROVINCE OF SUD-KIVU AND THE PREFECTURE OF THE TOWN OF KIGALI

At the invitation of the administration of the town of Kigali represented by its Prefect, Mr. Marc KABANDANA, a delegation of Sud-Kivu, headed by His Excellency Norbert BASENGEZI KATINTIMA, Governor of the Province, made a work visit at Kigali from August 21 to 24, 1999.

This visit was in connection to the twinning—cooperation of between both administrative entities.

The work took place at WINDSOR UMUBANO Hotel and the opening was by His Excellency Désiré NYANDWI, Minister of Local Administration of the Government of National Union of Rwanda, and in the presence of Madam Constance MUKYUHI RWAKA, General Secretary to the Ministry of Foreign Affairs and Regional Cooperation.

Present also were guests representing different institutions both administrative and socio-politic.

(*) Author's French-English translation

During the four working days, participants worked on the six key domains of intervention, namely:

- Economy, Trade and Industry;
- Transportation and Communication;
- Socio-cultural domain;
- Agriculture, Farming, Fishing, Tourism and Environment;
- Urbanism, Habitat; and finally;
- Politic and Security.

The opening ceremonies were followed by a plenary session during which a work methodology was adopted. Participants divided the work according to their domains of competence that constituted different committees. At the end of the work in committees, the following recommendations were given:

1. For the domain of Economy, Trade, and Industry

Both parties commit to:

-Facilitate customs formalities;
-Promote the training and exchange of experience;
-Cooperate in the research services of our customs administrations;
-Exchange all necessary information to fight fraud which only profits to individuals;
-Bring customs regimes into lines;
-Organize training seminars and colloquia in order to master customs techniques;
-Organize regular meetings between customs and economic operative authorities of both entities;

-Lessen administrative procedures at borders' posts of Sud-Kivu Province and Rwanda;
-Improve the accessibility in electricity for the benefit of our populations;
-Sign an agreement between Electogaz and the National Company of Electricity for the locality of Kamanyola;
-Exchange chemical products for the treatment of water;
-Boost research activities in the energy sector (methane gas of Kivu lake, turf, ethanol, bio-gas);
-Increase economic and trade exchanges between Sud-Kivu and the Prefecture of the town of Kigali;
-Boost industrial activities;
-Intensify cooperation between both Chambers of Commerce;
-Re-dynamize the sector banking, insurance services and others;
-Create opportunities to attract investments.

2. For the domain of Transportation and Communication

-Exchange experiences regarding rehabilitation of infrastructures;
-Bring norms of construction of roads into lines concerning the axle charges;
-Facilitate the use of existing infrastructures;
-Put in place a framework of collaboration in the field of Telecommunication.

3. For the Socio-Cultural Domain

a) Education

-Exchange of professors and researchers;
-Communicate the results of research;
-Exchange of students in training and trainees.

b) Health

-Exchange of medical personnel;
-Transfer of patients in the framework of over-medicating;
-Training of medical specialists at postgraduates' level (surgery, pediatric, internal medicine, and gynecology) at Kigali;
-Exchange of experiences in traditional medicine;
-Exchange of strategies in the field of the fight against HIV and other sexually transmitted diseases.

c) Woman and Family

-Organize meetings between mothers of Sud-Kivu and Rwandan associations of women, in particular the group Pro-women Twese Hamwe as to benefit of their experiences;
-Organize study travels.

d) Youth

-Study the feasibility of projects for the training and development of youth;
-Strengthen training centers for manual labor for those youth out of the school system;
-Organize summer vacations for the youth;
- Exchange and apply special programs for the training of vulnerable youth, streets, traumatized and handicapped children, etc.

e) Sports and Recreations

-Further the promotion, production, and circulation of cultural activities at sub-region level;
-Rehabilitate positive values of our cultures;
-Develop the press;
-Exchange experiences and information between journalists;
-Promote a culture of peace, justice, unity, and reconciliation.

4. For the Domain of Agriculture, Farming, Environment, and Tourism

-Creation of tourist sites, like zoos, museums, etc.;
-Creation of training centers in the field of conservation of nature;
-Establish a common politic of management of environment;
-Exchange of results and experiences in the field of agro-zootechnical research;
-Facilitate the distribution of animal, agriculture, and fishing products;
-Further the protection of fishing species.

5. For the Domain of Urbanism and Habitat

-Establish a national politic of habitat and accommodation and care about its application;
-Facilitate training, documentation, and information exchanges;
-Promote private companies or Para-static immovable companies in the

fields of planning and construction.

6. For the Domain of Politic and Security

-Educate the populations on general and politic plan;
-Encourage the principle of regional cooperation;
-Create a permanent joined committee on security;
-Encourage good governance and take energetic measures against impunity;
-That this twinning serve as a driving belt between respective States;
-Fight the mutual mistrust and suspicious climate by encouraging joint training in the fields of police, security, the training of political agents, and retraining of military;
-Organize seminars for the benefit of administrative agents of Sud-Kivu Province and those of the Prefecture of the town of Kigali.

Executed at Kigali on 24 August, 1999

E. UNIVERSAL DECLARATION OF HUMAN RIGHTS

Adopted and proclaimed by General Assembly resolution 217 A (III) of 10 December, 1948

On December 10, 1948 the General Assembly of the United Nations adopted and proclaimed the Universal Declaration of Human Rights, the full text of which appears in the following pages. Following this historic act the Assembly called upon all Member countries to publicize the text of the Declaration and "to cause it to be disseminated, displayed, read, and expounded principally in schools and other educational institutions, without distinction based on the political status of countries or territories."

PREAMBLE

Whereas recognition of the inherent dignity and of the equal and inalienable rights of all members of the human family is the foundation of freedom, justice and peace in the world,

Whereas disregard and contempt for human rights have resulted in barbarous acts which have outraged the conscience of mankind, and the advent of a world in which human beings shall enjoy freedom of speech and belief and freedom from fear and want has been proclaimed as the highest aspiration of the common people,

Whereas it is essential, if man is not to be compelled to have recourse, as a last resort, to rebel against tyranny and oppression, that human rights should be protected by the rule of law,

Whereas it is essential to promote the development of friendly relations between nations,

Whereas the peoples of the United Nations have in the Charter reaffirmed their faith in fundamental human rights, in the dignity and worth of the human person and in the equal rights of men and women and have determined to promote social progress and better standards of life in larger freedom,

Whereas Member States have pledged themselves to achieve, in co-operation with the United Nations, the promotion of universal respect for and observance of human rights and fundamental freedoms,

Whereas a common understanding of these rights and freedoms is of the greatest importance for the full realization of this pledge,

Now, Therefore THE GENERAL ASSEMBLY proclaims THIS UNIVERSAL DECLARATION OF HUMAN RIGHTS as a common standard of achievement for all peoples and all nations, to the end that every individual and every organ of society, keeping this Declaration constantly in mind, shall strive by teaching and education to promote respect for these rights and freedoms and by progressive measures, national and international, to secure their universal and effective recognition and observance, both among the peoples of Member States themselves and among the peoples of territories under their jurisdiction.

Article 1.

All human beings are born free and equal in dignity and rights. They are endowed with reason and conscience and should act toward one another in a spirit of brotherhood.

Article 2.

Everyone is entitled to all the rights and freedoms set forth in this Declaration, without distinction of any kind, such as race, color, sex, language, religion, political or other opinion, national or social origin, property, birth, or other status. Furthermore, no distinction shall be made on the basis of the political, jurisdictional, or international status of the country or territory to which a person belongs, whether it be independent, trust, non-self-governing, or under any other limitation of sovereignty.

Article 3.

Everyone has the right to life, liberty, and security of person.

Article 4.

No one shall be held in slavery or servitude; slavery and the slave trade shall be prohibited in all their forms.

Article 5.

No one shall be subjected to torture or to cruel, inhuman, or degrading treatment or punishment.

Article 6.

Everyone has the right to recognition everywhere as a person before the law.

Article 7.

All are equal before the law and are entitled without any discrimination to equal protection of the law. All are entitled to equal protection against any discrimination in violation of this Declaration and against any incitement to such discrimination.

Article 8.

Everyone has the right to an effective remedy by the competent national tribunals for acts violating the fundamental rights granted him by the constitution or by law.

Article 9.

No one shall be subjected to arbitrary arrest, detention, or exile.

Article 10.

Everyone is entitled in full equality to a fair and public hearing by an independent and impartial tribunal, in the determination of his rights and obligations and of any criminal charge against him.

Article 11.

(1) Everyone charged with a penal offense has the right to be presumed innocent until proved guilty according to law in a public trial at which he has had all the guarantees necessary for his defense.

(2) No one shall be held guilty of any penal offense on account of any act or omission which did not constitute a penal offense, under national or international law, at the time when it was committed. Nor shall a heavier penalty be imposed than the one that was applicable at the time the penal offense was committed.

Article 12.

No one shall be subjected to arbitrary interference with his privacy, family, home or correspondence, nor to attacks upon his honor and reputation. Everyone has the right to the protection of the law against such interference or attacks.

Article 13.

(1) Everyone has the right to freedom of movement and residence within the borders of each state.

(2) Everyone has the right to leave any country, including his own, and to return to his country.

Article 14.

(1) Everyone has the right to seek and to enjoy, in other countries, asylum from persecution.

(2) This right may not be invoked in the case of prosecutions genuinely arising from non-political crimes or from acts contrary to the purposes and principles of the United Nations.

Article 15.

(1) Everyone has the right to a nationality.

(2) No one shall be arbitrarily deprived of his nationality nor denied the right to change his nationality.

Article 16.

(1) Men and women of full age, without any limitation due to race, nationality, or religion, have the right to marry and to have a family. They are entitled to equal rights as to marriage, during marriage, and at its dissolution.

(2) Marriage shall be entered into only with the free and full consent of the intending spouses.

(3) The family is the natural and fundamental group unit of society and is entitled to protection by society and the State.

Article 17.

(1) Everyone has the right to own property alone as well as in association with others.

(2) No one shall be arbitrarily deprived of his property.

Article 18.

Everyone has the right to freedom of thought, conscience and religion; this right includes freedom to change his religion or belief, and freedom, either alone or in community with others and in public or private, to manifest his religion or belief in teaching, practice, worship, and observance.

Article 19.

Everyone has the right to freedom of opinion and expression; this right includes freedom to hold opinions without interference and to seek, receive, and impart information and ideas through any media and regardless of frontiers.

Article 20.

(1) Everyone has the right to freedom of peaceful assembly and association.

(2) No one may be compelled to belong to an association.

Article 21.

(1) Everyone has the right to take part in the government of his country, directly or through freely chosen representatives.

(2) Everyone has the right of equal access to public service in his country.

(3) The will of the people shall be the basis of the authority of government; this will shall be expressed in periodic and genuine elections, which shall be by universal and equal suffrage and shall be held by secret vote or by equivalent free voting procedures.

Article 22.

Everyone, as a member of society, has the right to social security and is entitled to realization, through national effort and international co-operation and in accordance with the organization and resources of each State, of the economic, social, and cultural rights indispensable for his dignity and the free development of his personality.

Article 23.

(1) Everyone has the right to work, to free choice of employment, to just and favorable conditions of work, and to protection against unemployment.

(2) Everyone, without any discrimination, has the right to equal pay for equal work.

(3) Everyone who works has the right to just and favorable remuneration ensuring for himself and his family an existence worthy of human dignity, and supplemented, if necessary, by other means of social protection.

(4) Everyone has the right to form and to join trade unions for the protection of his interests.

Article 24.

Everyone has the right to rest and leisure, including reasonable limitation of working hours and periodic holidays with pay.

Article 25.

(1) Everyone has the right to a standard of living adequate for the health and well-being of himself and of his family, including food, clothing, housing and medical care, and necessary social services, and the right to security in the event of unemployment, sickness, disability, widowhood, old age, or other lack of livelihood in circumstances beyond his control.

(2) Motherhood and childhood are entitled to special care and assistance. All children, whether born in or out of wedlock, shall enjoy the same social protection.

Article 26.

(1) Everyone has the right to education. Education shall be free, at least in the elementary and fundamental stages. Elementary education shall be compulsory. Technical and professional education shall be made generally available and higher education shall be equally accessible to all on the basis of merit.

(2) Education shall be directed to the full development of the human personality and to the strengthening of respect for human rights and fundamental freedoms. It shall promote understanding, tolerance, and friendship among all nations, racial or religious groups, and shall further the activities of the United Nations for the maintenance of peace.

(3) Parents have a prior right to choose the kind of education that shall be given to their children.

Article 27.

(1) Everyone has the right freely to participate in the cultural life of the community, to enjoy the arts, and to share in scientific advancement and its benefits.

(2) Everyone has the right to the protection of the moral and material interests resulting from any scientific, literary, or artistic production of which he is the author.

Article 28.

Everyone is entitled to a social and international order in which the rights and freedoms set forth in this Declaration can be fully realized.

Article 29.

(1) Everyone has duties to the community in which alone the free and full development of his personality is possible.

(2) In the exercise of his rights and freedoms, everyone shall be subject only to such limitations as are determined by law solely for the purpose of securing due recognition and respect for the rights and freedoms of others and of meeting the just requirements of morality, public order, and the general welfare in a democratic society.

(3) These rights and freedoms may in no case be exercised contrary to the purposes and principles of the United Nations.

Article 30.

Nothing in this Declaration may be interpreted as implying for any State, group, or person, any right to engage in any activity or to perform any act aimed at the destruction of any of the rights and freedoms set forth herein.

F. AMERICA'S COVERT OPERATIONS IN THE GREAT LAKES REGION

By Wayne MadsenWashington, DC05.17.01

Wayne Madsen is an Investigative Journalist On: "Suffering and Despair: Humanitarian Crisis in the Congo." Below is prepared testimony and statement presented before the Subcommittee on International Operations and Human Rights and Committee on International Relations (United States House of Representatives, Washington, DC on May 17, 2001.

My name is Wayne Madsen. I am the author of "Genocide and Covert Operations in Africa 1993-1999," a work that involved some three years worth of research and countless interviews in Rwanda, Uganda, France, the United Kingdom, United States, Belgium, Canada, and the Netherlands. I am an investigative journalist who specializes on intelligence and privacy issues.

I am grateful to appear before the Committee today (May 17, 2001). I am also appreciative of the Committee's interest in holding this hearing on the present situation in the Democratic Republic of the Congo. I wish to discuss the record of American policy in the DRC over most of the past decade, particularly involving the eastern Congo region.

It is a policy that has rested, in my opinion, on the twin pillars of military aid and questionable trade. The military aid programs of the United States, largely planned and administered by the US Special Operations Command and the Defense Intelligence Agency (DIA), have been both overt and covert.

Prior to the first Rwandan invasion of Zaire/DRC in 1996, a phalanx of US intelligence operatives converged on Zaire. Their actions suggested a strong interest in Zaire's eastern defenses. The number-two person at the US Embassy in Kigali traveled from Kigali to eastern Zaire to initiate intelligence contacts with the Alliance of Democratic Forces for the Liberation of Congo-Zaire (AFDL-CZ) rebels under the command of the late

President Laurent Kabila. The Rwandan embassy official met with rebel leaders at least twelve times.

A former US ambassador to Uganda—acting on behalf of the US Agency for International Development (USAID)—gathered intelligence on the movement of Hutu refugees through eastern Zaire. The DIA's second ranking Africa hand, who also served as the US military attaché in Kigali, reconnoitered the Rwandan border towns of Cyangugu and Gisenyi, gathering intelligence on the cross border movements of anti-Mobutu Rwandan Tutsis from Rwanda.

The Defense Intelligence Agency's African bureau chief established a close personal relationship with Bizima (alias Bizimana) Karaha, an ethnic Rwandan who would later become the Foreign Minister in the Laurent Kabila government. Moreover, the DIA's Africa division had close ties with Military Professional Resources, Inc. (MPRI), an Alexandria, Virginia private military company (PMC), whose Vice President for Operations is a former Director of DIA.

The political officer of the US Embassy in Kinshasa, accompanied by a CIA operative, traveled with AFDL-CZ rebels through the eastern Zaire jungles for weeks after the 1996 Rwandan invasion of Zaire. In addition, it was reported that the Kinshasa embassy official and three US intelligence agents regularly briefed Bill Richardson, Clinton's special African envoy, during the rebels' steady advance toward Kinshasa.

The US embassy official conceded that he was in Goma to do more than meet rebel leaders for lunch. Explaining his presence, he said, "What I am here to do is to acknowledge them [the rebels] as a very significant military and political power on the scene, and, of course, to represent American interests."

In addition, MPRI was reportedly providing covert training assistance to Kagame's troops in preparation for combat in Zaire.

Some believe that MPRI had actually been involved in training the RPF from the time it took power in Rwanda.

The Ba-N'Daw Report

The covert programs involving the use of private military training firms and logistics support contractors that are immune to Freedom of Information Act requests is particularly troubling for researchers and journalists who have tried, over the past several years, to get at the root causes for the deaths and mayhem in the DRC and other countries in the region. These US contractor support programs have reportedly involved covert assistance to the Rwandan and Ugandan militaries—the major backers of the Rassemblement Congolais pour la démocratie (RCD factions and—as reported by the UN's "Panel of Experts on the Illegal Exploitation of Natural Resources an Other Forms of Wealth of the DRC"—are responsible for the systematic pillaging of Congo's most valuable natural resources.

The UN panel—chaired by Safiatou Ba-N'Daw of Cote d'Ivoire—concluded that "Top military commanders from various countries needed and continue to need this conflict for its lucrative nature and for temporarily solving some internal problems in those countries as well as allowing access to wealth."

There is more than ample evidence that the elements of the US military and intelligence community may have—on varying occasions—aided and abetted this systematic pillaging by the Ugandan and Rwandan militaries. The UN Report named the United States, Germany, Belgium, and Kazakhstan as leading buyers of the illegally exploited resources from the DRC.

Sources in the Great Lakes region consistently report the presence of a US-built military base near Cyangugu, Rwanda, near the Congolese border. The base, reported to have been partly constructed by the US firm, Brown & Root, a subsidiary of Halliburton, is said to be involved with training RPF forces and providing logistics support to their troops in the DRC. Additionally, the presence in the region of black US soldiers supporting the RPF and Ugandans has been something consistently reported since the first invasion of Zaire-Congo in 1996.

On January 21, 1997, France claimed it actually recovered the remains of two American combatants killed near the Oso River in Kivu province during combat and returned them to American officials. The US denied these claims.

Covert American support for the combatants

As US troops and intelligence agents were pouring into Africa to help the RPF and AFDL-CZ forces in their 1996 campaign against Mobutu, Vincent Kern, the Deputy Assistant Secretary of Defense for African Affairs, told the House International Operations and Human Rights Subcommittee on December 4, 1996 that US military training for the RPF was being conducted under a program called Enhanced International Military Education and Training (E-IMET). Kathi Austin, a Human Rights Watch specialist on arms transfers in Africa, told the Subcommittee on May 5, 1998 that one senior US embassy official in Kigali described the US Special Forces training program for the RPF as "killers ... training killers."

In November 1996, US spy satellites and a US Navy P-3 Orion were attempting to ascertain how many Rwandan Hutu refugees were in eastern Zaire. The P-3 was one of four stationed at old Entebbe Airport on the shores of Lake Victoria. Oddly, while other planes flying over eastern Zaire attracted anti-aircraft fire from Kabila's forces, the P-3s, which patrolled the skies above Goma and Sake, were left alone.

Relying on the overhead intelligence, US military and aid officials confidently announced that 600,000 Hutu refugees returned home to Rwanda from Zaire. But that left an estimated 300,000 unaccounted for. Many Hutus seemed to be disappearing from camps around Bukavu.

By December 1996, US military forces were also operating in Bukavu amid throngs of Hutus, less numerous Twa refugees, Mai Mai guerrillas, advancing Rwandan troops, and AFDL-CZ rebels. A French military intelligence officer said he detected some 100 armed US troops in the eastern Zaire conflict zone.

Moreover, the DGSE reported the Americans had knowledge of the extermination of Hutu refugees by Tutsis in both Rwanda and eastern Zaire and were doing nothing about it. More ominously, there was reason to believe that some US forces, either Special Forces or mercenaries, may have actually participated in the extermination of Hutu refugees. The killings reportedly took place at a camp on the banks of the Oso River near Goma.

Roman Catholic reports claim that the executed included a number of Hutu Catholic priests. At least for those who were executed, death was far quicker than it was for those who escaped deep into the jungle. There, many died from tropical diseases or were attacked and eaten by wild animals.

Jacques Isnard, the Paris-based defense correspondent for Le Monde, supported the contention of US military knowledge of the Oso River massacre but went further. He quoted French intelligence sources that he believed that between thirty and sixty American mercenary "advisers" participated with the RPF in the massacre of hundreds of thousands of Hutu refugees around Goma. Although his number of dead Hutus was more conservative than the French estimates, the UN's Chilean investigator, Roberto Garreton, reported the Kagame and Museveni forces had committed "crimes against humanity" in killing thousands [emphasis added] of Hutu refugees.

It was known that the planes the US military deployed in eastern Zaire included heavily armed and armored helicopter gunships typically used by the Special Forces. These were fitted with 105mm cannons, rockets, machine guns, land mine ejectors, and, more importantly, infrared sensors used in night operations. US military commanders unabashedly stated the purpose of these gunships was to locate refugees to determine the best means of providing them with humanitarian assistance.

According to the French magazine, *Valeurs Actuelles*, a French DC-8 Sarigue electronic intelligence (ELINT) aircraft circled over eastern Zaire at the time of the Oso River massacre. The Sarigue's mission was to intercept and fix the radio transmission of Rwandan military units engaged in the military operations. This aircraft, in addition to French special ground units, witnessed US military ethnic cleansing in Zaire's Kivu Province.

In September 1997, the prestigious "Jane's Foreign Report" reported that German intelligence sources were aware that the DIA trained young men and teens from Rwanda, Uganda, and eastern Zaire for periods of up to two years and longer for the RPF/AFDL-CZ campaign against Mobutu. The recruits were offered pay of between $450 and $1000 upon their successful capture of Kinshasa. [17] Toward the end of 1996, US spy satellites were attempting to ascertain how many refugees escaped into the jungle by locating fires at night and canvas tarpaulins during the day. Strangely, every time an encampment was discovered by the space-based imagery, Rwandan and Zaire rebel forces attacked the sites. This was the case in late February 1997, when 160,000, mainly Hutu refugees, were spotted and then attacked in a swampy area known as Tingi Tingi.

There was never an adequate accounting by the Pentagon and US intelligence agencies of the scope of intelligence provided to the RPF/AFDL-CZ.

An ominous report on the fate of refugees was made by Nicholas Stockton, the Emergencies Director of Oxfam UK & Ireland. He said that on November 20, 1996, he was shown US aerial intelligence photographs which "confirmed, in considerable detail, the existence of 500,000 people distributed in three major and numerous minor agglomerations." He said that three days later the US military claimed it could only locate one significant mass of people, which they claimed were identified as former members of the Rwandan armed forces and the Interhamwe militia. Since they were the number one targets for the RPF forces, their identification and location by the Americans was undoubtedly passed to the Rwandan forces. They would have surely been executed. [19] Moreover, some US military and diplomatic personnel in central Africa said that any deaths among the Hutu refugees merely constituted "collateral damage."

When the AFDL-CZ and their Rwandan allies reached Kinshasa in 1996, it was largely due to the help of the United States. One reason why Kabila's men advanced into the city so quickly was the technical assistance provided by the DIA and other intelligence agencies. According to informed sources in Paris, US Special Forces actually accompanied ADFL-CZ forces into Kinshasa. The Americans also reportedly provided Kabila's rebels and Rwandan troops with high definition spy satellite photographs that permitted them to order their troops to plot courses into Kinshasa that avoided encounters with Mobutu's forces.

During the rebel advance toward Kinshasa, Bechtel provided Kabila, at no cost, high technology intelligence, including National Aeronautics and Space Administration (NASA) satellite data.

American military support for the second invasion of Congo

By 1998, the Kabila regime had become an irritant to the United States, North American mining interests, and Kabila's Ugandan and Rwandan patrons. As a result, Rwanda and Uganda launched a second invasion of the DRC to get rid of Kabila and replace him with someone more servile. The Pentagon was forced to admit on August 6, 1998 that a twenty-man US Army Rwanda Interagency Assessment Team (RIAT) was in Rwanda at the time of the second RPF invasion of Congo. The camouflaged unit was deployed from the US European Command in Germany.

It was later revealed that the team in question was a JCET unit that was sent to Rwanda to help the Rwandans "defeat ex FAR (Rwandan Armed Forces) and Interhamwe" units. US Special Forces JCET team began training Rwandan units on July 15, 1998. It was the second such training exercise held that year. The RIAT team was sent to Rwanda in the weeks just leading up to the outbreak of hostilities in Congo.

The RIAT, specializing in counter insurgency operations, traveled to Gisenyi on the Congolese border just prior to the Rwandan invasion.

One of the assessments of the team recommended that the United States establish a new and broader military relationship with Rwanda. National Security Council spokesman P.J. Crowley, said of the RIAT's presence in Rwanda: "I think it's a coincidence that they were there at the same time the fighting began."

Soon, however, as other African nations came to the assistance of

Laurent Kabila, the United States found itself in the position of providing military aid under both the E-IMET and the Joint Combined Exchange Training (JCET) programs. US Special Operations personnel were involved in training troops on both sides of the war in the DRC—Rwandans, Ugandans, and Burundians (supporting the RCD factions) and Zimbabweans and Namibians (supporting the central government in Kinshasa).

As with the first invasion, there were also a number of reports that the RPF and their RCD allies carried out a number of massacres throughout the DRC. The Vatican reported a sizable killing of civilians in August 1998 in Kasika, a small village in South Kivu that hosted a Catholic mission station. Over eight hundred people, including priests and nuns, were killed by Rwandan troops. The RCD response was to charge the Vatican with aiding Kabila. The Rwandans, choosing to put into practice what the DIA's PSYOPS personnel had taught them about mounting perception management campaigns, shepherded the foreign press to carefully selected killing fields. The dead civilians were identified as exiled Burundian Hutu militiamen. Unfortunately, many in the international community, still suffering a type of collective guilt over the genocide of the Tutsis in Rwanda, gave the Rwandan assertions more credence than was warranted.

The increasing reliance by the Department of Defense on so-called Private Military Contractors (PMCs) is of special concern. Many of these PMCs—once labeled as "mercenaries" by previous administrations when they were used as foreign policy instruments by the colonial powers of France, Belgium, Portugal, and South Africa—have close links with some of the largest mining and oil companies involved in Africa today. PMCs, because of their proprietary status, have a great deal of leeway to engage in covert activities far from the reach of congressional investigators. They can simply claim that their business in various nations is a protected trade secret and the law now seems to be on their side.

Profiting from the destabilization of Central Africa

America's policy toward Africa during the past decade, rather than seeking to stabilize situations where civil war and ethnic turmoil reign supreme, has seemingly promoted destabilization. Former Secretary of State, Madeleine Albright, was fond of calling pro-US military leaders in Africa who assumed power by force and then cloaked themselves in civilian attire, "beacons of hope."

In reality, these leaders, who include the current presidents of Uganda,

Rwanda, Ethiopia, Angola, Eritrea, Burundi, and the Democratic Republic of the Congo preside over countries where ethnic and civil turmoil permit unscrupulous international mining companies to take advantage of the strife to fill their own coffers with conflict diamonds, gold, copper, platinum, and other precious minerals—including one—columbite-tantalite or "coltan"—which is a primary component of computer microchips and printed circuit boards.

Some of the companies involved in this new "scramble for Africa" have close links with PMCs and America's top political leadership. For example, America Minerals Fields, Inc., a company that was heavily involved in promoting the1996 accession to power of Kabila, was, at the time of its involvement in the Congo's civil war, headquartered in Hope, Arkansas. Its major stockholders include long time associates of former President Clinton going back to his days as Governor of Arkansas. America Mineral Fields also reportedly enjoys a close relationship with Lazare Kaplan International, Inc., a major international diamond brokerage whose president remains a close confidant of past and current administrations on Africa matters.

The United States has a long history of supporting all sides in the DRC's civil wars in order to gain access to the country's natural resources. The Ba-N'Daw Report presents a cogent example of how one US firm was involved in the DRC's grand thievery before the 1998 break between Laurent Kabila and his Rwandan and Ugandan backers. It links the Banque de commerce, du developpement et d'industrie (BCDI) of Kigali, Citibank in New York, the diamond business, and armed rebellion. The report states: "In a letter signed by J.P. Moritz, general manager of Societe miniere de Bakwanga (MIBA), a Congolese diamond company, and Ngandu Kamenda, the general manager of MIBA ordered a payment of US$3.5 million to la Generale de commerce d'import/export du Congo (COMIEX), a company owned by late President Kabila and some of his close allies, such as Minister Victor Mpoyo, from an account in BCDI through a Citibank account. This amount of money was paid as a contribution from MIBA to the AFDL war effort."

Also troubling are the ties that some mining companies in Africa have with military privateers. UN Special Rapporteur Enrique Ballesteros of Peru concluded in a his March 2001 report for the UN Commission on Human Rights, that mercenaries were inexorably linked to the illegal diamond and arms trade in Africa. He stated, "Mercenaries participate in both types of traffic, acting as pilots of aircraft and helicopters, training makeshift troops in the use of weapons, and transferring freight from place to place."

Ballesteros added, "Military security companies and air cargo companies registered in Nevada (the United States), in the Channel Islands and especially in South Africa, are engaged in the transport of troops, arms, munitions, and diamonds."

In 1998, American Mineral Fields purchased diamond concessions in the Cuango Valley along the Angolan-Congolese border from International Defense and Security (IDAS Belgium SA), a mercenary firm based in Curacao and headquartered in Belgium. According to an American Mineral Fields press release, "In May 1996, American Mineral Fields entered into an agreement with IDAS Resources NV ("IDAS") and IDAS shareholders, under which the Company may acquire 75.5% of the common shares of IDAS. In turn, IDAS has entered into a 50/50 joint venture agreement with Endiama, the Angola state mining company. The joint venture asset is a 3,700 km mining lease in the Cuango Valley, Luremo, and a 36,000 km2 prospecting lease called the Cuango International, which borders the mining lease to the north. The total area is approximately the size of Switzerland."

American Mineral Fields directly benefitted from America's initial covert military and intelligence support for Kabila. It is my observation that America's early support for Kabila, which was aided and abetted by US allies, Rwanda and Uganda, had less to do with getting rid of the Mobutu regime than it had to do with opening up Congo's vast mineral riches to North American-based and influenced mining companies. Presently, some of American Mineral Fields' principals now benefit from the destabilization of Sierra Leone and the availability of its cut-rate "blood diamonds" on the international market. Also, according to the findings of a commission headed up by Canadian United Nations Ambassador, Robert Fowler, Rwanda has violated the international embargo against Angola's UNITA rebels in allowing them "to operate more or less freely" in selling conflict zone diamonds and making deals with weapons dealers in Kigali.

One of the major goals of the Rwandan-backed RCD-Goma faction, a group fighting the Kabila government in Congo, is restoration of mining concessions for Barrick Gold, Inc. of Canada. In fact, the rebel RCD government's "mining minister" signed a separate mining deal with Barrick in early 1999.[29] Among the members of Barrick's International Advisory Board are former President Bush and former President Clinton's close confidant, Vernon Jordan.

Currently, Barrick and tens of other mining companies are helping to stoke the flames of the civil war in the DRC Each benefits by the de facto partition of the country into some four separate zones of political control. First the mineral exploiters from Rwanda and Uganda concentrated on pillaging gold and diamonds from the eastern Congo. Now, they have increasingly turned their attention to coltan.

It is my hope that the Bush administration will take pro-active measures to stem the conflict in the DRC by applying increased pressure on Uganda and Rwanda to withdraw their troops from the country. However, the fact that President Bush has selected Walter Kansteiner to be Assistant Secretary of State for African Affairs, portends, in my opinion, more trouble for the Great Lakes region.

A brief look at Mr. Kansteiner's curriculum vitae and statements calls into question his commitment to seeking a durable peace in the region.

In an October 15, 1996 paper written by Mr. Kansteiner for the Forum for International Policy on the then-eastern Zaire, he called for the division of territory in the Great Lakes region "between the primary ethnic groups, creating homogenous ethnic lands that would probably necessitate redrawing international boundaries and would require massive 'voluntary' relocation efforts." Kansteiner foresaw creating separate Tutsi and Hutu states after such a drastic population shift. It should be recalled that the creation of a Tutsi state in eastern Congo was exactly what Rwanda, Uganda, and their American military advisers had in mind when Rwanda invaded then-Zaire in 1996, the same year Kansteiner penned his plans for the region. Four years later, Kansteiner was still convinced that the future of the DRC was "balkanization" into separate states.

In an August 23, 2000 Pittsburgh Post-Gazette article, Kansteiner stated that the "breakup of the Congo is more likely now than it has been in 20 or 30 years." Of course, the de facto break up of Congo into various fiefdoms has been a boon for US and other western mineral companies. And I believe Kansteiner's previous work at the Department of Defense where he served on a Task Force on Strategic Minerals—and one must certainly consider coltan as falling into that category—may influence his past and current thinking on the territorial integrity of the DRC. After all, 80 percent of the world's known reserves of coltan are found in the eastern DRC. It is potentially as important to the US military as the Persian Gulf region.

However, the US military and intelligence agencies, which have supported Uganda and Rwanda in their cross-border adventures in the DRC, have resisted peace initiatives and have failed to produce evidence of war crimes by the Ugandans and Rwandans and their allies in Congo. The CIA,

NSA, and DIA should turn over to international and congressional investigators intelligence-generated evidence in their possession, as well as overhead thermal imagery indicating the presence of mass graves and when they were dug. In particular, the NSA maintained a communications intercept station in Fort Portal, Uganda, which intercepted military and government communications in Zaire during the first Rwandan invasion. These intercepts may contain details of Rwandan and AFDL-CZ massacres of innocent Hutu refugees and other Congolese civilians during the 1996 invasion. There must be a full accounting before the Congress by the staff of the US Defense Attache's Office in Kigali and certain US Embassy staff members in Kinshasa who served from early 1994 to the present time.

As for the number of war casualties in the DRC since the first invasion from Rwanda in 1996, I would estimate, from my own research, the total to be around 1.7 to 2 million—a horrendous number by any calculation. And I also believe that, although disease and famine were contributing factors, the majority of these deaths were the result of actual war crimes committed by Rwandan, Ugandan, Burundian, AFDL-CZ, RCD, and military and paramilitary forces of other countries.

Summary

It is beyond time for the Congress to seriously examine the role of the United States in the genocide and civil wars of central Africa, as well as the role that PMCs currently play in other African trouble spots like Nigeria, Sierra Leone, Equatorial Guinea, Angola, Ethiopia, Sudan, and Cabinda. Other nations, some with less than stellar records in Africa—France and Belgium, for example—have had no problem examining their own roles in Africa's last decade of turmoil. The British Foreign Office is in the process of publishing a green paper on regulation of mercenary activity.

At the very least, the United States, as the world's leading democracy, owes Africa at least the example of a critical self-inspection.

I appreciate the concern shown by the Chair and members of this committee in holding these hearings.

Thank you.

G. COVERT ACTION IN AFRICA: A SMOKING GUN IN WASHINGTON, DC

Congresswoman Cynthia McKinney: OPENING STATEMENT:

I want to thank you all for coming today.

I especially want to thank our esteemed speakers for traveling, in some instances, quite a long way, to be with us today.

Our speakers are courageous individuals who have gone to many of Africa's most dangerous and desperately poor locations, not for wealth or riches, but in order to merely discover the truth. They provide us with a remarkable insight into what has gone on in Africa and what continues to go on in Africa today.

Much of what you will hear today has not been widely reported in the public media. Powerful forces have fought to suppress these stories from entering the public domain.

Their investigations into the activities of Western governments and Western businessmen in post-colonial Africa provide clear evidence of the West's long-standing propensity for cruelty, avarice, and treachery. The misconduct of Western nations in Africa is not due to momentary lapses, individual defects, or errors of common human frailty. Instead, they form part of long-term malignant policy designed to access and plunder Africa's wealth at the expense of its people. In short, the accounts you are about to hear provide an indictment of Western activities in Africa.

That West has, for decades, plundered Africa's wealth and permitted, and even assisted, in slaughtering Africa's people. The West has been able to do this while still shrewdly cultivating the myth that much of Africa's problems today are African made; we have all heard the usual Western defenses that Africa's problems are the fault of corrupt African administrations, the fault of centuries-old tribal hatreds, the fault of unsophisticated peoples rapidly entering a modern high technology world.

But we know that those statements are all a lie. We have always known it.

The accounts we are about to hear today assist us in understanding just why Africa is in the state it is in today. You will hear that at the heart of Africa's suffering is the West's, and most notably the United States', desire to access Africa's diamonds, oil, natural gas, and other precious resources. You will hear that the West, and most notably the United States, has set in motion a policy of oppression, destabalisation, and tempered, not by moral principle, but by a ruthless desire to enrich itself on Africa's fabulous wealth. While falsely pretending to be the friends and allies of many African countries, so desperate for help and assistance, many western nations, and I'm ashamed to say most notably the United States, have in reality betrayed those countries' trust and instead, have relentlessly pursued their own selfish military and economic policies. Western countries have incited rebellion against stable African governments by encouraging and even arming opposition parties and rebel groups to begin armed insurrection. The Western nations have even actively participated in the assassination of duly-elected and legitimate African Heads of State and replaced them with corrupted and malleable officials. Western nations have even encouraged and been complicate in the unlawful invasions by African nations into neighboring counties.

These accounts today are a public indictment of European and American governments and businessmen. Something must be done to right these wrongs. Something must be done to restore Africa to peace and prosperity.

I invite you to listen and learn first hand of the West's activities in Africa.

Prepared Statement of Janine Farrell Roberts. Author of the book, Blood Stained Diamonds.The Secret Story Behind the Bloody Diamond. How US Foreign Policy over decades was influenced by the Diamond Cartel. Maurice Tempelsman: The Convergence of Policy and Profit in Private:

May I first briefly introduce myself. I hold degrees in Sociology and Theology and have authored several books written about Australian Aborigines and their civil rights struggle, which were launched by their leaders. For many years I was funded by a coalition of US and European church to work on human rights frontiers internationally.

This work led me to De Beers—after it clashed with an Aboriginal community. The more I worked internationally the more I discovered about its human rights violations. I have now been researching and writing on De

Beers and the diamond trade for twenty years, during which time I have made several films—including: "The Diamond Empire," a feature length "Frontline," since suppressed by WGBH due to pressure from De Beers. The owners of Doubleday also commissioned a major work from me on diamonds—only to drop it at the very last moment as they wrote, "rich and important people" did not want it to come out.

De Beers is nothing if not secretive In the course of my investigation, De Beers banned me from its South African diamond mines where I was the guest of the National Union of Mineworkers (but I was smuggled in). Here I witnessed in De Beers' mines horrific conditions with wages paid at one third of the official union minimum and in very hazardous conditions. I also witnessed considerable natural resources being hidden from the SA Government. I went also to India and witnessed children as young as 8 cutting and polishing diamonds in workshops mostly supplied by De Beers through its favored merchants, working in what is defined as a form of slavery. The wages were slashed this year from 40c to 25c a diamond, causing riots. Workers get one dollar a day for cutting romantic gems. India cuts 55% by value of the world's gem diamonds.

De Beers tried to stop my film in the Canadian NW Territories diamond fields—but the Sierra Club and the Unions had it happen. On 5th Avenue, merchants were phoned telling them not to speak to me "as I worked with Blacks in Australia to make life difficult for De Beers." I was also the keynote speaker at the first post apartheid conference of Southern African mineworkers where I was funded by the World Council of Churches.

I have been told that a major reason for some of my difficulties is the fear publishers have of a certain Maurice Tempelsman, the former companion of Jackie Onassis who in 1998 was reported to be developing a romantic relationship with Secretary of State Albright. He is a leading international diamond merchant of unique power and influence—often he has helped shape US foreign policy in directions that favor De Beers. I have extensively researched his work. Much of this is in my forthcoming book, *Blood Stained Diamonds*. I have been asked to talk about Tempelsman's role in the confluence of public policy and private profit that happens in private. He is an excellent example. I have time only to summarize my findings.

Why was he uniquely important in the De Beers? In the 1940s De Beers was indicted by the US Justice Department for price fixing under the Sherman Act. The US also believed De Beers had rationed the supply of tool diamonds to the US during the Second World War severely damaging the war effort. It was determined never to let this happen again, and legislation was thus passed to set up a national diamond stockpile. De Beers needed a way to ensure it was the source of this stockpile despite being indicted. It sought a middleman to do the deals with the US. Early in the 1950s Tempelsman met with the Oppenheimers who rule De Beers and became this middleman. He was uniquely supplied with millions of diamonds to sell the US as its strategic reserve. Most of these diamonds came from the Congo.

The Congo

When Lumumba, Congo's first elected leader, spoke of using the Congo's resources to benefit the Congo, De Beers feared it would lose access to one third of the world's diamond supply in the Congo—as would also Tempelsman. Shortly after this, the CIA facilitated Lumumba's assassination. Evidence on this came before the Church Intelligence Commission. Immediately after Lumumba's death, the Acting Prime Minister of the Congo, Adoula, announced support for a very major Tempelsman diamond deal, telegramming this to President Kennedy. The historian, Richard Mahoney, claimed that the Adoula regime was receiving funds from Tempelsman. A State Department memo headed, "Congo Diamond Deal" stated, "The State Department has concluded that it is in the political interest of the US to implement this proposal." (2 August, 1961)

Immediately after Mobutu came to power, Tempelsman became an even bigger player in the Congo—recruiting his own staff from those CIA staffers that Mobutu most favored that put him in power. Mobutu also at this time gave Tempelsman, as a "Christmas Gift", rich mineral reserves.

According to Tempelsman's staff we interviewed, they had a wonderful time helping to run the Congo. One of the first acts by Tempelsman was to facilitate the return of the Oppenheimers to the Congo—and to secure funding for Mobutu. He succeeded in persuading the White House to secretly buy a vast number of diamonds for the US strategic reserve—at a time when Administration officials were protesting that the reserve was over full. The reason for this deal given in secret US government memos was to support Mobutu and his partner Adoula. This Tempelsman plan made much profit for him and for De Beers.

A State Department Cable of 23 December, 1964 warned about the need of secrecy over this Mobutu diamond and South African uranium deal because: "it could outrage the moderate Africans we are trying to calm down." It suggested South African Foreign Minister Muller would understand the need for secrecy since the US was "doing a job" in the Congo that South Africa could not do. This covert support for Mobutu gave the US a gross excess in the strategic diamond stockpile that was still being sold off in 1997.

In 1967 the State Department reported: "Tempelsman is playing an increasingly central role as GDRC (Congo's) technical advisor and mediator." But these deals and other deals done throughout the following decades with a corrupt Mobutu government left the Congolese people in absolute poverty.

Ghana

In the late 1950s democracy arrived in Africa with the election of President Nkrumah—who thought Black Africans should not have to sell diamonds to an apartheid company—so took Ghana's diamonds from the cartel. A short while later, the State Department wrote a furious letter to Maurice Tempelsman saying that his office, by using an unguarded phone line, had betrayed the identity of the plotters against Nkrumah and the identity of the CIA Head of Station. The plotters seemingly were communicating to the White House via Tempelsman's office. (Memorandum for the President from WW Rostow, 24 September, 1961.) Tempelsman clearly had advanced knowledge of this coup attempt. Shortly afterward President Kennedy decided not to "downgrade" (his word) Tempelsman for this error.

Sierra Leone

Tempelsman worked out a new diamond contract for President Stevens—under which Tempelsman got 27% of the country's diamonds—setting up an independent cutting factory—and De Beers bought shares in it. However, it was not set up to compete effectively. I have gathered ample evidence that historically Sierra Leone has been grossly exploited by fraudulent De Beers' practices, which I would be happy to give during question time.

Angola

In recent years Tempelsman has been trying to use US money and support to set up Savimbi of UNITA in the diamond trade with both De Beers and US support. On the side, he has also been setting up his own diamond cutting factory—here as in his other African cutting plants on terms that are likely to stop Africa getting a fully commercial cutting industry ... a De Beers aim.

Tempelsman, in 1996, persuaded the Assistant Secretary of State, George E. Moose to give him a letter suggesting that the US would finance Tempelsman's plans. On October 10th, 1996 he met with Tony Lake, the National Security Advisor, and with Lake's deputy, Shawn McCormick—and gained their support for Tempelsman's plans. In May 1997 the US Ambassador for Angola, Steinbach, met with Savimbi—to back the Tempelsman plan. This plan included UNITA, keeping its diamond mines—and selling them via De Beers. Again US foreign policy was being shaped to benefit De Beers.

Tempelsman's Independence of De Beers.

Tempelsman frequently poses as an independent diamond merchant, even as a rival to De Beers. This has enabled him to do such things as to advise the President of Namibia on his negotiations with De Beers.

But if he were truly such, he would lose his diamond supplies from De Beers as have other diamond merchants who tried to rival De Beers. He has never lost these supplies. He is rumored in the trade as having one of the very largest of the diamond "sights" supplied by De Beers It is easy for De Beers to pay him secretly. They simply put more and better stones into the box they send him. The US customs are unable to check if this has happened, as they are not the experts on staff.

Conclusion

Maurice Tempelsman served the De Beers diamond cartel by promoting foreign policy decisions that favored its access to and control of African diamond fields. This lead to the US covertly supporting undemocratic and corrupt regimes in Africa to the great detriment of the African people.

Information on Blood Diamonds Suppressed?

Why did WGBH suppress its Frontline program, "The Diamond Empire," refusing to sell it to many who asked for it. The owners of Doubleday were later scared off from publishing the "sensational, important, and accomplished" (their words) human rights book, *Glitter and Greed: The story of Blood Stained Diamonds.* They wrote, after promoting the book as due to come out in 3 months, saying that rich and powerful people were against it, and although we may win any legal battle, it is not worth the cost of such a fight. See my website, www.sparkle.plus.com

Prepared Statement of Ellen Ray:

Balkanization of Africa; Destruction of Congo.

In the last decade, an ancient tool of foreign policy has been raised by the United States to new heights. The Romans called it "divide and conquer;" since the late Nineteenth Century it has been called Balkanization.

With the collapse of the Soviet Union, Balkanization became a common occurrence, as former "enemy" states were pursued—attacked and occupied—by the only remaining superpower—sometimes alone, sometimes with one or another of America's allies. The USSR was quickly divided into a dozen new nations; Czechoslovakia was halved; and then Yugoslavia was shattered, piece by piece. And now there is a serious effort under way by the western powers to Balkanize and further plunder Africa. Indeed, three of the largest nations on the continent, Congo, Angola, and Sudan, for many years have faced violent struggles to divide their territories. Some geo-strategists suggest that Balkanization is not necessary when large targeted nations are led by strong, generally repressive, governments, installed by, or at least indebted to, the West, especially the US. This may explain why, during most of the Mobutu regime, there were no serious efforts to destabilize his government, a US client state for all its three decades. The ultimate departure of Mobutu was effected by his own greed, and perhaps a philosophical tilt toward France. Zaire outlived its usefulness to the US. The nation, now Congo, has ended up on the chopping block, its sovereign territory divided and subdivided by invaders, the prize offered by what the Clinton administration cheerfully dubbed, "Africa's First World War."

When a nation is targeted for Balkanization, the justification for the overt and covert operations such a campaign entails is almost always a "humanitarian" effort to control inter-ethnic strife. The media generate public confusion by fabricating, or exaggerating, ethnic, tribal, mini-wars, often stirred up and paid for by the agents of the would-be Balkanizers.

For example, nearly every article about the invasion of the Democratic Republic of Congo by the US-supplied and trained armies of Uganda and Rwanda referred to the invaders' local paid agents as oppressed Congolese ethnic groups or former members of Mobutu's army rebelling against the Kinshasa government. The articles often described "tribal warfare" in breathless detail, citing mini-wars like those being fostered by outsiders between the Hema and the Lentu.

The severe destabilization of a targeted nation or area of the world is a logical and necessary prerequisite to Balkanization. The media help to promote that destabilization by their demonization of targeted leaders. Such campaigns often carry overtones of ethnic persecution, along with accusations of corruption, communism, terrorism, or (but only when it suits the US) fundamentalism.

Even though the western press could not, in the end, continue to boost Mobutu, their grudging recognition of Kabila was at best cautious, suspicious, and extremely short-lived. After Kabila threw out the Tutsi officers (Rwandan and Ugandan) who had been installed in most key military and intelligence posts, usually over the strong objections of the local people, the press' honeymoon with Kabila was over. As Kabila heard the complaints of the Congolese people about Tutsi-led terror against Hutu refugees, as he traveled to independent nations like China, Libya, and Cuba, he began to be vilified as "corrupt," as a "thug."

Something should be said about the way in which a very shady peace process has furthered African Balkanization, just as it did in Yugoslavia. The Lusaka accord was not a good deal for the Congo government; Kabila was forced to accede by implicit and explicit threats of even greater assistance to the rebels, and an endless war. And in consequence, a divided Congo became an accepted, institutionalized reality, a solid line drawn through the country in every map that accompanies every news story. The negotiations, stage-managed by the US, intensified the demands for the pullout of all foreign troops from Congo, neatly equating the Ugandan and Rwandan invaders with the troops from Angola, Namibia, and Zimbabwe, invited by the invaded country to assist in repelling the invasion. There is no moral equivalency here. As President Dos Santos of Angola pointed out during the UN debate, the accord did not even recognize the legitimacy of the Kabila government.

A year later, Kabila has been murdered, the very first peacekeeping forces are arriving and setting up camp in Goma, while the de facto division of Congo has become conventional wisdom. The outsiders ensconced in the east, now behind the cease-fire line and protected by the peacekeepers, control some of the most valuable natural resources in the world, while the Congolese people suffer.

The western wire service headlines in the aftermath of the murder of Laurent Kabila hint candidly at Congo's future.

Reuters, January 17: "Copper, cobalt markets little moved by Congo news."

Reuters, January 19: "Kabila killing not seen hurting diamond industry."

Laurent Kabila's place in the spectrum of African politics, continues to be abraded, his death seen only as one less deterrent to ramming through the peace plan:

Reuters, January 18: "Kabila failed to live up to great expectations."

Reuters, January 18: "Holbrooke suggests Africans break from Non-Aligned." Holbrooke, the reporter admitted, "startled his listeners" with this one.

Reuters, January 19: "Congo rebels say young Kabila 'unacceptable.'"

And finally, the future of the current cease-fire remains in doubt:

Associated Press, March 21: "UN Says Congo Foes Pulling Back."

But, Reuters, March 28: "UN Says Congo armies delaying disengagement."

Prepared Statement of Keith Snow:

Thank you, Representative McKinney, for organizing this very important forum.

I find it particularly remarkable that the diamond exports from the Democratic Republic of Congo (DRC) were some US$897 million in 1997. Now this is a "country" which was in a major war. And then in 1998, DRC ranked second in diamond production at 25.7 million carats. Again, a country in a brutal war where hundreds and hundreds of thousands of people—and, in fact, I think it is millions of people—suffered the consequences through disease and despair and displacement and rape and hunger and robbery and often death.

Based on my research, this is a western syndicated proxy war, and like Sierra Leone, Angola and Sudan, it is war-as-cover for the rapid and unrestricted extraction of raw materials, and war as a means to totally disenfranchise the local people. Diamonds, gold, columbium tantalite, niobium, cobalt, manganese and petroleum, natural gas and timber—and possibly uranium—are a few of the major spoils being pillaged behind the scenes as war ravages DRC—and some of these minerals are almost solely found in DRC—especially cobalt, niobium, columbium tantalite.

Barrick Gold provides a convenient example using war-as-cover. According to testimony I took in western Uganda in November, Barrick Gold is operating in the Kilo Moto mines near Bunia. These mines are reportedly protected by UPDF. An Israeli General was awarded another Kilo Moto concession and UPDF and RCD operate others. And there is massive ivory poaching—again protection rackets—going on. Barrick Advisory Board member George Bush and his CIA connections certainly play into these mining deals and lay the groundwork—aka slaughter if necessary—to get the product. That includes long-time links to people like CIA station operative in Zaire, Lawrence Devlin, for example, and his associations with the Templesmans. Look at the CIA operations in Lumumbashi and you will probably find connections to the repression and massacres of students at the University of Lumumbashi in the early 1990's.

George Bush apparently telephoned Mobutu just prior to the first US supported invasion of Congo—August 1996—on behalf of Swedish Financier Adolph Lundin to negotiate a deal over the Kilo Moto fields. And the US Presidential Election outcome of 1996 was completely irrelevant to the invasion of Zaire and the replacement of Mobutu. Remember that Kagame was in Washington about August 1996 checking his battle plans with the Pentagon. Mobutu's days were numbered.

The US took all the right decisions to allow the Rwanda genocide to unfold. And Clinton's comment that, "we didn't know what was going on at the time," couldn't have been a bigger lie. Do you suppose it was coincidental that a Rwanda delegate rotated on to the security council early in 1994 and then worked with US representatives to block all subsequent attempts to deal appropriately with the unfolding slaughter?

The Lundin Group appears also to be involved in south Katanga, where they are into the Tenke Fungarume copper/cobalt concessions. This is near where America Mineral Fields International and Anglo American are operating as well. And these are a few of the many mining companies.

All these US military programs like IMET and E-IMET, ACRI and JCET are designed to consolidate US hegemony. UPDF and RCD and SPLA have conscripted child soldiers. They use sophisticated weapons—not only the machetes so widely advertised by the media propaganda front of 1994, which sowed indifference and apathy in the US public. Troops have been trained by US green berets, and US military personnel have worked to coordinate SPLA and RPF/UPDF/RCD military campaigns. This is according to Ugandan dissidents and/or Congolese refugees fleeing Congo and/or ex-patriots on the ground. And there are plenty of people who support these statements.

Weapons are reportedly shipped in through Entebbe. Again, people testified to seeing "American blacks"—quote Negroes unquote—traveling in the area, both in Uganda and in Eastern DRC, but they are always very clandestine and they don't mingle or talk to people. One refugee cited the locations of jungle camps where western—he said American—military advisors were training RCD or RPF or UPDF guerrillas in counterinsurgency and heavy artillery operations. Again, this was in November.

Note that the whole Tutsi contre-genocide against Hutus is off the radar screen of people in the US and that's because the media has covered for the powerful interests and US agenda of consolidating power in the region by any means necessary. In fact, the RPF have actually "turned" Interahamwe to their service in doing the dirty work of eliminating any dissidents and insurgents and creating a situation defined by the media as incomprehensible tribal warfare.

It was reported to me that UPDF will disguise themselves as their enemies and attack villages to provide justification to return and sweep—aka brutalize or rape or pillage—these villages. They have also reportedly used these tactics to substantiate their needs for international support—weapons and funds and military expertise—from US and UK backers, funds and equipment, which were often diverted to the secret US SPLA war against Khartoum, for example.

But war doesn't seem to be essential to the plan. Multinational corporations—a very significant constellation of US companies and/or US citizens included—are everywhere stripping the resources, leaving pollution and disease and environmental disasters in their wakes. And you might probe into the whole classified nuclear waste transshipments programs.

Nigeria, Cameroon, Gabon, Togo, Niger, Madagascar, and Burkina Faso provide examples, being massively exploited, where military repression and structural adjustment and the concomitant destitution suffice to enable lucrative western control and exploitation. Zambia, Tanzania, Namibia, Botswana, and Ghana are a few more examples where I have similarly witnessed profound human suffering amidst huge multinational profits and SAP. I mean, 120 years after the British invasion of western Zambia—this is an area heavily burdened by refugee flows out of Angola and DRC, and the concomitant insecurity of insurgent nomadic military forces—the people have absolutely no possessions. The schools don't exist and even if they do there are no books and the kids are so destitute that they often can't attend in any case. You can't buy basic staples. I mean absolutely no food, no medicine, no drugs for malaria. Some 30% of people in Zambia don't even know that malaria is caused by mosquitoes. But you can buy Coca-Cola and

Sprite and Fanta virtually everywhere, but there are usually no basic foodstuffs, no books, no medical supplies. You cannot imagine the suffering until you live it yourself.

And it is no coincidence that one of the directors of Coca Cola—now I think that's a US company—is also a Director of ELF, and ELF's corrupt practices have been mildly exposed but very, very mildly.

These wars are prosecuted by local warlords, military dictators and their elite intelligence and security networks, typically armed, funded, and trained by western intelligence and/or ex-military and/or private security companies. And these networks are particularly ruthless. However, again, they are directly associated with in-country western military and intelligence advisors and their programs. That includes Israel, US, British, German and French. But IMF/WB and OPIC and ADB funds continue to flow, and they support selective interests and projects and infrastructure, which helps their related industries further expropriate the resources and the people and the institutions.

Uganda provides a good example. Uganda is at war on three fronts and a significant percentage of the IMF/WB funding, which has gone into Uganda, has been diverted for military objectives. The banks which fund Uganda through the international monetary institutions are often associated with the multinationals involved in the plunder of raw materials. Uganda has supported the SPLA war in southern Sudan, and I took testimony from Uganda dissidents who insist that US military advisors have worked with the SPLA and UPDF against Khartoum.

In Cameroon, Benin, Burkina Faso, Gabon, and Niger in 1997, I found abundant evidence of unrestricted raw materials extraction by interests associated with the United States. The people of the oil-producing areas of the Niger River Delta are suffering horrendous atrocities. Again, on the Niger border with Burkina—famine, disease, despair, political repression for the most trifling reasons—and right next door there is a Barrick Gold mining operation. And Sumitomo and the Keidanren (Zaibatsu) out of Japan are all involved. And people in these (African) countries know what is going on, but they can't tell their stories because most westerners are completely caught up in the mental illness of colonialism and imperialism, which disallows the simple truth to be seen. And those who tell their stories are often brutalized or disappeared.

In Zimbabwe, the issue of land and elections and Mugabe's intransigence aside, the lasting repercussions of the Mugabe "five brigade" genocide against the Ndebele people in Matebelelands North and South and the Midlands provinces are heartbreaking. Here was this scorched earth campaign from 1981 to 1987 where hundreds and hundreds of thousands perished, where food was used as a weapon and rape prevailed, and the United States diverted its eyes. And the media knew about it but the media diverted its eyes. And this is all very current stuff in Zimbabwe. The 1990s were more of the same in a more subtle form. And the Ndebele people have suffered untold injustice and terror.

Meanwhile, there was plenty of mining and tobacco farming going on in Zimbabwe and the weapons for Mugabe's dirty little secrets came from where? The IMF and WB funded Mugabe, no matter, throughout his tenure and right up into the late 1990s. Again, these are big banks like Chase Manhattan and First Boston and Citicorp and the Morgan Banks—and their directors sit on some of the western media boards and they dictate relief operations at a certain level. And then, of course, there are all these supranational multinational corporations like Asea Brown Baveri (ABB) and Unilever, and Royal Dutch Shell and Lonrho, and Citibank and Bechtel. I mean, Bechtel gets away with raping the system in Boston—the 10 or 12 billion dollar overruns in the Harbor Tunnel project—never mind their tight CIA and US government interconnections, policy interventions of dictations, and the orchestration of coups, assassinations, disappearances, and wars.

Lonrho, of course, is Buckingham Palace and I contend that very powerful US citizens are tied in through companies like Brown & Root and Halliburton, to Lonrho and Lonrho interests. And please recall that Vice President Cheney is a former Halliburton executive. And Lonrho has a lock on British media. And it is no coincidence that Lonrho has the most elegant and modern skyscraper in downtown Nairobi.

And all this is hidden by the US media. Even the village idiot, if he opens his eyes, can see that the directors of the media corporations are the same directors of those corporations raping Africa. But too many people have a paycheck to worry about. And that includes humanitarian organizations and the United Nations and the OAU and the International Criminal Tribunal on Rwanda.

Special torture centers and death squads and massive repression of the population are the rule in Togo, Cameroon, Kenya, Gabon, Nigeria, Zimbabwe, Burkina Faso, and were so in Zaire. And these people—Eyadema, Biya, Bongo, Obasanjo, Abacha, Babangida, Mobutu, Compaore, Rawlings, Banda, Kaunda, Moi, Habyarimana, Kagame, Museveni, Garang,

Ratsiraka—they provide the environment for pillage, and they are duly rewarded, with power, with all the perks.

Charles Taylor was incarcerated in Charlestown, Massachusetts circa 1983 or 1984 and he is the only person, I believe, in the history of the Charlestown jail, to have been broken out. Apparently the records no longer exist of his stay there. And now he is President in Liberia?

And then you have the whole misery industry, which profits from the wars and repression and population displacement, which their affiliated institutions and their funding banks and materials-providing multinationals create. Again, you don't need a PhD to figure out that thousands of highly paid western AID workers would be out of a job if there were peace in Sudan. And Toyota wouldn't sell all those shiny 4-WD SUVs. And who would buy the US made weapons? And all that business of feeding and clothing and interning the refugees would be lost by these multinationals who get huge tax write-offs and subsidies and whose products are purchased by US AID or other government agencies. And some of these relief organizations also have close ties to the corporate media executives.

So I see it as a policy of depopulation in Africa. Because what I am talking about is access. That's all. Access to the animals. Access to the game parks and trophy fishing. Access to the minerals. Access to the cheap and replenished labor pool. Access to uninformed populations to dump inferior and toxic and outdated products on. Access for military adventurism and special forces training and PSYOPS operations. Access to biological and pharmaceutical testing grounds. Access to markets. And while at times it seems contradictory, at times it is, but it's all completely unethical, entirely arrogant and racist. It is driven purely by greed. And the profound human suffering is totally unnecessary.

End.

Prepared Statement of Mr. James R. Lyons:

Statement regarding the April 6, 1994 assassination of the Presidents of Rwanda and Burundi in addition to all others on board the Presidential Aircraft.

Sparta, New Jersey.April 6, 2001.

I am a retired Supervisory Special Agent with the Federal Bureau of Investigation (FBI) having served from November 1970 through July 1995. Most of my FBI career was spent in the area of counter-terrorism in the New

York Office. I was an original member of the FBI/New York Police Department (NYPD) Domestic Terrorism Task Force, which was formed in 1980. I was promoted to Supervisory Special Agent in 1987 with the task of forming a second task force to address the growing threat of international terrorism. In that capacity, I performed supervisory investigative duties in numerous terrorist bombing and political assassination cases committed by various international terrorist groups from all over the world. In addition, I was the FBI, New York Office on site supervisor following the bombings of the World Trade Center and was detailed as a supervisor to the post blast investigation following the bombing of the Murrah Federal Building in Oklahoma City.

In February 1996, I was contracted by the US Department of State as an investigator for the International Criminal Tribunal for Rwanda (ICTR). Shortly after my arrival in Kigali, I was appointed the Commander of Investigations, which was actually a United Nations staff post. At that time there was a Deputy Prosecutor, Honre Rokatomanana, a Director of Investigations, Al Breau and only twenty-three investigators. Seventeen of the investigators were police officers seconded to the ICTR by the Government of the Netherlands.

At that time, the strategy of the Director of Investigations with the approval of the Deputy Prosecutor, was to identify victims/witnesses to the genocide in the western and southern Prefectures such as Kibuye and Butare and obtain signed statements implicating the targets who were the Prefects, communal officials, local leaders of the Hutu Interahamwe militia, and local businessmen. The strategy was to charge these individuals in connection with the Genocide with the hope of gaining the cooperation of some in order to move up the ladder to the "Big Fish." There was a separate investigation into the role of the media in inciting the Hutu population to violence against the Tutsi and moderate Hutu. In view of the lack of manpower and other resources, other avenues, such as investigating the role of national political and military leaders, were put on hold.

In March/April 1994, more investigators began to arrive, including Michael Hourigan, a former Australian Crown Prosecutor. In view of the influx of a few more investigators, I and the Director of Investigations agreed that a new "National Investigative Team" be formed to target those responsible for the planning of and the eventual execution of the Genocide, and at my suggestion, Mr. Hourigan was appointed the Team Leader. The team began with three investigators but eventually grew to twenty members representing the nations of Holland, Germany, the United States, Canada, Senegal, Mali, Tunisia, Madagascar, and others.

The National Team was given the task of investigating a number of the ICTR's most important lines of inquiry. Principal among these tasks were:

1. The Investigation and prosecution of Colonel Theoneste Bagosora, considered to be the leading Hutu military force behind the Genocide.

2. The investigation and prosecution of persons with overall responsibility for the selected killings of Rwandan political leaders and intellegencia by elite Presidential Guard kill teams, which occurred during the first 48-72 hours of the downing of the president's airplane.

3. The investigation and prosecution of persons responsible for the rocket attack on April 6, 1994, which resulted in the downing of the Presidential Airplane, killing Rwanda President, Juvenal Habyarimana, Burundi President, Cyprien Ntaryamira, the French crew, and all others aboard.

As the Commander of Investigations, I believed that the investigation of the rocket attack was within the mandate of the ICTR. It was the spark that ignited all of Rwanda into a conflagration, which would ultimately take the lives of 700,000 to 1,000,000 men, women, and children. The UN Security Council had expressed its abhorrence at this terrorist attack and had directed that all information regarding the event be gathered. The ICTR Statute, Article 4, specifically included Acts of Terrorism in its list of offenses. In my view, there was more than ample justification for the ICTR to consider the rocket attack as an international criminal event falling well within its jurisdiction.

No member of the ICTR leadership ever suggested to me that this investigation was outside our mandate. On the contrary, discussions among senior personnel concerned the enormous challenge that lay ahead to identify those responsible.

The National Team's investigation was thorough but slow moving initially. The world community had long attributed the attack to hard line Hutus close to the President but there was no evidence supporting that theory. There was some speculation that the Rwandan Patriotic Front (RPF) was responsible and there were bits of information to support that view.

The National Team obtained information in 1996 that a United Nations Assistance Mission to Rwanda (UNAMIR) soldier had overheard a radio broadcast over an RPF network shortly after the plane crash saying that the target had been hit. In addition, there was a report that a soldier in the Armed

Forces of Rwanda (FAR) heard the same or a similar broadcast.

Mr. Hourigan regularly briefed me and other senior ICTR staff members on the progress of the investigations and that always included the plane crash investigation. Hourigan and some members of his team briefed Chief Prosecutor Louise Arbour during one of her few visits to Kigali. At no time did Judge Arbour relay to me, or to my knowledge, any other senior investigator, that the plane crash was outside the mandate of the ICTR.

I always worked closely with Mr. Hourigan and his team and was continually briefed on developments. In February 1997, there was a dramatic turn of events in the investigation when three potential cooperating witnesses came forward. Two of the witnesses knew of each other's cooperation. The third was independent and we believe, had no knowledge of the other two. The witnesses were all past or present members of the RPF and because of their duties were in a position to personally know the accuracy of information being furnished.

The information furnished, although untested, was extremely detailed to the point of naming individuals involved in the planning and the execution of the rocket attack. The sources advised that the then leader of the RPF, General Paul Kagame, formed a commando type group referred to as the "network" and that he and his senior advisors had put into affect the plan to shoot down the Presidential aircraft as it approached Kigali Airport.

During the last days of February 1997 I was present with Mr. Hourigan at the US Embassy in Kigali. He placed a call to Judge Arbour in The Hague on the Embassy secure telephone line. He briefed her on the latest developments in the plane crash investigation. It was obvious to me, from listening to Mr. Hourigan's side of the conversation, that Judge Arbour was pleased with the progress of the case and enthusiastic about continuing the investigation. Later, Mr. Hourigan advised me that Judge Arbour asked him to travel to The Hague so that they could further discuss this matter personally.

On the first Monday in March, 1997 I returned to the United States as my contract was finished and I did not choose to extend it. I later had a telephone conversation with Mr. Hourigan during which he advised me that during his meeting with Judge Arbour, she unexpectedly ordered him to shut down the investigation. She explained that the shooting down of the President's airplane was a crime outside the jurisdiction of the ICTR.

Prepared Statement of Wayne Madsen. Wayne Madsen is an

investigative journalist who has written for The Village Voice, The Progressive, CAQ, and The Intelligence Newsletter. He is the author of, Genocide and Covert Activities in Africa 1993-1999 (Lewiston, NY: Edwin Mellen, 1999), an expose of US and French intelligence activities in Africa's recent civil wars and ethnic rebellions. He served as an on-air East Africa analyst for ABC News in the aftermath of the 1998 US embassy bombings in Kenya and Tanzania. Mr. Madsen has appeared on "60 Minutes," "World News Tonight," "Nightline," "20/20," "MS-NBC," and "NBC Nightly News," among others. He has been frequently quoted by the Associated Press, foreign wire services, and many national and international newspapers.

Mr. Madsen is also the author of a motion picture screen play treatment about the nuclear submarine USS Scorpion. He is a former US Naval Officer and worked for the National Security Agency and US Naval Telecommunications Command:

I wish to discuss the record of American policy in Africa over most of the past decade, particularly that involving the central African Great Lakes region. It is a policy that has rested, in my opinion, on the twin pillars of unrestrained military aid and questionable trade. The military aid programs of the United States, largely planned and administered by the US Special Operations Command and the Defense Intelligence Agency (DIA), have been both overt and covert.

ACRI, ACSS, and the covert programs all involve the use of private military training firms and logistics support contractors that are immune to Freedom of Information Act requests. More troubling than these overt problems are those that involve covert assistance to the Rwandan and Ugandan militaries. Sources in the Great Lakes region consistently report the presence of a US-built military base near Cyangugu, Rwanda, near the Congolese border. The base, reported to have been partly constructed by the US firm Brown & Root, a subsidiary of Halliburton, is said to be involved with training RPF forces and providing logistics support to their troops in the DRC.

The increasing reliance by the Department of Defense on so-called Private Military Contractors (PMCs) is of special concern. Many of these PMCs—once labeled as "mercenaries" by previous administrations when they were used as foreign policy instruments by the colonial powers of France, Belgium, Portugal, and South Africa—have close links with some of the largest mining and oil companies involved in Africa today. PMCs, because of their proprietary status, have a great deal of leeway to engage in covert activities far from the reach of congressional investigators. They can simply claim that their business in various nations is a protected trade secret and the law now seems to be on their side.

The Destabilization of Africa

America's policy toward Africa during the past decade, rather than seeking to stabilize situations where civil war and ethnic turmoil reign supreme, has seemingly promoted destabilization. Former Secretary of State, Madeleine Albright, was fond of calling pro-US military leaders in Africa who assumed power by force and then cloaked themselves in civilian attire, "beacons of hope."

In reality, these leaders, who include the current presidents of Uganda, Rwanda, Ethiopia, Angola, Eritrea, Burundi, and the Democratic Republic of the Congo, preside over countries where ethnic and civil turmoil permit unscrupulous international mining companies to take advantage of the strife to fill their own coffers with conflict diamonds, gold, copper, platinum, and other precious minerals—including one that is a primary component of computer microchips.

Some of the companies involved in this new "scramble for Africa" have close links with PMCs and America's top political leadership. For example, American Minerals Fields, Inc., a company that was heavily involved in promoting the 1996 accession to power of the late Congolese President, Laurent-Desiré Kabila, was, at the time of its involvement in the Congo's civil war, headquartered in Hope, Arkansas. Its major stockholders included long-time associates of former President Clinton going back to his days as Governor of Arkansas. American Mineral Fields also reportedly enjoys a close relationship with Lazare Kaplan International, Inc., a major international diamond brokerage whose president remains a close confidant of past and current administrations on Africa matters.

One of the major goals of the Rwandan-backed Rassemblement Congolais pour la démocratie (RCD), a group fighting the Kabila government in Congo, is restoration of mining concessions for Barrick Gold, Inc. of Canada. In fact, the rebel RCD government's "mining minister" signed a separate mining deal with Barrick in early 1999. Among the members of Barrick's International Advisory Board are former President Bush and former President Clinton's close confidant Vernon Jordan.

Currently, Barrick and tens of other mining companies are stoking the flames of the civil war in the Democratic Republic of the Congo. Each benefits by the de facto partition of the country into some four separate zones of political control. First the mineral exploiters from Rwanda and Uganda concentrated on pillaging gold and diamonds from the eastern Congo. Now, they have increasingly turned their attention to a valuable black sand called columbite-tantalite or "coltan." Coltan is a key material in computer chips and, therefore, is as considered a strategic mineral. It is my hope that the Bush administration will take pro-active measures to stem this conflict by applying increased pressure on Uganda and Rwanda to withdraw their troops from the country. However, the fact that President Bush has selected Walter Kansteiner to be Assistant Secretary of State for African, portends, in my opinion, more trouble for the Great Lakes region. A brief look at Mr. Kansteiner's curriculum vitae and statements calls into question his commitment to seeking a durable peace in the region. For example, he has envisaged the splitting up of the Great Lakes region into separate Tutsi and Hutu states through "relocation" efforts and has called the break-up of the DRC inevitable. I believe Kansteiner's previous work at the Department of Defense where he served on a Task Force on Strategic Minerals—and one must certainly consider coltan as falling into that category—may influence his past and current thinking on the territorial integrity of the DRC. After all, 80 percent of the world's known reserves of coltan are found in the eastern DRC. It is potentially as important to the US military as the Persian Gulf region.

The US military and intelligence agencies, which have supported Uganda and Rwanda in their cross-border adventures in the DRC, have resisted peace initiatives and have failed to produce evidence of war crimes by the Ugandans and Rwandans and their allies in Congo. The CIA, NSA, and DIA should turn over to international investigators both signals intelligence and human intelligence evidence in their possession, as well as overhead imagery, including thermal imagery indicating the presence of mass graves and when they were dug. There must be a full accounting before the Congress by the staff of the US Defense Attache's Office in Kigali who served there from early 1994 to the present time.

A Lingering Question on Assassinations

The present turmoil in central Africa largely stems from a fateful incident that occurred on April 6, 1994. That was the missile attack on the Rwandan presidential aircraft that resulted in the death of Rwanda's Hutu President, Juvenal Habyarimana, his colleague, President Cyprien Ntaryamira of Burundi, Habyarimana's chief advisers, and the French crew.

This aerial assassination resulted in a genocide coordinated by the successor militant Hutu Rwandan government that cost the lives of some 800,000 Tutsis and moderate Hutus. This was followed by a counter-genocide orchestrated by the Tutsi-led Rwanda Patriotic Front (RPF) government that resulted in the deaths of 500,000 mostly Hutu refugees in Rwanda and neighboring Zaire/Congo.

No one has even identified the assassins of the two presidents let alone sought to bring them to justice. There have been a number of national and international commissions that have looked into the causes for the Rwandan genocide. These have included investigations by the Belgian Senate, the French National Assembly, the United Nations, and the Organization of African Unity. None of these investigations have identified the perpetrators of the aerial assassination. In 1998, French Judge, Jean-Louis Bruguière, launched an investigation of the aircraft attack. After interviewing witnesses in Switzerland, Rwanda, Tanzania, and Russia, Bruguière apparently has enough evidence to issue an international arrest warrant for President Kagame. A former French Judge, Thierry Jean-Pierre, now a Member of the European Parliament, in an entirely separate and private investigation, came to the same conclusion that Kagame was behind the attack. The United States government must come to its senses, as it did with past intelligence assets like Sadaam Hussein, Alberto Fujimori, General Suharto, Ferdinand Marcos, and Manuel Noriega, and support a judicial accounting by Kagame. If it is proven that US citizens were in any way involved in planning the assassination, they should also be brought to justice before the international war crimes tribunal.

Immediately after the attack on the presidential plane, much of the popular press in the United States brandished the theory that militant Hutus brought it down. I suggest that following some four years of research concentrating on the missile attack, there is no basis for this conclusion. In fact, I believe there is concrete evidence to show that the plane was shot down by operatives of the RPF. At the time, the RPF was supported by the United States and its major ally in the region, Uganda. Prior to the attack, the RPF leader, the current Rwandan strongman General Paul Kagame, received military training at the US Army Command and General Staff College at Fort Leavenworth, Kansas. Many of Kagame's subordinate's received similar training, including instruction in the use of surface-to-air missiles (SAMs) at the Barry Goldwater Air Force Range at Luke Air Force Base, Arizona. It was Soviet-designed SAMs that were used to shoot down the Rwandan president's airplane. By its own admission, the US Defense Department provided official military training to the RPF beginning in January 1994, three months before the missile attack on the aircraft.

In testimony before the French inquiry commission, former French Minister for International Cooperation Bernard Debré insisted that the two SAM-16s used in the attack on the aircraft were procured from Ugandan military stocks and were "probably delivered by the Americans ... from the Gulf War." He was supported by two former heads of the French foreign intelligence service (DGSE), Jacques Dewatre and Claude Silberzahn, as well as General Jean Heinrich, the former head of French military intelligence (DRM). Former moderate Hutu Defense Minister, James Gasana, who served under Habyarimana from April 1992 to July 1993, stated before the French inquiry that his government declined to purchase SAMs because they realized the RPF had no planes and, therefore, procurement of such weapons would have been a waste of money.

The contention by French government officials that the RPF was responsible for the aerial attack is supported by three former RPF intelligence officers who disclosed details of the operation to UN investigators. The three informants were rated as Category 2 witnesses on a 4-point scale where 1 is highly credible and 2 is "true but untested." The RPF informants claim the plane was downed by an elite 10-member RPF team with the "assistance of a foreign government." Some of the team members are apparently now deceased. A confidential UN report on the plane attack was delivered to the head of the UN War Crimes Tribunal, Judge Louise Arbour of Canada, but was never made public. In fact, Arbour terminated the investigation when details of the RPF's involvement in the assassination became clear. The UN now denies such a report exists. Michael Hourigan, an Australian lawyer who first worked as an International War Crimes Tribunal investigator and then for the UN's Office of Internal Oversight Services, confirmed that the initial war crimes investigation team uncovered evidence of the RPF's involvement in the attack but their efforts were undercut by senior UN staff.

After the former RPF intelligence team revealed details of the attack, they were supported by yet another former RPF intelligence officer named Jean Pierre Mugabe. In a separate declaration, Mugabe contended that the assassination was directed by Kagame and RPF deputy commander-in-chief James Kabarebe. The RPF, according to Mugabe, campaigned extensively for the regional peace meeting in Dar es Salaam from which Habyarimana was returning when he was assassinated. Mugabe claimed the idea was to collect the top Hutu leadership on the plane in order to easily eliminate them in the attack.

Yet another defector from the RPF, Christophe Hakizabera, in a declaration to a UN investigation commission, states that the "foreign power" that helped the RPF shoot down the airplane was, in fact, Uganda. According to Hakizabera, the first and second assassination planning meetings were held in Uganda in the towns of Kabale and Mbarara, respectively. A third, in which Kagame was present, was held in March 1994 in Bobo-Dioulasso, Burkina Faso. As it did with the three other RPF defectors, the UN took no action as a result of this complaint. It appears, and this is supported by private conversations I have had with former UN officials, that some other party is calling the shots in the world body's investigation of human rights violations in Africa.

The involvement of Uganda in the assassination tends to support the contention of the former French government ministers that the SAMs were provided to Uganda by the United States from captured Iraqi arms caches during Desert Storm. My own research indicates that these missiles were delivered to Uganda via a CIA-run arms depot outside of Cairo, Egypt. After the transfer, Uganda kept some of the missiles and launchers for its own armed forces and delivered the remainder to the Sudan People's Liberation Army (SPLA) and the RPF.

Other evidence pointing to an RPF role in the attack includes COMINT (communications intelligence) picked up by military units and civilian radio operators in Rwanda. A Rwandan Armed Forces COMINT listening station picked up a transmission on an RPF frequency, which stated "the target is hit." This was reported to a Togolese member of the UN Assistance Mission for Rwanda (UNAMIR). A Belgian amateur radio operator reported that after the attack, he heard someone on a frequency used by a Belgian PMC in Kigali state, "We killed Le Grand (Habyarimana)." The Belgian operator also stated that all Rwandan Armed Forces messages following the attack indicated the Rwandan army was in complete disarray—something that would not have been the case had the Rwandan government perpetrated the attack on its own president. Another source of COMINT was a French signals intelligence unit sent to Kigali from the French military base in Bangui, Central African Republic. According to French Judge, Jean-Pierre, copies of French intercepts of RPF communications indicate, beyond a doubt, the culpability of the RPF in the attack on the aircraft.

Some formerly classified US State Department cables, which I received following a Freedom of Information Act request, reveal that the US foreign policy establishment was of two minds over the April 6 attack. The US Embassy in Burundi kept a surprisingly open mind about its theories about the missile attack, even suggesting a Rwandan Patriotic Front (RPF) role in it. Other US diplomatic posts, most notably that in Kigali, seemed to follow the script that the aircraft was downed by hard-line Hutus who wanted to implement a well-planned genocide of Tutsis and moderate Hutus.

A May 25, 1994 Secret message from the Department of State to all African diplomatic posts also reports that "the RPF has summarily executed Hutu militia alleged to have been involved in the massacres and the RPF has admitted to such killings." The same message states that "Rwandan government officials who controlled the airport" or "French military officials" recovered the downed presidential aircraft's black box after securing the airport and removing the body of the French pilot from Habyarimana's plane. However, according to officials I interviewed who were involved with UN air movements in the region, the black box was secretly transported to UN Headquarters in New York where it remains to this day. Officially, the Rwandan government claims the black box went missing. According to the UN investigators, the black box was spirited away by UN officials from Kigali to New York via Nairobi. In addition, this shipment was known to US government officials. According to the UN sources, data from the black box is being withheld by the UN under pressure from our own government. The investigators also revealed that RPF forces controlled three major approaches to Kayibanda Airport on the evening of the attack and that European mercenaries, in the pay of the RPF and US intelligence, planned and launched the missile attack on the Mystere-Falcon. The CIA figured prominently in the UN investigation of the missile attack. According to the investigators, the search for the assassins ultimately led to a warehouse in Kanombe, near the airport. From this warehouse, during the afternoon of April 6, the missile launchers were assembled and readied for action by the mercenaries. As the UN investigation team was nearing its final conclusion and was prepared to turn up evidence indicating the warehouse had been leased by a Swiss company, said to be linked to US intelligence, its mandate was swiftly terminated.

Conclusion

It is clear that the United States, contrary to comments made by its senior officials, including former President Clinton, played more of a role in the Rwandan tragedy than it readily admits. This involvement continued through the successive Rwandan-and-Ugandan-led invasions of neighboring Zaire/ Congo. Speculation that Rwanda was behind the recent assassination of President Laurent Kabila in Congo (and rumors that the CIA was behind it) has done little to put the United States in a favorable light in the region. After all, the date of Kabila's assassination—January 16 this year—was practically 40 years from the very day of the CIA-planned and executed assassination of Congolese leader, Patrice Lumumba. The quick pace at which Kabila's son and successor Joseph Kabila visited the United States—at the same time of Kagame's presence, and his subsequent meetings with Corporate Council for Africa officials and Maurice Tempelsman (the majordomo of US Africa policy), calls into question what the United States knew about the assassination and when it knew about it.

Also, particularly troublesome is a conclusion the CIA is said to have reached in an assessment written in January 1994, a few months before the genocide. According to key officials I have interviewed during my research, that analysis came to the conclusion that in the event that President Habyarimana was assassinated, the minimum number of deaths resulting from the mayhem in Rwanda would be 500 (confined mostly to Kigali and environs) and the maximum 500,000. Regrettably, the CIA's higher figure was closer to reality.

Certain interests in the United States had reason to see Habyarimana and other pro-French leaders in central Africa out of the way. As recently written by Gilbert Ngijol, a former Assistant to the Special Representative of the Secretary General of the UN to Rwanda in 1994, the United States directly benefitted economically from the loss of influence of French and Belgian mining interests in the central Africa and Great Lakes regions.

There is also reason to believe that a number of people with knowledge of Kagame's plot against the presidential aircraft have been assassinated. These possibly include Tanzania's former intelligence chief, Major General Imran Kombe, shot dead by policemen in northeastern Tanzania after he was mistaken for a notorious car thief. His wife maintains he was assassinated. Kombe had knowledge of not only the planned assassination of the Rwandan and Burundian presidents but a plot against Kenya's President Moi and Zaire's President Mobutu, as well. There is a belief that Roman Catholic

Archbishop of Bukavu, Emmanuel Kataliko, was assassinated last October in Rome by members of a Rwandan hit team acting on orders from Kagame. Other Tutsi and Hutu leaders who oppose Kagame's regime continue to flee Rwanda to the US and France in fear of their lives. Rwanda's figurehead Hutu President, Pasteur Bizimungu, was forced to resign last year under pressure from the only power in Rwanda, his then-Vice President, Paul Kagame. Deus Kagiraneza, a former intelligence officer in Kagame's Military Intelligence Directorate (DMI), interim Prefect of the Ruhengeri province, and member of the Parliament, is now in exile in Belgium. He charges that Kagame's top government and military are responsible for torturing and executing their political opponents. Kagiraneza maintains that the RPF has pursued such policies since the time of the 1990 invasion of Rwanda from Uganda.

It is beyond time for the Congress to seriously examine the role of the United States in the genocide and civil wars of central Africa, as well as the role that PMCs currently play in other African trouble spots like Nigeria, Sierra Leone, Equatorial Guinea, Angola, Ethiopia, and Cabinda. Other nations, some with less than stellar records in Africa—France and Belgium, for example—have had no problem examining their own roles in Africa's last decade of turmoil. At the very least, the United States, as the world's leading democracy, owes Africa at least the example of a critical self-inspection.

H.

[as corrected by the procés-verbaux of 10 November, 1998 and 12 July, 1999]

PART 2:
JURISDICTION, ADMISSIBILITY, AND APPLICABLE LAW

Article 5
Crimes Within the Jurisdiction of the Court

1. The jurisdiction of the Court shall be limited to the most serious crimes of concern to the international community as a whole. The Court has jurisdiction in accordance with this Statute with respect to the following crimes:

(a) The crime of genocide;
(b) Crimes against humanity;
(c) War crimes;
(d) The crime of aggression.

2. The Court shall exercise jurisdiction over the crime of aggression once a provision is adopted in accordance with articles 121 and 123 defining the crime and setting out the conditions under which the Court shall exercise jurisdiction with respect to this crime. Such a provision shall be consistent with the relevant provisions of the Charter of the United Nations.

Article 6
Genocide

For the purpose of this Statute, "genocide" means any of the following acts committed with intent to destroy, in whole or in part, a national, ethnical, racial, or religious group, as such:

(a) Killing members of the group;

(b) Causing serious bodily or mental harm to members of the group;

(c) Deliberately inflicting on the group conditions of life calculated to bring about its physical destruction in whole or in part;

(d) Imposing measures intended to prevent births within the group;

(e) Forcibly transferring children of the group to another group.

Article 7
Crimes Against Humanity

1. For the purpose of this Statute, "crime against humanity" means any of the following acts when committed as part of a widespread or systematic attack directed against any civilian population, with knowledge of the attack:

(a) Murder;

(b) Extermination;

(c) Enslavement;

(d) Deportation or forcible transfer of population;

(e) Imprisonment or other severe deprivation of physical liberty in violation of fundamental rules of international law;

(f) Torture;

(g) Rape, sexual slavery, enforced prostitution, forced pregnancy, enforced sterilization, or any other form of sexual violence of comparable gravity;

(h) Persecution against any identifiable group or collectivity on political, racial, national, ethnic, cultural, religious, gender as defined in paragraph 3, or other grounds that are universally recognized as impermissible under international law, in connection with any act referred to in this paragraph or any crime within the jurisdiction of the Court;

(i) Enforced disappearance of persons;

(j) The crime of apartheid;

(k) Other inhumane acts of a similar character intentionally causing great suffering, or serious injury to body or to mental or physical health.

2. For the purpose of paragraph 1:

(a) "Attack directed against any civilian population" means a course of conduct involving the multiple commission of acts referred to in paragraph 1 against any civilian population, pursuant to or in furtherance of a State or organizational policy to commit such attack;

(b) "Extermination" includes the intentional infliction of conditions of life, *inter alia* the deprivation of access to food and medicine, calculated to bring about the destruction of part of a population;

(c) "Enslavement" means the exercise of any or all of the powers attaching to the right of ownership over a person and includes the exercise of such power in the course of trafficking in persons, in particular women and children;

(d) "Deportation or forcible transfer of population" means forced displacement of the persons concerned by expulsion or other coercive acts from the area in which they are lawfully present, without grounds permitted under international law;

(e) "Torture" means the intentional infliction of severe pain or suffering, whether physical or mental, upon a person in the custody or under the control of the accused; except that torture shall not include pain or suffering arising only from, inherent in or incidental to, lawful sanctions;

(f) "Forced pregnancy" means the unlawful confinement of a woman forcibly made pregnant, with the intent of affecting the ethnic composition of any population or carrying out other grave violations of international law. This definition shall not in any way be interpreted as affecting national laws relating to pregnancy.

(g) "Persecution" means the intentional and severe deprivation of fundamental rights contrary to international law by reason of the identity of the group or collectivity;

(h) "The crime of apartheid" means inhumane acts of a character similar to those referred to in paragraph 1, committed in the context of an institutionalized regime of systematic oppression and domination by one racial group over any other racial group or groups and committed with the intention of maintaining that regime;

(i) "Enforced disappearance of persons" means the arrest, detention or abduction of persons by, or with the authorization, support or acquiescence of, a State or a political organization, followed by a refusal to acknowledge that deprivation of freedom or to give information on the fate or whereabouts of those persons, with the intention of removing them from the protection of the law for a prolonged period of time.

3. For the purpose of this Statute, it is understood that the term "gender" refers to the two sexes, male and female, within the context of society. The term "gender" does not indicate any meaning different from the above.

Article 8
War Crimes

1. The Court shall have jurisdiction in respect of war crimes in particular when committed as part of a plan or policy or as part of a large-scale commission of such crimes.

2. For the purpose of this Statute, "war crimes" means:

(a) Grave breaches of the Geneva Conventions of 12 August 1949, namely, any of the following acts against persons or property protected under the provisions of the relevant Geneva Convention:

(i) Wilful killing;

(ii) Torture or inhuman treatment, including biological experiments;

(iii) Wilfully causing great suffering, or serious injury to body or health;

(iv) Extensive destruction and appropriation of property, not justified by military necessity and carried out unlawfully and wantonly;

(v) Compelling a prisoner of war or other protected person to serve in the forces of a hostile Power;

(vi) Wilfully depriving a prisoner of war or other protected person of the rights of fair and regular trial;

(vii) Unlawful deportation or transfer or unlawful confinement;

(viii) Taking of hostages.

(b) Other serious violations of the laws and customs applicable in international armed conflict, within the established framework of international law, namely, any of the following acts:

(i) Intentionally directing attacks against the civilian population as such or against individual civilians not taking direct part in hostilities;

(ii) Intentionally directing attacks against civilian objects, that is, objects which are not military objectives;

(iii) Intentionally directing attacks against personnel, installations, material, units or vehicles involved in a humanitarian assistance or peacekeeping mission in accordance with the Charter of the United Nations, as long as they are entitled to the protection given to civilians or civilian objects under the international law of armed conflict;

(iv) Intentionally launching an attack in the knowledge that such attack will cause incidental loss of life or injury to civilians or damage to civilian objects or widespread, long-term and severe damage to the natural environment which would be clearly excessive in relation to the concrete and direct overall military advantage anticipated;

(v) Attacking or bombarding, by whatever means, towns, villages, dwellings or buildings which are undefended and which are not military objectives;

(vi) Killing or wounding a combatant who, having laid down his arms or having no longer means of defense, has surrendered at discretion;

(vii) Making improper use of a flag of truce, of the flag or of the military insignia and uniform of the enemy or of the United Nations, as well as of the distinctive emblems of the Geneva Conventions, resulting in death or serious personal injury;

(viii) The transfer, directly or indirectly, by the Occupying Power of parts of its own civilian population into the territory it occupies, or the deportation or transfer of all or parts of the population of the occupied territory within or outside this territory;

(ix) Intentionally directing attacks against buildings dedicated to religion, education, art, science or charitable purposes, historic monuments, hospitals and places where the sick and wounded are collected, provided they are not military objectives;

(x) Subjecting persons who are in the power of an adverse party to physical mutilation or to medical or scientific experiments of any kind which are neither justified by the medical, dental or hospital treatment of the person concerned nor carried out in his or her interest, and which cause death to or seriously endanger the health of such person or persons;

(xi) Killing or wounding treacherously individuals belonging to the hostile nation or army;

(xii) Declaring that no quarter will be given;

(xiii)Destroying or seizing the enemy's property unless such destruction or seizure be imperatively demanded by the necessities of war;

(xiv) Declaring abolished, suspended or inadmissible in a court of law the rights and actions of the nationals of the hostile party;

(xv) Compelling the nationals of the hostile party to take part in the operations of war directed against their own country, even if they were in the belligerent's service before the commencement of the war;

(xvi) Pillaging a town or place, even when taken by assault;

(xvii) Employing poison or poisoned weapons;

(xviii) Employing asphyxiating, poisonous or other gases, and all analogous liquids, materials or devices;

(xix) Employing bullets which expand or flatten easily in the human body, such as bullets with a hard envelope which does not entirely cover the core or is pierced with incisions;

(xx) Employing weapons, projectiles and material and methods of warfare which are of a nature to cause superfluous injury or unnecessary suffering or which are inherently indiscriminate in violation of the international law of armed conflict, provided that such weapons, projectiles and material and methods of warfare are the subject of a comprehensive prohibition and are included in an annex to this Statute, by an amendment in accordance with the relevant provisions set forth in articles 121 and 123;

(xxi) Committing outrages upon personal dignity, in particular humiliating and degrading treatment;

(xxii) Committing rape, sexual slavery, enforced prostitution, forced pregnancy, as defined in article 7, paragraph 2 (f), enforced sterilization, or any other form of sexual violence also constituting a grave breach of the Geneva Conventions;

(xxiii) Utilizing the presence of a civilian or other protected person to render certain points, areas or military forces immune from military operations;

(xxiv) Intentionally directing attacks against buildings, material,medical units and transport, and personnel using the distinctive emblems of the Geneva Conventions in conformity with international law;

(xxv) Intentionally using starvation of civilians as a method of warfare by depriving them of objects indispensable to their survival, including wilfully impeding relief supplies as provided for under the Geneva Conventions;

(xxvi) Conscripting or enlisting children under the age of fifteen years into the national armed forces or using them to participate actively in hostilities.

(c) In the case of an armed conflict not of an international character, serious violations of article 3 common to the four Geneva Conventions of 12 August, 1949, namely, any of the following acts committed against persons taking no active part in the hostilities, including members of armed forces who have laid down their arms and those placed *hors de combat* by sickness, wounds, detention or any other cause:

(i) Violence to life and person, in particular murder of all kinds, mutilation, cruel treatment and torture;

(ii) Committing outrages upon personal dignity, in particular humiliating and degrading treatment;

(iii) Taking of hostages;

(iv) The passing of sentences and the carrying out of executions without previous judgement pronounced by a regularly constituted court, affording all judicial guarantees which are generally recognized as indispensable.

(d) Paragraph 2 (c) applies to armed conflicts not of an international character and thus does not apply to situations of internal disturbances and tensions, such as riots, isolated and sporadic acts of violence or other acts of a similar nature.

(e) Other serious violations of the laws and customs applicable in armed conflicts not of an international character, within the established framework of international law, namely, any of the following acts:

(i) Intentionally directing attacks against the civilian population as such or against individual civilians not taking direct part in hostilities;

(ii) Intentionally directing attacks against buildings, material, medical units and transport, and personnel using the distinctive emblems of the Geneva Conventions in conformity with international law;

(iii) Intentionally directing attacks against personnel, installations, material, units or vehicles involved in a humanitarian assistance or peacekeeping mission in accordance with the Charter of the United Nations, as long as they are entitled to the protection given to civilians or civilian objects under the international law of armed conflict;

(iv) Intentionally directing attacks against buildings dedicated to religion, education, art, science or charitable purposes, historic monuments, hospitals and places where the sick and wounded are collected, provided they are not military objectives;

(v) Pillaging a town or place, even when taken by assault;

(vi) Committing rape, sexual slavery, enforced prostitution, forced pregnancy, as defined in article 7, paragraph 2 (f), enforced sterilization, and any other form of sexual violence also constituting a serious violation of article 3 common to the four Geneva Conventions;

(vii) Conscripting or enlisting children under the age of fifteen years into armed forces or groups or using them to participate actively in hostilities;

(viii) Ordering the displacement of the civilian population for reasons related to the conflict, unless the security of the civilians involved or imperative military reasons so demand;

(ix) Killing or wounding treacherously a combatant adversary;

(x) Declaring that no quarter will be given;

(xi) Subjecting persons who are in the power of another party to the conflict to physical mutilation or to medical or scientific experiments of any kind which are neither justified by the medical, dental or hospital treatment of the person concerned nor carried out in his or her interest, and which cause death to or seriously endanger the health of such person or persons;

(xii) Destroying or seizing the property of an adversary unless such destruction or seizure be imperatively demanded by the necessities of the conflict;

(f) Paragraph 2 (e) applies to armed conflicts not of an international character and thus does not apply to situations of internal disturbances and tensions, such as riots, isolated and sporadic acts of violence or other acts of a similar nature. It applies to armed conflicts that take place in the territory of a State when there is protracted armed conflict between governmental authorities and organized armed groups or between such groups.

3. Nothing in paragraph 2 (c) and (e) shall affect the responsibility of a Government to maintain or re-establish law and order in the State or to defend the unity and territorial integrity of the State, by all legitimate means.

Article 9
Elements of Crimes

1. Elements of Crimes shall assist the Court in the interpretation and application of articles 6, 7 and 8. They shall be adopted by a two-thirds majority of the members of the Assembly of States Parties.

2. Amendments to the Elements of Crimes may be proposed by:

(a) Any State Party;

(b) The judges acting by an absolute majority;

(c) The Prosecutor.

Such amendments shall be adopted by a two-thirds majority of the members of the Assembly of States Parties.

3. The Elements of Crimes and amendments thereto shall be consistent with this Statute.

Article 10

Nothing in this Part shall be interpreted as limiting or prejudicing in any way existing or developing rules of international law for purposes other than this Statute.

Article 11
Jurisdiction Ratione Temporis

1. The Court has jurisdiction only with respect to crimes committed after the entry into force of this Statute. 2. If a State becomes a Party to this Statute after its entry into force, the Court may exercise its jurisdiction only with respect to crimes committed after the entry into force of this Statute for that State, unless that State has made a declaration under article 12, paragraph 3.

Article 12
Preconditions to the Exercise of Jurisdiction

1. A State which becomes a Party to this Statute thereby accepts the jurisdiction of the Court with respect to the crimes referred to in article 5.

2. In the case of article 13, paragraph (a) or (c), the Court may exercise its jurisdiction if one or more of the following States are Parties to this Statute or have accepted the jurisdiction of the Court in accordance with paragraph 3:

(a) The State on the territory of which the conduct in question occurred or, if the crime was committed on board a vessel or aircraft, the State of registration of that vessel or aircraft;

(b) The State of which the person accused of the crime is a national.

3. If the acceptance of a State which is not a Party to this Statute is required under paragraph 2, that State may, by declaration lodged with the Registrar, accept the exercise of jurisdiction by the Court with respect to the crime in question. The accepting State shall cooperate with the Court without any delay or exception in accordance with Part 9.

Article 13
Exercise of Jurisdiction

The Court may exercise its jurisdiction with respect to a crime referred to in article 5 in accordance with the provisions of this Statute if:

(a) A situation in which one or more of such crimes appears to have been committed is referred to the Prosecutor by a State Party in accordance with article 14;

(b) A situation in which one or more of such crimes appears to have been committed is referred to the Prosecutor by the Security Council acting under Chapter VII of the Charter of the United Nations; or

(c) The Prosecutor has initiated an investigation in respect of such a crime in accordance with article 15.

Article 14

Referral of a Situation by a State Party

1. A State Party may refer to the Prosecutor, a situation in which one or more crimes within the jurisdiction of the Court appear to have been committed requesting the Prosecutor to investigate the situation for the purpose of determining whether one or more specific persons should be charged with the commission of such crimes. 2. As far as possible, a referral shall specify the relevant circumstances and be accompanied by such supporting documentation as is available to the State referring the situation.

Article 15

Prosecutor

1. The Prosecutor may initiate investigations *proprio motu* on the basis of information on crimes within the jurisdiction of the Court.

2. The Prosecutor shall analyze the seriousness of the information received. For this purpose, he or she may seek additional information from States, organs of the United Nations, intergovernmental or non-governmental organizations, or other reliable sources that he or she deems appropriate, and may receive written or oral testimony at the seat of the Court.

3. If the Prosecutor concludes that there is a reasonable basis to proceed with an investigation, he or she shall submit to the Pre-Trial Chamber a request for authorization of an investigation, together with any supporting material collected. Victims may make representations to the Pre-Trial Chamber, in accordance with the Rules of Procedure and Evidence.

4. If the Pre-Trial Chamber, upon examination of the request and the supporting material, considers that there is a reasonable basis to proceed with an investigation, and that the case appears to fall within the jurisdiction of the Court, it shall authorize the commencement of the investigation, without prejudice to subsequent determinations by the Court with regard to the jurisdiction and admissibility of a case.

5. The refusal of the Pre-Trial Chamber to authorize the investigation shall not preclude the presentation of a subsequent request by the Prosecutor based on new facts or evidence regarding the same situation.

6. If, after the preliminary examination referred to in paragraphs 1 and 2, the Prosecutor concludes that the information provided does not constitute a reasonable basis for an investigation, he or she shall inform those who provided the information. This shall not preclude the Prosecutor from considering further information submitted to him or her regarding the same

situation in the light of new facts or evidence.

Article 16
Deferral of Investigation or Prosecution

No investigation or prosecution may be commenced or proceeded with under this Statute for a period of 12 months after the Security Council, in a resolution adopted under Chapter VII of the Charter of the United Nations, has requested the Court to that effect; that request may be renewed by the Council under the same conditions.

Article 17
Issues of Admissibility

1. Having regard to paragraph 10 of the Preamble and article 1, the Court shall determine that a case is inadmissible where:

(a) The case is being investigated or prosecuted by a State which has jurisdiction over it, unless the State is unwilling or unable genuinely to carry out the investigation or prosecution;

(b) The case has been investigated by a State which has jurisdiction over it and the State has decided not to prosecute the person concerned, unless the decision resulted from the unwillingness or inability of the State genuinely to prosecute;

(c) The person concerned has already been tried for conduct which is the subject of the complaint, and a trial by the Court is not permitted under article 20, paragraph 3;

(d) The case is not of sufficient gravity to justify further action by the Court.

2. In order to determine unwillingness in a particular case, the Court shall consider, having regard to the principles of due process recognized by international law, whether one or more of the following exist, as applicable:

(a) The proceedings were or are being undertaken or the national decision was made for the purpose of shielding the person concerned from criminal responsibility for crimes within the jurisdiction of the Court referred to in article 5;

(b) There has been an unjustified delay in the proceedings which in the circumstances is inconsistent with an intent to bring the person concerned to justice;

(c) The proceedings were not or are not being conducted independently or impartially, and they were or are being conducted in a manner which, in the circumstances, is inconsistent with an intent to bring the person concerned to justice.

3. In order to determine inability in a particular case, the Court shall consider whether, due to a total or substantial collapse or unavailability of its national judicial system, the State is unable to obtain the accused or the necessary evidence and testimony or otherwise unable to carry out its proceedings.

Article 18
Preliminary Rulings Regarding Admissibility

1. When a situation has been referred to the Court pursuant to article 13 (a) and the Prosecutor has determined that there would be a reasonable basis to commence an investigation, or the Prosecutor initiates an investigation pursuant to articles 13 (c) and 15, the Prosecutor shall notify all States Parties and those States which, taking into account the information available, would normally exercise jurisdiction over the crimes concerned. The Prosecutor may notify such States on a confidential basis and, where the Prosecutor believes it necessary to protect persons, prevent destruction of evidence or prevent the absconding of persons, may limit the scope of the information provided to States.

2. Within one month of receipt of that notification, a State may inform the Court that it is investigating or has investigated its nationals or others within its jurisdiction with respect to criminal acts which may constitute crimes referred to in article 5 and which relate to the information provided in the notification to States. At the request of that State, the Prosecutor shall defer to the State's investigation of those persons unless the Pre-Trial Chamber, on the application of the Prosecutor, decides to authorize the investigation.

3. The Prosecutor's deferral to a State's investigation shall be open to review by the Prosecutor six months after the date of deferral or at any time when there has been a significant change of circumstances based on the State's unwillingness or inability genuinely to carry out the investigation.

4. The State concerned or the Prosecutor may appeal to the Appeals Chamber against a ruling of the Pre-Trial Chamber, in accordance with article 82. The appeal may be heard on an expedited basis.

5. When the Prosecutor has deferred an investigation in accordance with paragraph 2, the Prosecutor may request that the State concerned periodically inform the Prosecutor of the progress of its investigations and any subsequent prosecutions. States Parties shall respond to such requests without undue

delay.

6. Pending a ruling by the Pre-Trial Chamber, or at any time when the Prosecutor has deferred an investigation under this article, the Prosecutor may, on an exceptional basis, seek authority from the Pre-Trial Chamber to pursue necessary investigative steps for the purpose of preserving evidence where there is a unique opportunity to obtain important evidence or there is a significant risk that such evidence may not be subsequently available.

7. A State which has challenged a ruling of the Pre-Trial Chamber under this article may challenge the admissibility of a case under article 19 on the grounds of additional significant facts or significant change of circumstances.

Article 19
Challenges to the Jurisdiction of the Court or the Admissibility of a Case

1. The Court shall satisfy itself that it has jurisdiction in any case brought before it. The Court may, on its own motion, determine the admissibility of a case in accordance with article 17.

2. Challenges to the admissibility of a case on the grounds referred to in article 17 or challenges to the jurisdiction of the Court may be made by:

(a) An accused or a person for whom a warrant of arrest or a summons to appear has been issued under article 58;

(b) A State which has jurisdiction over a case, on the ground that it is investigating or prosecuting the case or has investigated or prosecuted; or

(c) A State from which acceptance of jurisdiction is required under article 12.

3. The Prosecutor may seek a ruling from the Court regarding a question of jurisdiction or admissibility. In proceedings with respect to jurisdiction or admissibility, those who have referred the situation under article 13, as well as victims, may also submit observations to the Court.

4. The admissibility of a case or the jurisdiction of the Court may be challenged only once by any person or State referred to in paragraph 2. The challenge shall take place prior to or at the commencement of the trial. In exceptional circumstances, the Court may grant leave for a challenge to be brought more than once or at a time later than the commencement of the trial. Challenges to the admissibility of a case, at the commencement of a trial, or subsequently with the leave of the Court, may be based only on article 17, paragraph 1 (c).

5. A State referred to in paragraph 2 (b) and (c) shall make a challenge at the earliest opportunity.

6. Prior to the confirmation of the charges, challenges to the admissibility of a case or challenges to the jurisdiction of the Court shall be referred to the Pre-Trial Chamber. After confirmation of the charges, they shall be referred to the Trial Chamber. Decisions with respect to jurisdiction or admissibility may be appealed to the Appeals Chamber in accordance with article 82.

7. If a challenge is made by a State referred to in paragraph 2 (b) or (c), the Prosecutor shall suspend the investigation until such time as the Court makes a determination in accordance with article 17.

8. Pending a ruling by the Court, the Prosecutor may seek authority from the Court:

(a) To pursue necessary investigative steps of the kind referred to in article 18, paragraph 6;

(b) To take a statement or testimony from a witness or complete the collection and examination of evidence which had begun prior to the making of the challenge; and

(c) In cooperation with the relevant States, to prevent the absconding of persons in respect of whom the Prosecutor has already requested a warrant of arrest under article 58.

9. The making of a challenge shall not affect the validity of any act performed by the Prosecutor or any order or warrant issued by the Court prior to the making of the challenge.

10. If the Court has decided that a case is inadmissible under article 17, the Prosecutor may submit a request for a review of the decision when he or she is fully satisfied that new facts have arisen which negate the basis on which the case had previously been found inadmissible under article 17.

11. If the Prosecutor, having regard to the matters referred to in article 17, defers an investigation, the Prosecutor may request that the relevant State make available to the Prosecutor information on the proceedings. That information shall, at the request of the State concerned, be confidential. If the Prosecutor thereafter decides to proceed with an investigation, he or she shall notify the State to which deferral of the proceedings has taken place.

Article 20
Ne Bis in Idem

1. Except as provided in this Statute, no person shall be tried before the Court with respect to conduct which formed the basis of crimes for which the

person has been convicted or acquitted by the Court.

`2. No person shall be tried by another court for a crime referred to in article 5 for which that person has already been convicted or acquitted by the Court.

3. No person who has been tried by another court for conduct also proscribed under article 6, 7 or 8 shall be tried by the Court with respect to the same conduct unless the proceedings in the other court:

(a) Were for the purpose of shielding the person concerned from criminal responsibility for crimes within the jurisdiction of the Court; or

(b) Otherwise were not conducted independently or impartially in accordance with the norms of due process recognized by international law and were conducted in a manner which, in the circumstances, was inconsistent with an intent to bring the person concerned to justice.

Article 21

Applicable Law

1. The Court shall apply:

(a) In the first place, this Statute, Elements of Crimes and its Rules of Procedure and Evidence;

(b) In the second place, where appropriate, applicable treaties and the principles and rules of international law, including the established principles of the international law of armed conflict;

(c) Failing that, general principles of law derived by the Court from national laws of legal systems of the world including, as appropriate, the national laws of States that would normally exercise jurisdiction over the crime, provided that those principles are not inconsistent with this Statute and with international law and internationally recognized norms and standards.

2. The Court may apply principles and rules of law as interpreted in its previous decisions. 3. The application and interpretation of law pursuant to this article must be consistent with internationally recognized human rights, and be without any adverse distinction founded on grounds such as gender as defined in article 7, paragraph 3, age, race, colour, language, religion or belief, political or other opinion, national, ethnic or social origin, wealth, birth or other status.

I. OAU CONVENTION ON THE PREVENTION AND COMBATING OF TERRORISM, 1999

Adopted at Algiers on 14 July, 1999
Entry into force in accordance with Article 20
Depositary: Secretary-General of the Organization of African Unity

The Member States of the Organization of African Unity:

CONSIDERING the purposes and principles enshrined in the Charter of the Organization of African Unity, in particular its clauses relating to the security, stability, development of friendly relations, and cooperation among its Member States;

RECALLING the provisions of the Declaration on the Code of Conduct for Inter-African Relations, adopted by the Thirtieth Ordinary Session of the Assembly of Heads of State and Government of the Organization of African Unity, held in Tunis, Tunisia, from 13 to 15 June, 1994;

AWARE of the need to promote human and moral values based on tolerance and rejection of all forms of terrorism irrespective of their motivations;

BELIEVING in the principles of international law, the provisions of the Charters of the Organization of African Unity and of the United Nations and the latter's relevant resolutions on measures aimed at combating international terrorism and, in particular, resolution 49/60 of the General Assembly of 9 December 1994, together with the annexed Declaration on Measures to Eliminate International Terrorism as well as resolution 51/210 of the General Assembly of 17 December, 1996 and the Declaration to Supplement the 1994 Declaration on Measures to Eliminate International Terrorism, annexed thereto;

DEEPLY concerned over the scope and seriousness of the phenomenon of terrorism and the dangers it poses to the stability and security of States; 205

DESIROUS of strengthening cooperation among Member States in order to forestall and combat terrorism;

REAFFIRMING the legitimate right of peoples for self-determination and independence pursuant to the principles of international law and the provisions of the Charters of the Organization of African Unity and the United Nations as well as the African Charter on Human and Peoples' Rights;

CONCERNED that the lives of innocent women and children are most adversely affected by terrorism;

CONVINCED that terrorism constitutes a serious violation of human rights and, in particular, the rights to physical integrity, life, freedom and security, and impedes socio-economic development through destabilization of States;

CONVINCED FURTHER that terrorism cannot be justified under any circumstances and, consequently, should be combated in all its forms and manifestations, including those in which States are involved directly or indirectly, without regard to its origin, causes and objectives;

AWARE of the growing links between terrorism and organized crime, including the illicit traffic of arms, D.R.ugs and money laundering;

DETERMINED to eliminate terrorism in all its forms and manifestations;

HAVE AGREED AS FOLLOWS:

PART I
SCOPE OF APPLICATION

Article 1

For the purposes of this Convention:

1. "Convention" means the OAU Convention on the Prevention and Combating of Terrorism.

2. "State Party" means any Member State of the Organization of African Unity which has ratified or acceded to this Convention and has deposited its instrument of ratification or accession with the Secretary.

3. "Terrorist act" means: (*a*) any act which is a violation of the criminal laws of a State Party and which may endanger the life, physical integrity or freedom of, or cause serious injury or death to, any person, any number or

group of persons or causes or may cause damage to public or private property, natural resources, environmental or cultural heritage and is calculated or intended to: (i) intimidate, put in fear, force, coerce or induce any government, body, institution, the general public or any segment thereof, to do or abstain from doing any act, or to adopt or abandon a particular standpoint, or to act according to certain principles; or (ii) disrupt any public service, the delivery of any essential service to the public or to create a public emergency; or (iii) create general insurrection in a State; (*b*) any promotion, sponsoring, contribution to, command, aid, incitement, encouragement, attempt, threat, conspiracy, organizing, or procurement of any person, with the intent to commit any act referred to in paragraph (a) (i) to (iii).

Article 2

States Parties undertake to: (*a*) review their national laws and establish criminal offenses for terrorist acts as defined in this Convention and make such acts punishable by appropriate penalties that take into account the grave nature of such offenses; (*b*) consider, as a matter of priority, the signing or ratification of, or accession to, the international instruments listed in the Annexure, which they have not yet signed, ratified or acceded to; and (*c*) implement the actions, including enactment of legislation and the establishment as criminal offenses of certain acts as required in terms of the international instruments referred to in paragraph (b) and that States have ratified and acceded to and make such acts punishable by appropriate penalties which take into account the grave nature of those offenses; (*d*) notify the Secretary General of the OAU of all the legislative measures it has taken and the penalties imposed on terrorist acts within one year of its ratification of, or accession to, the Convention.

Article 3

1. Notwithstanding the provisions of Article 1, the struggle waged by peoples in accordance with the principles of international law for their liberation or self-determination, including armed struggle against colonialism, occupation, aggression and domination by foreign forces shall not be considered as terrorist acts.

2. Political, philosophical, ideological, racial, ethnic, religious or other motives shall not be a justifiable defense against a terrorist act.

PART II
AREAS OF COOPERATION

Article 4

1. States Parties undertake to refrain from any acts aimed at organizing, supporting, financing, committing or inciting to commit terrorist acts, or providing havens for terrorists, directly or indirectly, including the provision of weapons and their stockpiling in their countries and the issuing of visas and travel documents.

2. States Parties shall adopt any legitimate measures aimed at preventing and combating terrorist acts in accordance with the provisions of this Convention and their respective national legislation, in particular, they shall do the following:

(*a*) prevent their territories from being used as a base for the planning, organization or execution of terrorist acts or for the participation or collaboration in these acts in any form whatsoever;

(*b*) develop and strengthen methods of monitoring and detecting plans or activities aimed at the illegal cross-border transportation, importation, export, stockpiling and use of arms, ammunition and explosives, and other materials and means of committing terrorist acts;

(*c*) develop and strengthen methods of controlling and monitoring land, sea and air borders and customs and immigration check-points in order to pre-empt any infiltration by individuals or groups involved in the planning, organization and execution of terrorist acts;

(*d*) strengthen the protection and security of persons, diplomatic and consular missions, premises of regional and international organizations accredited to a State Party, in accordance with the relevant conventions and rules of international law;

(*e*) promote the exchange of information and expertise on terrorist acts and establish data bases for the collection and analysis of information and data on terrorist elements, groups, movements and organizations;

(*f*) take all necessary measures to prevent the establishment of terrorist support networks in any form whatsoever;

(*g*) ascertain, when granting asylum, that the asylum seeker is not involved in any terrorist act;

(*h*) arrest the perpetrators of terrorist acts and try them in accordance with national legislation, or extradite them in accordance with the provisions of this Convention or extradition treaties concluded between the requesting State and the requested State and, in the absence of a treaty, consider facilitating the extradition of persons suspected of having committed terrorist acts; and

(*l*) establish effective co-operation between relevant domestic security officials and services and the citizens of the States

Article 5

States Parties shall co-operate among themselves in preventing and combating terrorist acts in conformity with national legislation and procedures of each State in the following areas:

1. States Parties undertake to strengthen the exchange of information among them regarding:

(*a*) acts and crimes committed by terrorist groups, their leaders and elements, their headquarters and training camps, their means and sources of funding and acquisition of arms, the types of arms, ammunition and explosives used, and other means in their possession;

(*b*) the communication and propaganda methods and techniques used by the terrorists groups, the behavior of these groups, the movement of their leaders and elements, as well as their travel documents.

2. States Parties undertake to exchange any information that leads to:

(*a*) the arrest of any person charged with a terrorist act against the interests of a State Party or against its nationals, or attempted to commit such an act or participated in it as an accomplice or an instigator;

(*b*) the seizure and confiscation of any type of arms, ammunition, explosives, devices or funds or other instrumentalities of crime used to commit a terrorist act or intended for that purpose.

3. States Parties undertake to respect the confidentiality of the information exchanged among them and not to provide such information to another State that is not party to this Convention, or to a third State Party, without the prior consent of the State from where such information originated.

4. States Parties undertake to promote co-operation among themselves and to help each other with regard to procedures relating to the investigation and arrest of persons suspected of, charged with or convicted of terrorist acts, in conformity with the national law of each State.

5. States Parties shall co-operate among themselves in conducting and exchanging studies and researches on how to combat terrorist acts and to exchange expertise relating to control of terrorist acts.

6. States Parties shall co-operate among themselves, where possible, in providing any available technical assistance in drawing up programs or organizing, where necessary and for the benefit of their personnel, joint training courses involving one or several States Parties in the area of control of terrorist acts, in order to improve their scientific, technical and operational capacities to prevent and combat such acts.

PART III
STATE JURISDICTION

Article 6

1. Each State Party has jurisdiction over terrorist acts as defined in Article 1 when:

(*a*) the act is committed in the territory of that State and the perpetrator of the act is arrested in its territory or outside it if this is punishable by its national law;

(*b*) the act is committed on board a vessel or a ship flying the flag of that State or an aircraft which is registered under the laws of that State at the time the offense is committed; or

(c) the act is committed by a national or a group of nationals of that State.

2. A State Party may also establish its jurisdiction over any such offense when:

(*a*) the act is committed against a national of that State; or

(*b*) the act is committed against a State or government facility of that State abroad, including an embassy or other diplomatic or consular premises, and any other property, of that State; or

(c) the act is committed by a stateless person who has his or her habitual residence in the territory of that State; or

(*d*) the act is committed on board an aircraft which is operated by any carrier of that State; and

(*e*) the act is committed against the security of the State Party.

3. Upon ratifying or acceding to this Convention, each State Party shall

notify the Secretary General of the Organization of African Unity of the jurisdiction it has established in accordance with paragraph 2 under its national law. Should any change take place, the State Party concerned shall immediately notify the Secretary General.

4. Each State Party shall likewise take such measures as may be necessary to establish its jurisdiction over the acts set forth in Article 1 in cases where the alleged offender is present in its territory and it does not extradite that person to any of the States Parties which have established their jurisdiction in accordance with paragraphs 1 or 2.

Article 7

1. Upon receiving information that a person who has committed or who is alleged to have committed any terrorist act as defined in Article 1 may be present in its territory, the State Party concerned shall take such measures as may be necessary under its national law to investigate the facts contained in the information.

2. Upon being satisfied that the circumstances so warrant, the State Party in whose territory the offender or alleged offender is present shall take the appropriate measures under its national law so as to ensure that person's presence for the purpose of prosecution.

3. Any person against whom the measures referred to in paragraph 2 are being taken shall be entitled to:

(*a*) communicate without delay with the nearest appropriate representative of the State of which that person is a national or which is otherwise entitled to protect that person's rights or, if that person is a stateless person, the State in whose territory that person habitually resides;

(*b*) be visited by a representative of that State;

(c) be assisted by a lawyer of his or her choice;

(*d*) be informed of his or her rights under sub-paragraphs (*a*), (*b*) and (*c*).

4. The rights referred to in paragraph 3 shall be exercised in conformity with the national law of the State in whose territory the offender or alleged offender is present, subject to the provision that the said laws must enable full effect to be given to the purposes for which the rights accorded under paragraph 3 are intended.

PART IV
EXTRADITION

Article 8

1. Subject to the provisions of paragraphs 2 and 3 of this Article, the States Parties shall undertake to extradite any person charged with or convicted of any terrorist act carried out on the territory of another State Party and whose extradition is requested by one of the States Parties in conformity with the rules and conditions provided for in this Convention or under extradition agreements between the States Parties and within the limits of their national laws.

2. Any State Party may, at the time of the deposit of its instrument of ratification or accession, transmit to the Secretary General of the OAU the grounds on which extradition may not be granted and shall at the same time indicate the legal basis in its national legislation or international conventions to which it is a party which excludes such extradition. The Secretary General shall forward these grounds to the States Parties.

3. Extradition shall not be granted if final judgement has been passed by a competent authority of the requested State upon the person in respect of the terrorist act or acts for which extradition is requested. Extradition may also be refused if the competent authority of the requested State has decided either not to institute or terminate proceedings in respect of the same act or acts.

4. A State Party in whose territory an alleged offender is present shall be obliged, whether or not the offense was committed in its territory, to submit the case without undue delay to its competent authorities for the purpose of prosecution if it does not extradite that person.

Article 9

Each State Party undertakes to include as an extraditable offense any terrorist act as defined in Article 1, in any extradition treaty existing between any of the States Parties before or after the entry into force of this Convention.

Article 10

Exchange of extradition requests between the States Parties to this

Convention shall be effected directly either through diplomatic channels or other appropriate organs in the concerned States.

Article 11

Extradition requests shall be in writing, and shall be accompanied in particular by the following:

(*a*) an original or authenticated copy of the sentence, warrant of arrest or any order or other judicial decision made, in accordance with the procedures laid down in the laws of the requesting State;

(*b*) a statement describing the offenses for which extradition is being requested, indicating the date and place of its commission, the offense committed, any convictions made and a copy of the provisions of the applicable law; and

(c) as comprehensive a description as possible of the wanted person together with any other information which may assist in establishing the person's identity and nationality.

Article 12

In urgent cases, the competent authority of the State making the extradition may, in writing, request that the State seized of the extradition request arrest the person in question provisionally. Such provisional arrest shall be for a reasonable period in accordance with the national law of the requested State.

Article 13

1. Where a State Party receives several extradition requests from different States Parties in respect of the same suspect and for the same or different terrorist acts, it shall decide on these requests having regard to all the prevailing circumstances, particularly the possibility of subsequent extradition, the respective dates of receipt of the requests, and the degree of seriousness of the crime.

2. Upon agreeing to extradite, States Parties shall seize and transmit all funds and related materials purportedly used in the commission of the terrorist act to the requesting State as well as relevant incriminating evidence.

3. Such funds, incriminating evidence and related materials, upon

confirmation of their use in the terrorist act by the requested State, shall be transmitted to the requesting State even if, for reasons of death or escape of the accused, the extradition in question cannot take place.

4. The provisions in paragraphs 1, 2 and 3 of this Article shall not affect the rights of any of the States Parties or bona fide third parties regarding the materials or revenues mentioned above.

PART V
EXTRA-TERRITORIAL INVESTIGATIONS (COMMISSIONROGATOIRE) AND MUTUAL LEGAL ASSISTANCE

Article 14

1. Any State Party may, while recognizing the sovereign rights of States Parties in matters of criminal investigation, request any other State Party to carry out, with its assistance and cooperation, on the latter's territory, criminal investigations related to any judicial proceedings concerning alleged terrorist acts and, in particular:

(*a*) the examination of witnesses and transcripts of statements made as evidence;

(*b*) the opening of judicial information;

(c) the initiation of investigation processes;

(*d*) the collection of documents and recordings or, in their absence, authenticated copies thereof;

(*e*) conducting inspections and tracing of assets for evidentiary purposes;

(*f*) executing searches and seizures; and

(*g*) service of judicial documents.

Article 15

A commission rogatoire may be refused:

(*a*) where each of the States Parties has to execute a commission rogatoire relating to the same terrorist acts;

(*b*) if that request may affect efforts to expose crimes, impede investigations or the indictment of the accused in the country requesting the commission rogatoire; or

(c) if the execution of the request would affect the sovereignty of the requested State, its security or public order.

Article 16

The extra-territorial investigation (commission rogatoire) shall be executed in compliance with the provisions of national laws of the requested State. The request for an extra-territorial investigation (commission rogatoire) relating to a terrorist act shall not be rejected on the grounds of the principle of confidentiality of bank operations or financial institutions, where applicable.

Article 17

The States Parties shall extend to each other the best possible mutual police and judicial assistance for any investigation, criminal prosecution or extradition proceedings relating to the terrorist acts as set forth in this Convention.

Article 18

The States Parties undertake to develop, if necessary, especially by concluding bilateral and multilateral agreements and arrangements, mutual legal assistance procedures aimed at facilitating and speeding up investigations and collecting evidence, as well as cooperation between law enforcement agencies in order to detect and prevent terrorist acts.

PART VI
FINAL PROVISIONS

Article 19

1. This Convention shall be open to signature, ratification or accession by the Member States of the Organization of African Unity.

2. The instruments of ratification or accession to the present Convention shall be deposited with the Secretary General of the Organization of African

Unity.

3. The Secretary General of the Organization of African Unity shall inform Member States of the Organization of the deposit of each instrument of ratification or accession.

4. No State Party may enter a reservation which is incompatible with the object and purposes of this Convention.

5. No State Party may withdraw from this Convention except on the basis of a written request addressed to the Secretary General of the Organization of African Unity. The withdrawal shall take effect six months after the date of receipt of the written request by the Secretary General of the Organization of African Unity.

Article 20

1. This Convention shall enter into force thirty days after the deposit of the fifteenth instrument of ratification with the Secretary General of the Organization of African Unity.

2. For each of the States that shall ratify or accede to this Convention shall enter into force thirty days after the date of the deposit by that State Party of its instrument of ratification or accession.

Article 21

1. Special protocols or agreements may, if necessary, supplement the provisions of this Convention.

2. This Convention may be amended if a State Party makes a written request to that effect to the Secretary General of the Organization of African Unity. The Assembly of Heads of State and Government may only consider the proposed amendment after all the States Parties have been duly informed of it at least three months in advance.

3. The amendment shall be approved by a simple majority of the States Parties. It shall come into force for each State which has accepted it in accordance with its constitutional procedures three months after the Secretary General has received notice of the acceptance.

Article 22

1. Nothing in this Convention shall be interpreted as derogating from the

general principles of international law, in particular the principles of international humanitarian law, as well as the African Charter on Human and Peoples' Rights.

2. Any dispute that may arise between the States Parties regarding the interpretation or application of this Convention shall be amicably settled by direct agreement between them. Failing such settlement, any one of the States Parties may refer the dispute to the International Court of Justice in conformity with the Statute of the Court or by arbitration by other States Parties to this Convention.

Article 23

The original of this Convention, of which the Arabic, English, French, and Portuguese texts are equally authentic, shall be deposited with the Secretary General of the Organization of African Unity.

ANNEX
LIST OF INTERNATIONAL INSTRUMENTS

(*a*) Tokyo Convention on Offenses and Certain Other Acts Committed on Board Aircraft of 1963;

(*b*) Montreal Convention for the Suppression of Unlawful Acts against the Safety of Civil Aviation of 1971 and the Protocol thereto of 1984;

(*c*) New York Convention on the Prevention and Punishment of Crimes against Internationally Protected Persons, including Diplomatic Agents of 1973;

(*d*) International Convention against the Taking of Hostages of 1979;

(*e*) Convention on the Physical Protection of Nuclear Material of 1979;

(*f*) United Nations Convention on the Law of the Sea 1982;

(*g*) Protocol for the Suppression of Unlawful Acts of Violence at Airports Serving International Civil Aviation, supplementary to the Convention for the Suppression of Unlawful Acts against the Safety of Civil Aviation of 1988;

(*h*) Protocol for the Suppression of Unlawful Acts against the Safety of Fixed Platforms located on the Continental Shelf of 1988;

(*i*) Convention for the Suppression of Unlawful Acts against Maritime Navigation of 1988;

(*j*) Convention on the Marking of Plastic Explosives of 1991;

(*k*) International Convention for the Suppression of Terrorist Explosive Bombs of 1997;

(*l*) Convention on the Prohibition of the Use, Stockpiling, Production and Transfer of Anti-Personnel Mines and on their Destruction of 1997.

J. UNITED STATES ALIEN TORT CLAIMS ACT, 1789 (28 U.S.C. §1350)

The district courts shall have original jurisdiction of any civil action by an alien for a tort only, committed in violation of the law of nations or a treaty of the United States.

K. UNITED STATES TORTURE VICTIM PROTECTION ACT OF 1991

(Enrolled as Agreed to or Passed by Both House and Senate)

H.R.2092

One Hundred Second Congress of the United States of America AT THE SECOND SESSION

Begun and held at the City of Washington on Friday, the third day of January, one thousand nine hundred and ninety-two

An Act

To carry out obligations of the United States under the United Nations Charter and other international agreements pertaining to the protection of human rights by establishing a civil action for recovery of damages from an individual who engages in torture or extrajudicial killing.

Be it enacted by the Senate and House of Representatives of the United States of America in Congress assembled,

SECTION 1. SHORT TITLE.

This Act may be cited as the "Torture Victim Protection Act of 1991."

SECTION 2. ESTABLISHMENT OF CIVIL ACTION.

(A) Liability- An individual who, under actual or apparent authority, or color of law, of any foreign nation:

(1) subjects an individual to torture shall, in a civil action, be liable for damages to that individual; or

(2) subjects an individual to extrajudicial killing shall, in a civil action, be liable for damages to the individual's legal representative, or to any person who may be a claimant in an action for wrongful death.

(B) Exhaustion of Remedies- A court shall decline to hear a claim under this section if the claimant has not exhausted adequate and available remedies in the place in which the conduct giving rise to the claim occurred.

(C) Statute of Limitations- No action shall be maintained under this section unless it is commenced within 10 years after the cause of action arose.

SECTION 3. DEFINITIONS.

(A) Extrajudicial Killing- For the purposes of this Act, the term 'extrajudicial killing' means a deliberated killing not authorized by a previous judgment pronounced by a regularly constituted court affording all the judicial guarantees which are recognized as indispensable by civilized peoples. Such term, however, does not include any such killing that, under international law, is lawfully carried out under the authority of a foreign nation.

(B) Torture- For the purposes of this Act:

(1) the term "torture" means any act, directed against an individual in the offender's custody or physical control, by which severe pain or suffering (other than pain or suffering arising only from or inherent in, or incidental to, lawful sanctions), whether physical or mental, is intentionally inflicted on that individual for such purposes as obtaining from that individual or a third person information or a confession, punishing that individual for an act that individual or a third person has committed or is suspected of having committed, intimidating or coercing that individual or a third person, or for any reason based on discrimination of any kind; and

(2) mental pain or suffering refers to prolonged mental harm caused by or resulting from:

(a) the intentional infliction or threatened infliction of severe physical pain or suffering;

(b) the administration or application, or threatened administration or application, of mind altering substances or other procedures calculated to disrupt profoundly the senses or the personality;

(c) the threat of imminent death; or

(d) the threat that another individual will imminently be subjected to death, severe physical pain or suffering, or the administration or application of mind altering substances or other procedures calculated to disrupt profoundly the senses or personality.

L. THE UNITED NATIONS CONVENTION AGAINST TORTURE AND OTHER CRUEL, INHUMAN, OR DEGRADING TREATMENT OR PUNISHMENT

Adopted and opened for signature, ratification and accession by General Assembly resolution 39/46 of 10 December 1984

entry into force 26 June, 1987, in accordance with article 27 (1)

The States Parties to this Convention,

Considering that, in accordance with the principles proclaimed in the Charter of the United Nations, recognition of the equal and inalienable rights of all members of the human family is the foundation of freedom, justice and peace in the world,

Recognizing that those rights derive from the inherent dignity of the human person,

Considering the obligation of States under the Charter, in particular Article 55, to promote universal respect for, and observance of, human rights and fundamental freedoms,

Having regard to article 5 of the Universal Declaration of Human Rights and article 7 of the International Covenant on Civil and Political Rights, both of which provide that no one shall be subjected to torture or to cruel, inhuman or degrading treatment or punishment,

Having regard also to the Declaration on the Protection of All Persons from Being Subjected to Torture and Other Cruel, Inhuman or Degrading Treatment or Punishment, adopted by the General Assembly on 9 December 1975,

Desiring to make more effective the struggle against torture and other cruel, inhuman, or degrading treatment or punishment throughout the world,

Have agreed as follows:

PART I

Article 1

1. For the purposes of this Convention, the term "torture" means any act by which severe pain or suffering, whether physical or mental, is intentionally inflicted on a person for such purposes as obtaining from him or a third person information or a confession, punishing him for an act he or a third person has committed or is suspected of having committed, or intimidating or coercing him or a third person, or for any reason based on discrimination of any kind, when such pain or suffering is inflicted by or at the instigation of or with the consent or acquiescence of a public official or other person acting in an official capacity. It does not include pain or suffering arising only from, inherent in or incidental to lawful sanctions.

2. This article is without prejudice to any international instrument or national legislation which does or may contain provisions of wider application.

Article 2

1. Each State Party shall take effective legislative, administrative, judicial or other measures to prevent acts of torture in any territory under its jurisdiction.

2. No exceptional circumstances whatsoever, whether a state of war or a threat of war, internal political in stability or any other public emergency, may be invoked as a justification of torture.

3. An order from a superior officer or a public authority may not be invoked as a justification of torture.

Article 3

1. No State Party shall expel, return ("refouler") or extradite a person to another State where there are substantial grounds for believing that he would be in danger of being subjected to torture.

2. For the purpose of determining whether there are such grounds, the competent authorities shall take into account all relevant considerations including, where applicable, the existence in the State concerned of a consistent pattern of gross, flagrant or mass violations of human rights.

Article 4

1. Each State Party shall ensure that all acts of torture are offenses under its criminal law. The same shall apply to an attempt to commit torture and to an act by any person which constitutes complicity or participation in torture.
2. Each State Party shall make these offenses punishable by appropriate penalties which take into account their grave nature.

Article 5

1. Each State Party shall take such measures as may be necessary to establish its jurisdiction over the offenses referred to in article 4 in the following cases:
(a) When the offenses are committed in any territory under its jurisdiction or on board a ship or aircraft registered in that State;
(b) When the alleged offender is a national of that State;
(c) When the victim is a national of that State if that State considers it appropriate.
2. Each State Party shall likewise take such measures as may be necessary to establish its jurisdiction over such offenses in cases where the alleged offender is present in any territory under its jurisdiction and it does not extradite him pursuant to article 8 to any of the States mentioned in paragraph I of this article.
3. This Convention does not exclude any criminal jurisdiction exercised in accordance with internal law.

Article 6

1. Upon being satisfied, after an examination of information available to it, that the circumstances so warrant, any State Party in whose territory a person alleged to have committed any offense referred to in article 4 is present shall take him into custody or take other legal measures to ensure his presence. The custody and other legal measures shall be as provided in the

law of that State but may be continued only for such time as is necessary to enable any criminal or extradition proceedings to be instituted.

2. Such State shall immediately make a preliminary inquiry into the facts.

3. Any person in custody pursuant to paragraph I of this article shall be assisted in communicating immediately with the nearest appropriate representative of the State of which he is a national, or, if he is a stateless person, with the representative of the State where he usually resides.

4. When a State, pursuant to this article, has taken a person into custody, it shall immediately notify the States referred to in article 5, paragraph 1, of the fact that such person is in custody and of the circumstances which warrant his detention. The State which makes the preliminary inquiry contemplated in paragraph 2 of this article shall promptly report its findings to the said States and shall indicate whether it intends to exercise jurisdiction.

Article 7

1. The State Party in the territory under whose jurisdiction a person alleged to have committed any offense referred to in article 4 is found shall in the cases contemplated in article 5, if it does not extradite him, submit the case to its competent authorities for the purpose of prosecution.

2. These authorities shall take their decision in the same manner as in the case of any ordinary offense of a serious nature under the law of that State. In the cases referred to in article 5, paragraph 2, the standards of evidence required for prosecution and conviction shall in no way be less stringent than those which apply in the cases referred to in article 5, paragraph 1.

3. Any person regarding whom proceedings are brought in connection with any of the offenses referred to in article 4 shall be guaranteed fair treatment at all stages of the proceedings.

Article 8

1. The offenses referred to in article 4 shall be deemed to be included as extraditable offenses in any extradition treaty existing between States Parties. States Parties undertake to include such offenses as extraditable offenses in every extradition treaty to be concluded between them.

2. If a State Party which makes extradition conditional on the existence of a treaty receives a request for extradition from another State Party with which it has no extradition treaty, it may consider this Convention as the legal

basis for extradition in respect of such offenses. Extradition shall be subject to the other conditions provided by the law of the requested State.

3. States Parties which do not make extradition conditional on the existence of a treaty shall recognize such offenses as extraditable offenses between themselves subject to the conditions provided by the law of the requested State.

4. Such offenses shall be treated, for the purpose of extradition between States Parties, as if they had been committed not only in the place in which they occurred but also in the territories of the States required to establish their jurisdiction in accordance with article 5, paragraph 1.

Article 9

1. States Parties shall afford one another the greatest measure of assistance in connection with criminal proceedings brought in respect of any of the offenses referred to in article 4, including the supply of all evidence at their disposal necessary for the proceedings.

2. States Parties shall carry out their obligations under paragraph I of this article in conformity with any treaties on mutual judicial assistance that may exist between them.

Article 10

1. Each State Party shall ensure that education and information regarding the prohibition against torture are fully included in the training of law enforcement personnel, civil or military, medical personnel, public officials and other persons who may be involved in the custody, interrogation or treatment of any individual subjected to any form of arrest, detention, or imprisonment.

2. Each State Party shall include this prohibition in the rules or instructions issued in regard to the duties and functions of any such person.

Article 11

Each State Party shall keep under systematic review interrogation rules, instructions, methods and practices as well as arrangements for the custody and treatment of persons subjected to any form of arrest, detention or imprisonment in any territory under its jurisdiction, with a view to preventing any cases of torture.

Article 12

Each State Party shall ensure that its competent authorities proceed to a prompt and impartial investigation, wherever there is reasonable ground to believe that an act of torture has been committed in any territory under its jurisdiction.

Article 13

Each State Party shall ensure that any individual who alleges he has been subjected to torture in any territory under its jurisdiction has the right to complain to, and to have his case promptly and impartially examined by, its competent authorities. Steps shall be taken to ensure that the complainant and witnesses are protected against all ill-treatment or intimidation as a consequence of his complaint or any evidence given.

Article 14

1. Each State Party shall ensure in its legal system that the victim of an act of torture obtains redress and has an enforceable right to fair and adequate compensation, including the means for as full rehabilitation as possible. In the event of the death of the victim as a result of an act of torture, his dependants shall be entitled to compensation.

2. Nothing in this article shall affect any right of the victim or other persons to compensation which may exist under national law.

Article 15

Each State Party shall ensure that any statement which is established to have been made as a result of torture shall not be invoked as evidence in any proceedings, except against a person accused of torture as evidence that the statement was made.

Article 16

1. Each State Party shall undertake to prevent in any territory under its

jurisdiction other acts of cruel, inhuman or degrading treatment or punishment which do not amount to torture as defined in article I, when such acts are committed by or at the instigation of or with the consent or acquiescence of a public official or other person acting in an official capacity. In particular, the obligations contained in articles 10, 11, 12 and 13 shall apply with the substitution for references to torture of references to other forms of cruel, inhuman or degrading treatment or punishment.

2. The provisions of this Convention are without prejudice to the provisions of any other international instrument or national law which prohibits cruel, inhuman or degrading treatment or punishment or which relates to extradition or expulsion.

PART II

Article 17

1. There shall be established a Committee against Torture (hereinafter referred to as the Committee) which shall carry out the functions hereinafter provided. The Committee shall consist of ten experts of high moral standing and recognized competence in the field of human rights, who shall serve in their personal capacity. The experts shall be elected by the States Parties, consideration being given to equitable geographical distribution and to the usefulness of the participation of some persons having legal experience.

2. The members of the Committee shall be elected by secret ballot from a list of persons nominated by States Parties. Each State Party may nominate one person from among its own nationals. States Parties shall bear in mind the usefulness of nominating persons who are also members of the Human Rights Committee established under the International Covenant on Civil and Political Rights and who are willing to serve on the Committee against Torture.

3. Elections of the members of the Committee shall be held at biennial meetings of States Parties convened by the Secretary-General of the United Nations. At those meetings, for which two thirds of the States Parties shall constitute a quorum, the persons elected to the Committee shall be those who obtain the largest number of votes and an absolute majority of the votes of the representatives of States Parties present and voting.

4. The initial election shall be held no later than six months after the date

of the entry into force of this Convention. At least four months before the date of each election, the Secretary-General of the United Nations shall address a letter to the States Parties inviting them to submit their nominations within three months. The Secretary-General shall prepare a list in alphabetical order of all persons thus nominated, indicating the States Parties which have nominated them, and shall submit it to the States Parties.

5. The members of the Committee shall be elected for a term of four years. They shall be eligible for re-election if re-nominated. However, the term of five of the members elected at the first election shall expire at the end of two years; immediately after the first election the names of these five members shall be chosen by lot by the chairman of the meeting referred to in paragraph 3 of this article.

6. If a member of the Committee dies or resigns or for any other cause can no longer perform his Committee duties, the State Party which nominated him shall appoint another expert from among its nationals to serve for the remainder of his term, subject to the approval of the majority of the States Parties. The approval shall be considered given unless half or more of the States Parties respond negatively within six weeks after having been informed by the Secretary-General of the United Nations of the proposed appointment.

7. States Parties shall be responsible for the expenses of the members of the Committee while they are in performance of Committee duties. (amendment (see General Assembly resolution 47/111 of 16 December, 1992); status of ratification)

Article 18

1. The Committee shall elect its officers for a term of two years. They may be re-elected.

2. The Committee shall establish its own rules of procedure, but these rules shall provide, inter alia, that:

(a) Six members shall constitute a quorum;

(b) Decisions of the Committee shall be made by a majority vote of the members present.

3. The Secretary-General of the United Nations shall provide the necessary staff and facilities for the effective performance of the functions of the Committee under this Convention.

4. The Secretary-General of the United Nations shall convene the initial

meeting of the Committee. After its initial meeting, the Committee shall meet at such times as shall be provided in its rules of procedure.

5. The States Parties shall be responsible for expenses incurred in connection with the holding of meetings of the States Parties and of the Committee, including reimbursement to the United Nations for any expenses, such as the cost of staff and facilities, incurred by the United Nations pursuant to paragraph 3 of this article. (amendment (see General Assembly resolution 47/111 of 16 December, 1992); status of ratification)

Article 19

1. The States Parties shall submit to the Committee, through the Secretary-General of the United Nations, reports on the measures they have taken to give effect to their undertakings under this Convention, within one year after the entry into force of the Convention for the State Party concerned. Thereafter the States Parties shall submit supplementary reports every four years on any new measures taken and such other reports as the Committee may request.

2. The Secretary-General of the United Nations shall transmit the reports to all States Parties.

3. Each report shall be considered by the Committee which may make such general comments on the report as it may consider appropriate and shall forward these to the State Party concerned. That State Party may respond with any observations it chooses to the Committee.

4. The Committee may, at its discretion, decide to include any comments made by it in accordance with paragraph 3 of this article, together with the observations thereon received from the State Party concerned, in its annual report made in accordance with article 24. If so requested by the State Party concerned, the Committee may also include a copy of the report submitted under paragraph I of this article.

Article 20

1. If the Committee receives reliable information which appears to it to contain well-founded indications that torture is being systematically practiced in the territory of a State Party, the Committee shall invite that State Party to co-operate in the examination of the information and to this end to submit observations with regard to the information concerned.

2. Taking into account any observations which may have been submitted by the State Party concerned, as well as any other relevant information available to it, the Committee may, if it decides that this is warranted, designate one or more of its members to make a confidential inquiry and to report to the Committee urgently.

3. If an inquiry is made in accordance with paragraph 2 of this article, the Committee shall seek the co-operation of the State Party concerned. In agreement with that State Party, such an inquiry may include a visit to its territory.

4. After examining the findings of its member or members submitted in accordance with paragraph 2 of this article, the Commission shall transmit these findings to the State Party concerned together with any comments or suggestions which seem appropriate in view of the situation.

5. All the proceedings of the Committee referred to in paragraphs I to 4 of this article s hall be confidential, and at all stages of the proceedings the co-operation of the State Party shall be sought. After such proceedings have been completed with regard to an inquiry made in accordance with paragraph 2, the Committee may, after consultations with the State Party concerned, decide to include a summary account of the results of the proceedings in its annual report made in accordance with article 24.

Article 21

1. A State Party to this Convention may at any time declare under this article that it recognizes the competence of the Committee to receive and consider communications to the effect that a State Party claims that another State Party is not fulfilling its obligations under this Convention. Such communications may be received and considered according to the procedures laid down in this article only if submitted by a State Party which has made a declaration recognizing in regard to itself the competence of the Committee. No communication shall be dealt with by the Committee under this article if it concerns a State Party which has not made such a declaration. Communications received under this article shall be dealt with in accordance with the following procedure;

(a) If a State Party considers that another State Party is not giving effect to the provisions of this Convention, it may, by written communication, bring the matter to the attention of that State Party. Within three months after the receipt of the communication the receiving State shall afford the State which sent the communication an explanation or any other statement in writing clarifying the matter, which should include, to the extent possible and pertinent, reference to domestic procedures and remedies taken, pending or available in the matter;

(b) If the matter is not adjusted to the satisfaction of both States Parties concerned within six months after the receipt by the receiving State of the initial communication, either State shall have the right to refer the matter to the Committee, by notice given to the Committee and to the other State;

(c) The Committee shall deal with a matter referred to it under this article only after it has ascertained that all domestic remedies have been invoked and exhausted in the matter, in conformity with the generally recognized principles of international law. This shall not be the rule where the application of the remedies is unreasonably prolonged or is unlikely to bring effective relief to the person who is the victim of the violation of this Convention;

(d) The Committee shall hold closed meetings when examining communications under this article;

(e) Subject to the provisions of subparagraph (c), the Committee shall make available its good offices to the States Parties concerned with a view to a friendly solution of the matter on the basis of respect for the obligations provided for in this Convention. For this purpose, the Committee may, when appropriate, set up an ad hoc conciliation commission;

(f) In any matter referred to it under this article, the Committee may call upon the States Parties concerned, referred to in subparagraph (b), to supply any relevant information;

(g) The States Parties concerned, referred to in subparagraph (b), shall have the right to be represented when the matter is being considered by the Committee and to make submissions orally and/or in writing;

(h) The Committee shall, within twelve months after the date of receipt of notice under subparagraph (b), submit a report:

(i) If a solution within the terms of subparagraph (e) is reached, the Committee shall confine its report to a brief statement of the facts and of the solution reached;

(ii) If a solution within the terms of subparagraph (e) is not reached, the Committee shall confine its report to a brief statement of the facts; the written submissions and record of the oral submissions made by the States Parties concerned shall be attached to the report.

In every matter, the report shall be communicated to the States Parties concerned.

2. The provisions of this article shall come into force when five States Parties to this Convention have made declarations under paragraph 1 of this article. Such declarations shall be deposited by the States Parties with the Secretary-General of the United Nations, who shall transmit copies thereof to the other States Parties. A declaration may be withdrawn at any time by notification to the Secretary-General. Such a withdrawal shall not prejudice the consideration of any matter which is the subject of a communication already transmitted under this article; no further communication by any State Party shall be received under this article after the notification of withdrawal of the declaration has been received by the Secretary-General, unless the State Party concerned has made a new declaration.

Article 22

1. A State Party to this Convention may at any time declare under this article that it recognizes the competence of the Committee to receive and consider communications from or on behalf of individuals subject to its jurisdiction who claim to be victims of a violation by a State Party of the provisions of the Convention. No communication shall be received by the Committee if it concerns a State Party which has not made such a declaration.

2. The Committee shall consider inadmissible any communication under this article which is anonymous or which it considers to be an abuse of the right of submission of such communications or to be incompatible with the provisions of this Convention.

3. Subject to the provisions of paragraph 2, the Committee shall bring any communications submitted to it under this article to the attention of the State Party to this Convention which has made a declaration under paragraph I and is alleged to be violating any provisions of the Convention. Within six months, the receiving State shall submit to the Committee written explanations or statements clarifying the matter and the remedy, if any, that may have been taken by that State.

4. The Committee shall consider communications received under this article in the light of all information made available to it by or on behalf of the individual and by the State Party concerned.

5. The Committee shall not consider any communications from an individual under this article unless it has ascertained that:

(a) The same matter has not been, and is not being, examined under another procedure of international investigation or settlement;

(b) The individual has exhausted all available domestic remedies; this shall not be the rule where the application of the remedies is unreasonably prolonged or is unlikely to bring effective relief to the person who is the victim of the violation of this Convention.

6. The Committee shall hold closed meetings when examining communications under this article.

7. The Committee shall forward its views to the State Party concerned and to the individual.

8. The provisions of this article shall come into force when five States Parties to this Convention have made declarations under paragraph 1 of this article. Such declarations shall be deposited by the States Parties with the Secretary-General of the United Nations, who shall transmit copies thereof to the other States Parties. A declaration may be withdrawn at any time by notification to the Secretary-General. Such a withdrawal shall not prejudice the consideration of any matter which is the subject of a communication already transmitted under this article; no further communication by or on behalf of an individual shall be received under this article after the notification of withdrawal of the declaration has been received by the Secretary-General, unless the State Party has made a new declaration.

Article 23

The members of the Committee and of the ad hoc conciliation commissions which may be appointed under article 21, paragraph I (e), shall be entitled to the facilities, privileges and immunities of experts on mission for the United Nations as laid down in the relevant sections of the Convention on the Privileges and Immunities of the United Nations.

Article 24

The Committee shall submit an annual report on its activities under this Convention to the States Parties and to the General Assembly of the United Nations.

PART III

Article 25

1. This Convention is open for signature by all States.
2. This Convention is subject to ratification. Instruments of ratification shall be deposited with the Secretary-General of the United Nations.

Article 26

This Convention is open to accession by all States. Accession shall be effected by the deposit of an instrument of accession with the Secretary-General of the United Nations.

Article 27

1. This Convention shall enter into force on the thirtieth day after the date of the deposit with the Secretary-General of the United Nations of the twentieth instrument of ratification or accession.
2. For each State ratifying this Convention or acceding to it after the deposit of the twentieth instrument of ratification or accession, the Convention shall enter into force on the thirtieth day after the date of the deposit of its own instrument of ratification or accession.

Article 28

1. Each State may, at the time of signature or ratification of this Convention or accession thereto, declare that it does not recognize the competence of the Committee provided for in article 20.
2. Any State Party having made a reservation in accordance with paragraph I of this article may, at any time, withdraw this reservation by notification to the Secretary-General of the United Nations.

Article 29

1. Any State Party to this Convention may propose an amendment and file it with the Secretary-General of the United Nations. The Secretary-

General shall thereupon communicate the proposed amendment to the States Parties with a request that they notify him whether they favor a conference of States Parties for the purpose of considering and voting upon the proposal. In the event that within four months from the date of such communication at least one third of the States Parties favors such a conference, the Secretary-General shall convene the conference under the auspices of the United Nations. Any amendment adopted by a majority of the States Parties present and voting at the conference shall be submitted by the Secretary-General to all the States Parties for acceptance.

2. An amendment adopted in accordance with paragraph I of this article shall enter into force when two thirds of the States Parties to this Convention have notified the Secretary-General of the United Nations that they have accepted it in accordance with their respective constitutional processes.

3. When amendments enter into force, they shall be binding on those States Parties which have accepted them, other States Parties still being bound by the provisions of this Convention and any earlier amendments which they have accepted.

Article 30

1. Any dispute between two or more States Parties concerning the interpretation or application of this Convention which cannot be settled through negotiation shall, at the request of one of them, be submitted to arbitration. If within six months from the date of the request for arbitration the Parties are unable to agree on the organization of the arbitration, any one of those Parties may refer the dispute to the International Court of Justice by request in conformity with the Statute of the Court.

2. Each State may, at the time of signature or ratification of this Convention or accession thereto, declare that it does not consider itself bound by paragraph I of this article. The other States Parties shall not be bound by paragraph I of this article with respect to any State Party having made such a reservation.

3. Any State Party having made a reservation in accordance with paragraph 2 of this article may at any time withdraw this reservation by notification to the Secretary-General of the United Nations.

Article 31

1. A State Party may denounce this Convention by written notification to the Secretary-General of the United Nations. Denunciation becomes effective one year after the date of receipt of- the notification by the Secretary-General.

2. Such a denunciation shall not have the effect of releasing the State Party from its obligations under this Convention in regard to any act or omission which occurs prior to the date at which the denunciation becomes effective, nor shall denunciation prejudice in any way the continued consideration of any matter which is already under consideration by the Committee prior to the date at which the denunciation becomes effective.

3. Following the date at which the denunciation of a State Party becomes effective, the Committee shall not commence consideration of any new matter regarding that State.

Article 32

The Secretary-General of the United Nations shall inform all States Members of the United Nations and all States which have signed this Convention or acceded to it of the following:

(a) Signatures, ratifications and accessions under articles 25 and 26;

(b) The date of entry into force of this Convention under article 27 and the date of the entry into force of any amendments under article 29;

(c) Denunciations under article 31.

Article 33

1. This Convention, of which the Arabic, Chinese, English, French, Russian and Spanish texts are equally authentic, shall be deposited with the Secretary-General of the United Nations.

2. The Secretary-General of the United Nations shall transmit certified copies of this Convention to all States.

M. THE AFRICAN RENAISSANCE STATEMENT OF SOUTH AFRICAN PRESIDENT, THABO MBEKI, 13 AUGUST, 1998

A struggle for political power is dragging the Kingdom of Lesotho toward the abyss of a violent conflict. The Democratic Republic of Congo is sliding back into a conflict of arms from which its people had hoped they had escaped forever.

The silence of peace has died on the borders of Eritrea and Ethiopia because, in a debate about an acre or two of land, guns have usurped the place of reason.

Those who had risked death in Guinea Bissau as they fought as comrades to evict the Portuguese colonialists, today stand behind opposing ramparts speaking to one another in the deadly language of bazooka and mortar shells and the fearsome rhythm of the beat of machine-gun fire.

A war seemingly without mercy rages in Algeria, made more horrifying by a savagery which seeks to anoint itself with the sanctity of a religious faith.

Thus can we say that the children of Africa, from north to south, from the east and the west and at the very center of our continent, continue to be consumed by death dealt out by those who have proclaimed a sentence of death on dialogue and reason and on the children of Africa whose limbs are too weak to run away from the rage of adults.

Both of these, the harbingers of death and the victims of their wrath, are as African as you and I.

For that reason, for the reason that we are the disemboweled African mothers and the decapitated African children of Rwanda, we have to say enough and no more.

It is because of these pitiful souls, who are the casualties of destructive force for whose birth they are not to blame, that Africa needs her renaissance.

Were they alive and assured that the blight of human made death had passed for ever, we would have less need to call for that renaissance.

In the summer of light and warmth and life-giving rain, it is to mock the gods to ask them for light and warmth and life-giving rain. The passionate hope for the warming rays of the sun is the offspring of the chill and dark nights of the winters of our lives.

Africa has no need for the criminals who would acquire political power by slaughtering the innocents as do the butchers of the people of Richmond in KwaZulu-Natal.

Nor has she need for such as those who, because they did not accept that power is legitimate only because it serves the interests of the people, laid Somalia to waste and deprived its people of a country which gave its citizens a sense of being as well as the being to build themselves into a people.

Neither has Africa need for the petty gangsters who would be our governors by theft of elective positions, as a result of holding fraudulent elections, or by purchasing positions of authority through bribery and corruption.

The thieves and their accomplices, the givers of the bribes and the recipients, are as African as you and I. We are the corrupter and the harlot who act together to demean our Continent and ourselves.

The time has come that we say enough and no more, and by acting to banish the shame, remake ourselves as the midwives of the African Renaissance.

An ill wind has blown me across the face of Africa. I have seen the poverty of Orlando East and the wealth of Morningside in Johannesburg. In Lusaka, I have seen the poor of Kanyama township and the prosperous residents of Kabulonga.

I have seen the African slums of Surulere in Lagos and the African opulence of Victoria Island. I have seen the faces of the poor in Mbari in Harare and the quiet wealth of Borrowdale.

And I have heard the stories of how those who had access to power, or access to those who had access to power, of how they have robbed and pillaged and broken all laws and all ethical norms and with great abandon, to acquire wealth, all of them tied by an invisible thread which they hope will connect them to Morningside and Borrowdale and Victoria Island and Kabulonga.

Everyday, you and I see those who would be citizens of Kabulonga and Borrowdale and Victoria Island and Morningside being born everywhere in our country. Their object in life is to acquire personal wealth by means both foul and fair.

Their measure of success is the amount of wealth they can accumulate and the ostentation they can achieve, which will convince all that they are a success, because, in a visible way, they are people of means.

Thus, they seek access to power or access to those who have access to power so that they can corrupt the political order for personal gain at all costs.

In this equation, the poverty of the masses of the people becomes a necessary condition for the enrichment of the few and the corruption of political power, the only possible condition for its exercise.

It is out of this pungent mixture of greed, dehumanizing poverty, obscene wealth, and endemic public and private corrupt practice, that many of Africa's coups d'etat, civil wars, and situations of instability are born and entrenched.

The time has come that we call a halt to the seemingly socially approved deification of the acquisition of material wealth and the abuse of state power to impoverish the people and deny our Continent the possibility to achieve sustainable economic development.

Africa cannot renew herself where its upper echelons are a mere parasite on the rest of society, enjoying as self-endowed mandate to use their political power and define the uses of such power such that its exercise ensures that our Continent reproduces itself as the periphery of the world economy, poor, underdeveloped and incapable of development.

The African Renaissance demands that we purge ourselves of the parasites and maintain a permanent vigilance against the danger of the entrenchment in African society of this rapacious stratum with its social morality according to which everything in society must be organized materially to benefit the few.

As we recall with pride the African scholar and author of the Middle Ages, Sadi of Timbuktu, who had mastered such subjects as law, logic, dialectics, grammar, and rhetoric, and other African intellectuals who taught at the University of Timbuktu, we must ask the question—where are Africa's intellectuals today?!

In our world in which the generation of new knowledge and its application to change the human condition is the engine which moves human society further away from barbarism, do we not have need to recall Africa's hundreds of thousands of intellectuals back from their places of emigration in Western Europe and North America, to rejoin those who remain still within our shores?!

I dream of the day when these, the African mathematicians and computer specialists in Washington and New York, the African physicists, engineers, doctors, business managers, and economists, will return from London and Manchester and Paris and Brussels to add to the African pool of brain power, to enquire into and find solutions to Africa's problems and challenges, to open the African door to the world of knowledge, to elevate Africa's place within the universe of research, the information of new knowledge, education, and information.

Africa's renewal demands that her intelligentsia must immerse itself in the titanic and all-around struggle to end poverty, ignorance, disease, and backwardness, inspired by the fact that the Africans of Egypt were, in some instances, two thousand years ahead of the Europeans of Greece in the mastery of such subjects as geometry, trigonometry, algebra, and chemistry.

To perpetuate their imperial domination over the peoples of Africa, the colonizers sought to enslave the African mind and to destroy the African soul.

They sought to oblige us to accept that as Africans we had contributed nothing to human civilization except as beasts of burden, in much the same way as those who are opposed to the emancipation of women seek to convince them that they have a place in human society, but only as beasts of burden and bearers of children.

In the end, they wanted us to despise ourselves, convinced that, if we were not sub-human, we were, at least, not equal to the colonial master and mistress and were incapable of original thought and the African creativity which has endowed the world with an extraordinary treasure of masterpieces in architecture and the fine arts.

The beginning of our rebirth as a Continent must be our own rediscovery of our soul, captured and made permanently available in the great works of creativity represented by the pyramids and sphinxes of Egypt, the stone buildings of Axum and the ruins of Carthage and Zimbabwe, the rock paintings of the San, the Benin bronzes and the African masks, the carvings of the Makonde and the stone sculptures of the Shona.

A people capable of such creativity could never have been less human than other human beings and being as human as any other, such a people can and must be its own liberator from the condition which seeks to describe our Continent and its people as the poverty stricken and disease ridden primitives in a world riding the crest of a wave of progress and human upliftment.

In that journey of self discovery and the restoration of our own self-esteem, without which we would never become combatants for the African Renaissance, we must re-tune our ears to the music of Zao and Franco of the Congos and the poetry of Mazisi Kunene of South Africa and refocus our eyes to behold the paintings of Malangatane of Mozambique and the sculptures of Dumile Feni of South Africa.

The call for Africa's renewal, for an African Renaissance, is a call to rebellion. We must rebel against the tyrants and the dictators, those who seek to corrupt our societies and steal the wealth that belongs to the people.

We must rebel against the ordinary criminals who murder, rape and rob, and conduct war against poverty, ignorance, and the backwardness of the children of Africa.

Surely, there must be politicians and business people, youth and women activists, trade unionists, religious leaders, artists, and professionals from the Cape to Cairo, from Madagascar to Cape Verde, who are sufficiently enraged by Africa's condition in the world to want to join the mass crusade for Africa's renewal.

It is to these that we say, without equivocation, that to be a true African is to be a rebel in the cause of the African Renaissance, whose success in the new century and millennium is one of the great historic challenges of our time.

Let the voice of the Senegalese, Sheik Anta Diop, be heard:

The African who has understood us is the one who, after reading of our works, would have felt a birth in himself, of another person, impelled by a historical conscience, a true creator, a Promethean carrier of a new civilization and perfectly aware of what the whole earth owes to his ancestral genius in all the domains of science, culture and religion.

Today each group of people, armed with its rediscovered or reinforced cultural identity, has arrived at the threshold of the post industrial era. An atavistic, but vigilant, African optimism inclines us to wish that all nations would join hands in order to build a planetary civilization instead of sinking down to barbarism.

Thank you.

Issued by: Office of the Executive Deputy President

N. DEMOCRATIC REPUBLIC OF CONGO MAPS

Map Provided by GraphicMaps.com Reprinted with Permission.

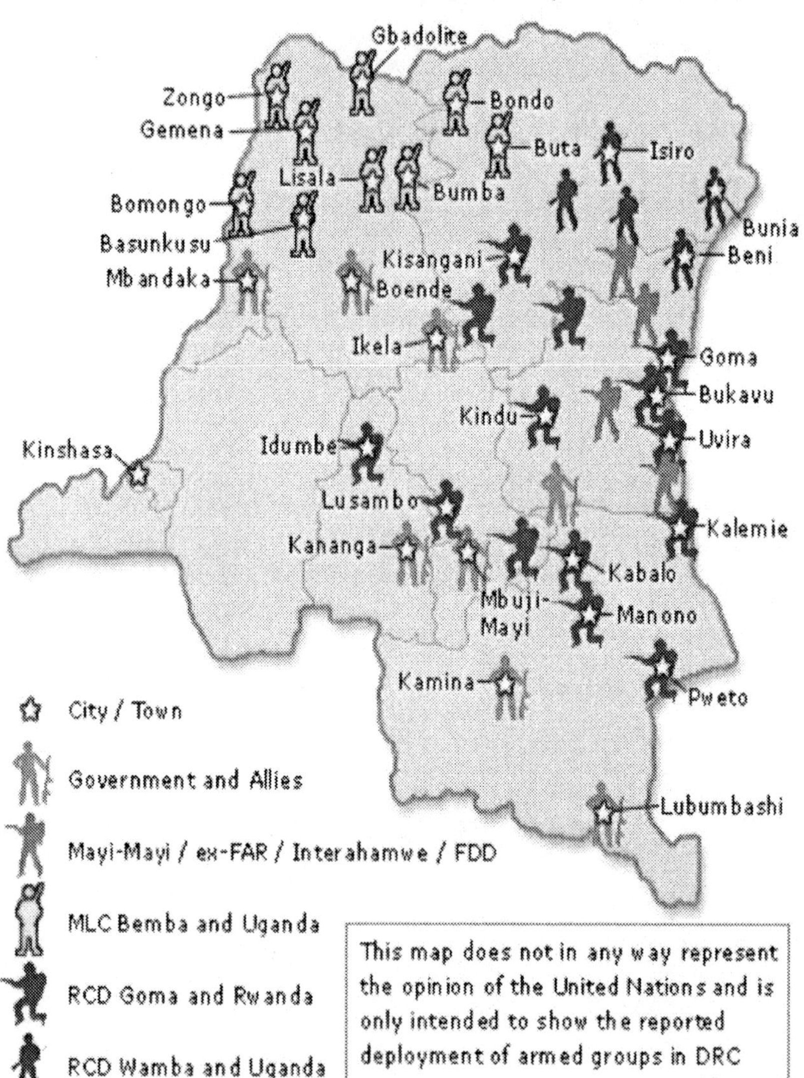
Approximate Deployment of Armed Groups in DRC
Source: IRIN-CEA, 28 March 2000
Gbadolite
Zongo
Gemena
Bondo
Buta
Isiro
Lisala
Bumba
Bomongo
Basunkusu
Bunia
Beni
Kisangani
Mbandaka
Boende
Ikela
Goma
Bukavu
Kindu
Uvira
Kinshasa
Idumbe
Lusambo
Kalemie
Kananga
Kabalo
Mbuji-Mayi
Manono
Kamina
Pweto
Lubumbashi
City / Town
Government and Allies
Mayi-Mayi / ex-FAR / Interahamwe / FDD
MLC Bemba and Uganda
RCD Goma and Rwanda
RCD Wamba and Uganda
This map does not in any way represent the opinion of the United Nations and is only intended to show the reported deployment of armed groups in DRC

C.A.R
SUDAN
GBADOLITE
CAMEROON
BUNIA
REP. OF CONGO
KISANGANI
GABON
GOMA
BUKAVU
KINSHASA
CONGO (DR)
MLC, UGANDA
RCD, RWANDA
CIRCA DEC 2002
LUBUMBASHI
ZAMBIA

O. AFRICA MAP

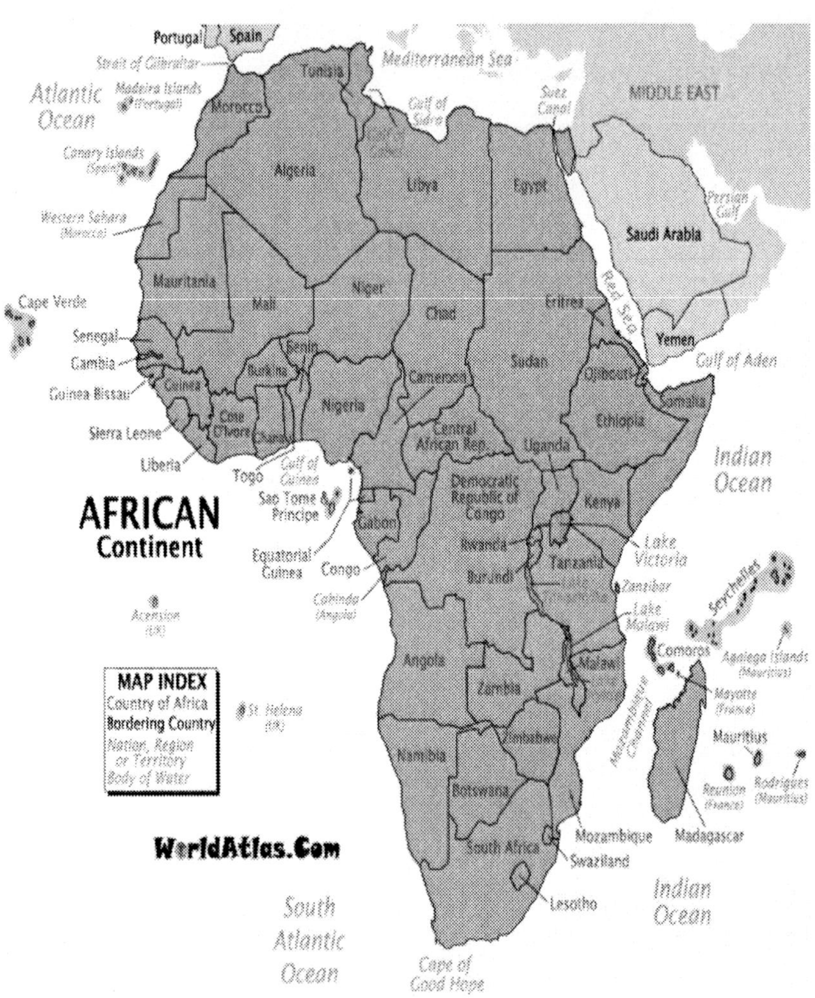

Map Provided by GraphicMaps.com Reprinted with Permission.

ABBREVIATIONS USED

ADF	Allied Democratic Forces
ADR	Alternative Dispute Resolution
AFDL	Alliance des forces démocratiques pour la libération du Congo-Zaïre (Alliance of Democratic Forces for the Liberation of Congo-Zaire)
AI	Amnesty International
AMF	American Mineral Fields
ATCA	Alien Tort Claims Act
AU	African Union
CIA	Central Intelligence Agency
COJESKI	Collectif des Organisations et associations des jeunes du Sud-Kivu en RDC (Group of Organizations and Associations of the Youth of South Kivu)
COLTAN	Columbo-tantalite
DGLI	Dara Great Lakes Industries
DRC	Democratic Republic of Congo
DR CONGO	Democratic Republic of Congo
DSP	Division Spéciale Présidentielle (Presidential Special Division)
ECOSOC	Economic and Social Council

EU	European Union
Ex-FAR	Ex-Forces Armées Rwandaises (Former Rwandese Armed Forces)
Ex-FAZ	Ex-Forces Armées Zaïroises (Former Zairean Armed Forces)
FAC	Forces Armées Congolaises (Congolese Armed Forces)
FDD	Forces pour la Défense de la Démocratie (Forces for the Defense of Democracy in Burundi)
FUNA	Former Uganda National Army
HCR-PT	High Council of the Republic-Parliament of Transition
HIPC	Highly Indebted Poor Countries
HIV/AIDS	Human Immuno Virus/Acquired Immuno Defiency Syndrom
ICC	International Criminal Court
ICJ	International Court of Justice
ICRC	International Committee of the Red Cross/Red Crescent
ICTR	International Criminal Tribunal for Rwanda
ICTY	International Criminal Tribunal for the Former Yugoslavia
ICU	Intensive Care Unit
IHL	International Humanitarian Law
IMF	International Monetary Fund

IRIN	Integrated Regional Information Network
JMC	Joint Military Commission
LRA	Lord's Resistance Army
MLC	Movement for the Liberation of Congo
MONUC	Mission des Nations Unies en République démocratique du Congo (United Nations Organization Mission in the Democratic Republic of Congo)
NALU	National Army for the Liberation of Uganda
NEPAD	New Partnership for African Development
NGO	Non-Governmental Organization
NRM	National Resistance Movement
OAU	Organisation of African Unity
OPIC	Overseas Private Investment Corporation
P-5	Five Permanent Members of the United Nations Security Council
PCNICC	Preparatory Commission for the International Criminal Court
RCD	Congolese Rally for Democracy
RCD/N	Congolese Rally for Democracy/National
RPA	Rwandan Patriotic Army
SADC	Southern Africa Development Community

SNEL	Societé Nationale d'Eléctricité (National Company of Electricty)
TVPA	Torture Victims Protection Act
UDF	Ugandan Defense Forces
UK	United Kingdom
UN	United Nations Organisation
UNHCHR	United Nations High Commissioner for Human Rights
UNITA	National Union for the Total Independence of Angola
UNRF II	Uganda National Rescue Front II
UNS/PRST	United Nations Security Council Presidential Statement
UNS/RES	United Nations Security Council Resolution
UNSC	United Nations Security Council
UPC	Congolese Patriotic Union
US	United States
USA	United States of America
USCA	United States Code Annoted
USSR	Union of Sovietics Socialist Republics
WB	World Bank
WHO	World Health Organization
WNBF	West Nile Bank Front

Endnotes

1. Literal translation: Man is a wolf to another man.

2. Moira Rayner, *History of human rights. History of Universal Human Rights - Up to WW2*, http://www.universalrights.net/main/histof.html.

3. NCN 2000, *The Democratic Republic of Congo: The Lusaka Peace Accords and Beyond.* The public hearings of the Subcommittee on Africa, Committee on International Relations, Us House of Representatives, Washington, DC. September 28, 1999. *Testimony of Mwabilu L.Ngoyi, assisted by Dr. Kanyand Matand.* wysigwyg:/255/http://www.marekinc.com/NCNLegislate092806.html.

4. Dr. Reginald Moreels, *"Boboto – Amani", A Report for Peace*, given at the "*International Conference on Armed Conflicts in the Democratic Republic of Congo on the Eve of the Inter-Congolese Dialogue in South Africa: Building a Sustainable Peace in the Great Lakes Region*", Pretoria, February 2002, at 4. Dr. Moreels is the Belgian Special envoy for Humanitarian Affairs for the Great Lakes region.

5. Kristin Connor, *Chaos in the Congo, Las Cruces Sun – News*, 123rd year, No.105, July 14, 2003.

6. Moira Rayner, ibid.

7. United Nations, *Report of the Secretary-General on the work of the Organization*, General Assembly, Official Records, Fifty-fifth session, Supplement No. 1, (A/55/1), New York, August 30, 2000.

8. Rigobert N. Butandu, in *The Causes and Legal Consequences of Military*

Coups d'Etat in Black Africa, and Their Implications on International Law: A Case Study of the Democratic Republic of Congo under Mobutu Regime (1965-1997), LL.M. Dissertation, J. Reuben Clark Law School, Brigham Young University, Provo, Utah, 2000, for a detailed discussion. The work has been improved for publication under the title "*The Coup that kills African and its Implications in Law*".

9. David Matas, *No More. The battle against human rights violations.* Toronto/Oxford: Dundurn Press, 1994, at 5.

10.NCN 2000, *The Democratic Republic of Congo: The Lusaka Peace Accords and Beyond. ibid.*

11.Several reports on the Rwandan genocide mentioned both the Hutus and Tutsis as the perpetrators, but not only the former as widely known.

12.Ellen Ray, *Us Military and Corporate Re-colonization of the Congo,* Covert action Quarterly Spring-Summer 2000 #9. http://www.covertaction.org. Copyright © 2000 by Ellen Ray; permission to reproduce granted by the Institute for Media Analysis, Inc.

13.*International Non-Governmental Commission of Inquiry into the Massive Violations of Human Rights Committed in the Democratic Republic of Congo (Former Zaire) 1996-1997.* Report prepared by the International Center for Human Rights and Democratic Development (Montreal Canada) (ICHRDD) and l'Association Africaine pour la Défense des Droits de l' Homme en République Démocratique du Congo (Kinshasa) (ASADHO), 1998.

14.David Matas, Ibid., at 19-20.

15.Ibid., at 20-21.

16.Ibid., at 21.

17.Organizations des Nations Unies, Mission de la République Démocratique du Congo. Great Lakes Policy Forum, Washington D.C., *Rwanda and Uganda Aggression Against the Democratic Republic of Congo.* http://rdcongo.org/frames/acp/UN_RDC03.html.

18.Human Rights Watch World Report, *Rwanda. Human Rights Developments*. http://www.hrw.org/hrw/worldreport99/africa/rwanda.html. © 1999 Human Rights Watch. Reprinted with Permission.

19.Human Rights Watch World Report 1999, *The Democratic Republic of Congo. The Role of the International Community.* http://www.hrw.org./hrw/worldreport99/africa/drc3.html. © 1999 Human Rights Watch. Reprinted with Permission.

20.The leaders of so-called rebellion from 1998 to 2003 masterminded, armed and trained by Rwanda and Uganda, claimed that they were fighting a second war of liberation in the DR Congo.

21.Interview with a Congolese national and political refugee in the US, November 1999.

22.Marguerite Michaels, *The Bleeding Heart of Africa.* In *Time Magazine*, March 15, 1999, at 63.

23.Kamanga Mutond, *Congo Imposes Curfew Amid Gunfire.* http://search.washingtonpost.com/wp-srv/WAPO/19980803/V000370-080398-idx.html

24.Human Rights Watch World Report 1999, *The Democratic Republic of Congo. Human Rights Development.* http://www.hrw.org/hrw/world Report99/africa/drc.html. © 1999Human Rights Watch. Reprinted with Permission.

25.Ellen Ray, ibid.

26.Colette Braeckman, *Politique. Jean-Charles Magabe, Sur la situation qui prévaut dans la province controleé par la rébellion et les sentiments de la population* . . . In Congonline (Le Soir-31/10/98). http://www.congonline.com/Actualite_Politique/Octobre98/Les12.html.

27.Kirungi F. Fideri, *D.R. Congo: Who is Museveni kidding?* African News Online. The Monitor - Kampala. http://www.africanews.org/central/c...inshsa/stories/19981010_feat1.html.

28.NCN 2000, *The Democratic Republic of Congo: The Lusaka Peace Accords and Beyond.* Ibid.
29.NCN 2000, Ibid.
30.UN, Annual Report of the Secretary-General on the Work of the Organization, A/53/1, par. 17 & 18, 27 August 1998.

31.Congonline, *Politique. Compte rendu de la Tripartite de Lubumbashi fait par le Président Mugabe.* http://congonline.com/Actualite_Politique/Novembre98/ACP01.html.

32.*Time Magazine*, Ibid.

33.NCN 2000, *The Democratic Republic of Congo: The Lusaka Peace Accords and Beyond.* Ibid.

34.Organisation des Nations Unies Mission de la République Démocratique du Congo, Great Lakes Policy Forum, Washington D.C. *Rwanda and Uganda Aggression Against the Democratic Republic of the Congo.* Ibid.

35.Colette Braeckman, Ibid.

36.NCN 2000, Ibid.

37.Ellen Ray, ibid.

38.*Organisation des Nations Unies Mission de la République Démocratique du Congo, 53ième Session de l'Assemblée Générale de l'Organisation des Nations-Unies*, New York, September 23, 1998. Speech of His Excellence Jean-Charles Okito, Minister of Foreign Affairs of the Democratic Republic of Congo.

39.Human Rights Watch World Report 1999, *The Democratic Republic of Congo. Human Rights Development.* Ibid. © 1999 Human Rights Watch. Reprinted with Permission.

40.Organisation des Nations Unies Mission de la République Démocratique du Congo, Great Lakes Policy Forum, Washington D.C. *Rwanda and Uganda Aggression Against the Democratic Republic of Congo*, Ibid.

41.Flory Kante, *Le Palmares Politique. Paul Kagame s'accroche aux diamants de la RDC: 20.000 soldats Rwandais largués dans notre pays!* Le Palmares no 1665, at 8, 20/10/1999.

42.République Démocratique du Congo, Ministère des Droits Humains, Cabinet du Ministre, *Livre Blanc, Tome 3, Sur les Violations Délibérées de l'Accord de Cessez-le-Feu de Lusaka du 10 Juillet 1999, de la Charte Internationale des Droits de l'Homme, des Régles de Base du Droit International Humanitaire ainsi que des Résolutions Pertinentes du Conseil de Sécurité de l'ONU par les Aggresseurs (Ouganda, Rwanda, Burundi) et leurs Complices Congolais du RCD et du MLC dans les Territoires Occupés de la République Démocratique du Congo, Couvrant la Période du 11 Juillet 1999 au 31 Décembre 1999*, Kinshasa, Janvier 2000, at 6.22.

43.Human Rights Watch World Report 1999, *Rwanda. Human Rights Developments*. Ibid. © 1999 Human Rights Watch. Reprinted with Permission.

44.Prepared Statement of Keith Snow at a roundtable discussion organized by Congresswoman Cynthia McKinney at the Rayburn House Office Building to discuss American Foreign Policy toward Africa, *Covert Action in Africa: A Smoking Gun in Washington*, 6 April 2001. See Annex G for entire text.

45.Marguerite Michaels, Ibid.

46.See the Report of the Panel of Experts on the Illegal Exploitation of Congolese Natural and Mineral Resources, and Form of Wealths, in Annexure B.

47.David Matas, ibid., at 17.

48.Ellen Ray, ibid.

49.Prepared Statement of Ellen Ray at a roundtable discussion organized by Congresswoman Cynthia McKinney at the Rayburn House Office Building to discuss American Foreign Policy toward Africa, ibid. http://www.marekinc.com/USPolicy05051C.html.

50.Congonline, Politique. *Solution à la guerre en RDC. Me Kamanda exhorte*

les Congolais à un ressaisissement. (La Référence Plus - 12/11/98). http://www.congoline.com/Actualite_Politique/November98/Refer45.html.
51.Ibid.

52.A/Res/2625 (XXV) http://ods-dds-ny.un.org/doc/RESOLUTION/GEN/NR0/348/90/IMG/NR034890.pdf?OpenElement. See also République du Congo, Ministère des Droits Humains, Cabinet du Ministre, *Livre Blanc, Tome 3,* at 21, par.93.

53.République Démocratique du Congo, Ministère des Droits Humains, Cabinet du Ministre, *Livre Blanc, Tome 3,* at 20, par. 88-89. See entire Twinning Agreement in Annex D.

54.See Annexure O.

55.A flawed Cease-fire Agreement between some warring parties in the DR Congo and their allies, which has "legitimated" the rebellion, which does not include and discriminate against other armed groups, and that fails to address the rights and interests of the Congolese people. See entire Agreement in Annexure A.

56.Prepared Statement of Ellen Ray, ibid.

57.Amos Yoder, The Evolution of the United Nations System, Third Edition, Taylor & Francis, 1997, at137. See also A/Res/2625 (XXV) of 24 October 1970.

58.Moira Rayner, *History of human rights. History of Universal Human Rights - Up to WW2*, Ibid.

59.Burns H. Weston, *Human Rights. International human rights: prescription and enforcement. Human Rights in the United Nations (from the Encyclopedia Britannica).* http://www.uiowa.edu/~hr98/resources/basics/weston4.html.

60.Kim Gleeson, *World influence of the UDHR. Worldwide Influence of the Universal Declaration of Human Rights and the International Bill of Rights.* http://www.universalrights.net/main/world.html. See also Universal Declaration of Human Rights in Annexure E.

61.Organisation des Nations Unies Mission de la République Démocratique du Congo, *53ième Session de l'Assemblée Générale de l'Organisation des Nations Unies. Speech by His Excellency Jean-Charles Okoto, Minister of Foreign Affairs of the Democratic Republic of Congo*, Ibid.

62.NCN 2000, *The Democratic Republic of Congo: The Lusaka Peace Accords and Beyond*. Ibid.

63.David Matas, Ibid., at 6.

64.*International Non-Governmental Commission of Inquiry Into The Massive Violations of Human Rights Committed in the Democratic Republic of Congo (Former Zaire) 1996-1997*. Ibid., at 15. Cited in Lexique de Géopolitique, Dalloz, Paris, 1998, at 10.

65.Henry J. Steiner & Philip Alston, *International Human Rights in Context. Law, Politics, Morals*. Oxford: Clarendon Press, 1996, at 100. By Permission of Oxford University Press.

66.*Preparatory Commission for the International Criminal Court, Working Group on the Crime of Aggression*. New York, 16-26 February 1999, 26 July-13 August 1999, 29 November-17 December 1999. *Discussion paper proposed by the Coordinator. Consolidated text of proposals of the Crime of Aggression*, 9 December 1999, at 1-2.

67.Bryan A. Garner, *Black's Law Dictionary*, Seventh Ed. , West Group, ST. PAUL, MINN., 1999, at 66.

68.Ibid., at 829.

69.République Démocratique du Congo, Ministère des Affaires Etrangères et de la Coopération Internationale, Cabinet du Ministre, Mémoire sur les Evénéments de Kisangani, Couvrant la Période d'Août 1999 à Mai 2002, Kinshasa, Septembre 2002, at 8, par. 49.

70.See UN S/RES/1078 (1996) 9 November 1996; UN S/RES/1097 (1997) 18 February 1997.

71.Rigobert N. Butandu, ibid.

72.Amos Yoder, ibid., at 123.

73.See Rigobert N. Butandu, ibid, for a detailed discussion on this issue, unedited.

74.In 1977 and 1978, for example, Mobutu called on French and Moroccan troops to back the Zairean armies fighting rebels' attacks in the Katanga province.

75.International Non-Governmental Commission of Inquiry into the Massive Violations of Human Rights Committed in the Democratic Republic of Congo (former Zaire) 1996-1997, Ibid., at 15.

76.Amos Yoder, ibid.

77.See also *Case Concerning Armed Activities on the Territory of the Congo (Democratic Republic of Congo v. Uganda). Request for the Indication of Provisional Measures, Order*, at Section 24, International Court of Justice, 1 July 2000. http://www.icj-cij.org/icjwww/idocket/ico/ico_orders/iCO_iOrder_20000701.htm.

78.David Matas, ibid., at 18.

79.Henry J. Steiner and Philip Alston, ibid., at 787.

80.Rome Statute of the International Criminal Court. *Adopted by the United Nations Diplomatic Conference of Plenipotentiaries on the Establishment of an International Criminal Court on 17 July 1998.* http://www.un.org/icc/part1.html. See also Annexure H.

81.Black's Law Dictionary, ibid., at 694-695. *The Draft Convention on the Prevention and Punishment of the Crime of Genocide was adopted by the General Assembly on December 9, 1948 and unanimously recommended for adherence to the members of the United Nations. It came into force in October, 1950 between twenty-four states. The term "genocide" was first proposed by Dr. Lemkin in the course of the war and incorporated on his suggestion on the Indictment of the Major German War Criminals. The Assembly Resolution on Genocide of December 11, 1946, and the Convention of 1948, are also the result of a remarkable one-man campaign." Georg Schwarzenberger, Power Politics: A Study of International Society 634 (2d ed. 1951).*

82.Kirungi F. Fideri, Ibid.

83.David Matas, ibid., at 19.

84.Congonline, Politique. *Des liberateurs pillards. Des soldats tutsi pillent l'archidiocèse de Bukavu et emportent USD 120.000 à Kigali.* Ibid.

85.United Nations Security Council Resolution 1355 of 15 June 2001.

86.The CIA World Fact Book: Uganda estimates for this country explicitly takes into account the effects of excess mortality due to AIDS, 1 August, 2003. http://www.cia.gov/cia/publications/factbook/geos/ug.html. See also An Overview of AIDS/HIV in Uganda-Presentation, Magnitude of the Epidemic. 1.9 millions Cumulative HIV infection has been reported since the epidemic started in Uganda in 1982. Of these 1.4 millions are living with HIV; about 500.000 have died of AIDS; 120.000 are living with AIDS; 7% of the adult population in Uganda is HIV infected. http://www.health.go.ug/index2.htm.

87.*International Non-Governmental Commission of Inquiry into Massive Violations of Human Rights Committed in the Democratic Republic of Congo (former Zaire) 1996- 1997*, ibid., at 71.

88.Today with reference to the CIA World Book Fact of 1 August, 2003, Botswana has an estimated population of 1,573,267; the Republic of Congo 2,954,258; Gabon 1,321,560; Gambia 1,501,050 (estimation of July 2003); Lesotho 1,861,959; Mauritius 1,210,447 (estimation of July 2003); and Swaziland 1,161,219. Given the fact that today the DR Congo tragedy has cost the lives of over 4,5000,000 victims, it should be considered that the premises that each of the populations in these countries taken individually were all destroyed. In addition, each combined pair of populations in these countries were killed during a war, and further to the following triple combination of the populations of these were also decimated: first, Botswana, Gambia and Swaziland; second, Botswana, Gabon and Gambia; third, Botswana, Gabon and Mauritius; fourth, Botswana, Gabon and Swaziland; fifth, Gabon, Gambia and Mauritius; sixth, Gabon, Gambia and Swaziland; seventh, Gambia, Mauritius and Swaziland; and eight, Lesotho, Mauritius and Swaziland. See also http://www.cia.gov/cia/publications/factbook/index.html.

89. Latin maxime meaning, "Matters will throw light upon (other) matters."

90. Henry J. Steiner & Philip Alston, ibid.

91. Black's Law Dictionary, ibid., at 1577. See also Article 8 of the Rome Statute of the International Criminal Court for the ICC definition of war crimes, Annexure H.

92. Henry J. Steiner & Philip Alston, ibid.

93. Black's Law Dictionary, ibid., at 378.

94. Rome Statue of the International Criminal Court, as corrected by the procés-verbaux of 10 November, 1998 and 12 July, 1999. www.un.org/law/icc/statute/99_corr/cstatute.htm.

95. IRIN, *Democratic Republic of Congo: 6,000 deaths in war's first year*. http://www.reliefweb.int/IRIN/cea/countrystories/D.R.c/19991104.html.

96. United Nations, General Assembly, A/RES/56/173, Distr.: General, Fifty-sixth session, par.2(c) (i). 27 February, 2002. See also United Nations, General Assembly, A/RES/57/233, Distr.: General, Fifty-seventh session, par. 2(b), 28 January 2003.

97. République du Congo, Ministère des Droits Humains, Cabinet du Ministre, *Livre Blanc, Tome 3,* at 48.

98. Ibid. at 59-63. Author's French-English translation.

99. République Démocratique du Congo, Ministère des Droits Humains,

Cabinet du Ministre, *Livre Blanc, Tome 2, Sur les Violations Massive des droits de l'Homme, des Régles de base du droit International Humanitaire, ainsi que des Normes Relatives à la Protection de l'Environnement par les Pays Agresseurs (Ouganda, Rwanda, Burundi) et leurs Complices Congolais à l' Est de la République Démocratique du Congo, Couvrant la Période du 06 Novembre 1998 au 30 Avril 1999, at 55.*

100. République Démocratique du Congo, Ministère des Droits Humains, Cabinet du Ministre, *Livre Blanc, Tome 3,* at 47.

101. Mail & Guardian, *Rape a Daily Horror in Eastern Congo*, Opinion, 24 May 2002; posted to the web by James Astill, Bukavu, D.R. Congo, 23 May 2002. See also http://www.guardian.co.uk/international/story/0,3604,717648,00.html?79%3A+International+news+-+guardian

102. Human Rights Watch, *Sexual Violence Rampant, Unpunished in DR Congo War*, June 20, 2002. http://www.hrw.org/press/2002/06/congo0620.htm © 2002Human Rights Watch. Reprinted with Permission. See the entire Human Rights Watch Report titled THE WAR WITHIN THE WAR, *Sexual Violence Against Women and Girls in Eastern Congo* at http://www.hrw.org/reports/2002/DRC/.

103. *International Non-Governmental Commission of Inquiry into the Massive Violations of Human Rights Committed in the Democratic Republic of Congo (former Zaïre) 1996- 1997.* Ibid., at 19.

104. Human Rights Watch World Report 1999, *the Democratic Republic of Congo. Human Rights Developments*. Ibid. © 1999Human Rights Watch. Reprinted with Permission.

105. IRIN, ibid.

106. Dr. Réginald Moreels, ibid., at 19.

107. IRIN, *Democratic Republic of Congo: Bleak picture of life along ceasefire line.* http://www.reliefweb.int/IRIN/cea/countrystories/D.R.c/19991011.html.

108. Dr. Réginald Moreels, ibid., at 7.

109. The official response of Rwanda is that they had a much disciplined and well-controlled army in the DR Congo, and therefore their troops had never committed any violation of international human rights and humanitarian international laws. But even though, many years had passed and none will remember what really took place in terms of atrocities and violations of the laws of nations. Still, Rwanda argued that those who have evidence of such violations should bring them forth.

110. See République Démocratique du Congo, Ministère des Droits Humains, Cabinet du Ministre, *Livre Blanc, Tome 3,* at 11, par. 43-45.

111. David Philip, *Nelson Mandela Speaks, Forging a Democratic, Non-racial South Africa,* Pathfinder, 1993 & David Philip Publishers & Mayibuye Books, 1994, at 85.

112. Colette Braeckman, ibid.

113. David Matas, Ibid.

114. Rich Mkhondo, *Terrorism, in Crimes of War; What The Public Should Know*, Edited by Roy Gutman and David Rieff, W.W. Norton & Company Ltd., New York/London, 1999, at 350.

115. Bryan A. Garner, ibid., at 1484.

116. Treaty on Cooperation among the States Members of the Commonwealth of Independent States in Combating Terrorism, 1999. See also, OAU Convention on the Prevention and Combating of Terrorism, 1999, Adopted at Algiers on 14 July, 1999. Entry into force in accordance with Article 20. http://untreaty.un.org/English/Terrorism/oau_e.pdf.

117. A/RES/49/60, ANNEX, *Declaration on Measures to Eliminate International Terrorism,* 84th plenary meeting, 9 December, 1994.

118. Nelson Mandela, ibid.

119. Inter-American Commission on Human Rights, Organization of American States, *Report on Terrorism and Human Rights,* OEA/Ser.L/V/II.116, Doc. 5 rev. 1 corr., 22 October, 2002. http://www.cidh.oas.org/Terrorism/Eng/toc.htm. © 2002 Inter-American Commission on Human Rights. Reprinted with Permission.

120. Human Rights Watch, Human Rights News, Human Rights Watch Response to Attacks on the Us , *Civilian Life Must Be Respected,* (New York, September 12, 2001). htpp://www.hrw.org/press/index.htm. ©2001 Human Rights Watch. Reprinted with Permission.

121. République Démocratique du Congo, Ministère des Droits Humains, Cabinet du Ministre, *Livre Blanc, Tome 2,* at 35, par. 135.

122. Kristin Connor, ibid.

123. République Démocratique du Congo, Ministère des Droits Humains, Cabinet du Ministre, *Livre Blanc, Tome 3,* at 64-66, 72-76.

124. Ed. Marek, ibid. Only very selective pictures are reproduced here for courteous to sensitive viewers. See more detailed photos of the Congolese tragedies in the three Livre Blanc of the Democratic Republic of Congo published both by the Ministers of Human Rights and Foreign Affairs and International Cooperation and listed herein in the bibliography. Visit also the following websites, but viewers discretion is advised for many of these are very graphic: http://www.congovision.com/massacres_files/frame.htm, http://www.worldrevolution.org/Projects/PhotoArchive/PhotoSlideshow.asp?Topic=africa

125. Henry J. Steiner & Philip Alston, ibid., at 787.

126. IRIN, *Democratic Republic of Congo. Government alleges UN inaction.* http://www.reliefweb.int/IRIN/cea/countrystories/D.R.c/19991019.html.

127. Human Rights Watch World Report 1999, *The Democratic Republic of Congo.* Ibid. © 1999 Human Rights Watch. Reprinted with Permission.

128. NCN 2000, *The Democratic Republic of Congo: The Lusaka Peace*

Accords and Beyond, Ibid.

129. B.Y., Congonline. Politique. *Solution à la guerre en DRC Me Kamanda exhorte les Congolais à un ressaisissement national*, Ibid.

130. From, *Preparing for power, Oliver Tambo Speaks*, by Adelaide Tambo. Reprinted by permission of Hacourt Education, 1987, at 64.

131. David Matas, Ibid., at 11.

132. Ibid., at 5.

133. Kurt Jonassohn with Karin Solveig Björnson, *Genocide and Gross Human Rights Violations in Comparative Perspective*. New Brunswick/ London: Transaction Publishers, at 133.

134. David Philip, ibid., at 196.

135. Bruce Hendrickson, *The Fate of the Congolese People is in Your Hands. A Message to Britain, France, and the United States*, in NCN 2000. http:// www. Marekinc.com/NCNEditorchoiceD.R.C111001.html.

136. Amos Yoder, ibid., at 121-122.

137. NCN 2000, *The rape of the Congo, blame the victim, and the rapist walks*, November 27, 2001.

138. There are at least twenty-three Security Council Resolutions from 2 August 1998 when the occupation of the D.R.C began to 15 November 2003 when the UN released the final Report on the Illegal Exploitation of Congolese Resources and other forms of Wealth: S/Res./1234 of 9 April 1999, S/Re./ 1258 of 6 August 1999, S/Res./1273 of 5 November 1999, S/Res./1279 of 30 November 1999, S/Res./1291 of 24 February 2000, S/Res./1304 of 16 June 2000, S/Res./1316 of 23 August 2000, S/Res./1318 of 7 September 2000, S/ Res./1323 of 13 October 2000, S/Res./1332 of 14 December 2000, S/Res./ 1341 of 22 February 2001, S/Res./1355 of 15 June 2001, S/Res./1376 of 9 November 2001, S/Res./1399 of 19 March 2002, S/Res./1417 of 14 June 2002, S/Res./1445 of 4 December 2002, S/Res./1457 of 24 January 2003, S/

Res./1468 of 20 March 2003, /Res./1484 of 30 May 2003, S/Res./1489 of 26 June 2003, S/Res./1493 of 28 July 2003, S/Res./1499 of 13 August 2003, and S/Res./1501 of 26 August 2003.

139. See also S/PRST/1998/26 of 31 August 1998; S/PRST/1998/36 of 11 December 1998; S/PRST/1999/17 of 24 June 1999; S/PRST/2000/2 of 26 January 2000; S/PRST/2000/15 of 5 May 2000; S/PRST/2000/20 of 2 June 2000; S/PRST/2000/28 of 7 September 2000; S/PRST/2001/13 of 3 May 2001; S/PRST/2001/19 of 24 July 2001; S/PRST/2001/22 of 5 September 2001; S/PRST/2001/29 of 24 October 2001; S/PRST/2001/39 of 19 Decemebr 2001; S/PRST/2002/5 of 25 February 2002; S/PRST/2002/17 of 24 May 2002; S/PRST/2002/19 of 5 June 2002; S/PRST/2002/22 of 23 July 2002; S/PRST/2002/24 of 15 August 2002; S/PRST/2002/27 of 18 October 2002; S/PRST/2003/6.

140. See integral Resolution in Annexure C.

141. Chapter VII of the UN Charter set forth the procedures that the Security Council must follow on the Action to be taken by this entity with Respect to The Threats to the Peace, Breaches of the Peace, and Acts of Aggression. See its articles 39, 41 and 42 above.

142. S/2003/1027, *Final Report of the Panel of Experts on the Illegal Exploitation of Natural Resources and Other Forms of Wealth of the Democratic Republic of the Congo,* 15 October, 2003, paragraph 16.

143. S/1999/815; see also Annexure A for full text.

144. UN S/Res/1279 of 30 November, 1999 and UN S/Res/1291 of 24 February, 2000.

145. UN S/Res/1304 of 16 June, 2000.

146. UN S/Res/1468, Art. 2, of 20 March, 2003.

147. UN S/Res/1304, Art. 4, of 16 June, 2000.

148. NCN 2000, *The Democratic Republic of Congo: The Lusaka Peace*

Accords and Beyond. Ibid.

149. David Philip, ibid., at 62.

150. The Star, in Opinion & Analysis, Thursday, September 19, 2002 Edition. Dr. Firoz Osman is the Secretary of the Media Review Network, an advocacy group based in Pretoria, South Africa.

151. Brendalyn P. Ambrose, *Democratization and the Protection of Human Rights in Africa.Problems and Prospects*. Westport: Praeger Publishers, 1995, at 163.

152. Marguerite Michaels, Ibid.

153. Kurt Jonassohn with Karin Solveig Björnson, ibid., at 118.

154. Prepared Statement of Ellen Ray, ibid.

155. Mr. Agrrey Awori is an Ugandan politician and Member of the Ugandan Parliament.

156. NCN 2000, *The rape of the Congo, blame the victim, and the rapist walks*, ibid.

157. Prepared Statement of Keith Snow, ibid.

158. Report of the Panel of Experts on the Illegal Exploitation of Natural Resources and Other Forms of Wealth of the Democratic Republic of the Congo, April 12, 2001. See full text in Annexure B.

159. Bruce Hendrickson, ibid.

160. Freddy Monsa Iyaka Duku, *Les dessous des cartes de l'instabilité en Afrique: La guerre en RDC: rivalité americano-européenne*, in le Palmares Politique, ibid., at 3.

161. Maitre Franco Luambo Makiadi, a modern figure of the Congolese musical family died in 1989.

162. NCN 2000, *UN says Tutsi community face imminent threat in DRC.* http://www.marekinc.com/Letters122502.html

163. Moreels, R., ibid.

164. Ellen Ray, ibid.

165. *The Star*, Ibid.

166. Joseph R. Biden Jr., US Senator, Foreign Relations Committee Ranking Member, *The National Dialogue on Iraq + One Year*, The Brookings Institute, Washington D.C., 31 July, 2003. http://biden.senate.gov/pressapp/record.cfm?id=207000

167. Mondli Makhanya, *True Power Lies in Critical Individuals*, Sunday Times, September 15, 2002, at 17.

168. Henry J. Steiner and Philip Alston, ibid., at 814-815.

169. *Accusations, Crimes against Humanity.* http://www.c-df.org/plaintes/mckinney.html.

170. *Covert Action in Africa, Opening Statement of Congresswoman McKinney*. See Annex G.

171. *Suffering and Despair: Humanitarian Crisis in the Congo,* Hearing Before the Subcommittee on International Operations and Human Rights of Committee on International Relations, House of Representatives, One HunD.R.ed Seventh Congress, First Session, May 17, 2001, Serial No. 107–16, US Government Printing Office Washington: 72-638PS 2001. http://www.house.gov/international_relations/107/726638.pdf. See also Testimony and Statement by Wayne Madsen in Annexure F.

172. Socrates, a Greek philosopher (469-399 B.C.E.).

173. Black's Law Dictionary, ibid.

174. Nelson Mandela, ibid.

175. Xavier Renou, *A Major Obstacle to African Unity: the New Franco-American Cold War on the Continent,* edited by Eddy Maloka in A United States of Africa?, Africa Institute of South Africa, 2001, at 432.

176. CNN, *Report: Rwanda genocide could have been prevented.* Ibid.

177. Xavier Renou, ibid., at 440.

178. NCN 2000, *Holbroke should not have gone to Africa.* http://www.marekinc.com/NCNEditornotesREG121001.html.

179. David Matas, ibid., at 6.

180. NCN 2000, *The Democratic Republic of Congo: The Lusaka Peace Accords and Beyond.* Ibid.

181. David Matas, ibid., at 215.

182. *United States Legislation on Military and Economic Aid: Human Rights Provisions. Human Rights and Security Assistance, Sec. 502B of the Foreign Assistance Act of 1961, as amended, 22 USC.A. §2304.*

183. Human Rights Watch Report 1999, *The Democratic Republic of Congo. Human Rights Developments*, ibid. © 1999 Human Rights Watch. Reprinted with Permission.

184. David N. Gibbs, *The Political Economy of the Third World Intervention. Mines, Money, and US Policy in the Congo Crisis.* Chicago & London: The University of Chicago Press, 1991, at 89-90. Reprinted with Permission of the University of Chicago Press.

185. David N. Gibbs, Ibid., at 93-94.

186. Ibid., at 95-96.

187. Ibid., at 99-100.

188. Allen Ray, ibid.

189. Congonline, *Politic. J.R. Boulle: ce chasseur de trésor qui en veut à Kabila. Les dessous des cartes de l'aggression rwando-ougandaise.* http://www.congonline.com/Actualite_Politique/Octobre98/Potentiel09.html.

190. David N. Gibbs, Ibid., at 100-101, 107-111, 142.

191. *The Star*, Ibid.

192. Xavier Renou, ibid. at 424-425.

193. Gibbs, ibid. at 165.

194. NCN 2000, *Genocide in Central Africa*, White House briefing on the interahamwe and the situation in the DR Congo, presented in the Washington foreign press center by Pierre Prosper, State Department Ambassador-at-large for War Crimes, on August 6, 2002. *www.marekinc.com/LooAds.html.*

195. NCN 2000, US Policies Toward Africa, *Uganda and Rwanda, two serious American policy failures*, November 09, 2001.

196. NCN 2000, *Genocide in Central Africa*, ibid.

197. Joseph R. Biden, Jr., ibid.

198. Restatement of the Law Third, The American Law Institute, Restatement of the Law, The Foreign Relations Law of the United States, Volume 2, St. Paul, Minn., American Law Institute Publishers, 1987, § 906, at 392. Copyright 1987 by the American Law Institute. All rights reserved. Reprinted with permission.

199. Kofi Annan, *"We The Peoples", The Role of the United Nations in the 21st Century*, Millennium Report of the Secretary-General of the United Nations, New York, April 3, 2000.

200. Kim Gleeson, *World influence of the UDHR. Worldwide Influence of the Universal Declaration of Human Rights and the International Bill of Rights.* http://www.universalrights.net/main/world.html.

201. Moira Rayner, cited by Kim Gleeson, ibid.

202. Moira Rayner, History of human rights. History of Universal Rights - Up to WW2, ibid.

203. Richard G. Wilkins, *Bias, Error, And Duplicity. The UN and the Domestic Law*, Manuscript notes, J. Reuben Clark Law School, Brigham Young University, 2000. See also in The World and I Magazine, Volume 11, Issue 12, December 1996.

204. Ibid.

205. Evelyn Leopold, *UN criticizes itself on keeping peace in Africa.* http://biz.yahoo.com/rf/991215/bjl.html.

206. Ibid.

207. Ibid.

208. Rome Statute of International Criminal Court, ibid.

209. See also Thomas A. Street, *The Theory and Principles of Torts Law*, Beard Books, 1999; Francis M. Burdick, *The Law of Torts: A Concise Treatise on the Civil Liability at Common Law and Under Modern Statutes for Actionable Wrongs to Person and Property,* Beard Books, 2000; Prosser and Keeton, *On Torts*, Fifth Edition, Horn Series, Student Edition, West Group, 2001. See also Barbri Bar Review, Thomson Company, 2002.

210. See Chapter V, Article 24, on the Security Council, of the UN Charter.

211. The UN followed and applied similar procedures to force Iraq out of Kuwait in 1991.

212. UN Charter, Chapter V, Articles 1 and 2.

213. See also Richard C. Wydick, *Professional Responsibility*, Barbri Bar Review, A Thomson Company, 2003, at 34.

214. Charter of the United Nations.

215. Rwanda, Uganda, and allies were disenchanted with Kabila who they accused of all evils and were already plotting to topple his regime.

216. Kofi Annan, "We The Peoples", ibid.

217. United Nations Report of the Secretary-General on the work of the Organization General Assembly Official Records Fifty-fifth session Supplement No. 1 (A/55/1), New York, August 30, 2000.

218. See also Richard Wydick, ibid., at 35.

219. Bryan A. Garner, ibid., at 660.

220. United Nations Report of the Secretary-General on the work of the Organization General Assembly, Official Records, Fifty-fifth session, Supplement No. 1 (A/55/1), ?New York, August 30, 2000. See also UN, *Annual Report of the Secretary-General on the Work of the Organization*, A/ 53/1, par. 26, 27 August 1998.

221. Kofi Annan, "We The Peoples", ibid.

222. UN, *The causes of conflict and the promotion of durable peace and sustainable development in Africa,* Report of the Secretary-General Kofi Annan to the UN Security Council, April 16, 1998.

223. A Latin dictum meaning that verbal language disappears but a written one remains. In the case of the DR Congo, the UN Charter, its resolutions, reports, and others documents shall stand as a testimony against itself and condemn it.

224. Latin maxim meaning that words of a strict signification can be given a wide signification if there is a reason for it.

225. Kofi Annan, "*We The Peoples*", ibid.

226. *United Nations Report of the Secretary-General on the work of the*

Organization, General Assembly, Official Records, Fifty-fifth session, Supplement No. 1 (A/55/1), New York, August 30, 2000. See also UN, *Annual Report of the Secretary-General on the Work of the Organization*, A/53/1, par. 62, 27 August 1998.

227. UN, *The causes of conflict and the promotion of durable peace and sustainable development in Africa,* Report of the Secretary-General Kofi Annan to the UN Security Council, April 16, 1998.

228. Kurt Jonassohn & Karin Solveig Björnson, ibid., 1998, at 101.

229. *United Nations Report of the Secretary-General on the work of the Organization*, General Assembly, Official Records, Fifty-fifth session, Supplement No. 1 (A/55/1), New York, August 30, 2000. See also UN, *Annual Report of the Secretary-General on the Work of the Organization*, A/53/1, par. 17, 18 & 180, 27 August 1998.

230. Michael N. Schmitt, *The Law of Belligerent Occupation*, Crimes War Project, April 15, 2003. http://www.crimesofwar.org/. Reprinted with Permission.

231. Ibid.

232. Carole Murphy, Occupation of Territory, in Crimes of War, ibid., at 263.

233. See also Article 24 of the Rome Statute Establishing the International Criminal Court.

234. Stuart E. Hendin, *Command Responsibility and Superior Orders in the Twentieth Century - A Century of Evolution,* Murdoch University Electronic Journal of Law, Vol.10 No.1 (March 2003). Htt://www.murdoch.edu.au/elaw/issues/v10n1/hendin101_text.html.

235. Ibid.

236. A.P.V. Rogers, *Command Responsibility Under the Law of War*. http://www.law.cam.ac.uk/rcil/COMD.R.ESP.doc. © A.P.V. Rogers. Reprinted with

Permission.

237. Nicole Barrett, *Holding Individual Leaders Responsible for Violations of Customary International Law: The US Bombardment of Cambodia and Laos*, 32 Colum. Hum. Rts. L. Rev. 429 (2001). http://www.icai-online.org/kissingerwatch/barrett.pdf.

238. Ibid.

239. Under pressure from the US government, Belgium was forced to repel this law and, subsequently the Supreme Court of Belgium on 24 June, 2003 dismissed all pending cases related to this law. Pursuant to the new law, only cases brought by Belgian citizens or long-term Belgian residents and with Belgian connection fall under this law. According to the Belgian government, the old law became so politicized that changes were necessary to have the law be in line with internationally recognized legal norms relating to international jurisdiction. See also Laurie King-Irani, *On Learning Lessons: Belgium's Universal Jurisdiction Under Threat*, International Justice, Common Dreams, June 25, 2003 http://www.globalpolicy.org/intljustice/universal/2003/0626gut.htm.

240. *Belgium Court Dismiss War Crimes Cases*, International Justice, Associated Press, September 24, 2003. http://www.globalpolicy.org/intljustice/universal/2003/0924bush.htm.

241. *Complaint.* http://www.informationclearinghouse.info/word/Complaint.doc. See also Glenn Frankel, *Belgium War Crimes Law Undone by Its Global Reach*, International Justice, *Washington Post*, September 30, 2003. http://www.globalpolicy.org/intljustice/universal/2003/0930univjstop.htm. See also US Commander Franks Faces Belgium "Genocide' Case, International Justice, Expatica, April 18, 2003. http://www.globalpolicy.org/intljustice/general/2003/0418franks.htm. © 2003 Expatica. Reprinted with Permission.

242. Restatement Third of the Law, §703, comment c, at 176. Copyright 1987 by the American Law Institute. All rights reserved. Reprinted with permission.

243. Ibid., §703 (3), at 174.

244. 28 US Code § 1350.

245. Anne-Marie Slaugther and David L. Bosco, *Alternative Justice, Crimes of War*, International Justice, Global Policy Forum, New York. http://www.globalpolicy.org/intljustice/atca/2001/altjust.htm. Reprinted with Permission.

246. See Filartiga v. Pena-Irala, 630 F.2d 876, 577 F.Supp 860 (filed in 1979, judgment for the plaintiffs in 1984). See also Forti v. Suarez-Mason , 672 F.Supp. 1531, 694 F.Supp. 707 (filed in 1987, won in 1990).

247. Jim Lobe, *Attorney-General Attacks Key Law, International Justice*, Inter Press Service News Agency, May 15, 2003. http://www.globalpolicy.org/intljustice/atca/2003/0515AshcroftATCA.htm. © 2003 Inter Press Agency. Reprinted with Permission. See also Trajano v. Marcos, 978 F.2d 493, Hilao v. Marcos, 25 F.3d 1467, 103 F.3d 767, 103 F.3d 789 (filed in 1986, judgment for the plaintiffs in 1995; some damage claims still being litigated).

248. Anne-Marie Slaugther and David L. Bosco, ibid.

249. Ibid. See also Doe v. Karadzic, Kadic v. Karadzic, 866 F. Supp. 734, 70 F.3d 232 (filed in 1994, judgment for the plaintiffs in 2000).

250. In 2000 while on visit for a UN Conference in New York both Li Peng, former Chinese premier, and Robert Mugabe, president of Zimbabwe, were both served with court papers for cases brought by victims claiming human rights abuses and torture. But the leaders could not be arrested because of in a 1989 decision, the US Supreme Court rejected the notion that a plaintiff could bypass the protection of sovereign immunity and sue a foreign government or a sitting foreign leader directly under the Alien Tort statute — a precedent that makes the Mugabe case very unlikely to succeed. In March of the same year Mugabe was granted provisionary State Immunity by the US Government.

251. In the Filartigas case, plaintiffs never collected the money because US Immigration officers deported the Defendant. Also in many cases, Defendants

run away out of the US before the reward is collected.

252. President George W. Bush at a Rose Garden press meeting with Japanese Prime Minister Junichiro Koizumi, referring on how to capture Osama bin Laden and the Taliban leaders and destroy the alleged terrorist network that they control in Afghanistan, 26 September, 2001.

253. Anne-Marie Slaugther and David L. Bosco, ibid.

254. Jim Lobe, ibid.

255. Alison Raphael, Apartheid Victims Sue Global Corporations, Social/ Economic Policy, One Word US, November 13, 2002. http:// www.globalpolicy.org/socecon/tncs/2002/1113apartheid.htm.

256. Kenny Bruno, De-Globazing Justice, The Corporate Campaign To Strip Foreign Victims of Corporate Induced in Human Rights Violations of the Right To Sue in US Courts, Social/Economic Policy, Multinational Monitor, March 2003. http://www.globalpolicy.org/socecon/tncs/2003/03justice.htm.

257. See Conclusion and Findings of the Panel of Experts on the Illegal Exploitation of Natural Resources and Other Forms of Wealth, §213-217.

258. Ibid., On the Continuation of the War, at 173, 175.

259. See S/2003/1027, par. 15.

260. Ibid., par. 11.

261. See Panel of Experts in Annexure B at par. 181-183.

262. See S/2003/1027, par.9-10.

263. Ibid., at par.12.

264. Ibid., at par. 51. See also Statement of Congresswoman Cynthia McKinney herein.

265. Ibid., at 52.

266. Doe v. Unocal Corp., 2002 WL 31063976 (9th Cir. (Cal.) Sep 18, 2002).
267. *Prosecutor v. Furundzija*, IT-95-17/1-T (Dec. 10, 1998), quoted from in *Doe v. Unocal*, ibid, at 14219.

268. Arlen Specter, *The Court of Last Resort, International Justice*, New York Times, 7 August, 2003. http://www.globalpolicy.org/intljustice/atca/2003/0807specter.htm.

269. Justice & The Generals, US-Law, Background. http://www.pbs.org/wnet/justice/law_background_torture3.html.

270. *Torture Victim Protection Act of 1991*, H.R. 2092, approved March 12, Public Law No. 102 – 256, *Equipo* Nizkor & Derechos Human Rights, 9 November, 2002. http://www.derechos.org/nizkor/econ/TVPA.html.

271. Justice & The General, ibid.

272. 28 USC 1350 of 12 March, 1992.

273. *Alien Tort Claims Act*. http://cyber.law.harvard.edu/torts3y/readings/update-a-02.doc.

274. See Justice and the Generals, ibid. The TVPA was first used in *Ortiz v. Gramajo*, a companion case to Xuncax. Diana Ortiz was an American citizen nun tortured and sexually abused while in Guatemala. As a citizen, she could not use the ATCA and had to rely on the TVPA. She sued Gramajo under the statute, arguing that it was retroactive to the time of her torture. (The statute was passed in 1992; Ortiz was tortured in 1989.) The court agreed with Ortiz and found that the TVPA could be applied retroactively.

275. Ibid. http://www.pbs.org/wnet/justice/law_background_torture4.html.

276. Hugo Grotius, *2 De Jure Belli ac Pacis* (Whewell trans.1853) at p. 88, quoted by William F. Pepper in *The End of Sovereign Immunity in Cases involving Human Rights Crimes of States, their Leaders and Officials*. http://tihrs.org/resources/online/wfp2001.html.

277. Human Rights Watch, *Le précédent Pinochet: Comment les victimes peuvent poursuivre à l'étranger les criminals de droit de l'homme, L'affraire Pinochet – Un rappel à l'ordre aux tyrans, une source d'espoir pour les victims* [7/9/2001]. http://wwwhrw.org/campaigns/chile98/precedent_french.htm. © 2001Human Rights Watch. Reprinted with Permission.

278. William F. Pepper, *The End of Sovereign Immunity in Cases involving Human Rights Crimes of States, their Leaders and Officials*, Oxford, 23June, 2001. See Lafontant v. Aristide, 844 F. Supp. 128, Saltony v. Reagan, 702 F. Supp. 319 (D.D.C. 1988) affd 886 F. 2d 438 (D.C. Cir. 1989).

279. Lynn D. Wardle, W. Sherman Rogers, & L. Lynn Hogue, *Interstate and International Conflict of Laws* (manuscript ed.), Provo, 2000. http://www.law2.byu.edu/Wadle/International_Conflicts/iicl_casebook/CHI2IJUR.html. See also Psinakis v. Marcos, Civ. No. C-75-1725 (N.D.Cal.1975), excerpted in 1975 Dig.UsPrac.Int'l L.344-45 (immunity granted to then-President Marcos following suggestion of immunity by the Executive Branch); Kendall v.Saudi Arabia 65 Adm. 885 (S.D.N.Y.1965), reported in 1977 Dig.UsPrac.Int'l L. 107, 1053-54; Kilroy v. Windsor, Civ. No C-78-291 (N.D.Ohio 1978), (Prince Charles, The Prince of Wales, granted immunity from suit alleging human rights violations in Northen Ireland), excerpted in 1978 Dig.UsPrac.Int'l L. 641-43; Mr. Saltany v. Reagan, 702 F. Supp. 319 (D.C.C.1988), order aff'd in part, reversed in part (on other grounds), 886 F.2d 438 (D.C.Cir.1989), cert. denied, 495 Us 932 (1990) (granting head-of-state immunity to Prime Minister of England in suit alleging violations of international law).

280. Virginie Ladish, *Liberian President Indicted for War Crimes*, War Crimes Project, 16 June, 2003. http://www.crimesofwar.org/. Reprinted with Permission.

281. Human Rights Watch, *Le précédent Pinochet, ibid.* © 2001Human Rights Watch. Reprinted with Permission.

282. Frederic L. Kirgis, *The Indictment in Senegal of the Former Chad Head of State*, The American Society of International Law, February 2000. wysiwyg://113/http://www.asil.org/insights/insigh41.htm. © 2001 American

Society of International Law. Reprinted with Permission.

283. William F. Pepper, ibid. See also Hilao v. Marcos (In re: Estate of Marcos Litigation) 25 F. 3d 1467 (9'" Cir. 1994) cert denied 115 S.Ct. 934 (1996); Paul v. Avril, 812 F. Supp. 207. See Kadic v. Karadzic, 70 F. 3d 232 (2d Cir. ' Q95) for denial of immunity to a non-governmental entity. See In re: Grand Jury Proceedings, Doe No 700, 817 F. 2d 1108 (4'" Cir. 1987); Estate of Domingo v. Republic of the Philippines, 694 F. Supp. 782, 786 (W.D. Wash. 1988); also Hilao v Marcos, supra, for denial of immunity to a former head of state. See Ex Parte Pinochet Ugarte, 2 WLR 827 (24 March, 1999), for waiver of immunity by a foreign state.

284. Ibid.

285. Ibid.

286. Steven R. Ratner & Jason S. Abrams, *Accountability For Human Rights Atrocities in International Law, Behind the Nuremberg Legacy, Second Edition,* Oxford Press University, 2001, at 161-162.

287. Restatement of the Law Third, ibid., at 176, comment b. Copyright 1987 by the American Law Institute. All rights reserved. Reprinted with permission.

288. Virginie Ladisch, *Argentine Military Officer Extradited To Spain On Genocide Charges*, Crimes of War Project, 10 July, 2003. (Ricardo Miguel Cavallo, a former captain in the Argentine Navy, was suspected of torturing and killing hundreds of people during the Argentine "Dirty War" in the seventies. He was living in Mexico in 2003 at the time of his arrest, when indicted by Spanish Court, and extradited to Spain to stand trial of torture, disappearances, and extrajudicial killings.) http://www.crimesofwar.org/onnews/news-argentina.html. Reprinted with Permission.

289. Adopted and opened for signature, ratification, and accession by General Assembly resolution 39/46 of 10 December, 1984 *entry into force* 26 June, 1987, in accordance with article 27 (1). http://www.unhchr.ch/html/menu3/b/h_cat39.htm.

290. Françoise Hampson, Universal *Jurisdiction, in Crimes of War, What The Public Should Know*, ibid., at 222.

291. Frederic L. Kirgis, ibid.

292. Steven R. Ratner & Jason S. Abrams, ibid., at 185.

293. Ibid., at 335-336.

294. Ibid., at 335.

295. Paul Kagame has succeeded in preaching to Rwandans and some Western countries that for Rwanda to avoid a repeated genocide of the caliber of 1994, he and only he can direct the affairs of this nation. This attitude is both a threat and an intimidation to all those who like to freely manifest their political views. In this atmosphere of fear, which Rwandan could have cast a ballot not having Kagame's picture and name on it? And how can the international community dare support a more credible and competent leader for the Rwandan people in those circumstances?

296. Kurt Jonassohn & Karin Solveig Björnson, ibid., at 134-135.

297. Burns H. Weston, *Global Focus: Human Rights '98. Human Rights*, from the encyclopedia Britannica. *Definition of Human Rights*. http://www.uiowa.edu/~hr98/resources/basics/weston2.html.

298. Ibid.

299. United Nations General Assembly, Distr. GENERAL, A/RES/53/156, Fifty-third session, par.3, 9 February 1999.

300. Human Rights Watch World Report 1999, *Rwanda. Human Rights Development*. Ibid. © 1999 Human Rights Watch. Reprinted with Permission.

301. Human Rights Watch World Report 1999, *Rwanda. Defending Human Rights*. http://www.hrw.org/hrw/worldreport99/africa/rwanda2.html. © 1999 Human Rights Watch. Reprinted with Permission. See also United Nations General Assembly, Distr. GENERAL, A/RES/53/156, Fifty-third session,

par.6, 9 February 1999.

302. Amnesty International Annual Report 2000, Rwanda. http://web.amnesty.org/web/ar2000web.nsf/countries/7d4208bcf86ce147802568f200552963?OpenDocument.

303. Ibid., 2001 Annual Report, Rwanda. http://web.amnesty.org/web/ar2001.nsf/webafrcountries/RWANDA?OpenDocument.

304. See Interview by Ambassador Prosper.

305. In June 2002, Rwandan President Paul Kagame officially launch the nationwide revival of gacaca courts, an ancient system of traditional justice to judge some of the 100,000 detainees accused of the 1994 genocide. But this is a very untested and flawed legal system where due process of the law is questioned. See also Agency France Press, *Rwanda To Resurrect Traditional Justice System*, International Justice, 17 June 2002. http://www.globalpolicy.org/intljustice/general/2002/0617ga.htm.

306. NCN 2000.com, The American political elite has been misled by faulty analysis regarding the Congo, June 27, 2002.

307. Human Rights Watch World Report 1999, *Uganda. Human Rights Developments*. http://www.hrw.org/hrw/world Report99/africa/uganda.html. © 1999 Human Rights Watch. Reprinted with Permission.

308. Human Rights Watch, *Uganda Human Rights Developments*, World Reports 2000. http://www.hrw.org/wr2k/Africa-12.htm#TopOfPage.

309. Human Rights Watch, *Uganda Humna Rights Developments*, World Reports 2003. http://www.hrw.org/wr2k3/africa13.html. © 2003 Human Rights Watch. Reprinted with Permission.

310. NCN 2000, *The Democratic Republic of Congo: The Lusaka Peace Accords and Beyond.* Ibid.

311. NCN 2000, US Policies Toward Africa, *Uganda and Rwanda, two serious American policy failures*.

312. Contra Costa Times.com, Editorials, *Africa's forgotten war*, May 05, 2003. © 2003 Contra Costa. Reprinted with Permission.

313. Henry J.Steiner & Philip Alston, ibid, at 824.

314. NCN 2000, *The Democratic Republic of Congo: The Lusaka Peace Accords and Beyond.* Ibid.

315. UN, *The causes of conflict and the promotion of durable peace and sustainable development in Africa,* Report of the Secretary-General Kofi Annan to the UN Security Council, April 16, 1998.

316. NCN 2000, *The American political elite has been misled by faulty analysis regarding the Congo*, June 27, 2002.

317. NCN 2000, US Policy Toward Africa, Uganda and Rwanda, two serious American policy failures, November 09, 2001.

318. Ibid.

319. Ibid.

320. See Rigobert N. Butandu, ibid.

321. Payan Akhavan, *Beyond Impunity: Can International Criminal Justice Prevent Future Atrocities?*, 95 AJIL 8, 2001. © 2001 American Society of International Law. Reprinted with Permission.

322. Jennifer Widmer, *Courts and Democracy in PostConflict Transitions: A Social Scientist's Perspective on the African case*, 95 AJIL 67, 2001. © 2001 American Society of International Law. Reprinted with Permission.

323. See for instance S/Res./1484 of 30 May, 2003.

324. Jennifer Widmer, ibid., at 65.

325. See S/2003/1027, par. 50.

326. French sentence meaning that the Chief resolves his subjects' disputes under the village meeting tree (tribal court).

327. Richard Wydick, ibid., at 116-117.

328. Adopted by the Security Council at its 4,723rd meeting, on 20 March, 2003.

329. Sorcerers or enemies have not yet given up, sang Me Franco Luambo Makiadi, ibid.

330. Payam Akhavan, ibid, at 7.

331. David Philip, ibid., at 45.

332. Sunday Times, Letters, September 8, 2002 Edition.

333. Mukanda M. Mulemfo, *Thabo Mbeki and the African Renaissance*, Actua Press (Pty.) Ltd., 2000, at 37.

334. UN, *The causes of conflict and the promotion of durable peace and sustainable development in Africa,* Report of the Secretary-General Kofi Annan to the UN Security Council, April 16, 1998.

335. The Star, Letters, When Africa Treats Its Life as Precious, the World Will Too, Friday September 20, 2002.

336. Ibid. , at 34.

337. David Philip, ibid., at 46.

338. *The Star*, Letters, ibid.

339. Makanda M. Mulemfo, ibid., at 52.

340. Philip Iya, *Globalisation and the African Renaissance: A Case of Incompability in Africa?*, edited by Eddy Maloka, ibid., at 327.

341. Mukanda M. Mulemfo, ibid., at 47.

342. See Annexure M for the Statement of President Thabo Mbeki, then Vice-President, on the African Renaissance.

343. Philip Iya, ibid., at 327-328.

344. Restatement of The Law Third, ibid., §901, comment a, at 340. Copyright 1987 by the American Law Institute. All rights reserved. Reprinted with permission.

345. Marguerite Michaels, ibid., at 64.

346. David Philip, ibid., at 193.

347. Burns H. Weston, *Global Focus: Human Rights '98*, ibid.

348. NCN 2000, *The Democratic Republic of Congo: The Lusaka Peace Accords and Beyond.* Ibid.

349. Brendalyn P. Ambrose, ibid., at 161.

350. United Nations, Report of the Secretary-General on the work of the Organization, General Assembly, Official Records, Fifty-fifth session, Supplement No. 1 (A/55/1), ibid.

351. Kofi Annan, "*We The Peoples*", ibid.

352. Kurt Jonassohn & Karin Solveig Björnson, ibid. , at 119.

353. Amos Yoder, ibid., at 129.

354. Réginald Moreels, ibid., p. 25.

355. See S/2003/1027, par. 49.

356. Ackson Kanduza, *Popular Struggles, Civil Society Democratic Governance in Africa*, Edited by Eddy Maloka, ibid., p. 109.

357. UN, *Annual Report of the Secretary-General on the Work of the Organization*, A/53/1, ibid.
358. Ibid, par. 183.

359. In the context of the Panel's mandate.

360. Cross-border commercial exchanges between people of the region have traditionally existed.

361. COMIEX is registered as follows: immatriculé No. 43797, identification nationale No. 31837T, Siège sociale Kinshasa/Gombé No. 4 Avenue de la Justice. Administrateur Directeur générale: Frédéric Kabarele.

362. The number of soldiers has fluctuated during the period of the war; the numbers used are therefore average estimates.

363. Uganda's GDP has been increasing since the early 1990s. However, a slight decrease was noted in 1999.

364. In 2000, the official exchange rate was one dollar for 23 Congolese francs.

365. According to some sources, Mwenze Kongolo is involved in most COMIEX dealings. Most importantly, it is said to the main bridge between Zimbabwean officials such as the influential Emmerson Munangagwa and the Government of the Democratic Republic of the Congo.

366. The distribution of shares is a follows: Oryx 49 percent, COMIEX 33 percent, MIBA 16 percent and Congolese partners 3 percent.

Printed in the United States
24167LVS00003B/79-81

9 781413 730821